The Culture & Civilization of China

中國文化与文明

Yale University Press

New Haven & London

Foreign Languages Press

Beijing

Angela Falco Howard

Wu Hung

Chinese Sculpture

Li Song
Yang Hong

Calligraphy for series title by Qi Gong, president of
the China National Calligraphers' Association

Frontispiece: Bas-relief of female attendants and musicians, painted white marble, unearthed in 1995 from the tomb of Wang Chuzhi (fig. 2.45).

Designed by Jerry Kelly, New York,
based on the original series design by Richard Hendel.
Set in Monotype Garamond type by Angela Taormina.
Chinese type by Birdtrack Press, New Haven, Connecticut.
Printed and bound in China by C & C Offset Printing Co., Ltd.

Library of Congress Cataloging-in-Publication Data

Chinese sculpture / Angela Falco Howard ... [et al.].
   p. cm. — (The culture & civilization of China)
Includes bibliographical references and index.
  ISBN 0-300-10065-5 (cloth : alk. paper)
  1. Sculpture, Chinese. I. Howard, Angela Falco. II. Series.
NB1040.C516 2003
730'.951—dc21

2003002733

A catalogue record for this book is available from the British Library.

10   9   8   7   6   5   4   3   2   1

Publication of this book

was made possible by the generous support of

RUTH AND BRUCE DAYTON

Yale University Press gratefully acknowledges

the financial support given to

The Culture & Civilization of China by:

Robert H. Ellsworth

The William and Flora Hewlett Foundation

J. S. Lee

The Henry Luce Foundation, Inc.

Patricia Mellon

The National Endowment for the Humanities

John and Cynthia Reed

The Rosenkranz Foundation

The Starr Foundation

THE CULTURE & CIVILIZATION OF CHINA

Each book in this series is the fruit of cooperation between Chinese and Western scholars and publishers. Our goals are to illustrate the cultural riches of China, to explain China to both interested general readers and specialists, to present the best recent scholarship, and to make original and previously inaccessible resources available for the first time. The books will all be published in both English and Chinese.

The partners in this unprecedented joint undertaking are the China International Publishing Group (CIPG) and Yale University Press.

CONTENTS

CHRONOLOGY

Exact dates may vary depending on scholars' interpretations.

1,000,000–10,000 B.C.E.	PALEOLITHIC PERIOD
10,000–ca. 2100 B.C.E.	NEOLITHIC PERIOD
ca. 2070–ca. 1600 B.C.E.	XIA DYNASTY
ca. 1600–ca. 1046 B.C.E.	SHANG DYNASTY
ca. 1046–256 B.C.E.	ZHOU DYNASTY

      Western Zhou ca. 1046–771 B.C.E.
      Eastern Zhou 770–256 B.C.E.
            Spring and Autumn Period 770–476 B.C.E.
            Warring States Period 476–221 B.C.E.

221–206 B.C.E.	QIN DYNASTY
206 B.C.E.– 220 C.E.	HAN DYNASTY

      Western (Former) Han Dynasty 206 B.C.E.– 9 C.E.
      Xin Dynasty 9–25
      Eastern (Later) Han Dynasty 25–220

220–265	THREE KINGDOMS

      Wei 220–265
      Shu 221–263
      Wu 222–280

265–420	JIN DYNASTY*

      Western Jin 265–317
      Eastern Jin 317–420

386–581	NORTHERN DYNASTIES*

      Northern Wei 386–534
      Eastern Wei 534–550
      Western Wei 535–556
      Northern Qi 550–577
      Northern Zhou 557–581

421–589	SOUTHERN DYNASTIES*

      Liu Song 421–479
      Southern Qi 479–502
      Liang 502–557
      Chen 557–589

581–618	SUI DYNASTY
618–907	TANG DYNASTY
907–960	FIVE DYNASTIES (in the north)

      Later Liang 907–923
      Later Tang 923–936
      Later Jin 936–946
      Later Han 947–950
      Later Zhou 951–960

907–979	TEN KINGDOMS (in the south)

      Former Shu 907–925
      Later Shu 934–965
      Nanping or Jingnan 924–963
      Chu 927–951
      Wu 902–937
      Southern Tang 937–975
      Wu-Yue 907–978
      Min 909–945
      Southern Han 917–971
      Northern Han 951–979

907–1125	LIAO DYNASTY
960–1279	SONG DYNASTY

      Northern Song 960–1127
      Southern Song 1127–1279

1038–1227	WESTERN XIA DYNASTY
1115–1234	JIN DYNASTY
1271–1368	YUAN DYNASTY
1368–1644	MING DYNASTY
1644–1911	QING DYNASTY
1912–1949	REPUBLIC
1949–	PEOPLE'S REPUBLIC

*The Western and Eastern Jin dynasties together with the Southern Dynasties are frequently referred to as the Six Dynasties. From 304 to 439 north China was ruled by nomadic tribes in what is called the Sixteen Kingdoms period.

EMPERORS OF THE SONG, YUAN, MING, AND QING DYNASTIES

Emperor's Posthumous Temple Name	Reign Dates
SONG DYNASTY	
Northern Song	
Taizu (Zhao Kuangyin)	960–976
Taizong	976–997
Zhenzong	998–1022
Renzong	1023–1063
Yingzong	1064–1067
Shenzong	1068–1085
Zhezong	1086–1100
Huizong	1101–1125
Qinzong	1126–1127
Southern Song	
Gaozong	1127–1162
Xiaozong	1163–1189
Guangzong	1190–1194
Ningzong	1195–1224
Lizong	1225–1264
Duzong	1265–1274
Gong	1275–1276
Duanzong	1276–1278
Dibing*	1278–1279
YUAN DYNASTY	
Shizu	1260–1294
Chengzong	1295–1307
Wuzong	1308–1311
Renzong	1312–1320
Yingzong	1321–1323
Taiding	1324–1328
Tianshun	1328
Wenzong	1328–1329
Mingzong	1329
Wenzong	1330–1332
Ningzong	1332
Shun*	1333–1368

Emperor's Posthumous Temple Name	Reign Title	Reign Dates
MING DYNASTY		
Taizu (Zhu Yuanzhang)	Hongwu	1368–1398
Hui*	Jianwen	1399–1402
Chengzu	Yongle	1403–1424
Renzong	Hongxi	1425
Xuanzong (Zhu Zhanji)	Xuande	1426–1435
Yingzong	Zhengtong	1436–1449
Daizong	Jingtai	1450–1456
Yingzong	Tianshun	1457–1464
Xianzong	Chenghua	1465–1487
Xiaozong	Hongzhi	1488–1505
Wuzong	Zhengde	1506–1521
Shizong	Jiajing	1522–1566
Muzong	Longqing	1567–1572
Shenzong	Wanli	1573–1620
Guangzong	Taichang	1620
Xizong	Tianqi	1621–1627
Sizong*	Chongzhen	1628–1644
QING DYNASTY		
Shizu	Shunzhi	1644–1661
Shengzu	Kangxi	1662–1722
Shizong	Yongzheng	1723–1735
Gaozong	Qianlong	1736–1795
Renzong	Jiaqing	1796–1820
Xuanzong	Daoguang	1821–1850
Wenzong	Xianfeng	1851–1861
Muzong	Tongzhi	1862–1874
Dezong	Guangxu	1875–1908
Puyi*	Xuantong	1909–1911

*No temple name; personal name or posthumous memorial title is listed instead.

CHINA

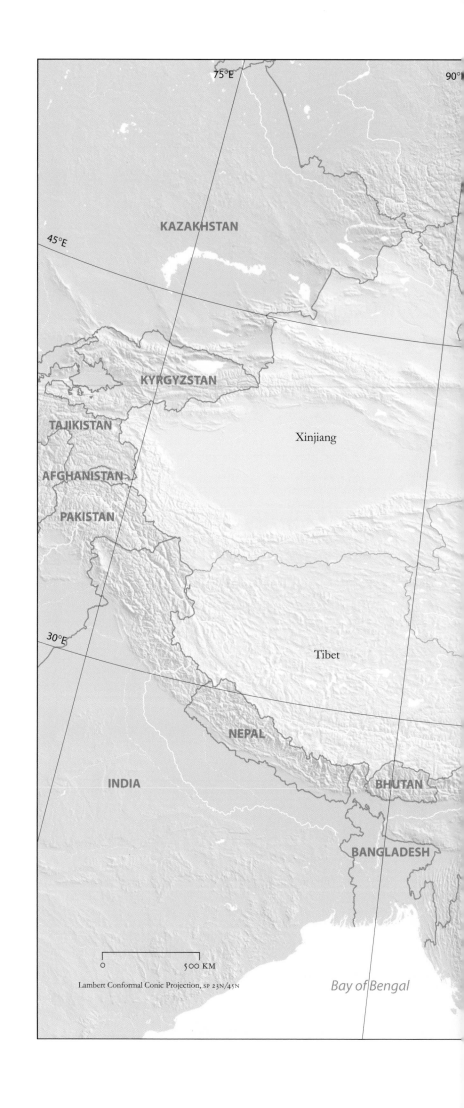

KAZAKHSTAN

KYRGYZSTAN

TAJIKISTAN

AFGHANISTAN

PAKISTAN

Xinjiang

Tibet

NEPAL

INDIA

BHUTAN

BANGLADESH

75°E

90°

45°E

30°E

0   500 KM

Lambert Conformal Conic Projection, SP 23N/45N

Bay of Bengal

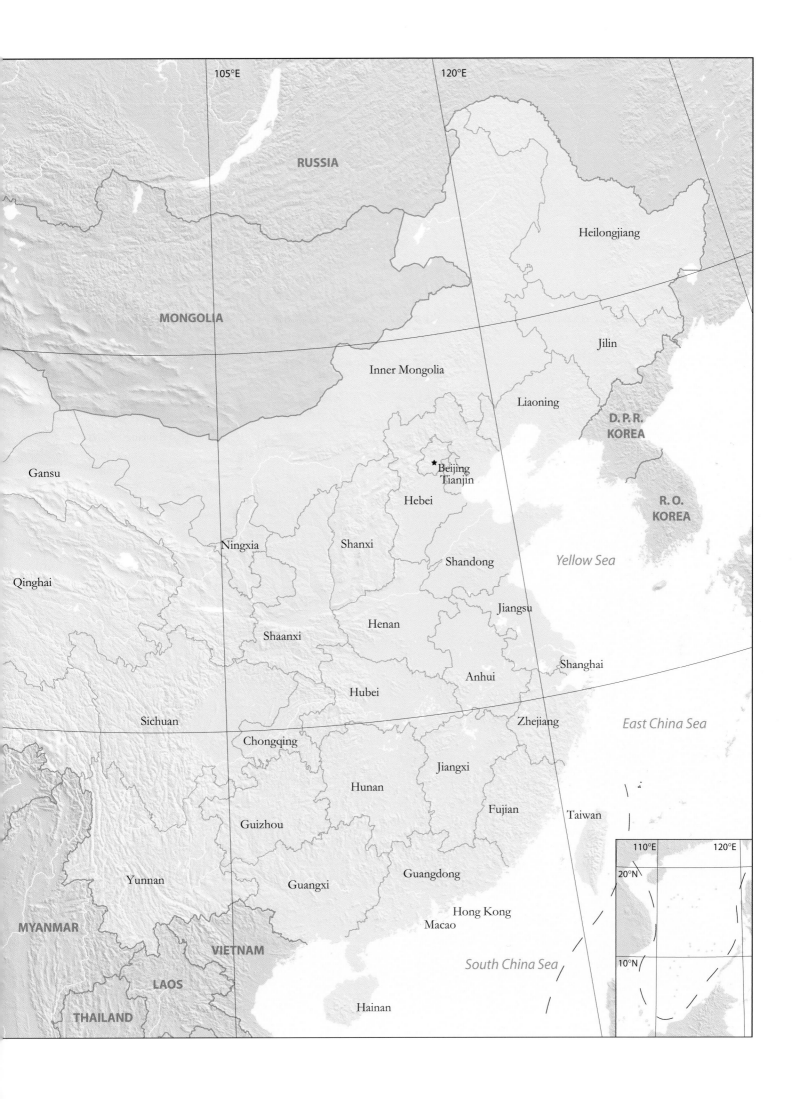

Introduction

LI SONG

Archaeological discoveries in recent decades have broadened and stimulated interest in Chinese sculpture by offering a stunningly beautiful and diverse world of objects to explore — objects that are amazing not just for their magnificence and range of styles but for sheer number. The head of a goddess from ruins of the Hongshan culture in Liaoning Province and the statue of a naked pregnant woman on the altar of a goddess temple display the vitality and creativity of early Chinese sculpture. The goddess head, with its broad forehead, raised eyebrows, high cheekbones, and large, sensuous mouth, is surprisingly naturalistic. It is life-size, and its component materials accentuate its lifelike quality: the eyes, made of bluish jade, stare forcefully ahead. On the naked woman — perhaps a representation of the goddess herself — the fragments of eyes, ears, and nose suggest that the statue was three times as large as a real person.[1]

In the autumn of 1986 one of the most spectacular archaeological finds of all time was made when excavators in Sanxingdui, Sichuan Province, came across two sacrificial pits containing thousands of rare art objects, including a staggering array of sculptural objects: more than one hundred bronze human and semi-human images, including a life-size statue; fifty or so heads with distorted noses, mouths, and ears; more than thirty masks; several dozen smaller figures; and a large bronze money tree. The art of casting large human figures was clearly well advanced by the late Shang dynasty (ca. 1200 B.C.E.).

No discovery was more breathtaking, however, than that of the underground burial of Qin Shihuang, the king of Qin who became the first emperor of China (r. 246–210 B.C.E.). Historical texts record that the First Emperor of Qin had arranged for the casting of Twelve Golden Men, each weighing 12,000 kilograms. These statues, which reportedly stood in the square fronting the palace complex used during the Qin and Han dynasties, were destroyed by King Fu Jian of the Former Qin in the fourth century. But an entire terracotta army remained buried underground until peasants accidentally discovered it in 1974. The size of the army is astonishing: there are more than seven thousand life-size warriors, along with chariots, horses, and thousands of weapons. The Qin warriors, many with broad foreheads, high cheekbones, large eyes, thick eyebrows, and stiff beards, show distinct personal features: some younger soldiers smile; weather-beaten veterans frown. In these sculptural creations of kneeling archers, rank upon rank of standing soldiers, generals in full panoply, horse-drawn chariots and cavalrymen, we see the military might of the Qin emperor who had once "swept over six rivals."[2]

Although China has a rich sculptural legacy dating

back more than seven thousand years, historical study of this distinctive art form did not begin until the early twentieth century, when Western sculptural terms were introduced. The recent discoveries have revolutionized our understanding of early Chinese sculptural achievements. Even the profoundly innovative and nontraditional methods of making large Buddhist statues, popular since the period of disunion — the division of the Northern and Southern Dynasties (386–589) — stemmed, it became evident, from a long tradition of monumental sculpture. Extraordinary finds of smaller art objects have expanded this historical perspective. Figurines of the Neolithic Shijiahe culture include a multitude of miniature animals and birds, among them elephants, apes, rabbits, tigers, dogs, pigs, tapirs, sheep, tortoises, owls, ducks, and hens. Other Neolithic finds, such as those at Dengjiawan, Hubei Province, include two full-bodied miniature human images wearing caps and earrings and sitting upright in a rigid, formal pose. They may be making offerings; one figure seems to be holding a fish, and the other is presenting an object with both hands. Not only the number of such ancient finds but the high artistry of the objects has been astounding. As a result, Chinese sculpture has become one of the most dynamic and exciting areas in the study of Chinese culture.

Major sculptural creations before the arrival of Buddhism in China can be divided into two main categories: works in imperial palaces and gardens, and burial items. Most sculptural works in imperial palaces and gardens have been lost; only a few are left to remind us of early splendor. A great number of sculptural works made for the royal tombs have survived, however, and archaeological excavations continue to bring many more sculpted tomb figurines and other funeral objects to light. Because in China tombs replicated the environment of the living, they provide us with many clues about palaces and gardens in the various dynasties.

Tomb architecture and sculpture also tell us a good deal about such core ethical concepts as filial piety and about religious beliefs and rituals. In ancient China people believed that the soul did not vanish when a person died; disembodied, it would continue to use clothing, food, utensils, and housing and enjoy social status — all the comforts of life. The choice of a tomb site was based on geomancy and the belief that five elements (water, fire, earth, metal, and wood) compose everything that exists. At the time of burial and then occasionally afterward, sacrifices were offered at ceremonies held in accordance with Confucian prescription.

The Qin army was underground, but many tomb sculptures are aboveground: mostly stone images of civil officials and military officers, carriages, and exotic birds and animals, all of which line the two sides of the Spirit Path — the road or walkway leading to the tomb mound. Their symbolic function was to protect the soul of the sovereign and drive away evil spirits. In essence, they were more ritualistic than religious, and their origin can be traced back to the Qin and Han dynasties.

After Qin Shihuang died, he was buried at Lishan (Mount Li, near present-day Xi'an), and "trees and grass were planted on and around the tomb mound to make it look like a mountain."[3] Huge sculpted stone tigers, horses, and elephants were erected around the tomb of Huo Qubing, a young and able general under Emperor Wu of the Western Han (r. 140–87 B.C.E.), to symbolically represent the Qilian Mountains, maybe because most of the battles he fought were in that area. Not far from Huo's tomb is that of Princess Qingyang, wife of Wei Qing, another famous general of the Western Han; her tomb was made to "resemble Mount Lu."[4]

Besides mountains, there were other obvious references to status and achievement. The six stone horses carved in relief in front of the Zhaoling mausoleum represent the famous chargers of Emperor Taizong (r. 627–649), while the stone statues of foreign chieftains and guests in the Qianling mausoleum, completed in 705, serve as memorials to diplomatic achievements of the Tang dynasty. In the following centuries, sculptural works lining the Spirit Paths of the imperial tombs became increasingly stylized in terms of imagery and the number of statues. The massive sculpted human and animal figures along Spirit Paths were meant to convey the solemnity and majesty of emperors, whose power to rule came from Heaven, it was said, but who did not seek religious piety. This distinction represents a clear difference between sculpture for tombs and sculpture for temples.

Although most sculptural works buried in tombs represent people performing various real-life tasks, other objects, used as talismans, were more fanciful. The sculptors, given considerable artistic freedom in creating tomb figurines, used different materials and generally, from the Han through the Tang dynasties — from the third century B.C.E. to the tenth century C.E.— produced images of high artistic quality.

The making of aboveground and underground tomb sculptures, particularly those in the tombs of imperial and noble families, was conducted mainly under government supervision.[5] As state-patronized projects, they were mostly done by professional sculptors or artisans following strict rules. In this, too, they differed somewhat from Buddhist and Daoist sculpture: although religious sculpture also followed rules of iconography, the rules were intended to enable sculptors to display religious devotion through their work.

In ancient China the offering of sacrifices to Heaven and Earth, the gods of land and grain, and one's ancestors was considered a great event, as significant as war. Later on, emperors and kings were the only ones considered worthy to offer sacrifices to Heaven and Earth, and in so doing they reinforced their claim to all religious, political, and military power. By the third century B.C.E. the author of the *Zuo Commentary* (*Zuo zhuan*), could write, "Of all major state events, sacrificial ceremonies and wars are the most important."[6]

The ancient rituals and sacrifice-offering ceremonies, which manifested a hierarchy based on clan lineages, were further systematized in the Eastern Zhou dynasty (ca. 770–256 B.C.E.) in such Confucian classics as the *Rites, Book of Rites,* and *Rites of Zhou,* which greatly influenced Chinese society in the following two to three thousand years. Another important stage in the development of religion and state ritual came during the Western and Eastern Han dynasties (206 B.C.E.–220 C.E.), when prevailing beliefs were combined with Confucian teachings to give birth to Confucianism, an integration of government with religion. Traditional beliefs also combined with alchemy, the practices of shamanism, and the theory of five elements to give rise to Daoism. Buddhism came into China in the first century via central Asia. As it spread through China, it came to embrace many Confucian beliefs, including some that contradicted its own tenets. The rise of numerous Buddhist schools and different interpretations of the Buddhist canon reflect this profound and continuous interplay between the alien faith of Buddhism and native Chinese traditions. Over the course of a long and complex history, Buddhism gradually became an integral part of Chinese culture.

Confucianism, Daoism, and Buddhism all used art to propagate their beliefs and in the process enriched the content and forms of artistic expression. The spread of Buddhist art revived traditional Chinese sculpture, and Buddhist sculpture was itself sinicized, largely between the fourth and tenth centuries, during the Southern, Northern, Sui, and Tang dynasties. Confucian art was mainly used in sacrifice-offering ceremonies and various ritual activities. The events were multimedia, employing painting and sculpture, together with music, dance, and other forms of art, to promote the educational role of culture and to cultivate sound human relationships. Buddhist and Daoist art, in contrast, were primarily concerned with showing the hierarchical order in Heaven. Artists painstakingly represented abstract religious tenets in easily accessible images, in the end providing worshipers with deities that matched sacred texts and rituals. Both faiths were greatly influenced over time by the powerful folk traditions and folk-god beliefs of the Chinese people.

Buddhist, Daoist, and Confucian beliefs conflicted at times, but they also coexisted, exchanging rituals, ideas, and revered persons. The same artist could create religious works celebrating each. In the Tang dynasty, for example, Yang Huizhi sculpted images of the Jade Emperor, a Daoist entity, as well as images of Vimalakirti, Vaishravana, and the five hundred arhats of Buddhism. In the Yuan dynasty, a time of religious tolerance, Anige, a Nepalese working for a Mongol patron, was commanded by imperial edict to sculpt statues of Confucius and the Ten Sages for the Imperial College in 1274 and a group of Daoist statues for the Chongzhen Wanshou Temple in 1295. In 1304–1305 he cast a 5-meter-high statue of Buddha for the Donghuayuan Monastery, along with a Thousand-handed and Thousand-eyed Guanyin and Buddhas of the Five Directions for the Shengshou Wanning Monastery. Liu Yuan, a student of Anige's, also made many famous Buddhist and Daoist statues.

If the major task of religious art in China was to create human images in line with doctrinal rules, making images of the founders of the three major belief systems became the foremost task of master sculptors. Guo Ruoxu of the Song dynasty provided guidelines for painters that would apply to sculptors as well: "The Buddhist images should show faces of benevolence and wisdom; the Daoist images must have the demeanor of immortality and divine deliverance; and the Confucian sages must have a manner evincing loyalty, faithfulness, and righteousness."[7]

For Buddhism, an imported religion, it was necessary to win Chinese believers by representing as truly as possible the features and tenets of the Buddha. At the same time, artists wished to follow orthodox guidelines, which guaranteed the spiritual efficacy of the icons. Starting in the Han dynasty, eminent and learned monks traveled to India for Buddhist scriptures and images, and foreign monks brought the same to China. To scholars today, these materials offer clues to the development of Buddhism in India, as well as to the sinicization of the Indian tradition as it moved east.

Buddhas of the highest echelon were highly stylized. Although standard representations of the Buddha underwent many changes in bodily form as they were made more Chinese, facial expressions, attire, and other features remained unchanged. The thirty-two major marks (*lakshana*) and eighty minor marks were fixed, as was the arrangement of grouped statues. Images of the bodhisattvas, disciples, Heavenly Kings, demigods, and arhats, however, were more realistic and were subject to considerable change. The famous example is the transformation over time of Avalokiteshvara, the Indian male bodhisattva, into Guanyin, a Chinese goddess, by, among other things, removing the moustache. An eminent monk in the Tang dynasty lamented that although Indian-style Buddhist images of the Southern Dynasties (specifically, the Liu Song and Southern Qi dynasties) had thick lips, high noses, slanting eyes, and full lower jaws that made them look powerful and manly, the same figures had been represented as gentle and fragile court ladies since the beginning of the Tang. Indeed, viewers today liken these bodhisattvas to palace maids. In such changes we can see the considerable imagination of Chinese artists, which reflected the evolving values and attitudes of Buddhists in China.

Daoist art undoubtedly borrowed from Buddhist art. But images of the founders of Daoism were also based in part on idealized images of Chinese scholar-officials. The pantheon of Daoist divinities contained government ministers, civil officials, and generals, as well as people from other walks of life. This connection with ordinary people fostered a realism in Daoist iconography that may have also filled a gap between Confucianism and Buddhism. Confucianism stresses self-cultivation through the classics, whereas Buddhism emphasizes the educational role of iconography. In early images, Confucius mainly appeared as either an aged scholar or an emperor wearing a crown and holding a jade tablet. In the Ming dynasty, after a debate broke out in the court over whether to allow statues of Confucius to be made, sculpted images of the famous scholar were replaced with wooden tablets for enshrinement and worship.

In China, sculpture and painting are closely related, and some early works combine the two — for example, Han stone and brick reliefs placed in tomb chambers. These reliefs are in fact paintings that can be touched in the dark. Reliefs produced later, such as the painted marble relief of female attendants and musicians in the tomb chamber of Wang Chuzhi of the Five Dynasties, are set off by mural draperies and include more painting elements than sculptural elements (see frontispiece).[8]

Because painting and painters enjoyed far more prestige than did sculptors, painters are often thought to have greatly influenced sculptural styles and designs. Some scholars counter that this view filters sculptural dynamics through our conception of painting and weakens our understanding of how sculptors developed their own art. Whatever the case, historical texts identify very few ancient sculptors by name, even though countless sculptures were produced in China.

We know of two sculptors who played a noteworthy role in promoting the sinicization of Buddhist images. Dai Kui and Dai Yong, father and son, who lived during the Eastern Jin (317–420) and Liu Song dynasties (420–479), produced a large number of Buddhist images made of wood, clay, and bronze — too many to keep a record of, as the seventh-century *Pearl Grove of the Dharma Garden* (*Fayuan zhulin*) notes. Because Buddhism was later suppressed, none of their works survive, yet their influence was enormous. They reinterpreted Buddhist iconography in a Chinese mode, giving their statues an individual look, and advanced new techniques for handling proportion in large Buddhist statues, along with other innovations.[9] Among Dai Yong's contributions was the use of molds for making ramie-reinforced clay and gilt-bronze statues of the Buddha and some bodhisattvas. Among Dai Kui's were the five "walking" statues in the Waguan Temple in Nanjing, which reportedly moved mechanically.

The Dais notwithstanding, most sculptors labored in obscurity, unlike many painters; and whatever the overall influence of painting on sculpture, it did lend certain qualities to sculpture, including a profound attention to outlines. Lines, an important means of representation in Chinese painting, became an essential component of sculpture. From the Northern Qi (550–577) through the Tang, two styles of painting in particular are thought to have influenced the making of Buddhist statues. In the first style, that of the famous Northern Qi painter Cao Zhongda, clothes appear to "cling as though wet."[10] His Indian-style Buddhist images may well have inspired the tight robes with decorative pleats unique to Buddhist statues of that era.

Wu Daozi, a famous Tang painter, contributed the second style: forceful strokes graced with simple, light touches of color.[11] Although none of his paintings survive, he reportedly loved to portray upper-class men and women in loose, flowing clothes. Dong Jiong, a scholar and art critic during the Song dynasty, once said that Wu's figures looked "sculpted," as if the viewer could walk around them and appreciate them from any angle. He described the brushstrokes as "thin and sweeping, looking like winding copper wires. The viewer is able to discern the depressions and bulges of the bones and muscles, which are touched lightly or coated heavily with red powder." Not only did Wu add a kind of anatomically correct three-dimensionality to his figure paintings; he also made Buddhist sculptures, once decorating the statues of Manjushri and Vimalakirti in the Great Xiangguo Temple in present-day Kaifeng.[12]

The styles shaped by Cao Zhongda and Wu Daozi probably influenced sculptural patterns of their respective ages. When people view the Northern Wei Buddhist statues in Cave 147 in the Maijishan caves or the large Tang statue of Vairocana in the Longmen grottoes, for example, many are touched not only by the kind, sympathetic, yet solemn faces of the Buddha, but also by the elegant and natural cloth patterns.

Yang Huizhi, a student of Wu Daozi's, was skilled in individualizing images of people. His creations were diverse, ranging from a statue of the Jade Emperor, ruler of Heaven, for the Taihua Daoist Temple (it was used during the Song dynasty as the model for the Jade Emperor of Yuqing Zhaoying Palace) to statues of the Buddha and Vimalakirti in the Great Xiangguo Temple. According to some traditional accounts, Yang Huizhi developed the model of both the Thousand-handed Guanyin and the mountain-water wall sculpture (made of mud dried on a wall and painted), later popularized by Guo Xi, a famous sculptor in the Song dynasty.[13]

A mid-Tang artist, Zhou Fang, who excelled at portraiture, made colorful paintings of plump court ladies. Again, some sculptures were probably modeled after his images, including his greatest contribution, the Water-Moon Guanyin, a painting of the bodhisattva looking at the moon reflected in water.

The connection between Chinese painting and sculpture is also clear in the pigmentation of sculptural art. Most sculptures from ancient China are colored, including those made from such materials as clay, timber, bronze, and stone. In sculpture, it was said, 30 percent of the effort was devoted to carving and 70 percent to painting. Although the ways of adding color to statues have not been handed down, the theory and methods governing the composition of paints and the methods of coloring developed by painters in the various dynasties reflect contemporary aesthetic tendencies.

Decorative coloring has particular importance in religious sculpture: skill was required to place gold foil on and add tints to Buddhist images. Wang Wenlie, who worked in the Five Dynasties period, decorated the sitting Amitabha Buddha cast by Yang Huizhi for the Great Xiangguo Temple. Because "the painted face of the gold [gilt-bronze] Buddha possesses all the features of great compassion," it was listed as one of the "ten superb views" at the monastery.[14]

Sculptural achievements, however beautifully executed, were overseen by political and religious leaders. Very early in Chinese history, in the Shang and Zhou periods, the state subsumed sculpture under architecture or handicrafts. It exercised complete control, providing working and living arrangements, raw materials, and tools. Quality was strictly measured and standards enforced; if a finished sculpture did not conform, punishments were meted out. Putting the name of a sculptor on a work was done only to indicate quality, not to give credit. Consequently there were few independent sculptural works, and those who made them were *baigong* (artisans in different trades), including managers of workshops, designers, and manufacturers. Among the seven kinds of tradesmen who served the rulers with their skills, the social status of the baigong was the lowest. Their skills were passed down from generation to generation, and they were not allowed to change to other professions.

Rulers did not encourage artistic invention, fearing that it might inspire heretical ideas and disrupt their quest for ideological uniformity: "major innovations should not be made." The *Book of Rites* repeatedly stressed that artisans should be forbidden to create "obscene and ingenious artifacts"; violators were to be severely punished. Such views failed, however, to smother artistic imagination. As the economy expanded, society underwent rapid, large-scale changes, and by the Eastern Zhou the restrictions set by Confucian doctrine largely vanished. Among the newly emerging elite the desire for material comfort grew, encouraging the development of "ingenious skills and rare artifacts."[15] Handicrafts flourished, and the baigong system collapsed, giving rise to a large number of individually known artisans, including sculptors. Still, for the next two thousand years, until the nineteenth century, large-scale sculptural projects remained under the control of the government, and the creators of sculptural works could never rise above their position as artisans. They were ranked from assistant artisan (*xiangjiang*) to ingenious artisan (*qiaojiang*) to artisan (*sujiang*), but even the most accomplished were held in contempt by scholars and officials, who continued to hold conservative ideas about the relative status of the various arts; music was thought to be of a higher status than art, and within the arts, calligraphy and painting were held in higher esteem than sculpture.[16]

Probably because of this bias against sculpture, Dai Kui and Dai Yong were among the few eminent scholars to create sculptural works.[17] Nor do we know of any scholars who studied or wrote about sculpture in ancient times. The artisans themselves seem not to have recorded their experiences and insights either. We might infer that Yang Huizhi's *Rhymes of Sculpture (Su jue)* sums up his practical experience, but the fragments are far from constituting a theoretical work. The extant ancient textual materials on sculpture, such as the *Record of Painting and Sculpture in the Yuan Dynasty (Yuandai huasu ji)*, mainly list the regulations for carving and decorating religious sculptural works and do not include any of the theory behind the art.[17]

Stone steles are of little help. Although they offer epigraphic records for some important sculptural creations of ancient times, they mainly record the reasons a work was created, the names of those who presided over its creation, and the date. The names of the artisans who actually produced such masterpieces as the huge statue of Vairocana in Fengxian Temple, Longmen, Henan Province, are not mentioned. Works that have been admired for centuries remain unattributed.

Today we study as high art the sculptures, large and small, left by nameless sculptors. Although they did not leave us treatises on approaches or principles, each outstanding sculpture they created offers clues to the secular and religious influences that shaped their work and the methods they used to make it. Mysteries remain in China's far too little explored world of sculpture. But if we can decipher the sculptures themselves, many questions about this marvelous legacy of Chinese art may be solved.

Introduction

ANGELA FALCO HOWARD

Over nearly two millennia foreign influences and imperial patronage propelled the development and spread of both secular and religious art in China. Indeed, sculpture as the result of cutting or carving into stone or wood was not an art form indigenous to the Han Chinese, the ethnic majority of Chinese. And although sculptural techniques were never applied exclusively to Buddhist images, once Buddhism was introduced into China in the first century, those techniques were closely linked to the evolution of Buddhist traditions and practices.

This dual dynamic — foreign inspiration and indigenous elite support — produced stunning three-dimensional art for at least a thousand years, from the time Buddhism took hold in the latter part of the Han dynasty to the end of the Song. During the Song (960–1279), Buddhism and its arts reached a pinnacle: Chinese Buddhism was rooted in social and intellectual life, and its maturity was regarded as truly representative of China's doctrinal and aesthetic attainments. Imperial patronage of religion and the arts achieved new heights as well.

Another example of this important dynamic of imperial patronage and non-Han influences came later, from Tibet, starting with the Yuan dynasty (1271–1368). Tibeto-Chinese sculpture, shaped by a multicultural Inner Asian perspective, was troubling to many Han

Chinese because its Yuan and, later, Qing patrons were the conquering Mongols and Manchus of those two dynasties. Tibetan-inspired sculpture during the Yuan dynasty was radically different in content and appearance from the sculpture achieved in the Song, which was the product of a great Buddhist synthesis. Indigenous sculpture lost its harmonious balance in the Yuan because the Mongol emperors' adoption of Tibetan Buddhism and its arts raised for the subject Chinese fundamental questions of self-identity.

To present China's rich and complex sculptural legacy, this book is divided into two parts: one devoted to mortuary sculpture — sometimes referred to as a secular art — and another dealing with Buddhist, Daoist, and Confucianist sculpture, or religious art. The first part of the book covers mortuary sculpture from prehistoric times to the Han (Chapter 1), bringing us into the Common Era, and tomb sculptures above and below ground from the Han up through the Qing, bringing us into the twentieth century (Chapter 2). The second part covers Buddhist sculpture — sculptures in cave temples, independent sculptures, gilt-bronze sculptures, and sculpted steles — from the introduction of Buddhism in China to the Song, that is, from the third century to the thirteenth (Chapter 3), as well as sculptures in monasteries, temples, and shrines from the Song through the Qing (Chapter 4).

The bipartite division into secular and religious art is designed to help present Chinese sculpture in its historical complexity, not to indicate a sharp distinction between the two sculptural traditions, for they clearly developed side by side. To interpret the one tradition of art as exclusively secular would be as profoundly misleading as to interpret the other as exclusively religious. All traditional Chinese sculpture is inseparable from powerful belief systems — systems that respond in different ways to interpretations of the supernatural, to visions of the afterworld, and to the demands of temporal political power. As Wu Hung and Yang Hong explain in their chapters, burial art of various sizes and mediums, both aboveground and belowground, was influenced by beliefs that date back to the Shang dynasty or perhaps earlier. At the same time, although such art had a religious quality, much of it can also be considered a manifestation of state rituals.

The art discussed by Angela Howard and Li Song in the second part of the book is the expression of Buddhism, Daoism, and Confucianism, three distinct systems of thought. Buddhism was a foreign religion, but the Han Chinese thoroughly assimilated most of its teachings (except Tibetan Esoteric developments) and made it an essential component of their culture. Buddhism was just as influential on art as were Daoism and Confucianism, China's native systems of thought.

Buddhist and Daoist sculptures were responses to firmly set beliefs, in contrast with tomb sculpture, which was a response to a rather amorphous ethos that evolved to suit the demands of a given social and political context. The interaction was mutual: as artisans kept pace with an ever expanding political-intellectual context, their efforts enriched both Daoism and Buddhism. Similarly, the two systems of belief reacted to each other and benefited mutually from their diverse teachings. Artistically, Buddhist art became a model to the other.

This distinction between burial sculpture as the expression of Chinese state ritual and Buddhist and Daoist sculptures as the products of well-articulated ideologies backed by an organized structure is reflected in other differences. The earlier, burial tradition, from its Neolithic to its later phases, did not give rise to jade artifacts, clay pots, metal vessels, or carved figures as self-contained artistic works — that is, as sculptures in their own right. Such creations were often remarkably beautiful and represent an extraordinary aesthetic sensibility. Nonetheless, they were primarily intended as tomb furnishings, utilitarian objects for drinking and cooking, or as architectural embellishments.

What most profoundly divides the earlier and later works, however, is not doctrine but technology — how the sculptures were made. As Wu Hung points out, the Chinese distinguished between "modeling" and "carving," two different approaches applied consistently over time. Which was used depended on the medium. Modeling with clay was predominantly an additive process that involved piecing together sections of the work, whether it was ultimately shaped like a container, a human being, or an animal. The same process was used to execute bronze vessels. But stone and wooden sculptures required carving, a taking away. To make jade objects the artist also used a reductive process, abrading and polishing the hard stone, but this was not comparable to the techniques later applied to sandstone, limestone, and marble. The carving of stone sculptures became popular in China with the spread of Buddhism: icons were needed to offer devotion to, and by making them, buying them, or providing them to places of worship, believers acquired merit. The icons were made initially according to iconographic and stylistic conventions established in India. With the introduction of stone carving, sculpture became figurative, and the stone figures were exhibited in temples and shrines. No doubt Chinese monuments carved in stone, such as the tomb of General Huo Qubing (d. 113 B.C.E.), antedate Buddhist statuary (see fig. 1.51); but such monuments cannot be regarded as the fountainhead of all the ensuing figurative sculptures linked to religious beliefs.

Whether modeled or carved, functional or figurative, not every three-dimensional work of art executed in China is a sculpture, however we define the word. In this book we use the word *sculpture* loosely, ignoring its Western origin and its specificity of reference, traditionally in the West, to statues and reliefs.

For many Westerners, *sculpture* conjures up the idea of great artists — of styles they forged that in turn inspired their followers. Before the modern period, however, the word also encompassed anonymously carved friezes on classical public buildings and statues of saints in medieval cathedrals executed according to prevailing modes in style and material — much as in China, where most works were produced anonymously and in strict conformity to function. Whether a matter of modeling or carving, sculpture in China was, on the whole, a nameless undertaking, and most Chinese sculptures were buried in tombs for the benefit of the dead. In contrast, typical Western practice through the ages has been to exhibit sculpture in churches, homes, plazas, and other living spaces. Chinese burial objects included bronze vessels decorated with figurines, carved jade ornaments, and so forth — kinds of works that are typically not part of the Western sculptural tradition.

From roughly the second century C.E. until the division of the country in 317, the production of religious artifacts was driven by a still incomplete reading of Buddhist doctrine and lacked the supervision of an established clergy; in addition, the rituals for which the artifacts were the focus were not yet organized. Even if the images resembled those used in Buddhist worship, they were not self-contained images with specific Buddhist antecedents, not sculptures proper, but everyday forms taken from customary Han burial objects. Their style was also tinged by popularized Daoist beliefs, which, like Buddhist beliefs, were at an initial stage of development. Burial objects — figurines, models of houses, mirrors, and soul urns (*hunping*) — were placed in the tombs of affluent members of society who held a view of Buddhism that was consistent with an ongoing interest in Daoist religion and art (see fig. 2.1).

During these early centuries both Buddhism and Daoism developed their respective iconographies. It is generally accepted that Buddhism was grafted onto preexisting Daoist beliefs and that the Buddha image became interchangeable with that of the Daoist goddess Xiwangmu, Queen Mother of the West. Sichuan Province, in the southwest, was a melting pot for the two diverse and nascent movements that evolved side by side and became two distinct Chinese religions. The surviving artifacts are noticeably ambiguous; indeed, it is difficult to distinguish the respective contributions of each belief system. Later on, Daoist sculpture relied heavily on the conventions established for statues of Buddhist deities.

Although the element of patronage is not recognizable in the artifacts themselves, it is clear that Buddhist beliefs and the associated ritual items came from abroad. Examples of proto-Buddhist sculpture have been found in Sichuan, along the upper reaches of the Yangzi River, and in the coastal provinces of Jiangsu and Zhejiang. All of these locations were linked to the outside world: Sichuan was at the confluence of roads and rivers that — through Yunnan Province and, in the north, through the Gansu corridor to central Asia (see map 3.2) — linked it ultimately to India. The coastal provinces communicated with India by sea.

During the period of disunion (317–589), when Buddhism first spread and developed, the Chinese were receptive to the newly imported teachings in part because Buddhism had not taken firm shape. At that time

as well, the issue of ethnicity did not surface, even though the rulers were non-Han Chinese. They were Xiongnu and Xianbei of Turkic and Mongolian stock, Qiang and Di related to Tibetans and Tanguts, and Jie people now believed to have been Indoscythians. Imperial patronage for the later Buddhism originating from Tibet was a different story, of alien dynasties penetrating the surface of Chinese society and, at some level, altering the Han character of Buddhist art. The split between Han or traditional Buddhist art and non-Han or Vajrayana (Esoteric) art derived from the central Asian model became a reality under the Yuan dynasty, with its Mongol rulers, and was thereafter a key element of the Buddhist sculptural legacy in China. Buddhist sculpture from the Yuan to the Qing developed within this quite changed context.

Emperors influenced the sculptural art of China in later years not merely through their wealth and patronage but also through their desire to transform the imported doctrines and images into truly Chinese expressions of belief. Imperial patronage repeatedly emerges as critical for understanding Buddhist sculptural developments. Kublai Khan, the second Yuan emperor, initiated the special relationship between the emperor as patron, his lama teachers, and foreign artists that persisted during the Yuan and the Qing dynasties. Equally important were the foreign Buddhist hierarchs who acted as preceptors to the emperors and established the doctrinal guidelines for producing the devotional art.

During the Ming dynasty personal and political ties between the Chinese emperors and the Tibetan prelates were again strong. During the reign of the Yongle emperor (r. 1403–1424), there was a proliferation of gilt bronzes bearing his reign mark that were fashioned jointly by Tibetan and Chinese artists and artisans. Many were given to lamas as tokens of respect when they returned to Tibet; others were kept for the devotional practices of the emperor and his court.

During the Qing dynasty patronage remained significant for the flowering of Tibetan Buddhism: the Kangxi emperor (r. 1662–1722) and his grandson, the Qianlong emperor (r. 1736–1795), for example, whom eminent lamas initiated into Vajrayana Buddhism, supported the faith vigorously. This late imperial period generated an important synthesis of several imported stylistic trends, as numerous artists from Tibet and equally talented Han Chinese artisans were brought together by the court and encouraged to follow the traditions of Vajrayana Buddhism.

Exciting new discoveries over the past fifty years

have profoundly transformed our understanding of how Buddhist sculpture developed in China from the late Han dynasty through the Song. Significantly, much of the great art, especially during the Tang and Song dynasties, was "peripheral" or regional, not produced under the supervision of the central government. A deep-seated regionalism controlled the dynamics of Buddhist art during the entire period of disunion, from the fourth to the sixth centuries, as Chapter 3 details. Innovations in style and doctrine usually originated at the periphery, then were absorbed at more powerful political and artistic centers, which were often connected with dynastic capitals.

A robust pluralism of aesthetic idioms and content can be seen, for example, in the artistic legacy of the Liang patrons who governed the Gansu corridor during the fourth and early fifth centuries; in the artistic traditions developed by the Qin rulers of Shaanxi Province; and in the manufacture of outstanding gilt bronzes in Hebei Province under the Zhao rulers. The art created at these three centers merged by 439 into the Northern Wei style practiced in Pingcheng (present-day Datong) and Luoyang, the capitals of the Northern Wei (386–534), a dynasty established by the non-Han Tuoba, who unified all the territories in the northern part of China from Shandong to Gansu Provinces.

The making of Buddhist art in the south paralleled that in the central plains of the north. Astonishing discoveries of Buddhist sculptures — manufactured at different times in areas administered by or having close contact with the southern capital of Nanjing — enable us to speculate about the style and content of this lost art of the south. The retrieval of two hundred pieces of sculpture from the site once occupied by the Longxing Temple in Qingzhou capped almost a decade of excavations in Shandong Province. Politically and culturally Shandong was under the influence of Nanjing, the capital of the Southern Dynasties. Among evidence found in Sichuan and Shandong are several steles dated to the Southern Liang dynasty (502–557) and Buddha images that we take as representative of the southern style (see figs. 3.75 and 3.77).

The northern and southern styles were dramatically different. The southern style emphasized realism and three-dimensionality in humanized images. Among other innovations, southern iconographies paired the Amitabha and Maitreya Buddhas, represented Avalokiteshvara as the central figure of a group (a distinction otherwise reserved for the Buddha), and placed deities in landscape settings — an important step toward representing paradises, or Pure Lands. In addition, Southern Liang art, as seen in Sichuan and Shandong, alerts us to the inclusion of the Gupta style of India, which superseded the introduction of the Gandharan style.

The Buddhist art of the period of disunion, then, is marked by splendid artistic syntheses. The various styles that emerged in the second half of the sixth century — during the short-lived Northern Zhou, Northern Qi, and Sui dynasties — reveal complex regional dynamics. The Northern Zhou style, for example, with its animated, ornate surface decor, was the outgrowth of an Indian style that had roots in Sichuan, whereas the sturdy, blocklike bodies of Northern Zhou statuary reflected a local preference in northwest Gansu, Ningxia, and Shaanxi (see fig. 3.88). Central Asian influences can be seen in recent discoveries in Taiyuan (Shanxi Province) and Xi'an (Shaanxi Province), where Persian deities and fire rituals practiced by Zoroastrian devotees were the subjects of sculpted marble slabs made for wealthy Sogdian merchants (figs. 2.22, 2.38).

An uninterrupted stream of religious teachings and icons reached China from various directions at this time. The Silk Road was the major conveyor of images and sacred architecture from India. The southwest route — from India through present-day Myanmar (once Burma) to Yunnan Province — and the maritime route from India to China's east coast also played an important role in transmission. Because of so many external influences acting at once, sculptural images — in gilt bronze, stone, clay, and wood — had an international character. The influx of foreign doctrines and artistic models, together with the infusion of patronage from both regional and imperial authorities, also produced enormous and lavishly ornamented cave temples.

During the roughly three centuries when China was split into north and south, Buddhism was gradually transformed into a native religion, one fully supported by a solid monastic and textual tradition. In contrast with the art of the preceding proto-Buddhist phase, the art of this period sprang from a theological body of work disseminated by foreign and native clergy. The images also reflected the proselytizing of monks preaching different aspects of Buddhism.

Once China was unified under the Tang dynasty (618–907), sculptural output reached new heights. The unobstructed expansion of the empire on the Asian continent, as well as the unprecedented commercial and cultural exchanges with many foreign countries, transformed the urban centers of China — especially Chang'an, the capital — into international metropolises. Sculptors, exposed to an array of styles, broadened their perspective, coming eventually to favor a more natural and realistic look over the highly stylized abstraction and linearity of earlier styles. Not to be underestimated is the possible influence of figure painting, which also reached maturity at this time.

The more realistic style suited the contemporary interpretations of Buddhist doctrines, which challenged sculptors and painters with their philosophical depth. The eighth-century marble sculptures of the Tianlongshan cave temples in Shanxi Province and the opulent statuary of Xi'an best embody the worldly realism of the Tang age. The group of sculptural works retrieved from the ruins of the Xiangguo Temple in Xi'an illustrate the doctrinal complexities of the newly imported Indian Esoteric Buddhism. The wrathful Esoteric images shown with multiple arms and heads, possibly benefiting from the development of illusionism in Buddhist painting (the Dunhuang murals specifically), were fully carved in the round and took on lively poses. The exclusively frontal views and static composure of earlier sculptures had been abandoned.

Although a rather uniform stylistic language prevailed during the Tang, experiment continued on the artistic fringe. Sichuan, for example, though an integral part of the empire, had unique aesthetic concerns because of its massive production of rock-cut sculptures. Local landowners and thriving commercial interests sponsored vast projects that rivaled the imposing cave temples of Longmen, built in Henan Province under imperial patronage. Secularism and materialism even informed Sichuanese interpretations of Pure Lands, where deities gathered, as if patrons wished to affirm that their earthly comforts were fit for the spiritual world.

Another area of innovation was the Nanzhao monarchy, located in present-day Yunnan, which was cut off from the cultural activity of the Tang capital. At its apogee during the late ninth century, the Nanzhao produced lavish gilt bronzes and even gold images quite distinct from other northern artifacts (see fig. 3.156). (Yunnanese Esoteric deities indicate a possible Himalayan derivation.) Not only is the formal language of Nanzhao sculpture independent of and dissimilar to the contemporary imperial Tang style, but its subject matter is exclusively indigenous: it celebrates the monarchy of Yunnan and its tutelary deities.

The roughly three hundred years of Song rule, beginning in the tenth century, was a time of profound change as China interacted with and adapted to ethnically diverse Inner Asian tribal nations that had eroded China's territorial integrity along its northern borders. Foreign influence and imperial patronage took on a novel relevance as three conquest dynasties ruled over portions of northern China side by side and at the same time as the native Song. The Khitan of the Liao dynasty (907–1125) and the Jurchen of the Jin dynasty (1115–1234) occupied China's northeast and a part of the central plains, while the Tangut of the Western Xia (Xi Xia; 1038–1227) extended their rule over the northwest and parts of present-day Xinjiang. Although the three groups were primarily Buddhist, their perspectives on matters of art and faith were distinct. The influence of the Tangut Western Xia was undoubtedly the strongest and most profound because it introduced new developments in Tibetan Buddhism. The Western Xia, moreover, advocated a non-Han model of rulership in which the emperor and his adviser, the Imperial Preceptor, held temporal and spiritual authority, respectively.[1] This form of government later became a model for the Mongol Yuan dynasty.

These political and religious developments challenged China's existing Buddhist tradition both doctrinally and artistically. The spread of Tibetan Buddhist teachings and its related art gave rise to a dual system. Chinese now had at their disposal traditional Buddhist teachings that by the Song era had reached a brilliant stage of maturity, as well as an alien body of doctrines and art that had matured in Tibet. From this time on, the two systems coexisted, but because they addressed the needs of ethnically diverse peoples, they never merged.

Traditional Song sculpture was innovative in several ways. The building of cave temples diminished, especially in the central plains of the north, possibly in part because of an increase in opulently decorated temples like the imperially sponsored Great Xiangguo Temple in Kaifeng, known to us only through literary sources.[2] Where cave temples continued to be carved out, as in the provinces of Sichuan and Shaanxi, profound stylistic and structural changes took place. Sichuan sculpture became monumental, with expanded niches throughout a site. In addition, cave sculptors seemed to be striving for an all-encompassing doctrinal message. At Baodingshan, in Dazu County, Chongqing, for example, which was completed around 1249, the idea of compartmentalized niches was abandoned; instead, the site featured about thirty enormous reliefs grouped together and linked thematically.[3] The huge sculptural compositions described the major schools of Buddhism thriving during the autumnal years of the Song: the Huayan School, whose teachings derived from the

Garland Sutra; the Pure Land School; Chan (Zen) Buddhism and its related cult of the arhat (*luohan*); the teaching of the Full Enlightenment sect; and the widespread cult of Guanyin (the Chinese incarnation of Avalokiteshvara). In addition to traditional deities there were often Esoteric ones, such as the Brilliant Kings of Wisdom, the Great Peacock King, and the Thousand-headed, Thousand-handed Guanyin, which had been introduced to the Chinese during the initial Tang transmission, not through subsequent Tibetan Western Xia teachings.

The Shaanxi cave temples built during the Northern Song and Jin dynasties also offered startling new features. Many are situated in the northwest of the province, isolated from urban centers; a few are in and around Yan'an. These grottoes, which were often built with the support of the local elite (often military leaders), were constructed according to similar plans and use an iconography suggestive of a grand temple interior. At the center of the squarish cave is a huge tripartite altar on which appear a Buddha triad with their retinue. Above them is an ornately carved well-ceiling, receding into space. The sturdy pilasters that divide the altar into three parts, along with the surrounding walls of the cave, are covered with thousands of carved images of varying sizes depicting the One Thousand Buddhas, the arhats (generally in sets of sixteen), Wenshu (Manjushri) and Puxian (Samantabhadra), the Water-Moon Guanyin, the Parinirvana, and the charismatic monk Sengie (a manifestation of Guanyin). The depictions amount to a local grouping of traditional deities.

Song sculpture in general, especially the images of bodhisattvas, achieved an idealized, urbane portrayal of the divine figure that fit the climate of humanism pervading elite culture. Only in the portrayal of the arhats can a trace of the realism promoted by Tang patrons be seen.

Liao and Jin sculptors distanced themselves from Song aesthetic ideals, though not completely. The Liao clay images adorning the five-storied Shakyamuni Pagoda built in 1056 as part of the Fogong Temple at Yingxian County, Shanxi Province, betray an awareness of Tibetan style in the increased formalism of their appearance and in the diminished naturalism of the body and the facial expressions. Similar influences are visible in Jin temple sculptures.

Western Xia sculpture, which radically moves away from the coeval Song style, was not a derivation of Tibetan models but an independent interpretation of Tibetan Buddhism. Deities unknown to the Chinese were fashioned for the temples of the Hui Autonomous Region (as it is today called), where the Western Xia had their capital, and for the Yulin caves, near Anxi, in Gansu Province.[4]

Tangut Western Xia Buddhist sculpture was directly nourished by ideas and images carried by Tibetan missionaries on their way to the Liao and Jin courts. It also found models in the illustrations of the canon sponsored by the court. The Western Xia emperor Renzong (r. 1139–1193) asked the Tibetan lama Tsang Popa of the Karmapa School to reside at court and teach him about Buddhism. Thus came into being the special bond between lama and patron subsequently instituted by the Mongol and Manchu emperors. The merging of temporal and spiritual power gave patronage a new meaning.

Buddhist sculpture of the Yuan dynasty broke unequivocally with the past as Tibetan Buddhism became the official religion of the Mongols. Finalizing a situation initiated by the Western Xia court, Kublai Khan (r. 1260–1294) invited the lama Phagspa to Beijing. Phagspa became the Imperial Preceptor, and he in turn invited a group of Nepalese artists to court. They set up a workshop to create the images needed for Tibetan-tradition Buddhist rituals. Anige, their leader, was enormously influential across the entire spectrum of Tibetan-related art — sculpture, architecture, and painting.[5]

After Kublai, numerous Chinese emperors — Mongol, Han Chinese (during the Ming), and Manchu — relied on foreign artists for the production of Tibetan Buddhism–related art, setting up court workshops where artists of different nationalities could collaborate. The Imperial Preceptors established guidelines on how the images were to be made. For two of the last three dynasties (Yuan and Qing), then, the patron emperors of China were not Chinese, and non-Chinese artists were creating non-Chinese images that often required imported alloys and techniques. Yet this artistic production was an integral part of China's culture and, during the Yuan dynasty, defined traditional sculptural art.

Mongol emperors might have displaced Han Chinese emperors, but Tibetan Buddhism images simply took their place alongside Chinese Buddhist images, whose style had developed since the introduction of Buddhism in China. Although the political situation was perhaps not unlike that after northern China fell under alien Tuoba rule, the reaction to Tibetan Buddhism was completely different from the earlier reaction to Indian Buddhism. Chinese Buddhism was still incipient in the fourth and fifth centuries, but by the thirteenth century doctrine and art had reached such a mature and brilliant level that the Chinese regarded them as the embodiment of their intellectual and artistic ideals. The Chinese were consequently not interested in the religion of the Mongol rulers — who had usurped China's independence and drawn China into an Inner Asian empire. Then and now the Chinese have been reluctant to assess the effect of Tibetan Esoteric Buddhism on their art, although it is a facet of Chinese culture that shone resplendently until the end of the imperial age.

Between 1368 and 1644, during the Ming dynasty, imperial rule reverted to native Chinese emperors. Imperial patronage and interest in Tibetan Buddhist art continued, however, albeit with different degrees of intensity, depending on the emperor. Some emperors established very close ties with Tibetan hierarchs. Foremost among them was the Yongle emperor, of the early fifteenth century, whose interest was shared by the imperial household and the official elite. Some historians have interpreted the imperial leaning toward the alien religion as a diplomatic choice designed to maintain harmony between China's central government and a polycentric Inner Asian world. Yet the Han Chinese emperors may also have been genuinely interested in the faith.

Meanwhile, lama teachers and foreign artisans kept arriving in the capital. Among the most illustrious visitors was Helima, the Fifth Karmapa, who at the Yongle emperor's request officiated at special funerary rites for his father and his mother, Empress Ma, at the Linggu Monastery in Nanjing. The Fifth Karmapa became the Yongle emperor's guru and was so favored that the emperor lavished on him gifts of bronzes modeled on the Tibetan bronzes given earlier to the Ming envoy.

The exchange of gifts — characteristic with this type of Buddhist art — perpetuated the imported style. Indeed, Tibeto-Chinese gilt bronzes of the last three imperial dynasties (Yuan, Ming, and Qing) are fairly uniform in style, in contrast with the profoundly evolved style of those made earlier. Gift giving may also be partly responsible for the abundance of modestly sized gilt bronzes and the scarcity of sculptures executed in stone and wood, especially bulky or heavy ones, which could not have been transported easily. In addition, it is possible that the rules governing Tibetan Buddhism required that many icons be displayed in a specific formation. For the average temple or sacred building, a plethora of icons could be on display only if they were of modest proportions.

Generally Tibeto-Chinese bronzes of the fifteenth century follow their foreign models closely. Those bearing the mark of the Yongle reign, however, show traits that we can ascribe to imperial taste — namely, intricate ornamentation, exquisitely precise manufacture, and a mannered elegance. The deities' faces are unnaturally round and are accented by heavy eyelids, rounded cheeks, diminutive chins, and sensuously protruding lips. These formal qualities are also visible in the gilt bronzes made for the Xuande and Chenghua emperors later in the century.

In addition to gilt bronze, traditional Buddhist sculptures were executed in various mediums, and the finished works, which were placed in city temples or more secluded mountain spots, were inspired by the teachings of the major schools — Pure Land, Tiantai, Huayan, and Chan — or celebrated the compassion of Guanyin in her numerous manifestations (see fig. 4.65). Throughout the Ming dynasty the imperial largess for and interest in Tibeto-Chinese art did not diminish, although most Chinese supported the more "native" kind of Buddhism. Tibeto-Chinese and traditional sculpture remained distinct. A merging of the two or interchange between them at the doctrinal and artistic levels never occurred. Indeed, they met the needs of different groups of followers.

During the latter part of the Ming, Altan Khan (ca. 1507–1582), leader of the Chahar federation in Inner Mongolia, reasserted the Mongol influence in Inner Asia. Altan Khan not only embraced Tibetan Buddhism as the official religion of his people but also established a special relationship with Tibet by instituting the religious and political authority of the Dalai Lama and the Panchen Lama. The relationship with Tibet's highest spiritual leaders gave Altan Khan enormous power among the entire Mongol population. When the Manchus of northeast Asia prevailed over the Mongols and defeated the Ming ruler, thereby founding the Qing dynasty in China in 1644, they continued this special relationship with Tibet.

During the Qing dynasty (1644–1911), much more than during the preceding Ming, Tibetan Buddhism had an enormous influence on the imperial court. Indeed, the Manchus acted as cultural mediators across Inner Asia (as the Mongols of the Yuan dynasty had done during the thirteenth and fourteenth centuries). Imperial patronage remained enormously important to the arts. One artist who benefited from patronage was the prelate and sculptor Zanabazar (1635–1723) of the Khalkas Mongol federation. Zanabazar's family belonged to the elite of Urga, the capital of the federation, and his father was a Gelug hierach. This exceptionally talented artist was sent to Tibet as a youth for training in religious matters. Recognized as a Living Buddha, Zanabazar received the special teachings of the fifth Dalai Lama and the Panchen Lama. He returned to Khalka accompanied by fifty painters and bronze casters. The parallels with Anige at Kublai's court are striking.[6]

In Khalka, with the splendor of the icons used in Tibet's great temples fresh in mind, Zanabazar undertook his two roles: as the highest prelate in the land and as its supreme artist. Although the style of his gilt bronzes had roots in the Nepali-Tibetan tradition, it was transformed by his own Mongolian taste (see p. 463). This style, one more version of Tibeto-Chinese art, pleased the Kangxi emperor of China, who became his devout and devoted patron.

The Kangxi emperor's grandson, the Qianlong emperor, was also deeply involved with Tibetan Buddhism during his long reign, an involvement that seems to have been sincere and personal as well as expedient — a way to keep a multiethnic and overextended empire at peace.[7] His longtime preceptor, Zhangjia Khutukhtu Rolpay Dorje, was, like Phagspa before him, extremely knowledgeable about religious matters (see fig. 4.93). At the age of eight Rolpay Dorje was recognized as a Living Buddha and assigned to reside in a monastery near Inner Mongolia. But most of his life was spent at the Beijing court as the emperor's adviser and close friend. The Qianlong emperor and Rolpay Dorje oversaw many projects — cataloguing iconographic images, building temples, producing images, graphic images, building temples, producing images, and reprinting the classical canon. The numerous gilt bronzes bearing the Qianlong mark derive from the iconographic sources or compendia commissioned by the emperor and his preceptor together. In these compendia the characteristics and identity of each deity were listed in four languages — Chinese, Manchu, Tibetan, and Mongolian, and these notes became guidelines for making art.[8] The art was displayed in the many sacred buildings erected by the emperor to celebrate Tibetan rituals, such as the Yonghegong, Palace of Eternal Harmony — formerly the residence of the Yongzheng emperor, father of the Qianlong emperor — which in 1744 became the most prominent Tibetan Buddhist temple and monastery in Beijing. Together Rolpay Dorje and the emperor were the prime movers behind the brilliant flowering of Tibetan Buddhism – inspired faith and Tibeto-Chinese art.

Their joint work encapsulates the history of sculpture in China, influenced as it was in various ways at different times by imperial patronage and by alien or external ideas, as well as by regional developments. If the full story of Chinese Buddhist sculptural art — its link to doctrine, its evolution over hundreds of years, and its connections with imperial art — has yet to be fully told, the same is true of other sculptural art. With both the religious and the secular traditions, new archaeological discoveries and scholarly interpretations add constantly to our understanding. Behind the terminology and the explanations, the time lines and the histories, however, stand the sculptures themselves: an amazingly diverse and beautiful creative legacy for us all to enjoy.

Part I   The Secular Tradition

BURIAL ART AND SPIRIT PATHS

CHAPTER I

From the Neolithic to the Han

WU HUNG

Two sets of traditional terms in the Chinese language describe the fundamental methods of sculpture by which an artist can turn a block of stone or a pile of clay into a desirable three-dimensional shape. One set, including *diao* and *ke,* has the general meaning of "carving"; the other, including *dui* and *su,* pertains to different ways of modeling. These basic technical definitions also hark back to the origin of sculpture: this art could have emerged only during the Neolithic period, when human beings learned to make polished stone objects and pottery artifacts. Although some perforated ornaments from the late Paleolithic period (ca. 50,000–10,000 years before the present) had begun to reflect concern with certain formal attributes of an object, such as color and shape, the typical manufactured items of that period were rough stone implements formed from natural pebbles or rocks.[1]

Carving and modeling represent two very different sculptural approaches, however. For a carver, a block of stone or a jade boulder can provide the material substance for the work of art and determine the spatial framework within which the work is conceived. Carving requires tools with which to "reduce" a given mass of raw material to a sculpted form. Sculptures in a hard and precious substance like jade — a material that the ancient Chinese favored from prehistoric times — are necessarily small but demand laborious work and specialized skill. All these features distinguish carving from modeling, which is the most immediate of all sculptural techniques.

Full view of figure 1.2 (*opposite*) and detail of figure 1.35 (*above*)

The artist is free to determine the scale of a modeled sculpture. The material is cheap: natural clay, the most widely used malleable material, can be found in almost every part of China. When clay is moistened and kneaded, it becomes extremely plastic, easily manipulated by hand. For durability, a clay sculpture can be baked in the sun or fired. Whereas the spatial and material limitations of carving both challenge and stimulate the artist's creative response, modeling provides even a nonspecialist with the freedom to experiment with extended forms, varied compositions, and expressive textures.

Carving and modeling are therefore not simply different techniques; they in fact define two basic modes of artistic creation, each associated with particular art mediums and manufacturing processes and implying particular design concepts and modes of artistic imagination. Carved or modeled works often serve specific purposes, and they may be created by artists of different professional status, as carving often requires specific professional knowledge and training. Because of such differences, carving and modeling can never replace each other; rather, they have developed side by side in China since the beginnings of sculpture.

Prehistoric Cultures

Archaeological excavations in China have identified numerous regional Neolithic cultures, most of which developed along small and large rivers. Beginning about 5000 B.C.E., many of these cultures began to form two major regional cultural complexes, which scholar David N. Keightley has named the eastern tradition and the northwestern tradition.[2] Each tradition produced carved and modeled sculptures. Typical works from the eastern tradition include carved jades and monochromic pottery, whereas the northwestern tradition is known for painted pottery and stone sculptures. Within each tradition, sculptors from various regions often fashioned particular kinds of carved and kneaded works, whose distinctive forms and functions signaled indigenous cultural conventions. It would be mistaken, however, to consider these regional differences absolute. In fact, interactions and exchanges often took place between different regions, and archaeologists have observed that during the late Neolithic period, from about 4000 to 2100 B.C.E., an extensive cultural network gradually took shape across much of the continent and laid the foundation for the emerging Chinese civiliza-

tion.[3] In studying the sculpture of this period, therefore, it is important to pay attention to both indigenous forms and broader artistic conventions that increasingly pertained.

The creation of small clay figures probably emerged with pottery making. Early examples of such small figures have been found in many parts of China. A sculpted human head from Mixian County in Henan Province and a human torso from Baoji in Shaanxi Province have both been dated to the late sixth to early fifth millennium B.C.E.[4] Unlike these two examples, which were made in the Yellow River valley in the north, two sculpted human heads found at Hemudu in Zhejiang Province were products of a southeastern culture that flourished in the lower Yangzi River delta around 5000 B.C.E. Both heads feature an elongated face with exaggerated cheekbones. But one head has almond-shaped eyes and a half-open mouth delineated in incised lines. The other head, a grotesque image with an unnaturally pronounced forehead and deep eye sockets, exhibits no linear incisions. Rather, the artist worked exclusively by molding the clay.[5] Besides human forms, images of animals and birds, including pigs, sheep, dogs, swallows, and fish, have also been excavated from various Neolithic sites dating from the sixth to the fifth millennium B.C.E.[6]

Such solid miniature pottery figurines constituted an early tradition of Chinese sculpture that continued throughout the Neolithic period. Another kind of pottery sculpture — hollowed-out vessels shaped like animals or birds — has also been found in several regions. Early examples of such vessels, dating from the fifth to the fourth millennium B.C.E., include a bird-shaped tripod from Huaxian County, Shaanxi Province (fig. 1.1), and a number of animal-shaped jars from Dawenkou in Shandong Province. The Huaxian tripod, in particular, is an exceptionally powerful sculpture in the round. It is quite large — 36 centimeters high — and the artist ingeniously shaped it into an eagle whose body, the hollowed container, is supported by a tail and two strong legs. The real achievement of this work, however, is not its clever shape but the extraordinary impression of volume and weight it conveys. The few details — eyes, beak, and a suggestion of talons — only add to the sense of wholeness. This tripod was from the northwest, but pottery vessels of comparable artistic quality in zoomorphic shapes have been found in the east and south as well. Several vessels from the Dawenkou culture in Shandong Province are in the shape of animals. Standing on all four legs, the animals raise their heads and seem to roar at the sky.[7] Another example, excavated at a Liangzhu-culture site at Wuxian County, Jiangsu Province, resembles a hybrid of a seal and a bird — a fantastic combination that enables the artist to contrast the smooth, swelling outline of a seal's body with the angular bone structure of a bird's head.[8]

By contrast, in the third tradition of Neolithic pottery sculpture the main body of the object is a conventional-looking vessel, and only the elements protruding from it are sculpted. Some relief images found at Hemudu in the southeast, for example, have been identified as decorations from pottery vessels. A majority of these excavated examples were associated with the northwestern tradition, which first flourished along the middle stretch of the Yellow River during the fifth millennium B.C.E. and over the next two millennia gradually shifted its center to the upper Yellow River valley. Three kinds of sculpted images — low-relief, high-relief, and three-dimensional forms — appear on vessels from this vast region. Even the low-relief images were often made separately, from rolls of clay, and then attached to the wall of the vessel. Some of these images are playful: a pottery shard from Miaodigou in Shanxian County, Henan Province, represents a lizard sticking its head over the rim of a basin.[9] Other images may have had particular religious or shamanistic implications. A pottery jar excavated at Liuwan in Ledu, Qinghai Province, for instance, is decorated with a naked woman on one side. Modeled in relief, she has an enormous head, a round belly, prominent breasts, and an emphasized vagina, which she seems to be exposing with both hands.[10] Although it is difficult, if not impossible, to comprehend the precise meaning of this figure, its relation to the image on the reverse side of the vessel is worth noting: instead of a similarly sculpted human figure, we find there a painted, semiabstract image whose arms and legs are suggested by zigzag lines joined to a vertical spine.

A different combination of these two contrasting visual forms — one sculptural and figurative, the other painted and geometric — decorates some other vessels: these feature a painted figure with a high-relief or three-dimensional head protruding from the shoulders of the vessel.[11] Objects with high-relief decoration have been found in various locations in the northwestern provinces of Shaanxi and Gansu. Normally, such sculpted human heads have only rudimentary facial features, but occasionally more careful treatment reflects the attempt to represent a specific person. A pottery fragment from Beishouling in Shaanxi, for example, bears a head of

1.1 Eagle-shaped tripod, earthenware, unearthed in 1957 in Taipingzhuang, Huaxian County, Shaanxi Province. Yangshao culture, 5th–4th millennium B.C.E. 36 cm. National Museum of China, Beijing.

considerable size (7.3 centimeters high). The figure is that of a middle-aged male with a broad face and high cheekbones. His small, slanting eyes and half-open mouth are pierced into the clay, while the strong eyebrows and beard are painted in black pigment.[12]

In a variation on this type of vessel with sculpted elements, the likeness of a human head atop a jar or vase transforms the vessel itself into an analogue of the human body.[13] Some of the heads, which have tattooed faces and snakelike braids winding down from short horns, may represent supernatural beings; others are naturalistic images of men and women. A red pottery vase excavated at Luonan County in Shaanxi best exemplifies this second type (fig. 1.2). The head, possibly that of a young woman, which surmounts the plain, gourd-shaped vase, is unusually large, about one-third the total height of the object, and is arguably one of the best sculpted human images from prehistoric China. The head is covered with hair, represented by pricked patterns. The face is complex and sensitive in its contours, with a broad forehead, rounded cheeks, and a pointed chin; all the features are well proportioned. What really makes this image lifelike, however, is the extraordinary facial expression: slightly raising her head and narrowing her gently smiling eyes, the figure seems to be whistling or singing. Although we do not know the potter's intention, the work clearly reflects an effort to represent motion and emotion. It is this attempt to capture evanescent human feeling that continues to arouse so strong a response from us five to six thousand years later.

Evolving alongside the northwestern tradition, the eastern tradition produced not only solid pottery figurines and sculptural pottery vessels but also, and more significantly, carved jades, which represent a radical departure from ordinary craft and a step toward ritual art.[14] The extreme hardness of jade makes it a difficult medium for sculpture. In fact, *carving* may not be the right word to describe the technique for making a work out of jade, because the material is too hard to be cut even by steel tools and must instead be shaped entirely by means of abrasives. Even a jade carving that is simple in shape undergoes a complex manufacturing process consisting of at least five steps: (1) splitting the jade boulder and wearing away the rough surface, (2) cutting the raw material into roughly the desired shape, (3) elaborating the shape, boring holes, or both, (4) executing details and decorative patterns, and (5) polishing the surface to make it smooth and shiny. The whole process, effected with a tool to which an abrasive has been applied, is extremely slow and tedious. Such work must thus have emerged during an era when specialized human labor could be controlled and "squandered" on artistic production.

Although discussions of early Chinese sculpture have generally focused on human and animal images, such a focus reflects the notion of sculpture defined in the context of Western art history and has often turned the history of early Chinese sculpture into a poor facsimile of its Western counterpart. It is true that in ancient Egypt, the rest of the Middle East, and Greece, numerous statues and reliefs — many of which were monumental in scale — attest to a strong interest in the human form from a very early era. But in China, especially in the prehistoric eastern tradition, there was a similarly intense interest in creating objects in abstract shapes and in devising composite zoomorphic images.

1.2 Human-headed pot, red earthenware, excavated in 1953 in Luonan County, Shaanxi Province. Neolithic period. 23 x 13.5 cm. Banpo Museum, Xi'an.

Some of these works, which had a ritual use, imitated certain formal attributes of weapons or agricultural instruments while exaggerating them; others were designed specifically as religious symbols. This art was unique in the world during the prehistoric and early historical periods. Although sculpted images of human figures and animals also existed during that time, they must be understood in relation to the more abundant ritual objects and composite zoomorphic images created by the same people.

The tendency to fashion nonrepresentational forms and symbolic images is most evident in a series of late Neolithic cultures located along the lower reaches of the Yellow and Yangzi Rivers. The Dawenkou culture, which flourished on the Shandong Peninsula during the fourth millennium B.C.E., produced some exquisite jade axes, found only in the most opulent graves belonging to the culture.[15] The contours of these beautiful objects are both precise and subtle. Rich in color, the meticulously polished surface of each ax gleams with changing reflections and offers physical delight to the touch, for it is simultaneously smooth, moist, and unyielding. Originally held by the warrior in his right hand, the expensive ornamental weapon symbolized his social status and political authority. Jade axes and other ritual symbols were further embellished with imaginary zoomorphic images. Excavations have yielded an example of this sort from the Shandong Longshan culture, which dominated Shandong after the Dawenkou culture.[16] A jade tablet engraved with mask motifs, one on each side, it has enabled scholars to identify a large group of jade carvings in public and private collections as Longshan products from the third and second millennia B.C.E. Two of the principal images that appear in these carvings are a "monster" mask with sharp, protruding teeth and an eagle with outspread wings. Executed in low relief or in fine raised lines, these two images sometimes appear back-to-back on a ceremonial tablet — perhaps in keeping with an ancient legend about a kingdom in Shandong that had various birds as its ministers and the eagle as its ruler.[17] That the eagle image sometimes grasps human heads in its sharp claws may reflect the institutionalized violence — war or human sacrifice — that emerged during the Longshan period and foreshadowed the beginning of centralized power and organized religion.

Like their contemporaries in Shandong, the people of the Liangzhu culture in the lower Yangzi River region were fascinated by mask motifs, and they often decorated their ritual jades with two complementary masks. One image, more human, has an angular face adorned with an enormous feathered headdress. The other image, more animal-like, centers on a pair of huge round eyes connected by a horizontal bar.[18] These two images enjoyed enormous popularity in Liangzhu art, but they seem to have never been realized as three-dimensional forms: although thousands of Liangzhu jades have been found, the masks only appear in relief, line engravings, or openwork patterns. The decorations are applied, either individually or in combination, to various kinds of ritual paraphernalia and ornaments, but these objects never take a three-dimensional zoomorphic or anthropomorphic form. The works illustrate a growing trend in early Chinese art to favor ritual symbols over realistic icons and to develop a symbolic language based on abstract, nonmimetic formal elements.

The three most important kinds of Liangzhu ritual jades are the ax, the *bi* disk, and the *cong* tube. Continuing the Dawenkou tradition, huge and exquisitely polished jade Liangzhu axes were symbols of authority: only men of the highest social status were buried with them. The bi disk probably evolved from ornamental rings, but a Liangzhu bi is so large and heavy that its function could only have been symbolic or ceremonial. Unlike these two types of ritual jades, which are both somewhat flat, a tall tubular cong is a magnificent three-dimensional sculpture with an abstract design (fig. 1.3). The exterior of a typical cong is a truncated square prism with masks placed along the four corners. This design thus completely destroys the concept of a two-dimensional visual field: to comprehend the whole image, the viewer's gaze must shift to the adjacent side to find the other half of the mask.

Although generally classified as a branch of the eastern tradition, the northern Hongshan culture developed a strong interest in three-dimensional organic forms from an early date. Located in present-day Liaoning Province and Inner Mongolia, this Neolithic regional culture flourished approximately from the mid-fourth to the mid-third millennium B.C.E. Jade carvings from Hongshan sites include objects of abstract design such as hoof-shaped tubes and plaques in cloud patterns, miniature images of birds and turtles, hybrid figures with buffalo horns or deer antlers, and imaginary animals.[19] A popular image of this last kind is the "pig-dragon." Along with a ring-shaped body, the pig-dragon has a pair of large eyes framed by finely modulated ridges; the large, rounded ears connect smoothly with the face. The pig-dragon often accompanied the dead, being placed on the chest of the deceased at burial, in an act of symbolism that we can no longer comprehend.[20] The importance of this peculiar form in the Hongshan culture is attested by its frequency as well as by its influence on other sculptures. The largest jade carving from this culture known to us — an elegant dragon 26 centimeters high — has an elongated body and head (fig. 1.4), but its circular contour and square nose disclose its kinship to the stout pig-dragon.

Like jade carvings from other branches of the eastern tradition, Hongshan jades regularly — and sometimes exclusively — furnished large graves. But another type of ritual structure in this culture — the temple or shrine — was equipped with groups of clay sculptures of varying sizes. At Niuheliang in western Liaoning, archaeologists have discovered an enormous ritual complex, consisting of stone platforms with alternate circular and square ground plans, as well as a multichambered structure built of mud brick.[21] Remains of this structure include fragments of painted wall surfaces, which suggest that the chambers were originally decorated with colorful murals. Other fragments found inside the

structure are from clay statues; the largest surviving piece is a head 22.5 centimeters tall (fig. 1.5). Amazingly naturalistic, the figure has a broad forehead, raised eyebrows, high cheekbones, and a large, sensuous mouth. The image is life-size, and the use of different materials makes it look even more real: the pair of eyes made of bluish jade disks, for example, stare intensely at the onlooker. Sculpted clay fragments found near this head represent bare shoulders and arms; on the basis of their smooth shapes, scholars have suggested that the statue may have been of a female nude.[22] The assumption is further supported by the fact that none of the sculptural fragments from the structure can be identified as parts of male bodies. Instead, many of them represent female breasts of varying shapes. On the basis of the different sizes of body parts in these fragments, the excavators have concluded that the architectural structure must originally have housed a group of female statues, the largest of which were double or triple normal human size. The structure has thus acquired the name Temple of the Goddesses.

1.3 Prismatic *cong* tube, nephrite jade, unearthed in 1982 in Wujin district, Changzhou, Jiangsu Province. Liangzhu culture, Neolithic period, ca. 3600–ca. 2000 B.C.E. 29.7 × 6.1 cm. Nanjing Museum.

1.4 Dragon, jade, unearthed in 1971 at Sanxingtala, Ongniud Banner, Inner Mongolia. Hongshan culture, ca. 3500 B.C.E. 26 cm. Ongniud Banner Museum.

The separate discovery of a Hongshan-culture site at Dongshanzui in Liaoning has further linked such female statues to a fertility cult.[23] The site is again a large architectural complex consisting of square and round stone foundations. Some female clay figures originally installed there, quite large, sat cross-legged, holding their left wrists in their right hands. Their modeling technique and art style are identical to those of the Niuheliang figures. Two miniature statues from Dongshanzui, however, are absent from Niuheliang: one is 5.8 centimeters and the other 5.0 centimeters high; their surviving torsos, with large bellies and fleshy hips, possibly represent pregnant women, and their genitalia are marked with incisions. Scholars have related these images to the so-called fertility-goddess images produced across much of Europe and northern Asia during a long period from the late Paleolithic to the early Bronze Age. In China, the tradition of female figures as fertility symbols can be traced back to a group of six stone statuettes discovered at Houtaizi in Luanping County, Hebei Province, which have been dated to 5000 B.C.E. One image in this group, 34 centimeters high, is of a naked woman squatting while holding her swollen belly with both hands. A smaller image in this group is similar, but the woman's legs are wide open, leading scholars to propose that she is "in the position of childbirth."[24] It is understandable that such figures could have appeared in northern Hebei around 5000 B.C.E. and in Liaoning in the fourth to third millennium B.C.E.: both areas were connected with the Eurasian steppes. The location of the Hongshan culture between the steppes and China proper also explains the coexistence of the clay fertility figures and carved jade in zoomorphic or geometric shapes. While the clay "goddess" images originated in the west of China, the carved jades reflect strong influence from branches of the eastern tradition south of Hongshan, along the east coast. Interestingly, these two kinds of sculptures of divergent origins seem to have been associated with different genders and rites in the Hongshan culture: at Dongshanzui, clay female figures have been found only near a round platform, but jade plaques in the shape of a dragon and a bird appeared next to a large square foundation at the center of the site.

The Hongshan culture continued until the mid-third millennium B.C.E. Jade carvings of the period, both from Hongshan and from other regions, demonstrate distinct regional innovations and the interaction among cultures. One of the innovations is a nude statuette made of pale green nephrite. Discovered in 1987 at

1.5 Face from a life-size statue, clay and stone, excavated in 1983 from the temple structure at Niuheliang, Liaoning Province. Hongshan culture, ca. 3500 B.C.E. 22.5 × 16.5 cm. Liaoning Provincial Institute of Archaeology and Cultural Relics, Shenyang.

Lingjiatan in Hanshan County, Anhui Province, the carving has a well-proportioned silhouette; the subtly curved outline of the hips contrasts with the angular shoulders. The more detailed facial and bodily features are represented in relief or line incision. The figure stands straight while holding its hands in front of its chin — possibly a gesture of ritual significance.[25]

It has been suggested that the eastern tradition is an "oceanic" cultural tradition — that its people traveled by boat and its cultural influences spread along the coast and rivers.[26] This contention has recently gained important support from jade carvings excavated at sites of the Shijiahe culture along the Han River, a tributary of the Yangzi River in Hubei Province. The designs of these carvings reflect the borrowing of images typical of other regional cultures in the eastern tradition that were often located hundreds of kilometers away. Some works are reminiscent of the Hongshan pig-dragon; others recall the Longshan "monster" mask and eagle; still others are variations of the Liangzhu cong tube.[27] Created toward the late third millennium B.C.E., these works document the increasing interaction among different regions and the assimilation of regional art forms into an interregional cultural entity.

In addition to its exquisite jade carvings, the Shijiahe culture is famous for its miniature pottery sculptures, which may reflect influences from the northwest. Indeed, this culture in central China must have been the meeting place of the two main Neolithic traditions from the east and the west. Since the mid-1950s, thousands of terra-cotta figurines have been discovered at Shijiahe, Dengjiawan, and other sites along the Han River.[28] Unlike clay sculptures from isolated finds, Shijiahe figurines formed large assemblies that include an impressive range of miniature animals and birds, such as elephants, apes, rabbits, tigers, dogs, pigs, tapirs, sheep, tortoises, owls, ducks, hens, cockerels, and a variety of small birds. Most images are less than 10 centimeters high and are intended to be lifelike. Among the finds at Dengjiawan are two full-length miniature human images made by kneading and joining individual body parts. Both figures wear caps and earrings and sit upright in a rigid, formal pose (fig. 1.6). One figure seems to be holding a fish, and the other is presenting something with both hands. That these two figures seem to be making offerings suggests that the clay animals and birds were probably also symbolic offerings to spirits or the dead.

The Shang Dynasty

The end of the Chinese Neolithic era coincided with a powerful expansion of the eastern tradition represented by the Longshan culture. As a result, various regional Longshan cultures emerged in the central plains, while other branches of the eastern tradition continued to develop in the south and southeast. This change brought about the dominance of a highly symbolic art over a broad region. Carved jades appeared in the traditional territory of the northwestern tradition, artisans produced monochromic pottery vessels in great quantity in various locations in central China, and in the east the art of ceremonial pottery reached its highest stage of development. Although a black Longshan cup from Shandong is not always recognized as sculpture, it reflects the ideal three-dimensional image from the period of its creation. Such a vessel amazes us with both its technical and its artistic achievements: the wall of the vessel has been reduced to a critical point, 2 to 3 millimeters in thickness; the subtle curves of its contours are meticulously calculated; and the monochrome, often entirely black, exaggerates the sharpness of its silhouette. Instead of the pursuit of a round and solid form, the aesthetic goal here seems to be fragility and immateriality. Whereas such ritual vessels are either

1.6 Groups of terra-cotta figures of humans and animals, excavated in 1978 at Dengjiawan, Tianmen County, Hubei Province. Shijiahe culture, Neolithic period, ca. 2400–2000 B.C.E. Jingzhou Regional Museum, Hubei Province.

undecorated or ornamented only with simple geometric patterns, artisans embellished ritual jades — another focus of the Longshan artistic imagination — with increasingly complex mask motifs. Against this background the Chinese Bronze Age began.

The invention of bronze casting was undoubtedly the most significant phenomenon in Chinese art during the second millennium B.C.E. Although in other ancient civilizations bronze was used for making tools to improve production, the ancient Chinese reserved this "precious metal" almost exclusively for weapons and ceremonial vessels — instruments used to exercise power through warfare and ritual.[29] The art of ritual objects, or *liqi,* first appeared in the prehistoric eastern tradition: many aspects of bronze art, especially the emphasis on ritual vessels and mask motifs, can be traced to earlier ritual pottery and carved jades. But once ritual vessels became the primary form of artistic expression in bronze, their synthesis of features from pottery and jade sculpture gave rise to a new artistic tradition.

The earliest known bronze vessels — seven *jue* cups from Erlitou, Henan Province — resemble Longshan pottery vessels in both typology and aesthetics. Here we find the same emphasis on slenderness and delicacy, as well as the same pursuit of a complex silhouette even at the expense of volume and usefulness. Also like Longshan pottery vessels, these three-dimensional bronze forms, made at the end of the Xia dynasty before 1600 B.C.E., are without significant surface decoration.[30] The situation changed during the early to middle Shang dynasty (ca. 1600 to 1400 B.C.E.). An effort emerged to create "monumental" bronzes — ritual vessels that would impress people not by their fragility but by their impressive size and imposing appearance. Several such vessels — large square *ding* a meter tall and weighing almost 100 kilograms — have been found in the mid-Shang capital at Zhengzhou, Henan Province.[31] These and other vessels from the period also demonstrate an important blending of artistic traditions. Almost all mid-Shang bronzes derived their shape from pottery types, but masks, previously the exclusive province of jade art, were now translated into bronze as well.

The most popular image on middle and late Shang bronzes was the zoomorphic mask traditionally called the *taotie,* sometimes shaped like a pair of "dragons" standing nose to nose to form a frontal mask. On early and mid Shang bronzes, this motif was expressed largely by abstract scroll patterns surrounding a pair of round eyes, executed either in thin relief lines or in thicker ribbons. But toward the late Shang, the taotie gradually came into its own and achieved increasing prominence. The image of this mythic animal, which often integrates elements of animals and birds, stands out forcefully and vividly against the densely incised ground.[32] Bronze vessels from the late Shang increasingly bore such powerful relief images and sometimes took the form of three-dimensional representations of mythical animals or birds. Such animal- or bird-shaped vessels, which we may call sculptural bronzes, continued the prehistoric tradition of sculptural pottery vessels and have been classified into three major categories — *guang, zun,* and *you*—all used for containing or serving sacrificial wine. A guang is an asymmetrical covered pitcher. The front end of the lid, which covers the spout, is modeled into the head of a dragon or tiger, whose body is sometimes shown on the lid and is sometimes represented on both sides of the vessel. The rear of the vessel is frequently transformed into the image of an owl, with its upturned face and outspread wings shown on the lid and the vessel, respectively (fig. 1.7). Unlike the relatively uniform guang, the animal- and bird-shaped zun and you include a large variety of vessels of different shapes and ornamentation. It seems that the only feature these vessels have in common is their use of three-dimensional zoomorphic images, which shape either an entire vessel or certain sections. Relatively frequent subtypes include vessels portraying such quadrupeds as buffalo, rams, rhinoceroses, and elephants; owl-shaped vessels; and vessels combining two identical images of an owl or a ram back-to-back.

It is important to keep in mind that to make a sculptural bronze a Shang craftsman had first to make an equivalent form in clay. Unlike ancient bronzes from western Asia and Europe, which were cast from very early times by the lost-wax method, Shang and Western Zhou bronzes were made by the piece-mold technique, consisting of at least five basic steps: (1) making a clay model of the manufactured vessel and baking it dry, (2) making a clay impression from the model and dividing the "mold" into sections, (3) modifying the model into a casting core by slightly shaving its surface, (4) assembling the mold and the core and pouring molten bronze into the empty space between them, and (5) breaking the mold after cooling and polishing the bronze product. It is difficult to say whether this technique determined the fundamental symmetry of Shang-Zhou bronzes or whether a desire to achieve symmetrical forms led to the development of the technique. In any event, the piece-mold casting technique is integral to the visual appearance of Shang-Zhou bronzes. In

1.7 Covered ritual wine-pouring vessel (*guang*) with tiger and owl decor, cast bronze with pale green patina. Late Shang dynasty, 13th century B.C.E. 25 × 31.5 × 10.6 cm. Arthur M. Sackler Museum, Harvard University Art Museums.

sculptures produced by this technique, even animals and birds must remain frontal and still.

Bronzes excavated in 1976 from Yinxu Tomb 5 best exemplify the development of late Shang bronze art in several different directions.[33] This burial complex belonged to the Shang queen Fu Hao, who lived at the end of the thirteenth century B.C.E. Merely 4 meters wide and 5.6 meters long, this tomb nevertheless yielded 210 ritual vessels, including many monumental ones. Several vessels weigh more than 100 kilograms each; even a *jia* drinking cup is 68 centimeters high and weighs 18 kilograms.[34] The shapes of most vessels resemble those of standard ritual bronzes, and they bear in relief decorative motifs prevalent at the time. Some Fu Hao vessels fall into the category of sculptural bronzes. A pair of guang vessels, for example, are almost identical to the one illustrated in figure 1.7.[35] Another guang belongs to the quadruped type; it is shaped like a horse or ram standing on all four legs.[36] The animal has a pair of large horns and bears coiled dragons on its back, chest, and forelegs. When viewed from behind, the beast is transformed into the frontal image of a bird, standing erect and spreading its wings. This bird image resembles an owl zun found in the same tomb (fig. 1.8).[37] Standing on two strong legs and propped up by a flat tail, the owl's upright body and domed head are again decorated with relief or projected images of snakes, dragons, and smaller birds. The goal in creating this and other sculptural bronzes from the Fu Hao tomb was apparently not to represent real animals or birds or to capture movement or lifelikeness, but to forge composite mythical images for ancestor worship. The quadruped guang, in particular, bears the posthumous title of Fu Hao inside both the lid and the body of the vessel, which demonstrates that this sculptural bronze was made specifically for the queen's funeral.

Fu Hao's tomb also yielded more than eight hundred jade and stone carvings, many of which are miniature sculptures of animals and birds. Some are again mythical creatures, such as dragons and taotie. But many others, though often embellished with stylized surface patterns, vividly represent different species of real animals and birds, including rabbits, tigers, elephants, fish, buffalo, bears, monkeys, horses, eagles, swallows, and swans.[38] Some of these examples demonstrate the sculptors' clever use of the variation in color of a piece of natural jade or stone. Two turtles, for example, have black shells but translucent bodies, and a duck has dark eyes and wings but a white neck.[39] Many of these jades are three-dimensional sculptures; the thinner pieces either have small holes for hanging or were originally erected on stands (as is indicated by the unpolished protrusions at the lower end).[40]

A distinct group of jade and stone carvings from Fu Hao's tomb are human and semihuman images. These include full-length figures in kneeling-sitting positions, sculpted human heads, and a horned standing figure showing a different gender on either side.[41] Again, these examples exhibit a wide range of iconographic and stylistic variation, from composite mythical images to naturalistic portrayals of human figures, and from incised or relief images on flat pieces to round statuettes. A surprisingly naturalistic figurine, made of stone rather than fine jade, represents a middle-aged male wearing a long robe and a ring-shaped cap.[42] Probably an official or a courtier, he kneels on the ground while placing both hands on his knees — the formal sitting posture during the Shang. His facial features — the high cheekbones, large nose, and full lips — are represented with unprecedented sensitivity, even evoking an impression of individuality. The careful attention paid to the face may also explain the figure's disproportionately large head and the relatively simple treatment of his body.

Some other kneeling or squatting figures from the tomb, however, have human torsos but birds' claws or combine a human image and a bird image back-to-back.[43] The royal clan of the Shang dynasty traced its origin to Pan Geng, whose birth was connected to a "divine bird," sometimes identified as a swallow. It was said that this bird was sent down by the God on High (Shang Di). After a woman named Jiandi ate the bird's egg, she became pregnant and subsequently gave birth to Pan Geng, the founder of the Zi clan, which eventually established the Shang. Ceremonial hymns recounting this legend were performed in the clan's ancestral temples long after the Shang perished. In addition to possibly explaining the symbolism of these bird-man images, the legend may also relate to one of the most interesting objects from Fu Hao's tomb — an exquisite miniature sculpture carved out of a piece of yellow-brown jade (fig. 1.9). Not quite 7 centimeters high, it represents a figure in the formal kneeling-sitting posture. Both the tubelike crown and the elaborate gown, with its wide embroidered belt and sash — features of the most prestigious ritual costumes in ancient China — give some indication of the extraordinary status of the figure. His (or her) facial features and clothing are rendered rather naturalistically, but a strange shape protrudes from the lower back. Unable to identify this shape exactly, some researchers have hypothesized that it may represent a certain kind of weapon.[44] This assumption can be ruled out: not only does the protrusion not resemble any Shang weapon we know, but its surface patterns extend to the figure's left thigh, thus indicating that it is part of the figure's body. In comparing the shape of this protrusion with images

1.8 Owl-shaped vessel, excavated in 1976 from Tomb 5 at Anyang, Henan Province. Late Shang, ca. 1200 B.C.E. 46.3 cm. Institute of Archaeology, Beijing.

and pictographs from the late Shang, it becomes clear that it represents a bird's, perhaps a swallow's, tail. The figure may even be a "portrait" of Fu Hao: just as the names of Shang royal ancestors were sometimes combined with bird graphs in divinatory inscriptions, an attribute of the "divine bird" here may again allude to the divine origin of a member of the Shang royalty.[45]

Sculptures of various forms and materials from Fu Hao's tomb can be related to examples collected from other places in Anyang, where the Shang established its last capital. Long before the discovery of this tomb, for example, images of human figures in either kneeling or squatting postures had been found in Xiaotun village and in one of the royal tombs at Houjiazhuang.[46] The largest sculptures from Fu Hao's tomb include an egret made of pure white marble.[47] It is 40 centimeters long and has a deep, rectangular trough cut in its back, a feature that has led the excavators to identify it as an architectural ornament. Similar marble carvings were found during the Anyang expeditions between 1928 and 1937. In Tomb 1001, the largest Shang royal mausoleum, which may have belonged to Fu Hao's husband, King Wu Ding, archaeologists found a series of marble sculptures of both realistic and mythical types, representing tur-

tles, frogs, eagles, egrets, owls, a double-faced monster with an elephantine proboscis, and a tiger-headed monster with a human body (fig. 1.10).[48] Nearly every one of the larger stone animals has either a vertical trough in its back or a hole in its middle. These have also been identified as architectural elements. Because the tomb had been looted and the carvings were found amid the debris in the plundered tunnels, however, it was impossible to determine their original positions and function.

Early and mid Shang clay sculptures of animals, birds, and human figures found at Zhengzhou and Shanxian County in Henan, Yumen in Gansu, and Gaocheng in Hebei demonstrate the continuation of this older art form into the Bronze Age.[49] There are two especially notable specimens of late Shang sculpture from Anyang now in the Institute of History and Philology, Academia Sinica, Taibei.[50] Although sketchily modeled, each figurine vividly depicts a prisoner whose hands are fettered either before or behind him and whose neck is banded by some kind of shackle. Both wear long robes that conceal their lower limbs. The two figures' heads are shaved clean (such shaving may have been a form of punishment). A different kind of realism is evident in a remarkable bronze mask from Tomb 1400, a royal

1.9 Jade figurine, excavated in 1976 from Tomb 5 at Anyang. Late Shang, ca. 1200 B.C.E. 6.9 cm. Institute of Archaeology, Beijing.

1.10 Tiger-headed monster, white marble, excavated from Tomb 1001 at Houjiazhuang, Anyang. Late Shang, ca. 1200 B.C.E. 36.3 cm. Institute of History and Philology, Academia Sinica, Taibei, Taiwan.

mausoleum in Houjiazhuang (fig. 1.11).[51] At 25.4 centimeters in height, it approaches the size of a real person's face, and its sculptural style is also unusually naturalistic by comparison with most Shang bronze images. The image has high cheekbones, a narrow forehead, and a pointed chin. The rounded cheeks and fine, slanting eyes convey a sense of youthfulness. The broad nose contrasts with the thin lips, and the figure seems to be smiling at the onlooker. The amazing realism of this bronze face has led some observers to speculate that it portrays a deceased Shang king or that it is a death mask from a corpse. But we should note that the generally realistic representation in this mask blends with many stylized features, such as the thick eyebrows formed by parallel lines or the disproportionately large ears with conventional cloud patterns. Although its function in the tomb remains uncertain, a large loop cast on the top of this mask suggests that it hung on a wall. A more recent find — a clay mold for casting a bronze face — demonstrates that the Tomb 1400 mask was not the only such sculpture made in late Shang Anyang. Again executed in a stunningly naturalistic style, the negative image of a human face inside the mold is only 11.8 cm high and thus much smaller than a real person's face.[52]

Last but not least, a bronze vessel in the shape of a rhinoceros in San Francisco's Asian Art Museum indicates a new direction in Shang sculpture at the very end of the dynasty (fig. 1.12). A lengthy inscription cast inside the vessel documents that it was made to commemorate an event during the southern expedition of the last Shang king, Di Xin. Unlike the ram-shaped guang or bird-shaped zun from Fu Hao's tomb, the vessel represents a real animal rather than a composite mythical one. Moreover, it lacks the surface ornamentation that often clutters earlier vessels; the artist limits the vocabulary to the three-dimensional shape — a baby rhinoceros with short legs, a round belly, and a curious expression on its face. The long narrative inscription and plain appearance of the vessel identify it as a new type of bronze that became fashionable at the end of the Shang.[53] Its realistic style may have been influenced, however, by bronze sculptures created in the south.

One of the most important achievements in Chinese archaeology during the past thirty to forty years is the finding of a number of highly advanced regional Bronze Age cultures contemporary with the late Shang and early Western Zhou. The finds are especially crucial to the study of early Chinese sculpture because they show that toward the end of the second millennium B.C.E., at least two of these regional cultures had devel-

1.11 Bronze mask, excavated from Tomb 1400 at Houjiazhuang, Anyang. Late Shang, 12th century B.C.E. 25.4 cm. Institute of History and Philology, Academia Sinica, Taibei, Taiwan.

oped an interest in three-dimensional sculptural forms and that the bronze sculptures these cultures produced often surpassed Shang metropolitan products in both scale and iconographic diversity.

These bronze-oriented cultures were centered in eastern Hunan and central Sichuan. Late Shang bronzes from several adjacent locations along the Xiang River in eastern Hunan Province, including Ningxiang, Hengyang, and Liling, are not only spectacularly large and ornate but also frequently have the shape of elephants, buffalo, and even a boar.[54] Like the animal-shaped bronzes from Fu Hao's tomb, these vessels are covered with profuse and varied geometric and zoomorphic motifs rendered in high relief. Unlike the Fu Hao examples, however, they resemble real animals, rather than being imaginary composites of zoomorphic forms. Some Ningxiang vessels even represent human images. A square ding, for example, exhibits seemingly identical images of a large human face on all four sides. Closer observation, however, reveals that the designer subtly altered the proportions of the face to fit it into two different frames of unequal sizes and shapes. Tiny horns and claws attached to these imposing faces identify the subject as a supernatural being.[55] Connected with such supernatural images is a pair of identical wine jars shaped like round sculptures. Both works — one

1.12 Rhinoceros-shaped bronze vessel, commissioned by Yu, unearthed in Liangshan County, Jining, Shandong Province. Late Shang, 12th century B.C.E. 24.5 cm. Asian Art Museum of San Francisco.

of which is in the Musée Cernuschi in Paris and the other in the Sumitomo Collection in Japan — represent a powerful tigerlike beast holding a man in its arms and seemingly about to devour him (fig. 1.13). Different interpretations have been proposed to explain the image: to some scholars the beast and the man are "alter egos" in a harmonious relationship; to others the man is a human sacrifice to be consumed by a deity. A more reliable interpretation may have to wait, however, until the discovery of written materials from Ningxiang, which might reveal the religious or shamanistic practices of that southern region.

Compared with Hunan bronzes, sculptures from the Sanxingdui culture in the southwest signify an artistic custom even further removed from the Shang metropolitan tradition.[56] Although archaeological finds prove that there was communication between the culture of this inland region and that of the middle Yangzi River valley during the late Shang, bronze was used here mainly to make monumental statues, not ritual vessels.

In 1986 at a place called Sanxingdui, Sichuan archaeologists discovered, in one of the most spectacular archaeological excavations of all time, two sacrificial pits containing thousands of rare art objects.[57] Particularly important to the history of sculpture are the more than a hundred bronze human and semihuman images in the pits, including a life-size statue, fifty or so individual heads, more than thirty masks, several dozen smaller figures, and a large bronze "divine tree." The unprecedented scale of these sculptures and their unusual forms have made Sanxingdui world famous.

All bronze figures from Sanxingdui have extremely exaggerated noses, mouths, and ears. One likely reason for their grotesque appearance is that they are wearing masks: on some examples a clear demarcation separates the presumably masked face from the rest of the head, and on some examples this masked face is covered by an additional gold mask (fig. 1.14). With a single exception, all Sanxingdui figures have a uniform sculptural style, which forgoes smooth transitions and defines every facial feature through sharply angular ridges connected with deep grooves. The different shapes of the eyes, however, divide these figures into two general groups. In a majority of the examples, including all individual heads, all full-length figures, and some masks, a pair of slanting almond-shaped eyes, with large brows above and deep sunken grooves below, dominates the whole face. The most distinctive feature of these eyes is a horizontal ridge in the middle that transforms the eyeball into an angular geometric form. Figures belonging to this group are distinguished by their varied hairstyles and headdresses, which may indicate different identities. The only standing figure from Sanxingdui, an imposing statue 262 centimeters high, also has this type of eye (fig. 1.15). Wearing an elaborate crown and dressed in a long robe, he stands on an altar embellished with an openwork design combining four elephant heads. His tall, slender body has been given a semiabstract, columnlike shape covered with ornate decorative patterns. His hands are transformed into two large loops: they were originally holding something in front of his chest, possibly an elephant tusk, an object that held special significance for the Sanxingdui people and was found in abundant quantities in the two pits.

The second type of eyes is even more fantastic: the pupil projects on a stalk from the surface of the eye. Three enormous, grotesque masks from Pit 2 feature such eyes. These masks were probably originally installed on huge wooden columns. The largest mask is 138 centimeters wide and 65 centimeters high; each of the tubelike pupils is 16.5 centimeters long and 13.5 centimeters in diameter, with a flat "hoop" in the middle. As is indicated by the hole between the eyebrows, the figure probably had a soaring, scroll-shaped projection installed here, such as we find in a smaller Sanxingdui mask with the same eyes.

Since no contemporary written records have been found from Sanxingdui culture sites, evidence on the meaning of these bronze images has been sought in later documents. Scholars have found an interesting passage from *Records of the Huayang Kingdom* (*Huayang-guo zhi*) — a fourth-century text containing valuable information about ancient Sichuan history — which indicates that Cancong, the legendary ruler of the Shu kingdom, "had a pair of 'vertical eyes' (*zong mu*) and made himself king." It has been proposed that the term *zong mu* may in fact describe the tubelike eyes on some Sanxingdui masks and that these masks thus represent Cancong.[58] Regardless of the reliability of this theory, the text clearly documents a belief that an

1.13 Bronze vessel in the shape of a beast holding a man. Late Shang, ca. 12th century B.C.E. 35.3 cm. Musée Cernuschi, Musée des Arts de l'Asie de la Ville de Paris.

extraordinary ruler is distinguished by the extraordinary shape of his eyes. This belief seems in full agreement with the Sanxingdui bronze figures, whose unusual eyes are their most distinctive feature and signify their supernatural power.

Additional evidence for the meaning of these bronze images can be adduced by comparing them with another type of human image from Sanxingdui, a much smaller, naked figure, part of a group of sculptures. So far, all scientifically excavated examples of this image are from Sanxingdui culture sites in central Sichuan: two were discovered at Sanxingdui, one at Chengdu, and eight at Jinsha village.[59] The most beautiful example, however, is now in the Art Institute of Chicago (fig. 1.16). Carved from a block of black stone and polished to a sheen, the figure kneels in a frontal pose. His hands are tied behind his back with what appears to be a thick rope. The pressure on his wrists forces him to bend his upper body slightly, but he still

1.14 Bronze head with a gold mask, from Pit 2, Sanxingdui, Guanghan, Sichuan Province. Sanxingdui culture, late 13th century B.C.E. 46.6 × 12.7 cm. Sanxingdui Museum.

raises his head high and faces forward. The statue is not a tiny mannequin: about 20 centimeters tall, it is considerably larger than most known jade figures from the Shang-Zhou period. What is truly remarkable about this work, however, is the quality of artistic representation. The proportions of the figure are surprisingly naturalistic for a work from such a remote age. No clothes are shown, yet neither the genitals nor other bodily details are represented. The planes on the torso are so simplified that the sculpture takes on an almost abstract character; the unbroken smoothness of the subtly swelling surfaces seems to reflect the conscious pursuit of a plastic rendering of form and volume.

Although this figure is perhaps the most sensitive representation of the human body from Bronze Age China, it has no eyes. On either side of the straight bridge of the nose are two slightly sunken surfaces, curving smoothly to connect raised cheekbones with a pronounced forehead. It is possible that the statue originally had painted eyes, however. Similar stone figures recently discovered at Jinsha village in Chengdu provide strong evidence for this possibility. Among the four examples from Jinshacun on which research has been published, two have painted eyes and two have eyes delineated by faint sunken lines. It is interesting that the methods the Sanxingdui artists employed for the eyes were different from those used to depict other facial features, for the ears, mouths, noses, and hair of the statues are all rendered in bold, three-dimensional form. The rendering of these stone figures' eyes further distinguishes them from the bronze statues, whose eyes are all sculpted in dramatic manner. It may be said that both groups of Sanxingdui sculpture reflect a heightened awareness of the significance of eyes but in opposite ways, with one exaggerating the eyes and the other repressing them. Scholars of religious art frequently discuss the extraordinary significance of the eyes of sacred icons. They have also noticed that a universal expression of iconoclasm is to destroy the eyes of an image; the unspoken premise behind this practice is that to deprive the image of its eyes is to deprive it of power and life.[60] It is possible that in Sanxingdui culture, different representations of eyes highlighted the images' different social and religious identities: whereas the eyes of slaves or captives were downplayed, the deities most forcefully demonstrated their power through their extraordinary eyes.

1.15 Bronze statue, from Pit 2, Sanxingdui. Sanxingdui culture, late 13th century B.C.E. 262 cm. Sanxingdui Museum.

1.16 Kneeling figure, chlorite/serpentinite?, probably from Guanghan, Sichuan Province. Sanxingdui culture, late Shang, 13th–12th century B.C.E. 19.6 × 7 × 9.8 cm. The Art Institute of Chicago.

The Zhou Dynasty

Established by the Ji clan, the Zhou dynasty originated in the northwest, in what is today part of Shaanxi Province. As a regional cultural and political organization, the Zhou developed its own bronze industry, beginning no later than the fifteenth century B.C.E., and maintained a relationship with the Shang as both competitor and ally. After its army conquered the Shang in the eleventh century B.C.E., the Zhou continued to absorb and modify Shang metropolitan art, including various forms of Shang sculpture. A recently discovered animal-shaped vessel demonstrates this twofold development. Excavated from Tomb 163 at Zhangjiaopo in Xi'an, Shaanxi, the unconventional shape of this rare early Zhou sculptural bronze seems to have resulted from a Shang prototype modified by the distinctive local sense of taste.[61] The main body of the vessel is a mythical horned beast of unknown identity, with an enormous head but thin legs. An array of smaller sculpted animals and birds are attached to its head, chest, back, and rear, giving the object a fractured silhouette. What is absent here is the strong evocation of three-dimensionality and organic energy that a Shang animal-shaped bronze often has. Instead the object generates an impression of eclecticism, of synthesizing existing art forms while distorting them.

We find the same tendency in Zhou modifications of other types of sculptural bronze, including guang and animal-shaped you and zun. A considerable number of guang were made during the early Western Zhou. But a guang of this new generation rarely has an organic, unified animal form, such as we have found in some Shang examples (see fig. 1.7). Rather, Western Zhou guang makers adopted and developed a particular late Shang design, which transformed the body of the guang into a standard wine container, either round or square; only the front part of the lid retains the form of an animal head.[62] Animal-shaped zun and you survived likewise, but in altered form. An important bird you commissioned by a top early Zhou minister resembles an eagle, but it is constructed of semiabstract shapes.[63] Sculptural bronzes became increasingly abstract and simplified during the mid-Zhou. A buffalo zun excavated at Qishan, Shaanxi, for example, has a nearly cylindrical body covered with bold geometric decorative patterns.[64] Similar patterns were also applied to a contemporary zun from the tomb of Yu Bo; the animal shape of the vessel is recognizable as an "elephant" only because of an awkwardly upturned trunk.[65]

Taken together, these examples signify a general decline in sculptural bronze in early and middle Western Zhou art. It is interesting to speculate on the causes of this decline. One reason may be the discontinuation of important bronze cultures in the south and southwest. After the early Zhou, both the Sanxingdui culture and the bronze manufacturing center in Hunan stopped producing monumental sculptural bronzes in animal and human forms. These cultures had existed during the late Shang as major centers of bronze sculpture and provided important stimuli for the development of that art in the Shang metropolitan area. With their disappearance, such stimuli no longer existed. In addition to sculptural bronzes, other forms of Shang sculpture,

such as jade figurines and bronze masks, also survived into the Zhou.[66] Like sculptural bronzes, however, these works reflect no new kind of creative energy or imagination, whether derived from inside the metropolitan area or outside it.

This observation then leads us to another and more important reason for the decline of sculpture. During the Western Zhou, ritual art was further systematized, and many bronze vessels were created for ancestral rituals held in the temples of aristocratic families. Lengthy inscriptions on these bronzes commemorating important political events constituted written histories of such families. As bronze vessels became merely bearers of such texts, their forms often ceased to convey independent meaning. The decoration was gradually simplified, geometric patterns came to predominate, and sculptural forms became a rarity. In fact, this movement in bronze art toward textualization and abstraction had started in the late Shang; but it came to control the entire development of ritual art only during the Western Zhou.[67] Initiated in the Zhou metropolitan center, this process was carried on to the Zhou vassal states in different regions of the country, established through a system of enfeoffment. An important mechanism in this system was the investiture ceremonies held in the Zhou royal temple, during which a Zhou king bestowed official titles, land, people, and ritual symbols upon royal relatives and meritorious ministers. Many Western Zhou bronzes were in fact made to record and commemorate the granting of such royal favors.

Occasionally, however, an investiture could also inspire the creation of a bronze sculpture. One such rare result is a bronze zun in the shape of a pony, created for Li, a high official who lived in the tenth century B.C.E. (fig. 1.17). Excavated at Meixian County in Shaanxi, the bronze horse bears a long inscription on its chest that details the circumstances of its creation. The text records that Li participated in a special ceremony held by a Zhou king during which young ponies were sent into the royal stable. When the ceremony was over, the king gave Li two ponies as gifts. Li then commissioned this vessel to express his gratitude to the king and to honor his deceased father. Interestingly, this vessel has two lids for a single opening on the horse's back. The lid installed on the vessel is cast with a short inscription on its reverse side, identifying one of the two ponies Li received from the king as black and white. The second lid, stored inside the vessel, identifies the other pony as white with a black mane. The vessel was therefore made specifically to represent — indeed, to

1.17 Horse-shaped vessel, bronze, commissioned by Li, excavated in 1955 from a hoard at Licun village, Meixian County, Shaanxi Province. 10th century B.C.E. 32.4 × 34 cm. National Museum of China, Beijing.

immortalize — the king's gifts in precious bronze. This purpose explains the sculpture's naturalistic form and plain decoration, which sharply contrast with the style of the other Li bronzes unearthed together with the horse, which are without exception covered with dense and ornate semiabstract patterns.[68]

Although this bronze horse demonstrates the capability of Western Zhou bronze casters in designing and working with naturalistic forms, it was an isolated attempt; no significant artistic movement ever developed along those lines. Toward the end of the Western Zhou, however, a new kind of bronze with sculpted accessories in human and animal form did mark a new direction for bronze sculpture. Such objects have mainly been found in the Zhou capital area in southern Shaanxi or excavated from cemeteries of the Jin state in southern Shanxi. Given that the two areas were closely connected both geographically and politically, the bronzes must reflect a taste prevalent among some Zhou aristocrats, and constitute a relatively independent development of a particular type of sculptural bronze within Zhou art. Two examples from southern Shaanxi seem to indicate an earlier stage in this development, one from Fufeng

and the other from Baoji. Each object is a variation on a square ding vessel, consisting of a rectangular pot cast onto a small stove.[69] The stove is modeled after an architectural structure, with windows on two sides and a latched door in front. Most interestingly, the door is guarded by a round, naked human figure, whose left leg is cut off at the knee. A textual reference to this image is found in the *Rites of Zhou* (*Zhou li*): "A tattooed criminal can be used to guard a gate; a cut-nose criminal can be used to guard a pass; a cut-foot criminal can be used to guard a park." An ancient commentary further specifies that this last duty meant to watch over the animal pens in the Zhou royal park.[70]

The amputated watchman reappears on a boxlike bronze object from a Jin tomb at Shangguo in Shanxi (fig. 1.18).[71] But the much fancier design of this object must indicate a later date, probably around the middle to late eighth century B.C.E. in the early Eastern Zhou. A mere 9.1 centimeters high, it has one human figure and as many as fifteen sculpted animals and birds attached on all sides. On its flat top are four birds surrounding a monkey; around the object are four dragons and three tigers; and on the front side the watchman stands next to a pair of double-paneled doors. Although this human image reflects the cruel custom in Zhou society of severing a slave's leg, among Western Zhou bronzes the object is uncharacteristically playful in design. In fact, it may not be totally wrong to call it a toy. Six wheels installed at the bottom of the boxlike object transform it into a miniature carriage. The front wheels are shaped like a pair of tigers, so when the carriage is pulled around, the tigers seem to be running and carrying all the other sculpted animals and birds on their backs.

The rectangular shape, the miniature scale, and the three-dimensional accessories of this object relate it to a group of bronzes recently excavated from the Jin royal cemetery at Tianma-Qucun, a village in Beizhao. Rather than the amputated guardian, however, the sculpted human images on the Beizhao bronzes are naked figures in a kneeling or squatting posture who carry the vessels.[72] Human-shaped accessories of this second type appeared fairly widely on late Western Zhou and early Eastern Zhou bronzes, often functioning as the feet of an otherwise conventional vessel. The figures' nudity may indicate their lowly social status as slaves; but an interesting bronze object found in Tomb 306 at Potang in Shaoxing, Zhejiang Province, also suggests that nudity may have a certain ritual significance. This is a unique miniature sculpture representing an architectural structure, perhaps a temple or shrine, with a group of six musicians inside (fig. 1.19). The structure has a square floor and three walls, and is densely decorated on every surface with repeated geometric patterns. A post, which is disproportionately tall and thick, rises from the middle of the peaked roof to support the image of a giant bird. From ancient times a cult centered on birds had existed in the eastern coastal area where this architectural model was found.[73] This bronze sculpture may therefore indicate the continuation of the cult into the sixth century B.C.E. The interior also suggests that the building had a religious function: devoid of any furnishing, the structure houses only an orchestra of six naked musicians playing various musical instruments. This sculpture probably shows a musical performance inside a ritual building to entertain or invoke gods or spirits, which was a widespread religious or shamanistic practice in ancient China.

The development of such sculpted accessories and architectural models heralded the gradual emergence and consolidation of a new interest in sculptural forms from the eighth to the early fifth centuries B.C.E., traditionally known as the Spring and Autumn period.[74] Bronze objects and clay molds from an important foundry site at Houma City, Shanxi, show that this development is related to some important technical innovations, especially the increasingly frequent and sophisticated use of the "cast-on" technique. In this technique, a three-dimensional accessory, often either a serpentine handle or a human-shaped base, was made first and then cast onto a larger bronze. The manufacture of the individual parts, from the shaping of a model to the casting of the bronze, employed all the essential techniques and necessary steps for creating a freestanding bronze image. Not coincidentally, some of the accessories began to look like independent sculpture. Although not completely self-contained, the three-dimensional forms of human figures or mythical animals impress the viewer; their artistic style is often independent from that of the works to which they are attached.

A famous example of this kind is a pair of magnificent bronze *hu* from Lijialou at Xinzheng, Henan.[75] Each hu, more than a meter high and weighing close to

1.18 Miniature carriage with human guardian, monkey, birds, and crouching tigers, bronze, excavated in 1989 at Shangguo village, Wenxi County, Shanxi Province. Ca. middle to late 8th century B.C.E. 9.1 × 13.7 × 11.3 cm. Shanxi Provincial Institute of Archaeology, Taiyuan.

64 kilograms, combines a wide range of zoomorphic images, from semigeometric dragon patterns on the body to mythical animals with openwork designs on the handles to an amazingly realistic image of a crane on the top. Raising its head and spreading its wings, this crane seems on the verge of flying away. The openwork patterns on the dragon-shaped handles also reflect the influence of the lost-wax casting technique, which began to be employed in China around this time for creating complex shapes and intensely textured surfaces. Probably introduced from western Asia, this technique substitutes a wax model of the object to be produced for a clay model. The wax model is packed in fine clay and then heated, thereby producing a hollow pottery mold when the wax runs out. Unlike the traditional piece-mold casting method, which is suitable mainly for making symmetrical forms and blocklike constructions, the lost-wax technique can produce infinitely complex forms, as seen in even the earliest products of this technique in China.[76]

One group of these products consists of a pair of identical sculptures from Tomb 9 at Xujialing in Xichuan County, Henan, which together may have formed a drum stand (fig. 1.20).[77] Each sculpture is brilliantly inlaid with green-blue stones and features an imaginary animal as its principal image. Firmly planted on the ground with four flattened legs, the creature turns its head to the side, opening its large mouth and sticking out a long tongue. The top of its head is crowned with serpents whose writhing bodies form energetic, branching patterns. A handle-like accessory protrudes from the animal's back and supports a smaller animal, a replica of the main one. This second animal also sticks out a long tongue, from which sprouts the horned head of a third imaginary animal. The animal images in this work seem to be reproducing themselves, in the process giving the sculpture a liveliness that is as disturbing as it is fascinating. Diverging from the tradition of realistic human and animal figures, this work exemplifies a distinctive sculptural tradition of fantastic animals. Both traditions, along with the technical progress made in the sixth century B.C.E., paved the way for a major advance in bronze sculpture during the Warring States period that followed.

The Warring States period was a magnificent era of artistic creation and renewal in Chinese history. By the end of the Spring and Autumn period in the early fifth century B.C.E., changes within traditional ritual art and architecture had reached a critical mass. Many new art and architectural forms, styles, and genres that appeared during the following centuries redefined the whole visual vista. In architecture, tall platforms and terrace buildings found great favor with political patrons. Thanks to their monumental appearance and dazzling ornamentation, these forms supplied the powerful visual symbols that the new elite needed. In art, solemn, monochromic vessels had gone out of fashion; lacquers and inlaid objects began to enjoy great popularity, reflecting a fascination with fluid imagery and coloristic effects. Lamps, screens, tables, and other utilitarian objects were created as serious works of art. These objects, which combined expensive materials, exquisite workmanship, and exotic images, documented the desire for material possessions and the taste for extravagance. The interest in three-dimensional images related to all these phenomena stimulated the development of sculpture, an art form that had languished during the Western Zhou and most of the Spring and Autumn period, during which ritual vessels dominated artistic production.

Works from a single tomb — Leigudun Tomb 1 of Marquis Yi of Zeng — exemplify the impressive development of sculpture in the early Warring States period. An inscription dates this tomb, located at Suixian County in Hubei Province, to 433 B.C.E. or slightly later.[78] The numerous bronze vessels, bells, and other objects buried in the tomb, however, were almost certainly made prior to Yi's death, around the middle of the fifth century B.C.E. One striking feature of these objects is their uniform inscription — "Marquis Yi himself makes [the object], using it forever" — a straightforward declaration of ownership. Unlike many earlier ritual bronzes, including some Zeng examples dating from the Spring and Autumn period, these objects neither commemorated important historical events nor facilitated routine ancestral sacrifices.[79] Most likely they were made to fulfill the needs of the extravagant life at court, as well as to assist in the new kinds of rituals that prevailed during the Eastern Zhou.[80]

Many bronzes from Leigudun Tomb 1 integrate three-dimensional images. These images, however, are no longer tiny figures or animals attached to a ritual vessel; rather, they have increased in size enormously, becoming statues in their own right. Among these sculpted bronze images, the three most important are all associated with musical instruments: the human-shaped caryatids of a bell set, the two-winged monsters supporting a set of chime stones, and a hybrid creature with a bird's body and a deer's antlers, which may have been the stand of a drum.[81] Let us consider the set of

1.19 Model of a structure with musicians, bronze with gold inlay, excavated in 1982 from Tomb 306 at Potang in Shaoxing, Zhejiang Province. 6th–5th century B.C.E. 17 × 13 × 11.5 cm. Zhejiang Provincial Cultural Relics Bureau, Hangzhou.

1.20 Imaginary creature, bronze with hard stone inlay, excavated in 1990 from Tomb 9 at Xujialing in Xichuan County, Henan Province. 6th–5th century B.C.E. 48 cm. Henan Provincial Institute of Cultural Relics and Archaeology, Zhengzhou.

bells as our chief example. Its value lies not only in its inscriptions, which document a sophisticated musical system, or in the complex shape and decor of each bell, sometimes produced by as many as thirty-eight molds: the three-tiered wooden frame from which the bells are suspended is itself a work of art. Fitted with intricate bronze finials, its horizontal wooden beams are supported by six standing bronze figures, who are giants compared with the tiny figures found on earlier bronze vessels. Each of the three figures on the lower level weighs 359 kilograms and stands approximately a meter high on a hemispherical base 0.35 meters high. The three figures on the second level are slightly shorter, about 80 centimeters each; tenons extending from the upper and lower ends secure these figures in position. The statues must represent people of rank: their identical clothes consist of a tight jacket and a long skirt, both originally painted with black lacquer and embellished with bands of red floral patterns. All of the six wear swords, a detail that has led some scholars to call the figures warriors or palace guards.

The modeling of the figures shows that artistic concerns were given as much weight as functional ones. Although in actuality the straight bodies function as columnlike caryatids, the artist created the illusion that these "warriors" are effortlessly supporting the heavy frame with their bent arms. Each figure has a rather large head, but it is not so disproportionately large as in some earlier or contemporary examples. What makes these bronze figures truly outstanding works of sculpture, however, is their faces, which were created with a surprisingly sophisticated understanding of human anatomy. The nonslanted eyes and closed lips are defined by sharp contours, which lend contrast to the smooth and subtler transition between the broad forehead and the high cheekbones, and between those and the pointed chin. This naturalistic sculptural style must have been intentional, because an entirely different style has been employed to decorate the hemispherical base of each statue. Densely covered with undulating curls and volutes derived from dragon motifs, these bases resemble many ritual objects from the tomb stylistically — but in this case the prickly surfaces also set off the naturalness of the figures they support.

These and other works from Leigudun Tomb 1 confirm that two large categories of Warring States sculpture — human figures and mythical animals — followed quite separate paths of development. The naturalistic representation evident in the caryatids is also apparent in a large group of human figures from the Warring States period. The famous Houma foundry debris has yielded complicated section molds for casting such figures; finished products from such molds have been excavated from other sites in Shanxi dated to the late sixth and early fifth centuries B.C.E.[82] Even though these Shanxi figures often raise their arms to support certain objects (and hence are similar to the Leigudun figures), many other bronze figures, in kneeling, squatting, or standing positions, extend their arms to hold hollow tubes or clasp a tube with both hands. Several examples of this kind reportedly came from the Eastern Zhou capital site Jincun village; others have been found in archaeological excavations and in these a lamp holder has sometimes been inserted in the tube held by a figure.[83] All these figures are in stiff frontal poses, with extended arms like bent cylinders. The detailed rendering of their costumes, especially their headdresses, however, reveals the attempt to achieve a naturalistic effect.

Sculptures of mythical animals from the Warring States period, by contrast, emphasize a very different set of qualities. Like the hybrid drum stand from Leigudun Tomb 1, these works show little effort to portray actual animals. Instead, their images originated in fantasy and aimed to stir the imagination. A famous bronze dragon, reportedly from Laomu Terrace outside Wuyang, the capital of the state of Yan, may originally have decorated the pavilion standing on this famous platform.[84] Half-feline and half-reptilian, the dragon has dorsal spikes and pinioned wings. Linear volutes filled with dots cover its body, but its sharp wings, horns, and fins convey a strong sense of three-dimensionality. The exaggerated curves of the projecting parts even create a feeling of movement: the mythical animal, bending its cylindrical neck and tightening its sinews and muscles, seems about to leap into the air.

The only large group of sculptures of both human figures and mythical animals from the middle to late Warring States period was found in the royal mausoleums of the Zhongshan kingdom at Pingshan in Hebei. Like the earlier Zeng state of the fifth century B.C.E., the Zhongshan kingdom of the fourth century B.C.E. was one of the smaller peripheral states that contended for survival with surrounding superpowers. The Zeng probably perished not long after Marquis Yi's death; the Zhongshan was destroyed by the state of Zhao in 296 B.C.E., some ten years after the construction of the last major mausoleum (Tomb 1) near the state capital, Lingshou. From 1974 to 1978, extensive archaeological work at the site resulted in the discovery of more than thirty tombs dating from the Eastern

Zhou period.[85] Tomb 1 belonged to King Cuo, and the occupant of Tomb 6 was probably his father. A combined group of sculptures from these two tombs includes two bronze lamps with human and animal figures; an inlaid bronze table supported by dragons and phoenixes; three screen stands in the shapes of an ox, a rhinoceros, and a tiger; and a pair of winged mythical beasts without apparent practical function.

Three essential features of these sculptural works are a strong three-dimensionality, vivid images, and brilliant ornamentation. Most important, they no longer just exhibit stiff frontal views of men and animals; rather, it is possible to appreciate the sculptures from various angles. They also portray a far wider range of subjects. A bronze lamp from Tomb 1 takes the shape of a gigantic tree, whose individual branches support thirteen lamp holders. The spiraling dragon climbing the central branch may be the mythological *zhulong,* meaning literally "lamp dragon." Other images on this tree-lamp, however, are derived from the observed world: singing birds perch on the tree, and monkeys reach out toward two men who stand under the tree to feed the animals. The artist has captured a moment in life and created a lively and delightful atmosphere. A different visual strategy was employed in the design of a lamp from Tomb 6 (fig. 1.21). Instead of emphasizing dramatic interactions between people and animals, the artist has arranged to have a single standing male figure, an individual statue, dominate the visual field. The serpents that he grasps in both hands support lamp holders. The rich inlay of this work serves both decorative and representational functions. The man's face is made of silver and his eyes of a black gem. Inlaid patterns also represent the scales of the serpents and the fabric of the figure's elegant long robe.

Other sculpted works from the Zhongshan mausoleums, mostly animal images, have equally exquisite inlays but show more exotic or foreign features. Among these, a small table stand consists of four dragons and four phoenixes; their bodies, wings, and horns intertwine, forming one of the most ingenious interlaced designs from ancient China. With their square horned heads, gaping mouths, and winged feline bodies, a pair of mythical beasts from Tomb 1 resemble the four dragons on this table stand but differ from three other animal sculptures, which show definite influences from the steppes. Originally the bases of a tripartite screen, these three animal images must have been arranged in a row, with the ox and rhinoceros flanking the tiger biting a deer (fig. 1.22). It is the tiger stand that best reveals

the origin of these animal images: both the animal-combat motif and the emphasis on life-motion are trademarks of steppe art. This stylistic connection had a historical reason: it was widely believed that the Zhongshan people had descended from the nomadic White Di tribes and made incursions into the area of northern Shaanxi and northwestern Shanxi around the eighth century B.C.E.[86] It would be a mistake, however, to view the tiger stand as merely a copy of steppe art. Created in the fourth century B.C.E. in central China, the object transforms a steppe combat scene on a small plaque into one on a monumental scale, half a meter long and weighing 26 kilograms. The scene has been molded into a brilliantly colored three-dimensional form, in place of the original two-dimensional representation. The cultural and artistic fusion is also reflected in the creative use of inlay decoration. Instead of forming abstract designs, the gold and silver inlays accentuate the patterns of the animal's skin.

Both the bell set from Leigudun Tomb 1 and the sculpted lamps, tables, and screens from the Zhongshan mausoleums originally belonged to the palaces of deceased lords. It is clear that palaces served as a center for the art of sculpture in the Warring States period. Another focal point for the creation and supply of sculptural works during this period was the graveyard. The growing importance of the tomb was closely related to the country's social and political transformation. During this period, the Zhou royal house further declined, and the local rulers waging political struggles derived their power from the control of economic resources and military forces. Tombs belonging to such individuals came to symbolize the strength and status of the new social elite.[87] Two important manifestations of this transformation were the increasing grandeur of mortuary monuments and the rise of an art tradition of spirit articles (*ming qi*), which were made specifically as tomb furnishings and which included funerary figurines, a new type of sculpture.

According to an ancient definition of spirit articles, such objects were distinct from both utilitarian objects and ritual temple vessels.[88] A major feature of spirit articles was that they had to be nonfunctional. The *Book of Rites* (*Li ji*) states that spirit articles made of "bamboo should not be suited for actual use; those of earthenware should not be able to contain water; those of wood should not be finely carved; the zithers should be strung, but not evenly; the mouth organs should be prepared, but not in tune; the bells and chime stones should be there but have no stands."[89] Following this

1.21 Lamp bearer, bronze with lacquer and silver inlay and black gemstone, excavated in 1976 from Tomb 6 of the royal Zhongshan tombs, Pingshan County, Shijiazhuang, Hebei Province. 4th century B.C.E. 66.4 cm. Hebei Provincial Institute of Archaeology and Cultural Relics, Shijiazhuang.

logic, grave figurines (*muyong*) could not be put to real use; they merely symbolized the people who would follow the dead into the afterlife. Although sculpted human figures have been found in Shang and Western Zhou tombs and even in prehistorical burials, it is unclear whether such images were produced specifically for funerary purposes, and their chance occurrences do not confirm any ritual convention. Only in the late Spring and Autumn and early Warring States periods did grave figurines become a regular, though still minor, component of tomb furnishings in both the north and the south. The 209 tombs at Changsha, Hunan, for example, which have been dated to this period, yielded fourteen figurines.[90] The appearance of such objects in other Chu burial sites in the south tends to be later, though. Among the eighty-four tombs discovered at Deshan in Changde, none of the early Warring States tombs contained figurines, and only two tombs dating from the middle Warring States period yielded (seven) figurines. The largest group of figurines, twenty-three in all, came from five late Warring States tombs.[91]

Funerary figurines have frequently been interpreted as a substitute for human sacrifices, widespread during earlier periods. Archaeological excavations generally support this theory. First, in Warring States tombs, figurines were often placed next to or around the deceased; this arrangement followed the burial pattern of human sacrifices. Second, Niujiapo Tomb 7, a late Spring and Autumn burial at Changzi in Shanxi, contained three human victims along the eastern and southern walls and two pairs of wooden figurines near the western and northern walls. These seven "figures" together surrounded and protected the dead person in the middle.[92] Third, figurines are identified in the grave inventory from Wangshan Tomb 2 as "dead servants" (*wang tong*) of the deceased master in the underworld.[93] Fourth, the appearance and popularity of tomb figurines were coupled with a general decline in human sacrifices for funerary purposes.

Other archaeological excavations also show situations in which human sacrifices and figurines coexisted in a burial. In a fifth-century tomb at Langjiazhuang near Linzi, for example, twenty-six skeletons in all were found outside the main burial chamber.[94] Seventeen of them, all young females, were in wooden coffins in individual tombs surrounding the man buried in the middle. These women wore jewelry and possessed personal belongings; two were accompanied by human sacrifices; and six had small pottery figurines. A similar arrangement was found in another Qi tomb, excavated more

1.22 Stand in the shape of a tiger biting a deer, bronze with gold and silver inlay, excavated in 1977 from the tomb of King Cuo of Zhongshan in Pingshan County, Shijiazhuang, Hebei Province. 4th century B.C.E. 21.9 × 51 cm. Hebei Research Institute of Cultural Relics, Shijiazhuang.

recently at Zhangqiu and dating from the mid–Warring States period.[95] This repeated phenomenon seems to suggest that even if the death of a prestigious nobleman might still have required human sacrifices, lower-ranking people could substitute figurines.

The Linzi tomb, on the other hand, also challenges the general categorization of human sacrifices. Unlike the seventeen young women who had been given their own burials, nine other victims in the tomb, including both men and women, had suffered violent deaths, having been either executed or buried alive. Scholars have thus made the distinction between two types of human victims: "companions in death" (*ren xun*) and "human offerings" (*ren sheng*).[96] It is possible that when funerary figurines first appeared, they were made to substitute for both types of human victims. Most figurines represent servants, drivers, and musicians and were therefore replacements of companions in death. The features of a small number of examples, however, imply specific ritual or magical functions. In Changtaiguan Tomb 1, for example, a transverse front room extends for the width of the entire structure (fig. 1.23).[97] Behind that room, five small rooms surround the coffin chamber in the center. Grave furnishings in each room indicate the room's function, thereby suggesting the identities of the figurines stored there. The front room resembles an audience hall, furnished with bronze vessels and musical instruments for a ceremonial orchestra. Behind it, the deceased, wearing jade ornaments and a gold-inlaid belt hook, was buried in a double coffin in the central room. This coffin chamber is flanked by a "stable" to

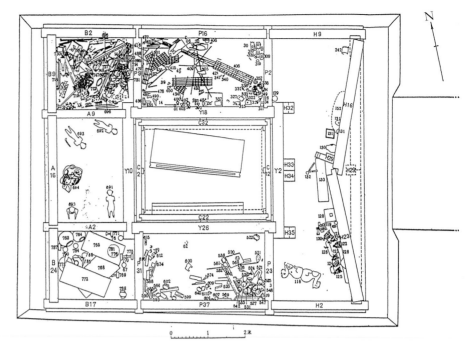

1.23 Layout of Changtaiguan Tomb 1, Xinyang, Henan Province.

the left and a "kitchen" to the right: the stable contained two driver figurines; the kitchen, two cook figurines. The far left room behind the stable was probably a study, equipped with a large couch as well as a box of writing equipment and bamboo slips to write on. Two exquisite figurines found in this room probably represent secretaries. Their black clothes are painted with extremely fine patterns; hair is glued to their heads, and their sleeves are made of fabric. To the far right behind the kitchen is a storage room, in which a kneeling servant is guarding large jars. The most mysterious room is the one at the rear center, directly behind the coffin chamber: a long-tongued creature with deer antlers, conventionally called a tomb guardian beast (*zhen-mushou*), stood in the middle of the room, surrounded by four human-shaped figurines at the four corners. Unlike other figurines in the tomb, these four figures have no robes and their bodies are crudely carved. Most intriguingly, one of them has a bamboo needle piercing its chest. It is possible that these signify human sacrifices dedicated to the deity whose statue is in the center.

Two kinds of Warring States figurines generally correspond to the geographical divisions of north and south. All figurines from the Chu region in the south are made of wood, while most figurines from the northern states are of clay.[98] The eleven figurines from Changtaiguan Tomb 1 exemplify one of three major types of Chu figurines. Each of the eleven figures is carved from a single block of wood, but some figures' outstretched arms and hands were made separately and then attached to the body with dowels. Facial features were not carved but painted on; the same method was

used to represent the patterns on clothes. Some figures are more carefully designed then others, as suggested by their well-proportioned bodies, the subtle modeling of their round shoulders, the flowing robes, the richly painted fabric patterns, and their unconventional postures. An extraordinary group of two figurines of this type came from Tomb 6 at Yidi in Jiangling County, Hubei (fig. 1.24). More than half a meter in height, the figures have identical faces and costumes but different gestures: one stretches both arms out to hold something, while the other folds her arms in front of her body. Arguably the most naturalistic renderings of human forms in Warring States sculpture, they have a realistic look that has been achieved through a combination of sculpture and painting. In fact, the figures' oval faces and cylindrical bodies are rather simple forms of sculpture, but the exquisitely painted facial features, long robes, and elaborate pendants make them unforgettable works of art.

A more stylized figurative type is found in Changsha. Again often made of a single piece of wood, figures of this type have a shield-shaped face, with a broad forehead and a pointed and slightly protruding chin. The neck is greatly elongated and connected to sloping shoulders. The figures are sometimes dressed in robes drawn up in front. The stylization of these Changsha examples stands in contrast to the third type of Chu figurine, which reflects the most assiduous effort to imitate living persons. Two large figures from Baoshan Tomb 2, for instance, are more than a meter high each. Not only were their arms made of separate pieces of wood, but their ears, hands, and feet were also all carved individually and then attached to achieve more complex shapes and gestures. The head and face are subtly modeled and finely painted, with a mustache and a braid of real hair attached. The sculpted body, however, only served as a mannequin for silk dresses — the torso below the neck is crudely carved.

A radically different style characterizes the majority of figurines from the north. Most of them are handmade from soft clay and painted either in bright red, yellow, and brown or entirely in black. Many are tiny: the figurines from Langjiazhuang Tomb 1 are about 10 centimeters tall, and examples of similar size have been found at Fenshuiling in Shanxi, Huixian County and Luoyang in Henan, and several locations in Shandong.[99] The faces are rudimentary; what make the figures special are their dramatic poses and gestures, which identify them as performers. The most significant group of this type of figurines was discovered in 1990 in a large tomb at Zhangqiu in Shandong.[100] Both human offerings and companions in death accompanied the deceased in this tomb, and a group of thirty-nine figurines further accompanied a female companion in death. Consisting of twenty-six figures, five musical instruments, and eight birds, these miniature sculptures originally constituted a large assemblage of musicians and dancers. There are ten female dancers and one female singer, ranging from 7.7 to 7.9 centimeters high. Their varying costumes and gestures indicate finer groupings in a dance formation. Two male performers are drummers; the other three are playing bells, chime stones, and a zither (fig. 1.25). Ten additional figures have their hands folded in front of them, a pose that has led excavators to identify them as the audience.

Figurines from the north and south thus attest to quite different artistic and religious concerns. Most Chu figurines were identified with their household roles as servants, cooks, drivers, and secretaries in the underworld. They rarely formed a larger group on their own. Instead, each was associated with a specific type of tomb furnishing — daily utensils, horse and chariot, kitchenware, or writing equipment — and was installed in a particular chamber in a tomb. We can thus consider these figurines individual "puppets" on a series of stages that imitated various parts of a household. The Zhangqiu figurines, on the other hand, demonstrated no definable relationship with other grave goods at the burial site. Instead, the crudely modeled miniatures were integral elements of a large, self-contained representation of dance and musical performances, which possessed a definable meaning in the mortuary context:

with performers, props, and audience, this group of figurines portrayed a delightful aspect of the afterlife. In this sense, a group of clay figurines from a small Qin tomb is similar to these Qi examples, though it has a different focus. By representing an ox-drawn carriage and a granary, the figurines reveal a specific interest in economic life, an interest that may have been related to the low social status of the patrons who were buried there.[101]

Generally speaking, all these styles and types reflect regional and cultural variations in a single category of artwork known as the grave figurine. Other types of sculpture, however, were strictly regional productions. The best known of these is the tomb guardian beast. Although the identity and meaning of this sculpture has been the focus of an intense debate among scholars, a definitive interpretation still eludes us. Many different kinds of beast sculptures seem to fall into this category of tomb guardian. One style, exemplified by a remarkable carving in the British Museum, is distinguished by the human face of the beast, concisely but forcefully defined by a series of angular, semigeometric planes.[102] Other examples, such as the one from Changtaiguan Tomb 1, have an animal form, representing a strange beast with a powerful torso, two disklike eyes, a gaping mouth, a long tongue hanging down to its stomach, and a pair of deer antlers (fig. 1.26). Kneeling, it grasps a snake with both hands and devours it. Examples of a third kind are more abstract: erected on a wooden base, the beast is shaped by a series of square blocks; but carved and painted details still indicate its round eyes and hanging tongue.[103] Because these divergent forms were relatively contemporaneous, they probably reflect regional differences within the Chu cultural sphere.

Examples of the tomb guardian beast have been found in Henan and Hunan, but this type of sculpture seems to have enjoyed its greatest popularity during the Warring States period in the Jiangling area in Hubei, where a single cemetery at Yutaishan yielded as many as 156 examples.[104] Without direct textual references, a study of the objects must rely on formal archaeological evidence. Common features of this style of sculpture, including the long tongue, the deer antlers, and the action of grasping and devouring snakes, seem to reflect shamanistic elements.[105] Archaeological excavations suggest that it was associated with higher-ranking tombs (those with wooden encasements and ritual vessels), that only one such sculpture appeared in a tomb, that it usually appeared in conjunction with drums, and that it was regularly positioned in the front or the rear tomb chamber.[106] While some of the contextual fea-

1.24 Tomb figurines, painted wood, excavated in 1978 from Tomb 6 at Yidi, Wuchang, Jiangling County, Hubei Province. 4th–3d century B.C.E. 52.5 cm (*left*) and 56.6 cm (*right*). Jingzhou District Museum, Jiangling County.

1.25 Tomb figurines, painted earthenware, excavated in 1990 from Nülangshan, Zhangqiu, Shandong Province. 4th century B.C.E. 7.4–7.9 cm. Shandong Provincial Institute of Archaeology and Cultural Relics, Ji'nan.

tures (such as its coexistence with the drum) seem to support the shamanistic connection, others may confirm the sociological and religious significance of the statue as a symbol of social privilege and as the representation of a deity worshiped in a large household.

The tomb guardian beast is related to other types of sculpture from the Chu culture, both technically and iconographically. As regards material and manufacture, these objects are all made of wood and covered with a thick layer of lacquer (and hence are generally classified as "lacquer sculpture"). To make such a lacquer object was a long process, beginning with gathering the sap of the lacquer trees. The raw sap was then made into a clear, viscous liquid through repeated filtering. Mixed with cinnabar or carbon, colored lacquer was applied to a core, which gave the object a protective coating, transformed the core material into a much stronger substance, and offered the artists a surface to decorate with colorful patterns and images.[107]

Although lacquer objects appeared long before the Warring States period in China, they gained great popularity during this period.[108] By 1986, more than three thousand lacquer objects, most dating from the Warring States period, had been found in the Chu area.[109] Unlike bronze vessels, which appeared only in the tombs of the rich and powerful, lacquer objects were almost ubiquitous in Chu burial sites. Even a small grave might contain several dozen of them; a large tomb such as Leigudun Tomb 1, in Hunan, often had more than two hundred. Some of the Leigudun lacquer objects have sculptural forms. There are two round sculpted deer,

one with a coiled black body and the other, more naturalistic, with exquisitely painted facial features and minutely detailed skin patterns.[110] Although these two deer have no apparent practical function, another object, a duck-shaped box, marries a utilitarian purpose with a sculptural form. It also highlights a main advantage of a lacquer object: it can easily include both sculpture and painting. Well proportioned and with a voluminous body, the duck displays two miniature paintings on either side, one a dance scene and the other a musical performance, each framed in a rectangular "window" surrounded by dense decorative patterns.

This duck-shaped box exemplifies one way of integrating sculptural and pictorial elements in a single work. A small screen from Wangshan Tomb 1 at Jiangling, in Hubei, offers a different combination of these two art forms, in a row of deer, birds, and snakes appearing in a continuous, openwork design. While these sculpted images are unified on a two-dimensional plane almost like a painting, additional brushwork has been used to show the features of the animals in detail. Another extraordinary example of painted sculptures from Chu is a lacquer phoenix from Lijiatai Tomb 4 at Jiangling. The phoenix, as well as the tiger-shaped base on which it stands, is painted with bold, abstract patterns of contrasting colors. The tiger is predominantly black, whereas blocks of red, silver, and yellow cover the bird's body. A pair of deer antlers planted on the back of the phoenix and likewise painted in these colors possibly indicates the magical power of this mystical bird.[111]

Any discussion of Warring States sculpture should

1.26 Tomb guardian beast, wood and lacquer, excavated from Changtaiguan Tomb 1 at Xinyang, Henan Province. 4th century B.C.E. 128 cm. Henan Provincial Institute of Cultural Relics and Archaeology, Zhengzhou.

also touch on jade carvings and other types of ornament, which testify as well to the increasing interest in sculptural forms during this period. This development was again related to the secularization of ritual art. During the Warring States era, the production of personal ornaments finally superseded that of ritual paraphernalia, not only in number but, more importantly, in the creative energy that they inspired. An early Warring States example of extraordinary workmanship again comes from Leigudun Tomb 1. Forty-eight centimeters long, this beltlike jade ornament consists of sixteen openwork segments lashed together with mortises and bronze hooks. Found next to the head of the deceased, it was probably part of an elaborate headdress. Other jade ornaments of the Warring States period included pendants, garment hooks, and rings, as well as fittings on daggers and swords. Different kinds of dragon pendants, with their gracefully curved bodies and projecting spiral fins, became widespread during the fourth century B.C.E.[112] A famous necklace from Jincun is formed of three such dragons, tubes with scroll patterns, and a pair of dancers. Made of highly polished white jade, the two dancers exemplify the increasing use of human images in personal ornamentation, a phenomenon that parallels the use of bronze figures in interior furnishing.

Like such pendants, garment hooks during the Warring States period were lavishly decorated. The early hooks were small and lacked significant surface decoration. This situation changed dramatically during the fourth and third centuries B.C.E., when garment hooks acquired various sculpted shapes, technical finishes, and colors. Some of the most beautiful hooks are said to have come from the Eastern Zhou capital Luoyang; their provenance is confirmed by the recent finding of an extraordinary gilded hook in that area.[113] Among the splendid garment hooks found in other places is an example from Guwei village Tomb 5 in Huixian County, Henan, on which intertwined animals, cast in bronze openwork designs, surround three jade rings fitted on the surface. The round back of the object is marked by a large animal mask seen head-on; the hook itself, on the front, represents a slender animal head made of jade.[114] Richly inlaid with precious metals and stones and embellished with mythical or realistic animal images, these objects best exemplify the tradition of "extravagant art" at the time. Together with the revolutionary developments in palatial architecture and funerary art, this extravagant artwork provided an essential condition for the advance of sculpture in the Warring States period.

The Qin Dynasty

Historians consider the founding of the Qin dynasty in 221 B.C.E. the single most important event in traditional Chinese history. Not only did the Qin bring about China's territorial unification, but they also redefined the country. China before that time was a society based on clan ties and lineage; afterward, it was an empire governed by a central government. Under different dynasties, this Chinese empire was to endure for more than two thousand years.

The arrival of the Qin marked a turning point in the country's cultural history as well. The bloody battles that made possible the initial unification were followed by a political, social, and intellectual unification on several levels. Relying on his powerful army as well as his administrative genius, the First Emperor of Qin broke down the stubborn regionalism of the Zhou feudal system by replacing it with a bureaucratic system in which the central government had direct control over thirty-six commanderies. Sima Qian, the Grand Historian of the Han dynasty that followed, recorded many other reforms that the First Emperor carried out as soon as the country was unified, including the standardization of laws and regulations, weights and measures, written characters, and the length of carriage axles. This last measure also led to the creation of a system of imperial roads of uniform width. In the intellectual sphere, philosophers and politicians of the Eastern Zhou had all made their own proposals about the coming society; Confucians, Daoists, and members of the other "One Hundred Schools" had all developed their own political visions and theories. The First Emperor dismissed all of these but one — Legalism — a political school whose fundamental agenda was to promote an autocratic state.

All these reforms implied simultaneous construction and destruction, and the new order established by the Qin had one man at its head. The First Emperor personified the new political entity: his ideas *were* the law, his beliefs *were* the state religion, and his personal activities *were* the most important political, religious, and artistic events. As a result, all state-sponsored sculpture projects during this period were by nature linked to the destruction of the old society, the establishment of the new system, and the interests and ambitions of the First Emperor himself. Moreover, because the Qin lasted only twenty-six years and all major sculpture projects were carried out in the capital, the projects were closely linked in time and space and must be examined within a common context. For this reason, this section on Qin sculpture will not start from a discussion of individual works such as the famous terra-cotta soldiers. Rather, the soldiers will be examined as belonging to a large underground army, which in turn constituted a section of the emperor's mausoleum. The mausoleum, too, was a counterpart to the emperor's palaces in the capital, Xianyang, where huge statues standing aboveground served different functions.

Although no longer extant, the most frequently documented sculptural works commissioned by the First Emperor were not the terra-cotta soldiers but a group of bronze statues known as the Twelve Golden Men (*shi'er jinren*). Sima Qian first recorded their creation in his *Historical Records* (*Shi ji*): in 206 B.C.E., after the First Emperor had just successfully united China, "all the weapons in the country were collected and brought to Xianyang. They were melted down to make bronze bells and the Twelve Golden Men. These bronze figures, each of which weighed a thousand catties, were placed in front of his palace."[115]

The timing of their creation was crucial. Fashioned immediately after the destruction of the rival kingdoms, they commemorated a single historical moment: Qin's victory. Sima Qian listed the making of the Twelve Golden Men among the unification measures that the First Emperor announced on the day he assumed the imperial title. The implication was unmistakable: the country had been pacified and no further wars were necessary. The former Six Kingdoms had been destroyed and assimilated into the new political entity; their weapons had been melted down to make new monuments, just as the rival powers had been transformed into submissive subjects. Standing along the Imperial Way leading to the throne hall of the First Emperor's Xianyang Palace, the Twelve Golden Men formed six pairs of figures, which, one may imagine, represented the six defeated kingdoms.[116] This monument must have also reminded contemporary Chinese of the legendary Nine Tripods, said to have been created in antiquity when Chinese history first began. According to ancient records, these sacred objects were also made of bronze collected from different regions and also symbolized the assimilation of these regions into a political entity, the Xia.[117] But in the case of the Qin, the chief visual signifier of such a political process was not a group of ritual vessels but statues of human figures.

It is possible that the Twelve Golden Men still existed during the Han and were on display in front of the Changle Palace, the throne hall of the Western Han in Chang'an. When the country fell into chaos at the end of the second century, the warlord Dong Zhuo melted down ten of the twelve figures to make coins. The last two were moved in and out of Chang'an by different regimes and finally destroyed in 384 by Fu Jian, the founder of the Former Qin. During the six hundred years from the Qin to the Former Qin, stories in circulation about the Twelve Golden Men yielded contradictory information on their size, weight, and meaning. Some Han and post-Han writers named them after the Qin general Weng Zhong, or identified them as portraits of some giant "barbarians" who came to China when the First Emperor unified the country. The recorded weight of each statue ranges from 240,000 to 340,000 *jin* (about 54.4 to 90.6 tons).[118] Since such records can hardly be taken as reliable historical accounts, the appearance of the Twelve Golden Men can only be imagined, on the basis of some actual Qin bronze figures discovered in recent archaeological excavations.

One of the finds is the head of a bronze statuette, discovered in 1982 in Xianyang (fig. 1.27). Its Qin date is secured by an accompanying bronze edict issued by the First Emperor in 221 B.C.E.[119] Although only 11 centimeters tall, this head attests to a major advance in the art of bronze sculpture. It surpasses all pre-Qin three-dimensional figurative sculptures in both technical sophistication and artistic representation. The image does not belong to any established figurative type, and it seems to represent an individual. He has a rounded but well-structured face, with high cheekbones and a broad forehead. Wearing a sensitive, inward-looking expression, he seems to be smiling at the onlooker. The sculptor clearly had a superb understanding of human anatomy; the face was modeled in an unprecedentedly complex way, as a series of hard and soft (convex and concave) surfaces smoothly connected to create a three-dimensional form. The remarkable subtlety of the face contrasts with the figure's slick hair and tall, elaborate headdress. The hair is delineated by clear, parallel flowing lines, and the headdress, which is angular in contour, is decorated with sharply defined whorls. The unusual shape of this multi-layered headdress seems to identify the figure as a man of high rank. Although we can in no way link this work with the Twelve Golden Men, it suggests the high level of artistry a Qin bronze sculptor could master.

Other examples of Qin bronze sculptures have been found next to the First Emperor's grave. These include

1.27 Head of warrior, bronze with traces of gilding, excavated in 1982 at Xianyang, Shaanxi Province. 3d century B.C.E. 11 × 7.5 cm. Xianyang Museum.

1.28 Chariot no. 1, bronze with gold and silver inlay and painting, excavated in 1980 from a pit west of the tomb of the First Emperor of Qin, Lintong County, Shaanxi Province. 3d century B.C.E. 152 × 225 cm. Museum of Terra-Cotta Warriors and Horses, Lintong County.

two amazing bronze chariots, probably the most ambitious and sophisticated bronze sculptures to have survived from ancient China (figs. 1.28, 1.29).[120] The chariots represent two different types of vehicle, even though both have four horses and a driver. The first, 225 centimeters long and 152 centimeters high, is a canopied "lead chariot" (*dao che*) with a shallow carriage; the second, 317 centimeters long and 106.2 centimeters high, is a closed wagon covered with a broad and slightly rounded roof. The driver of each chariot, also made of bronze, is about half life-size. The driver of the first chariot is 92 centimeters high. Wearing a long robe and a tall cap, he stands under the umbrella in the carriage while holding the reins with both hands (fig. 1.28). The driver of the second chariot also holds the harness, but instead of standing, he kneels in the front of the roofed vehicle before the carriage. The sculptors clearly intended to create highly realistic images of contemporary figures. Not only are the two drivers accurately proportioned, but the modeling of their faces, clothes, caps, shoes, belts, and swords imitates the textures of different materials. Moreover, the driver of the first chariot wears a jade pendant, and both figures were painted in their entirety. Although most of the paint has peeled off, traces have allowed archaeologists to reconstruct their original appearance: each driver wore a green robe over a pink shirt, while their caps, scarves, and trousers were all white.

An important feature of the two chariots is their sec-

tional construction. Unlike a conventional one-piece sculpture, each chariot consists of numerous individual parts, made independently and then assembled. The manufacturing process thus imitated the production of real chariots. The second chariot in particular is a marvel of bronze technology: an assemblage of 3,462 individual parts weighing 1,241 kilograms altogether, it renders with amazing accuracy a fully equipped chariot in half size (fig. 1.29).[121] To replicate in bronze a wooden-structured vehicle, as well as its driver and horses, the sculptors developed a system of extremely complex casting techniques and employed various "cast-on" methods. The driver's body, head, and cap, for example, were made separately and cast together in three steps. Each horse's four legs, two ears, and tail were also made individually and then cast onto the body. To make a wheel, the sculptors first fashioned a hub and thirty individual spokes. Next, they assembled them, and finally they cast the loose ends of the spokes into the cog. After casting each part, the sculptors used additional carving to represent details such as the eyebrows and mustache of the driver and the details of the horses' bodies. Many pieces of the horses' fittings are inlaid and gilded with — or made entirely of — silver or gold. (The gold parts weigh 3,033 grams, and the silver parts 4,342.1 grams.) The carriage itself is shaped like a small room, with movable windows on either side and a door at the rear. Like the driver, the chariot was originally painted in brilliant colors. The horses were

1.29 Chariot no. 2, bronze with gold and silver inlay and painting, excavated in 1980 from a pit west of the tomb of the First Emperor of Qin. 3d century B.C.E. 106.2 × 317 cm. Museum of Terra-Cotta Warriors and Horses.

entirely white; only the tongue and nostrils were pink. The wagon was decorated with intricate geometric designs and cloud patterns, which are still largely preserved inside the carriage.

One puzzling feature of these bronze chariots is the absence of the passenger in the second vehicle, whose unusually extravagant construction and decoration have convinced many scholars that it must be a bronze copy of the First Emperor's private sleeping wagon (*wenliang che*).[122] What was the ritual role or religious symbolism of these two chariots? Where in the First Emperor's grave were they buried, and why? What was their relation to other sculptures from the emperor's mausoleum? These questions lead us to investigate the overall structure of the First Emperor's tomb, where many other kinds of sculpture have also been found.

The First Emperor's necropolis, called the Lishan Mausoleum (*ling*), is considered the pinnacle of monumental mortuary architecture, which had been in development since the Eastern Zhou.[123] According to Sima Qian, the emperor began building his tomb the very day he mounted the throne. The project employed at least seven hundred thousand convicts, many of whom died while laboring at the construction site. Archaeological surveys and excavations of the Lishan Mausoleum have been carried out at full speed since the mid-1970s. The results have begun to show the general plan of the

tomb and also to allow us to speculate on its architectural symbolism (fig. 1.30).[124] Located near Xi'an, north of Lishan and south of the Wei River, the central portion of the mausoleum was a rectangular "funerary park" (*ling yuan*) surrounded by double walls. (The outer walls measure 2,165 meters north to south and about 940 meters east to west; the inner walls measure 1,355 meters north to south and about 580 meters east to west.) Separated by a wide space, these two walls divided the whole mausoleum into three zones: the central enclosure within the inner walls, the space between the two walls, and the area outside the funerary park.

A huge pyramid-shaped tumulus occupied the southern half of the central enclosure. The grave chamber underneath this artificial hill has not been excavated, but Sima Qian recorded that this secret space was transformed into a physical representation of the universe for the deceased emperor: "With mercury the myriad rivers and ocean were created, and a specially designed mechanism made them flow about. Above were all the Heavenly constellations and below all the creatures on Earth."[125] A large architectural complex, which stands north of the tomb mount and the grave, has been identified as containing the sacrificial halls where ritual offerings to the deceased emperor were placed. Surrounding the tumulus are many individual storage pits, sometimes connected to the tomb chamber by underground passageways. A walled area in the northeast corner of this central enclosure contains rows of small and mid-size tombs, probably belonging to the emperor's sonless consorts, who were forced to follow their lord into death.

In the space between the two walls, archaeologists have found foundations of several groups of buildings; pottery vessels unearthed there bear inscriptions such as "the sacrificial officer of the Lishan Mausoleum," suggesting that these buildings housed ritual administrators and imperial servants. The sections on either side of the tumulus are especially rich in archaeological deposits. Large pottery figurines found in the west section can be divided into two groups with different functions. The first group of figurines comes from two underground structures containing skeletons of several hundred horses. Clearly the structures imitated royal stables, and the pottery figures represented officials in charge of the palace and royal grooms. Figurines in the second group flanked a row of individual pits containing the remains of various animals and birds. These creatures constituted an underground zoo, and the pottery figures represented zookeepers.

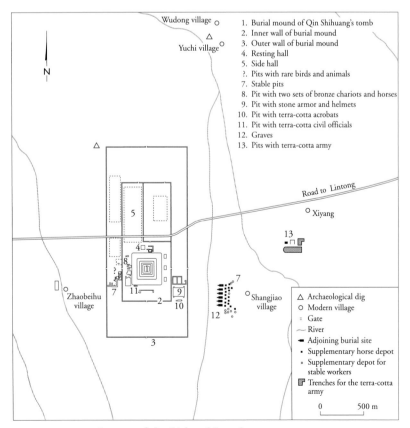

1.30 Layout of the Lishan Mausoleum.

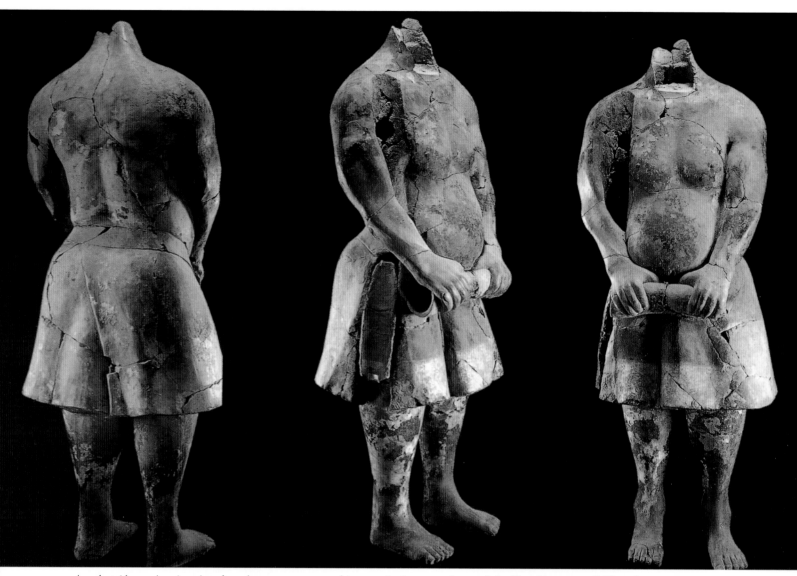

1.31 Acrobat (three views), painted earthenware, excavated in 1999 in the mausoleum of the First Emperor of Qin. 3d century B.C.E. 171 cm. Shaanxi Provincial Museum, Xi'an.

To the east of the tumulus, more sculptures have been found in two large underground structures.[126] One group again includes life-size pottery figures. A few of the figures, who are wearing only short skirts, are making dramatic gestures. These characteristics have led the excavators to identify them as acrobats (fig. 1.31). Another unexpected discovery in the First Emperor's mausoleum took place about 35 meters north of the pit containing these pottery acrobats. There, archaeologists found an underground timber structure 130 meters east to west and 100 meters north to south. Amazingly, it contained numerous sets of armor and helmets made of stone lamella in rectangular, square, trapezoid, scale-like, and irregular shapes (fig. 1.32), as well as stone harnesses.

When we synthesize these finds inside the funerary park, it becomes clear that the area within the inner wall was the First Emperor's inner court, and the space between the two walls symbolized his palace.[127] Archaeological excavations beyond the two walls reveal a different symbolism. Buried in a broad area surrounding the walled mausoleum district were a replica of the Qin Imperial Guards, graves of Qin courtiers as well as slaves, and a subterranean "water park." Sculptures installed at these locations seem to have divergent meanings, either symbolizing the political institution of the Qin empire or mirroring the First Emperor's hunting park outside the royal palace. About 350 meters east of the funerary park lay a straight row of seventeen tombs of considerable size. Their occupants were of noble rank but appear to have suffered an unnatural death: some of them were cut into pieces before burial. On the basis of historical records, scholars have suggested that the deceased were probably the princes and

1.32 Stone armor, excavated in 1998 in the mausoleum of the First Emperor of Qin. 3d century B.C.E. 125 × 43 cm. Shaanxi Provincial Museum, Xi'an.

ministers who were executed in 208 B.C.E., after the death of the First Emperor. Buried in front of the emperor's tomb, these men constituted a special kind of human sacrifice. Slightly to the east of these tombs is another huge underground horse stable, and farther to the east and northeast are the famous underground terra-cotta army and a group of newly discovered pottery figures and bronze birds. All three sites yielded abundant ceramic sculptures of human figures, to which we will return. West of the funerary park, almost symmetrical in layout with the seventeen noble burials and the horse stable on the east side, lay the burials of numerous convicts — some of whom were executed or buried alive.

Against the foregoing general structure of the Lishan Mausoleum we can map the distribution of various groups of sculptures and try to understand their meaning. A number of factors are important for this investigation, including the specific location of a sculpture in the mausoleum and its relative proximity to the First Emperor's burial chamber; the relation between a sculpture and accompanying burials of animals or objects; and the material, size, and construction method of a sculpture. On the basis of these factors we can classify the sculptures so far excavated from the Lishan Mausoleum into three categories: (1) bronze chariots and drivers possibly made for the emperor's posthumous journey, (2) stone armor, helmets, and harnesses, and (3) terra-cotta figurines representing administrators and servants in royal stables and parks; acrobats; and generals, officers, and soldiers in the Imperial Guards.

The bronze chariots and drivers were buried within the central enclosure of the funerary park. The underground wooden chamber that housed them was attached to the western ramp of the tomb and was therefore connected to the emperor's grave. These two chariots, made of bronze, differ not only from the wooden-structured battle chariots in the underground army but also from the chariots buried in the adjacent chambers, which, though elaborately painted, were still made of wood and have almost entirely disintegrated. In fact, it is possible that the bronze and wooden chariots from these adjacent chambers together formed a special procession, stationed immediately outside the First Emperor's tomb. Ancient ritual books instruct that a funerary procession to a grave should include an empty chariot for the departing soul of the dead; this chariot thus acquired the name "soul carriage" (*hun che*).[128] Pictures painted or carved in Han-dynasty tombs abundantly illustrate such processions — a validation of this record. Other pic-

tures and actual chariots found in Han tombs, however, disclose an alternative belief that a soul carriage would also transport the soul of the deceased to an immortal world after entombment.[129] Significantly, carriages serving this function were always pointed toward the outside of a tomb, as if they were about to leave the burial with the soul. This position is shared by the Qin bronze chariots, which faced west, away from the First Emperor's tomb chamber. It is possible, therefore, that these two chariots and their drivers belonged to a ritual entourage, and that the roofed wagon was the emperor's soul carriage. This hypothesis would explain not only the special location, orientation, type, material, and decoration of that chariot but also the absence of any passenger. Chinese archaeologists have recently reported the discovery of a second group of bronze and wooden chariots on the north side of the burial mound.[130] Perhaps multiple soul carriages existed. Stationed at all four sides of the tomb, they would have facilitated the emperor's posthumous journey in any direction.

Sculptures in the second category — stone armor, helmets, and harnesses — were also symbolic. Weighing more than 21 kilograms each, the sets of stone armor with helmets were clearly not created for practical use (see fig. 1.32). It is possible that stone, a durable material denoting immortality and eternity, was considered suitable to equip the army of "stone soldiers" who guarded the emperor's grave. As we will see later in this chapter, not long after the Qin — during the Western Han — this significance made stone a popular material for funerary monuments and burial chambers.

The first subgroup in the third category of Qin sculpture includes terra-cotta statues of male figures in standing or kneeling-sitting postures. Most of these figures were buried to accompany animals and birds, either sacrificed horses in several subterranean stables, deer and birds in an underground zoo, or bronze cranes in the subterranean water park. Two large stables and the zoo are located to the west of the tumulus between the two walls, while a newly discovered subterranean park is situated northeast of the mausoleum precinct. One stable, 117 meters long, is a wooden gallery containing several hundred horses killed before their burial. Eleven pottery figures found inside this stable are all life-size statues, ranging from 1.82 to 1.9 meters tall. Either holding weapons to guard the place or simply standing and watching, they represent the stable's administrators of different ranks. In the space between this stable and the inner wall of the funerary park, fifty-one individual pits in three rows constitute the underground zoo. Each pit

1.33 Kneeling figure, painted earthenware, excavated in 1973 in the mausoleum of the First Emperor of Qin. 3d century B.C.E. 65 cm. Shaanxi Provincial Museum.

in the middle row contained an animal or bird, along with a pottery basin to symbolize the continuing supply of food and drink. Fourteen pottery figures, each buried in a square pit 2 meters deep, were found on either side of the middle row. Clearly representing zookeepers or animal trainers, without caps or any weapon, they all wear simple clothes. A pottery jar buried with each figure perhaps served as a reminder of his duty to feed the animals in the afterlife. In contrast to the rigid arrangement of this underground zoo, the F-shaped subterranean park northeast of the mausoleum precinct seems to have been designed to mimic a natural environment. The timber-framed trench that housed this park has a sloping passage, which may have been used to guide water to the bottom of the structure. A dozen or so life-size birds, including several cranes and other water fowl, were unearthed there. While animals in the underground zoo were all real creatures, these birds are made of bronze. But they were still accompanied by terra-cotta human figures; this feature differentiates this group of sculptures from the bronze chariots and drivers buried next to the emperor's grave.

Not all terra-cotta figures from the Lishan Mausoleum are life-size. At about 65 centimeters tall, for example, the zookeepers in a kneeling position are considerably smaller than the administrators of the royal stable next to them. (In such a kneeling position, a person 1.85 meters tall would be about a meter high.) Pottery figures in similar sizes and postures have also been found outside the walls of the funerary park (fig. 1.33). Most of them represent stable boys or grooms working in the underground stable on the east side. It is possible that the smaller sizes of these figures correspond to their lower official status. According to an estimate, this stable, probably representing a "government stable" rather than a "royal stable," consisted of three hundred to four hundred individual pits, each containing a real horse, a pottery groom, or both. As with the zoo, the horses here were buried with pottery basins and jars, and the grooms were accompanied by oil lamps and iron tools. These animals and figures were clearly supposed to continue providing services to the First Emperor after his death. This belief must have underlain the highly realistic images of the grooms. No trace of negligence is detectable in the representation of these low-ranking servants: each figure's head, hands, and torso were made separately and then assembled. The sculptural language, too, is both concise and expressive. Quiet and dignified, these figures have inspired more than one modern scholar to praise their "serenity and elegance."[131]

The discovery in 1999 of the life-size acrobats — the second subgroup of pottery figures in the Lishan Mausoleum — was an important event in Chinese art history: the astonishing achievement of ancient Chinese sculptors in representing the human body came to light. These Qin figures challenge a conventional view that traditional Chinese art eschewed any realistic rendering of the human body. Take the statue illustrated in figure 1.31, for example. It represents a powerful male, 171 centimeters tall, standing firmly on his bare feet. The image impresses us with both the sculptor's mastery of human anatomy and his superb artistry: omitting excessive details, he endowed the figure with not only a convincing masculine torso but also an air of inner strength.

The third subgroup of pottery figures found in the Lishan Mausoleum constitutes the famous underground army, separated from the two previous categories by some major differences: this subgroup formed a relatively independent unit at the outer rim of the mausoleum district; not only people but also animals are represented in clay, alongside actual battle chariots and bronze weapons.

Accidentally discovered in 1974 by local farmers, the underground army has become known as the eighth wonder of the ancient world. It is astonishing, first of all, for its sheer scale. The four excavated pits, including an unfinished one, contained some eight thousand life-size statues of men and horses, each exquisitely sculpted and painted. Different theories have been proposed to identify this army and its components. The prevailing opinion among Chinese archaeologists is that the four pits together formed a replica of the Qin Imperial Guards. Pits 1 and 2 and the unfinished Pit 4 represented the three branches of the guards, called the Right Army, the Left Army, and the Middle Army, respectively, whereas the smaller Pit 3 was the headquarters of the whole army (fig. 1.34).[132]

The largest military formation in Pit 1 probably imitated the Right Army (fig. 1.35). The enormous rectangular pit, extending 210 meters east to west and 62 meters north to south, was surrounded by a continuous gallery on all four sides.[133] Within this rectangle was a series of nine corridors running east to west, each 3.5 meters wide. Separated by thick walls of rammed earth, these tunnel-like subterranean chambers had paved brick floors; their wooden roofs were supported by timber pillars and cross-beams. The terra-cotta legions, some six thousand warriors and 160 horses, were interred standing in a very orderly fashion. Two rows of infantry soldiers dressed in armor or plainclothes protected the regiment on each side. The soldiers in the east gallery, including nearly two hundred sharpshooters equipped with crossbows, formed the vanguard of the whole regiment and were followed by a total of thirty-eight single-file columns of warriors in the nine corridors. The infantry squads, the main components of this pit, were regularly reinforced by battle chariots, each pulled by four terra-cotta horses and manned by a charioteer and one or two soldiers. Some of the chariots, equipped with drums and bells, seem to have been command vehicles. By striking either instrument, the officer riding in such a chariot could order his section of the regiment to advance or retreat. Facing east in uniform, the army seems to be waiting on alert before marching out along the earthen ramps leading to the surface.

Pit 1 contains predominantly an infantry regiment, but the regiment in Pit 2 is a unit of war chariots and cavalry, possibly a representation of the Left Army of the Qin Imperial Guards.[134] Situated about 20 meters north of Pit 1, this roughly L-shaped pit held some 939 pottery warriors and 472 horses, divided into four groups: a square group of kneeling archers on the eastern side, a square group of war chariots in the southern half, a rectangular group of chariots and foot soldiers at the center, and a rectangle composed of mounted cavalry in the northern half. Like the horses in Pit 1, the horses found in this pit have their tails knotted. The manes are short, standing straight at the crest of the neck, except for the forelocks, which are left long and parted in the middle to curl around the front of each ear. The ears are set forward and appear tense and alert. The highest-ranking officer found in this pit, probably the head of the regiment, commands a chariot at the rear of the military formation (fig. 1.36). At 196 centimeters tall, he stands to a magnificent height. Wearing a long, double-layer military uniform and an armored vest decorated with tassels, he is also distinguished from other officers by his unique headdress, which is in the form of a double-tailed bird, said to be a symbol of bravery and skill on the battlefield. He rests his hand on a bronze sword in front of his abdomen (missing in the photo). Instead of showing him in a more predictable domineering manner, the sculptor represented him in a state of contemplation. Looking slightly downward, he appears resolute, steadfast, and highly intelligent.[135]

Because the regiment for Pit 4 was never installed, its identification as the Central Army of the Qin Imperial Guards remains hypothetical. Pit 3, the smallest of the four, clearly replicated a military command post, where the commander in chief of the underground army was

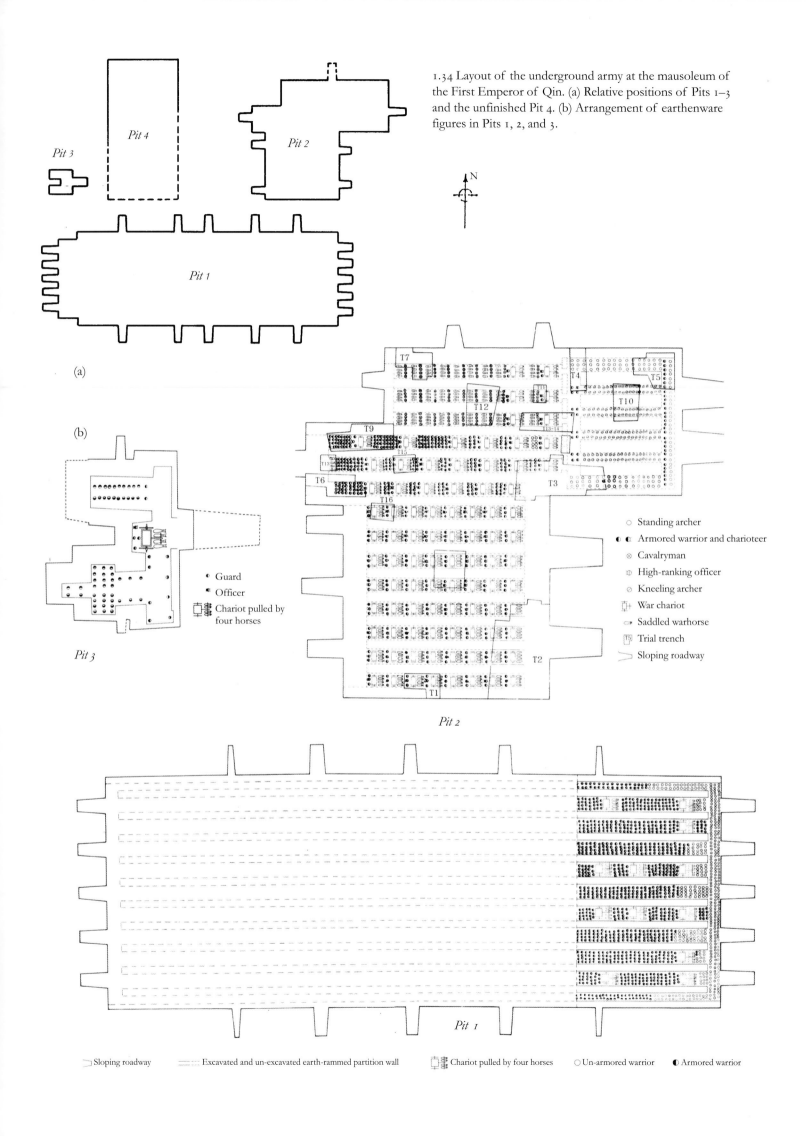

1.34 Layout of the underground army at the mausoleum of the First Emperor of Qin. (a) Relative positions of Pits 1–3 and the unfinished Pit 4. (b) Arrangement of earthenware figures in Pits 1, 2, and 3.

(a)

(b)

Pit 4

Pit 3

Pit 2

Pit 1

N

Pit 3

● Guard
■ Officer
⊞ Chariot pulled by four horses

○ Standing archer
● ● Armored warrior and charioteer
⊗ Cavalryman
⊕ High-ranking officer
⊘ Kneeling archer
⊡ War chariot
⊸ Saddled warhorse
T5 Trial trench
＼ Sloping roadway

T7 T4 T5 T10 T12 T9 T15 T13 T6 T3 T16 T2 T1

Pit 2

Pit 1

＼ Sloping roadway   ⋯ Excavated and un-excavated earth-rammed partition wall   ⊞ Chariot pulled by four horses   ○ Un-armored warrior   ● Armored warrior stationed.[136] Indeed, his war chariot, yoked to four terra-cotta horses, dominated the center of this irregularly shaped subterranean chamber (fig. 1.37). Richly painted with lacquer patterns, this canopied vehicle was originally attended by four unusually tall guards and flanked by sixty-eight officers in two kinds of armor. These officers were stationed in two side rooms that were originally separated by curtains from the central room, which contained the commander's chariot. Most of the officers held long spearlike weapons with blunt blades, whose function was more ceremonial than practical. Archaeologists have also found animal bones and deer antlers in this pit, possibly left over from certain religious or divinatory practices related to military operations. The figure of the commander in chief, however, was not found in the pit. Some scholars have hypothesized that he is the occupant of a large Qin-period tomb just 15 meters to the west. Another possibility, however, is that this absent commander in chief was the First Emperor himself. As with the empty bronze wagon found next to the First Emperor's tomb chamber, the emperor's likeness was beyond representation, and his posthumous existence could be indicated only by his physical absence.

Distinguished by their different uniforms and military functions, the several thousand terra-cotta figures in this underground army included foot soldiers in battle array, archers bending their bows, cavalrymen leading their horses, charioteers driving their chariots, and generals standing at attention, sword in hand. All the men have strong and resolute faces, powerfully structured, with a determined expression that imparts a dignified martial air.

Much research has been devoted to the manufacturing procedures for these sculptures. Generally speaking, each statue was produced by making and then assembling three separate parts of the body: the head, hands, and torso. The torso was modeled by hand, while the other two parts were fashioned with molds. Whether modeled or molded, the rudimentary form of each part was first made of a rather coarse, sandy clay. When the rough form had dried slightly, layers of finer clay were applied, in which were then carved the details of hair, beards, eyes, mouths and chins, muscles and tendons, collars, pleats, belts and belt hooks, leg bindings, and armor plates. It was at this stage of production that each figure's individual features and personality were articulated and the numerous details represented: the varying hairstyles, the tissues and ribbons on the armor, the thousand grooves on a shoe sole. The sculptors demon-

strated extraordinary skill in imitating various materials, whether the soft fabric of a gown (fig. 1.38) or the hard surface of leather armor (notice the differences, for example, between figures 1.36 and 1.38). After such modeling and carving, the entire figure was mounted on a base and fired. Finally, it was brilliantly painted in contrasting hues of red, black, blue, white, and yellow and outfitted with real weapons or bronze trappings.

This technical reconstruction helps clarify the representational status of these sculptures: Are they portraits of individual Qin warriors or artistic renderings of generic figure types? The same question arises with the pottery grooms and zookeepers found in other sections of the Lishan Mausoleum. It is true that each figure differs from the others, but the production process summarized earlier makes it clear that each statue cannot be an individual portrait. Rather, Qin sculptors used a limited number of molds to produce a repertoire of standardized components. The distinctive appearance of each statue resulted from assembling a different set of components and from hand finishing at the final stage. Thanks to this assembling and modeling process, however, the sculptures are more than mere figure types: although the sculpted warriors fall into several classifications based on their costumes and weaponry, the subtle variations in their faces defy a rigid typology. These figures are therefore "neither realistic portraits of individuals nor idealized types" but correspond to "the goal of creating a reality of a different order," one that could serve the emperor in death.[137]

This goal, as well as the material and context of the figures, reveals their debt to several regional traditions of pre-Qin funerary figurines. As discussed in the preceding section, it was customary to bury wooden figurines in a Chu tomb together with other grave goods, including real objects made of different materials, to form representations of social life, such as a chariot stable or a kitchen scene. The tradition seems to have had its continuation in the Qin terra-cotta figures, which were also accompanied by real animals, chariots, weapons, and utilitarian objects. In fact, as scholars have pointed out, the Qin terra-cotta figures exemplify one of several modes of representation found in the Lishan Mausoleum. Each mode represents a different degree of figuration — real human

OVERLEAF: 1.35 View of Pit 1, mausoleum of the First Emperor of Qin. 3d century B.C.E. Museum of Terra-Cotta Warriors and Horses.

1.36 General, brown and gray clay, originally painted, excavated in 1976–1977 from Pit 2, mausoleum of the First Emperor of Qin. 3d century B.C.E. 196 cm. Museum of Terra-Cotta Warriors and Horses.

1.37 View of Pit 3, mausoleum of the First Emperor of Qin. 3d century B.C.E. Museum of Terra-Cotta Warriors and Horses.

1.38 Military officer, brown and gray clay, originally painted, excavated in 1976–1977 from Pit 1, mausoleum of the First Emperor of Qin. 3d century B.C.E. 191 cm. Museum of Terra-Cotta Warriors and Horses.

1.39 Scale drawings of a Warring States figurine from Zhangqiu, Shandong Province (*left*), and a warrior figure from the mausoleum of the First Emperor of Qin.

and animal sacrifices, clay figures and animals, or bronze figures and horses. Together these real and manufactured images constituted "a reality appropriate for the emperor's eternal sleep."[138] It is also significant to note that in this posthumous "reality," those most closely associated with the emperor — his consorts, courtiers, and relatives — were represented by human sacrifices, while those of lower status who performed more general governmental and military roles were represented by clay statues. We can trace this convention back to some of the Eastern Zhou tombs discussed earlier, in which human sacrifices and clay figurines appeared within a single mural context to connote a social hierarchy.

This connection points to the relation between the Qin terra-cotta figures and the northern tradition of Warring States figurines. I have mentioned that most pre-Qin figurines from the north, including those from the pre-dynastic Qin kingdom, were made of clay, but their tiny size — they were often only 7 to 10 centimeters high — allowed only rudimentary representation of faces and costumes. While continuing the tradition of clay sculpture, the terra-cotta figures in the Lishan Mausoleum reflect the First Emperor's desire to impress — that is, his wish to have the figures both dwarf pre-Qin terra-cotta figurines (fig. 1.39) and astonish human observers with their large size (see fig. 1.35). Indeed, visitors to the site often find themselves surrounded and overwhelmed by the rows upon rows of this enormous army. It is at this juncture that we can link the underground army with Qin politics and the First Emperor's personal ambitions. In particular, it reminds us of the inscriptions that the emperor engraved on China's sacred mountains during his expeditions:

[The emperor's] great rule purifies the folkways; the whole empire acknowledges its sway; it blankets the world in splendid regulation.

All honor his rules and maxims, harmonious, peaceful, and diligent; there are none who do not heed his command.

The commoners are orderly and virtuous, individuals delighting in a common rule, rejoicing in and guarding the great peace.

Posterity will obey his laws, his constant governance knowing no end, like carriages and boats that never overturn.

The officials in his retinue praise his brilliance, begging to inscribe this stone; may its glorious message shine through the ages.[139]

The Western Han Dynasty

The absolute monarchy created by the Qin did not endure long. The death of the First Emperor in 210 B.C.E. was followed by four years of struggle between the two main contenders for the throne. Then, in 206 B.C.E., Liu Bang defeated his rival, Xiang Yu, and founded the Han dynasty, or more precisely, the Western Han, or the Former Han, which remained in power for the next two centuries. The beginning years of the Han were a period of consolidation. The bureaucratic system was restructured; the country's damaged economy was repaired; and the capital Chang'an was built south of the Wei River, not far from the First Emperor's Lishan Mausoleum. Of the palaces constructed to symbolize the regime's mandate from Heaven, none were even remotely comparable to the extravagant architectural projects the First Emperor had pursued a few decades before.[140] The third and fourth Western Han emperors, Wen (r. 179–157 B.C.E.) and Jing (r. 156–141 B.C.E.), especially discouraged costly construction work. During their rule, an economic policy was introduced that drastically reduced taxation and government spending, and Chang'an's expansion halted. Indeed, the policy gave these two emperors a reputation as frugal sovereigns ready to sacrifice personal luxury for the public good. Emperor Wen, in particular, "made no move to increase the size of the palaces or halls, the parks or enclosure, or the number of dogs and horses, vestments and carriages. Whenever a practice proved harmful, he immediately abandoned it in order to ensure benefit to the people."[141] We will see later that the two emperors did not exercise quite the same self-control in preparing their own burials, but their public image as moral exemplars may explain the absence of monumental architecture and sculpture during their reigns.

This situation changed dramatically with the enthronement of the next emperor, Wu, who ruled China from 140 to 87 B.C.E. The extraordinary length of his tenure and the abundant wealth accumulated during the peaceful reigns of his predecessors provided him with more than enough time and resources to attain his many goals. It was during this period that the Chinese empire attained a height of power that was to be equaled only by the Tang dynasty in the eighth century. A new kind of energy sent the Chinese armies driving across the wastes of central Asia to the fringe of the Western world. Ambitious efforts were also undertaken in the domains of culture and art. A strong-willed ruler who commissioned many monumental structures,

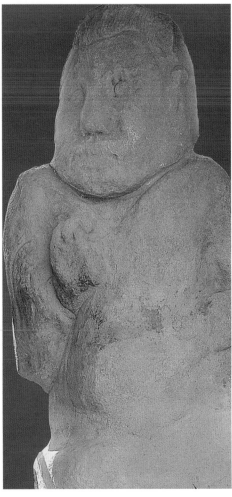

1.40 Cowherd (*right*) and Weaving Maid, granite, found at Caotangsi, Chang'an district, Xi'an, Shaanxi Province. 258 cm (Cowherd) and 228 cm (Weaving Maid).

Emperor Wu, so unlike his frugal forebears, may be compared to the First Emperor of Qin. The sculptures he initiated, however, were not the kind of political monuments fashioned during the Qin. Rather, all related to the Han ruler's personal pursuit of longevity and immortality.

One central location of these sculptures was Shanglin Park, the famous imperial park southwest of Chang'an. Partly inspired by a prose poem of Sima Xiangru (179–117 B.C.E.), Emperor Wu decided the year he ascended the throne to rebuild this park as a microcosm of the universe.[142] All sorts of "strange and precious" animals, birds, plants, and objects, acquired through tribute, confiscation, and conquest, were brought into the park. In addition to real animals, the park also housed structures dedicated to imaginary ones. One of these buildings was the Pavilion of Feilian (Feilian guan) established in the first year of the Yuanfeng reign (110 B.C.E.). Feilian was an imaginary beast with the body and antlers of a deer, the head of a pheasant, and the tail of a snake. It was believed to be a wind god who could facilitate people's communication with Heaven.[143] That was probably why Emperor Wu ordered its statue to be made and placed above the

pavilion. Significantly, 110 B.C.E. was the year that Emperor Wu held an important ceremony on Mount Tai. Known as *fengshan,* this ceremony aimed to connect the emperor with Heaven and to seal his mandate to rule the world — a symbolism consistent with the Feilian statue in Shanglin Park.

Inside the park, the emperor created the huge Kunming Lake. Stone statues of the Weaving Maid (the constellation Vega) and the Cowherd (the constellation Altair) were placed on opposite shores of the lake to turn it into a replica of the Milky Way.[144] This arrangement re-created an old legend, which tells how the couple came to be separated by the celestial river and were able to cross it only once a year with the help of magpies, who would construct a bridge for them. Both statues were found in recent years (fig. 1.40).[145] Made of hard granite, the Cowherd is 258 centimeters tall, and the Weaving Maid 228 centimeters tall. These two images were among the earliest large-scale stone sculptures created in China, a fact that explains the rather naive treatment of their bodies and the disproportionately large heads. Nevertheless, the sculptor was able to bestow different facial features and even a certain measure of individuality on the husband and wife: the Cowherd appears intense and impatient, whereas the Weaving Maid sits quietly, her hands concealed in wide sleeves.

Another and more important center for Emperor Wu's sculptures was the Jianzhang Palace west of Chang'an, constructed during the later part of his reign to imitate on earth the palace of heavenly deities. For this reason the main gate of this palatial complex was named Changhe ([the gate of the] Heavenly Palace) and the principal hall was called Yutang (Jade Hall). The Changhe Gate had three layers and was reportedly 60 meters high. Within it, a labyrinth with "a thousand doors and ten thousand windows" surrounded the Jade Hall, which soared over this architectural maze. Rather than being a conventional wooden structure, this hall was appropriately built of translucent white stone. More than one ancient historian testified that the palace was so tall that it overlooked the throne hall of the Weiyang Palace, inside Chang'an. Further emphasizing its amazing height was the gilded sculpture of a phoenix on the roof, shining in the sun and turning in the wind.[146]

The Jianzhang Palace was an enormous architectural complex. In addition to the Jade Hall, an artificial lake was created inside the palace area and given the name of Taiye (Cosmic Liquid). A giant stone whale was partially submerged in the water, and in the center of the lake was a replica of an immortal island, surrounded by other sculpted sea creatures. The shape of this island may correspond to that of an incense burner from the contemporaneous tomb of Prince Liu Sheng, a stepbrother of Emperor Wu (fig. 1.41). An exquisite miniature sculpture in its own right, this bronze censer is inlaid with precious metals and constructed in three parts. The conical top exhibits deeply undercut, fingerlike mountain peaks, decorated with relief images of animals, birds, and travelers. Apertures concealed between the peaks released the incense. This mountaintop is set over a deep bowl, inlaid with swirling gold and silver patterns representing ocean waves. A pin secures the bowl to an openwork base composed of three intertwining dragons.

It is possible that this island-shaped censer and the artificial island in the Jianzhang Palace both represented

1.41 *Boshan* incense burner, bronze with gold and silver inlay, excavated in 1968 from Tomb 1, Mancheng County, Baoding, Hebei Province. From before 113 B.C.E. 26 cm. Hebei Provincial Museum, Shijiazhuang.

1.42 Horse, gilded bronze, excavated in 1981 from a pit near Tomb 1 on the east side of the Maoling mausoleum of Emperor Wu, Xi'an. 2d century B.C.E. 62 × 76 cm. Maoling Museum.

Penglai in the Eastern Sea, a mysterious place that had been the most alluring destination for seekers of immortality since the Warring States period. Several necromancers (*fang shi*) who frequented Emperor Wu's court told him that if he could reach this place, he would never die. They described Penglai as consisting of three individual island-mountains, where all the birds and animals were pure white and all the palaces and gates were made of gold and silver. From afar, the islands looked like clouds, but as one drew closer, they seemed instead to be submerged beneath the water.[147] These and other fantasies inspired vivid sculptural images.

The Jianzhang Palace housed another famous sculpture: an immortal standing on a 46-meter-high bronze pillar and raising a plate above his head. Sweet dew falling into the plate would be mixed with powdered jade — a kind of elixir for spirits that would now be served to Emperor Wu. It is interesting to compare this statue with the Twelve Golden Men. Although both were bronze sculptures commissioned by emperors, the creation of the Han figure had little to do with the state and politics; instead it was inspired by a ruler's desire for personal longevity. The two works had a similarly tragic ending, however. After the fall of the Han in the early third century, Emperor Wen of the succeeding Wei dynasty decided to transport Emperor Wu's statue from Chang'an to his new capital, Ye. It was said that when the plate was broken off and the bronze immortal was about to be loaded in a cart, tears gushed from the statue's eyes — a melancholy image that inspired the Tang poet Li He to write these famous lines:

Withered orchids escort the departing statue along
    the Xianyang road:
If Heaven too had passions, even Heaven would
    grow old.
With plate in hand, the statue comes forth alone
    under the desolate moon:
The city on the Wei [that is, Chang'an] far back
    now, quiet the waves.[148]

As the idea of immortality came to dominate the design of imperial gardens and palaces, it also inspired smaller sculptures of bronze and jade, which often represented fairy mountains, immortals, and divine animals. Bronze censers in the shape of an immortal mountain, known as *boshanlu,* gained wide popularity around this time and demonstrate inexhaustible artistic ingenuity.[149] It is therefore not surprising that one of the earliest known sculptors in Chinese history was associated with this type of object: the Chang'an master craftsman Ding

Yuan designed a "nine-layered *boshan* incense burner," with vivid images of animals and immortals that seemed to be "naturally moving."[150] Ding's design has been linked to Prince Liu Sheng's censer, discussed earlier, on which nine layers of mountain peaks are arranged in concentric circles (see fig. 1.41). The prince's censer was one of a small group of exquisite examples of the type created during the second century B.C.E. Another boshanlu of comparable artistic quality was found in the tomb of Liu Sheng's consort, Dou Wan. Although less ornate and lacking inlaid patterns made of precious metals, the mountain-shaped burner has a base that is imaginatively shaped like a half-naked giant riding on a mythical animal while holding up the immortal mountain with a single arm. Because the bronze plate under the censer was filled with water when the censer was in use, the giant on the mythical animal would have seemed to emerge from a pool. Interestingly, ancient texts relate that a divine turtle carried Penglai on its back; as the beast moved, the fairy island would emerge from or sink back into the ocean.[151]

A good example of the third boshanlu design is a gilded censer originally used in the Weiyang Palace, an important structure in Chang'an that replaced the Changle Palace as throne hall soon after the founding of the Qin dynasty.[152] Probably made in 136 B.C.E., the censer has a mountain-shaped burner supported by a tall stem in the shape of a long stalk of bamboo. The upper end of the stem branches into three dragons; around the censer itself parades a series of mythical animals in relief, gilded with silver and contrasting with the gold surface of the immortal mountain. This beautiful object was part of a large group of luxurious goods buried in a sacrificial pit near one of the "satellite tombs" of Emperor Wu's mausoleum, Maoling. Another extraordinary sculpture from the group is a large bronze-gilt horse (fig. 1.42). Unlike the stout terra-cotta battle horses of the First Emperor, this Han sculpture represents an animal with a slender body and long legs whose smooth, elegant contour contrasts with its strong musculature. This new horse image does not merely reflect a new artistic taste or style, however: we see here a different breed of horse, introduced from the distant western region of Ferghana (Dayuan). Such horses were highly praised during Emperor Wu's reign as *tianma,* "celestial steeds" or "horses of Heaven," and indeed were so highly regarded that they became a subject for mythology. Emperor Wu believed that a tianma could help him obtain immortality, and he wrote a hymn praising it:

... The horse of Heaven has come
Open the far gates
Raise up my body
I go to the immortal Kunlun Mountains
The horse of Heaven has come
Mediator for the dragon
He travels to the gates of Heaven
And looks on the Terrace of Jade.[153]

It has been suggested that both this horse statue and the Weiyang Palace censer belonged to Princess Yangxin, the elder sister of Emperor Wu.[154] The suggestion seems plausible because several objects from the sacrificial pit bear a "Yangxin Household" (Yangxin *jia*) inscription and because the occupant of a "satellite tomb" was often a royal relative. Following this argument, the princess should have received the censer from the emperor as an imperial gift when she was alive, then brought the prized object with her into the afterlife. A similar situation may explain the finding of an imperial bronze-gilt lamp in Dou Wan's tomb, Mancheng County, Baoding, Hebei (fig. 1.43). A series of six inscriptions on this lamp reveal the history of its possession: originally made by a Han prince before the mid-second century B.C.E., it was confiscated around 151 B.C.E. and entered the Changxin Palace of Empress Dowager Dou, a powerful political figure during Emperor Jing's reign. It happened that this empress not only was the grandmother of Prince Liu Sheng but also had the same surname as Liu Sheng's wife, Dou Wan. It is thus possible that after obtaining the precious object, she in turn gave it to Dou Wan, a younger lady of her own clan who had also married into the royal household.[155]

Considered one of the finest early Chinese sculptures, the lamp is in the shape of a young girl raising a cylindrical lantern with both hands. The girl, perhaps a palace servant, appears dignified; her slightly downcast eyes and sharply defined eyebrows convey a rather timid expression. Yet her pose is natural and relaxed, and her simple robe both conceals and reveals her round shoulders and curving waist. This beautiful sculpture is ingeniously functional. The lantern has a movable circular base. The two vertical "doors" of the lantern can be adjusted to control the direction of light and to regulate brightness by changing the size of the opening. And the girl's raised right arm also served as a chimney, channeling the smoke from a burning candle into her hollow body. Combining utility with the beauty of a sculpted human image, this lamp continued an old tradition that can be traced back to before the Eastern

1.43 Lamp in the shape of female attendant, bronze, excavated in 1968 from Tomb 2, Mancheng County, Baoding, Hebei Province. Early 2d century B.C.E. 48 cm. Hebei Provincial Museum, Shijiazhuang.

Zhou (see figs. 1.2, 1.21). But it was also associated with other small bronze sculptures created during the Western Han, which often represented servants, storytellers, dancers, acrobats, or foreigners. Many of the figures decorate practical objects; others are independent sculptures that furnished a nobleman's residence with playful and amusing images. Among the entertaining kind are a pair of partially gilded bronze figures from Liu Sheng's tomb that represent two men engaged in storytelling. One of them, probably the principal storyteller, raises his right hand close to his head and seems to be emphasizing his point; the other slightly lowers his head and listens. Both figures have exaggerated, wide cheeks, small pointed chins, narrow eyes, and mustaches resembling a cat's whiskers. Their unusual physiognomy has led some scholars to identify them as foreign entertainers serving at the Han court.[156]

The most popular Western Han statuettes, however, were of the immortals, especially a kind of fairy known as *yuren,* or "feather-men." One yuren image, a bronze statue of a winged figure, only 15.3 centimeters tall, was

1.44 Winged immortal, bronze gilt, excavated in 1987 from a tomb near Luoyang, Henan Province. 2d century B.C.E. 15.5 × 9.5 cm. Cultural Relics Bureau, Luoyang.

found in 1964 in a place adjacent to the Changle Palace in Chang'an.[157] The figure is barefoot and has a slender body covered with feathers extending across its back and down to the lower legs. Its otherworldly origin is evident also in its extraordinary face, with raised eyebrows shadowing a pair of sunken eyes, a sharply pointed nose, and protruding lips, and especially in the large ears on top of the head. Never before have we seen such an angular, bony figure in ancient Chinese sculpture — the immortal seems to have been reduced to near immateriality. The figure grins wickedly. Stretching out both arms, he appears to be holding something, but the object he originally held is now gone. An almost identical yuren image, discovered more recently in an Eastern Han tomb at Luoyang, is fortunately complete: the missing part is a small container with two separate compartments, one round and one rectangular (fig. 1.44). Probably this intricately decorated box originally contained Daoist elixir or talismans — secret keys to immortality. This second statuette is also better preserved; much of the gilded surface and richly inlaid patterns remains on both the figure's body and the container. Although it came from an Eastern Han tomb, it should be dated to

the Western Han on the basis of its decorative style; moreover, the first yuren image was found at a Western Han site with a group of Western Han objects.

A feather-man is also the subject of an exquisite jade carving excavated near the Weiling mausoleum of Emperor Yuan (r. 48–33 B.C.E.). Here the immortal is riding on a heavenly horse, which also has wings and is roaming the sky.[158] This work thus integrates figurative and zoomorphic motifs and reflects an important feature of Western Han animal sculptures: the melding of naturalistic forms with imaginary elements. The most striking example of such a hybrid image is perhaps a wine container in the shape of a rhinoceros, discovered in 1963 near Emperor Wu's tomb (fig. 1.45). Clearly continuing the old tradition of animal-shaped vessels (for example, figures 1.1, 1.7, 1.8, 1.12, 1.17), it has been dated to the late Eastern Zhou or Qin. Its sophisticated realism and lively cloud patterns, however, betray a later date, probably around the early second century B.C.E. There is no question that the sculptor modeled this image after a real rhinoceros, because the vessel shows the animal's anatomic details, down to the soft upper lip and the hard forehead, in an amazingly realistic manner. Yet a purely naturalistic representation is not the purpose of this work. Densely scalloped cloud scrolls swirl around the animal's body with extraordinary energy and vigor. These intaglio scrolls were once inlaid with precious metals, but now only fine gold strokes are visible on the raised areas between the cloud patterns. Combinations of clouds and auspicious animals are frequently seen in Han art, in both painted and sculpted forms. Such images reflect the Han belief in *yuan qi* (cloud breath), which would appear when Heaven sent down unusual animals or birds to announce its blessing to human beings.[159]

The bronze and jade sculptures just discussed were created to be seen and used in royal palaces and aristocratic households. Another major group of Western Han sculptures belong to the category of spirit articles made especially for tombs. These works thus continued the tradition of Warring States wooden figurines and Qin terra-cotta warriors (see figs. 1.24, 1.25, 1.31, 1.36, 1.38) while revitalizing this old art tradition with many innovations.

Among the eleven Western Han royal tombs constructed around Chang'an, nine were located north of the Wei River. This river therefore became a natural symbol of death, separating the mausoleums of individual emperors from the capital city, the collective administrative center of the state.[160] Most of the impe-

1.45 Rhinoceros-shaped vessel, bronze with gold inlay, excavated in 1963 in Xingping County, Shaanxi Province. Tang dynasty, early 2d century B.C.E. 34.1 × 58.1 cm. National Museum of China, Beijing.

rial tombs, dominated by a four-sided, truncated pyramidal mound of pounded earth, owe a clear debt to the First Emperor's Lishan necropolis. Instead of burying executed princes and ministers in front of the ruler's grave, however, as we observed with the Lishan Mausoleum, the Han emperors developed a *peiling* (satellite burial) system, according to which imperial consorts, royal relatives, and meritorious ministers and generals were allowed to attach their own tombs to the tomb of a deceased emperor. A present-day visitor to Changling, for example, would find some sixty-three pyramid-shaped tumuli crowded east of this mausoleum of Emperor Gaozu, the founder of the dynasty; sixteen tumuli near the Anling mausoleum of the second emperor, Hui; and seventy-two satellite tombs around Emperor Wu's tomb, Maoling. So far archaeologists have not opened any of the eleven imperial tombs, but some of their auxiliary sacrificial pits and the accompanying satellite tombs have been excavated. These excavations have yielded a great many tomb figurines, allowing us to outline the development of this type of sculpture under the patronage of the Western Han elite.

Several groups of early Western Han figurines continued the Qin tradition of constructing a large under-

ground army. A group consisting of 1,965 infantrymen and 583 mounted cavalrymen was found at Yangjiawan near Xi'an.[161] These terra-cotta figurines were buried in eleven sacrificial pits in five rows, which accompanied two satellite tombs near Emperor Gaozu's Changling mausoleum. The occupants of the two tombs have been identified as Zhou Bo and his son Zhou Yafu, both of whom were famous early Han generals. Their official capacity as commanders of Han imperial armies explains the exclusively military content of their tomb figures: among the eleven pits, four were for foot soldiers, six were for cavalrymen, and one was for war chariots. The infantrymen were in the vanguard, with the mounted cavalry bringing up the rear. This arrangement is reminiscent of the First Emperor's underground army, but the Han terra-cotta warriors are much smaller: the standing soldiers are about 45 centimeters tall, and even the mounted cavalry figures never exceed 68 centimeters in height. Lacking are the minute attention to detail and the effort to create individual faces; the Yangjiawan examples are nearly identical mannequins with large heads, masklike faces, and still poses. These mass-produced figurines are evidence of the popularization of a specific type of symbolic image:

now that warrior figurines were no longer created exclusively for emperors, an entire manufactured army could accompany a general into the afterlife.

Large groups of tomb figures were made for many burials during this period. As a consequence, the early Western Han witnessed the most abundant production of funerary figurines in Chinese history. As the Yangjiawan examples demonstrate, the impressive quantity of these works often came at the expense of artistic quality. This was especially true during the early second century B.C.E. Only later, around the mid-second century B.C.E., did a new sculptural style begin to emerge, one that brought a better balance between mass production and artistic expression.

In contrast to the Yangjiawan figurines, some other assemblages of Western Han tomb figures combined military personnel with domestic figures and animals, thereby bringing the various components of the Lishan Mausoleum — warriors as well as grooms and servants — into a single context. One such group was discovered in one of the sixteen satellite burials (Tomb 11) near Emperor Hui's mausoleum, Anling. Here the central tomb chamber was surrounded on all sides by a square auxiliary trench built of brick, in which grave goods and spirit articles were installed. In the middle of the southern trench archaeologists found eighty-four ceramic human figures and herds of animals, including 46 oxen, 125 sheep, and 23 pigs.[162] In retrospect, we realize that no terra-cotta sculptures of domestic animals except for battle horses have been found in the Lishan Mausoleum, and all the horses buried in the underground stables at Lishan were real ones. Perhaps the rendering of herds of livestock in clay was an early Han invention, one that expanded the subject of funerary sculpture to represent the economic aspect of social life.

Much more ambitious than this single assemblage were various kinds of figurines and grave goods buried in at least twenty-four sacrificial pits south of Yangling, the tomb of Emperor Jing.[163] These pits — actually underground trenches supported by timber structures — range from 25 to 291 meters long. Located close by in a well-defined area, their uniform orientation and parallel positioning suggest that they were designed as a unit, and indeed their differing contents mirrored various aspects of a Han royal household. The southern section of Pit 17, for example, was filled with grain and can be identified as an underground granary. The seventy terra-cotta soldiers marching behind two carriages in the northern section may have been created to protect this important source of food. The square Pit 21 was divided into three sections for a variety of sculptured domestic animals, including oxen, dogs, sheep, pigs, and chickens, all carefully modeled and painted to achieve a lifelike effect. Stoves and cooking utensils were also unearthed from this pit, along with domestic servants. A third component of the pit was a group of terra-cotta guards, equipped with short- and long-range weapons and stationed at the four corners of the subterranean building.

These finds show several major changes in funerary figurines in the early Western Han. The first change concerns the size of tomb sculpture. I have emphasized that a crucial aspect of the Qin terra-cotta warriors is their size: they are giants compared with pottery figurines from the Warring States period. But the early Han rulers abandoned the First Emperor's quest for monumentality in favor of moderation in sculptural representation. Figurines from Yangling, though among the largest from the early Han, are only about a third as tall as a Qin warrior sculpture; those from Houloushan in Xuzhou and other places are even smaller, about one-ninth the size of a Qin figure. Although the Han figurines are still larger than pre-Qin examples, they can be called miniatures because they are much smaller than their natural models and because their limited size resulted from a conscious decision to reduce the scale of tomb figures drastically. It must have been a conscious decision, because these works were made not long after the Qin warriors in the Xianyang-Chang'an area, when the memory of creating thousands of life-size statues must have still been alive in the region.

Why did the Han emperors not follow the Qin example and furnish their tombs with life-size figurines? Some scholars have postulated that the decision stemmed from frugality or other economic concerns, but this reasoning hardly explains why *no* Han emperors ever attempted life-size figurines, even after accumulating great wealth after the initial years of the dynasty. It is important to realize that Han figurines were not just smaller and less elaborate versions of the Qin warriors. Instead, the basic purpose of these clay images was to fashion a miniature world, not a gigantic one. The sacrificial pits south of Yangling best illuminate this miniature world. They contained not only small figures and domestic animals but *everything* needed to create a miniature version of reality — including buildings, chariots,

1.46 Female dancer, pottery with slip and pigments, probably from Xi'an. Western Han, 2d century B.C.E. 53.3 cm. The Metropolitan Museum of Art, New York.

weapons, stoves, pots, measuring cups, and many other objects. We wonder why these tiny imitations conform painstakingly to a uniform scale of reduction. The answer must be found in the specific artistic goals of the miniature. It has been suggested that miniature representations consciously create an interior space and time in a fictional world.[164] Unlike life-size figures, which are an attempt to map art upon life, the metaphorical world of the miniature skews the temporal and spatial relations of the everyday world. Buried underground, the miniatures in Yangling and other Han tombs not only "substituted" for the real human world but also constituted a world free from the natural laws of that human world, thereby extending life in perpetuity.

The second important change in tomb figurines during the Western Han concerns the social roles of the figures being represented. Whereas the Lishan Mausoleum was furnished mainly with images of warriors and administrators, a growing interest in domestic life during the early Han led to the popularity of other types such as attendants, servants, guards, and performers — people who were indispensable for a comfortable afterlife. This was indeed a nationwide phenomenon, observable not only in the metropolitan area but all over Han China. In the south, the famous Mawangdui Tomb 1, constructed before 168 B.C.E., contained 162 wooden figurines, of which 154 represent household roles. In the east, a large rock-cut tomb at Beidongshan near Xuzhou consisted of a 55-meter-long passageway and nineteen chambers. Inside the tomb, 422 painted pottery figurines occupying the different sections include armed guards stationed in shallow niches along the passageway, male and female attendants serving in various tomb chambers, and dancers and musicians performing in a "music and dance hall."[165] Indeed, although some Han underground armies have been found, excavated figurines of domestic types vastly outnumber them. This general shift in the subject matter of tomb sculpture led to the creation of some especially beautiful images as new cultural icons of the period. One such image, found at Beidongshan and other contemporaneous tombs, is a graceful dancer caught during a formal performance (fig. 1.46).[166] Her tight-fitting robe and extremely long sleeves accentuate her elegant outlines. Bending her upper body slightly, she flings her right sleeve over one shoulder while dangling the left sleeve in a relaxed way. It is this kind of "indoor" image, not the miniature soldiers from Yangjiawan, that best illustrates the achievement of Western Han tomb sculpture.

The interest in representing domestic and private life also affected the emergence of a new sculptural style and changes in figurines' facial expressions. A group of early examples of this style came from sacrificial pits associated with the tomb of Empress Dou (d. 135 B.C.E.), wife of Emperor Wen.[167] The forty-two pottery figurines from these pits are mostly female attendants (fig. 1.47). Nothing about them is dramatic or overwhelming. These graceful figures stand or kneel quietly in simple but natural poses. Their gentle faces wear contemplative expressions. Ornamentation and detail are largely omitted for the sake of visual simplicity and harmony. The subtle curves of every surface — the oval-shaped faces, the round shoulders and calves, and the smooth draperies of their robes — evoke a feeling of serenity. The same sculptural style characterizes contemporary figurines from several locations in the Han metropolitan area, including Langjiagou and Lintong.[168] Examples of this style include figurines from Emperor Jing's Yangling mausoleum, built before 141 B.C.E. (fig. 1.48). Markedly different from the heroic warriors of the First Emperor of Qin, these Han sculptures show youthful figures with classic smiles and dreamy expressions. Although we cannot explain this expression precisely, it seems to reflect a new attitude toward the afterlife: the dark underworld now promised to be a realm of eternal happiness.

A third major change in Western Han tomb figures is more specific: the figurines from Yangling were found naked. These nude figures demonstrate a keen interest in the physicality of the human body rarely seen in Chinese art: each figure was carefully molded and modeled to represent the slightly bulging muscles on the chest, the subtly protruding collarbones, the round buttocks, and certain often hidden bodily features, such as the navel and sexual organs. The entire surface of the body was polished smooth and covered with orange paint to imitate the color of the skin. So far, such naked figurines, predominantly male but also including a limited number of female images, have been found in several burials associated with members of the royal family. Excavations of a group of twenty-one official kilns located 300 meters from Chang'an's northern wall have also yielded unfinished and abandoned examples of such figures.[169] To judge from the dates of the burials and kilns, this type of figurine, as exemplified by those from Yangling, may have been invented around the mid-second century B.C.E. The figures remained in limited use till the mid-first century B.C.E., as shown by those from a sacrificial pit (Pit 1) near Emperor Xuan's (r. 73–49 B.C.E.) mausoleum, Duling.[170]

1.47 Female attendants, clay, excavated in 1966 from pits associated with the tomb of Empress Dou, at Renjiapo village, Xi'an. Mid-2d century B.C.E. 33–53 cm. Shaanxi Provincial Museum, Xi'an.

All these naked figurines are armless; next to each shoulder is a flat circular surface with a round hole in the center running through the chest. Scholars believe that the hole permitted the installation of movable arms on the body, arms that have completely decayed because they were made of perishable material. The traces of fabric that remained on the surface of some figures prove that they were originally clothed. But why should these tomb figures have been sculpted without clothes and then dressed? And why should their bodies have been so painstakingly sculptured and painted if they were going to be covered in the end? The goal could not have been simply to imitate the external appearance of a clothed figure. Rather, the artist must have tried to duplicate the process of *fashioning* human forms — that is, to evoke the way that real people look after putting on layer after layer of clothing and ornamentation. The body had to be made first and then dressed, because this was how it was in real life. In retrospect, we realize that the sectional construction of the First Emperor's bronze chariots already implied this particular notion of realism; otherwise, it would have been unnecessary to create the four horses individually and then put fittings on them, and it would have been unnecessary to assemble 3,462 parts for a single chariot. Many miniature bronze objects found in Yangling followed this tradition. To take a bronze crossbow as an example, its mechanism is only 3.9 centimeters long, but all its parts, including a sight, a trigger, an arrow holder, and several connectors, were made separately, engraved with serial codes, and assembled so that they could be freely moved.[171] A major difference between the Lishan Mausoleum and Yangling, however, is that the tomb figures in the Han mausoleum were granted individual bodies to be dressed and undressed. In this way they could elicit more vividly the image of an animated underground world where soldiers, attendants, and others, dressed in miniature clothes and equipped with miniature instruments, carried out their respective duties.

People of the Han conceived the goal of mimicking a fashioning process in relation to divine creativity. Significantly, it was around this period that a creation myth developed in China. The central figure, Nü Wa, was an ancient goddess who attained the status of a fashion-ing deity during the period from the late Eastern Zhou to the Han. Indeed, she was credited with the creation of human beings, as described in a second-century text, *Explanations of Customs (Fengsu tong)*: "People say that when Heaven and Earth opened up, mankind did not yet exist. Nü Wa kneaded yellow earth and fashioned human beings. Though she worked feverishly, she did not have enough strength to finish her task, so she drew her cord in a furrow through the mud and lifted it out to make human figures. That is why the rich and the noble are those men of yellow earth, whereas the poor and the lowly — all ordinary people — are the human beings made from the cord's furrow."[172] This myth, thanks to which the making of funerary figurines by anonymous artisans could be likened to the creation of humankind at the hands of a supreme deity, clearly derives its imagery from contemporaneous artistic production.

When we shift our focus from tomb figurines made in the metropolitan area to those produced in the provinces, we find a more complex situation: the earlier regional traditions of mortuary art persisted more in these places, even as the metropolitan styles gained acceptance. The social group that most readily adopted the metropolitan style of figurine included the rulers of principalities, established in the early Western Han through enfeoffment. Such local rulers, often members of the royal clan, constructed enormous tombs for themselves near their capitals. The excavation of some of the tombs and auxiliary sacrificial pits has yielded a huge number of figurines that closely resemble those from metropolitan areas. A local underground army of more than six thousand figures, for example, found in subsidiary pits near the tomb of a Chu prince at Shizi-shan in Xuzhou, mirrors the Yangjiawan underground army of Chang'an.[173] And shortly after naked figurines began to appear in metropolitan art (around the mid-second century B.C.E.), some examples also turned up in the tomb of a Liang prince at Mangshan in Yongcheng, Henan.

The imported metropolitan styles never replaced regional styles of tomb figurines, however. Rather, during the early and middle Western Han, local traditions continued to develop, enriched by elements from metropolitan art. In Shandong, an earthenware tableau of performers and spectators excavated from an early Western Han tomb at Ji'nan clearly continued the tradition of Warring States figurines from the same region; but in this Han work individual figures were arranged on a rectangular platform, thus revealing a stronger desire to construct a coherent setting for a miniature

1.48 Naked figurines, ceramic, originally dressed in clothes made of fabric, excavated in 1992–1993 from pits near the Yangling mausoleum of Emperor Jing. Mid-2d century B.C.E. Ca. 60 cm. Shaanxi Provincial Institute of Archaeology, Xi'an.

presentation (see fig. 1.25). Here, an orchestra provided musical accompaniment for a singer, dancers, and a troupe of acrobats, while an audience of proud dignitaries stood watching in two rows.[174]

In the south, southeast, and southwest, the Chu tradition of wooden figurines was still all-powerful in Hunan, Hubei, Anhui, Jiangsu, and Sichuan. Many such tomb figures were found in 1972 in Mawangdui Tomb 1 at Changsha, Hunan.[175] This tomb from the early second century B.C.E. belonged to Lady Dai, the wife of a chancellor of Changsha principality.[176] Her tomb was constructed as a large wooden box divided into five compartments or chambers, with the coffin chamber in the center and the others — one marking each of the four cardinal directions — surrounding it. A total of 154 figurines, together with more than a thousand household articles and food items, were found in the side chambers. The varying sizes of the tomb figures — as well as their different costumes, methods of manufacture, sculptural styles, and positions in the tomb — provide rich information about southern figurines at this time in Chinese sculptural history.

Of the four side chambers, the northern one imitated Lady Dai's private resting room. Silk curtains hung on the walls, and a bamboo mat covered the floor. Eating and drinking vessels stood in front of an empty couch backed by a screen — a seat prepared for Lady Dai's posthumous use. From this couch, the invisible soul could watch a musical and dance performance staged in the western section of the chamber. Several groups of figurines found in this chamber — musicians, dancers, singers, and attendants — are of different sizes and materials. Five kneeling figures, made entirely of wood, with painted facial features and clothes, represent musicians playing various musical instruments in a miniature orchestra (fig. 1.49). Eighteen other figurines, dressed in silk clothes, can be divided into two subgroups according to their size and degree of elaboration. Ten of them are much larger — 69 to 78, as compared with 48 to 49, centimeters high — and wear wigs made of human hair. They appear to represent Lady Dai's personal attendants. The other eight have been identified as singers and dancers. Compared with these images in the northern chamber,

1.49 Five musicians, painted wood, excavated in 1972 from Mawangdui Tomb 1, Changsha, Hunan Province. Early 2d century B.C.E. 32.5–38 cm. Hunan Provincial Museum, Changsha.

most of the hundred figurines stored in the eastern and southern chambers are much simpler, each made of a flat piece of wood and sketchily painted. Since these figurines were found together with most of the domestic utensils and food in the tomb, they probably represent servants in Lady Dai's underground home. Two large figurines — chief servants — are poised to lead the others out of the eastern and southern chambers. Almost twice as high as other images, these two figures wore tall caps and silk robes. A title inscribed on one of them, *Guan ren,* or "Capped Man," identifies them as the administrators of Lady Dai's household.[177]

Although the coexistence of several figurine styles as found in the Mawangdui tomb was unprecedented in the south, each style developed from a previous type of Chu figurine. Wooden figurines from a roughly contemporary burial (Tomb 167) at Fenghuangshan in Jiangling, Hubei, however, show the influence of the prevailing metropolitan style to a greater degree. This tomb, also belonging to a lady of noble birth, was constructed some time before 141 B.C.E.[178] The twenty-seven figurines discovered there represent different household roles, including supervisors holding halberds and agricultural laborers equipped with the tools of their trade. Unlike the Mawangdui figures, however, these images show definite similarities as regards sculptural style to terra-cotta figurines popular in the Chang'an area around the mid-second century B.C.E. In particular, the rounded contours and strong three-dimensionality have much in common with the shapes of figurines from Renjiapo, Langjiagou, and Lintong near Xi'an (see fig. 1.47). Figurines of similar styles have also been found in other southern areas, such as Lianyungang in Jiangsu and Mianyang in Sichuan.[179]

All these examples reveal the interplay among sculptural traditions within China. Another important aspect of Han art is the relation between Chinese art traditions and those of the outside world. Many new elements in Han art can be traced to foreign cultures brought into closer contact with the Han Chinese through the country's territorial expansion. Military conquest also caused peripheral non-Chinese cultures to lose their own artistic heritage after becoming part of the Han empire. One such culture was the Dian (in present-day Yunnan), which had maintained an independent sculptural tradition until its submission to Han rule in 109 B.C.E. The achievement of Dian sculpture before this date is most effectively exemplified by bronze works from the necropolises at Shizhaishan, Lijiashan, and Taijishan, all located near Lake Dian in central Yunnan.[180] A gold seal of the "king of Dian," supposedly awarded by Emperor Wu to a Dian ruler, has been found in a Shizhaishan tomb and substantiates the written history of the area. Most of the sculptures from this and other sites belong to the second century B.C.E., but some have been dated to as early as the Warring States period. Many sculpted images appear on the flat top of a kind of cylindrical bronze object used to contain cowry shells. Found only in the richest tombs, the containers symbolize the extraordinary importance of the tombs' occupants. The images on these cowry containers, sometimes populated with as many as 127 figures, often constitute large tableaus of social events. The scene on one cowry container, for example, depicts a ritual centered on a pillar with a snake coiling around it and a tiger on top. Surrounding the pillar, a large crowd of people are making human sacrifices. Tableaus on other cowry containers represent a golden image of a Dian ruler surrounded by bulls, battle scenes, and the ceremonial killing of cattle.[181] With their lively and finely modeled human and animal figures, these dramatic scenes provide vivid visual records of Dian society and religion.

A different kind of realism characterizes sculptures of individual human and animal figures from the same Dian tombs. A statue from Shizhaishan Tomb 20, for example, portrays an older man. The power of the image lies both in its anatomical accuracy and in its psychological depth: while holding a ceremonial umbrella, the man stares at the void before him with a complex, intense expression. A "sacrificial altar" discovered at Lijiashan is 76 centimeters long and is dominated by the magnificent image of a bull (fig. 1.50). The animal's head was modeled in the round with a pair of sweeping horns thrusting forward. Its body, however, was transformed into a ritual altar — its back was scooped away to form a smooth surface and its belly hollowed out to allow a young bull to rest between its legs. These two bulls are joined by the third image in this sculpture — a tiger marked with intaglio stripes on its skin — which clutches the hind end of the big bull with all four paws and holds the bull's tail in its teeth. Although we have little idea of the function of this object or the meaning of the images, we cannot help admiring the work's powerful imagery and clever design.

These and other Dian sculptures reflect the strong influence of steppe art. As mentioned earlier, steppe influences had been a factor in Chinese art long before the Han. Genuine examples of steppe sculpture during the Western Han period, found in several northern locations in present-day Inner Mongolia and Liaoning,

1.50 Ritual altar in the form of two bulls and a tiger, bronze, excavated in 1972 at Lijiashan, Jiangquan, Yunnan Province. 3d–2d century B.C.E. 43 × 76 cm. Yunnan Provincial Museum, Kunming.

include bronze openwork plates representing hunting and battle scenes, bronze finials with three-dimensional animal images, and a gold crown decorated with a sculptured eagle on the top.[182] Works of Han art bearing clear signs of the influence of steppe art also appear over a much wider region. The finding of animal images corresponding to steppe types in Xi'an as well as in Hubei and Hunan provides evidence of intensified artistic interaction between China and the outside world. It is clear that on the heels of the expansion of the Han empire and the development of international trade, steppe influences penetrated more deeply into many parts of China.[183]

A subtler but no less important outside influence on Han art was the use of stone as an architectural and sculptural material. This Chinese "discovery," which took place around the end of the second century B.C.E., was to change the course of sculpture in China over the following centuries. Before the second century B.C.E., the Chinese seldom used stone to make human or animal images.[184] Until this time the main materials for sculpture had been clay, bronze, and jade. Even the ambitious First Emperor of Qin seemed satisfied with

his terra-cotta soldiers and bronze chariots; the stone carvings found in the Lishan Mausoleum up until now represent only suits of armor and helmets, not figures or animals. This situation changed fundamentally with the appearance of several groups of monumental stone sculptures in the Han metropolitan area, all created in the later part of the second century B.C.E. We have discussed the stone statues that Emperor Wu commissioned for his Shanglin Park and Jianzhang Palace (see fig. 1.40). The same emperor sponsored another group of stone sculptures for the graveyard of General Huo Qubing, who died in 117 B.C.E. at the age of twenty-four. The tomb of Huo, one of the chief commanders of Emperor Wu's western expedition army, is one of the satellite burials attached to the emperor's Maoling mausoleum. It is recorded that to commemorate General Huo's achievement, Emperor Wu ordered his tomb built to resemble the Qilian Mountains on the northwest frontier, where the general had led a series of brilliant campaigns against the Huns.[185] This record is difficult to verify because the appearance of the tomb has changed considerably over the past two thousand years. Yet even today, the many large stone boulders

1.51 Leaping horse, granite sculpture, tomb of Huo Qubing, Xingping County, Shaanxi Province. 117 B.C.E. 150 × 240 cm.

scattered on the tumulus suggest that irregularly shaped natural stones originally covered this earthen mound. Some stone boulders with suggestive shapes were slightly modified to represent a toad, a frog, a wild boar, an elephant, a monster devouring an animal, and a strange man hugging a bear. The sculptor preserved large portions of the natural stone surface and created the images by using as few strokes as possible. These modified stones are now displayed in a sculpture museum in General Huo's graveyard, but in 1914, when the French sinologist Victor Segalen visited the site, most of them were still scattered over the tumulus, mixed in with unmodified natural stones. As part of a simulated wild mountainscape, the sculptures, so unexpected or even bizarre in appearance, took visitors by surprise.

Another group of sculptures dedicated to General Huo was designed to be displayed on the ground, probably along the ritual path leading to the tumulus. Each of these heavy, three-dimensional statues is about 2 meters long, with a flat bottom for stability. The images they represent include a tiger, a reclining ox, and three horses in different positions. Each image is confined within the framework of a large stone boulder; but with limited effort the sculptor was able to transform his material into something exceedingly powerful and lifelike. The three horses, for example, whose heads and shoulders are sculpted in the round, are otherwise represented as relief carvings on solid stone blocks. The horses seem to represent three consecutive stages leading to a triumphant moment. The first horse, still in a reclining position, has lifted its head and one leg and is about to stand up. The second, perhaps the most forceful image in the whole group, is leaping into the air; its head stretches forward and its arching forelegs almost touch its chin (fig. 1.51). The third horse stands steadfast over a barbarian soldier who is holding an empty bow. Confident and victorious, the animal displays total dominance over the prostrate enemy. While reminding visitors of General Huo's military achievement, these horse images may also summarize the life of the young general. Moreover, from the broader perspective of art history, the sculptures announced the first appearance of stone funerary monuments, which were to spread throughout China during the following dynasty.

The Eastern Han Dynasty

After the brief interval of the Xin dynasty (9–23 C.E.), the Han was restored by General Liu Xiu, a distant member of the Western Han royal clan, who came to be known in Chinese history as Emperor Guangwu (r. 25–57). Because Chang'an had been repeatedly sacked by rebels during the unrest, Liu Xiu moved the capital eastward to Luoyang and so won the name of Eastern Han for his dynasty, which lasted through thirteen emperors and 195 years. None of these emperors, though, even the most adventurous, could remotely equal the First Emperor of Qin or Emperor Wu in historical vision and ambition; none of them sponsored architectural and sculptural works significant enough to leave a distinctive mark on art history. A few surviving public sculptures from this period were connected with local water projects. Among them was a nearly 3-meter-high stone statue of Li Bing, erected by local people in 168 C.E. at Dujiang Weir in Guanxian County, Sichuan, to commemorate that Qin magistrate (fig. 1.52).[186] In other parts of China, large statues representing "barbarian" images and believed to have the ability to quell floods through supernatural power stood on riverbanks.[187] All these statues present a frontal and formal view. Their static appearance may have served a ceremonial or magical function well, but it signifies little artistic innovation.

The most important developments of sculpture in the Eastern Han were in the domain of funerary art. During this period, when the construction of stone mortuary structures and statues became a nationwide phenomenon, many new kinds of sculptures were designed for the tomb. No single ruler was responsible for these developments. Rather, the proliferation of stone funerary monuments during the Eastern Han was the by-product of vast religious, social, and artistic movements, which can be traced back at least to the Western Han. Encouraged by Eastern Han rulers, these movements converged in the practice of filial devotion, which in turn stimulated funerary art and architecture to an unprecedented degree.

The center for ancestor worship shifted from temples of clans to the burial places of families and individuals.[188] Closely related to changes in the social structure, this shift had begun with the Eastern Zhou, but it took a decisive step forward during the Qin, when so much energy went into construction of the First Emperor's Lishan Mausoleum. During the Western Han, a temple was constructed for each deceased emperor near his mausoleum and was connected with the memorial shrine inside the mausoleum by a special road. Each month, a ritual procession conveyed the emperor's royal crown and costume from the shrine to the temple as a way of escorting the emperor's soul to the temple to receive offerings. The road thus became known as the costume-and-crown avenue (*yiguan dao*). During the Eastern Han, this and other temple rituals were largely abolished and transferred to mausoleums. The second Eastern Han ruler, Emperor Ming (r. 58–75 C.E.), established the ceremony of "mausoleum sacrifice" (*shangling li*) as the most important ritual in royal ancestor worship and ordered in his will that no temple except a funerary shrine be built for him. All later Eastern Han emperors followed this arrangement, and their subjects, in turn, followed the royal example. As the Qing scholar Zhao Yi remarked: "Taking the imperial 'grave sacrifice' as their model, all officials and scholars erected funerary shrines. Commoners, who could not afford to establish shrines, also customarily held sacrifices to the ancestors in the family graveyard."[189]

Another reason for the flourishing of mortuary monuments during the Eastern Han lay in the gradual changes in funerary structures. All pre-Qin burials were vertical earthen pits containing wooden encasements. The main purpose of this design was to preserve the corpse and to enable the storage of grave goods, not to create an underground architectural space for the departed soul to live in. Beginning in the mid–Western Han, however, tombs were increasingly built of stone or brick, and their designs began to imitate those of domiciles with a live-in household. Shrines for offerings were placed in front of the tumuli, and stone sculptures were sometimes erected in a graveyard. Funerary structures further increased in size and number of types during the Eastern Han. One important reason for this inflation was the heightened emphasis on filial piety. Under the slogan "To govern the country with filial piety" (*yi xiao zhi guo*), the special official rank of "filial and uncorrupted" (*xiao lian*) was awarded to those who distinguished themselves through outstanding filial practices, and filial piety was taken as a primary criterion for selecting and promoting officials. To dedicate lavish funerary monuments to one's deceased ancestors became a conventional way of expressing one's filial devotion — a motivation frequently expressed in the inscriptions carved on funerary monuments.[190]

A third factor that contributed to the florescence of funerary monuments was the introduction of stone as an architectural and sculptural material. In addition to the stone armor buried in the First Emperor's mausoleum, we have discussed the stone statues in Shanglin Park and Huo Qubing's cemetery as the earliest evidence for this development. Another early example is Prince Liu Sheng's tomb, constructed before 113 B.C.E., in which the "living quarters" — a stable, a banquet hall, and a storage room — were timber structures containing pottery figurines, but the coffin chamber was built entirely of stone with stone figurines inside.[191] This arrangement shows clearly that stone was employed symbolically. Stone's natural characteristics — strength, plainness, and especially endurance — represented eternity or immortality. Wood, which was relatively fragile and vulnerable to the elements, was associated with temporal, mortal existence. From this dichotomy emerged two kinds of architecture and sculpture: those made of wood and used by the living, and those made of stone and dedicated to gods, the immortals, and the dead. When this idea became widespread, all sorts of structures, objects, and images associated with death began to be fashioned of stone. Significantly, it seems that the imperial clans of both the Western and Eastern Han were behind this development; for example, the earliest stone sarcophagi and masonry tombs, dating from the mid-first century B.C.E. to the early first century C.E., were concentrated in two areas, one in southern Shandong and northern Jiangsu and the other in Henan, centered on Nanyang. The first area was the homeland of the Western Han royal clan; Nanyang was the spot where the Eastern Han royal house originated. We are thus not surprised to read that Emperor Ming's mausoleum, constructed before 71 C.E., included a "stone sacrificial hall." From this time through the second century, textual records as well as extant buildings and statues confirm that it had become common practice to erect aboveground stone funerary monuments throughout the country.

The most valuable textual reference to Eastern Han stone funerary monuments is Li Daoyuan's *Annotated Canon of Waterways (Shuijing zhu)*, written in the fifth century. A great geographer and naturalist, Li recorded the location, condition, and attribution of these monuments. His description of Zhang Boya's graveyard allows us to imagine these monuments in their original architectural context.

The You River flows southeastward and passes the tomb of Zhang Boya, Grand Administrator of Hongnong under the Han. A stone wall was built to surround the graveyard, located in a spot where a

1.52 Statue of Li Bing, stone, excavated in 1974 at Dujiang Weir, Guanxian County, Sichuan Province. 168 C.E. 290 cm. Sichuan Provincial Museum, Chengdu.

mountain slope gradually descends and reaches the north bank of the Sui River. The gate of the graveyard is marked by a pair of stone *que* towers, under which two stone animals flank the entrance. In front of the tomb is a stone shrine, and three steles stand in a row. The inscriptions on the steles state that Boya is the style name of Zhang De, a native of Mixian County in Henan. Two stone figures stand beside the steles. There are also several stone columns and other stone animals in the graveyard. In the past, the Zhang family diverted water into the cemetery from the south side and made a pond to correspond to the *chou* position. Stone toads were made to spurt water out of their mouths, and stone drains were installed to receive rainwater. The family also built a stone pavilion south of the pond, and arranged various stone animals in two rows to flank the stone shrine. But as time passed, things deteriorated — all these buildings and sculptures are almost completely destroyed.[192]

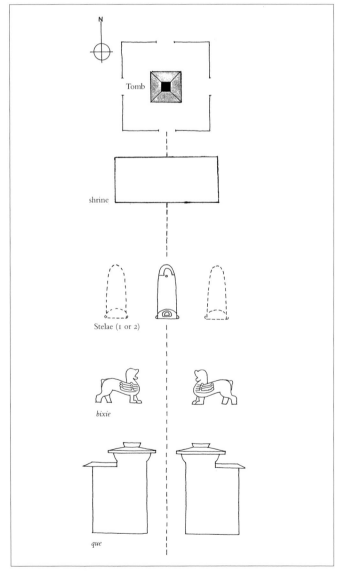

1.53 Standard layout of an Eastern Han cemetery.

Zhang Boya's graveyard and its stone sculptures have long since vanished, and in fact no Eastern Han cemetery has survived intact. The best preserved include the Wu family cemetery at Jiaxiang in Shandong and the Gao Yi cemetery at Ya'an in Sichuan. The Wu cemetery consists of stone carvings dedicated by and to different members of a family from the local gentry during the twenty years from 147 to 168, including a pair of stone que towers that formed the gate of the graveyard, two stone lions below the towers, several stone steles inscribed with biographies of deceased family members, and beautifully carved stone slabs from at least four collapsed memorial shrines.[193] Located hundreds of kilometers away, Gao Yi's tomb was constructed for him in 209, when he died while governor of Yizhou — the highest official post in southwest China at the time. Stone carvings surviving in his graveyard include a pair of que towers, a memorial stele, two mythical winged beasts, and a round base embellished with the image of an animal in relief.[194] Together with textual records, these extant structures and sculptures demonstrate the standard layout of an Eastern Han cemetery (fig. 1.53).[195] The boundary of a graveyard is marked symbolically by a gate formed by a pair of stone towers. (Both the gate and towers are called que.) Inscriptions on the towers identify the path running through the gate as a *shen dao* — Spirit Path, or Path of the Soul — which determines the central axis of the graveyard. Flanking the Spirit Path and close to the gate stand pairs of sculptured stone animals; at the end of the path is the tomb. The shrine for offerings in front of the tumulus is accompanied by one or more memorial steles and occasionally by stone figures and animals as well. These different features of a graveyard — gate towers, statues of animals and figures, shrines, steles, and the underground grave chambers — are either three-dimensional sculptures or architectural forms decorated with bas-relief or high-relief images.

Remains of twenty-nine Eastern Han stone que gates exist here and there throughout Henan, Shandong, Beijing, and Sichuan.[196] All but three belonged to graveyards. Yet even these three were not constructed for the living; instead, they were dedicated to deities on the sacred mountain Songshan, south of Luoyang. The largest surviving stone structures from this period, the twin towers of these gates, measure 4 to 6 meters high. Constructed of stone blocks, they were then carved with bas-relief or high-relief images. The simplest form of tower consists of little more than a rectangular shaft crowned with a sloping roof of stone pantiles. A more elaborate kind has an additional wing attached to the outer side of the main shaft. Han texts record that the number of wings indicated the status of a deceased person; the highest number, three wings, was reserved for emperors. That is perhaps why we find no three-winged towers among the twenty-six surviving examples of funerary que gates, which were all dedicated to deceased local officials and gentry.

These gate towers, all located outside a Han city, are stone imitations of gate towers built inside a city; they take different forms, depending on their models. The twenty-nine existing que towers can generally be divided into two regional types. Those in Henan and Shandong are simpler and geometric in appearance: the body of the gate tower is a solid monolith, reaching up to a small overhanging roof, carved to imitate pantiles. It is possible that this form was modeled on a gate tower built of bricks. The twenty que gates found in Sichuan exemplify the second type: their prototype was a wooden structure. Although the gate towers differ widely in their degree of elaboration, each has a complex capital consisting of overlapping layers of stone slabs carved like roof brackets, supplemented by stone imitations of entablatures, sculptural panels, and machicolations. The difference in prototype for the two groups of gate towers also explains their different decorative styles. On a Henan or Shandong tower, the flat surface of the vertical shaft is divided into schematic horizontal friezes, which are carved in low relief to look like "stone pictures." It has been suggested that this type of architectural decoration originated with images stamped on clay bricks.[197] Sculptural elements on a Sichuan tower concentrate on a different architectural section and are altogether more exuberant. Instead of exclusively decorating the rectangular shaft of the tower, most images on a Sichuan tower are applied to the capital. The styles of sculpture are much richer, including not only low-relief but also high-relief and three-dimensional images.

The most beautiful and best-preserved Sichuan gate tower is in the graveyard of Gao Yi outside Ya'an (fig. 1.54).[198] This is the right tower of a pair; the left one, though still extant, is severely damaged. Made of red sandstone, the intact tower is almost 6 meters high and retains its base, shaft, and capital. The capital — the most complex and striking section of the monument — is actually taller than the body of the tower, 280 centimeters, as compared with 264 centimeters. It consists of as many as eight layers of architectural forms representing brackets, rafters, eaves, a tiled roof, and, at the pinnacle, a sculptured bird — all stone imi-

tations of timber elements. The capital also contrasts with the shaft in visual effect and symbolic significance. The shaft provided a smooth surface on which to inscribe the name and title of the deceased and carve shallow images of a chariot procession to accompany the inscription. In sharp contrast to those, the images on the capital are all animation and activity. The forms are deeply incised, irregular, and intriguing. The people and animals that have been fitted in between, behind, and around the imitation brackets figure in historical narratives or hold out the hope of an immortal paradise.

Some of the historical tales illustrated on this tower are political. One depicts the young King Cheng of the Zhou flanked by his uncles, who served as regents and helped the king establish his authority. Carved on this funerary monument, this and similar pictures may have offered historical underpinning for the late governor's good political standing. Other stories illustrated on the tower, however, seem more personal. The subject of a

1.54 A que gate tower in Gao Yi's graveyard, sandstone, Ya'an, Sichuan Province. 209 C.E. 590 cm.

moving scene on the west side of the tower is the story of Yu Boya and Zhong Ziqi, one of the most beautiful legends about friendship from ancient China (fig. 1.55):

> Boya played the zither, and Zhong Ziqi was the audience. As soon as Boya started playing, his mind was transported to Mount Tai, and Ziqi sighed: "How wonderful the music is! It is as imposing as Mount Tai!" In a little while, Boya's mind shifted to the flowing river, and Ziqi was moved: "How graceful the music is! It is as vast as a flowing river!" After Ziqi died, Boya smashed his zither, cut the strings, and never played again in his life. He no longer had a soul mate in this world worthy of his music.[199]

Interestingly, the scene on the tower gives this story a new twist: here the musician and his friend both raise their sleeves to cover their faces and seem to be weeping. Perhaps, thanks to the inclusion of this gesture, the carving better suited the funereal mood of the occasion; or perhaps it conveyed the sentiment of Gao Yi's friends upon his death. A similar sentiment is expressed in another scene on the tower, in which a weeping figure represents Ji Zha, who hung his precious sword on a tree next to the tomb of his friend Xu. Responding to people's questions about this act, he said: "In my heart I had long promised Xu this sword. How can I change my mind because now he is dead?"[200]

These historical scenes appear on decorative panels between brackets and are framed by images of supernatural beings above and below. Below them, four legendary strongmen embellish the lower corners of the capital. Unlike the other figures, which are mostly relief images, these are sculpted almost in the round. With expressive faces and bulging eyes, they bow their half-naked, muscular bodies beneath the weight they support. Above the historical scenes, a series of images on the highest level of the capital represent mythical animals and immortals. The focal image on the south side is a half-open gate with a figure emerging from behind it. Frequently seen on funerary towers as well as in tomb chambers and on stone coffins, this scene represents the Gate of Heaven (Tianmen), through which the soul of the deceased would ascend to eternal paradise.[201]

Statues of figures and animals constitute a second group of stone sculptures in an Eastern Han graveyard. So far, fewer than ten stone figures have been found; the known examples always appear in pairs.[202] One of the better-preserved pairs, now in the Confucius Temple at Qufu, Shandong, was originally dedicated to a

1.55 The story of Yu Boya and Zhong Ziqi, relief carving on the Gao Yi que tower. 209 C.E.

magistrate of Le'an named Piao, as the inscriptions carved on one of the front sides make clear.[203] One of the two figures is further identified as the "Head of a *Ting* Station" (*Ting zhang*); the companion figure is labeled "Guardian of the Main Gate" of Magistrate Piao's mansion. During the Han, one type of *ting* in real life was a wayside inn for travelers. Depicted in funerary art, however, the image of a ting symbolized a tomb — a liminal space that the deceased would pass through before continuing on to the immortal realm. Thus, a pictorial carving in an Eastern Han tomb at Cangshan, Shandong, depicts a funerary procession delivering a hearse to a ting station, where it is greeted by a Ting zhang; the attendant carvings represent a comfortable afterlife and images of immortals.[204] The official duties of a Ting zhang also included the maintenance of public security in his jurisdiction. This role explains why a Ting zhang was paired with a guardian to protect the underground "mansion" of a deceased official, and why large stone figures of ting officials were sometimes installed inside grave chambers, as in the case of a pair of stone statues found in an Eastern Han tomb at Shimaba in Lushan County, Sichuan.[205]

Sometimes more than 2.5 meters tall, these tomb statues are imposing in size, but the sculptors seem to have consciously employed an old-fashioned sculptural style to render their subjects in an extremely rigid manner. In fact, these works show little attempt to represent believable human forms. Columnlike and motionless, each figure is restricted within a rough-hewn block of stone. Slightly lowering his massive head, a Ting zhang or tomb guardian stands in a frozen frontal position and folds both arms in front of his chest. Facial features are indicated summarily by reliefs or incisions, and so are the costumes and weapons. It would be mistaken, however, to judge the artistic abilities of their creators on the basis of this seemingly primitive style, because the crude technique and the awkward shapes of the figures resulted from a particular stylistic choice. Long before the Eastern Han, certain tomb figurines were deliberately coarse, the artist having avoided any attempt at a naturalistic representation of the human form. Their crude appearance contrasts sharply with that of other figurines from the same tomb, which were often beautifully manufactured to represent servants, performers, and other household assistants.[206] Made of wood or stone, these semi-figurative images functioned as talismans, thought to be able to protect the deceased through their magical powers. Fulfilling a similar protective function and executed in a similarly naive style, the Eastern Han stone Ting zhang and guardians were products of this sculptural tradition.

The deliberate archaism of these stone figures also becomes evident when they are compared with contemporaneous animal statues, which display a wide range of stylistic choices. It is also probably true that more animal statues than human figures were erected in Eastern Han cemeteries: the surviving examples of animal statues far outnumber the human, and traditional texts provide many more references to animal statues as protectors of graveyards and as status symbols of the deceased. The animal subjects of such statues mentioned in literature include the elephant, horse, ram, sheep, ox, camel, tiger, lion, and imaginary beasts, with the elephant and horse seemingly reserved for imperial mausoleums.[207] The largest surviving animal sculpture from this period, a partially damaged stone elephant 2.4 meters high and 3.5 meters long, now stands near the ruins of the Eastern Han capital, Luoyang. It has been identified as a marker of the entrance to the imperial burial district located 2 kilometers to the north. While opinions about this identification differ, the animal's pose — it is walking with one forefoot before the other — seems to confirm its Eastern Han date, because later elephant statues in imperial graveyards normally stand or kneel in still poses.[208]

This stone elephant exemplifies a naturalistic tendency in animal sculpture in Eastern Han funerary art. Free from fantastic elements, it is well proportioned and massive. Some sensitive details — the folded edges of the ears and its bulging forehead — seem to indicate that the sculptor had observed a real elephant. Unlike the Western Han statues in front of Huo Qubing's tomb, where the animals' legs appear in low relief on solid monoliths, this elephant stands on all four legs — the stone between its belly and the ground has been cut away, making the image entirely round. This style is one that other animal sculptures share, including those fantastic creatures which constitute by far the largest category of Eastern Han animal funerary statues. Again, these winged and horned animals appear in a walking pose. Always created in symmetrical pairs and oriented to face the Spirit Path, each figure stretches out a different forefoot, depending on its position in relation to the road. They are generally shown in an energetic moment: lifting their heads and opening their mouths, they advance roaring.

Despite their similar postures, the fantastic animals show impressive variations in iconography. Some of them distinctly retain the features of tigers or lions, others are more conceptual and "minimalist," and still others are fanciful — products of the imagination. Their wide range of sculptural styles — from simple geometric shapes to carefully rendered three-dimensional forms — attest to divergent artistic goals as well as different regional traditions. Winged felines in Gao Yi's graveyard, for example, belong to the more conceptual kind. Their forms are compact and blocky, each presenting a narrow body frame flattened on both sides. Details such as the wings are rendered in relief. The sculptor was primarily concerned with the silhouette of the statues, which in itself conveys the fierce pose of the beasts. This conceptual style gives way to a more naturalistic approach in the sculpture of a lion in the graveyard of Yang Jun at Lushan County, Sichuan (fig. 1.56). Still focusing on the solidity of stone and not bothering with the finer details, the sculptor no longer relied on the silhouette to convey his intention. Rather, through his modeling of the subtle curves of the animal's body, he was able to represent convincingly hunched shoulders, muscular back, and powerful legs. The image is clearly one of a lion, as indicated by the large mane framing the head — the only surface carving on the statue. The pose of the beast generates an impression of suppressed strength: stretching out its left paw but drawing back its heavy head, the lion seems to be gathering its tremendous force for the next movement.

Even more naturalistic in style is a pair of male and female stone lions from Shenjia village in Xianyang, Shaanxi. Instead of displaying physical strength, they display agility and nimbleness. Each lion has a sinuous body, with an elongated torso and narrow hips. The muscular legs are almost like scientific studies of animal anatomy. Striding forward, the beasts also turn their heads to one side, in a pose that demonstrates the sculptor's attempt to represent complex movement. Once equipped with wings, horns, and beards, however, such naturalistic creatures are readily transformed into fantastic beasts. A famous pair of winged felines excavated in Yichuan, Henan, reflects just such a transmutation. Their basic shape is almost identical to that of the Shenjia village pair, and they turn and roar in a similar manner. But each of them sports two short horns and a long beard hanging from its chin (fig. 1.57). Wings protrude from their shoulders. Relief patterns of feathers covering the entire torso, thighs, and even tail complete the transformation of a lion into the fabulous beast named *qilin, bixie,* or *tianlu.*

Located at the heart of an Eastern Han cemetery is the third group of funerary structures, comprising the tomb, the shrine, and the stele(s). The tomb contained the physical remains of the dead; the shrine was a memorial hall and housed offerings. Either the patriarch or the descendants in a family that owned a burial plot usually constructed two such structures. By contrast, social relations of the deceased — former friends, colleagues, or students — usually erected the stele. Originating from a timber prototype like other stone mortuary structures, the stele developed into an independent architectural and sculptural form during the Eastern Han. A stele, essentially a tall rectangular stone slab erected on a square or a tortoise-shaped base, has only a minimum of relief decoration on its pointed or rounded crown. Its main function in a graveyard was to bear an epitaph on the front; the back was often inscribed with the names of the donors.

Like the que gate at the entrance to a graveyard, the shrine and tomb imitate wooden or brick buildings. A que, however, has sculpted images only on the outside, whereas a shrine or tomb is carved only on the inside. Rich images transform the interior space of a shrine or tomb into a symbolic universe in which Heaven is represented on the ceiling by gods and spirits, omens, celestial bodies, or mythical animals. Two other symbolic spaces in this universe include eternal paradise and the human world. Each tomb or shrine makes use of different pictorial and sculptural motifs to construct these symbolic spaces, but the varied images always reflect the fundamental longing for eternal happiness in the afterlife. What one finds in the carvings, therefore, is a realm that not only extends the life the dead formerly led but also fulfills all dreams of an ideal world. It seems that death was meant to permit the deceased to enjoy what he or she had been deprived of during life. The deceased would live in elaborate halls served by numerous attendants and feast on delicacies while watching colorful performances; ancient sages and paragons of virtues would supply companionship; in that destination, the eternal paradise, death would never occur again. This symbolic universe was also the subject of carvings on stone sarcophagi, which enjoyed popularity in Sichuan during the second century. On a sarcophagus, a que gate always appears on the front side, the celestial scenes on the top, and cosmic symbols on the back. The two long sides are carved with images representing feasting and entertainment, the world of immortality, and Confucian moral tales.[209] With such carvings, a single sarcophagus epitomizes the symbolic structure of a typical graveyard: through the

1.56 Stone lion from the tomb of Yang Jun. 2d century C.E. Ca. 160 cm. Lushan Cultural House, Lushan County, Sichuan Province.

1.57 Fantastic beast, stone, excavated at Yichuan, Henan Province. 2d century c.e. 114 × 175 × 45 cm. Guanlin Stone Sculpture Museum, Luoyang, Henan Province.

que gate the departing soul would enter an eternal realm of happiness.

Although Eastern Han funerary carvings shared many images, they employed a wide range of styles and techniques. At one end of the stylistic and technical spectrum are line carvings — images rendered exclusively in incised lines on a smooth or rough surface. In style as well as spirit, such works are closer to painting than to sculpture; and it has been suggested that stone line carvings actually copy painted murals in buildings with a wooden structure.[210] At the other end of the stylistic and technical spectrum are nearly three-dimensional images, found only in a few second-century tombs in Shandong. The vast majority of carvings in Eastern Han tombs and shrines fall between these two extremes, in stylistic and technical variations that have been classified into as many as six types and twelve sub-types.[211] All these variations, however, are the product of three different relationships between the image and its background: (1) sunken images cut away from a smooth or striated surface, (2) bas-relief images with flat surfaces rising above a smooth or striated background, and (3) relief images with rounded surfaces rising above a smooth or striated background. Generally the first two kinds — exemplified by the carvings in the famous Xiaotangshan shrine in Changqing County in Shandong and the Wu family shrines, respectively — are two-dimensional images and can be viewed as works of pictorial art. Images of the third kind, which show greater three-dimensionality, should be considered together with high-relief and three-dimensional images as sculptural works.

Many different techniques and styles are found in a large second-century tomb at Dongjiazhuang in Anqiu, Shandong.[212] Most unusual in this tomb are the open-work carvings on three columns arranged roughly along the tomb's central axis. These hollow, nearly three-dimensional images represent embracing figures, nursing mothers and babies, and intertwining snakes (fig. 1.58). Rough chiseling adds a certain charm to the rudimentary human and animal forms. Similar images and scenes are represented in a contemporary tomb at Pingyin in Shandong, where one finds a larger number of embracing couples and even figures with exposed genitals. Scholars have interpreted these images as representations of an ancient fertility rite called *gaomei* or *jiaomei*, during which men and women freely copulated at a designated ritual site.[213] It is possible that through the depiction of fertility scenes in a tomb, death was symbolically rejected and framed within the chain of human reproduction. The same idea seems to underlie a moving relief carving, which represents a couple in an intimate moment, embracing and kissing each other (fig. 1.59).[214] Originally carved above the entrance to a cliff tomb in Pengshan County, Sichuan, this image transformed the dark grave behind the tomb door into a promised land of eternal joy.

This last image leads us to Sichuan, a region in China's southwest that grew into a major center of funerary sculpture during the second half of the Eastern Han. We have discussed a number of Sichuan sculptures — Gao Yi's tower (see fig. 1.54), animal statues, carved sarcophagi, and the Pengshan relief image (see fig. 1.59). These examples attest to the many connections between this regional tradition and Han metropolitan art but also give an idea of its unique media and sculptural styles. In addition to stone sarcophagi and cliff tombs, which existed only in this area, a type of funerary object called a money tree (*qian shu* or *yaoqian shu*) provided local artists with an unparalleled opportunity to experiment with sculptural forms.

The origin of the money tree can be traced to the Sanxingdui culture, which flourished in Sichuan in the late Shang and has left us an amazing 4-meter-tall bronze "divine tree."[215] An Eastern Han money tree always consists of two sections: a sculpted ceramic or stone base and a bronze tree whose branches are densely decorated with a coin motif and mythological images. Because of the fine openwork design of a bronze tree, very few examples have survived intact.[216] The tree from Guanghan illustrated here (fig. 1.60) is not only the best preserved but also the largest and most elaborate among all known examples. Perched on top of the tree is a large bird with an elaborate peacock tail. This image is derived from a Chinese sun myth: in the Eastern Sea grew a gigantic tree, on top of which the golden sun-bird would perch every morning, presenting the world with light and warmth. Underneath this bird image are six layers of branches, each comprising four identical branches pointing to the four directions. Each ornate branch has a pointed tenon at one end, for insertion into a mortise on the tree trunk, so the whole work could be taken apart or assembled at will. The design of the top layer differs from the others, but all the branches are decorated with two prominent motifs: the Queen Mother of the West and coins. The Queen Mother — the most prominent immortal in Han mythology — is seated on her dragon-and-tiger throne, surrounded by animals and humans who are performing acrobatics, music, or dances; riding on

heavenly horses; or playing the magical game *liubo*. Imitations of the *wuzhu* coin hang down in rows from the branches. Embossed with leaf and stamen patterns, these coins appear to be flowers or fruit growing from the tree. It is not difficult to imagine that placed in a tomb, an object like a money tree would symbolize the world where people hoped to abide — a world full of sunlight, riches, and eternal life.

Compared with the scarcity of intact bronze trees, money tree bases have survived in much greater quantity and in a variety of sculptural forms. Most of them are terra-cotta and exhibit images related to immortality. Many are rather crudely made, but a considerable number show ingenious designs and artisanry. Among this second group is a base from the suburbs of Chengdu whose intricate spatial construction reinforces its rep-

resentation of a spiritual journey (fig. 1.61). The clay sculpture is modeled into a columnlike mountain. Men and women are climbing this mountain and appear on three levels. Those on the first level still have a long way to go; those on the third level are about to reach the top of the mountain and join the deity on the summit. This second-century C.E. design thus translates into visual expression a passage from a second-century B.C.E. Daoist text, the *Writings of Master Huainan* (*Huainan zi*): "He who climbs onto the Chilly Wind Peak of Kunlun will achieve deathlessness; he who climbs twice as high, into the Hanging Garden, will become a spirit...; he who climbs twice as high again will reach Heaven and become a god." Interestingly, caves appear regularly on all three levels. Punctuating the journey, each of them marks a particular stage in the search for immor-

1.59 Figures embracing and kissing, stone relief from Pengshan County, Sichuan Province. 49 cm. Palace Museum, Beijing.

1.60 Bronze money-tree with pottery base, from Liangshan, Guanghan, Sichuan Province. 2d century C.E. 153 cm. Guanghan County Cultural Center.

1.61 Image of the search for immortality, clay money-tree base, unearthed in 1978 in the vicinity of Chengdu, Sichuan Province. 2d century C.E. 60.5 × 42 cm. Chengdu Museum.

tality. This is arguably the earliest representation of a *dong tian*, or cave heaven, an important concept in religious Daoism.

Other mountain images in Sichuan sculpture are more naturalistic. A rare stone money-tree base from Lushan County, for example, fleshes out supernatural tales with a realistic setting.[217] The whole work takes the shape of a solid mountain formed by layers of rocks and embellished with carved trees, animals, and human or supernatural figures in various poses, behind rocks or inside caves. Among the figures is the Queen Mother of the West, who appears as a hermit on a terrace. Mountain images also dominate a pottery relief from Chengdu, but the subject of the elegant tomb tile is no longer religious — rather, it illustrates the salt-mining industry (fig. 1.62). Indeed, its portrayal of a brine well and human activities relating to it has helped historians reconstruct an important staple of Sichuan's regional economy. The significance of the work, however, lies not merely in the visual documentation it provides but also in its successful rendering of a three-dimensional landscape in a two-dimensional relief composition. In fact, one might argue that the salt-mining scene depicted in the lower left-hand corner only elaborates on a larger landscape, in which hunters and animals are scattered over silhouetted, undulating mountainsides that overlap and extend into the distance.

Tomb tiles and figurines were not unique to Sichuan art during the Eastern Han, but it was in this region that the two art forms achieved a highly sophisticated blending of naturalism and fantastical representation. A large group of Sichuan tomb figures represent performers — musicians, dancers, and especially storytellers — whose poses and expressions differ in accordance with their arts. The flute player, for example, wears a dreamy expression on his gentle face. He crouches on his knees and holds a vertical flute; but instead of playing, he lifts his head with a tranquil smile, as though he has just finished a piece of music and is still listening to the melody echoing in the air. The remarkable subtlety of this image contrasts sharply with the dramatic atmosphere generated by the storyteller found in Pixian County in 1964 (fig. 1.63). This striking pottery sculpture is quite large, at 67 centimeters high. The figure, who holds a small drum in his left hand and a drumstick in his right, is portrayed in near caricature. His grimacing face borders on the grotesque as he sticks his tongue out to lick his upper lip. Half naked, he throws out his stomach and shoves his hip backward, to the point that his pants are about to fall off. What we see here is the exaggerated

image of a versatile entertainer like a court jester, who amused his audience with his songs, jokes, and comic acting.[218] Another storyteller from a cliffside tomb in Xindu, by contrast, shows an engaging figure captured in mid-performance, who is kicking out a bare foot and raising his right hand high to beat his drum (fig. 1.64).

Among the portable sculptures created in the late Eastern Han, the impressive vitality of these Sichuan figurines is perhaps matched only by a bronze sculpture from a late second-century tomb at Leitai, Wuwei, Gansu Province. Excavated in 1969, this multichambered brick tomb divulged a large procession of bronze tomb figures, consisting of nearly one hundred horses, chariots, attendants, and guards. One image stands out in this assemblage: a galloping horse (fig. 1.65). Whereas all the other horses in the procession are standing or walking, this horse alone is running or, more accurately, flying. Tilting its head to one side, it stretches its legs out almost horizontal to the ground. Arrested in a dramatic gesture, one of its hoofs rests lightly on a swallow with wings outstretched, a beautiful and imaginative way of suggesting the otherworldly nature of the journey.

For funerary sculptures to be enormous, as in the Leitai tomb, was rare during this period. Generally speaking, the number of figurines, whether bronze, pottery, or stone, diminished significantly in Eastern Han tombs. Whereas it was not rare for an early Western Han burial to contain more than a hundred tomb figures, no more than ten figurines were usually buried

1.62 Salt mining, pottery tomb relief, unearthed in 1975 at Chengdu. Eastern Han. 39.5 × 48 cm. Chengdu Museum.

1.63 Storyteller, pottery tomb figurine, unearthed in 1964 in Pixian County, Sichuan Province. 2d century C.E. 67 × 26 cm. Sichuan Provincial Museum, Chengdu.

1.64 Storyteller, painted earthenware, excavated in 1982 from Majiashan Tomb 23 in Xindu district, Chengdu, Sichuan Province. 2d century. 50 cm. Xindu Administrative Department for Cultural Relics.

1.65 Flying horse, bronze, excavated in 1969 from Leitai, Wuwei, Gansu Province. Late 2d century C.E. 34.5 × 45 cm. Gansu Provincial Museum, Lanzhou.

in an Eastern Han tomb. One reason for this phenomenon was the popularity of tomb carvings and murals: two-dimensional images had assumed the function that figurines alone had served earlier — constructing an idealized afterlife for the deceased. Another reason concerns the changing subject matter of tomb sculpture. As discussed earlier, most Western Han figurines depicted people who had household roles, primarily servants, guards, and entertainers. From the late Western Han on, however, an increasing number of tomb sculptures began to represent the material possessions of a wealthy household, including land, buildings, grain, and livestock.[219] Often modeled with uncanny realism, such tomb sculptures integrated images of human figures, animals, and architectural forms into large tableaus, thereby reducing the number of individual figurines and shifting the focus of representation from figural

images to their architectural settings. The same change can also be described as a shift from indoors to outdoors. Western Han figurines, with their colorful representations of banquets and entertainment, were created to construct a comfortable domestic life, whereas Eastern Han tomb sculptures, with their barns, rice paddies, watchtowers, and pigpens, were designed to represent large estates.[220]

We can therefore understand why architectural models developed into a major type of pottery tomb sculpture during the Eastern Han, especially in the metropolitan centers in Henan and adjacent Hebei and Shaanxi. Often mass-produced, these works were straightforward representations of property for the afterlife. The many models of watchtowers further attest to a strong concern with security — a natural outcome of the heightening desire for material possessions. A multichambered

1.66 Watchtower, glazed earthenware, from Sangzhuang, Fucheng County, Hebei Province. Late 2d century C.E. 216 × 82.8 cm. Hebei Provincial Institute of Archaeology and Cultural Relics, Shijiazhuang.

1.67 Buddha, stone relief, Mahao Cliff Tomb 1, Leshan, Sichuan Province. Eastern Han dynasty, late 2d–early 3d century C.E.

brick tomb at Sangzhuang in Fucheng County, Hebei, had been seriously robbed prior to the excavation, but still yielded a large group of pottery sculptures, including images of domestic animals, a well, a granary, a kitchen, and three watchtowers.[221] One of the watchtowers is perhaps the largest and most elaborate of its kind (fig. 1.66). More than 2 meters in height, it is a magnificent construction five stories high, rising from an abbreviated courtyard with its front gate tightly shut. It faithfully duplicates all the complex brackets and openwork window frames of a timber tower. The military function of the structure is indicated by the bows and shields displayed on each story. Guards survey the area from openings under the intermittent eaves. And a large gong hangs on the top level; two men standing underneath the gong hold sticks in their hands, prepared to strike it if anything goes wrong.

This watchtower is also significant in connecting Eastern Han art and architecture with those of later periods. Scholars have long identified Han-dynasty watchtowers as an indigenous prototype of the Buddhist pagoda, a type of religious architecture that was to enjoy enormous popularity in later Chinese history. This contention gains strong support from the Sangzhuang watchtower, whose design bears a close resemblance to that of later Buddhist pagodas.

It is appropriate to end this survey of early Chinese sculpture with the arrival of Buddhism. In traditional Chinese historiography, the introduction of this foreign religion to China from India is presented as the introduction of a new religious image. *The Sutra in Forty-Two Sections* (*Sishi'er zhang jing*), one of the earliest Buddhist texts, written in China around the second century, relates that Emperor Ming of the Eastern Han had a dream in which a divine figure flew to his palace. The figure had a golden body, and sunlight emanated from his neck. Other texts supply more details about the figure's extraordinary physique: he was said to be sixteen *chi* tall and able "to assume countless forms and enter anything at will." These various accounts all end the same way: the next day the emperor told his ministers about the divine figure and demanded an identification. A learned man named Fu Yi replied that this must be a sage in India called the Buddha. His answer led to the emperor's sending envoys to the west in search of Buddhism. Upon their arrival in India, the envoys learned that the Buddha had entered Nirvana long ago. They nevertheless found an old image of the Buddha commissioned by King Udyana and brought it back to China. Emperor Ming found it "to look just as in his dream" and made copies of it for his capital and mausoleum.

Regardless of how reliable these records are, archaeological evidence has proven that images of the Buddha did reach China no later than the second century and were reproduced there. The meaning of the images, however, changed greatly when they were transplanted from their original context into new religious and artistic traditions. One such new tradition was Chinese funerary art, which immediately absorbed Buddhist imagery. Carved on a tomb or decorating a money tree, an image of the Buddha no longer accompanied Buddhist worship but came to symbolize the Chinese ideal of immortality.[222] Archaeologists have found various Buddhist art motifs in Eastern Han tombs in Shandong, Sichuan, and Inner Mongolia.[223] Among them, the two most faithful copies of Indian images of the Buddha both came from Sichuan and have been dated to the late second century or the early third century. One of them is a relief image from a large cliff tomb at Mahao, Leshan (fig. 1.67; see also fig. 3.2). The figure is seated, with the left hand holding a portion of its gown and the right hand raised in a gesture known as the *abhaya mudra.* The face is unfortunately damaged, but an extra protuberance, the *ushnisha,* on top of the head — one of the Buddha's holy marks — is still visible, ringed by a halo. All these features, as well as the heavy folds in the robe, can be traced to Indian images of the Buddha created in Mathura and Gandhara in the second century.[224] Carved above the entrance to the burial chambers, this Buddha is the focal image in the Mahao tomb. Its basic iconography appears again in the second one, a high-relief image positioned in front of a stump on a money tree base found in a cliff tomb at Pengshan County.[225] A major difference, however, is that this second Buddha is flanked by two standing figures, identified by some scholars as bodhisattvas.

Hundreds of kilometers away from Sichuan, in Lianyungang near the Yellow Sea, archaeologists have found a group of Buddha images carved into a mountain cliff. Seated or standing, these figures have the ushnisha and halos. One figure raises his right hand in the fear-not gesture, or *abhaya mudra* (fig. 1.68, image on the left); another is in meditation and has his hands in the pensive gesture, or *dhyana mudra*. These Buddhist images, however, are intermingled with typical Chinese figures wearing traditional costumes and holding ritual instruments (fig. 1.68, image on the right). It has been suggested that the images in the second group represent Daoist deities, which were often worshipped together with the Buddha during the Eastern Han. The location of these carvings lends support to this opinion. In the foothills of Mount Kongwang lie the remains of a huge stone platform, which contains the base of a lost stele, mentioned in ancient texts as the Stele of the Eastern Sea Temple, erected in 172 C.E. Both archaeological and textual evidence have led some scholars to believe that the carvings on the cliffs of the

Kongwangshan hills were originally part of this temple, an important center of Daoism mentioned in many early Daoist texts.[226]

There are different opinions about the date and subject of the Kongwangshan carvings, but it is clear that during the Eastern Han, Daoism and other indigenous religious traditions made use of Buddhist images to further their own needs. A later legend, about the arrival of Buddhist statues in China from India, relates a version of this episode in history: Some fishermen in eastern China saw two stone figures standing above the water far out to sea. Taking them to be sea gods or immortals, the fishermen asked local shamans to offer a sacrifice in welcome. But the wind grew stronger, the waves rose higher, and the people were frightened away. Then some Daoists, saying, "They are Heavenly Masters of our religion," went to welcome the statues by offering a Daoist ceremony. The wind and the waves would not subside, however, and the Daoists, too, were scared away from the shore. Finally some followers of Buddhism came to pray on the beach. Only then did the sea become calm and the two figures wash in with the tide. They turned out to be statues of the Buddha and his disciple Ananda.

This incident is of course no more than a legend. Yet it represents symbolically the three different ways through which Buddhist sculpture entered Chinese culture — as part of the immortality cult, as part of Daoist worship, and as an independent artistic tradition in its own right. Only through this complex process could a foreign art gain a foothold in a vast alien land.

1.68 Buddhist and Daoist images, stone cliff carving, Kongwangshan, Lianyungang, Jiangsu Province. 2d–3d century C.E.

CHAPTER 2

From the Han to the Qing

YANG HONG

The ancient Chinese burial system that had emerged by the end of the Han dynasty inspired developments in Chinese secular sculpture for millennia. Structures both aboveground and belowground, burial objects and furnishings, as well as murals, mosaics, and ornamental paintings, became part of a vast funerary tradition altered to suit the style of the dynasty in power. Among these many works of art, sculptures, both those lining the great Spirit Paths and those found inside tombs and mausoleums, are of particular interest, in part because they highlight some of the regional variations and artistic innovations that occurred during this rich historical period.

In ancient Chinese history, the Wei, the Jin, and the Southern and Northern Dynasties marked a transition between two periods of national unification. Preceding the Wei dynasty the national unification of China had taken place under the auspices of the Han imperial court, which founded an empire of unprecedented power and prosperity. The Han empire began to wane early in the second century C.E., but it was the rebellion of the Yellow Turbans in central China, which erupted in 184, that caused the emperor's power and authority to erode and the country to descend into years of political chaos and the unbridled supremacy of warlords. The subsequent emergence of the Three Kingdoms of Wei, Shu, and Wu marked the beginning of a fragmented rule that lasted several centuries. At last, in 280, the Western Jin unified the nation, but only thirty-six years later the dynasty was overcome by internal revolt and foreign invasion. During this period of social turmoil and economic recession, tomb sculpture went into decline.

After the downfall of the Western Jin, the Xiongnu (Huns), Xianbei (Sienpi), and other nomads from the north and the west established the Sixteen Kingdoms (304–439). The Sima family, which had once ruled the Western Jin, fled across the Yangzi River and restored their rule under the dynastic title of Eastern Jin (317–420). The real confrontation between the north and south came only much later, however, after the Sima family had been overtaken by Liu Yu, who founded the first Song dynasty (420–479), and after the Tuoba clan of Xianbei nomads had unified the north under the Northern Wei dynasty. The subsequent political and military conflict between the Northern Wei and the Liu Song across the Yangzi characterized the Southern and Northern Dynasties. Before long, the Northern Wei split into the Eastern Wei (534–550) and Western Wei (535–556), with the Eastern Wei subsequently replaced by the Northern Qi (550–577), and the Western Wei by the Northern Zhou (557–581). The Northern Zhou unified the north by annihilating the Northern Qi — only to be toppled by Yang Jian, who founded the Sui (581–618) and proclaimed himself Emperor Wen. In south China, the fall of the Liu Song was followed by a quick succession of regimes: the Southern Qi (479–502), the Liang (502–557), and the Chen (557–589). It was not until the troops of the Sui vanquished the Chen in 589 that national unification was restored. In short, for nearly four centuries from the late Eastern Han to the Sui, the Chinese political structure was in persistent turmoil. The political and social culture of China was repeatedly disassembled and re-created as people of different ethnic backgrounds made the gradual transition from internecine strife to unification under a single Chinese state.

Amid such social and political uncertainty and change, social life in general, as represented by literature and art, remained in a state of upheaval that provided the opportunity for elements from various ethnic contingents and the outside world to influence Chinese culture as a whole. While the traditions of the Han and the Jin dynasties persisted, the Chinese arts of painting, sculpture, and calligraphy burgeoned, culminating in a thriving culture during the Sui and the Tang. Major changes in the imagery and content of stone sculpture that adorned the exteriors and interiors of mausoleums and tombs — and in particular, of terra-cotta figurines used as burial objects — illustrate the development of Chinese plastic art during this period. During the Sui and the Tang, or, to be exact, beginning with the rule of Empress Wu Zetian of the Tang, Chinese sculpture reached a new zenith. New assemblages of stone figures, with characteristics that varied by historical period, region, and the social status of the interred, began to appear along the Spirit Paths leading to tombs. Innovations in the materials and techniques used to make terra-cotta figurines (which were buried in formations inside tombs) eventually led to the emergence of Tang-style tricolor pottery, glazed and fired at low temperatures and still appreciated to this day.

Nascent stone sculpture ensembles and images appeared along the Spirit Paths of the mausoleums of Northern Song emperors (960–1127). Although they exhibited the influence of the Tang tradition of funerary sculpture, the flourishing commerce in cities, emergence of an urban citizenry, changes in social mores, and newfound popularity of *zaju* (poetic drama set to music) combined to bring a new look to the works of sculpture that decorated even ordinary people's tombs.

As terra-cotta figurines became less popular as burial objects, inner-tomb brick carvings reflecting the luxurious courtyard dwellings of the deceased during their lifetimes came into vogue, as did brick reliefs and figurines depicting zaju characters — to such a degree that even theaters appeared in brick relief. Stories of dutiful sons were another major theme of inner-tomb brick reliefs and stone sculpture during this period. This was the case with inner-tomb sculpture under the Liao regime of the non-Han Khitans and the Jin regime of the non-Han Jurchens (Nüzhen). The practice of gracing the Spirit Paths to an emperor's mausoleum with stone statues continued during the Ming and the Qing as a means of showing his position and authority as the supreme ruler in his lifetime. Yet even though such statues were made of quality stone and were monumental in size, their forms were stereotyped and lifeless.

Over time, inner-tomb sculpture became a luxury reserved for imperial tombs. Terra-cotta figurines were found only in the tombs of aristocrats and senior ministers. Even there, their artistic attainment was so unimpressive that they were eclipsed by counterparts from the Northern Dynasties, the Sui, and the Tang. The decline of terra-cotta figurines as burial objects seems to have been due to changes in burial rites and the newfound popularity of paper furnishings for burial purposes.

Our story begins near the end of the Han dynasty. During this period of decline, times became harder and funds for burials scarce. The Wei kingdom (220–265), one of the Three Kingdoms founded by Cao Cao, advocated simple burials. The once popular practice of using beautiful jade burial suits for the deceased members of the royal house of Han ended, luxury funerary objects disappeared entirely, and the exquisitely made funerary figurines often seen in Han tombs fell out of vogue.

The sudden decline in attention to funerary "spirit articles" is evident in Wei tombs around Luoyang. Instead of large groups of funerary figurines, only a few terra-cotta figurines and pottery models of domestic animals appear. A Wei tomb built in 247 in Jianxi County, Luoyang, for example, yielded only two miniature terra-cotta figurines, a male attendant and a house maid.[1] Both stand with their hands clasped in front of their chests. Their design is rather dull and rigid; there is no trace of the liveliness and vividness demonstrated by terra-cotta figurines of the Eastern Han (25–220). Two chickens and a dog, which accompany the attendant and maid, are both sketchily modeled with simple contour lines.

Funerary terra-cotta figurines in tombs of the Wu kingdom (222–280), the one of the Three Kingdoms that was founded by Sun Quan, have fascinating and distinctive regional features. There, clay figurines of naked people sitting on their heels, absent from the tombs of central China, have frequently been found. Crudely modeled, they are often covered with a blue glaze. Four such figurines were excavated from a tomb built in 262 in Wuchang, Hubei Province.[2] Each figure has a round growth between its eyebrows that is similar to the *urna,* the luminous tuft of hair or dot appearing between the eyebrows of the Buddha.[3] In a passageway in a Wu tomb at Tangjiaotou in Ezhou, Hubei, an important Buddhist relic was discovered: a statue of a sitting Buddha flanked by barefoot clay figurines.[4] Many of the tomb guardian beasts found in Wu tombs have four claws, similar to those of crocodiles, and backs carved with circular scales — a typical regional feature. In Wu tombs, there are also many glazed terra-cotta figurines in zoomorphic shapes. Mostly small with simple contours, these include chickens, ducks, sheep, dogs, and pigs. Often, too, pottery coops of chickens and ducks, sheep pens, and pigsties are present. Given that many clay models of granaries, millstones, mortars, and stoves have also been unearthed, these models may well document the increasing significance and prosperity of agriculture as practiced in the Yangzi River delta.

Another type of funerary object unearthed in a Wu tomb, a granary jar, or "soul urn," also has distinct regional features. Spirit articles of this type, usually made of clay or celadon, first began to appear in the Yangzi River delta during the Wu period. The design originated with the urn with five openings, a funerary object of the Eastern Han in the Yangzi River delta. Essentially an urn in the shape of a barrel, it has four smaller urns attached to its bulging middle. On the rims and upper parts of the five jars appear buildings, tiny human figures, birds, and beasts. Attached to the middle part of this complex, ornate piece are various images of immortals, magical beasts, and even fish and turtles. The human figures and animals are sketchily sculpted; aside from the facial features, no other details are shown. Though the modeling methods are simple and coarse, the figures give quite a lively impression and have a kind of antique beauty and simplicity (fig. 2.1). Most noteworthy among these soul urns is an early Buddhist work from the Yangzi River delta, with a small statue of Buddha sitting on top.

Funerary terra-cotta figurines unearthed at tombs in Sichuan Province from the period of the Shu kingdom (221–263) are somewhat similar to those of the East-

2.1 Granary jar (soul urn), clay, unearthed in 1955 from a Wu tomb in Zhaotugang, Nanjing, Jiangsu Province. Three Kingdoms period. 34.3 cm. Nanjing Museum.

2.2 Ox-shaped tomb guardian beast, clay, unearthed in 1984 in Yanshi County, Henan Province. Western Jin dynasty. 23.6 × 36 cm. Arthur M. Sackler Museum, Peking University.

2.3 Tomb guardian (armored warrior), clay, unearthed in 1984 in Yanshi County, Henan Province. Western Jin dynasty. 57 cm. Arthur M. Sackler Museum, Peking University.

ern Han in that region. The human figurines primarily represent household servants, such as male attendants or housemaids holding all sorts of objects, cooks working at carving boards, musicians playing various musical instruments, and dancers with flowers in their hair. By comparison with Han figurines, though, they appear simple and almost haphazardly posed. The most typical representative works are those excavated from Shu tombs on cliff faces in Tujing in Zhongxian County, Sichuan.[5] The site features a pottery house with miniature figurines in various postures — a kind of sculpture rarely seen in Han tombs.

Fifteen years after the founding of the Western Jin dynasty (265–317), the whole country was unified. Though the simple burial system of the Wei continued to be practiced, new traditions emerged. In particular, when prosperity returned to China, the burial of funerary clay figurines with the deceased was once again in vogue. Finds unearthed since the 1950s in Western Jin tombs in the region of Luoyang, the capital at that time, reveal four types of Western Jin clay funerary figurines.[6] First we find two styles of tomb guardian: a fierce beast with tufts in its mane resembling a dragon's scales, which leans forward menacingly (fig. 2.2); and a warrior guardian, wearing armor and a pointed cap surmounted by a ball and holding a shield in his left hand. In our example (fig. 2.3), he holds his right hand as if to attack, but the weapon, believed to be a long knife, is missing. Second are figurines of honor guards in a procession with ox-drawn carriages and horses with saddles, which perhaps illustrate the preferred mode of travel for the upper class in the Western Jin. Third are figurines of servants, attendants, and performers in the service of the deceased, although, unlike in Han times, normally only one representative male figurine and one female figurine were placed in a tomb. Fourth are figurines of cooks, usually accompanied by clay models of stoves, wells, and millstones, as well as models of livestock and domestic fowl. Artistically, though, these Western Jin clay figurines do not rival the Han figurines in delicacy and nimbleness. The lively human figures so characteristic of the Han became stiff in design, the robust horses of the Eastern Han were rendered in the Western Jin with short torsos and thick legs, and the Western Jin livestock and domestic fowl are simplistically portrayed. In general, the Western Jin clay figurines were crudely modeled and rigid in appearance. This style persisted throughout most of the Southern and Northern Dynasties period, until around 589.

In vast areas of northern China around Luoyang,

clay figurines found in Western Jin tombs basically followed the same rules, an indication that the centralization of power had influenced burial practices. In the Yangzi River delta, however, which had been a part of the Wu, works with the traditional Wu modeling could still be seen. The human figurines are naked or barefoot; some also sport the growth on the forehead similar to the Buddha's *urna*. Among the most striking finds is a group of Western Jin tombs excavated in Changsha, Hunan Province.[7] In one of the tombs, bricks carved with the characters "Second Year of the Yongning Reign" (302) were discovered, and some thirty pieces from various clay figurines were unearthed. In addition to naked warriors holding big knives, there appear officials with high hats who are riding on horses and holding official plaques in their arms, members of an equestrian orchestra playing musical instruments, and servants holding various utensils. This collection is a realistic illustration of a local dignitary's subordinate officials and troops. It also indicates that although the Western Jin had wiped out the Wu, a uniform funerary system was not yet completely in place in the Yangzi River delta. Two celadon sculptures from the Western Jin tomb in Changsha are particularly noteworthy. One depicts two officials sitting face to face, each holding a tablet in one hand and a brush in the other. As each writes on his own side of the tablet, the eyes of the two remain locked, as if in challenge (fig. 2.4). This lifelike representation is of great historic value because it seems to illustrate how people during the Han and the Western Jin wrote or kept records. The other sculpture is a small, triangular stirrup dangling from the left side of a saddle. This is the earliest stirrup ever discovered in China. Historians believe that a rider would have used the single stirrup for mounting the horse but not while riding; this single-stirrup arrangement only later evolved into the two-stirrup saddles we know today. Such works thus are immensely valuable not only because they show the artistic achievements of the ancient Chinese but also because they illuminate aspects of their daily lives.

The burial system and funerary practices of the Eastern Jin (317–420), which had its capital at Nanjing in the Yangzi River delta, continued the style of the earlier Western Jin, as well as local traditions inherited from the Wu. Celadon works, in particular, predominated among funerary objects, though figurines still looked much like those from the Western Jin. Examples can be found in the tombs of the prestigious Wang clan of Langya in Xiangshan, Nanjing, which have been exca-

vated since 1970. Terra-cotta figurines from Tomb 7 are representative of funerary figurines of the Eastern Jin period.[8] In the passageway to the tomb were fourteen clay human figurines, an ox-drawn carriage facing the entrance to the tomb, and a saddled horse. Beside the carriage stood a groom with a pointed hat, who was holding the reins of the ox, and to the right of the carriage waited a robust harnessed steed with a saddle who was also accompanied by a groom. In front of the carriage, another man with a pointed hat prostrated himself on the ground to greet the owner of the carriage. The other figurines stood on either side of the carriage, except for two who stood on the inner side of the entrance. All the figurines wear long robes and either flat-topped hats that are low at the front and high at the back or *liangguan* (hats with strips in front to indicate official ranking). They also all hold tablets or other objects in both hands. The composition of this group of figurines — with the carriage and the horse at the center — is identical to that of Western Jin figurine groups from Luoyang. All that is missing by comparison with groups from Western Jin tombs in Luoyang are the tomb guardian figures and house cooks.

The way they were made was also inherited from the Western Jin. The rudimentary figurines were obviously kneaded and pushed into shape. Lines were then cut; traces of incisions remain on the surface of some figurines. Although a few figurines have separate legs, the lower part is more often modeled in one trumpet-shaped piece without detailed carving. All were made of gray clay and covered with white powder; none were painted with colors. In some other tombs from the Eastern Jin in the region of Nanjing, terra-cotta figurines were also made almost entirely of gray clay, but for most of them molds were used. The basic design is similar to that of the figurines discovered at Jin tombs in Shandong. The standing figures, particularly the female ones, have only a trumpet-shaped piece below the waist. They all hold their hands in front of their chests. Only the hairstyles vary: some have hair in a fan shape, and some have hair arranged in a floral pattern at their temples. The terra-cotta figurines holding shields that are often seen in Western Jin tombs are also found in Eastern Jin tombs; however, the Eastern Jin figures wear no armor or helmets. Instead, they have *xiaoguan* hats (small hats with several parallel vertical ridges at the front) and robes with wide collars. Terra-cotta warriors from Eastern Jin tombs at Hongmao Hill in Shimenkan, Nanjing, sport a bun on the very top of their heads. In their left hands they raise their shields, while

2.4 Two officials sitting face to face to write records, celadon, unearthed in 1958 in Changsha, Hunan Province. Western Jin dynasty. 17.3 cm. Hunan Provincial Museum, Changsha.

with their right hands they reach forward, a posture that lends them an animated look.[9]

Terra-cotta figurines of the Eastern Jin are generally from 20 to 30 centimeters in height; almost none are more than 40 centimeters. The only exceptions are the four figurines holding shields from the Great Tomb in Fugui Hill in Nanjing. They are 52.8 centimeters in

height and exquisitely modeled. The left hand and the shield, separate pieces, are connected at the torso (fig. 2.5). The lips are painted vermilion, and the front of the shields is a vibrant red.[10] These tall, meticulously made clay figurines are believed to have been created as funerary objects for royal mausoleums of the Eastern Jin, and they represent the highest artistic attainment at the time in the manufacture of terra-cotta figurines. This belief is supported by the presence of a stone stele created in memory of Emperor Gong of the Song period in the Eastern Jin dynasty and erected in 421, during the Song period of the Southern Dynasties.[11] The stele was found some 400 meters from the site of the Great Tomb, indicating that the royal mausoleums of the Jin had been built in that area.

Funerary clay figurines of the Southern Dynasties (which include the Song, Southern Qi, Liang, and Chen) continued in the pattern of the Eastern Jin. The facial designs, however, began to change as social aesthetics evolved. When the "lean face and serene features" advocated by the artist Lu Tanwei gained popularity in other art forms during the reign of Emperor Ming of the Song (465 to 472), the faces of clay figurines began to reflect this trend. Examples include the female figurines unearthed at a late Song tomb at Xishanqiao, Nanjing.[12] Their heads, framed at the temples by hair, seem too small for their torsos, and their faces are lean and severe, with high cheekbones and pointed chins. The women's slightly upturned mouths smile mysteriously. By the early sixth century, however, around 502–519, a different painting style, that of the artist Zhang Sengyou, became popular: plump faces delineated with round brushstrokes gradually replaced the lean faces with sharp lines. Chinese art historians have a saying to describe these two styles of the Southern Dynasties: "Zhang excels in flesh; Lu excels in bones."[13] As a result of Zhang's influence, the lean faces of figurines became softer and rounder, like those unearthed at Liang tombs at Nanjing's Yaohua Gate.[14] Figurines at tombs built in Yanziji in 521 are even chubbier.[15]

Crudely modeled clay figurines with distinct regional characteristics from the Wu kingdom to the Western Jin still existed during the Southern Dynasties, but such figurines appear mostly in Guangxi, which is far to the south. The best examples are clay figurines discovered in two Southern Dynasties tombs in Daoshui in Cangwu and Shoucheng in Yongfu County.[16] The figurines, made of either clay or celadon, include rows of warriors holding halberds, axes, or drums, men on horseback wearing high hats, and, at the center, an official in a sedan-chair carried by two people and an ox-drawn carriage. There are also models of workshops and plowing oxen. Although the carving technique used to create these models was crude, they are significant because they reflect the lifestyle of the people living in remoter areas of the Southern Dynasties (fig. 2.6).

Although the rulers of the Eastern Jin were able to keep peace in the south, the people of northern China suffered from continuous conflict. The Xiongnu and Xianbei peoples gradually entered central China, control was in flux, and the area entered into a chaotic period of struggle among the Sixteen Kingdoms.[17] Rapid turnover in local political leadership, as well as the introduction of various customs of different nationalities, challenged the established traditions and rituals. The burial system that had developed during the Western Jin collapsed, and funerary traditions came to differ from area to area and from nationality to nationality. In particular, the practice begun in the Han and Western Jin of burying figurine groups at the burial ground declined. Excavation of tombs from the Sixteen Kingdoms period in the northeast, northwest, and central areas of China show no sign of funerary figurines.[18] Only in Guanzhong (the area around present-day Xi'an) have such funerary figurines been found in tombs from that era.

In Tomb 1 at Caochangpo in Xi'an, Shaanxi Province, for example, some 120 clay figurines were found.

2.5 Armored warrior with shield, clay, unearthed in 1956 in Nanjing. Eastern Jin dynasty. 52.8 cm. Nanjing Museum.

2.6 Honor guard attendants, porcelain, unearthed in 1981 in Yongfu County, Guangxi Zhuang Autonomous Region. Southern Dynasties. 13.5 cm. Yongfu County Cultural Relics Storeroom.

2.7 Cavalryman in armor, clay, unearthed in 1953 in Xi'an, Shaanxi Province. Sixteen Kingdoms period (Northern Dynasties). 37.5 × 35 cm. Shaanxi Museum of History, Xi'an.

Unlike with the Western Jin figurines, no tomb guardian figures were among them, and as for the other three types of figurine, although the general features remain the same, the details are quite different.[19] The stone figures in the group of honor guards in procession, the ox-drawn carriage, and the saddled horses are still in the center, but joining them is a cavalry horse, entirely covered with armor except for its ears, mouth, eyes, nose, and legs (a missing piece that shielded the horse's rump is presumed to have rotted away). In addition, the array of clay figurines comprises armored cavalrymen, a military orchestra on horseback — two drummers and two buglers — and infantrymen, some carrying bows and arrows and others armored and holding long-pole weapons. (Although the spears and possibly other long weapons are missing, holes on the figurines indicate where they were held.) The fully armed cavalrymen and the soldiers seem to protect the procession of the ox-drawn carriage and saddled horses. Such a demonstration of force gives an indication of the tense situation that prevailed during the warring period of the Sixteen Kingdoms.

Among the figurines of servants, attendants, and dancers are female figures that sit plucking strings of the zither or sing and clap their hands. Colorfully dressed servants wear buns arranged in floral patterns just like those of the women figurines in Eastern Jin tombs. This hairstyle was evidently in vogue in both the south and the north at the time. Models of kitchen furnishings, and of pigs, dogs, chickens, stoves, and wells, all by and large follow the designs from the Western Jin, though the rendering is cruder. The four legs of a horse, for instance, are like four posts, without a trace of joints or hoofs. Human figures are generally rigid (fig. 2.7). The terra-cotta armored horses and fierce-looking cavalrymen found here were made throughout the Northern Dynasties period.

As the Tuoba clan of the Xianbei people grew stronger and established the Northern Wei dynasty (385–535), which finally unified north China, funerary figurines again flourished. Originally, the Xianbei had no tradition of using funerary figurines. As the Tuoba regime gained political control and its territory expanded, however, Tuoba customs and traditions gradually merged with those of the Han and the Jin. Such adaptations were necessary to them; in their quest for power, they needed to garner the respect of peoples in the vast northern regions of China. This pressure to adapt also contributed to both the decision to move the capital during the Taihe reign of Emperor Xiaowen of the Northern Wei (477–499) and the reform of the traditional ritual system. The reintroduction of funerary figurines was one such reform. Early Northern Wei clay figurines have been discovered in Northern Wei tombs in Hohhot, in the Inner Mongolia Autonomous Region. They are believed to have been crafted in the first half of the fifth century.[20] The Hohhot site has yielded fifteen clay funerary figurines, as well as models of an ox-drawn carriage, saddled horses, livestock, domestic fowl, and cooking utensils. The tomb guardian figures, which look like armored warriors, are twice as tall as the other figurines. The ox-drawn carriage and saddled horses are still in the center of the procession. New to the Northern Wei figurine groups are camels, grooms, and servants with cowl-like hats.

Along with the servants, other attendants, dancers, and musicians is a group of seven seated musicians (unfortunately, all the musical instruments are missing). A dancer with both arms outstretched gracefully sways to their music. In addition to models of domestic animals, including sheep, pigs, dogs, and chickens, there are kitchen utensils, stoves, millstones, wells, granaries, and pestles. Both human figures and animals are sketchily modeled, with few details, and on many the body parts are disproportionately large or small. The head of one of the tomb guardian figures, for example, is almost one-third of its total height; its legs are very short, and its hands are outsized (fig. 2.8). Similarly, some of the animals have unrealistically large, thick limbs. The human figurines are dressed in the Xianbei style. The dancers wear dresses with tight sleeves and sport buns piled high and wrapped in head scarves. Horse and camel grooms mostly wear the small cowled hats or round hats typical of early Northern Wei pottery figurines.

As the customs of the Xianbei people under the rule of the Tuoba clan increasingly absorbed the Chinese influence, the appearance of funerary figurines began to change. Human figurines began to be made more in proportion, and manufacturing techniques matured. Terra-cotta figurines excavated from the joint tomb of Sima Jinlong and his wife, buried in the village of Shijia, Datong, Shanxi, in 474 and 484, respectively, are representative works.[21] The total number of funerary figurines at the burial ground is around 360; half of these are armored military men, light cavalrymen without armor, armored cavalrymen, and horses. Together with packhorses and camels, they form a large military assemblage. In addition, there are figurines of crouching beasts with human faces and tomb guardian beasts, attendants, servants, and musicians. Among the livestock and domestic fowl are cows, sheep, pigs, dogs, and chickens, in addition to camels and horses.

2.8 Tomb guardian warrior, clay, unearthed in 1975 in Hohhot, Inner Mongolia Autonomous Region. Northern Wei dynasty. 39.5 cm. Museum of the Inner Mongolia Autonomous Region.

Sima Jinlong had been a member of the royal house of the Eastern Jin before he gave his allegiance to the Northern Wei.[22] He and his family became favorites of the Northern Wei emperors, and during his lifetime he bore the hereditary title Prince of Langya. Sima Jinlong died in 484. His popularity was emblematic of the coalescence of the elites of the Xianbei and prestigious Han clans, and the funerary objects at his tomb suggest this merging of traditional Han culture with Xianbei culture. The realistic clay figurines in the tombs, for example, which also show the indirect influence of Western Jin figurines, illustrate the Xianbei style in costumes and masks. For instance, the human figures have pointed noses and mustaches; they also wear tight-sleeved costumes, belts, and cowled hats. The women figures wear their hair piled high in buns and wrapped in scarves. Furthermore, the large number of clay armored horses, cavalrymen, packhorses, and camels indicates that heavily armored cavalrymen were the mainstay of Xianbei military might and that horses were one of the primary means of transporting military goods.

After the Northern Wei moved its capital to Luoyang, Emperor Xiaowen gradually introduced a transformation in rituals and art: the styles began to resemble those of the Han people. The burial system underwent further reform, and the types of funerary figurines again changed. In addition to the four categories from the Western Jin mentioned previously, figurines of armored cavalrymen and camels now made their appearance. The design and costuming of figurines took on a new look as well. The funerary figurines of this period can be classified into several basic types, according to their pattern and basic structure.

First were the tomb guardian figures. Among the sculptures that have been excavated are a pair of human guardians and a pair of squatting beasts with heads held high. One of the beasts has a human face, the other a lion's head. Their shoulders sprout wings with flame-shaped feathers, and their manes are arranged in three tufts. The pair of human figures are warriors wearing two-piece armor, helmets, shoulder plates, trousers, and leggings. Presumably, each of them once held a weapon in the right hand, although only a small hole in the hand remains where the weapon was. They make an awe-inspiring impression (fig. 2.9). This group of figurines is taller than the others, and the modeling is more elaborate.

Second was a representative funerary scene comprising a large procession of honor guards, on both foot and horseback, with an ox-drawn carriage and saddled horses in the center. Among the human figures are drummers and trumpeters on horses, armored cavalrymen, musicians on foot, soldiers holding shields or carrying bows and arrows, officials with *longguan* (hats covered in lacquer) or xiaoguan hats, and warriors with swords and with cloaks draped over their shoulders. Apart from military gear, costumes include items which officials might wear (such as the longguan); a long gown with a wide belt; trousers with leggings in the style of the Hu people, a national minority then living in the north or northwest of China; and a small hat and cloak typical of the Xianbei. (Historical records state that after Emperor Xiaowen's reforms, the Northern Wei "combined customs of the Hu and the Han").[23] At the end of the procession are figurines of pack donkeys and camels.

Third, we find figurines of male and female atten-

2.9 Tomb guardian warrior in armor with shield, clay, unearthed in 1965 in the tomb of Yuan Shao, Luoyang, Henan Province. Northern Wei dynasty. 30.5 cm. Luoyang Museum.

dants, servants, dancers, and musicians, including some looking exactly like the Hu people, with their curly hair and big mustaches, deep eye sockets, and high-bridged noses.

Figurines of women make up the fourth group; they are seated and they either carry a baby or hold a winnowing basket or a basin. Domestic animals and fowl, along with wells and kitchen objects, are present, but they are small and coarsely modeled by comparison with the other figurines at the site. Northern Wei figurines were made mostly of gray clay. After being produced in molds, they were then fired and covered with white powder. Finally, they were painted with colors, although these have faded with time.

In the late Northern Wei, the contemporary painting style of the Southern Dynasties again influenced the design of terra-cotta figurines. One of the most noticeable changes was in the depiction of human faces: leanness fell out of fashion, in favor of fleshiness. The best examples of such sculpture come from the excavations at the base of a pagoda in Yongning Monastery, Luoyang (see figs. 4.7–4.10).[24] The nine-story wooden pagoda, erected in 516 by Empress Dowager Hu, mother of Emperor Xiaoming of the Northern Wei, housed a statue of Buddha sculpted in 519.[25] The wooden pagoda was destroyed by lightning fifteen years later. Some 1,560 fragments of painted pottery sculptures have been discovered among the ruins of the pagoda. Though none is intact, some of the small human figurines that had been attached to the surface of walls retain fairly complete heads and torsos. Once fired, the clay of which they were made became as hard as porcelain, but the original pigments have since faded almost completely. Instead of being angular like those which mimicked the painting style of Lu Tanwei, the faces are plump, with healthy complexions, fine eyebrows, and beautiful eyes, and the outlines neat and precise. These are masterpieces of sculpture in the new artistic style of Zhang Sengyou of the Southern Dynasties, which is known for realistically round faces and robust, carefully rendered bodies.[26] The terra-cotta figurines unearthed in Panlongzhong village at Yuan Shao's tomb, built in 528, are of this kind.[27] Though the tomb had been robbed early on, some one hundred pieces of pottery figurines were found during excavation of the tomb. They are made of gray clay, their heads and torsos having been molded separately and then assembled. After a few rudimentary touches here and there, the figurines were fired. Afterward, white powder and, later, colored pigments to depict costum-

ing, armor, and other details were applied. Except for the armored tomb guardian figures, which are 30.8 centimeters high, all the figurines measure between 16 and 23 centimeters in height. Most are standing in natural poses, though their postures vary. The creases in their costumes are neat, and the incised lines are simple and sweeping. Some warriors have bulging eyes and big beards; in design they are very similar to figurines unearthed from the ruins of the pagoda base at Yongning Monastery. The modeling is slightly inferior to that of the exquisite figurines at the royal monastery, but the clay horses, donkeys, and camels are lifelike and their postures animated. Clay human figurines with curly hair and mustaches, deep eye sockets, and high-bridged noses were also found. A squatting boy is a rare masterpiece among the clay figurines of the Northern Wei. He wears a red robe with a belt around the middle, red trousers, and a pair of knee-high boots. He is burying his head in both arms, and only his curly hair is showing (fig. 2.10).

When the Northern Wei split into the Eastern Wei (534–550) and the Western Wei (535–556), the Eastern Wei moved its capital from Luoyang to Ye (in the northwestern part of present-day Linzhang, Hebei Prov-

2.10 Squatting boy with his head buried in his arms, painted clay, unearthed in 1965 in the tomb of Yuan Shao, Luoyang, Henan Province. Northern Wei dynasty. 9.6 cm. Luoyang Museum.

2.11 Warrior in armor, clay, unearthed in 1987 from a tomb in Wanzhang, Cixian County, Hebei Province. Northern Qi dynasty. 28.1 cm. Arthur M. Sackler Museum, Peking University.

2.12 Armored warrior on horseback, clay, unearthed in 1987 from a tomb in Wanzhang. Northern Qi dynasty. 33 cm. Arthur M. Sackler Museum, Peking University.

ince).[28] Many artisans and artists from the Northern Wei moved to Ye. As a result, the Eastern Wei inherited the painting and sculpture traditions of the late Northern Wei. During the period that followed, the greater the rank of the deceased, the greater the number of funerary figurines. In one case there were about one thousand pieces.[29] After the Northern Qi (550–577) replaced the Eastern Wei, funerary figurines in Northern Qi tombs in the area of Ye followed the style that had flourished during the Eastern Wei. The best-known examples are the 1,500 clay figurines unearthed at a large tomb in Wanzhang, Cixian County, Hebei Province.[30] Two figurines of officials, 28.1 and 33 centimeters high, each placed on one of the outer sides of the stone gate of the tomb, are the tallest clay figurines ever discovered from the Northern Dynasties period (figs. 2.11–2.12).

The most vivid clay figurines created in the period from the Eastern Wei to the Northern Qi are dancers. Dancing female figurines were excavated from the tomb of Princess Ru Ru (also known as Lüchi Dilian), built

in 550, during the Eastern Wei. Wearing long skirts and their hair piled high, the dancers are lifting their left feet. The thirteen figurines of female dancers excavated at the large tomb in Wanzhang are exquisite. Most of the dancers, captured in various graceful poses, are wearing longguan hats, and all have red dresses with crossed lapels and wide sleeves. An even more interesting piece unearthed from the same tomb is a figurine of an elderly male dancer with a tall hat and a long beard. His floor-length robe seems to sway as he moves. Remarkably, his appearance is almost identical to that of an old dancer carved on a brick in a Southern Dynasties tomb in Dengxian County, Henan. The musical instruments used to accompany the male dancer include a waist drum, cymbals, and a *sheng* (reed pipe), and the melody to which he dances may be the "High Cloud Dance" of the Liang dynasty.[31] This figurine of the elderly dancer unearthed at the tomb of Ru Ru is the most lifelike piece of sculpture excavated from it (fig. 2.13).

Other details of clay figurines were modified during this period. The armor of the tomb guardian figures,

2.13 Old dancer from tomb of Princess Ru Ru, clay, unearthed in 1979 in Cixian County, Hebei Province. Eastern Wei dynasty, 550 C.E. 29.8 cm. Handan Area Cultural Hall, Hebei Province.

for instance, became "shining armor" (with one shining circular plate in front and another in back), which was in vogue at the time. And the plain shield changed into one with a central ridge and a lion's head pattern. Another political center of the Eastern Wei and the Northern Qi was Jinyang (present-day Taiyuan, Shanxi). It was the base of the clan of Gao Huan, who first held military power in the Eastern Wei and then replaced the Eastern Wei with the Northern Qi. Funerary figurines unearthed at tombs in Jinyang are similar in pattern and design to those found in the area of Ye, but the details of the figurines reveal regional stylistic influences. The faces tend to be fleshier and rounder with heavy chins, the figures have paunches, and their lower limbs are short and thin. The details of the costumes are simple. The most typical of the works are the figurines unearthed in Shouyang, Shanxi, from She Diluo's tomb, built in 562, and in Taiyuan, Shanxi, from Lou Rui's tomb, built in 570 (fig. 2.14).[32] An intriguing exception

to this style was an exceptionally crafted figurine of a dancer with a tall hat found in She Diluo's tomb. Note the expressive, smiling mouth (fig. 2.15).

The capital of the Western Wei, a rival of the Eastern Wei, was Chang'an (present-day Xi'an in Shaanxi). The actual military and political power of the Western Wei was in the hands of the Yuwen clan. Later on, the Yuwen clan founded the Northern Zhou to replace the Western Wei. Terra-cotta figurines unearthed from tombs of these periods resemble those created during the Northern Wei era, but again strong regional characteristics can also be found. A Western Zhou burial site, known as the Xiaoling mausoleum of Emperor Wu (also known as Yuwen Yong), has been excavated in recent years.[33] The tomb, located to the southeast

2.14 Armored warrior with shield, clay, unearthed in 1980 from the tomb of Lou Rui, Taiyuan, Shanxi Province. Northern Qi dynasty, 570 C.E. 63.5 cm. Shanxi Provincial Institute of Archaeology, Taiyuan.

of Chenma village, in the township of Dizhang in Xian-yang, Shaanxi, having been seriously damaged by grave robbers, has yielded only 150 terra-cotta figurines — fewer than one might have hoped, but enough to help understand the skills required to manufacture these important funerary objects.

As in the Eastern Wei and Northern Qi periods, these figurines of gray clay were made in molds. Except for the horses, few were made in the two-piece molds so ubiquitous in earlier periods. Instead, standing figurines and figurines on horseback were all manufactured in a half mold, so each piece is solid and the back side is smooth and flat. After the clay figurines were fired and completed, they, like earlier versions, were decorated with white powder and colored pig-ments. As for the tomb guardian beasts of the Northern Zhou, one has a human face and a beast's body, the other has a lion's head and the body of another beast. But they are all prostrate on the ground instead of squatting. The tomb guardian figures are armored human figurines, but without elongated shields in their hands. All have paunches (fig. 2.16). The clay horses, either saddle horses or cavalry horses, have heads that seem too small and legs that appear surprisingly thick (fig. 2.17). They are primitively made. On the whole, the clay sculptures of the Western Wei and the Northern Zhou are less refined than those of the Eastern Wei and the Northern Qi, although all groups followed designs developed during the Sixteen Kingdoms period in areas around Xi'an.

2.15 Old foreign dancer with tall hat, clay, unearthed in 1973 from the tomb of She Diluo, Shouyang, Shanxi Province. Northern Qi dynasty, 562 C.E. 25.3 cm. Shanxi Provincial Institute of Archaeology, Taiyuan.

2.16 Armored tomb guardians with paunches, clay, unearthed in 1983 from the tomb of Li Xian, Guyuan County, Ningxia Hui Autonomous Region. Northern Zhou dynasty. 18.2 and 19.2 cm. Guyuan Museum.

2.17 Soldiers on horseback, clay, unearthed in 1983 from the tomb of Li Xian. Northern Zhou dynasty. 17.5 × 17 cm. Guyuan Museum.

Stone Funerary Sculpture in the Northern Dynasties

Early Northern Dynasties tombs consisted of a long earthen ramp, a brick passageway, and an inlaid brick chamber. In later years, a few patios and cave openings were added between the passageway and the chamber. Colored murals have frequently been discovered on their walls, but stone sculptures have rarely been found. The only stone funerary sculpture discovered so far is in the large Yongguling mausoleum of Empress Dowager Feng (Wenming), who was in power during the Northern Wei. Construction of the tomb at Mount Fang in Datong, Shanxi, began in 481, and the empress was buried there in 490.[34] A pagoda in front of the mausoleum lends a Buddhist atmosphere to the place. The stone gates and door frames of the tomb passageway are carved with patterns in bas-relief; beneath these are arched shrine posts with patterns of lotus petals (fig. 2.18). Each shrine post is carved in relief with a smiling, plump, barefoot boy holding a lotus bud and wearing a sweeping dress and belt; the effect is lifelike and joyful (fig. 2.19). Beneath each boy is a long-plumed peacock with a pearl in its beak. The blocks supporting the pivot of the door are in the shape of a tiger's head, implying solidness and strength. Stylistically, this group of sculptures is similar to those of the same period in the grottoes of Yungang. Though obviously influenced by Buddhist art, the Yongguling mausoleum works are particularly notable because they are non-Buddhist sculptures, seldom seen from the Northern Wei.

Northern Dynasties tombs are also known for carvings on the sarcophagus platform and pictures scored into the surface of the sarcophagus. One such platform was laid horizontally in the western part of the rear chamber of Sima Jinlong's tomb in Datong. It is 2.41 meters long, 1.33 meters wide, and 0.51 meters high, and it is made of six pieces of gray slate. The bottom of the slate in front is carved with three base stands, each in the shape of a warrior supporting the weight. The stand in the center shows two warriors, while those on the left and right sides each have one. Between the stands are wavy patterns, above which appear carvings of interlocking acanthus designs. In the center of this slate are carved images of performers, a dragon, a tiger, a phoenix, a bird with golden wings, and a bird with a human face. Of the thirteen performers, the one in the middle is a dancer, flanked by two equal rows of musicians holding various instruments, such as a *pipa* (tradi-

tional plucked string instrument), a pipa with a crank handle, panpipes, a vertical flute, a transverse flute, cymbals, a drum, and a waist drum with a narrow center. The figures are exquisitely scored with flowing lines.[35] The human figures very closely resemble carvings in the Yungang grottoes from the same period. Standing on four pedestals behind the sarcophagus before the grave was ransacked by robbers was a lacquer screen with colorful paintings praising filial sons and loyal wives. One pedestal was found on top of the base of the sarcophagus. The other three were scattered in the passageway linking the front and the rear chambers, where the screen boards were left on the ground as well. Each pedestal is made of gray stone; its lower part is a square-shaped base, carved with acanthus designs and performing boys in bas-relief. Above the base is an inverted basin in the form of upside-down lotus petals surrounded by carvings of dragons and mountains in high relief. On the top of the pedestal is another upside-down lotus blossom with a hole in the middle into which the screen stand fitted. On the four corners of the square base of two pedestals are four animated, three-dimensional sculptures of boys either dancing or playing the *bili* (an ancient bamboo pipe with a reed mouthpiece), the drum, or the pipa.[36] The facial outlines are very similar to those of the boys carved in bas-relief on the shrine posts of stone gates in Yongguling mausoleum at Fangshan. Both illustrate the playful, ornate style and distinctive themes of stone carvings during the early years of the Taihe reign of the Northern Wei.

After the Northern Wei moved its capital to Luoyang, Mangshan became a favorite place for burials of the royal family and nobles. Unfortunately, these graves have been robbed repeatedly. Though some sarcophagus platforms with carvings from the period have been kept in place, others have been moved out of the country. Remaining in Luoyang today are only a few incomplete sarcophagus platforms. But one can still see that the structure of those platforms is identical to that used for the platform of the sarcophagus of Sima Jinlong.

A relatively complete stone sarcophagus platform from the Northern Dynasties period has been found in recent years in Qinyang County, Henan. It is 2.23 meters long, 1.12 meters wide, and 0.51 meters high — measurements much like those of the sarcophagus platform of Sima Jinlong — but the carvings at the bottom of the stone platform are somewhat different. The central stand is carved mostly with door knockers. The other stands are incised with images of magical beasts, guardians, or Law protectors (fierce guardians of Buddhism). The horizontal bar over the stands is carved with rhomboid patterns reminiscent of those on the back of a tortoise and reminiscent too of a *kunmen* (a round arch design with a downward chip in the middle of the top arch line) decorated with designs of lotus blossoms and acanthus. Between the plants are all sorts of magical birds and weird beasts. The whole bar is edged with etchings of lotus petals and strings of pearls.[37] It is quite similar to Northern Dynasties sarcophagi with carvings.

During the Northern Dynasties period in the area of Luoyang, the sarcophagus itself was used as a ritual funerary object. In the tomb of Wang Yuanwei, King Nanping, for example, a stone coffin made of six pieces of polished slate has been found.[38] It is said that grave robbers made away with no fewer than ten stone sarcophagi, some elaborately painted and carved, from tombs in this area.[39] Some have surfaced in other countries. The one housed in the Nelson-Atkins Museum of Art in Kansas City has pictures in praise of filial sons incised on both sides of the coffin. Each side has pictures under three separate headings. On the one side are "Son Shun," "Son Guo Ju," and "Filial Grandson Yuan"; on the other side are "Son Dong Yong," "Son Cai Shun," and "Wei" (fig. 2.20). Each of these headings applies to one to three pictures, partially separated by images of trees or rocks, to present a story. The pictures are very well composed. The human figures in them are tall, slim, and finely rendered, clearly showing the influence of the Southern Dynasties artistic style.

In addition, the Luoyang Ancient Stone Carving

2.18 Carvings and bas-reliefs on stone doorway, unearthed in 1976 from the Yongguling mausoleum of Empress Dowager Feng, Fangshan, Datong, Shanxi Province. Northern Wei dynasty. 182 × 159 cm. National Museum of China, Beijing.

2.19 Detail of doorway in figure 2.18 showing a boy holding a lotus bud. 37 cm.

2.20 Stone sarcophagus with "filial piety" motif, engraved gray limestone, from Luoyang. Northern Wei dynasty. 62.2 × 223.5 cm. The Nelson-Atkins Museum of Art, Kansas City, Missouri.

2.21 Offering shrine with engraved figures and inscriptions, limestone. Northern Wei dynasty, early 6th century. 138 × 200 × 97 cm. Museum of Fine Arts, Boston. Anna Mitchell Richards and Martha Silsbee Funds, 37.340.

Art Museum has some carved sarcophagi, fragments of sarcophagi, and especially sarcophagus lids. Both ends of the lid are often engraved with a full frontal view of a beast, which holds in its mouth a horizontal pole decorated with lotus blossoms on either end. The inside of the lid is incised with a picture of the sky with the sun, the moon, the Milky Way, and other constellations. There are also pictures of Fuxi and Nü Wa in the shape of entwined snakes holding up the sun and the moon.

Another well-preserved sarcophagus was unearthed in the 1970s in Shangyao village in the suburbs of Luoyang.[40] Made of bluish limestone, its panels were held together with dovetails. The carving technique is exceptional. First, the images were given prominence through carving in relief; then additional details were incised onto those carvings. Both the right and the left sides of the slate in front depict two doormen holding knives and wearing xiaoguan hats and two-piece armor. Above them is a vermilion bird. The back is carved with three pictures telling three stories. The ones on the left and right sides are indistinct, but the one in the center is about the filial grandson Yuan Gu. Interestingly, it is quite different stylistically from other pictures on the sarcophagus and seems to have been taken from another sarcophagus altogether. The left and right sides of the sarcophagus are incised with images of large dragons and tigers with immortals riding on them. Carved on the bottom are strange beasts with human figures, dragons, tigers, and rare birds. Mosaics with similar motifs are used in other tombs of the Southern Dynasties period, for example, some tombs found in Nanjing and Dantu, Jiangsu Province.[41] The animals may be a reference to a popular belief during the Han dynasty that the dragon, the tiger, and assorted deities led the deceased in their ascent to Heaven.

Finally, a masterpiece must be mentioned: Ning Mao's offering shrine, now in the collection of the Museum of Fine Arts, Boston. It was allegedly unearthed from a tomb, but its shape suggests that it might be a Northern Wei stone shrine and not a burial sculpture after all (fig. 2.21).

Ornately carved sarcophagi and stone screens for sarcophagus platforms have also been excavated from burials of the Northern Qi and the Northern Zhou. A Northern Qi sarcophagus with incised pictures has been discovered in Qingzhou, Shandong Province. The incised pictures are of people riding on horses, ox-drawn carts, or pack camels and of a man offering a gift to his master. Unfortunately, the tombs were seriously damaged and the sarcophagus fragments were scattered. Despite efforts to collect the many pieces, a complete sarcophagus could not be assembled.[42]

A related discovery is that of a stone screen from the Northern Zhou, found in a tomb in Kangdizhai village in Xi'an. The deceased was called An Jia, probably a native from the part of central Asia belonging to China. He served both as an administrator in charge of matters concerning the Hu businessmen who stayed in China and as a Zoroastrian priest. He died in 579.[43] An altar carved into the lintel on the stone gate of his tomb is flanked on each side by a magical bird with the face of a human being and the talons of an eagle. Inside the burial chamber is the platform of his sarcophagus, whose stands feature distinctively west Asian patterns. A stone screen made of eleven pieces of bluish gray stone stands behind and on either side of the coffin. Each panel of the screen is carved with two groups of pictures in bas-relief, one on the upper part and one on the lower. They include renderings of chariots, horses, hunting scenes, banquets, and dance performances, all painted with gold and other pigments. When they were unearthed, they still looked resplendent. That was the first time that such a masterpiece of Northern Zhou art had ever been discovered (fig. 2.22).

2.22 Relief carving, bluish gray stone with gilt and pigment, unearthed in 2000 from the tomb of An Jia, Xi'an. Northern Zhou dynasty. Shaanxi Provincial Institute of Archaeology, Xi'an.

Sculptures in Tombs from the Sui, the Tang, and the Five Dynasties

In 581, Yang Jian overthrew the Northern Zhou and founded the Sui dynasty. Eight years later, the Sui army crossed the Yangzi River and wiped out the state of Chen. For more than 272 years, ever since the fall of the Western Jin, China had been fragmented; now it was united again. Artists and craftsmen from all over the country came to the Sui capital, Daxing (near present-day Xi'an), where they learned about one another's regional artistic styles and techniques. The dynamic mix enabled artists and craftsmen to use others' strong points as a springboard for their own new ideas.[44] Yet because the Sui dynasty lasted just less than forty years, ending in 618, there was too little time for the different art schools to produce a new, cohesive style of any historical significance.

The designs of funerary figurines during these years reflect the incomplete amalgamation of styles. Archaeological finds from Sui tombs in Shaanxi, Shanxi, and Henan, for example, show distinct regional features. Funerary figurines found in Sui tombs within the boundaries of what had been Northern Zhou territories are still Northern Zhou in style. The clay figurines excavated at the tomb of Liu Wei, who died in 583 in Liujiaqu in the city of Sanmenxia in Henan, are typical of those sculpted during the Sui dynasty.[45] Two pairs of the tomb guardian figurines are identical in design to those created for Northern Zhou burials. One is a pair of beasts crouching on the ground, their heads slightly lifted, without manes or bristles on their backs. Figurines of horses with riders on their backs have four thick, postlike limbs. The riders are carved only on the front; their backs are flat.

Similarly, funerary figurines unearthed in the region previously ruled by the Northern Qi show a clear continuation of the Northern Qi style. Terra-cotta figurines unearthed at Sui tombs in Anyang, Henan, obviously follow a design that was popular for figurines manufactured near Yecheng, capital of the Northern Qi (near present-day Anyang). Among the tomb guardian figurines at Tomb 103, built in Nandi, Xiaotun, in 603, are a pair of standing warriors in shining armor who are holding shields, and a pair of squatting beasts with tufted manes.[46] Both reflect a style inherited from the Northern Qi, as do the designs of the xiaoguan hats, trousers, cowl hats, and cloaks of the honor guard figurines excavated from that tomb. As might be expected, pottery horses and camels found at the site

are lifelike, with details such as hoofs and knee joints, another Northern Qi characteristic.

Clay figurines unearthed at Sui tombs in Taiyuan proper follow designs of the Northern Qi centered on Jinyang. Clay figurines unearthed from Hulü Che's tomb, built in 597, during the Sui dynasty, in Shagou village, Taiyuan, are good examples.[47] The tomb guardian figurines still include both standing armored warriors, holding elongated shields carved in the shape of a lion's head in their left hands, and squatting beasts with tufted manes. The limbs of the clay horse are well proportioned and realistic, unlike those of clay horses from the Northern Zhou. Figurines of horsemen wearing both black flat-topped hats with upturned rims and black coats with a pattern of pointed leaves are often seen in Northern Qi tombs in the region of Jinyang: the Lou Rui tomb from the Northern Qi has yielded two such clay figurines riding red horses. The horsemen wear black coats and hats, white trousers, and black boots.[48] Nearly identical figurines of horsemen have also been

2.23 Warrior riding a horse, clay, unearthed in 1980 from the tomb of Hulü Che, Taiyuan, Shanxi Province. Sui dynasty. 29.5 cm. Shanxi Provincial Institute of Archaeology, Taiyuan.

2.24 Civil officials, white porcelain, unearthed in 1959 from the tomb of Zhang Sheng, Anyang, Henan Province. Sui dynasty. 70 cm. Henan Museum.

found in the Hulü Che tomb. The only difference is that the horsemen are painted vermilion (fig. 2.23).

The design of funerary clay figurines unearthed from Sui tombs in a place near Daxing is a remarkable, albeit awkward, combination of the Northern Zhou and Northern Qi styles. A typical group of such works comes from Li He's tomb (582) in Shuangsheng village, Sanyuan County, Shaanxi.[49] Among the funerary figurines that were unearthed is a pair of tomb guardian warriors in shining armor, each, in Northern Qi style, holding an elongated shield carved in the shape of a lion's head. The figurines of armored honor guards, however, were made with half molds, for their backs are flat. The horse, too, in perfect Northern Zhou style, has stiff limbs and a head that is totally out of proportion. As if to emphasize the incomplete merging of styles, some of the warrior figurines that have been found have flat-topped hats with upturned brims and coats with a pattern of pointed leaves — clearly representing design elements from the Northern Qi. The figurines eloquently suggest that so quickly was the Northern Qi followed by the Sui that significantly new sculptural styles did not have a chance to emerge.

Particularly notable are the designs of the ninety-five Sui funerary figurines unearthed from Zhang Sheng's tomb in Anyang, Henan, from 595.[50] In addition to the clay figurines, there are some extremely rare porcelain figurines. Especially worthy of mention are four 60-centimeter-high porcelain figurines each standing on a pedestal shaped like an upside-down lotus. The other masterpieces are two finely detailed porcelain figurines of civil officials (fig. 2.24) and two of warriors. In the center of the clay figurines is a ceremonial procession with an ox-drawn carriage, but the armored cavalrymen and soldiers holding shields or carrying arrow bags, so popular in the Northern Dynasties period, are absent. Moreover, many more figurines of well-dressed women and women holding objects have been found; to date, female figures make up more than 40 percent of the figurines discovered at the burial. Also unearthed at the tomb are two figurines of monks, one short, the other tall (fig. 2.25). One of them holds an incense burner in his hand. Those figurines and the pedestals on which the porcelain figurines stand, which are in the shape of an upside-down lotus flower, display a strong Buddhist influence. Also notable are new Sui figurine designs, such as those seen in the figurine known as Qianqiu Wansui (literally, "a thousand autumns" and "ten thousand years," or "longevity"), figurines of birds with human heads, and twelve well-dressed figurines representing the signs of the zodiac, each with the head of a beast, discovered at Sui burials in Hubei, Anhui, and Jiangsu Provinces. But no trace of such Sui figurines has been found in northern China.[51]

2.25 Monks, clay, unearthed in 1959 from the tomb of Zhang Sheng. Sui dynasty. 16.5 cm and 24 cm. Henan Museum.

Tang Figurines

In the early years of the Tang dynasty, the burial system still followed the Sui system. Terra-cotta funerary figurines in tombs look much the same as Sui figurines. The figurines of warriors or tomb guardian figures that have been unearthed at burials from the reign of Emperor Taizhong (627–649) near Xi'an are standing and holding elongated shields in their left hands. Occasionally, armored cavalrymen have been discovered. Figurines of buglers on horseback, riders, attendants and servants, and honor guards all are similar in design to their Sui counterparts. (Representative figurines can be found at the tomb of Li Shou, Prince Jing of Huai'an [631] in Jiaocun village, Sanyuan County, Shaanxi, as well as at the tomb of Princess Changle [643] in Guangcun village, Quanling.)[52] Celadon funerary figurines in tombs of that period created by the Tang in Wanzhou district, Chongqing, represent a regional twist on this theme.[53] They depict mostly armored cavalrymen and musicians on horseback in a procession (fig. 2.26). The shape of a camel included in the group, however, is rather strange, perhaps because the craftsmen there had no real camel to imitate. Also

among this group of celadon figurines are Qianqiu Wansui figurines and twelve zodiac signs in the form of beasts with human heads (fig. 2.27). The inclusion of these thematic figurines probably reflects the existence of material and cultural connections between Sichuan and peoples from the lower reaches of the Yangzi River.

By the time Emperor Gaozong had risen to power (he reigned from 650 to 683), terra-cotta figurines had begun diversify in pattern and design. The art of modeling developed rapidly, and soon Sui designs had completely fallen from favor. Tomb guardian figurines show this evolution well. Figurines of standing warriors in armor holding elongated shields in their left hands, popular in the Northern Dynasties and in the Sui and early Tang, were replaced by new models. The tomb guardian figurines from the tomb of Zheng Rentai at Mazhai village, Liquan, Shaanxi, built in 664, no longer hold shields, for example, even though they still wear shining armor and are in standing poses with their feet on mountain rocks.[54] Before long, the tomb guardian figurine had been transformed from a warrior in armor to the kind of armored Heavenly King familiar from Buddhist art, very often with a reclining ox underneath its feet. Such a figurine was discovered at

2.26 Cavalryman in full armor, celadon, unearthed in 1978, Chongqing. Tang dynasty. 24.9 cm. Sichuan Provincial Museum, Chengdu.

2.27 Qianqiu Wansui (Longevity), celadon, unearthed in 1978, Chongqing. Tang dynasty. 8 cm. Sichuan Provincial Museum, Chengdu.

the tomb of Li Shuang (built in 668) in Yangtou Township, Xi'an.[55]

Later the tomb guardian figure in the form of the Heavenly King lost its rigid standing posture and instead acquired a lively pose with one hand reaching out and upward, the other hand on his side, and one leg bent, his foot often crushing a little devil. Figurines with such designs have been found in the auxiliary tomb of Li Xian, Prince Zhanghuai, in the Qianling mausoleum. The deceased in this tomb were buried between 706 and 711.[56]

The pair of tomb guardian beasts also changed during this period. In the tomb of Zheng Rentai, they still have tufted manes, but their two front limbs and both shoulders sprout wings in a flame pattern. In the later tomb of Li Shuang, the tomb guardian beasts have no manes, the wings are stretched out, and the feet rest on mountain rocks. The tomb guardian beasts in the tomb of Li Xian have two pricked-up ears and long, upturned horns: one horn on the beast with the human head, and two on the one with the head of a beast. Their flame-shaped feathery wings are larger and stretched out. Standing on mountain rocks, these guardians look very different from those created between the Northern Dynasties and the Sui. Figurines of fully dressed civil officials and military generals, as tall as the tomb guardian figure in the form of the Heavenly King, also appear among the groups of terra-cotta figurines. The civil officials wear erect headdresses, and the generals comblike hats. The ox-drawn carriage, at the center of processions since the Western Jin, has lost its pivotal position to a saddled horse with a rider. The horse looks more real and animated than the rigid horse with four postlike limbs so common since the Western Jin. Many hunting eagles, dogs, and cheetahs are in the procession, an indication that hunting was popular with noblemen of the time (fig. 2.28). Large numbers of formally dressed drummers and buglers, wearing scarves and xiaoguan or *weimao* hats (hats with a neck flap to keep out the wind) create a grand and celebratory atmosphere. The strong military air that was a feature of Northern Dynasties figurine processions has receded. There are only a few guards, and these no longer wear armor: now they have uniforms made of brocade painted to look like armor. Figurines of cavalrymen in armor have been found only in the tomb of Crown Prince Yide. Again, the armor of these honor guards is made of resplendent brocade. Their horses have protective plates over their faces, but they are ornamented with gold foil (fig. 2.29).[57] All these changes herald the high point in artistic inno-

vation, and in particular sculptural creativity, that accompanied the appearance of the prosperous Tang dynasty.

This artistic peak is also evident in the appearance of tricolor glazed pottery. The tombs of Prince Zhanghuai and Prince Yide have yielded male and female standing tricolor figurines and tricolor tomb guardian figures, as well as tricolor horses and grooms (fig. 2.30). It seems that this new method of firing pottery first appeared in the era of Emperor Gaozong and matured under the reign of Empress Wu Zetian. The so-called Tang tricolor refers to a special kind of pottery painted with mixed colored glazes and heated by a slow fire.[58] Except for a few bases still made of ordinary clay that turned red after firing, figurines during this era were created with refined, white clay (kaolin), which was used for manufacturing porcelain. The temperature needed for firing such pottery is lower than that for porcelain, however. It is correctly fired at about 800–1,100 degrees centigrade, whereas porcelain requires firing at temperatures of at least 1,300 degrees centigrade. Another distinction of kaolin is that its glaze is bright but not transparent like that of porcelain. The basic colors are yellow, green, and ochre (hence the name *tricolor*). In fact, there are more than three colors; blue and black, for example, are also used. These pigments were created by mixing differently colored metals in various proportions.

During the Kaiyuan and Tianbao reigns of Emperor Xuanzong (713–756), the art of Tang figurines reached its height. Human models were carefully crafted to show off attributes that were valued in society at large. Figurines of women, for example, round-faced and ample of figure, look stately and poised with their high-piled hair and long dresses. The famous imperial concubine Yang was thought to represent perfect beauty in her time. In all cases, the human figures are well proportioned, and contour lines are precise and varied. As the economy flourished, members of the ruling class laid great stress on burial. The number and size of funerary figurines entombed in each burial grew throughout the period, and the figurines were ever more elaborately ornamented. The pairs of tomb guardian figures and tomb guardian beasts from this time are gorgeously decorated, and the beasts seem to be prancing about rather than squatting motionless. The helmet

2.28 Mounted hunter, with a cheetah jumping onto the horse's hindquarters, painted clay, unearthed in 1960 from the tomb of Princess Yongtai in Qianxian County, Shaanxi Province. Tang dynasty. 30.5 × 21 cm. Shaanxi Museum of History, Xi'an.

2.29 Armored cavalryman, clay with gold foil, unearthed in 1971 from the tomb of Prince Yide in Qianxian County, Shaanxi Province. Tang dynasty. 34 cm. Shaanxi Museum of History, Xi'an.

of a tomb guardian figure in the guise of the Heavenly King is often decorated with meticulously designed peacock or phoenix patterns. His shoulders are often ornamented with decorative motifs such as splendid-looking beast's heads or pearls in flames. Artistically, the most vivid group consists of painted figurines that range in height from 1.10 to 1.42 meters. The figurines were unearthed in the tomb of Madame Song, wife of Lei Jun, who was buried in the village of Hansen, Xi'an, in 745.[59] From written sources, we know the names of the figurines: Dangkuang, Dangye, Zuming, and Dezhou.[60] The pair resembling the Heavenly King are Dangkuang and Dangye (fig. 2.31), whereas the pair in the form of beasts have been determined to be Zuming and Dizhou.[61] In addition to tomb guardian figures, there are figurines of the same size representing officials and military officers. Grand processions have disappeared.

Figurines during this period primarily depict well-dressed maids, orchestra members, beautifully decorated horses and their grooms (fig. 2.32), and pack camels and their grooms. Occasionally, we find polo players and acrobats and even models of residential courtyards. These figurines are mostly tricolor pieces. Representative tricolor figurines can be found at the tomb of Xianyu Tinghui, who was interred in Nanhe village, Xi'an, in 723.[62] One rare piece is a figurine depicting a camel carrying a stage on which sit many musicians and a Hu dancer with a beard (fig. 2.33). It is believed to represent the convergence of the best in the sculptural art and ceramic technology of the time.[63] Another, similar piece has been found in a Tang tomb in the village of Zhongbao, Xi'an.[64] This figurine is smaller, but the camel is carrying seven performers, including six musicians and one girl dancer with a tall

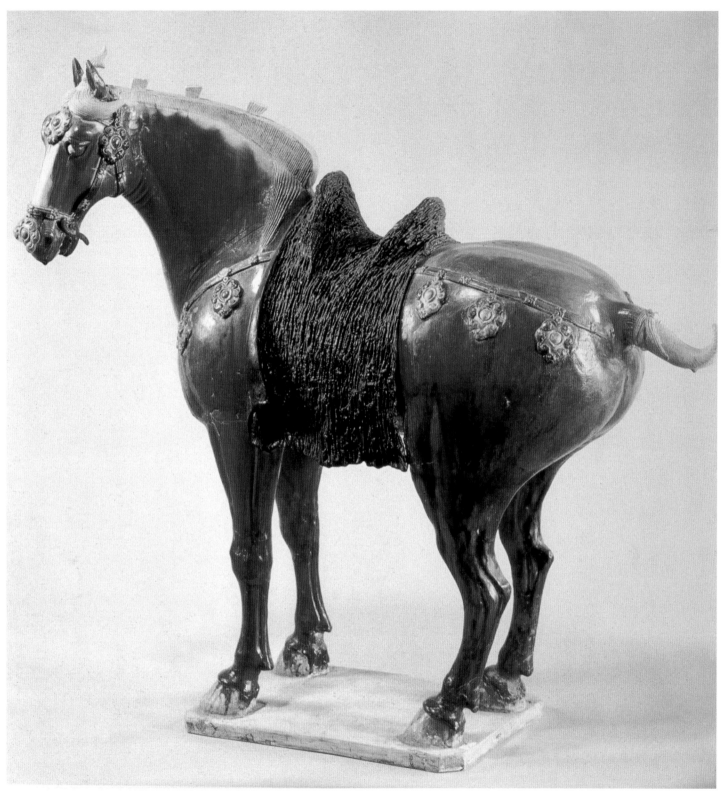

2.30 Tricolor horse, glazed kaolin, unearthed in 1971 from the tomb of Prince Yide. Tang dynasty. 79.5 cm. Shaanxi Museum of History, Xi'an.

2.31 Heavenly King tomb guardian with peacock or phoenix, glazed clay, unearthed in 1996 from the tomb of Madame Song, wife of Lei Jun, in Xi'an. Tang dynasty, 745 C.E. 92 cm. Shaanxi Provincial Institute of Archaeology, Xi'an.

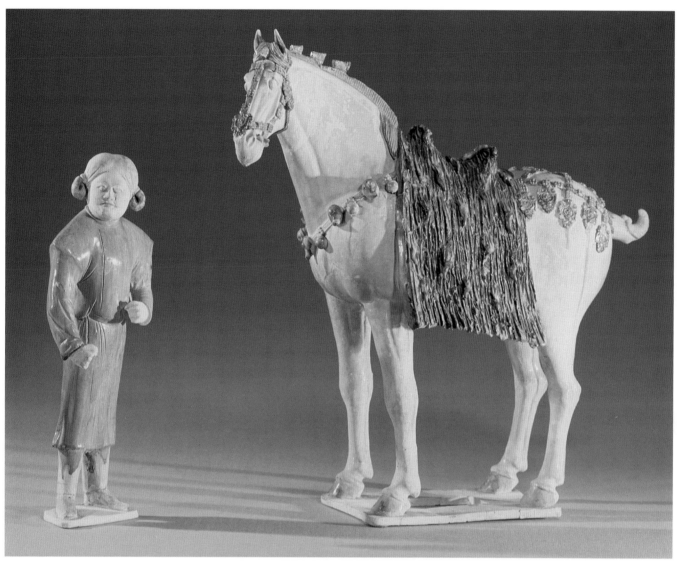

2.32 Tricolor horse led by figure of Hu nationality, glazed kaolin, unearthed in 1957 from the tomb of Xianyu Tinghui, in Xi'an. Tang dynasty. 54.6 cm (horse) and 39.8 cm (person). National Museum of China, Beijing.

headdress (fig. 2.34). It is a witty, imaginative master-piece of pottery art.

The Tang tricolor figurines were popular not only in the capital Xi'an, but also in Luoyang, the secondary or eastern capital of the Tang. Although the artistic designs and firing techniques used in Luoyang were not as advanced as those in Xi'an, unique innovations emerged there that cannot be found in the tricolors of Xi'an. The application of glaze, in particular, is extremely bold and vigorous. Take, for example, the renderings of horses. The tricolor horses of Chang'an have primarily brown and white coats. Some of the horse figurines from Luoyang, however, have black coats, which some viewers believe makes the figurines look even more elegant and powerful. Furthermore, a blue horse has been found that is unique (fig. 2.35).[65] In 755, shortly after the armed rebellion led by An Lushan and Shi Siming, craftsmanship in Xi'an and Luoyang

began to decline. But tricolor funerary figurines became a popular component of Tang tombs in towns of the Yangzi River delta, such as Yangzhou. Occasionally, tri-color funerary figurines have also been discovered in Tang tombs in Gansu, Shanxi, Liaoning, Anhui, Hubei, and Hunan; however, these are not nearly as finely crafted as those found in Xi'an and Luoyang, and they are fewer in number.

Although Tang figurines (including tricolor figurines) are made primarily of clay, a few marble figurines were created. The two that are most exquisitely carved both portray soldiers wearing head scarves and carrying weapons (fig. 2.36). They were unearthed at the tomb of Yang Sixu, a general, who was interred in Dengjiapo village, Xi'an, in 740.[66]

After An and Shi's rebellion, Tang figurines changed. For a time, a type of figurine with a clay bust, wooden limbs, and a silk dress was in vogue. The effect was no

2.33 Tricolor camel carrying musicians and dancer, glazed kaolin, unearthed in 1957 from the tomb of Xianyu Tinghui, in Xi'an. Tang dynasty. 58.4 cm (camel) and 25.1 cm (musicians). National Museum of China, Beijing.

2.34 Tricolor camel carrying musicians and dancer, glazed kaolin, unearthed in 1959 in Zhongbao village, Xi'an. Tang dynasty. 56.3 × 41 cm. Shaanxi Museum of History, Xi'an.

2.35 Tricolor horse, glazed kaolin, unearthed in 1965 in Guanlin, Luoyang, Henan Province. Tang dynasty. 36 × 32.5 cm. Luoyang Cultural Relics Team.

2.36 Soldier with weapons and head scarf, carved marble with traces of gilding and pigments, unearthed in 1958 from the tomb of Yang Sixu, in Xi'an. Tang dynasty. 40.1 cm. National Museum of China, Beijing.

doubt beautiful at the time, but today only the clay busts remain. On some of them, traces of silk and wood have been found. This type was also popular for a time in the tombs of Astana in Xinjiang. There, painted wooden figurines showing a strong regional influence were also in style (fig. 2.37).

Line Carvings on Sui and Tang Sarcophagi

In addition to their many funerary figurines, a remarkable feature of Sui and Tang tombs is pictures incised on the stone gates of tomb chambers or on stone sarcophagi. Such artistic works are usually found in tombs of royal families, nobles, or high-ranking officials, and most were discovered in auxiliary tombs of imperial mausoleums near the capital of Chang'an. A typical piece is the sarcophagus in the tomb of Li He in Shuangsheng village, Sanyuan County, Shaanxi, sealed in 582.[67] As in tombs from the Northern Dynasties period, the sarcophagus was placed on the western side of the chamber. The front of the sarcophagus is incised with an image of a gate with a lock, flanked by two armored guards. A vermilion bird has been carved on top of the gate. The back of the sarcophagus depicts a turtle riding on clouds. The left and right sides of the sarcophagus are incised with pictures of a blue dragon and a white tiger, respectively, each bearing a deity. In front of the dragon and the tiger are four honor guards, each holding a knife. What is most attractive is the picture on the lid, which features figures with human heads and bird bodies, like the Qianqiu Wansui figurine, and strings of carved pearls. Beneath these are *apsaras* (flying celestials) with flowing dress belts. The background features designs of lotus, acanthus, and clouds. More strings of pearls are carved on the four edges, as are all kinds of pictures — most of human faces, but others of elephants, tigers, horses, and other animals. The pearls, reminiscent of a pattern on Sassanian silk, indicate that the carvings were influenced by the art of western Asia. The gates of the tomb chamber bear line carvings as well. Incised on each panel are four rows of five round-headed decorative nails each. Each row has a warrior doorkeeper, and on each side under the doorpost squats a carved stone lion.

A good example of another type of sarcophagus is found at the tomb of Li Jingxun (Li Xiaohai), com-

pleted in 608. in Liangjia village, Xi'an.[68] Buried in this tomb is Li Jingxun, the nine-year-old granddaughter of Yang Lihua, who was the eldest daughter of Emperor Wen of the Sui dynasty and the wife of Emperor Xuan of the Northern Zhou. In the tomb chamber is an outer stone coffin made of bluish gray rock, inside which lies a unique inner stone coffin shaped like a palace. The lid is sculpted to resemble two sloping house roofs joined at the middle by a horizontal ridge. Fixed at both ends of this ridge are ceramic decorations shaped like an owl's tail, and in the center of the ridge is a pearl. The facade of the coffin is a three-bay hall with four pillars in front. *Dougong* brackets were used for the top of the pillars. Brackets in the shape of an upside-down V support the ceilings between bays. The central room has a stone gate. Each panel of the gate is carved with two rows of five round-headed decorative nails (a round *pushou* is also found in each row). On each side of the gate appears an engraving of a young servant girl. The front of the two side rooms is carved with latticed windows. The beam, rafter, posts, and dougong brackets are all incised with exquisite floral designs. Beneath the windows are carved pictures of a blue dragon and a vermilion bird. The inner panels of the coffin were adorned with painted murals, which have faded; indeed, so few traces remain that they cannot be restored.

Another unique sarcophagus sculpted in the form of a Sui palace has been discovered in Taiyuan, Shanxi. Buried in the sarcophagus was not a member of the royal family or a nobleman, but an official named Yu Hong from the state of Yu in central Asia (the actual location of the state is still unknown) who lived in China. He was interred in 592.[69] Although the sarcophagus looks like a miniature Chinese palace with sloping, ridged roofs and a three-bay hall, the depiction of a human figure and the composition of the picture carved in bas-relief on both the inner and outer sides have a distinctively exotic style, undoubtedly owing to cultural exchanges between China and other countries during this time. The patterns, in particular, are unique to the Sassanian art of Persia. The front of the sarcophagus is incised with a banquet scene. The host, in a Sassanian robe, is flanked by vivid hunting scenes. Hunters on one-humped camels are shown shooting at lions (fig. 2.38). On the base of the sarcophagus is engraved an altar of flame supported by two magical birds with human heads: a symbol of Zoroastrian fire worship. The paint colors and gilding on the bas-relief carvings are well preserved, making the sarcophagus a rare masterpiece of its kind from the Sui dynasty.

2.37 Heavenly King tomb guardian, painted wood, unearthed in 1973 in Turpan, Xinjiang Uygur Autonomous Region. Tang dynasty. 86 cm. Xinjiang Uygur Autonomous Region Museum.

Stone gates and stone outer coffins with incised pictures of royal families and high-ranking officials of the Tang have been discovered here and there in the area of Xi'an. The earliest work of this type has been unearthed in the tomb of Li Shou, Prince Jing of Huai'an, built in 631 under Emperor Taizong of the Tang. The stone gate and its lintel in the tomb chamber are carved in bas-relief with large pictures of beasts, painted in color, and covered with gilding. An encircling vine is carved onto the two posts by the gate and the threshold. The two stone blocks supporting the posts of the gate are sculpted to resemble squatting lions. The outside of the door panels is carved in bas-relief with a picture of a vermilion bird, painted and covered with gold foil, and the inner side bears intaglio pictures of six kings. Along the east wall of the tomb chamber lies the stone coffin, which has two sloping roofs joined by a ridge in the middle and a three-bay front. The room in

2.38 Relief carving from the inner wall of the stone coffin of Yu Hong, bluish gray stone, unearthed in 1999 from his tomb in Taiyuan, Shanxi Province. Sui dynasty. 96 × 66 cm. Shanxi Provincial Institute of Archaeology, Taiyuan.

the middle has a stone gate that can be opened. The coffin, made of twenty-eight pieces of bluish gray stone, is 2.2 meters high.[70] Inside the coffin, on the outer wall of the sarcophagus, are pictures carved in bas-relief and covered with gold foil. They include portraits of the four directional deities, armed guards, both military and civil officials and servants, immortals riding dragons, and phoenixes (fig. 2.39). The inner side of the sarcophagus is incised with refined pictures, too, including a portrait of six dancers in three rows (fig. 2.40) and one of twelve sitting female musicians in three rows. The musical instruments they hold include the *konghou* (a plucked string instrument held vertically like a harp), five-stringed fiddle, pipa, zither, pipes, transverse flute, panpipes, cymbals, drum, waist drum, and conch. The eastern side is carved with twelve standing female musicians in three rows. Their musical instruments include panpipes, a large bamboo pipe with a reed mouthpiece, cymbals, the transverse flute, a small bamboo pipe with a reed mouthpiece, pipas, and a konghou. The inside wall is also carved with two pictures of standing servants holding all kinds of daily objects. One illustration shows eighteen servants in three rows; another depicts twenty servants holding items used in games like catapult, go, and chess, as well as a mattress, a cushion, a Hu-style bed, a creel-shaped stool, a low table, an urn, a cup, a jar, a bottle, a bowl, a plate, a stove, and so on.[71] Many of these are meticulously incised, and so it is possible to tell that some come from foreign regions. The tapered glass, the cup made of an animal's horn, and the tall crooked glass are probably objects from Sassania, Sogdia, and Byzantium, of great interest to modern historians. On the inner side of the coffin lid is incised a zodiac. On the edge along the bottom are carved twelve animals, signs of the years in which a person may be born. These pictures, engraved with lines, clearly show the influence of the periods from the Northern Dynasties to the Sui; they are found in tombs of the early Tang, which were created before the new burial system developed.

The Tang burial system came to maturity after the reign of Emperor Gaozong (d. 683) of the Tang. The use of stone coffins, for instance, was determined strictly by the social status of the deceased. Consequently, only prominent people like Li Chongrun (also known as Prince Yide), Li Xianhui (also known as Princess Yongtai), and Li Xian (also known as Prince Zhanghuai) were entitled to a stone outer coffin with a *wudian* roof — four sloping roofs, front, back, and sides, joined by a ridge in the center. The tombs of

2.39 Sarcophagus of Li Shou, stone, unearthed in 1973 from his tomb in Turpan, Xinjiang Uygur Autonomous Region. Tang dynasty. 86 cm. Xinjiang Uygur Autonomous Region Museum.

Prince Yide and Princess Yongtai were known as mausoleums, suggesting that these persons were of higher status than other princes or princesses.[72] All the sarcophagi in those three tombs are in the shape of a three-bay palace hall with a facade featuring four posts. As before, there is a gate to the middle room, while the two side rooms have windows with vertical lattices incised with portraits of human figures, mostly attendants and servants of the royal palace. The door frames are also carved with beautiful line drawings. The lintel of the gate to Prince Zhanghuai's sarcophagus, for example, is incised with a lotus design and a pair of vermilion birds. Its panels are carved with round-headed nails, as well as images of a eunuch and a maid-in-waiting.[73] The lintel of the gate of the stone coffin of Prince Yide is carved with two phoenixes. The "nails" carved on the door panels are in the shape of six-petaled flowers, together with a pushou on a floral base. On each panel is carved a well-dressed woman official with a high headdress showing both ends of a long phoenix-shaped hairpin.[74] In a departure from Tang portraiture, the officials wear long dresses with low-cut necklines and belts from which jade pendants dangle.

From the three stone coffins, the most vivid pictures of maidservants are those incised on the sarcophagus of Princess Yongtai. Fifteen such pictures appear on the coffin, inside and outside, each of which shows one or two.[75] Altogether, there are twenty-one maidservants, most of whom wear long dresses, large shoes, and their hair piled high. One occasionally sees maidservants dressed as men and wearing *futou* (a kind of headscarf worn by men in ancient China), and some hold in their hands a jar with a phoenix-headed lid, a fruit plate, or a *ruyi* (an S-shaped wand, usually made of jade, symbolizing good fortune). The two most vividly rendered maidservants are carved inside the coffin. One lowers her head and sniffs a bouquet, while the other throws a shawl over her shoulders (fig. 2.41). Given the artistry required to make these movements seem so natural and lifelike, these carvings rank as masterpieces among the portraits of Tang women.

The sarcophagi with wudian roofs excavated both at the tomb of Wei Jiong, governor of Huaiyang, in Wangcun village, Nanli, Chang'an (present-day Xi'an), Shaanxi, and at the tomb of General Yang Sixu, or Lord Guoguo, in Dengjiapo village, Xi'an, in 740 are unusual

2.40 Line drawing of dancers from the inner wall of Li Shou's sarcophagus.

2.41 Line drawing of maidservant from the coffin in the sarcophagus of Princess Yongtai, stone, unearthed in 1960, Qianxian County, Shaanxi Province. Tang dynasty. Qianling Mausoleum Museum.

in that the occupants were not royals.[76] Exceptions were made by the emperor, who showed favor toward these two men. Wei Jiong was the brother-in-law of Emperor Zhongzong and so was given the privilege of having a sarcophagus with a wudian roof. The images of the eunuch and the maid-in-waiting incised on his sarcophagus are exquisite, similar to the portraits on the sarcophagus of Princess Yongtai. Yang Sixu was a favorite eunuch of Emperor Xuanzong and once commanded the army for the entire country. When he died, he therefore was granted the privilege of being laid to rest in a stone sarcophagus; but the engraved pictures on his sar-

cophagus are not as refined as those on Wei Jiong's: only the lions beneath the window with the vertical lattice are lifelike. Sarcophagi are also found in the tombs of some generals who made important contributions to the founding of the Tang dynasty. Those stone coffins are not, however, ornamented to the same extent as that of Princess Yongtai: generally, they have arched roofs, and carvings on them are rather simple. One example is the sarcophagus of Grand General Zheng Rentai, buried in Mazhai village in Liquan County, Xi'an, in 664.[77] And outside Xi'an, in Huangpu village, Wanrong County, Shaanxi, a stone coffin has been unearthed in the tomb of Xue Jing, the husband of Princess Xiguo, eldest daughter of Emperor Ruizong. Buried in 721, Xue Jing also had a coffin with a facade boasting four posts and a three-bay hall. The gate in the middle room is engraved with two maids. Each of the wing rooms has a window with a vertical lattice. The sarcophagus is incised both inside and outside with pictures of seventeen standing maids, some of whom wear men's clothes. The carved lines are smooth and neat, and the design of human figures is clearly an imitation of those in the capital at Chang'an.[78]

Generally, a sarcophagus was not provided for a deceased prince or a princess during the Tang dynasty, but a stone gate incised with some pictures would be created for the entrance to his or her tomb. Often the door panels of these gates were incised with portraits of civilian courtiers, military generals, and palace officials. The lintel was carved with images of a vermilion bird and double dragons, and the doorposts were engraved with interlocking flowers and clouds. Designs of this sort can be seen in the tomb of Prince Huizhuang, interred in 714 in Qiaolin village, Pucheng County, Shaanxi, and the tomb of Princess Tang'an, who was buried in 784 in Wangjiafen, Xi'an.[79] This style of stone gate was also provided for officials above a certain rank. On those gates are incised portraits of ministers and generals, as well as male and female attendants and servants. The carving technique and designs are similar to those found in tombs of princes or princesses, though the craftsmanship is not as good. There are many such works, but three examples will help to illustrate the main features of the style. One comprises the carved portraits of a male attendant on the eastern door panel and of a maid on the western door panel of the stone gate in the tomb of Zhang Shigui, interred in the second year of the Xianqing reign (657), in Mazhai village, Liquan, Shaanxi.[80] Another such stone gate, the second example, is found in the tomb of Yuchi Jingde, also in Mazhai village, created in 659.[81] On one side is the portrait of a standing official wearing a head scarf and holding a ceremonial knife in both hands. On the other side is the profile of a man who is also holding a knife. The third example is the stone gate of the tomb of Su Sixu, interred in 745 in the eastern suburbs of Xi'an.[82] On one side of the gate is incised an official holding ceremonial plaques made of either ivory or jade; the other side features a warrior with a hat that resembles a bird crest; he also holds a ceremonial knife. Their appearances match those of officials or warriors of the period. The lintel of the gate is sculpted in a semicircle

and incised with exquisite vines and two phoenixes, each holding a straw in its bill. Apart from the capital Chang'an, other regions have also yielded carved stone gates from Tang tombs. Stone gates engraved with pictures have been discovered, for instance, in Tang tombs in the region of Guyuan in Ningxia, such as the tomb of Shi Suoyan and his wife, from 664, and the tomb of Shi Kedan and his wife, from 670.[83] Meriting particular attention is a stone gate unearthed in a Tang tomb in Yanchi, Ningxia. It is incised with the picture of a man from western Asia who on two circular rugs is performing the Whirling Dance, an ancient dance performed in the northwest of China for many kinds of celebrations.[84]

Sculptures in Tombs of the Five Dynasties

The Tang dynasty came to an end in 907, and ancient society was once again divided into rival factions, each controlling a small part of the country. This period is known in history as that of the Five Dynasties and Ten Kingdoms.[85] Since the 1940s, many mausoleums of the Ten Kingdoms have been excavated, such as those of Li Bian and Li Jing of the Southern Tang, Qian Yuanguan and his families of the Wu-Yue, Wang Jian of the Shu, Meng Zhixiang of the Later Shu, and Liu Hua, wife of King Wang Yanjun of the state of Min.[86] Because they are from different regions and systems, they have distinctive features. Yet they all have stylistic elements common to the inherited Tang tradition — for example, the multichambered structure. Normally, a mausoleum has front, central, and rear chambers, all built of rock. The mausoleum of Wang Jian is built of red sandstone, the mausoleum of Meng Zhixiang of gray rock, and the mausoleum of Liu Hua of granite. The two mausoleums from the Southern Tang are made of bricks and rock. The rear chamber of Li Bian's mausoleum is made entirely of bluish gray limestone. As regards the tomb of Qian Yuanguan of the Wu-Yue, the sarcophagus was built of gritty red rock and surrounded by an arched brick chamber. Sculptures in those mausoleums are distinctive, yet similar in content. In each, armored warriors guard the gate of the tomb chambers. The four directional deities, twelve signs of the zodiac, and the astronomical map were also found. In addition, they all have stone gates and structures created to look as though they were made of wood.

The main bas-relief carvings in the mausoleum of Li Bian are stunning examples of Five Dynasties tomb sculptures. There, two armored warriors carved into a gate on the northern wall of the central chamber stand at attention on clouds, holding long swords and wearing helmets and armor edged with meticulously carved plum blossom designs, much as the real armor of the day was (fig. 2.42). Traces of gilding and pigments can still be found on their bodies. Yet although they must have been quite resplendent and are masterfully carved, they are rigidly depicted, unlike Tang sculpture generally. Another example appears in the mausoleum of the Qian family of the Wu-Yue, where part of the upper inner side of the outer stone coffin is incised with a peony design. In the middle of the same surface are the four directional deities, blue dragon, white tiger, vermilion bird, and turtle, and in the lower part the twelve zodiac signs, which take the form of human figures, each holding a little animal in both hands (each beast is the symbol for a particular period of time) — all of this enclosed in a carved shrine with a pointed top. In the tomb of Qian Yuanguan, an astronomical map is carved on the vault of the rear chamber. The gilding on it can still be made out. Another astronomical map is carved on the vault of the tomb chamber of his wife, Wu Hanyue. Though not highly artistic, they are, to date, the most ancient astronomical maps in China, of high scientific value.[87] The stone walls of the tomb chambers of Liu Hua of the state of Min, by contrast, bear no carvings, and the walls are flat and plain. In the mausoleums of Wang Jian of the Shu and Meng Zhixiang of the Later Shu, the stone sculptures that can be regarded as having the greatest artistic value are the carvings on the stone platforms of the sarcophagi.

The platform of the sarcophagus in the tomb of Wang Jian, in Chengdu, Sichuan, is 7.45 meters long, 3.35 meters wide, and 0.84 meters high. It was placed in the central chamber, in the middle but slightly toward the rear. Of red sandstone, it was fashioned in the shape of Mount Sumeru, traditionally used for the pedestal of statues of the Buddha. The top of the platform is covered with a whole piece of a jadelike stone. The upper cornice of the pedestal was engraved with flaming jewels, flowing dragons, and clouds on the eastern, southern, and western sides. The northern side is carved only with clouds. All four sides of the platform are incised with kunmen containing human figures. Above these are upside-down lotus flowers, and then the cornice, beneath which are more inverted lotuses. The stands of the platform are engraved with lotus blossoms, and the base is engraved with inverted lotuses as well.

Each of the two sides of the platform has ten kunmen, and the front and back have four each. Engraved pictures appear in each. Except for the four kunmen at the rear, which contain lotus blossoms, all the kunmen feature seated female performers. The two of the arches at center front show two dancers: the one on the right is a woman performing with castanets; the one on the left is a female performer playing the pipa. The inside of the ten kunmen on the left-hand side of the

2.42 Carving on the mausoleum door, stone, unearthed in 1950 from the Qinling mausoleum of Li Bian, Nanjing. Southern Tang dynasty. 445 cm. Nanjing Southern Tang Two Mausoleums Storeroom.

platform is incised with performers sitting and playing musical instruments, including panpipes, the zither, a bamboo pipe with a reed mouthpiece, a vertical stringed instrument, the conch, cymbals, and a drum. The right-hand side also depicts ten female performers. Their musical instruments include drums of all kinds, the flute, a bamboo pipe with a reed mouthpiece, and castanets. In the tradition of Tang figurines, the musicians all have plump faces. Their headdresses vary, and their bearing is stately — although there are certain variations. Originally, they were colorfully painted; even today we can see their red dresses, yellow skirts, and beautiful collars painted red, green, and blue. This large orchestra with dancers faithfully illustrates an ensemble of the time.

This stone platform is unique in that it is encircled by twelve half-busts of deities arranged as though they have just emerged from the ground on which the platform rests. Each of them appears strong and awe-inspiring. All are in armor; half of them wear helmets,

2.43 Stone carvings of twelve deities on platform, rear chamber of the Yongling mausoleum of King Wang Jian, unearthed in 1943, Chengdu, Sichuan Province. Shu dynasty. 84 × 745 × 335 cm. Chengdu Wang Jian Tomb Museum.

2.44 King Wang Jian, painted stone, from the Yongling mausoleum of Wang Jian. 86 cm. Chengdu Wang Jian Tomb Museum.

the other half have elaborate coiffures, but each helmet or hairstyle is unique. According to historical documents, the twelve figures are the deities of the mausoleum, namely, the Flying Snake, Vermilion Bird of the South, the Deity of the Six Directions (Liuhe), the Unicorn, or Qilin (Gouchen), the Green Dragon of the East, the Heavenly Queen (Tianhe), the Grand Sun Deity (Taiyang), the Black Warrior of the North, The Grand Norm Deity (Taichang), the White Tiger of the West, the Deity of Heaven (Tiankong), and the Deity of the North Pole (Tianyi). This stone platform with its twelve deities is the only one of its kind so far discovered in China. It is indeed a unique piece of burial art from the Shu (fig. 2.43).

Another extraordinary piece from this tomb is a stone statue of Wang Jian in the rear chamber, 86 centimeters high. It is a realistic work: the thick eyebrows, deep-set eyes, high-bridged nose, broad forehead, thin lips, and large ears match the descriptions of Wang Jian in the historical records. The statue of Wang wears a black head scarf, a long, bright red robe with sleeves, into which his hands are tucked, and a wide red belt that is similar in shape to the jade belt unearthed in this mausoleum. He wears red boots and sits on a four-legged stool shaped like a crescent moon (fig. 2.44). In front of the statue originally was a lacquered cabinet housing a white jade basin. The stone statue of Wang Jian, sculpted in the Shu, is indeed very precious because in ancient China (unlike in Western countries), it was unheard of to make a statue of a ruler and display it in public. It is the only Chinese work of its kind found to date.

The tomb of Meng Zhixiang of the Later Shu has also yielded a large sarcophagus platform cut in the form of Mount Sumeru. It is 5.1 meters in length, slightly shorter than that of Wang Jian, and its carvings are not as beautiful — no performers in bas-relief, no busts of twelve deities around the platform. The base of the platform, however, is carved with pictures of naked, muscular men kneeling on the ground in preparation for hoisting the stone platform onto their shoulders. Beneath the men are lotus seats. The gate of Meng's tomb is like that of Li Bian of the Southern Tang — that is, each of its sides is incised with the portrait of an armored warrior.

Sarcophagi with refined carvings have been found not only in mausoleums of those kings of small states; they have also been found in the tombs of such high-ranking officials as Sun Hanshao, governor of Le'an of

2.45 Bas-relief of female attendants and musicians, painted white marble, unearthed in 1995 from the tomb of Wang Chuzhi, Quyang County, Hebei Province. Five Dynasties period (Later Tang). 82 × 136 × 17–23 cm. Hebei Provincial Bureau of Cultural Relics, Shijiazhuang.

the Later Shu, and Zhang Qianzhao, teacher of the crown prince of the Later Shu.[88] Their sarcophagi are also mounted on platforms shaped like Mount Sumeru. As in Meng's mausoleum, the corner posts are incised with robust naked men kneeling to lift the platform. Inside each kunmen are images of all sorts of beasts such as the unicorn (qilin), *xiezhi* (a legendary animal able to tell right from wrong), lion, deer, horse, and sheep, most of which are portrayed in animated, running postures.

The tombs of Song Lin and Gao Hui have yielded sarcophagi with pictures of the four directional deities.[89] The front side of the platform beneath the sarcophagus of Song Lin is also carved with three dancers, reminiscent of the stone carvings of Wang Jian's sarcophagus platform. The splendid stone carvings in the tombs of the Shu and the Later Shu reflect the high level of artistic achievement in Sichuan during that era.

The most remarkable funerary carvings of the Five Dynasties period are the painted white-marble carvings in bas-relief unearthed in the tomb of Wang Chuzhi, prince of Beiping, who was buried in Quyang, Hebei, in 924, during the Later Tang.[90] They are inlaid on the lower part of the eastern and western walls of the rear chamber. Each work, 136 by 82 centimeters, is carved from a single piece of white marble.

On the western wall are carvings of twelve female musicians, who all stand facing the coffin (fig. 2.45). A girl dressed as a man leads the way, followed by two dancing children, and then the female musicians in two columns. They are all in long dresses with draping shawls, their high hairstyles adorned with hairpins. All their faces are plump, in accordance with the Tang paradigm of beauty. The musical instruments held by performers in the front row are a konghou, a zither, a pipa with a crooked handle, clappers, and a big drum. The konghou and zither lie on low tables. The big drum is set on a drum stand. The musicians in the back row hold the reed pipe, a *fangxiang* (an ancient percussion instrument consisting of sixteen iron pieces of the same size but different thicknesses), a hand drum, two bili, and two transverse flutes. Both the drum and the fangxiang are on stands. The picture is so meticulously carved, and the portraits of female musicians are so lively, that one can almost hear performers playing in concert.

Carved on the eastern wall are fourteen female attendants, also in two columns, whose hairstyles and dresses are similar to those of the musicians. In their hands they hold objects like pots, plates, square boxes, and feather fans. At the lower front is a picture of a boy with two hair buns, holding a narrow-necked bottle. The two carvings in bas-relief, which resemble the famous painting *A Galaxy of Girls* by Zhou Fang of the Tang, are stunning. Quyang, where Wang Chuzhi's tomb is located, was known for its white marble sculpture, and the two painted carvings in bas-relief and painted carvings of the twelve signs of the zodiac in bas-relief in the front chamber of this tomb, all original creations of Quyang, heralded the painted brick pictures that would be inlaid on the walls of tomb chambers of the late Northern Song period.[91]

Figurines from the Five Dynasties and Ten Kingdoms

The practice of including figurines in burials varied from place to place in the Five Dynasties and Ten Kingdoms periods. The largest number of terra-cotta funerary figurines has been found in the two mausoleums of the Southern Tang in Niushou Hill, Jiangning district, Nanjing, Jiangsu Province. Even though the graves had been robbed repeatedly, the sites still yielded more than two hundred terra-cotta figurines and models of beasts, including 190 standing male and female figurines, likenesses of the male and female attendants, eunuchs, guards, and dancers at the palace. The bases for the figurines are made of sandy clay mixed with chopped straw. The head and the body were manufactured separately and then assembled; details such as creases in the garments were carved with a scoring tool. After firing in the kiln, a white powder was applied; afterward, the figurines were painted with pigments. Generally, the faces are rouged with red powder, the lips of the women are painted vermilion, and the dresses are painted red. Traces of white flowers on the dresses and metal ornaments in the women's hair can still be seen. The figurines' attire is resplendent, and most of the eunuchs and other attendants hold objects in their hands. The guards in armor are holding small shields. The dancers comprise both men and women, and even an elderly man with a beard (fig. 2.46). They are all plump, with smooth, fleshy faces, a further continuation of Tang figurine style. They may lack the vitality and strength often seen in Tang figurines, and there is not much variety in design among the replicas, but their contours are smooth and natural. The fully dressed female dancers, in particular, seem delicate and pretty, even fragile (fig. 2.47). Among the terra-cotta animals unearthed are a horse, a camel, a lion, a dog, a chicken, and a frog. Both the horse and the camel lie prostrate on the

2.46 Male dancer, fired and painted terra-cotta, unearthed in 1950 from the Qinling mausoleum of Li Bian, Nanjing. Southern Tang dynasty. 46 cm. Palace Museum, Beijing.

covered once in the Northern Dynasties tombs in Shandong, but none have been found in central China, along the Wei River in Shaanxi, or in the region of Chang'an or Luoyang, the capitals of the Sui and the Tang.[92] Only in the Tang tombs of Shanxi have such figurines occasionally been found. Here, however, they appeared in royal mausoleums. As many as thirteen figurines with the head of a human and the body of a fish have been discovered in the two mausoleums from the Southern Tang. In both mausoleums, some have two human heads, and each of the heads wears the hat of a Daoist priest.[93] These must be the "grave dragons" mentioned in the historical record. The appearance of such figurines may be an indication of political instability during the Ten Kingdoms period and the rise of sorcery. Funerary figurines, formerly symbols of the social status of the deceased, became objects for protecting the tomb and warding off evil.

In addition to these two mausoleums of the Southern Tang royal mausoleums of the Wu-Yue were found in the Lin'an (present-day Hangzhou) area; however, grave robbers carried away most of the relics; no figurines have been found. Only in the clan burial ground of Qian Yuanliao, King Guangling of the state of Wu-Yue in Qizi Hill, Suzhou, have terra-cotta and bronze figurines of male and female attendants and servants been discovered. Their presence confirms the continued importance of figurines at burials during this time. The bronze figurines were roughly cast, whereas the clay figurines are quite exquisite and refined. They are standing with their hands either crossed in front or held up, clasped. Their faces are round, in the Tang tradition.

The burial, believed to be the tomb of Princess Xunyang of the state of Wu (892–937), in Caizhuang village, Hanjiang, Jiangsu, has yielded a group of wooden figurines.[94] Besides male and female figurines are replicas of the twelve zodiac animals, as well as creatures with a human head and the body of an animal. The similarities to figurines from the two mausoleums of the Southern Tang are obvious. The limbs of some of the wooden female figurines are movable. The high hairstyles of some female figurines include lavish silver ornaments, and all the women originally wore dresses.

Funerary figurines have also been excavated at the tombs of the state of Min along the southeast coast. In Lianhuafeng, Fuzhou, Fujian, at the tomb of Liu Hua, wife of Wang Yanjun, the third king of the state of Min, only forty or so terra-cotta figurines have survived. Most of them are standing male and female atten-

ground, with no sign of the vigor and power so typical of the Later Tang; this may be a reflection, in part, of the political and military weakness of the Southern Tang people at the time.

In addition to these animals, some figures of demons with unusual bodies, which were supposed to guard the tomb and ward off evil spirits, have been found in the two mausoleums of the Southern Tang: a creature with a human head and the body of a fish, one with a human head and the body of a snake, and one with two human heads and the body of a snake. Such figurines were dis-

2.47 Female dancer, fired and painted terra-cotta, unearthed in 1950 from the Qinling mausoleum of Li Bian. 49 cm. National Museum of China, Beijing.

2.48 Mural with motif of family banquet, brick, unearthed in 1951 from Song Tomb 1, Yuxian County, Henan Province. Northern Song dynasty. Approx. 100 cm square.

dants and servants. A few tall, well-dressed female figurines are believed to be female palace officials. There are also some figurines of demons, which must be grave dragons or grave fish, as well as a figurine of an old man with a cowl hat and a walking stick in his hand, probably a reference to the "Old Man of Haoli," an image that some believe may symbolize the wish for eternity, because Haoli is the place where the souls of the dead were thought to gather.[95] Figurines of the four directional deities were also present; still extant today are the dragon, the tiger, the vermilion bird, and the turtle, along with twelve signs of the zodiac. The heads and bodies were molded separately, then assembled. After firing, they were covered with a white powder, painted with colorful pigments, and finally adorned with gilding, pasted on. The design and craftsmanship are somewhat less refined than those seen in terra-cotta figurines unearthed at the two mausoleums from the Southern Tang.

Funerary figurines in mausoleums of the Shu and the Later Shu in the region of Chengdu, Sichuan, are rare indeed, probably owing to grave robbers. Only a cast-iron ox and a pig have been found, in the central chamber of the tomb of Wang Jian of the Shu. The iron ox weighs 60 kilograms. Presumably, it represents a variation on the Later Tang practice of burying a "golden ox and an iron pig" with the deceased to drive away evil spirits.

There is no doubt that figurines were used as funerary objects in Sichuan during the Five Dynasties and Ten Kingdoms period. They have been found in the tombs of two men buried in 955: Song Lin of the Later Shu in Pengshan County, Sichuan, and Sun Hanshao of the Later Shu in Xicun village, Chengdu. Sun Hanshao's tomb has yielded, in addition to figurines of male and female attendants, servants, and armored warriors, a group of terra-cotta models, rare for their time, of architectural forms such as a screen wall, a kiosk, a passageway, a pavilion, a rock garden, a plain wall, and the wall of a rock garden.

Brick Sculptures and Stone Carvings in Tombs from the Song and the Jin

Brick sculptures began to appear in tomb chambers in the early Northern Song. At first, they were only simple imitations of wooden structures, such as the pillars and door panels found in a Song tomb in Bolin village, Shijiazhuang, Hebei.[96] By about the eleventh century, however, such sculpture had matured into an independent art form.

At the tomb of an unknown occupant in Nanguanwai, Zhengzhou, Henan, sealed in 1056, during the Northern Song, the corner pillars of the chamber are built of brick.[97] The top of each pillar is supported by a dougong bracket that juts out underneath. The back wall has been ornamented with carved bricks in the shape of door panels. On the lintel is a brick carving of a decorative cross in a floral pattern. On both sides of the door are four brick "windows" with slanted elliptical lattices; brick carvings of furniture in bas-relief can be seen on the side walls. On the right wall is a table flanked by two chairs. On the table are carvings of bowls and vessels holding food and drink, and behind the chair on the right side is a tall lamp. On the left wall, in the middle, is a dress rack, beneath which are carvings of a pair of scissors, a ruler, an iron, and other household objects. On the left-hand side of the dress rack is a small cabinet with a lock, on which lie a brush rack and an ink slab. On the right of the dress rack is a side table on which lies a mirror with a long handle. On the sides of the front gate of the tomb are carvings of a basin rack and part of a dress rack. The brickwork gate itself is sculpted to look as though it is made of wood. Colors are also important here. The whole chamber was first painted white, after which pigments were applied. The pillars, dougong brackets, and so on, which were sculpted to look like wooden ones, were painted ochre, and the brackets and the spaces between brackets were painted in black, red, green, and yellow floral patterns. On the side walls of the passageway are some murals portraying horses and human figures that have unfortunately eroded away.

Even more elaborate works have been discovered in Baisha, Yuxian County, Henan, in the tomb of Zhao Daweng, buried in 1099, during the Northern Song.[98] This tomb contains both a front and a rear chamber. The front chamber is square-shaped with a caissonlike cloister vault, whereas the rear chamber is hexagonal with a conelike vault made of eight pieces. The whole structure, made of bricks, is an imitation of a wooden building. At this site, the dougong bracket has five elaborate layers, meticulously and resplendently painted. Painted murals depicting scenes from the dwelling of the deceased are carved on wall bricks. The one in the front chamber shows a banquet at which the host and the hostess of the tomb sit facing each other. The chairs, table, and utensils on the table are all carvings in bas-relief made of brick (fig. 2.48). Carvings like these in the tomb, as well as the richly colored murals discovered there, demonstrate the maturation of these art forms and the free rein given to the artists' imaginations.

In another brick tomb in Baisha imitating a wooden building are two groups of brick carvings depicting a zaju.[99] One group shows four performers staging a zaju, and another group depicts seven musicians playing *sanyue* (music based on folk tunes). The groups are separately inlaid on the two side walls. In addition, small carvings on single pieces of brick depict scenes of human life. One is of a horse and a groom, another depicts a boy attendant emerging from behind a door carrying a box in his hands, and the third shows a maid emerging from behind another door carrying a bronze mirror.

In another tomb with brick carvings that imitate wooden structures, in Jiuliugou, Yanshi County, Henan, both sides of the chamber are covered with brick carvings of door panels.[100] Inlaid on the back wall is a row of six brick carvings. The three on the right are beautiful, realistic images of three maidservants with hair piled high and long dresses. One stands by, looking on. The other two are busy cooking; one rolls up her sleeves, preparing to cook in a cauldron on the fire a fish that is on the table. The three panels on the left show five persons. One of them, in an open-necked robe, his hair knotted with a head scarf, is unfolding a small painted scroll. This must be the "narrator" of the zaju. On another panel are two performers. One of them is in an open-necked robe with wide sleeves, with his hair done up in a bun and tucked under a scarf. Holding in his left hand a *hu* tablet (which officials usually held in front of their chests when the emperor was holding audience), the man lowers his head and seems to listen to the other. The other person wears the same kind of robe, but it is tucked up at the bottom in front. He holds a package in his right hand and points to the other person, behind him, with his other hand, while apparently speaking. Both men's expressions and gestures are vividly carved and rich in meaning. Most scholars believe that they are acting out an episode in a formal zaju, but the name of the opera is unknown.

The third panel also shows two people. One wears a soft head scarf and an unbuttoned long coat, which reveals his chest and belly. His trouser legs are tied at the ends. He stands in splayed stocking feet and, while talking to someone in front of him, points to the bird in a cage he holds in his left hand. The other one, with his hair askew, also in a soft head scarf and a long coat, tied at the waist with a cloth belt, whistles with his thumb and forefinger in his mouth. He also stands with his feet apart. Both seem to be rocking their bodies to the same beat in what researchers believe is a performance of the final part of a zaju.[101] The entire group of brick sculptures represents work of the highest artistic level in the Song dynasty.

In the region of Sichuan, many Song tombs have chambers of stone carved to resemble wood, and very often warriors are carved on the sides of the gate, the four directional deities on the four walls, and on the back wall women emerging from behind half-open doors. The principal theme of such carvings is usually a family banquet scene. Other stone carvings tell stories about filial sons.[102] The most exquisite carvings, to our knowledge, are found in the clan burial ground of An Bing, who was buried in 1221, during the Southern Song, in Huaying, Sichuan. This burial ground has five tombs, each a stone chamber with a vault.[103] Stone sculptures found in these tombs include pillars, beams, and dougong brackets, all of which look as though they are made of wood, as well as door guards in armor, the four directional deities, musicians, and a large number of floral designs. On the back wall of An Bing's tomb chamber is a niche with carved portraits of An Bing and his wife in the center. The side walls are carved with images of subordinate officials standing quietly, holding hu tablets in their hands.

Another refined stone carving was found in the joint tomb of Yu Gongzhu and his wife, from 1226, during the Southern Song, in Pengshan County, Sichuan.[104] It is a tomb with two stone chambers side by side. In the western chamber, in addition to armed warriors holding knives and bows and arrows who guard the door and maids carrying objects in their hands, we find two large carvings in bas-relief on the side walls. One depicts a procession with a sedan-chair (fig. 2.49); the other is a scene where liquor or tea is being served (fig. 2.50). The sheer number of people and the grandeur of the scenes make an impression. In the niche in the back wall, too, is a rare stone carving of a landscape. Scattered on the mountain peaks are pavilions and kiosks, cranes and deer. The back wall of the eastern chamber bears a similar illustration. On the mountaintop, surrounded by thick foliage, is a cave, on top of which is carved "Penglai" (mountain of the immortals, or fairyland). An elderly man with a long beard and a long gown is also in the picture, facing the mountain path as if he is going to climb it. The scene illustrates the Southern Song idea of a fairy mountain. It also suggests that people of that time longed for immortality.

The Northern Song practice of creating tomb chambers built like wooden structures and murals made of bricks continued at Jin tombs in Houma City, Xinjiang, and Xiaoyi in Shanxi Province. Fine murals completely composed of brick carvings fill entire tombs there in many cases.[105]

2.49 Relief sculpture on the motif "Getting Ready for the Sedan-Chair and Banners," stone, unearthed in 1982 from the tomb of Yu Gongzhu, Pengshan County, Sichuan Province. Southern Song dynasty. 108 × 97 cm.

2.50 Relief sculpture on the motif "Getting Ready for Tea and Wine," stone, unearthed in 1982 from the tomb of Yu Gongzhu. 108 × 97 cm.

2.51 Carving of a stage and five zaju performers, painted brick, unearthed in 1959 from the tomb of the Dong brothers, Houma City, Shanxi Province. Jin dynasty. Height of stage: 101 cm. Houma Workstation, Shanxi Provincial Institute of Archaeology.

The most interesting tomb of this kind is that of the Dong brothers, sealed in Houma City in 1210.[106] The tomb chamber of Dong Qijiansu is built on two flat squares juxtaposed to form a caisson-like octagon. The four walls are covered with astonishingly elaborate brick sculptures. On the back wall is a brick carving of a three-bay hall; in the central room is a large table with crooked legs on which sits a large pot of peonies in bloom. On another table are a plate of fruit, a vase, and an incense burner, from which fragrant smoke wafts. The host and the hostess sit on chairs at the table, and boy and maid servants wait in screened wing rooms on either side, ready to serve their masters. Six door shutters with small lattices are carved into the walls on both the eastern and western sides. Flowers and human figures are carved on the lower part of the boards, some of which illustrate stories of filial sons.

On both sides of the front door to the second chamber of the tomb, carved lions stand guard. The upper parts of all four walls are carved with ornamental roofs supported by dougong brackets. Most interesting of all is the sculpture of a miniature stage with a low balustrade, which appears between two dougong brackets in the middle of the back wall. On the stage are five painted brick figurines, all in a row, performing roles in a zaju.[107] This work is valuable evidence for historians studying the evolution of ancient Chinese drama. It also gives viewers a beautifully detailed picture of how costumed actors looked on stage during the Jin dynasty (fig. 2.51).

Figurines from the Song to the Qing

The use of burial figurines began to wane in popularity after the Five Dynasties period. Recent excavations at Northern Song burials in central China indicate that figurines were virtually no longer used as funerary objects by then. The change is probably due to the rise of the new practice of burning paper articles for the deceased. Although in general fewer and fewer terracotta figurines were buried in tombs during this era, there were exceptions, including two Northern Song tombs, one in each of the neighboring villages of Yandian and Jintang in Fangcheng, Henan.[108] According to the epitaphs, the deceased were parents of someone named Fan Zhixu. The tomb in Jintang village is his father's, built during the Shaosheng reign (1094–1098), whereas the tomb in Yandian village is that of Fan Zhixu's mother, built during the Xuanhe reign (1119–1125). The father's tomb may have been built as much as twenty-five years earlier than the mother's.

Both stone figurines and stone models of furniture were used as funerary objects in the two tombs. Because the Jintang tomb had been robbed, only twelve figurines were discovered there. Four figures, of maids and female attendants with locks of hair over their temples, stand on square pedestals. The other eight pieces are of male honor guards holding parasols and other objects in both hands. Their pedestals, also square, are carved with such phrases as "Guides for the mansion of Fan in the Song" or "Grooms for the mansion of Fan in the Song." The stone figurines are meticulously carved, but their postures are rather rigid. In addition to the figurines, stone sculptures of dragons, chickens, horses, and furniture such as screens and chairs were found. There are more stone figurines in the tomb of Fan's mother in Yandian village, altogether more than thirty pieces. Similarly, the stone sculptures are of standing male and female attendants and servants, as well as honor guards holding parasols, staffs, and so forth. The craftsmanship is not as good as that in the stone carvings in the Jintang village tomb. The figurines are even stiffer and less lifelike. Also present are stone carvings of unicorns and the twelve zodiac signs in the form of beasts, as well as models of bridges, tables, chairs, incense burners, ink slabs, bowls, pots, and other items.

Stone figurines from the Song have also been found in Fujian, a province on the southeastern coast of China. Fujian produces Shoushan stone (agalmatolite), a fact that explains the popularity of such pieces; their appearance in Fujian has nothing to do with the stone figurines in the Henan region. A fairly large Song tomb with a tomb chamber was found in Yanzhi Hill in the northern suburbs of Fuzhou.[109] Some thirty-four stone figurines remain in this chamber, all carved from Shoushan stone. The stone is mostly gray; only a few examples have a purple color. The carving is meticulous. In addition to officials with hu tablets in hand, armored warriors, servants carrying objects, and dancers, the pieces include Futing (a servantlike figure always ready to take orders from his master) lying prostrate on the ground, a long-bearded, hunchbacked Old Man of Haoli, and a tiger (one of the four directional deities). At another Song tomb in Huai'an village in Minhou County, forty-six stone figurines remain.[110] Accompanying the usual officials, warriors, attendants, and servants is a grave dragon with a human head and snake's body.

The two-pit tomb of Zhu Zhu from the Southern Song discovered in Maotou Hill, Fuzhou, has also yielded funerary stone figurines of officials, warriors, attendants, and servants, as well as an Old Man of Haoli, a Futing, and the four directional deities (although only the turtle remains).[111] In addition to stone sculptures, many terra-cotta figurines were also used as funerary objects in Song tombs in Fujian. Some forty clay figurines were found in two Song tombs in Hutou Hill, Lianjiang, including officials, warriors, and the twelve zodiac signs in the form of human figures in robes, each bearing the character *wang* (king) on his forehead, and each holding a hu tablet.[112] On top of each headdress is the image of a tiger or dragon. Also found was a grave dragon with two heads and an Old Man of Haoli. These finds indicate that stone sculptures as well as clay figurines were in vogue in the Fujian region during the Song. The most common objects are the four directional deities, twelve zodiac signs, and demons, as well as officials, warriors, attendants, and servants.

Such zodiac figure and demon figurines were also popular in the region of Jiangxi. Twenty-one porcelain figurines have been unearthed in the shrine and the chamber of the tomb of Liu Zong from 1047 in Caojialong, Pengze, including twelve zodiac figures, each holding an animal in both hands, as well as a grave fish with a human head and the body of a fish.[113] They are more refined than ordinary pottery figurines. Porcelain figurines became quite popular in Jiangxi, which was already a porcelain production center.

Porcelain figurines have intermittently been discovered in Song tombs, particularly in the suburbs of Jingdezhen, known as the capital of porcelain. Un-

2.52 Woman dressed in Khitan style, white porcelain, unearthed in 1973 from the tomb of Zha Zengjiu, Jingdezhen, Jiangxi Province. Southern Song dynasty. 14 cm. Jingdezhen Porcelain Exhibit Hall.

2.53 Woman with her hair in a coil, painted clay, unearthed in 1986 in Changping district, Beijing. Liao dynasty. 51.5 cm. Beijing Changping District Cultural Relics Storeroom.

earthed in Shujia village in the tomb of a woman with the surname of Shu, wife of a man called Shi Lin, from 1065, were four directional deities made of shadowy blue porcelain: namely, a turtle (on a plain base), a vermilion bird, a blue dragon, and a white tiger.[114] All twelve of the zodiac figures, each holding a symbolic animal, have their foreheads carved with the character *wang*. A Futing, also sporting a *wang* on his forehead, a Dangkuang, and a Dangye in armor all have plain bases. Also unearthed in this tomb were the model of a sedan-chair and a porcelain figurine sitting on a chair, types rarely found elsewhere.

In another Song tomb, in Maopengdian (on the outskirts of Jingdezhen), the figurines that were unearthed are covered with a shadowy blue glaze, or such a glaze over a dark reddish-brown layer. In addition to figurines of the four directional deities and twelve zodiac figures, there are demon figurines such as a grave fish and a grave dragon, a model of a sedan-chair carried by four

male figurines, and models of a group of eight structures, including a hall and a warehouse. Song porcelain figurines unearthed in Jiangxi are believed to be connected with the performance of drama. The joint tomb of Hong Zicheng and his wife, sealed in 1264, during the Southern Song, in Boyang, Jiangxi, has yielded twenty-one figurines in different clothes, with different postures and expressions.[115] Some appear joyful, others sad. Some look up while others bow their heads in contemplation. Their poses suggest that they are performing a drama, although the content of the drama is as yet unknown.[116] Similar figurines have also been found in Jingdezhen proper (fig. 2.52).

In the area of north China once ruled by the Liao dynasty, it is rare to find terra-cotta figurines in tombs; the Khitan people who established the dynasty had a different burial tradition. One example, however, appears in a Liao tomb in Chenzhuang, Changping district, Beijing, where two half-meter-high standing

2.54 Maidservant, painted clay, unearthed in 1978 from the tomb of the He clan, Huxian County, Xi'an. Yuan dynasty. 30.5 cm. Huxian County Cultural Hall.

dimensional paintings and murals. The woman has been shaved around the back of the skull, while the hair on top is coiled into a bun. A fringe of hair around the bun falls from the temple to the ears (fig. 2.53). The man's head has been shaved, except for his temple hair, which dangles behind his ears.

During the Yuan dynasty, clay funerary figurines were again used at burials, but the demon figurines that had been popular from the Five Dynasties to the Song had disappeared. The traditional procession, with the carriage and horses at the center and figurines of male and female attendants and servants as the principal funerary objects, was restored. There were also models of granaries, domestic animals, and fowl. Significant discoveries from the period have been made at the burial ground of the He clan in Huxian County, which includes the tomb of He Renjie from 1308 and the tomb of He Sheng, which was relocated, from 1327 (fig. 2.54). Other clan tombs are those of Duan Jirong in West Qujiangchi village, Xi'an, from 1265; and a tomb in Baoji, also in Shaanxi Province.[118]

Although the presence and arrangement of the figurines in these tombs are similar to those from earlier periods, the dress and coiffures followed styles in vogue during the Yuan period. Pottery horses, too, had changed by then: they no longer looked like the tall and robust steeds of central Asia but like Mongolian horses, which have short legs and long manes. Even the stirrups were changed to the Mongolian style. Unfortunately, the figurines created during this era were rigidly carved, with no trace of the animated, flowing style seen in late Tang figurines. Funerary objects unearthed at the Yuan tomb in Baoji, particularly the figurines in a standing posture, are not well proportioned. Their heads are small, the necks thin. Yet the garments and hairstyles are meticulously carved: the hair plaits of the warriors and the buns of the women, for example, are depicted in great detail. It is important to note that no such funerary objects have been found in the tombs of Mongolians, the rulers of the country at that time. The people buried in the Yuan tombs in Shaanxi were high-ranking Han officials of the Yuan court. He Sheng was one of the prime ministers; He Renjie was a Dafu, an important senior official in Shaanxi; and Duan Jirong was an official of the Office of the Governor in the capital. Indeed, as far as we know, only Yuan tombs of deceased persons of Han nationality in the region of Shaanxi have yielded clay figurines, which are rarely found in Yuan tombs in other regions. This is an indi-

figurines made of gray clay were found near a niche in the back wall of the tomb, in which ashes were stored.[117] One of the figurines is male, the other female. Both are attired in Khitan style and have the shaved heads typical of the Khitan, seen elsewhere only in two-

cation that the practice, common since the Han and Tang dynasties, of entombing large numbers of funerary figurines had declined significantly.

By the time of the Ming, the production of figurines, unique artistic funerary objects in ancient China, had further declined; however, figurines were still used to indicate one's social status, whether emperor, member of the royal family, or high-ranking official. In the Dingling mausoleum of Emperor Zhu Yijun of the Ming, four trunks filled with wooden figurines were found at the southern and northern ends of the bed in the rear chamber of Xuangong Palace.[119] At the foot of the eastern wall at the southern end of the rear chamber lay another three trunks filled with wooden figurines and one trunk filled with wooden horses equipped with leather saddles and bronze stirrups. The figurines were made of poplar, dragon spruce, larch,

and other woods. About 20 centimeters high, they are mostly standing, with their hands joined in front of their chests. Originally there were more than a thousand figurines in the mausoleum. But when it was excavated, only 248 remained intact. It is supposed that those figurines are likenesses of eunuchs, runners, and intimate court officials at the palace. The shoddy construction of wooden figurines for an imperial mausoleum marked the final phase of the use of figurines in Chinese burials.

With regard to mausoleums of kings from the Ming, wooden figurines have been excavated in Jiulong Hill in Zouxian County, Shandong, in the mausoleum of Zhu Tan, Prince Luhuang, who died in 1389 (fig. 2.55); and terra-cotta figurines have been excavated from the mausoleum of Zhu Yuelian, the eldest son of the king of Shu, interred in Chengdu, Sichuan, in 1410.[120] Some 406

2.55 Honor guard figurines, wood, excavated in 1970 from the tomb of Prince Luhuang, Zouxian County, Shandong Province. Ming dynasty. 29 cm. Shandong Province Museum, Ji'nan.

intact wooden figurines, twenty-four models of horses, two model wooden carts, and various wooden models of furniture and daily utensils have been discovered at the mausoleum of Zhu Tan. Apart from two armored door guards holding "golden melons" (long clubs whose ends are shaped like golden melons — this ancient weapon was later carried by honor guards), they are mostly figurines of attendants, honor guards, and orchestra performers. Most are carved out of pine, and most of the painted colors have faded, but it is still possible to see that the hats, belts, and boots had been painted black. Moreover, the figurines are exquisitely carved and their postures are lively. Even the weapons they hold are meticulously carved.

The figurines in the mausoleum of Zhu Yuelian, eldest son of the king of Shu, are made of glazed clay. Except for a few that had been moved and damaged, most of the figurines were in a state of good preservation when they were excavated. All told, there are more than five hundred glazed clay figurines. Two figurines of warriors and three models of horses (one on the right side is missing) stand on both sides of the front hall right behind the gate of the tomb. Three rows of honor guards stand on each side of the main hall. Those in the first row are horse grooms; the next row is composed of figurines beating drums or gongs, playing painted military bugles, or holding various objects in their hands; and the third row is made up of warrior figurines carrying bows and arrows and shields. In front of the entrance to the main chamber of the main hall are two rows of warriors. On each side of the central hall are more than 150 members of the honor guard, nine of them with an imperial carriage (figs. 2.56, 2.57). Behind the main chamber in the central hall are four figurines carrying a large drum. One beats the drum with a stick. On the terrace of the rear chamber of the central hall stand four figurines, all clasping their hands in front of their chests. Another forty-eight figurines of attendants wait in the central room of the rear chamber. The glazed pottery figurines in this group seem lifeless and stiff. Nevertheless, because they illustrate the ceremonial system of the early Ming kings, they are of tremendous historical value.

After the middle of the Ming dynasty, the number of terra-cotta figurines in tombs diminished year by year, until, by the time of the mausoleums of Zhu Youbin, Prince Yiduan (built in Jiangxi in 1540), and Zhu Houye, Prince Yizhuang (completed in 1557 in Nancheng, Jiangxi), only 110 and 202 pieces, respectively, were found.[121] Moreover, the design of those figurines seems uninspired.

Ordinarily, no funerary figurines were buried in tombs of Ming officials, but there were certain exceptions. The tomb of Liao Ji in Fucheng County, Hebei, from 1534,[122] for example, was built by the Ministry of

2.56 Glazed figurines, unearthed from the tomb of the crown prince of Shu, Chengdu, Sichuan Province. Ming dynasty.

2.57 Imperial carriage and honor guard figurines, glazed porcelain, excavated in 1970 from the tomb of the crown prince of Shu, Chengdu. Ming dynasty. 70 × 78 × 34 cm (carriage) and 31 cm (honor guard). Sichuan Provincial Museum, Chengdu.

Works by order of the emperor. In front of the stone sarcophagus is a pit for spirit articles, and in the front part of this pit lie two groups of honor guard figurines surrounding sedan-chairs, an allusion to the Board of War and the Board of Civil Office. Models of a sitting-room, bedroom, and kitchen, as well as figurines of maids and facsimiles of daily utensils, were placed in the central and rear chambers. The clay figurines look dull and perhaps hastily carved.

Another exception is the burial ground of the Pan clan in the Luwan district of Shanghai, where exquisitely carved wooden models of furniture and figurines have been found.[123] In the tomb of Pan Yunzheng, from 1589, in the space between the inner and outer coffins, lay forty-five wooden figurines and many facsimiles of furniture. The two models of sedan-chairs in particular — one with a top, the other without — imitate real sedan-chairs of the time. The ends of the car-

rying poles of the sedan-chairs are covered in bronze. Among the wooden figurines, two hold up placards inscribed with characters meaning "Silence" and "Keep out"; another pair hold up parasols. The rest are performers, runners, attendants, sedan-chair carriers, and so forth. Pan Yunzheng was a minor official, but the beauty of the wooden figurines at his burial suggests that the practice of burying funerary figurines with the deceased still thrived in the region.

Few funerary figurines have been found in Qing tombs. A large group of figurines was recently unearthed in the tomb of Wu Liuqi of the early Qing in Guangdong.[124] There 137 clay figurines and models of furniture were found in a square chest divided in three by two partitions laid in front of the tomb chamber. Although all the figurines in the early years of the Kangxi reign (1662–1722) were crudely fashioned, they do offer a glimpse of the local customs of the time.

Stone Sculpture on Spirit Paths from the Wei to the Qing

As was mentioned earlier, during the Wei kingdom (220–265), the ruling Cao family eschewed the Han-dynasty obsession with elaborate funerals and instead advocated more frugal burials. One reason was that the economy had been so weakened by incessant war and turmoil that people could no longer afford lavish burials during the waning years of the Eastern Han (25–220). Also, during the war rival warlords had resorted to digging up and looting old tombs in the search for gold and treasure to replenish army provisions. In Cao Cao's own army, a Chamberlain of the Palace Guard in Charge of Tomb Excavation and Gold-Seeking Commandants had been appointed for the purpose. Even Cao Cao himself had personally inspected sites where coffins had been pried open, corpses taken out, and gold and other treasures removed.[125]

The Wei rulers, believing that the looting had been precipitated by the wasteful burials that had been practiced during the Han, laid down the rule that after an emperor had died, his funeral should be simple and that "neither tumulus nor stone tablets should be erected" at his tomb. In this way, they hoped to hide forever the location of the emperor's remains. In 205, Cao Cao issued an order banning lavish funerals and the erection of stone tablets at tombs. Making arrangements for his own funeral in 220, he reiterated that after his death his tomb should be marked by neither a tumulus nor a tombstone.[126] After Cao Pi inherited the throne, he carried out his father's idea of a simple burial. On his deathbed, he instructed that no enclosure, memorial hall, Spirit Path, or any other surface buildings should be built at his tomb.[127]

With the emperors setting the example, the ban on elaborate burials was carried out to the letter in all royal families, thus ending the large-scale construction of tomb enclosures, memorial halls, and Spirit Paths that had been fashionable during the late Eastern Han. Archaeological surveys and excavations have so far revealed neither a single trace of Spirit Path sculpture in the Cao family's Wei kingdom nor the exact location of the family's imperial mausoleums. The whereabouts of the Gaoling mausoleum of Emperor Wu (Cao Cao) and the Shouyangling mausoleum of Emperor Wen (Cao Pi) — a favorite theme of storytellers through the ages — remain undiscovered to this day.[128]

The Sima family, which succeeded the Wei and established the Western Jin (265–317), continued the Caos' tradition of simple burials that dispensed with tumuli, stone pillars, and other surface structures on and around tombs. That is why the exact location of Western Jin imperial tombs has also mystified archaeologists for generations.[129] In 276, Emperor Wu of the Western Jin issued an edict that reiterated the ban on stone animals and pillars at tombs: any tomb statues and steles built in violation of this edict were to be torn down.[130] By the time that Emperor Hui had ascended the throne in 290, however, the government had become corrupt and decadent, and enforcement of the ban was lax. This was why Han Shou, the son-in-law of an influential courtier by the name of Jia Chong, was able to have a stone pillar erected in front of his tomb.[131]

A 113-centimeter fragment of that pillar is housed today in the Luoyang Museum. Originally a piece of the upper part of the pillar, the fragment consists of a squarish section with an inscribed epitaph connected with the upper shaft that surmounts it and with part of the lower shaft of the pillar below. The tenons atop the upper shaft indicate that it was once connected with the capital. The upper and lower shafts are engraved with

2.58 Remaining section of a stone pillar with inscription in front of the tomb of Han Shou. Western Jin dynasty. 113 cm. Luoyang Ancient Arts Museum, Henan Province.

2.59 Zoomorphic image, stone, along the Spirit Path to the Chuningling mausoleum of Liu Yu, Jiangning district, Nanjing. Five Dynasties. 256 × 318 cm.

2.60 Inscription on stone pillar by the Spirit Path to the tomb of Xiao Hong, Prince Jinghui, Linchuan, Xianhe Gate, Jiangning district, Nanjing. Southern Dynasties.

2.61 Bas-relief on the side panel of a stele at the tomb of Xiao Hong.

vertical bamboo slip patterns and encircled with two rounds of rope patterns above and below the squarish section.

Inscribed in official script on the facade of the square section, whose edges are damaged, was a text of twenty Chinese characters arranged in four rows. Only the two middle rows are discernible, and only ten Chinese characters are left: "The [Spirit Path to the Mansion of Master] Han from Duyang Township, Nanyang, [the Deceased Cavalier Attendant-in-Ordinary]" (fig. 2.58). Both the shaft and the squarish section inscribed with the epitaph bear a close resemblance to the stone pillar for the Spirit Path to the tomb of Qin, the Han-dynasty administrative clerk of Youzhou Prefecture, an indication that the design of Han Shou's pillar drew on the tradition of Han tomb pillars.[132]

Another Western Jin Spirit Path stone pillar was found in 1987 in Bo'ai County, Henan Province.[133] The capital of the pillar is missing, but its square pedestal and shaft are still there. On the pillar's squarish facade are inscribed twelve Chinese characters in four lines: "The Spirit Path to the Mansion of the Late Prefect of Le'an, Master [Surname] of Henei, of the Jin Dynasty." So far, no other Western Jin tombstone carvings have been found.

In the year 311, the Xionghu army headed by Liu Yao sacked Luoyang, capital of the Western Jin. Crown Prince Sima Ye fled to Chang'an and ascended the throne as Emperor Min. When Liu Yao conquered Chang'an in 316 and annihilated the Western Jin, Sima Rui, prince of Langya and Grand General of the East (the Western Jin's top-ranking commander of the five prefectures south of the Yangzi River), established the Eastern Jin (317–420) in Jianye (present-day Nanjing, Jiangsu Province) with the support of aristocrats who had fled across the river and noble families that had already established themselves in the south.

The Eastern Jin carried forward all the traditions of its predecessor, including frugal funerals and burials and the ban on steles and stone animals on and in front of tombs. Enforcement of the ban gradually fell away, however, and by 318, Emperor Yuan had made at least one exception by approving the erection of stone tablets at the tomb of a major court official.[134] By the time Liu Yu had overthrown the Eastern Jin and founded the Song dynasty (420–479), the system of building a Spirit Path and erecting stone statues for tombs had been revived. Yet because the old Eastern Han burial system had been forgotten in the two intervening centuries (from 205, the tenth year of Cao Cao's Jian'an reign, to

the establishment of the Liu Song by Liu Yu), the Spirit Path stone statues that began to reappear looked, especially in their modeling, more like throwbacks to old models. The few extant tombstone carvings from the Song under the rule of the Lius are zoomorphic images. One pair was found in front of the Chuningling mausoleum of Liu Yu (Emperor Wu) at Qilinpu, in Jiangning (fig. 2.59), and another in front of the Changningling mausoleum of Liu Yilong (Emperor Wen) at Shizichong, south of Ganjia Lane in Nanjing.

It was not until the Southern Qi (479–502) that Spirit Path stone sculpture once again came into its own. Most of the sculptures have been found in Danyang County, and most are of animals. By the Liang dynasty (502–557), stone tomb sculpture was flourishing as never before: the use of Spirit Path figures and pillars had spread from imperial mausoleums to the tombs of princes and marquises. Complete ensembles of tombstones, epitaph pillars, and stone animals remain intact at some tombs built during that period (figs. 2.60, 2.61, 2.62).

The popularity of stone tomb sculpture, however, faded by the time of the Chen (557–589), as the nation's strength declined. Only one extant pair of stone animals are attributed to that period; they are at the Wan'anling mausoleum of Chen Baxian (Emperor Wu) in the town of Shangfang, Jiangning district. Stone tomb figures from the Southern Dynasties (420–589) have been found at thirty-one sites in and around Nanjing (including the counties of Jiangning, Jurong, and Danyang). These include twelve imperial mausoleums and nineteen tombs in which the remains of princes and marquises are buried. Tombstones, pillars bearing epitaphs, and stone animals in relatively complete ensembles, however, can be found only at three sites — the Jianling mausoleum of Xiao Shunzhi (Emperor Wen) at Sanchengxiang in eastern Danyang, the tomb of Xiao Xiu (Prince Kang of Ancheng) at Ganjia Lane, Yaohua Gate, in Nanjing, and the tomb of Xiao Hong (Prince Jinghui of Linchuan) at Xianhe Gate, Qilinmen, in Jiangning. At the Jianling mausoleum, though, only a pedestal of the tombstone remains, and at Xiao Hong's tomb, only one stone stele stands where a pair should be. Only at the tomb of Xiao Xiu is the assemblage of three pairs of stone sculptures in good shape (fig. 2.63).[135]

A Southern Dynasties assemblage of tombstone sculpture generally consists of tombstones, steles, and animals arranged symmetrically on both sides of a Spirit Path. All are massive. The imposing stone animals, for example, are about 3 meters in length and height (figs. 2.64, 2.65, 2.66). One notable stele from the

2.62 Zoomorphic image, stone, in front of the tomb of Xiao Hong.

period, featuring a round top and a decorative round hole, stands on the back of a colossal stone turtle. The turtle, its four strong legs digging into the ground, its bulging eyes wide open, cranes its neck and steadfastly strives forward under its heavy load. The stone pillars, which had their origins in ancient Chinese road signs and marked the Spirit Path to a tomb, differ totally in form and function from their foreign counterparts, which serve only to prop up a building. The vertical ridged grooves on the shaft of such a pillar are patterned after those on the traditional Chinese pillar; the design shows a number of bamboo slips with both ends "bundled" with hemp-rope patterns. The facade of the pillar assumes the shape of a rough square, in the Han tradition, and the text of an epitaph is inscribed on it vertically; the Chinese characters line up horizontally as well. The epitaph, inscribed in most cases in the conventional way on one side and in reverse on the other,

and mostly carved in intaglio in the regular script, indicates the dynastic title, as well as the name and official title, of the deceased to whom the Spirit Path is dedicated. The pillar is topped by a round capital graced by lotus patterns, and standing atop the capital is a tiny stone animal identical in appearance and posture to one of the pair of large stone animals guarding the Spirit Path (fig. 2.67). The base of the pillar is a square stone block on which two dragons coil together, and a round socket chiseled into the center of the base holds up the shaft of the stone pillar. The sturdy design of the pillar and its exquisite ornamental carvings accentuate the mournful atmosphere of the tomb.

In a Southern Dynasties assemblage of tombstone figures, more animals are represented than anything else. A complete array of stone animals attributed to the Liu Song, Southern Qi, Liang, and Chen dynasties has been preserved to this day, making it possible to study the

2.63 Assemblage of stone sculptures in front of the tomb of Xiao Xiu, Prince Kang of the Liang dynasty, in Nanjing. Southern Dynasties.

2.64 Zoomorphic image with one horn, stone, in front of the Yongningling mausoleum of Chen Qian, Emperor Wen of Chen, Jiangning district, Nanjing. Southern Dynasties. 313 × 319 cm.

2.65 Zoomorphic image with double horns, stone, in front of the Yongningling mausoleum, Nanjing. Southern Dynasties. 300 × 311 cm.

2.66 Zoomorphic image, stone, in front of the tomb of Xiao Jing, Marquis Zhong of Wuping, Jiangning district, Nanjing. Southern Dynasties. 350 × 380 cm.

zoomorphic imagery of tombstone sculpture of the Southern Dynasties. Some of these animals, 9 cubic meters each, are fantastic winged creatures. Those guarding the tombs of emperors or empresses have horns protruding from their heads; they are known as *tianlu* (heavenly deer) or qilin (unicorns). Those standing before the tombs of princes and dukes are hornless *bixie* (exorcising animals). With a pair of wings sprouting from their shoulders, the images of both the tianlu and the bixie follow rather closely the tradition of the winged celestial beasts seen during the Warring States, Han, and Wei periods. A mere glance at the gold- and silver-inlaid statues of winged mythological animals unearthed from the tomb of Prince Jing of Zhongshan from the Warring States period (476–221 B.C.E.) is needed to divine the origin of the stone tomb animals from the Southern Dynasties — they exhibit the same heroic posture and natural charm, limbs slightly bent and paws pressed into the earth, chests thrown out and heads held high. The only differences between them lie in the raw materials used, their size, and the spirit of the time.

The Southern Dynasties models show a remarkable improvement in chiseling techniques, especially in open-work skills, over Western and Eastern Han stone animals such as those guarding the tomb of the Western Han general Huo Qubing; they also demonstrate considerable maturity in the execution of monumental sculpture in the round as compared with the Eastern Han zoomorphic stone statues discovered in Sichuan and Henan. The massive bodies of these celestial creatures, lying low in the green fields and craning their necks toward the sky, give the impression that they are mustering all their strength for a takeoff. Because they were wrought in different ages, their style varies. There is a full-bodied solidity about those done during the Liu Song dynasty, although they may appear simple and crude at first sight.

The stone tomb animals dating back to the Southern Qi and the Liang show more freedom and ease of composition, and those gracing the tombs of princes and marquises seem to possess a latent power in their condensed forms (achieved through economy of ornamentation on their bodies). By the Chen, the deteriorating political and economic situation of the nation had unfailingly left its ugly mark on works of art. Stone animals created during that period have heads so big that they look bloated, on necks sinking in between hunched shoulders — their predecessors' dignified poses are nowhere to be found. Moreover, their limbs are short and feeble; the claws on their paws turn up, and they no

2.67 Stone pillar in front of the tomb of Xiao Jing, Marquis Zhong of Wuping. Southern Dynasties. 245 cm in circumference.

longer seem poised to soar: indeed, the wings on their shoulders have degenerated into useless ornaments and would be incapable of assisting the poor beasts to fly. These stone animals, appearing enervated despite their massive bodies, seems fit only to lash out with exaggerated ferocity in a last-ditch fight. Fierce of mien but faint of heart, they are a fitting emblem of a doomed dynasty.

The stone sculpture of Spirit Paths north of the Yangzi River is entirely different. Because careful archaeological surveys and studies have yet to be carried out on the imperial tombs of the separatist regimes of the Sixteen Kingdoms, a stone horse in the stele museum of Shaanxi Province is perhaps the only known representative of the north China stone sculpture of that period. The horse, attributed to the Xia kingdom, resembles the one standing over a fallen warrior in front of the Western Han general Huo Qubing's tomb, in that the areas between the forelegs and between the hind legs are not cut through (fig. 2.68).

After the Northern Wei unified north China, its monarchs gradually turned their attention to the construction of imperial mausoleums. Emperor Xiaowen had the Yongguling mausoleum built at Fangshan near the capital city of Pingcheng (present-day Datong, Shanxi Province) for his grandmother, the Empress Dowager Feng. Historical records indicate that in front of the mausoleum once stood Yonggu Temple, whose front court was arrayed with steles and animals hewn out of stone, a pagoda called Picture of Yearning for Souls Drifting Far Away, and two masonry que towers.[136] None of these have survived save for the pedestal of the pagoda and the foundations of a few buildings; thus there is no way of knowing the designs of the stone steles and animals that once stood by the Spirit Path of the mausoleum.

After the Northern Wei moved its capital to Luoyang, all the imperial mausoleums for the dynasty were built on Mangshan to the north of the city, but only the Jingling mausoleum of Yuan Ke (Emperor Xuanwu, who reigned from 500 to 515) has been excavated.[137] When digging began in 1991, a stone statue was found lying toppled, its head damaged, on the western side of the Spirit Path and 10 meters from the tumulus. The statue is cast in the image of an imperial attendant standing in state in a formal pose, with loose sleeves, his hands raised to his chest and holding a sword. The fragment of this statue stands 289 centimeters tall (fig. 2.69). An identical one should have been positioned opposite this partially surviving statue on the eastern side of the Spirit Path, but it is nowhere to be found. A survey conducted previously of the Jingling

mausoleum of Yuan Ziyou (Emperor Xiaozhuang, r. 528–530) revealed a 314-centimeter-high stone statue of a man looking dignified and sedate wearing a crown and a robe and holding a sword in hands that are raised to his chest (fig. 2.70).[138] Once again, no stone animals or pillars were found at the site. When a large tomb that should be attributed to a Northern Qi emperor was excavated at Wanzhang in Cixian County, Hubei Province, another stone figure was discovered to the south of the tumulus, but no other stone carvings were found.[139] Thus, we can conclude that most imperial tomb sculptures during the Northern Dynasties were cast as human images, even though such figures were rare on imperial Spirit Paths of the Southern Dynasties.

Tomb Sculpture from the Tang

In 618 Li Yuan established the Tang dynasty, which ushered Chinese culture and art into an age of unprecedented prosperity. Previously, the Sui had replaced the Northern Zhou and brought reunification to the nation by eliminating the Chen south of the Yangzi. Yet the Sui rule was so short-lived — it was toppled by peasant uprisings barely thirty years after it had wiped out the Chen — that little information is available about the stone sculpture for mausoleums of the Sui emperors. The Tang empire, by contrast, lasted 298 years, enough time for luxurious mausoleums to be built for all of its monarchs.

So far, eighteen Tang imperial mausoleums have been verified in the counties of Qianxian, Liquan, Jingyang, Sanyuan, Fuping, and Pucheng in Shaanxi Province. Dispersed from west to east across these six counties, they are known collectively as the Eighteen Tang Tombs in Central Shaanxi. Chronologically, they are (1) the Xianling mausoleum of Li Yuan (Emperor Gaozu); (2) the Zhaoling mausoleum of Li Shimin (Emperor Taizong); (3) the Qianling mausoleum of Li Zhi (Emperor Gaozong) and Empress Wu Zetian; (4) the Dingling mausoleum of Li Xian (Emperor Zhongzong); (5) the Qiaoling mausoleum of Li Dan (Emperor Ruizong); (6) the Tailing mausoleum of Li Longji (Emperor Xuanzong); (7) the Jianling mausoleum of Li Heng (Emperor Xiaozong); (8) the Yuanling mausoleum of Li Yu (Emperor Daizong); (9) the Chongling mausoleum of Li Shi (Emperor Dezong); (10) the Fengling mausoleum of Li Song (Emperor Shunzong); (11) the Jingling mausoleum of Li Chun (Emperor Xianzong); (12) the Guangling mausoleum of Li Heng (Emperor Muzong); (13) the Zhuangling mausoleum of Li Zhan (Emperor Jingzhong); (14) the Zhangling mausoleum of Li Ang (Emperor Wenzong); (15) the Duanling mausoleum of Li Yan (Emperor Wuzong); (16) the Zhenling mausoleum of Li Chen (Emperor Xuanzong); (17) the Jinling mausoleum of Li Cui (Emperor Yizong); and (18) and the Jingling mausoleum of Li Huan (Emperor Xizong).

Along the Spirit Paths to these mausoleums, the stone sculptures remain largely intact.[140] Stone figures have also been found at the Shunling mausoleum at Chenjia village, Xianyang, built by Empress Wu Zetian for her mother, Lady Yang.[141] And in the town of Goushi in Yanshi County, Henan Province (the site of the Gongling mausoleum of Li Hong, who was posthumously honored as Emperor Xiaojing), most of the stone figures have been well preserved.[142]

All these mammoth Tang imperial mausoleums are awe-inspiring. A few are underground tombs made visible as gigantic earth tumuli in the shape of truncated pyramids. Most are hollowed out of rocky mountainsides, and each is encircled by an extensive garden adorned with a vast assemblage of stone figures. Most of those, with their richly varied motifs, are positioned along the Spirit Path. A pair of awesome, majestic stone lions stands at each of the four gates of the garden, which correspond to the four directional deities.

These stone figures are representative of the Tang tradition of ceremonial groups of larger-than-life stone sculptures. Stone figures have been found along other Spirit Paths to the auxiliary tombs of aristocrats and major courtiers around the imperial mausoleums, but the figures are fewer in number and of lesser quality than those guarding the imperial mausoleums. At the tomb of Li Xianhui (Princess Yongtai), for example, an auxiliary tomb at the Qianling mausoleum, the two stone lions, four stone warriors, and two stone pillars greatly resemble the stone sculptures at the Qianling mausoleum, although they are smaller in scope and number.[143]

The stone sculpture of Tang imperial mausoleums underwent four stages of development: a formative stage, a period of maturation, a stage of continuity, and a period of decline. In the course of this development its artistic form went from bold and vigorous to solemn and ponderous before degenerating into crude, lackluster stereotypes. That progression reflected the history of a dynasty that, born of war in the early seventh century, grew in strength and built itself into the most prosperous and powerful empire in the east, and, after declining in the wake of the armed rebellion led by An Lushan and Shi Siming in 755, expired in war and turmoil.

An unmistakable grandeur characterizes the stone sculpture of the imperial mausoleums of the Tang during its formative years. Representative works include the Six Thoroughbreds of Zhaoling mausoleum, a group of bas-relief stone carvings modeled on the six favorite battle chargers of Li Shimin (Emperor Taizong). These horses, depicted in lithe and prancing postures, stormed the enemy line during the Sui-Tang interregnum and, braving showers of arrows and stones, carried Li, the commander in chief, from victory to victory. The bas-reliefs, done on six gigantic stone slabs, present a lateral view of the six heroic steeds in different trotting or galloping poses. Realism is a hallmark of these works, so much so that the ornamentation and the saddles — and even the arrow wound on one of the horses — are depicted in eloquent and accurate linear detail. Their names are Saluzi (Valiant purple-haired horse), Quanmaogua (Curly-haired yellow horse with a black mouth), Baitiwu (Black horse with white hoofs), Telebiao (Yellowish-white steed called Tele), Qingzhui (Piebald steed), and Shifachi (Red steed with the name of Chifa). All of them are captured in motion except Saluzi, which is standing still while Qiu Xinggong, a general in full armor, pulls out the arrow that has pierced its side. This was exactly what happened to the horse during the Battle of Mangshan against Wang Shichong (fig. 2.71).[144]

The Six Thoroughbreds reliefs of Zhaoling mausoleum were created in memory of Emperor Taizong's military exploits. Significantly, unlike Western sculptural eulogies of heroes, these six statues do not depict the hero himself — though his presence is felt in the heroic poses of his personal mounts. In this sense, Six Thoroughbreds of Zhaoling mausoleum is a masterpiece of symbolism typical of Eastern art, a symbolism without exaggeration or arrogant affectation. It can be said that this group of sculptures is rooted in the tradition of the statuary of Huo Qubing's tomb, where the Western Han general's distinctive service is also portrayed in the gallant forms of the stone horses that adorn the Spirit Path to his tomb. Sadly, they were stolen from the Zhaoling mausoleum and broken into pieces in order to be spirited out of China. Four of them, fortunately, were intercepted and are now on display in the Forest of Steles Museum of Xi'an, but the two finest ones, including the one depicting General Qiu Xinggong pulling the arrow out of Saluzi, have never been returned to China.[145] All that remains where these six sculptural works stood in front of the Zhaoling mausoleum are a few pedestals, crumbling with age.

2.68 Stone horse of the kingdom of Xia, Chang'an district, Xi'an. Sixteen Kingdoms period. 225 × 200 cm. Forest of Steles Museum of Xi'an.

Among the Tang-dynasty stone mausoleum sculptures older than the Six Thoroughbreds of Zhaoling mausoleum are those adorning the Xianling mausoleum of Li Yuan (Emperor Gaozu) and the stone figures he had erected at the tomb of his grandfather Li Hu when he renamed it Yongkangling mausoleum (in 618, the first year of the Wude reign of the Tang dynasty he had just founded). The lively stone lions squatting in front of the Yongkangling mausoleum bear vestiges of the sculptural tradition of the Northern Dynasties.[146] At Emperor Gaozu's Xianling mausoleum, each of the four deity gates of the garden was guarded by a pair of stone tigers, while the Spirit Path in the south was flanked by a pair of stone rhinoceroses and a pair of stone pillars. Both the tigers and the rhinoceroses stand at attention, looking valiant and ferocious despite their simple, almost crude, contours (fig. 2.72).[147] The stone pillars are octagonal columns with tiny stone lions

squatting on their round capitals. The standing stone animals and the octagonal stone pillars are reminiscent of Southern Dynasties traditions. Yet the realistic stone tigers and rhinoceroses indicate conceptual and technical breakthroughs by Tang sculptors, who nevertheless stopped short of creating an entirely new style. Indeed, Tang imperial mausoleums built after the Xianling and Zhaoling mausoleums have no large sculptural works such as the Six Thoroughbreds of Zhaoling mausoleum or the rough, compact images of the tigers and rhinoceroses from the Xianling mausoleum. Lions have replaced the guardian tigers. One reason for this discontinuity is that the design and construction of both the Xianling and Zhaoling mausoleums were the brainchild of the renowned painter Yan Lide. According to the biography of Yan Lide in the *Old Tang History (Jiu Tang shu)*, Yan was given the title Virtuoso Craftsman of a General's Caliber for his outstanding contribution

2.69 Imperial attendant, apparently partly re-created, in front of the Jingling mausoleum of Yuan Ke, Emperor Xuanwu. Northern Wei dynasty. 289 cm. Luoyang Museum of Ancient Tombs.

2.70 Imperial attendant at the Jingling mausoleum of Ziyou, Emperor Xiaozhuang, Mangshan, Luoyang. Northern Wei dynasty. 314 cm. Luoyang Ancient Arts Museum.

2.71 Saluzi (Valiant purple-haired horse), limestone relief, one of the Six Thoroughbreds that stood in front of the Zhaoling mausoleum of Emperor Taizong, Qianxian County, Shaanxi Province. Tang dynasty, 7th century. 176 × 207 cm. University of Pennsylvania Museum, Philadelphia.

2.72 Stone rhinoceros from the Xianling mausoleum of Li Yuan, Emperor Gaozu, Sanyuan County, Shaanxi Province. Tang dynasty. 230 × 300 cm. Forest of Steles Museum of Xi'an.

to the mausoleum for Emperor Gaozu and was put in charge of building the Zhaoling mausoleum in 636. It is safe to say, therefore, that the imposing and magnificent characteristics of the stone sculpture from Tang mausoleums were intimately related to this man's artistic style and concepts.

The group of stone figures of the Qianling mausoleum represents Tang funerary sculpture at its most advanced. Buried in this mountainside mausoleum are the remains of Li Zhi (Emperor Gaozong) and Wu Zetian, the empress who once changed the title of the dynasty to Dazhou. Stone lions guard each of the four deity gates to the mausoleum enclosure, but at the northern gate six stone horses are also stationed. All the major stone figures face each other in pairs, being placed symmetrically along both sides of the Spirit Path (fig. 2.73). Behind a pair of stone gateways are arrayed a pair of stone pillars, a pair of winged horses, a pair of ostriches, five pairs of ceremonial horses and grooms

(fig. 2.74), ten pairs of stone men (fig. 2.75), and two stone tablets — the Wordless Stele and the Stele Recording the Exploits of the Sacred Emperor. There are also sixty-one headless stone statues of diplomatic envoys from vassal countries (fig. 2.76). A comparison shows that the stone sculpture of the Qianling mausoleum lacks both the realism and technical excellence found in the Six Thoroughbreds of the Zhaoling mausoleum and the solidity and grandeur of the crude-looking stone figures of the Xianling. The Qianling sculpture marked the beginning of a standardization of style to ensure that each motif was portrayed in what was believed to be the most sedate and solemn fashion possible. Some of the stone statues, for example, were fashioned to stand straight-legged with their heads bowed. The composure of such statues is enhanced by the presence of a groom standing in docile attendance. Among the stone sculptures at the Qianling, the five pairs of horses and their grooms strike the same poses, in an attempt to inspire awe and reverence for the dead in an archetypal way. Docility and submission are even more salient characteristics of the ten pairs of imperial attendants who are attired impeccably in crowns and robes, standing upright, and clasping long swords to their chests. The sixty-one diplomatic envoys from vassal countries standing in two straight lines embody the same formal solemnity. An agreeable sense of stability and timelessness is palpable in this dignified, imposing, and somewhat melancholy congregation of massive stone men and horses and soaring stone pillars and tablets, as they combine to form a visual eulogy to the monarch of a burgeoning empire. The stone sculpture of the Qianling may lack the kind of exuberance and pioneering spirit that characterize the Six Thoroughbreds of the Zhaoling mausoleum, but it more than makes up for that with its serene and strictly stylized designs and its emphasis on minute detail, which reflect the dignity of imperial power and the dynasty's great prosperity. Special mention should be made of the pair of winged horses in this cluster. Standing erect, with heads held high and eyes fixed on the sky, they seem ready to soar (fig. 2.77).

The stone figures flanking the Spirit Path to the Gongling mausoleum, built in 675, were created contemporaneously with, or a bit earlier than, those gracing the Qianling mausoleum and are generally like them in style. The Gongling figures, however, especially the winged horses and lions, are smaller and look a bit stiffer and duller. The stone pillars at the Xianling mausoleum still displayed a round capital with a lion standing atop it in the style of the Southern Dynasties period — but by the time of the Gongling and the Qianling, the lion on the capital had been replaced with a more stylish design: a pearl-like lotus flower. This device was adopted for stone pillars erected for nearly all the late Tang mausoleums, in much the same way that the forms found in stone sculpture of the Qianling became the standard for the models during the mature stage of development of Tang tombstone sculpture, which also covered the Dingling mausoleum of Emperor Zhongzong and the Qiaoling mausoleum of Emperor Ruizong (fig. 2.78). These highly stylized sculptures worked in perfect harmony with the magnificence of surface buildings and the immensity of imperial mausoleums to create an atmosphere of classical sanctity.

Following the armed rebellion launched by An Lushan and Shi Siming toward the end of the Tianbao reign (742–756), Tang tombstone sculpture entered into

its stage of continuity. The empire might still have been able to build more mausoleums, but as the political power and economic vigor of the Tang empire waned with each passing day, Tang society became less able to support such endeavors. Consequently, the stone figures sculpted during this period were gradually robbed of their artistic appeal, though the craftsmen still observed the traditions and formulas adopted during the mature period. The stone figures of the Tailing, Jianling, Yuanling, Chongling, Fengling, Jingling, Guangling, and Zhuangling mausoleum were the products of this stage of continuity. Generally speaking, they were shabby in craftsmanship, lifeless and dull in imagery, and more lax and undisciplined in linear depiction. The glory of Tang funerary sculpture was no more. Although the stone figures along the Spirit Paths of the five late Tang mausoleums — the Zhangling, Duanling, Zhenling, Jianling, and Jingling — still appeared in the same formation as had those adorning earlier mausoleums of that dynasty, they bear unsightly indications of the debilitation of the dynasty; for example, they look considerably thinner, and the chisel work is cruder and more haphazard. It was during this stage of gradual decay that Tang tombstone sculpture lost its aesthetic appeal.

Having considered the course of development and artistic characteristics of funerary sculpture during the Tang, we naturally want to know who crafted that dynasty's wealth of stone figures. Because masons were on the bottom rung of the social ladder at the time, historians never went out of their way to name them in their books. That is why most of the works remain anonymous. Careful examination of the figures, however, enables us to identify at least one of the artists. A line engraved on a stone tiger at the Xianling mausoleum reads: "Done by Little Tang Er on the eleventh of the ninth month in the tenth year of the Wude reign." This Little Tang Er is perhaps the only creator of Tang tomb sculptures to have left his name for posterity.[148]

Finally, it should be noted that among the monumental works of sculpture created during the Tang, only a group of cast-iron men and oxen unearthed from a marshland of the Yellow River at the Pujin ferry crossing in Yongji County, Shanxi Province, can rival the army of imperial tombstone figures in magnitude and forcefulness of presentation.

This cluster, cast in 724 to hold a pontoon in place, comprises four iron oxen in two pairs, facing westward toward the river, with four iron herders, one standing beside each ox, as well as two cast-iron hills and a number of star-shaped iron pillars.[149] The oxen are bulky

2.73 Stone sculpture along the Spirit Path in front of the Qianling mausoleum of Li Zhi, Emperor Gaozong, Qianxian County, Shaanxi Province. Tang dynasty.

2.74 Horse decorated for imperial processions, with groom, stone, along the Spirit Path of the Qianling mausoleum of Li Zhi, Emperor Gaozong. 190 cm (horse) and 133 cm (groom).

2.75 Imperial attendant, stone, along the Spirit Path of the Qianling mausoleum of Li Zhi, Emperor Gaozong. 410 × 286 cm.

2.76 Diplomatic envoys from vassal countries, stone, in front of the Qianling mausoleum of Li Zhi, Emperor Gaozong. 142–160 cm.

2.77 Winged horse in front of the Qianling mausoleum of Li Zhi, Emperor Gaozong. 345 × 350 cm.

2.78 Ostrich image, stone relief, at the Qiaoling mausoleum of Li Dan, Emperor Ruizong, Pucheng County, Shaanxi Province. Tang dynasty. 232 × 198 cm.

and heavy, standing 1.9 meters high and 3 meters long and weighing 55 to 75 tons each. The casting is superb. The oxen's full-bodied forms, which exude a sense of masculine power and endurance, are fitting emblems of human beings' determination to try their mettle against nature and invaluable examples of the monumental metal sculpture of the Tang dynasty (fig. 2.79).

In the frontier regions, the tombs of rulers of non-Han regimes were often adorned with stone sculptures in imitation of Tang imperial mausoleums. Excavation of the graveyard of the imperial family of the Bohai kingdom at Liudingshan in Dunhua County, Jilin Province, brought to light a pair of stone lions from the underground passageway to the burial chamber in the tomb of Princess Zhenhui, the second daughter of King Da Qingmao.[150] More than 50 centimeters high, these lions are finely crafted and strike exactly the same poses as the squatting lions found at some Tang imperial mausoleums — obviously, the sculptor had accepted the cultural tradition of the Tang. At the eight imperial tombs of the Tufan kingdom (seventh to ninth century) that were found during an archaeological expe-

dition in the late 1950s in Qonggyai County, Tibet Autonomous Region, a pair of squatting stone lions in the same pose as the Tang prototype, along with an iron ox, were discovered flanking the front of a terrace below the square rammed-earth rampart atop Tomb 1's high and extensive rammed-earth tumulus.[151] To the left of the 8-meter-high tumulus of Tomb 6 stands a stone tablet inscribed with twenty-five lines in archaic Tibetan that record the exploits of the Tufan king Tride Tsungtan (793–815). An entasis is carved on the upper section of the tablet, whose sides are ornamented with cloud-and-dragon patterns in relief. The crowning part of the tablet is in the form of a truncated pyramid with a stone ball on top. Its lower part is engraved with patterns of scudding clouds and flying apsaras, and the entire tablet stands on the back of a stone turtle.

Both the shape and the ornamentation of the stone tablet are reminiscent of Tang models. These discoveries provide solid evidence of the significant influx of Han Chinese culture into Tibet during the days of the Tufan kingdom.

2.79 Oxen and oxherd, cast iron, unearthed in 1989 at the site of the Pujin ferry crossing of the Tang dynasty, Yongji County, Shanxi Province. Tang dynasty. 190 × 300 cm.

Tomb Sculpture from the Song

The fall of the Tang in 907 plunged all of China once again into disunity for a period that is known in Chinese history as the Five Dynasties (907–960) and Ten Kingdoms (902–979). The term *Five Dynasties* refers to the Later Liang (907–923), founded by Zhu Wen; the Later Tang (923–936), founded by Li Cunxu; the Later Jin (936–946), founded by Shi Jingtang; the Later Han (947–950), founded by Liu Zhiyuan; and the Later Zhou (951–960), founded by Guo Wei. The Ten Kingdoms were tiny regimes that emerged during this period in southeast and southwest China. It was not until Zhao Kuangyin toppled the Later Zhou in a mutiny and established the Song dynasty in 960 that these separate political powers were eliminated and China was once again under the control of a single ruler.

The kings of the Five Dynasties and Ten Kingdoms had luxurious tombs built for themselves. Imperial tombs of the Shu (907–925), the Later Shu (934–965), the Southern Tang (937–975), the Wu-Yue (907–978), the Southern Han (917–971), and the Min (909–945) have been excavated in Sichuan, Jiangsu, Zhejiang, Fujian, and Guangdong Provinces since the 1940s. No surface structures have been found at most of these sites, however, and little is known about any tombstone sculpture that may have existed there. The only evidence so far of tomb sculpture during this period is a piece found 300 meters south of the Yongling mausoleum of Wang Jian, king of the Shu, in present-day Chengdu, Sichuan Province. The stone statue of a man was excavated, depicted wearing the same style of robe and standing in the same solemn pose as the stone renditions of courtiers in the Tang imperial mausoleums. Believed to have been associated with the Yongling mausoleum, the stone man may indicate that tomb sculpture of the Five Dynasties and Ten Kingdoms, if it ever existed, carried on the Tang tradition.

The first imperial tomb built after the founding of the Northern Song (960–1127) was the Yong'anling mausoleum dedicated to Zhao Hongyin, father of Zhao Kuangyin, or Emperor Taizu. At first, a site was chosen near the capital city of Dongjing (present-day Keifeng, Henan Province), but construction actually took place in Gongxian County, Henan Prefecture (present-day Gongyi City, Henan Province) in 964. In the ensuing years, until the Jin (Jurchen) troops sacked the Northern Song capital of Dongjing and Zhao Gou (Emperor Gaozong) established the Southern Song dynasty south of the Yangzi in 1127, seven imperial mausoleums were built for Song emperors in Gongxian County: the Yongchangling mausoleum of Zhao Kuangyin (Emperor Taizu), the Yongxiling mausoleum of Zhao Guangyi (Emperor Taizong), the Yongdingling mausoleum of Zhao Heng (Emperor Zhenzong), the Yongzhaoling mausoleum of Zhao Zhen (Emperor Renzong), the Yonghouling mausoleum of Zhao Shu (Emperor Yingzong), the Yongyuling mausoleum of Zhao Xu (Emperor Shenzong), and the Yongtailing mausoleum of Zhao Xu (Emperor Zhezong). Local people say of these tombs and the Yong'anling mausoleum, "Seven emperors but eight mausoleums." It took the Northern Song empire 150 years to complete this immense necropolis, which also included one thousand auxiliary tombs in which the remains of twenty-two empresses and many imperial family members and important courtiers were buried. Regrettably, most of these tombs were found by robbers and reduced to ruins. Only the steadfast-looking stone figures that once lined their Spirit Paths have managed to survive in large numbers.

Recent archaeological surveys suggest that the Northern Song imperial mausoleums followed a unified system and layout. All of them ran due north and south. Each consisted of an upper palace, a lower palace, the tomb of the empress, and auxiliary tombs. The upper palace was the centerpiece of the entire cluster and was composed of auxiliary structures, arrayed from south to north, that included the Oriole Altar (Quetai), the Sacrificial Altar (Rutai), the Spirit Path flanked by stone sculptures, the platform of the mausoleum, and the palace wall around the platform. The lower palace, whose southern gate was guarded by a pair of stone lions, lay to the northwest of the upper palace. The tomb of the empress, situated in the northwest corner of the upper palace, featured the same layout as her husband's mausoleum, except that it was smaller and had fewer stone figures. Behind the empress's tomb was a group of auxiliary tombs, and those dedicated to noblemen and courtiers were adorned with stone figures in the number prescribed by the imperial hierarchical system. More than eight hundred stone figures remain in this immense imperial necropolis, including 407 (33 damaged to varying degrees) at the emperors' tombs, 336 (51 of them broken) at the empresses' tombs, and 69 (19 of them broken) at the auxiliary tombs.[152] The survival of so many monumental works of carved stone enables us to gain some idea of the artistic achievement of Northern Song funerary sculpture.

The stone statuary for Northern Song imperial mausoleums differed from its Tang counterpart in that it evolved much more quickly into its mature form. From the very beginning, the Song had formulated a system for its mausoleums, set the standards for the Spirit Path stone sculpture (including the content and number of stone figures for each assemblage), and established a hierarchical system for the tombs of empresses, aristocrats, and key ministers. By the Northern Song the bureaucracy of the feudal Chinese autocracy had reached near perfection, with an advanced system of legislation and ceremonial rituals and rites. That is why the mausoleums of the dynasty were built to a uniform blueprint. The stone figures along the Spirit Path for each imperial mausoleum were the same in arrangement and number and placed in the same prescribed positions. The only differences lay in minute details and in the patterns of ornamentation, which changed to reflect the style of the day. Generally speaking, each Northern Song imperial mausoleum contained sixty stone figures, and all of them were in the upper palace. With the exception of the stone lions placed outside the eastern, western, and northern gates of the enclosure, most of the statues were arranged in symmetrical pairs along both sides of the Spirit Path that lay between the Sacrificial Altar in the south and the palace wall in the north. Facing each other in pairs, and arrayed along the Spirit Path from south to north, they included a pair of pillars, a pair of elephants, each with a handler, a pair of stone screens each carved with an auspicious bird in relief, a pair of mythological animals, two pairs of horses, each with two grooms, two pairs of tigers, two pairs of goats, three pairs of foreign envoys, two pairs of warriors, and two pairs of civil officials (figs. 2.80, 2.81). The southern gate was guarded by a pair of lions and a pair of warriors; also there were a couple of stone steps for mounting a horse. An empress's tomb was graced with thirty stone figures — a pair at each of the four gates — and the Spirit Path was lined with statues: a pair of stone pillars, a pair of horses with two grooms each, two pairs of tigers, two pairs of goats, a pair of warriors, a pair of civil ministers, and a pair of servants. An auxiliary tomb was generally decorated with six stone carvings: a pair of pillars, a pair of tigers, and a pair of goats; if the deceased held one of the three top ranks during his lifetime, then a pair of stone men appeared too. An examination of the stone sculpture at Northern Song mausoleums and tombs indicates that rules and regulations were carried out to the letter when they were constructed — the feudal hierarchy was so rigid that not a single exception was made. Both the content and the number of stone figures in front of a Northern Song

tomb were more accurate indicators of the status of the deceased than had been the case during the Tang.

An obvious historical affinity existed between the Northern Song and the Tang with regard to imperial stone funerary sculpture, but there were many dissimilarities in content and design. Elephants and their handlers, armored warriors, palace servants, and celestial unicorns were new additions to Northern Song tomb sculpture; the number of ceremonial horses was also increased to two pairs, and the number of grooms escorting each horse became two instead of one. No Northern Song lineup was without its foreign envoys, goats, tigers, and auspicious birds, which gave the procession along the Spirit Path a more striking and awesome appearance than it had had during the Tang. In terms of artistic conception, the Northern Song school of stone funerary sculpture was more institutionalized; or, rather, the images had become so stereotyped that the robust, masculine quality of Tang stone tomb sculpture during its formative stage was totally absent from Song archetypes; nor does one find renditions as lifelike as the militaristic-looking Six Thoroughbreds of the Zhaoling mausoleum or images as dynamic and valiant as the Qianling mausoleum's winged horses, which distinguished tomb sculpture during the height of the Tang. All the stone men posted at Northern Song imperial mausoleums assume humble and submissive poses — especially those guarding the southern gate of a tomb enclosure, who stand meekly at attention with their hands crossed on their chests. Even the animals look dull and inert in their highly stylized poses, standing, squatting, or reclining. The lions by the southern gates were featured differently, in a walking stance, but their ferocity is subdued by long chains fastened to their collars, and their mouths merely gape. The entire assemblage of stone figures was at best a pale reflection of the pomp and pageantry the emperor enjoyed in his lifetime. In the care taken with detail, however, Northern Song stone sculpture was certainly more exquisite than its Tang predecessor. The costumes and draperies of a court official or servant, the helmet and armor of a warrior, and the saddle and bridle of a horse are without exception rendered in finely crafted low relief and careful lines.

Judging from the subtle differences in the plastic style and details of ornamentation, Northern Song stone tomb sculpture fell by and large into three stages of development: the early stage, from the late tenth to the early eleventh century, covering the Yong'anling, Yongchangling, Yongxiling, and Yongdingling mausoleums;

2.80 Stone sculpture along the Spirit Path of the Yongtailing mausoleum of Zhao Xu, Emperor Zhezong, Baling village, Gongyi City, Henan Province. Northern Song dynasty.

2.81 Civil official, stone, at the Yongyuling mausoleum of Zhao Xu, Emperor Shenzong, Baling village, Gongyi City, Henan Province. Northern Song. 306 × 84 cm.

2.82 Military general, stone, at the Yongyuling mausoleum of Zhao Xu, Emperor Shenzong. 434 × 144 cm.

the intermediate stage, spanning the first half of the eleventh century, including the Yongzhaoling and Yonghouling mausoleums; and the late stage, from the latter half of the eleventh to the early twelfth century, including the Yongyuling and Yongtailing mausoleums.

Vestiges of Tang tomb sculptural style are evident in the sturdy build of early stone men from the Song tombs, but they look stiff in their dutiful stances. This is especially true of the armored warriors, who present a rather ungainly sight as they stand with shoulders hunched and heads hanging low. The fist-sized weapons in their hands look ceremonial, so that in and of themselves they rob the warriors of their valor — thereby giving rise to the opinion that the stone warriors reflected the Northern Song imperial court prejudice against soldiers (fig. 2.82). The images of envoys from vassal countries, however, are more pleasing to the eye. Variations in facial expression, attire, and personality make these stone figures interesting and impressive, in spite of their standardized poses (fig. 2.83). The same is true of horse grooms and elephant handlers. Although all were generally portrayed in the same attire

and posture (fig. 2.84), the handlers look livelier, with their earrings, their bracelet-shaped arm bands, and their curly hair tied back with string; together with the lavishly adorned elephants, they add a distinctively foreign touch to the procession.

The stone pillars and auspicious birds also exemplify the change from Tang to Northern Song style. By the Tang dynasty, the pillars standing along the Spirit Path of an imperial mausoleum bore no sign of the squarish stone block for the epitaph inscription. Their round capitals were smaller, and the animal on top had been replaced by a stone ball: the shaft became a decorated prism. By the Northern Song, the round capital on such pillars had become invisible, having been subordinated to the stone ball above it, and the linear patterns of interwoven flowering branches on the prism-shaped pillar had become more elegant and elaborate. As a result, Northern Song pillars looked impressive but lacked the flamboyance of Tang tomb pillars.

Among the Northern Song stone tomb figures, only the auspicious bird, patterned on the ostrich imagery found in Tang stone sculpture, was represented in relief.

The Tang ostrich had been depicted realistically: it turned its head and gazed over its shoulder, its feet resting on a mountain crag against a blank background (see fig. 2.78). In the Northern Song version the bird sported an animal's head and a tail with an ostentatious plume and wings lifted for flight. The background of the relief was engraved with undulating mountains, adding a touch of mystery and splendor (fig. 2.85). Sitting next to this relief of the celestial bird was another Northern Song addition, a unicorn with its upper lip curling upward to reveal protruding fangs, and with wings attached to its shoulders. Known as the xiezhi (or *jiaoduan*), the legendary animal credited with the ability to distinguish between good and evil, it joined the array of imperial tombstone figures as a symbol of the righteousness of imperial power. The works of sculpture done during this stage are marked by an abundance of ornamental patterns. The pedestals for stone figures at the Yongxiling and Yongdingling mausoleums are engraved with finely chiseled designs on all four sides.

By the intermediate stage, human figures in Northern Song stone funerary sculpture no longer adhered to the Tang tradition. Sculptured bodies had turned from stocky to slender, faces from round to oblong, and heads and bodies were well proportioned. The clothing and caps became more realistic, and no ornamental patterns were carved on the sides of pedestals.

Tang traditional style was totally eclipsed in works produced during the late stage of Northern Song stone sculpture. Human figures were slim, as a rule — even their faces were long and skinny — and their facial features and expressions more vivid. The faces of envoys from vassal states, in particular, bore distinctive ethnic and individual characteristics. Soon after the mature stage in Northern Song sculpture had begun, however, the collapse of the dynasty brought the construction of imperial mausoleums to an abrupt end.

After the Southern Song was established, its emperors dreamed of restoring their rule over the north. Wishing to be buried after their death with their forefathers who occupied the Northern Song imperial mausoleums in Henan, they had temporary tombs built near the capital city Lin'an (modern Hangzhou). As before, the tombs also featured upper and lower palaces, but now the coffins were placed inside the polygonal-roofed hall behind the Hall of Sacrifices of the upper palace. No renaissance of funerary sculpture in the style of the Northern Song took place, however, because the practice of commissioning stone carvings for the imperial tombs had been abolished.[153] Yet although the

2.83 Envoy from a vassal country, stone, at the Yongyuling mausoleum of Zhao Xu, Emperor Shenzong. 220 × 87 cm.

2.84 Horse decorated for imperial procession, with grooms, stone, at the Yongtailing mausoleum of Zhao Xu, Emperor Zhezong. 204 × 260 cm (horse) and 268 × 305 cm (grooms).

Southern Song emperors decided to forgo stone sculpture in their own tombs, stone carvings were still erected in the tombs of certain officials. Some of these have survived to this day. The sculptures are mainly likenesses of court ministers, warriors, goats, and tigers; the images and style are inherited from the Northern Song, but there are occasional new additions as well. As an example, along the Spirit Path leading to the tomb of Shi Zhao, built in 1130 at Lake Qian, east of Ningbo in Zhejiang Province, the usual procession of goats, tigers, horses, court officials, and warriors is rounded out by a pair of carved stone chairs unlike anything found elsewhere. They are life-size renditions of the "wooden chair for lantern hanging" in Southern Song style. Both the seat and the back of the chair are impeccably carved, as is the footstool in front of it, providing valuable insight into not only Song-dynasty stone work but also furniture styles of that era.[154]

On the eastern side of Mount Jiangjun in Yunxiao County, Fujian Province, ten stone imperial attendants, accompanied by ceremonial horses, reclining goats, lions to guard the gates, and pillars, were erected in pairs along the Spirit Path of the tomb of Chen Zheng of the Tang dynasty in 1240, during the Southern Song.[155] The two horses are of different designs. One is saddled and bridled in the conventional manner. The other, however, is wearing a complete set of armor, its head is veiled, and on the buckle of its neckband is carved a fairly large tiger's head, its mouth yawning wide as if to bite the horse on the neck. The armor extends below the belly, and the saddle is finely engraved with an unusual ornamental relief pattern of a flying phoenix chasing a deer. This style of armored horse, found nowhere else and obviously not in keeping with the Song ceremonial system, may well be a local innovation in an area that during the Song years was still considered a frontier.

To the north and northwest of the Song territory were a number of political regimes established by non-Han peoples. These included the Western Xia (1038–1227), established by the Dangxiang people; the Liao (916–1125), formed by the Khitans; and the Jin (1115–1234), established by the Jurchens. Notwithstanding their distinctive cultural characteristics, these non-Han regimes show evidence in their imperial tombs of familiarity with Tang and Song burial traditions: specifically, they all are adorned with stone sculptures.

After annihilating the Western Xia, Genghis Khan's Mongol horde largely destroyed the nine imperial tombs and 207 auxiliary tombs that formed the imperial

2.85 Auspicious bird with the head of an animal, stone relief, at the Yongtailing mausoleum of Zhao Xu, Emperor Zhezong. 227 × 165 cm.

necropolis of the Western Xia at the foot of the Helan Mountains west of Yinchuan, capital of the Ningxia Hui Autonomous Region.[156] The invading troops smashed to pieces the stone tomb figures positioned in the "moon city" of each of the imperial tombs. Only fragments of the pedestals were left scattered about the site.

One theory puts the number of stone figures for each of these imperial tombs at about thirty, but there is no telling what the figures might have looked like.[157] Fragments of sculpted heads and bodies discovered at Tomb 1 and Tomb 6 suggest that there were human figures among them. Stone figures unearthed from the tombs shed some light on the sculptural techniques of the time. These include a reclining stone horse, 130 centimeters long, from the underground passageway to auxiliary Tomb M177.

The horse appears dull and inert, and all sculptural details were omitted save for the mouth, nose, eyes, and two wisps of hair below the ears. The techniques used were crude and almost childish. It can be inferred that the forms and techniques were of about the same caliber for all the other stone tomb animals on the premises as for this reclining horse. From the stele pavilions of

2.86 Stone statues along the Spirit Path of the Huangling mausoleum, Fengyang County, Anhui Province. Ming dynasty.

imperial Tombs 3, 6, and 8, too, archaeologists have found a number of huge sandstone pedestals with flat tops; on their sides are carved images of people on their knees carrying heavy burdens. The bodies, nude except for armbands and bracelets, have sagging breasts, rounded bellies, flat noses, round eyes, and protruding teeth. The techniques are crude and naive, and there is something puzzling about the entire composition.

As is true of imperial tombs from the Western Xia, few stone funerary figures from the Liao and the Jin have survived to this day. When an investigation was conducted of the tomb of Yelü'abaoji, or Emperor Taizu of the Liao, at Ju Ud in Inner Mongolia, a fragmented figure was found: a stone man wearing a robe with tight sleeves and a waistband and a long pigtail hanging down his back, who was standing with his hands crossed in front.[158] This could be one of the attendants that stood along the Spirit Path to this Liao imperial tomb. During the Liao and the Jin, the Spirit Paths at the tombs of officials were also decorated with stone figures. Seven pairs of them, consisting of pillars, tigers, goats, civil officials, and warriors, are preserved at the tombs of the family of Wanyan Xiyin, Left Grand Councillor of the Jin, in Shulan County, Jilin Province. The stone tigers are squatting, the goats are lying down, and the court officials are standing on the eastern side of the Spirit Path, facing the warriors positioned opposite them. Their forms hark back to Northern Song

models, but their poses are less interesting and animated. Moreover, the chiseling techniques used to make them were primitive.[159]

Tomb Sculpture from the Ming and the Qing

When the Yuan defeated the Southern Song, its emperors chose not to follow the Song funerary traditions with regard to stone figures. After Zhu Yuanzhang established the Ming, he began building a tomb for his parents in 1369. The tomb, known as the Zuling mausoleum of the Ming, is situated to the southwest of the seat of Fengyang County, Anhui Province, or about 5 kilometers from the Ming capital city of Zhongdu (literally, "middle capital"). Stone figures there, unlike those of the Tang and Song, were placed in the tomb's inner city, arrayed from north to south (the front gate of the Zuling mausoleum was unusual among those of ancient Chinese tombs: instead of facing southward, it was in the north so that it could face the capital city of the dynasty). Altogether, the tomb boasted thirty-two pairs of animals (including horses accompanied by grooms), court officials, warriors, and attendants (figs. 2.86, 2.87).[160] In 1385 the emperor had tombs built for his great-great-grandfather, great-grandfather, and grandfather in Yangjiadun to the north of Sizhou, in

2.87 Stone horse and grooms along the Spirit Path of the Huangling mausoleum.

2.88 Stone statues along the Spirit Path of the Zuling mausoleum, Xuyi County, Jiangsu Province. Ming dynasty.

2.89 Stone statues along the Spirit Path of the Xiaoling mausoleum of Zhu Yuanzhang, Emperor Taizu, Zhongshan, Nanjing. Ming dynasty.

2.90 Stone animals along the Spirit Path of the Thirteen Tombs of the Ming, Changping district, Beijing. Ming dynasty.

Fengyang Prefecture (now Mingling village, in Renji Township, Xuyi County, Jiangsu Province). Two years later, Zhu Yuanzhang had the Hall of the Memorial Tablet and Ancillary Hall built and imperial attendants carved from stone erected at the site.

In 1680 the Zuling mausoleum of the Ming was submerged during a devastating flood; it would remain under Lake Hongze for almost three centuries. When it finally resurfaced in the 1960s, after the lake had dried up, all the buildings had vanished except for their foundations. The stone figures from the Spirit Path, however, though they had toppled over, were by and large well preserved.[161] They offer examples of pillars, squatting lions, horses and their grooms, courtiers, and generals. The stone pillars and lions are similar in shape to those of the Song, and the presence of a groom on either side of a horse is definitely a reversion to Song style. Indeed, the discovery of stone figures from the Zuling mausoleum of the Ming indicates that a resurgence of Spirit Path stone sculpture took place two and a half centuries after the fall of the Northern Song (fig. 2.88). It also shows that, during the Hongwu reign of the early Ming, the various systems were still in their formative stage, and that even though the tradition of stone tomb sculpture had been restored, it did little more than assimilate the forms of its Northern Song

predecessors, given that new standards and forms had yet to be invented in the new dynasty.

It was not until the Xiaoling mausoleum was built for Zhu Yuanzhang, or Emperor Taizu, at Dulongfu, south of Mount Zhong (Zhijin) in the eastern suburbs of present-day Nanjing, that the Ming established their own standards for imperial tomb sculpture.[162] Though the buildings of the Xiaoling mausoleum were demolished by the Taiping rebels in the waning years of the Qing, its stone figures remained somewhat intact. They include lions, xiezhi, camels, elephants, unicorns, and horses, two pairs of each, with one pair standing and the other squatting or reclining (fig. 2.89). There are also a pair of stone pillars, two pairs of court officials, and two pairs of generals. Envoys from vassal countries and auspicious birds found among Song imperial tomb figures are conspicuous by their absence in the assembly at the Xiaoling mausoleum, and no longer was any distinction made between generals wearing court robes and warriors in armor: all the generals were depicted in full armor and holding a golden melon (the long club described earlier). Meanwhile, the stone grooms found at the imperial tombs built in the early days of the Ming had been abolished, and stone horses, having lost their unique ceremonial status, were placed with the other animals. The stone attendants, of stocky build, were depicted in traditional stances. Elaborate attention was paid to detail: the helmet and armor worn by the generals, for example, were carved meticulously and accurately. The stone animals, however, are so highly stylized in their poses that they look hackneyed and phony. Chisel work was used sparingly on these stone animals, so only the contours of bodies are brought out, and there are no detailed treatment of the heads — ears, noses, and manes are simple linear patterns. Standing ponderously by the Spirit Path, where they were intended to inspire solemnity and reverence, these figures speak volumes about an age defined by the increasingly cruel autocracy of the Ming imperial court.

After Zhu Di, or Emperor Chengzu, moved the Ming capital from Nanjing to Beijing, the deceased emperors of the dynasty were buried in tombs that covered an area 40 kilometers in circumference at the foot of the Tianshou Mountains in Changping district, Beijing. The remains of thirteen emperors were buried there — hence the description "Thirteen Tombs of the Ming."[163] Unlike the imperial necropolis of the Northern Song, the imperial tombs of the Ming were enclosed behind one wall, which followed the contours of the surrounding foothills, and they shared one front gate. A huge marble archway, along with stone tablets, stood in front of the front gate to mark the place where visitors were to stop and dismount. Inside the front gate are Spirit Paths leading to various tombs.

Though each of the tombs had its own garden and Spirit Path, only the Spirit Path of the Changling mausoleum of Emperor Chengzu was adorned with stone sculptures, which may well be regarded as having been intended to serve for the entire Ming necropolis. Entrance to the Spirit Path is by a stele pavilion with a ceremonial marble column at each of its four corners. Under the roof of the pavilion is a tall stele that bears the inscription "Tablet of the Divine Merit and Sage Virtue of Changling of the Great Ming." Behind the stele pavilion, twelve pairs of impressive stone animals line both sides of the Spirit Path. Following the model of the Xiaoling mausoleum of Nanjing, the procession includes four lions, four xiezhi, four camels, four elephants, four unicorns, and four horses. In each group one pair is standing and the other kneeling. They are

2.91 Civilian official, stone, standing next to the Spirit Path of the Thirteen Tombs of the Ming.

2.92 General, stone, standing next to the Spirit Path of the Thirteen Tombs of the Ming.

2.93 Official who did great deeds, stone, standing next to the Spirit Path of the Thirteen Tombs of the Ming.

2.94 Stone statues along the Spirit Path of the Fuling mausoleum of Nurhachi, Emperor Taizu, Shenyang, Liaoning Province. Qing dynasty.

2.95 Stone statues along the Spirit Path of the Yuling mausoleum of the Qianlong emperor, Eastern Qing tombs, Zunhua, Hebei Province. Qing dynasty.

2.96 Stone lion at the Yuling mausoleum of the Qianlong emperor.

2.97 Stone lion at the Yuling mausoleum of the Qianlong emperor.

2.98 Stone *qilin* at the Yuling mausoleum of the Qianlong emperor.

2.99 Commemorative stone pillar at the Tailing mausoleum of Emperor Yongzheng, Western Qing tombs, Yixian County, Hebei Province. Qing dynasty.

2.100 Decorative stone pillar at the Tailing mausoleum of Emperor Yongzheng.

identical to the Xiaoling forms in every sculptural aspect. The series of stone animals is followed by twelve stone attendants in six pairs, including four military officials, four civil courtiers, and four meritorious officials, who strike the same stately pose and wear the same kinds of robes and armor as those standing by the Xiaoling mausoleum — capturing exactly the ethos of the Ming empire (figs. 2.90, 2.91, 2.92, 2.93).

Shortly after Zhu Yuanzhang came to power, he enfeoffed his sons in different parts of the country. Spirit Path stone figures have been found in front of the tombs of these princes. The stone sculptures at the tomb of the prince of Jingjiang, southwest of Mount Yao in Guilin in the Guangxi Zhuang Autonomous Region, are of a lower grade than those adorning the imperial tombs, but the local style is unmistakable. In and around Nanjing, stone steles and sculptures have also been found at the tombs of famous courtiers who made outstanding contributions to the nascent Ming empire, including Duke Chang Yuchun of Kaiping, Duke Deng Yu of Ninghe, Duke Li Wenzhong of Qiyang, and Duke Xu Da of Zhongshan.[164] The sculptures at the tombs of Deng Yu, Li Wenzhong, and Xu Da are still in relatively good condition. Mostly created during the Hongwu reign (1368–1398), earlier than those found at the Xiaoling mausoleum, these stone sculptures have strong affinities with those of the Zuling mausoleum, and they usually include grooms and saddled and bridled horses. Narrower in scope and smaller in number than those adorning imperial mausoleums, they generally consist of pairs of pillars, courtiers, generals, horses and grooms, goats, and tigers. Those erected at Xu Da's tomb are larger and more finely crafted than those at the other courtiers' tombs. The patterns of clouds and cranes, the S-shaped scepter, and the Chinese character for "longevity" carved on the cloaks of the courtiers, for example, are all rendered in finely incised detail.

The stone sculpture for imperial mausoleums of the Qing (1644–1911) closely followed Ming imperial models in both content and form. The stone sculptures along the Spirit Paths to the Fuling mausoleum north of the Great Wall (fig. 2.94) and the eastern Qing tombs (figs. 2.95, 2.96, 2.97, 2.98) and western Qing tombs south of the Great Wall (figs. 2.99, 2.100), had the same lineup of courtiers, generals, horses, unicorns, elephants, lions, camels, and *suanni* (ferocious-looking mythological beasts resembling lions). The main differences are to be found in the attire and hairstyle of the stone men — the Qing stone men all have pigtails and official headdresses with accessories differentiated to indicate their rank.

The demise of the Qing dynasty brought several thousand years of Chinese feudal monarchy to an end. In the early years of the Republic (1911–1949), the notorious Yuan Shikai attempted to crown his success on the Chinese political scene by founding a new dynasty and declaring himself emperor, but his restoration campaign, under the dynastic title of Hongxian, ended in utter failure. After his death, the Spirit Path to his tomb was decorated with a series of stone figures. Among these sculptures the attendants, stout, short, and unattractive, were depicted wearing the army uniform of Yuan's time. This unfortunate collection of stone figures forms a rather inglorious coda to the rich history of Chinese tombstone sculpture — a history that adds a unique three-dimensional perspective to our understanding of the funerary rituals, political and social customs, and daily lives of the ancient Chinese.

Part II   The Religious Tradition

BUDDHAS, SAGES, AND HEAVENLY WORTHIES

CHAPTER 3

From the Han to the Southern Song

ANGELA FALCO HOWARD

The initial spread of Buddhism during the Eastern Han (25–220 C.E.) in Sichuan, the southern provinces along the Yangzi River, and China's coastal regions dramatically influenced the development of Chinese sculpture. During this formative stage, Buddhist representations did not correspond to canonical teachings; instead, they described popular Daoist beliefs. This art, called *proto-Buddhist* because the Chinese had not yet completely absorbed Buddhist principles, was composed chiefly of funerary items — displays in tombs or burial objects such as money trees, mirrors, and urns.

Gautama Siddhartha, the founder of Buddhism, was born in 563 B.C.E. in Kapilavastu (in present-day Bihar, northeast India). His religious fervor grew out of his desire to explain and avoid the cycle of endless reincarnation due to karma, whereby a good cause produces a good effect, and a bad cause an evil one. According to Brahmanic beliefs of the time, these effects of karma determine whether, upon death, one will be reborn into a good or evil destiny. At age twenty-nine Gautama Siddhartha renounced his princely status and began practicing the most rigorous asceticism in order to resolve this metaphysical problem. He was thirty-five when he attained Buddhahood, that is, when he understood how to extinguish reincarnation. After a long life of preaching in the Gangetic Plain of northeast India, in 483 the Buddha died attaining Parinirvana, the final release. Posthumously he was addressed as Shakyamuni, alluding to his birth in the Shakya tribe, a name that also came to mean the historical Buddha.

Full views, figure 3.19 (*opposite*) and figure 3.31 (*above*)

In general terms, to become a Buddha (or to become Enlightened) meant to clearly discern that human existence is characterized by suffering and that one must find the root of suffering, eradicate it, and pursue enlightenment through a set of rules fostering meditation and spiritual discipline. By the middle of the third century B.C.E., under King Ashoka of the Mauryan empire, Buddhism had spread from the Ganges River basin throughout India. During this pre-Mahayana stage (also called *Hinayana,* meaning Smaller Vehicle), marked by the rise of numerous sects, Buddhist teaching centered on the life of the deified founder and his original message.

By approximately the second century B.C.E., Buddhism had evolved into a second phase, the *Mahayana* (Great Vehicle), which professed the universal character of enlightenment and promised the practitioner the help of bodhisattvas. Mahayanists believed that bodhisattvas were supernatural beings who had reached such a high spiritual level as to be able to become Buddhas but who had, out of extreme compassion, forgone Buddhahood in order to help sentient beings perfect themselves and follow in their footsteps. In Mahayana Buddhism, the quest for spiritual salvation became a shared journey.

In the Kushan empire of the first and second centuries C.E., chiefly Mahayana Buddhism spread eastward beyond India. Mahayanists believed in a plurality of Buddhas: the historical Buddha, Shakyamuni, was thought to be merely one manifestation, because he had been preceded by several Buddhas and was to be followed by one. They were also devoted to the idea of Pure Lands, or paradises, where a meritorious Buddhist could reside for a given length of time, temporarily postponing, but not renouncing, the final goal of entering Nirvana.[1]

During the Mahayana phase the fashioning of images for the dual purposes of worship and attaining merit became central to Buddhism. The Prajnaparamita Sutra laid out a central precept of the era: "The reason that Buddha images are fashioned is merely the wish to enable men to gain merit.... After the Buddha's Parinirvana, it will be in recollection of the Buddha that His images shall be fashioned, out of the wish to enable sentient beings to make offerings to them and gain the merit thereof."[2] This canonical demand had a tremendous effect on the figurative arts of China and generated a great tradition of sculpture as this foreign religion extended its reach throughout the country.

Two historical factors led to the introduction of Buddhism to China: the expansionist policies of the Han empire during the first half of the dynasty (206 B.C.E.–9 C.E.) and the erosion of Han power and traditional Confucian ideology during the second half of the dynasty (25–220 C.E.). Han imperial expansion during the two centuries preceding the Common Era opened and consolidated several routes of communication linking China to the rest of the world. The Silk Road extended through central Asia to the Mediterranean; a maritime route connected China's southwest coast to Indochina and India; and the "southern Silk Road" linked the province of Sichuan to India via Yunnan and Myanmar (Burma). Buddhism eventually reached China through these conduits.[3] The weakening Han empire on the eve of the first millennium also favored and hastened the reception of Buddhism by the Chinese. Gradual political and economic instability generated a loss of confidence in the administrators and the Confucian ideology they represented.

During the Han empire, Confucianism and Daoism were the two traditional philosophies. Confucianism, a rather pragmatic moral and ethical code designed to maintain harmony between the ruler and the ruled, did not consider the possibility of an afterworld, although court ritual and ancestor worship were basic duties of the elite. In fact, in the *Analects* of Confucius (*Lunyu*), Confucius defined Wisdom as dedicating oneself to serving the needs of others, and respecting spirits and gods while keeping one's distance from them. As for Death, Confucius believed that people do not understand Life and so could not possibly fathom its opposite.

Daoism, on the other hand, encouraged individualism and withdrawal from society, when necessary, to pursue the Dao — that is, the supreme principle that governs the universe. Although very interested in the prospect of immortality attainable through alchemy, as well as through dietary, breathing, and sexual practices, the Daoists had not yet systematized a pantheon of gods nor forged soteriological theories.[4] These missing elements were soon to be provided by the imported religion of Buddhism, which offered concrete notions on the afterlife and on specific gods.

Disaffection for the dynasty and its Confucian administrators likely caused the Chinese to turn for solace to Daoism, especially its popularized forms. Buddhism entered China at this time of internal weakness. In its earliest phase Buddhism was embraced, not because of its doctrine but rather because it was perceived as an offshoot of Daoism, particularly in the popular cult of the Queen Mother of the West (Xiwangmu). The Five Pecks of Rice (Wudoumi) Dao, one of the earliest Daoist sects, became active in Sichuan during the late Eastern Han contemporaneously with the introduction of Buddhism in the same region.[5] The images produced by the two religions mingled.

In its formative stage during the Eastern Han, Buddhism was a hybrid religion, neither practiced according to the scriptures nor supported by a monastic body. This situation contrasted sharply with the state of Buddhism in India, where the religion was based on an extensive canon, supported by numerous monastic communities, and practiced by means of elaborate rituals centering on numerous deities.

Through numerous literary sources, we know that members of the Eastern Han court and imperial family practiced Buddhism alongside Daoist rituals known as Huang-Lao. The *History of the Later Han* (*Hou Han shu*) and several post-Han sources, for example, relate the prophetic dream of Emperor Ming (r. 58–76 C.E.), in which the Indian god appeared as a golden being, prompting the emperor to seek the foreign religion. The *History of the Later Han* also records that Liu Ying, king of Chu (the half brother of Emperor Ming), sponsored a vegetarian feast for Buddhist monks and laymen at his court in Pengcheng, Jiangsu, in 65 C.E.: "The Prince of Chu recites the obscure words of the Yellow Emperor and Laozi, he does honor to the Buddha's temples of forbearance. Having purified himself and fasted for three months, he makes a vow to his god." Similarly, "Emperor Huan (r. 147–149) planned the Palace of the Gleaming Dragon and equipped it with flowered canopies/honorific umbrellas for the worship of Buddha and Laozi."[6]

A more popular type of Buddhism developed parallel to the "court" religion. Isolated proto-Buddhist notions were combined with the earliest Daoist beliefs such as those of the aforementioned Wudoumi Dao, in particular the thriving cult of the Queen Mother of the West. By the first century C.E., this cult was well established in China, particularly in the southwest province of Sichuan.[7] It centered on a goddess, the Queen Mother, said to reside in the Kunlun Mountains, west of China. As a divine savior and helper in times of crisis, the Queen Mother was believed to bestow immortality through an elixir concocted by her retinue of strange animals: hare, three-legged crow, nine-tailed fox, and frog.

The Queen Mother was the first deity to be represented by the Chinese. Her image was carved on stone or modeled on brick and adorned the tombs of the wealthy, along the upper part of the wall below the ceiling, to indicate a heavenly space. Typically she is shown frontally, seated on a throne under a baldachin, guarded on each side by a dragon and a tiger, typical symbols in Han funerary art. In the 40-centimeter-high brick relief housed in the Sichuan Provincial Museum, she wears a special headdress (a jade bar across her forehead), is wrapped in an all-enveloping robe, and is attended by her motley crew of helpers (fig. 3.1).

As the Queen Mother's cult gained in popularity, notions and descriptions of the Buddha began to circulate in China. According to these legends, Buddha also was a deity from the West, appearing in the form of a golden body, endowed with supernatural powers like an immortal sylph (moving through the heavens and able to assume different guises), and, most important, willing to help people in need. For the Chinese, several aspects of this foreign god were similar to the divine attributes of the Queen Mother; hence Buddha was mistakenly regarded as a relative of the goddess and incorporated into her cult. During the second century C.E., in Sichuan, the two deities' images became very closely linked, if not interchangeable.

Many proto-Buddhist images have been found in Sichuan tombs. The best known is the Buddha relief in the Mahao tomb of Leshan, along the eastern bank of the Min River, which is ascribed to the late second century C.E. (fig. 3.2; see also fig. 1.67). (A similar carving is found in the Shiziwan tomb of Leshan.)[8] The Buddha, 37 centimeters high, was carved on the lintel above the door leading to the inner burial chamber — the place normally occupied by a depiction of the Queen Mother of the West. The image of Buddha was fashioned after an Indian model from the Bactro-Gandharan region (present-day Pakistan) during the Kushana period (late first to third century C.E.). The Mahao Buddha is shown strictly from the front, his head surrounded by a nimbus, and is marked by one of the essential physical traits symbolizing his enlightened nature: the *ushnisha*, the cranial protuberance denoting superhuman wisdom.[9] He wears a monastic robe held by his left hand; his right hand gives the fear-not gesture.[10]

The Mahao and Shiziwan tomb Buddhas cannot be linked to any text source translated in Han China, and thus are most likely the product of copying from an imported icon, not a result of evangelization. Fur-

3.1 Queen Mother of the West, brick relief. Eastern Han dynasty. Sichuan Provincial Museum, Chengdu.

3.2 Buddha, stone relief, Mahao Cliff Tomb 1, Leshan, Sichuan Province. Eastern Han dynasty, late 2d–early 3d century C.E.

thermore, the use of Buddhist motifs in China was inconsistent with standard Buddhist practice. The Mahao and Shiziwan Buddha reliefs, for example, are part of an underground burial and share that space with other non-Buddhist images. In orthodox Buddhism, such icons were never placed in burial sites, because they were intended for worship in temples or private dwellings.

Gilt-bronze money trees — also linked to the Wudoumi Dao movement — marked a further development in the cult of the Queen Mother and reflected how Buddhism was grafted to local religious beliefs during its initial hybrid phase in China. Money trees have been found in Sichuan at the sites of Mianyang, Pengshan, Guanghan, Zhongxian, and Xichang, suggesting that the cult was widespread in the province and followed fluvial arteries, the Yangzi River and its tributaries. These artifacts are dated from the late second to early third century, which corresponds to the late Eastern Han–early Three Kingdoms period.[11] The money tree excavated from Tomb 2 at Hejiashan, Mianyang (1.98 meters high), is the largest known tree, and it is made of twenty-nine parts that form the stand, trunk, and crown (fig. 3.3). The branches stretching in the four cardinal directions carry birds, deer, elephants with their keepers, and *wu* coins, together with the immortals and the Queen Mother — the most important feature — who is seated on her throne. A large bird, possibly a solar symbol, crowns the alluring and mysterious tree.[12]

At this stage the cult of the Queen Mother became associated with "land-god" worship, in which material goals seem dominant. (Alternatively, the profuse use of coins may allude to generous offerings to the Mother by her worshipers.) In some of the money trees discovered in Sichuan, another feature is present. In the Mianyang artifact, for example, as many as five Buddhas are attached to the trunk of the tree (fig. 3.4), each one strikingly similar to the Buddha carved in the Mahao tomb. Here the two deities, Buddha and the Queen Mother of the West, coexist: Buddha is placed on the axial trunk, the Queen Mother on the branches.

Moreover, the two deities became interchangeable. The clay base of the money tree was usually decorated with a representation of the mountainous world over which the Queen Mother presides from the summit (see fig. 1.61). Occasionally, however, the image of the Buddha replaces that of the goddess, as in the artifact excavated from a Pengshan tomb showing the Buddha flanked by two foreign figures, one of them possibly a monk.

3.3 Money tree, bronze, from Tomb 2, Hejiashan, Mianyang, Sichuan Province. Eastern Han dynasty, late 2d century. Cultural Relics Bureau, Sichuan Province.

3.4 Schematic drawing of Buddha attached to trunk of Mianyang money tree.

During the late Han to early Three Kingdoms period, a variety of Buddhist motifs adorned Sichuan tombs. On a tile from the Shenfang burial near Guanghan, Buddhist traces consist of stupas (Buddhist funerary monuments) enclosed by *bodhi* trees, under one of which Buddha attained enlightenment. At the Tujing burial near Zhongxian, pottery figurines use fear-not hand gestures, lotuses (symbols of purity and the transcendental state) adorn their headdress, and the *urna* (a special Buddhist mark, a dot or tuft of hair between the eyebrows) is visible. These motifs reveal that the deceased or his descendants were conversant with Buddhism and its symbols. The tomb makers, however, placed such symbols in a non-Buddhist context, distorting them into propitious safeguards for the afterworld.[13]

A pottery house model (61 centimeters high and 68 centimeters long), one of a set of five retrieved from Tomb 5 of Tujing, Zhongxian, is another example of proto-Buddhist motifs used in an unusual way (fig. 3.5). Its roof and corner posts are decorated with lotus flowers, and, more interestingly, inside the house are foreign-looking figures, such as a flutist making music and others possibly engaged in prayer for the benefit of a recumbent image, perhaps the deceased.[14]

Although these pottery homes remain an enigma, they probably served to protect the spirit of the deceased. Furthermore, they may reflect an emerging belief in a Buddhist Pure Land. As discussed above, when Buddhism started to spread in China, it did not rely on profound theological teachings, but caught the imagination of people at large with its exotic ceremonies and the novelty of its icons. The occupants of the house are perhaps engaged in a Buddhist religious ceremony, praying for the deceased so that he may enjoy prosperity in the afterworld. The imagery suggests that Buddhist rites increasingly coexisted with Daoist rites.[15]

The use of Buddhist symbols and the clear allusion to foreigners in the Sichuan burials raise the question of which route was most active in the transmission of Buddhism. It could have been the southern route (India, Myanmar, Yunnan, Sichuan), although almost no archaeological discovery in Yunnan has yet confirmed this. Traditionally, scholars have favored the transmission of Buddhism to Sichuan via the central Asian route or the Silk Road. But more recently the Chinese scholar Wu Zhuo has proposed an alternative route. He believes that travelers entered China from central Asia, but rather than proceeding along the Hexi corridor in Gansu they deviated toward Qinghai, then moved eastward into Sichuan near the present region of Aba and southward along the Min River to its confluence with the Yangzi River. The retrieval of numerous proto-Buddhist artifacts in several burial sites along the Min River supports this hypothesis. Furthermore, documents such as *Three Kingdoms* (*Sanguozhi;* the biographies of Hou Zhu in the *Book of Shu* and of Guo Huai in the *Book of Wei*) relate that rival factions of Cao Wei occupied the Hexi corridor in the late third century, at the time of the famous Shu general Zhuge Liang, making it impossible to use.[16]

Proto-Buddhist Images of the Coastal Provinces

The mingling of images of the Queen Mother of the West and representations of Buddha also occurred in the northeast province of Shandong, in the well-known tomb at Yinan, built approximately during the second half of the second century C.E. One encounters there the same mixture of popular Daoist motifs and Buddhist symbols taken out of context. On the surface of an octagonal stone pillar are various reliefs, including those of the Queen Mother accompanied by her consort, Dongwanggong, the Duke Father of the East, and a seated personage with strong affinities to the Buddha flanked by two figures (fig. 3.6).[17]

Furthermore, during the Three Kingdoms period (222–265) and the Jin dynasty (265–317), bronze mirrors found chiefly in Zhejiang and Jiangsu treated these deities interchangeably. These mirrors, known as *shenshoujing* (immortals and mythical animals mirrors) were decorated on the axis with the Queen Mother and her consort. When the couple were replaced with repre-

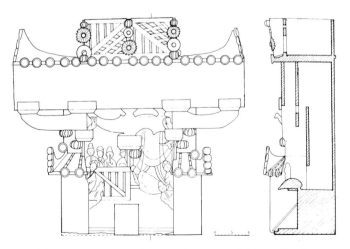

3.5 Schematic drawing of pottery house model from Tomb 5, Tujing, Zhongxian County, Sichuan Province, from the 3d century.

sentations of Buddha seated or standing, the mirrors were named *Foshoujing* (Buddha and mythical animals mirrors). Several examples dated to the fourth century also have been found in Japan, where they may have been imported from China or manufactured after a Chinese model.[18]

The ceramic soul urns (*hunping*) found exclusively in Zhejiang and Jiangsu are also extraordinary examples of a cultural synthesis between traditional Chinese beliefs regarding burial and Buddhist practices and teaching. These green-glazed soul urns were manufactured between 250 and 300. The urn excavated in 1955 in the outskirts of Nanjing (46 centimeters high) is ascribed to the Western Jin period. The decoration of its upper part — possibly a re-creation of a celestial setting — consists of pavilions and *que* towers and birds drinking from squat, round vases (fig. 3.7). Small, seated Buddhas are attached at the waist (and above the waist) of the urn. In other examples, rows of Buddhas occupy the summit of the urn — thus displacing the celestial landscape.[19]

These containers may express shamanistic beliefs found throughout southern China since the time of the kingdom of Chu (Eastern Zhou period). The urns would entice the soul of the deceased by representing a pleasurable place in which to reside. Moreover, the urns may have had a specific burial purpose. When a body was lost, such as that of a soldier who was killed in battle and whose remains never were recovered, the family would make an urn and place it in the deceased's tomb. If the soul came back, it would live in the urn.[20]

The Buddhist practice of placing ashes in reliquaries also may have been incorporated in the making of soul urns. In fact, the type of Buddha attached to the urn is reminiscent of the Buddha used in the famous Kanishka reliquary of the Kushan king (ca. second century C.E.) from the Shah-ji-ki-Dheri stupa, near Peshawar.[21] Furthermore, the depiction of a wonderland inhabited by humans, with pavilions surrounded by trees and animals, may have been a very early attempt to render a Buddhist Pure Land. The monk Zhi Qian, in fact, translated the Larger Sukhavativyuha Sutra (The Land of Bliss), one of the earliest texts to describe such a paradisiacal setting, into Chinese between 223 and 253 in the coastal kingdom of Wu, where the urns were made.[22]

The link to Buddhism is strengthened by the wording of the inscriptions sometimes accompanying an urn. The inscription on a soul urn in the collection of the Shanghai Museum, for example, expresses the wish that

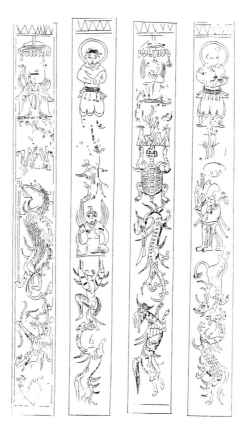

3.6 Drawings of octagonal stone pillar, Yinan tomb, Shandong Province, from the second half of the 2d century.

this funerary receptacle be beneficial to the progeny and procure endless happiness and accumulation of merits.[23] This citation reflects a synthesis of traditional Chinese beliefs (that the urn protects the deceased and benefits his offspring) and Mahayana concerns with gathering merits.

Other dramatic examples of the fusion of popular Daoism and Buddhism in art are the approximately 105 representations incised on large boulders at the site of Mount Kongwang, near Lianyungang, northern Jiangsu. As this technique was used during the Han, they are generally dated to the second to third century C.E.[24] The representations on these boulders of monks, seated images (among them the Queen Mother of the West), and a crowded Mahaparinirvana (the great release from the reincarnation cycle) superficially resemble Buddhist images, but they could also be the product of Daoist circles, which exercised a strong influence in this area. Because Daoists considered Buddha a manifestation of Laozi, their founder, they may have appropriated Buddhist images as well. The specific meaning of this art is still debated; nevertheless, Kongwangshan certainly demonstrates the imprecise boundaries between popular Daoism and Buddhism at the end of the Han and immediately after, a phenomenon that profoundly marks this earliest phase of Chinese Buddhism.

The earliest "orthodox" Buddhist art has not been found in China (in this sense, *orthodox* means responding to Buddhist teaching). No material traces remain of the so-called court Buddhism, for example, which manifested itself at the highest levels of society according to various records. Nevertheless, foreign merchants and Buddhist monks are known to have traveled to Luoyang; the Parthian monk Anshigao arrived in the Eastern Han capital in 128 C.E. and taught chiefly non-Mahayana and meditational practices. The Scythian monk Lokakshema arrived in Luoyang in 167 to teach Mahayana, especially the doctrine of emptiness.

Even though travelers along the Silk Road journeyed to the northern metropolitan centers, it is perplexing that no Buddhist art made during the Eastern Han has been found in northern China near Xi'an and Luoyang, the two Han capitals. Foreigners (monks and laymen) must have imported Buddhist images for their own devotional use; educated Buddhists may have made additional Buddhist images in northern China, though they probably were not blended with indigenous Chinese religions and local cults like those images previously described. As orthodox Buddhist images placed in temples or households for private devotion, they were probably much more susceptible to destruction than those fashioned for underground burials — a usage never intended by the Buddhist ritual. This could explain why no orthodox Buddhist art has been found in northern China.

Significantly, the proto-Buddhist artifacts discussed here are rather crudely executed and do not rise above the level of copying imported models. The makers' goal remained that of supplying images for worship. Indeed, the techniques and styles used in the clay reliefs, bronze money trees, incised boulders, and clay tablets continue in the style of Han funerary art. Even the few stone reliefs of Buddha, such as the Mahao image, are still rooted in the former Han mode, which in one sense cannot be termed sculptural because the idea of volume had not yet been mastered.

The crucial innovation of proto-Buddhist art was the subject matter itself, a divine image that was the focal point of the new religion. From tentative beginnings the few Buddha reliefs fashioned in the late Han proved to be the important foundation of a craft that would soon become three-dimensional and evolve through the centuries into a highly sophisticated art form. The key role played by images in Buddhist devotion forced the Chinese to forge a sculpture independent of burial practices, to abandon their penchant for abstraction (which had dominated the metal age), and to turn to figurative art. Stone sculpture was the gift of Indian Buddhism to China, as it became the medium par excellence of the imported faith, just as jade and metal had been the favorite medium for indigenous, pre-Buddhist rituals.

Cave-Temple Sculpture in Gansu During the Liang and Qin

In the early fourth century, the collapse of China's central government was imminent. Nomadic invaders, who for centuries had loomed on the northern and northwestern borders, conquered Luoyang in 311 and took Chang'an six years later. From the viewpoint of the native Chinese elite, the former Middle Kingdom had plunged into the Dark Ages. Yet this was also the period in which Buddhism was gradually transformed into a Chinese religion. During the fourth century, Buddhist art of Gansu Province in northwest China evolved into a fully fledged Buddhist form.

Unlike the art of the southwest and south, Gansu's Buddhist art was neither proto-Buddhist nor strongly influenced by Daoist cults. This art, typically situated in cave temples — sacred spaces carved into the rock — was one result of the evangelical activity of foreign monks. Significantly, the Buddhist figures did

3.7 Green-glazed soul urn (*hunping*), Zhejiang Province. Western Jin dynasty, 280. Quzhou Municipal Museum, Zhejiang Province.

not have fully Chinese features. Undoubtedly central Asia (present-day Xinjiang) acted as the mediator of Indian iconography and of structural and stylistic aspects integral to Buddhist devotionalism.

The Xinjiang Uygur Autonomous Region, part of the People's Republic of China, is formidable and desolate. Covered largely by harsh desert and steep mountains, it seems inhospitable to human settlement and creativity. Yet archaeologists have recently found that people have traveled across this region since Neolithic times, and by the second century B.C.E., especially under the aegis of Emperor Wu (r. 140–87 B.C.E.), a trade route connected the Chinese capital of Chang'an with the Mediterranean world (map 3.1). As the route crossed out of China at the Jade Pass, it divided into northern and the southern routes, which joined again at Kashgar before crossing the Pamirs at over 6,000 meters on the way to present-day Afghanistan. Because the major item traded by the Chinese was silk, the road became known as the Silk Road.[25]

Active trade fostered the development of small kingdoms in oases along the major northern and southern passages. These kingdoms depended on the waters of the Tarim River and its tributaries, as well as on an ingenious system of underground canals fed by the melting snows of the surrounding mountains. When traveling from China to the West along the northern Silk Road, one encountered first the kingdom of Turpan, then the more modest caravan centers of Sorchuq and Karashar, the prominent kingdom of Kucha, and, finally, Kashgar. Along the southern Silk Road, the important stopping places were Niya, Loulan, Miran, Endere, Khotan, and Yarkand.

These small kingdoms and caravan centers had their own cultural and ethnic identities, but a belief in Buddhism was common to all. By the first century C.E., missionaries carrying Buddhist texts and icons were spreading Buddhism in this area. The conversion to Buddhism of the upper classes encouraged others in the region to follow suit. In keeping with the Indian tradition, monastic communities were established with their own living and sacred spaces built on the side of mountains, especially alongside the northern Silk Road. The powerful and pious converts contributed generously to this effort and sponsored the sacred art that embellished monasteries and temples. In addition, the many innovations

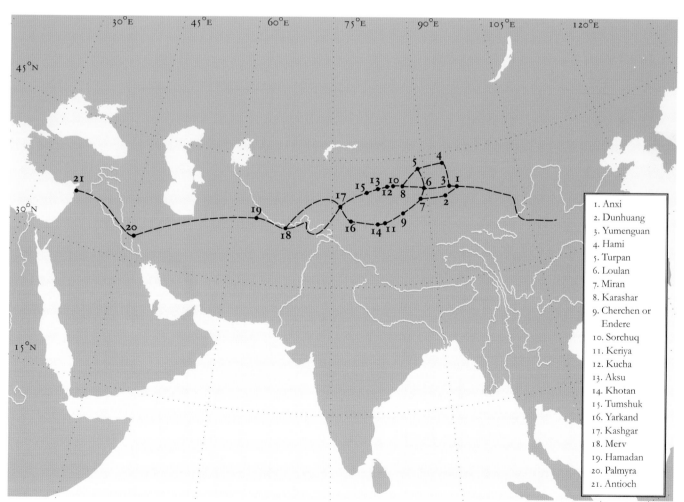

Map 3.1 The Silk Road in central Asia.

1. Anxi
2. Dunhuang
3. Yumenguan
4. Hami
5. Turpan
6. Loulan
7. Miran
8. Karashar
9. Cherchen or Endere
10. Sorchuq
11. Keriya
12. Kucha
13. Aksu
14. Khotan
15. Tumshuk
16. Yarkand
17. Kashgar
18. Merv
19. Hamadan
20. Palmyra
21. Antioch

3.8 Central pillar of Cave 38 (detail), Kizil, Xinjiang Uygur Autonomous Region. Early 4th century.

3.9 Entrance to Cave 38 (detail), Kizil.

of these creative local central Asian cultures shaped religious and artistic impulses that in turn influenced the cultures of other major Asian countries, including China.

Some scholars believe that institutionalized Buddhism on the southern Silk Road developed by the mid-third century, especially under the guidance of Indian Kushan monks, whereas the northern Silk Road developed slightly later and resulted from the evangelical work of Parthian and Sogdian clerics. In general, Buddhists along the northern route seem to have preferred pre-Mahayana teaching, whereas those along the southern route preferred Mahayana. According to such a chronology, the foreign monks who arrived in Luoyang, the Han capital, by the late second century merely passed along the Silk Road without spreading Buddhism. During the late Han, central Asia was a neutral buffer between India and China.[26]

Immediately after the Han dynasty, however, an intensified wave of evangelism promoted the rise of institutionalized Buddhism — that is, monastic communities patronized by wealthy donors. In fact, by 350

C.E., when the influential monk Kumarajiva began his career in his native Kucha, Buddhism had already reached its golden age there.[27]

The Buddhist art of the northern Silk Road is found in caves hewn out of mountainsides. In response to the needs of the clergy, caves were built specifically for performance of rituals, habitation, and assembly. These sacred places were adorned with clay sculpture and mural paintings that illustrated Buddhist teachings. The art is highly eclectic because the inhabitants of the Silk Road came into contact with many cultures, namely the classical world of Rome and Greece, India, and Persia under the Sassanian monarchy (ca. 300–600).

Among the Buddhist sites developed along the northern Silk Road, Kizil in the kingdom of Kucha was particularly influential; it in many ways shaped the Buddhist art of Gansu. This influence extended to cave structure and imagery, as well as to the styles and techniques used to create the clay statues and murals. During the past twenty years there have been several breakthroughs in the study of the Kizil caves. Carbon dating places the beginning of Kizil cave art as early as 300 C.E., possibly even earlier, and supports the theory that the making of Buddhist art in Gansu benefited immensely from the central Asian experience.[28]

Cave 38 illustrates typical features of Kizil Buddhist art in its earliest phase. The structure uses a stupa pillar layout with a large shaft of uncut rock occupying the rear space of the grotto. The Kizil stupa represents a departure from the Indian tradition and was possibly a local development; in India, stupas were freestanding with domical tops in a large, cathedral-like space carved out of the rock. This setting was designed presumably for performing the rite of circumambulation (*pradakshina*), in which devotees walked clockwise around the stupa pillar (fig. 3.8).

Although the clay sculpture of Cave 38 was destroyed, the wall frescoes are partially extant. In contemporary Chinese caves, such as Dunhuang, the iconography used in the painting is identical to that of the sculpture. The murals in Cave 38 therefore likely suggest the appearance of the former statues. The paintings that span the barrel-vaulted ceiling and the side walls focus on Theravada or other non-Mahayana themes, such as stories of Shakyamuni's last and previous lives (*jatakas*) and glorious representations of Shakyamuni assisted by *devatas*, or *devas* (heavenly beings); monks; and celestials.

The jatakas and devotionalism to Shakyamuni and Maitreya (the Buddha of the Future) are the most developed decorative themes at Kizil. Maitreya is the only bodhisattva singled out for representation in the cave. He is shown seated with crossed legs in Tushita Heaven (future Buddhas reside in this heaven prior to their final birth), where he waits to become Shakyamuni's successor in the world. This representation is placed in the lunette above the entrance door, suggesting that, fittingly, the last icon worshipers would see on their way out was that of the Buddha to come (fig. 3.9). All around the upper section of the lateral walls are painted niches that hold painted celestial musicians and are framed by ogival arches, which suggest hanging balconies.

Cave 38 exemplifies the Indo-Iranian painting style influenced by Sassanian Persia. This style, one of several coexisting at Kizil, is characterized by a vivid contrast between intensely brilliant ultramarine and green colors. The style's overall effect is decidedly two-dimensional, with flat figures placed against the once colorful background. Reduced to splendid abstractions of color on a single plane, the figures lack corporeality. A similar design of the cave's iconography, an obvious derivative of this prototype, was later used in Gansu.

By 317, at the start of the period of disunion, non-

Chinese rulers, originally nomads from the northern and northwestern borderlands, administered all of the provinces of China north of the Yellow River. The defeated Chinese Jin ruler migrated south to establish the "legitimate" Han dynasty in Jianye, near present-day Nanjing. Thus began an extremely turbulent period of history from 304 to 439 known as the Sixteen Kingdoms of the Five Nomadic Tribes, during which sixteen short-lived political entities, led by five ethnically differentiated rulers, governed northern China. These five ethnic tribes were the Xiongnu, Xianbei, Jie, Qiang, and Di. (Xiongnu and Xianbei were from Turkic and Mongolian stock, the Jie are believed to be Indoscythians, while the Qiang and Di were related to Tibetans and Tanguts.) After settling in the north, they intermarried with Chinese and, to an extent, adopted Han customs. This period of early medieval history was also marked by a tremendous increase in Buddhist devotionalism, and it represented the first stage in the sinification of Buddhism.[29]

During the Sixteen Kingdoms period, Gansu played a crucial role in the development of cave sites and Buddhist art. Local rulers in Gansu, assisted by numerous central Asian monks, undertook the transformation of central Asian Buddhist models. Between 317 and 439, the two major clans, the Liang (Xiongnu) and Qin (Xianbei, Di, and Qiang), ruled over Gansu and part of Shaanxi, respectively. The Liang and Qin, like the cen-

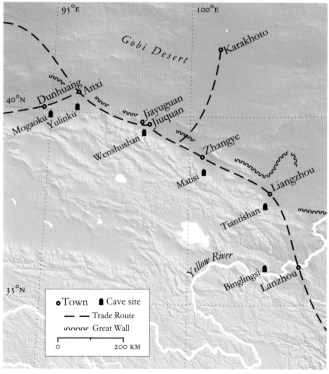

Map 3.2 Gansu's highway (Hexi corridor).

3.10 Detail of central pillar with clay images, east side, Eastern Cave of Jintasi Monastery, Zhangye, Gansu Province. 4th century.

tral Asian rulers on the Silk Road, were receptive to the teachings of visiting foreign Buddhist monks and promoted the establishment of religious communities.

Gansu's highway, known as the Hexi corridor, spanned 1,600 kilometers, or most of the province's length. A constant flow of foreigners, traders, and monks used this route on their way to China's metropolitan centers. They stopped in Dunhuang, Jiayuguan, Jiuquan, Zhangye, Wuwei, Lanzhou, and Tianshui, all of which had been set up as command posts during the Western Han (first century B.C.E.) and had become prosperous trading centers (map 3.2). As a result of local patronage, important Buddhist sites were established near these towns during the second half of the

fourth century. Of the five Liang dynasties (the Former Liang, 314–376; Later Liang, 386–403; Southern Liang, 397–414; Western Liang, 400–421; and Northern Liang, 397–439), the Former Liang was particularly important in western Gansu, because its rulers governed the area between Jiuquan and Dunhuang (and helped develop it into a Buddhist center).

During the Northern Liang, Gansu was gradually unified under the able leader Juqu Mengxun, who also had a decisive role in the development of Buddhism. During Mengxun's prestigious and lengthy reign (397–433), he played a prominent role in sponsoring work on several of the Northern Liang caves.[30] The *Collection of Miraculous Tales on Buddhism in China (Ji Shenzhou sanbao*

3.11 Detail of central pillar with clay images, west side, Eastern Cave of Jintasi Monastery.

gantong lu, compiled by Daoxuan between 596 and 667), which probably refers to the Tiantishan site, confirms his importance: "A hundred *li* to the south of his [Mengxun's] city [Wuwei], there is a line of cliffs that runs a great distance east and west. There he [Mengxun] excavated caves and installed the holy likenesses; some being of stone and others molded in clay, in so infinite a variety of forms, that those who worship are amazed and dazzled in mind and eye."[31]

I have questioned the dating of all the corridor's Buddhist art to the Northern Liang; artists of the Former Liang and Western Liang may have contributed substantially to this process, or projects initiated by an earlier Liang dynasty may have been reworked or com-

3.12 Schematic drawing of central pillar, west side, Eastern Cave of Jintasi Monastery.

3.13 Central pillar, east side, detail of upper tiers, Eastern Cave of Jintasi Monastery.

pleted by a later Liang dynasty.[32] Regardless of their date of creation, all of these Liang art sites were excavated in the coarse red sandstone of the Qilian Mountains. Caves were built near the corridor's major centers at Wenshushan (south of Jiuquan), Matisi and Jintasi Monasteries (south of Zhangye), and Tiantishan (near Wuwei). Despite damage from both natural and human causes, Wenshushan, Matisi, and Jintasi still offer significant evidence to those seeking to reconstruct Liang art. (Tiantishan was heavily damaged by an earthquake in 1927. In 1959 its remaining contents were brought to the Gansu Provincial Museum, Lanzhou.)[33]

In his pioneer study, the art historian Su Bai used the term *Liangzhou art* to characterize the Northern Liang artistic style and content, after the name of Juqu Mengxun's early territorial domain (centered on present-day Wuwei and Zhangye).[34] But here the term is used more broadly to include the contribution of earlier Liang patrons. The primary characteristics of Liangzhou (Liang) art include the use of the stupa-pillar plan, which was popular in early Kizil art; the use of iconographies, which also came from Kizil; and the embellishment of a cave with frescoes and clay sculpture. Even though

Kizil no longer has extant statues, based on other iconographic affinities we can suppose that these lost statues resembled the sculpture of Liangzhou.

Evidence from Jintasi illustrates the extent to which the Liangzhou style was influenced by the art of Kizil, while retaining distinctive characteristics. The two extant caves are the Eastern and Western Caves of Jintasi (figs. 3.10, 3.11). Although the two are very similar, the Eastern is larger (9.70 meters wide, 7.65 meters deep, and 6.05 meters high). The imposing squarish shaft (4.5 meters square) features a striking crowd of deities and blessed beings, all executed in painted clay over a wooden armature (fig. 3.12). It is centrally placed in the cave and totally separated from the surrounding walls. It may have been built in part to be circumambulated, like a stupa.

Throughout, Jintasi's iconography displays patterns common to central Asian cave sculpture. In particular, the pillar's iconography stresses the historical Buddha, Shakyamuni, and the future Buddha, Maitreya, his spiritual heir. Different manifestations of Buddha appear — as Shakyamuni, as the bodhisattva prior to the Enlightenment, as Maitreya, and even as the bodhisattva

Maitreya. Bodhisattva images, monks, flying celestials (*apsarases*), and heavenly beings (devas, or devatas) are represented in three ascending tiers, and some are enclosed in niches. Representations of jataka tales are conspicuously absent, but they may have been painted on the walls. The choice of imagery, thus, is still consonant with that of Kizil.

The sculptors' choice of different sizes for the images according to their placement on the pillar indicates sophisticated planning. Seated Buddhas occupying the first tier are 1.60 meters high, while those in the second tier are reduced to 1.25 meters. Likewise, the standing bodhisattvas vary from 1.60 to 1.85 meters in height, whereas the topmost figures are only half a meter tall. Significantly, this variation in size enhances the effect of the icons' apparent recession in space and distancing from the realm below. The receding planes also express the religious hierarchy; the major Buddhist figures occupy the bottom rows, while secondary images are placed farther up (fig. 3.13).

The images are also characterized differently: the Buddhas' hand gestures and expressions vary, as do the costumes and jewels of the bodhisattvas. The bodhisattvas, which are either partially or completely draped, are robust with fairly well modeled bodies and heavy jewels that accentuate their sturdy physiques (fig. 3.14). The apparel, in particular the triple-disk crowns worn by the bodhisattvas, is taken from Kizil painted figures. The wide, round faces, with their pronounced noses and tiny mouths, suggest non-Han features; perhaps they were modeled after central Asian or nomadic peoples who had settled along the trade route. Although crudely modeled, the celestials and the supernatural beings are the most lively creatures represented in the caves: the former assume daring midair poses, and the latter are visible only from the waist up as they lean from the summit to peek below. Caves with similar layout and decor, deemed typically Liang, were created at Tiantishan, Matisi, and Wenshushan.

The choice of certain iconographies at Jintasi and other Liangzhou sites, especially those of the Maitreya and Parinirvana cults, was influenced by the doctrines promoted by prominent monks active in Gansu. Even before the Northern Liang, Dharmaraksha (active ca. 266–308), a native of Dunhuang who often traveled through the Hexi corridor on his way to Chang'an, gave great impetus to the cult of Maitreya. Dharmaraksha translated at least three different versions of the sutra describing Maitreya's last incarnation.[35]

The most prominent monk at the court of Juqu Mengxun was Dharmakshema, who also acted as political adviser to the ruler. He left his mark instead on the diffusion of the Mahaparinirvana Sutra. According to the *History of the Wei* (*Weishu*) by Wei Shou (550–575), "There was a Jibin shramana or monk, Tanmo-chen (Dharmakshema) who conned scriptures and treatises. In Guzang, with the shramana Zhisong and others he translated the Nirvana and other scriptures, more than ten in number. . . . Mengxun always consulted him on affairs of state."[36] Because of the prominence given to the Nirvana scripture by Dharmakshema, the highest cleric of the time, the art of the corridor is widely believed to have placed particular emphasis on stupa worship.[37] In Gansu, in addition to the ever-present stupa pillar inside the caves are miniature stone pillars, traditionally also called stupas and manufactured exclusively during the Northern Liang. Because their shape is

3.14 Bodhisattva, east side, Western Cave of Jintasi Monastery.

3.15 Miniature pillar, stone brick, donated by Gao Shanmu, from Jiuquan, Gansu Province. Northern Liang dynasty, 428. Gansu Provincial Museum, Lanzhou.

not that of a stupa, however, the term *miniature pillar* seems more fitting.[38]

These votive artifacts (twelve are known at present) are all executed in black granite, a stone seldom used in sculpture. All are products of western Gansu, the area between Dunhuang and Jiuquan (the two found in Turpan were most likely exported from Gansu). They are similar in structure, decor, and, to an extent, their inscribed texts.[39] The artifact from Jiuquan (44.6 centimeters high), donated by Gao Shanmu and dated 428, remains one of the best preserved and most important of the Northern Liang miniature pillars (fig. 3.15). It consists of five parts: the tall octagonal base with incised images; the cylindrical shaft with the Chinese inscription, surmounted by a section decorated with the reliefs of seven Buddhas and the bodhisattva Maitreya; shapes suggestive of a spire with disks; and the round summit, which can be interpreted as a lotus or jewel. In this particular example, the top carries an incised representation of the Big Dipper constellation.

The Jiuquan miniature pillar combines the architectural and sculptural influences of a wide geographical region. In opting for a predominantly vertical shape, the structure modifies the Indian model and transforms it to suit Han Chinese tradition. Stylistically, the Buddha reliefs suggest the Indian art of Gandhara, whereas the incised images of the base and the billowing scarves framing the figures reflect the influence of central Asia, especially Kizil.

The inscribed text is a passage on the teaching of the twelve links of causality from the Ekottoragama Sutra, a pre-Mahayana scripture translated in 384 by the monk Dharmanandi at the request of Zhao Zheng, the governor of Wuwei. The stupa carries an additional and unusual textual reference: trigrams from the *Yijing* (Book of changes) — which are drawn from Daoist philosophy — are carved in the base alongside each of the incised figures.

In blending Buddhist and Daoist beliefs, the miniature pillars are culturally composite works that are different from the earlier mingling observed in Sichuan. In these Gansu artifacts, the two traditions are correctly understood (not debased or vulgarized) and used by erudite clerics who were conversant with China's philosophical and religious heritage. The use of Daoist symbols in the miniature pillar's decor reflects the local merging of traditional Chinese and Buddhist beliefs. It is the concrete expression of the so-called Abstruse Learning (*xuanxue*), proof of the erudite eclecticism present in fourth-century Gansu and the interaction of Buddhist and Daoist ontological processes.

Northern Liang Patronage at Dunhuang

The Mogao cave complex at Dunhuang is the most important Buddhist site in China. With almost five hundred caves extant, the site displays about one thousand years of stylistic and iconographic development. It is generally accepted that the first caves were opened in 366 during the Former Liang by the monk Lezun (also known as Yuezun), but these initial grottoes are no longer extant. The earliest viewable caves are those identified as Caves 268, 272, and 275, which both Chinese and Western scholars ascribe to Northern Liang patronage. According to this dating, these caves were built after the Northern Liang conquered Dunhuang in 421.[40]

Cave 268 is unusual in that it has four small rooms (two on each side), which may have been used for meditation. The main image is a seated bodhisattva Maitreya with legs crossed, a pose that means he is in Tushita Heaven waiting for his final reincarnation.

Cave 272, square in plan, displays an almost life-size

3.16 Maitreya Buddha, painted clay, Cave 272 (rear niche), Dunhuang, Gansu Province. Northern Liang dynasty.

3.17 Seated bodhisattva Maitreya, painted clay, Cave 275 (rear wall), Dunhuang, Gansu Province. Northern Liang dynasty.

3.19 Seated Buddhas, clay, Cave 169 (niche 23, south wall), Binglingsi Monastery. Western Qin dynasty, 420.

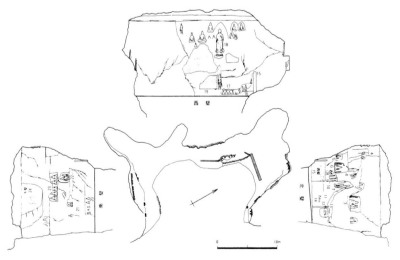

3.18 Plan of Cave 169, Binglingsi Monastery, Yongjing, Gansu Province.

seated Buddha (whose head is a replacement) in the niche of the rear wall facing east (fig. 3.16). He is possibly the incarnated Maitreya Buddha because he sits according to Western custom. The sculpture, which is backed by a many-ringed aureole filled with Buddha emanations, is complemented by the surrounding wall painting: two bodhisattvas sway gracefully on either side of him, and numerous miniature images — including blessed beings and monks in ecstatic and frenzied poses — hold audience. The naive freshness that distinguishes the throng of images modeled in clay and attached to the Jintasi stupa pillar is also noticeable in these paintings. Where the walls and ceiling join, painted balconies are filled with musicians that are shown from the waist up, like those in early Kizil caves.

The decor of the rectangular Cave 275, the largest

and most accomplished of the three, also celebrates the cult of Maitreya (fig. 3.17). The large bodhisattva shown with knees spread wide in the crossed-leg position is fashioned closely on a Kizil prototype, specifically the Maitreya painted in the lunette of Cave 224 (now at the Berlin Museum).[41] The similarity of dress and crown is particularly noticeable. The sculpture's wide, non-Chinese face and thick-set modeling also resemble the Jintasi style. In the upper section of the lateral walls are smaller but identically fashioned Maitreyas. The frescoes of the cave are representations of jatakas and episodes of Shakyamuni's last life; they carry the message of karmic retribution and impel the believer to attain spiritual perfection in order to be admitted to Maitreya's Pure Land.

The style used in the modeling of Maitreya and the motif of the balconies in these three caves seem to have come from Kizil. The caves do not, however, use the central stupa pillar, which is considered the leitmotif of Liang cave art. Of course, the modest size of the caves may have imposed the layout of a rectangular, unobstructed space. The emphasis on the Maitreya cult is also consonant with doctrinal developments in the Hexi corridor, mentioned earlier.

A further link between Liang Buddhist sculpture and central Asia lies in the patronage of Buddhist art and the influence of eminent clerics. Most notably, the famous monk Kumarajiva, a descendant of Kucha's ruling family, was taken prisoner by Lü Guang of the Former Qin in 384 and kept in Liangzhou for seventeen years before he was allowed to move to Chang'an (where he resided at the Later Qin court). Kumarajiva must have been an important source of information on the doctrine and rituals practiced in Kucha. Besides Kumarajiva — and even before his time — numerous other monks, some foreign and others native to Gansu, maintained contact between central Asia and the Liang.

Although Kucha's impact on Liang art of the corridor was significant, Khotan was also very influential. This link is harder to establish because much of Khotan's Buddhist art has been destroyed. Records exists indicating that several native Liangzhou monks — the most notable being Mengxun's paternal cousin, the prince Jingsheng — traveled to Khotan to gather scriptures and information about the country. Liangzhou's prominence during the fourth century as a bustling Buddhist center is confirmed by Dao An's *Comprehensive Catalogue of Sutras* (*Zong li congjing mu lu*), compiled by 374 into fifty-nine titles in eighty rolls. This record demonstrates how Liangzhou contributed to the growth of Buddhism in northwest China and the parallel development of its devotional art.[42]

The three Qin dynasties were the other established powers in Gansu, contemporaneous with the Liang. They represented chiefly Xianbei peoples, with the exception of the Former Qin (351–394), who were Tibetans. Qin territorial power extended beyond Gansu: under Fu Jian of the Former Qin, it had practically unified northern China; under the Yao of the Later Qin (384–417), Chang'an (present-day Xi'an, Shaanxi Province) was the major Buddhist center outside Liangzhou. The three dynasties vied for power and fought occasionally with the Liang. Each Qin dynasty contributed to the growth of Buddhism, but this chapter focuses on the Qifu rulers of the Western Qin dynasty (385–431), because their patronage led to two of the most important cave temples in Gansu: Binglingsi and Maijishan.

The establishment of Buddhist caves at Binglingsi Monastery near Yongjing may have occurred at the end of the fourth century, but the earliest inscription at the site, found in Cave 169, is dated 420.[43] This naturally formed space at the highest point of the cliff (60 meters above the ground) is of grand proportions (15 meters high, 26.75 meters wide, and 8.56 meters deep); inside the cave, clay images and frescoes are laid out rather freely, suggesting that their execution did not follow a preestablished pattern (fig. 3.18). Chinese scholars have catalogued the objects within the cave according to numbered niches (although this is something of a misnomer, as no niche as such exists). Some of the clay sculpture is built on an interior armature, but for a few pieces clay was used over a stone core.

Two important and novel features of Cave 169 are the stylistic link of some of its sculpture with the Buddhist art of Khotan on the southern Silk Road and the presence of numerous inscriptions that identify the sculpture and painted images. The five seated Buddhas in niche 23, in the south side of the cave, closely resemble the clay sculpture of Rawaq, Khotan (fig. 3.19). The Buddhas are wrapped in their monastic robes and performing the pensive (*dhyana*) hand gesture, and they are backed by large aureoles. The imposing standing Buddha (2.45 meters high), the only extant one of the original triad, in niche 7 in the northern side of the cave, is covered by a robe, is performing the giving (*varada*) and fear-not (*abhaya*) hand gestures, and is backed with a sizable aureole (fig. 3.20). But other styles are also apparent in the cave: in niche 6, in the northern side of the cave, the image of a seated Buddha assisted on either side by a standing bodhisattva (fig. 3.21) is closer to the Liangzhou aesthetic, and thus to Kucha.

The explanatory inscriptions occur most notably in niche 6, which, significantly, is dated 420, the earliest extant record in the cave. The triad of sculptures includes the Wuliangshou Buddha (which means either Buddha of Measureless Light or Buddha of Measureless Life, also known as Amitayus), assisted by his canonical helpers Guanyin (Avalokiteshvara) and Dashizhi (Mahasthamaprapta), who preside over the Western Pure Land. The painted images of niche 6 are also identified: the Buddhas of the Ten Directions, the

donors, members of the Qifu dynastic house, and the venerable monks in residence at the Western Qin court (fig. 3.22). Among these historical personages is the National Teacher — monk Tanmopi (Dharmapriya), a follower of the famous Chang'an-based monk Xuan Gao — who preached meditational practices in secluded surroundings such as Binglingsi. "At the time of Qifu [leader of the Western Qin], the foreign monk Dharmapriya arrived in the Western Qin where he had many followers who were instructed by him in *chan* [meditational] practices."[44] These clerics likely were involved with the construction of Cave 169, or at least

3.20 Standing Buddha, clay, Cave 169 (niche 7, north wall), Binglingsi Monastery.

3.21 Amitayus Buddha with two bodhisattvas, clay, Cave 169 (niche 6, north wall), Binglingsi Monastery.

with some of its votive images, and the cave probably was for contemplation.

Identifying inscriptions are also used in the cluster of rather crude paintings of different deities in niches 10–13 on the northern side of the cave (fig. 3.23). In the group at the upper left — in addition to the Shakyamuni Buddha with two bodhisattvas — is a foreign-looking monk leading two ladies of the Qin elite in worship. Additional scenes of iconographic interest were painted below and to the side, all identified by inscription. Two prominent examples are the debate between Wenshu (Manjushri) and Weimojie (Vimalakirti), and the co-presence of the Shakyamuni and Duobao (Prabhutaratna) Buddhas.

These representations originated in the sacred books

Vimalakirti Sutra and the Lotus of the Wonderful Law (Saddharmapundarika Sutra), respectively, which were given their definitive translation in Chang'an by Kumarajiva in approximately 400–410.[45] Kumarajiva's translation of the Small Sukhavativyuha Sutra (Amituojing) during this same period also inspired the sculpture of Wuliangshou in niche 6.[46] These works, derived from the most influential Mahayana teachings, received their first visual interpretation in Binglingsi and would serve as important precedents for the Northern Wei sculpture at Yungang and Longmen. The art of Cave 169 of Binglingsi is an unrivaled example of the interaction of patrons and clerics in the formation of Buddhist art.

The cave temple of Maijishan, near Tianshui, established at roughly the same time as Binglingsi, was also

3.22 Schematic drawing of Cave 169 (niche 6, north wall), Binglingsi Monastery.

3.23 Schematic drawing of Cave 169 (niches 10–13, north wall), Binglingsi Monastery.

used for meditation; both sites had the same Chan monk, or meditation master, in residence, most notably Xuan Gao.[47] (Chan Buddhism later became Zen Buddhism in Japan.) Opinions on Maijishan chronology vary. Some scholars attribute its construction to the Later Qin dynasty under the Yao Xin family (396–416), the same family that hosted Kumarajiva; their claim is based on the finding of an inscription in Cave 76 with a date that can be transposed to 407. Other scholars prefer to attribute the site to the Western Qin, arguing that if this site was chosen by the monk Xuan Gao, he could have started his residence at the site no earlier than 420. The monk's biography, however, does not mention him as the site's founder. Whether Maijishan was opened by the Later Qin or the Western Qin implies a difference of scarcely a decade. More important is the consensus that a few caves precede the conquest by the Northern Wei dynasty in 439.[48]

In general, the structure of the Maijishan caves is very different from that of all the other sites in Gansu.

These caves are rather small and do not use the central stupa-pillar structure. Moreover, the decor (painting and sculpture) creates a more intimate effect as a result of the softer modeling of the clay images and their quaint expressions. Although the cave paintings are heavily damaged, the sculpture is better preserved. Caves 74 and 78, which form a pair, are the earliest caves. The arrangement of Cave 78 (4.5 meters high, 4.7 meters wide, and 3 meters deep) consisted of three large, seated Buddhas (approximately 2.5 meters high) placed on the tall dado running along the walls, but the one along the right wall is lost (fig. 3.24). The Buddha on the rear wall, shown in the fear-not pose, is assisted by two standing bodhisattvas (one original, the other of a later date and from another cave). The Buddha on the left wall, shown in the pensive pose, has no attendants. The three may have alluded to the belief in the Buddhas of Past, Present, and Future. In the two small niches of the rear wall are placed the bodhisattva Maitreya and Shakyamuni in the pensive pose. The remaining two Buddhas overwhelm the tight space. The modeling of the bodies creates smooth and flat planes devoid of naturalism. The wide base formed by the interlocked legs imparts stability, the Buddhas' countenances are uncommonly dignified and serene, and their foreign faces (round, open eyes and pronounced noses) are similar to those of the Binglingsi images.

The build of the two standing bodhisattvas (each about 2.20 meters high) in the twin Cave 74 emphasizes columnar verticality, yet the images also convey a sense of movement: their asexual, lithe bodies seem to sway toward the Buddha, an effect enhanced by the billowing scarves that elegantly frame their bodies. This style, as well as the three-disk crown, is Kizilian. The Maijishan sculpture uses the Gansu adaptation of the central Asian model that is evident at all the sites along the corridor, but produces a local and unique interpretation of it, perhaps grounded in the aesthetic demands of the patrons. The Maijishan bodhisattvas — exemplified by the one in Cave 80—are highly original and endearing: they display unusually small heads with a gracious mien, and limber bodies draped in flowing robes (fig. 3.25).

The importance of Gansu art during the fourth century, before the Northern Wei takeover in 439, is clear. The caves opened along the Hexi corridor demonstrate the artistic synthesis of different central Asian influences as well as the interpretation of numerous iconographies derived from the sutras whose translation by famous foreign ecclesiastics had been sponsored by the native Liang and Qin dynasties. Moreover, the cave art of the corridor is not uniform, because it interprets different central Asian modes. The intense effort made in Gansu to create a language suited to local Buddhism generated this Liangzhou art, which heavily influenced the development of later Northern Wei artistic styles.

In addition to their artistic contribution, the short-lived dynasties in Gansu forged a very special rapport between institutionalized Buddhism and their dynastic patrons. Under this new relationship, the ecclesiastics became advisers to the rulers (for instance, Dharmak-shema to Juqu Mengxun of the Northern Liang, and Kumarajiva to Yao Xin of the Later Qin); the rulers, in turn, used Buddhism to enhance political prestige. The Northern Wei rulers did not invent this formula but further developed it; both artistically and politically, the Northern Wei rulers were indebted to the earlier rulers of the Sixteen Kingdoms period.

Early Buddhist Gilt Bronzes

The earliest Buddhist metal images were gilt bronzes produced during the fourth and early fifth centuries, primarily in northern China (in present-day Hebei). Many predate the Gansu clay sculptures discussed above. Unlike those clay sculptures, however, the gilt-bronze Buddhas executed from about 300 C.E. represent orthodox images imported from India, instead of proto-Buddhist artistic expressions with links to popular indigenous cults.

Although clay and wood may have been used, the existing evidence suggests that the first Chinese Buddha images were made of bronze. (Stone Buddhist sculpture, which became so important to the genre, had not yet been developed.) For two millennia Chinese artisans had made three-dimensional objects in clay and metal

3.24 Two seated Buddhas, clay, Cave 78, Maijishan, Gansu Province. Later Qin or Western Qin dynasty, early 5th century.

3.25 Standing bodhisattva, clay, Cave 80, Maijishan. Northern Wei dynasty, after 439.

by adding parts to a base, rather than by cutting away from a larger piece to make sculpture (as is done with stone). By 300, Chinese craftsmen were drawing upon this tradition and technology to make Buddhist icons, innovating in ways that were later copied in stone and painting.

The earliest extant gilt bronzes form a very small group, a handful of examples that vary widely in style. In fact, some are unique pieces, because the craftsmen were still experimenting with formulas to satisfy the demands of clergy and patrons. These earliest images were also probably copied from imported icons used by foreigners for private devotion. Only one bronze from the group is dated by inscription, to 338. Given that the others retain even more Indian characteristics, they have been dated to about 300 (or slightly earlier).[49]

Despite their many differences, the gilt bronzes do share certain characteristics. The bronzes are hollow, and most of them were cast in one piece with the addition of a halo or an aureole attached by tenon to the head or back. Furthermore, the Buddhas (only one is a bodhisattva), portrayed seated or standing, have not been transformed yet into Chinese-looking deities. Their facial characteristics and expressions are instead markedly Indian; note their prominent noses, pointed chins, and round, open eyes staring directly ahead. The standing bodhisattva Maitreya (33.1 centimeters high), if not the most alien-looking and exotic gilt bronze of the group, is certainly a contender (fig. 3.26). Thought to come from Sanyuan County, a suburb of Xi'an, Shaanxi, it is now in the collection of the Fujii Saiseikai Yurinkan, Kyoto. The bodhisattva is portrayed as a Brahmin: he wears a royal costume that partially reveals his body, conspicuous and heavy jewelry, and sandals. His hair is rendered with striations (a device common to the earliest bronzes) and is piled on top of his head in the style of the caste in which Maitreya will be reborn in his last reincarnation. His right hand, which is webbed — a trait indicative of Buddhahood — performs the fear-not gesture, and in his left hand he carries a bottle, as ascetic Brahmins do. In each of the details, the image accurately reflects the Gandharan norm and

3.26 Standing bodhisattva Maitreya, gilt bronze, Sanyuan County, Shaanxi Province. Late Western Jin dynasty, ca. 300. Fujii Saiseikai Yurinkan, Kyoto.

3.27 Seated Shakyamuni Buddha in meditation with hands in pensive gesture and with flaming shoulders (Gandhara type), gilt bronze, presumably from Hebei Province. Six Dynasties period, ca. 300. 32 × 24 × 13 cm. Arthur M. Sackler Museum, Harvard University Art Museums.

3.28 Seated Buddha, gilt bronze, Hebei Province. Later Zhao dynasty, 338.
Asian Art Museum of San Francisco.

portrays a sturdy strength, through the vigorously spread
fingers and firmly set feet, as well as through the deeply
incised pleats of the weighty robe, which end in rounded
patterns suggestive of animal ears. If fashioned in
Shaanxi about 300, the bronze would have been created
during the late Western Jin dynasty.

A seated Buddha (31.8 centimeters tall), presumably
from Hebei Province, is a contemporary of the standing bodhisattva Maitreya and is now in the Sackler
Museum, Cambridge, Massachusetts (fig. 3.27). This is
a superb, well-preserved statue; its gilded surface is still
intact. It is also a richly complex work. The Buddha sits
with interlocked legs and the hands palms-up, one on
top of the other in the pensive gesture. In a state of
deep meditation, the Buddha leans slightly forward.
Above the wide face is a conspicuous ushnisha (cranial
protuberance) resting on striated hair. The throne is a
low Indian-style dais adorned with two lions in the corners, a variation of a lion throne. On each side, cast in
miniature but finely detailed, stand a monk and a nun
who carry a lamp and a lotus flower, respectively. In
front of the throne is a flower container holding lotuses.
The motif of the lotus is repeated yet again on the large,
detachable halo. The image, thought to have been created in the late third to early fourth centuries, is sensitively executed.[50]

The seated Buddha follows closely the Gandharan
aesthetic. Facial features include broad eyebrows,
prominent and deeply set eyes, a pronounced nose, and
a moustache. Moreover, the clothing is Gandharan, as
exemplified by the draping of the robe. The flaming
shoulders are also seen in royal portraits of Kushan
kings. A naturalism is apparent in the modeling of the
chest and abdomen, the tense arms and thighs underneath the draping robes, and the strong and carefully
depicted fingers. In short, the Fujii Yurinkan Maitreya
and the Sackler seated Buddha are finely crafted reproductions that do not seem to deviate from their foreign
models.

The only dated gilt bronze of the group, the seated
Buddha (39.7 centimeters high) made in Hebei in 338
under the Later Zhao dynasty, retains a Gandharan
flavor but unmistakably shows the evolution toward a
Chinese style (fig. 3.28). When this gilt bronze was first
cast, the tall pedestal was embellished with a central
lotus vase or an incense burner, with a lion on each side.
No round halo is visible. The bronze is now in the
Asian Art Museum of San Francisco.

In part, the gilt bronze's historical value lies in its
inscription, which records its date and provenance. The

fragmentary text reads: "Jianwu year 4 [338 of the Later Zhao], in the year of *wuzi*, eighth month, thirtieth day, the monk . . . karma image." Furthermore, the iconography of this particular bronze became a favorite Chinese depiction during the period of disunion. This type of Buddha, seated in the pensive pose (*dhyana*) and wrapped in the monastic robe, was fashioned in bronze in northern and southern China for at least a century after its inception. Its popularity extended to stone; for instance, it was carved on the Liangzhou miniature pillars described earlier. Paintings, such as the frescoes of Cave 169 in Binglingsi, also conspicuously feature the image.

The pensive gesture is an essential component of this iconographic type, though in a slight deviation from the canonical norm the hands are placed against the stomach instead of palms-up on the lap. Buddha's ushnisha and head are defined with striations. The

3.29 Seated Buddha, gilt bronze. Liu Song dynasty, 437. Eisei Bunko Foundation, Tokyo.

bronze's facial features and garment point to a process of artistic sinicization. The face is not completely Chinese, yet it has changed and softened since the two preceding gilt bronzes. It has become rounder, while the eyes are more elongated, and there is an inkling of a smile around the mouth. The nose, however, is still markedly foreign. Perhaps the most Chinese part of the image is its robe. In the uniquely Chinese style of the time, which disregards naturalism, stylized surface designs are prominent in the pleats.

The influence of this gilt bronze, which became a Chinese prototype, transcended the limited political domain of the ruling house. The bronze was cast in the Later Zhao (319–351), which was only a minor dynasty of the Sixteen Kingdoms period. Nevertheless, the controlled territory of present-day Hebei in northern China took the lead in the production of Buddhist images because of the availability of superb metalworkers (see, for example, artifacts from the tomb of Prince Liu Sheng and his wife at Zhongshan, Mancheng County [113 B.C.E.]). Nor is it surprising that Hebei remained a leading center in the production of Buddhist gilt bronzes in subsequent centuries, given the energizing presence in Hebei of an important foreign missionary, the monk Fotudeng, who greatly influenced the Zhao leaders.[51]

Like the patrons of Buddhism in the Gansu corridor, influential clerics served the local ruler while carrying on their evangelical mission. Fotudeng, one of these clerics, was probably a native of Kucha, although some believe he came from Kashmir. He preached pre-Mahayana Buddhism and strictly observed monastic discipline. He arrived in Luoyang in 311, on the eve of the collapse of the north. Supposedly he was already in his eighties when he settled with the Zhao's illiterate ruler Shi Le and his nephew and successor, Shi Hu. The two Shis converted to Buddhism ostensibly out of self-interest. They believed that Fotudeng had supernatural powers that they could use to achieve military success. Indeed, under the Shi rulers, Zhao territory — which initially consisted of Henan, part of Hebei, and Shandong — spread westward to include Shanxi and Shaanxi Provinces. For his part, Fotudeng, while advising the Shis in matters of politics, also trained several monks and some nuns who would succeed him in proselytizing in other parts of China (especially Shandong, Guangdong, and Sichuan). It is tempting to think that the gilt-bronze Buddha dated 338 was cast as a result of Fotudeng's mission to Zhao.

In contrast, gilt bronzes manufactured in southern

China are extremely rare. None have been found from the fourth century, and only two cast between 400 and 450 are extant. Both represent the 338 pensive-pose Buddha type, confirming the importance of this iconography to the Chinese. The gilt bronze (11.8 centimeters high without its pedestal), dated to 437 (Liu Song dynasty, a century after the Hebei prototype) and now held by the Eisei Bunko Foundation, Tokyo (fig. 3.29), is noteworthy for its superior craftsmanship and well-preserved state. The bronze is cast in two pieces: the Buddha seated on the high pedestal, and an aureole attached to the Buddha's back. As in the Hebei bronze, the Buddha sits in the pensive pose. The monastic robe is also interpreted in a stylized linear fashion.

In contrast with the earlier icon, the southern Chinese Buddha sits on a special throne called *sumeru* (in reference to the Buddhist axis of the world), which constricts at the middle and flares out at both ends. The Liu Song Buddha is fully Chinese, with elongated eyes, highly arched eyebrows, and less-pronounced nose and chin. The sensitively modeled face is more elongated and leaner than the Indian-style face of the Buddha from 338. The large aureole, embellished with a dynamic fire pattern darting out toward the rim, is a superb example of pictorial abstraction. The level of skill demonstrated in the sculpting of the Liu Song bronze exceeds that of the northern work. The rich culture and high artistic level at the southern court of Nanjing during the period of disunion no doubt provided a supportive environment for the casting of such a superb object.

The political situation of the early fifth century was shaped by the gradual emergence of the Tuoba tribe, a branch of the Xiongnu that originated from the Inner Mongolian area around Shengle. In 396, the leader Tuoba Gui marched into China and in 398 founded the Wei dynasty with its capital at Pingcheng (present-day Datong) in northern Shanxi. Over the following fifty years the tribe unified northern China, annexing Gansu in 439 and part of the northeast (Shandong, Anhui, and a portion of Jiangsu) in 469.

The gilt bronzes executed in the first half of the fifth century (400–450) differ markedly from the fourth-century ones. A new Buddha type was introduced: a standing Buddha dressed in a monastic garment, with his hands raised to his chest. Judging from contemporary reproductions in clay along with paintings in cave temples, this type was as popular as the one from 338. Although the Buddha remains Gandharan in attire and facial expression, Chinese traits are also detectable. Extant examples vary in size, but some are conspicuously large and, more importantly, are dated and identified by inscription. Significantly, the makers used the names Shakyamuni and Maitreya interchangeably (although one refers to the historical Buddha, the other to the future Buddha), indicating both that the distinction between the two had not yet been drawn and that their respective iconographies had not yet been firmly set.

The near-life-size Buddha (140.3 centimeters high) reputedly from Mount Wutai, in Shanxi, that is presently in The Metropolitan Museum of Art, New York, remains the outstanding representative example of the period (fig. 3.30). The inscription identifies the image as Maitreya and dates it to 486 (Northern Wei dynasty), but the inscription is generally regarded as a later and misleading addition. It is more accurate to date the gilt bronze to the years 420–443, that is, between the creation of the imposing Binglingsi clay Buddha in Cave 169 (see fig. 3.20) and the creation of a smaller (53.5 centimeters) gilt-bronze Maitreya — dated to 443 (Northern Wei) — that was manufactured in Hebei and is currently in a private collection in Osaka, Japan.[52] Stylistically, these three images are closely related.

In the Metropolitan gilt bronze, the Gandharan style is visible in the facial expression and in the adherence to strict canonical requirements. The major marks are prominently displayed: the ushnisha embedded in a whorled hairstyle, the dot or tuft of hair (*urna*), the conspicuously elongated earlobes, and the large, webbed hands. The Buddha correctly wears the three prescribed monastic garments — dhoti and inner and outer robes — that, in Indian style, are draped to suggest the well-formed body underneath.

The evolution toward a Chinese Buddha is recognizable by the drape of the robe and by the Buddha's hand position. On the front and back of the Buddha the cloth forms decorative concentric patterns similar to ripples of water, whereas on the sides it falls in strong vertical folds. This emphasis on linear contrasted embellishments and abstractions follows a Chinese aesthetic. In all three images, Buddha is shown with the fear-not gesture performed by the right hand and the giving gesture performed by the left, which is incorrectly raised to chest level in order to balance the other hand. This variation (or misunderstanding), perhaps motivated by the Chinese penchant for symmetry, resulted in a compassionate, friendly icon that invited the believer with its open arms and outstretched hands. These serene and smiling Buddhas were considerably more accessible and engaging than their Gandharan inspiration.

3.30 Standing Maitreya Buddha, gilt bronze, reputedly from Mount Wutai, Shanxi Province. Northern Wei dynasty, 486. 140.3 × 48.9 cm. The Metropolitan Museum of Art, New York.

3.31 Buddha group, sandstone, Cave 20, Yungang, Shanxi Province. Northern Wei dynasty, 460–470.

Dynastic Art of Pingcheng, the First Capital of the Northern Wei

Although stone became the prevalent medium in fashioning Buddhist cave-temple images or independent objects of worship, it was only toward the mid-fifth century that stone sculpture began to be produced in China regularly. The making of stone images set in grandiose cave temples was linked in the north to the imperial patronage of the Northern Wei dynasty, and the first such imperially sponsored cave temple during the Northern Wei was Yungang. This imposing complex was rooted in an artistic and doctrinal framework established in the three Buddhist centers of northern China: Liangzhou in the Gansu corridor, Chang'an in Shaanxi, and Hebei. The works in Yungang elaborated on the relationships among text, audience, and art. Sculpture was often used as a means to illustrate the sacred texts; in turn, the visual aspects were shaped in accordance with the tastes of the local devout. Yungang also drew upon an emerging tradition in which eminent monks and rulers forged mutually beneficial relationships, and the success of Buddhism was linked tightly to that of the dynastic family.

Yungang was the first of three grand Buddhist projects sponsored by the Northern Wei dynasty (the other two were Longmen and Gongxian). As such, it represents a preliminary stage of an ongoing process of acculturation that involves not only the art but also its patrons. Yungang shows how the Tuoba culture evolved from a nomadic culture into a culture of settlers through the people's increasing reliance on Chinese

institutions and customs and on their active sponsorship of Buddhist culture. Just as one cannot ignore the surroundings of the sculptures, which are literally embedded in the cave, it is impossible to discuss the art of Yungang without considering the political circumstances that brought about this massive undertaking.

As an act of atonement for the persecution of Buddhism enforced by his predecessor in 446, Emperor Wencheng in 452 ordered the restoration of Buddhism and subsequently established the initial five caves and their respective colossal Buddhas at Yungang. Chinese scholars believe that the Imperial Five (as the caves are commonly referred to) were built during the reign of Wencheng and completed before his death in 465. The traditional chronology, set by Japanese scholars and shared by Western historians, varies slightly; they date the caves from 460 to 470.[53] The project undoubtedly drew upon the mass deportation to Datong of Gansu laborers, craftsmen, and scholars after the annexation of Gansu in 439: they were employed to build the Northern Wei capital and its surroundings. The influence of the northwest on the iconography, architecture, and style at Yungang is undeniable.

Notwithstanding the immense scope and importance of the project, there are no inscriptions to help secure the details of the site's creation. Information from the *History of the Wei,* however, can be used to reconstruct the history regarding the caves' sponsorship. There are two salient events: the 454 imperial edict ordering the casting of five colossal Buddhas (no longer extant), each one in memory of the former Tuoba emperors; and the petition by the monk Tanyao (appointed in 460 by the emperor to oversee the Buddhist church) to have five Buddha caves carved in the Wuzhou mountain ridge, where Yungang is located. Undoubtedly, these caves are the Yungang Imperial Five; each cave's Buddha honors a prior Tuoba emperor much as the five bronzes had. In this way, the caves not only represent an act of repentance for the persecution of Buddhism but also illustrate how Northern Wei power sought legitimacy in, and the blessing of, Buddhism. The Northern Wei rulers used Buddhism to strengthen the government's control over unified northern China. To this end, equating the Buddha with the emperor meant merging political with religious power and establishing a theocracy.

The initial five caves — 16, 17, 18, 19, and 20—are characterized by colossal images (14–16.5 meters high) scooped out of the solid sandstone mountain. Each cave is a gigantic elliptical south-facing Buddha-niche protected by walls and a roof. The five towering images, placed at the center of rather tight spaces, eloquently convey both spiritual and temporal power. In building these colossal Buddhas, the Tuobas were likely aware of similar central Asian examples, such as the earliest of the Bamiyan Buddhas (approximately 38 meters high; now destroyed) in Afghanistan, or the 10-meter-high clay images (no longer extant) in some of the Kizil caves. In this respect, the Northern Wei followed an established Buddhist tradition.

The construction of the enormous caves at Yungang was also linked to the practice of ancestor worship.[54] The Tuoba Xianbei believed that their ancestors would emerge from a Sacred Cave, where their descendants had worshiped them. Chinese scholars have recently identified this as the Ganxian County cave site, situated at the northern side of the Xing'anling mountain chain in Inner Mongolia. The cave even has an inscription commemorating the visit in 443 of a certain Li Chang, sent by the Northern Wei emperor to verify the existence of the site. The Tuobas' prolific building of Buddhist caves may have been derived from this ancestral custom.

The main images of the Imperial Five were partially influenced by iconographic and stylistic features present in northwest China. The images consist of a seated Buddha in Cave 20, a seated Buddha in Cave 19, a standing Buddha in Cave 18, a seated Maitreya in Cave 17, and a standing Buddha (recut) in Cave 16. The Buddhas of Caves 18, 19, and 20 likely represent the three Buddhas of Past, Present, and Future, a canonical group already portrayed in northwest China.[55]

Cave 20 is totally exposed since the collapse of the surrounding walls and ceiling (fig. 3.31). Originally the seated Buddha was flanked by two standing Buddhas (half the size of the seated one) and by two standing bodhisattvas (half the size of the standing Buddhas), an arrangement that accentuated their hierarchical relationship. Today, of the standing figures, only the Buddha to the viewer's right remains. In spite of modern restoration and alteration, the face of the colossal Buddha (as that of the other imperial four) suggests that it originally looked quite foreign, similar to the Buddhas sculpted at Cave 78 at Maijishan, in Gansu (see fig. 3.24).

Although there are ties to the Buddhist art of Gansu, Cave 20 is unprecedented in its display of the Buddha's might as a symbol of imperial power. The rendering of the body is blocklike and powerful; its surface is sparsely enlivened by abstract, linear embellishments. The dominant feature of the work is its huge size; the massive body conveys a feeling of heroic monumentality that illustrates the dual power of Buddha and the emperor. In my view, this was intentional and not the result of a lack of skill. In fact, the ability of the Northern Wei artisans is evident in the refined detailing of the Buddha's aureole, which is reminiscent of metalwork of the time. In the aureole, the stone is worked to suggest lacy, fine ornamentation, and the celestials and kneeling adorers are sensitively carved.

The structure of Cave 18 magnifies the presence of the Buddha. The cave has retained its pristine structure: its walls and ceiling are extant, and above the entrance is a window exactly as high as the head of the standing Buddha. The window lights a rather dark interior. Moreover, visitors approaching the outside of the cave can see the head of the overpowering Buddha through this opening. Inside the cave, the lack of proportion between width and height is apparent, and the cramped space surrounding the Buddha accentuates its towering presence.

The iconography of Cave 18 is quite unusual. The standing Buddha is attended by two Buddhas, two smaller smiling and friendly bodhisattvas, and the ten disciples, which are unusually lifelike and expressive. The monumental Buddha, unlike any other at the site (or anywhere else in China), is shown undergoing countless Buddha transformations in his upper body (fig. 3.32), a reflection, in my view, of the teaching expressed in the *guan*—the visualization sutras translated in the Gansu corridor.[56]

The Imperial Five were created according to a formula that stressed the central image in a sparsely ornamented interior architectural setting. The Northern Wei used this austere approach to express the solemnity and

grandeur of an icon that combined the identities of Buddha and the emperor. Embellishing the surrounding space would have only distracted from this foremost concern. Caves belonging to a second phase of development, however, were conceived as architectural spaces. According to Chinese chronology, these caves were begun circa 470 and completed by 494 when the capital was moved to Luoyang. A fascinating aspect of the construction of this group of equally imposing caves — which began immediately after completion of the Imperial Five — is that they were carved according to completely different guidelines.

The majority of these second-phase caves are paired chambers built in memory of members of the imperial family. (These include Caves 1 and 2, 5 and 6, 7 and 8, and 9 and 10.) The earliest of this group are 7 and 8, while 5 and 6, the most sumptuous, were created in the 480s. Caves 1 and 2 may have been the last of the paired chambers to be built. The most notable individual caves are Caves 3 (left unfinished), 11, 12, and 13.

The caves of the second phase suggest more complex and well-articulated architectural structures. Many have a front room with a columned porch as well as an inner room. The interiors, too, as in Cave 10, are enriched with imposing gates, windows, and elaborate ceilings, all executed in stone (fig. 3.33), and the walls are imaginatively divided into levels of ordered niches for the display of images. It is a dazzling setting for figura-

3.33 Gate (detail) of Cave 10 (inner room), painted sandstone, Yungang. Northern Wei dynasty, 470–480.

3.32 Standing Buddha, sandstone, Cave 18, Yungang. Northern Wei dynasty, 460–470.

3.34 Buddha of Cave 5 (inner room), sandstone, Yungang. Northern Wei dynasty, 480s.

3.35 Cave 6 (inner room), painted sandstone, Yungang. Northern Wei dynasty, 480s.

tive sculpture, even if these caves are more suggestive of architecture than true architectural forms themselves.

The Yungang stone carvers and builders may have found inspiration in the frescoes of the Dunhuang caves, but they may also have been responding to foreign models. Figured sculpture displayed in architectonic settings was often depicted on the facades of Roman and Hellenistic buildings. Because monumental stone buildings embellished with sculpture were previously unknown in China, the Northern Wei may have acquired knowledge of the classical tradition through the Silk Road.[57]

Several structural elements of these caves are Han in origin, however. The tiled roofs with acroteria, which were used to surmount the wall niches, were modeled after houses in the southern urban areas of China. The heavily curtained niches suggest the comfortable alcoved beds of rich households, and the gates framed

with sumptuous decoration are reminiscent of palatial entrances. In short, some of the architectural components used in these lavishly decorated caves resemble those in Chinese homes. The patrons of the caves — Tuoba courtiers and leaders — sought to emulate a Chinese setting. The Northern Wei annexation between 466 and 469 of Shandong, Anhui, and part of Jiangsu — territories formerly under the southern Liu Song dynasty — probably accelerated this sinification. The conquest certainly enriched the capital of Pingcheng (Datong) with artisans and scholars who had been living in a Chinese environment.

Caves 5 and 6, the most representative in style of these second-phase caves, are also the most lavish. The creativity is astonishing: architectural forms are fantastically conceived, and the walls are animated with highly ornamented images that are stylistically controlled to achieve a continuous, harmonious effect throughout.

The sculpture of Cave 6, furthermore, reflects a fully developed Northern Wei style.

It has been suggested that the Empress Dowager Feng, the de facto ruler between 479 and 490, had the two caves built on behalf of her deceased father and herself.[58] The taste and personality of the empress, who was known to be intensely pro-Chinese, may have determined the splendor of these interiors. The use of colors and gold on the surface of the sculptures made them seem even more opulent and festive.

Although paired, Caves 5 and 6 differ in layout: Cave 5 is trapezoidal and dominated by a colossal Buddha (that can be circumambulated) with attendants on each side (fig. 3.34), whereas Cave 6 is a square box containing a massive central shaft still connected to the ceiling and profusely ornamented on all sides with many sculptures (fig. 3.35). The shaft of Cave 6, which can also be circumambulated, is one of the most intriguing creations at the site. Because of its uniqueness and the audacity of its construction, the shaft may not be a symbolic stupa, like those created by the Liang in Gansu, but a replica of another Buddhist structure (fig. 3.36).

The central shaft was built on a platform and consists of two levels. The bottom level has four deeply cut, trabeated niches, one for each cardinal direction; these are sheltered by a tiled roof supported by square pillars. The top level, an open space delimited at the four corners by nine-storied towers on top of elephants, reaches to the ceiling and is quite radical in design. Within this level are four Buddha images standing back to back and facing the cardinal directions (they have been recently restored and gilded). The standard central shaft, rather than being symbolic of a stupa, may be a replica of the "image cart" used on Buddha's birthday to parade Buddhist icons in a religious festival that began in India. The monk Faxian writes in his diary (ca. 415) of having witnessed this joyous event both in the city of Pataliputra, India, and in Khotan, central Asia. The *History of the Wei* likewise describes the celebration, taking place in Luoyang, the second Northern Wei capital, and relates that the emperor would greet the floats with offerings of flowers and incense as they neared the palace.[59]

The use of a completely Chinese, Northern Wei style to depict Buddhas and bodhisattvas was an equally

3.36 Central pillar of Cave 6 (inner room), Yungang.

important innovation of Cave 6. The second tier of the rear wall contains excellent examples of this style. Three standing Buddhas, rather than being dressed in Gandharan-style monastic robes, wear the formal costume of court officials: all-enveloping bulky dress with ample sleeves resting on top of other layers of heavily pleated clothes (fig. 3.37). Because most of the body is hidden beneath these layered robes, the head and hands become major focal points of the sculpture — an emphasis also seen in Byzantine art. In this sculpture, the head has the marks of a Buddha, and the hands convey a specific didactic message. The style is insistently geometric; note the triangular shapes throughout.

The bodhisattvas depicted on the same wall of Cave 6 also display a new mode: their noticeably elongated bodies are covered by a dhoti and wrapped in a wide scarf, whose ends cross in front with pronounced loops and hang gracefully along the sides. The faces are no longer Gandharan but Chinese: they are sharply cut and rather angular, somewhat softened by a smile. Any number of reasons could explain this stylistic choice. Chinese features became popular under the pro-Chinese influence of Empress Dowager Feng and her step-grandson, Emperor Xiaowen (d. 499). From 472 until 499, many of their reforms and decrees steered Tuoba culture toward a purely Chinese lifestyle. The most prominent of these reforms were the abolition of Tuoba shamanistic rituals (472), the requirement that courtiers dress in Chinese clothes (486), the offering of sacrifices to legendary Chinese rulers (492), and the

banning of non-Chinese languages at court (495).[60] During the last quarter of the fifth century, therefore, the Northern Wei court (but not all the Tuobas) consciously rejected its ethnic roots to embrace the Han Chinese culture.

The stylistic innovations present in the second phase of Yungang were also certainly influenced by the annexation of Liu Song territories in 467. Alexander Soper has argued that the exposure to and availability of southern images (which were of a higher aesthetic and technological quality) shaped the Northern Wei style. His argument rests on the assumption that the south had already achieved a purely Chinese formula for the images of Buddhas and bodhisattvas — a formula that the north subsequently appropriated.[61] Most likely, however, the Northern Wei style was shaped by a combination of factors. Northern Wei artisans' improved skills, the patrons' acquired taste, and political circumstances certainly influenced the style of the sculpture of Yungang's second phase, as did the leaders of the Southern Dynasties and those who migrated into and through the Gansu corridor.

After the Northern Wei moved the capital south to Luoyang, Henan, in 494, artistic activity continued at the Yungang site, but no longer under imperial sponsorship. The side of the mountain west of the Imperial Five caves was developed on a much smaller scale, and private donors had images of various sizes carved within niches. The new style was applied, but in the modified, more linear manner that was to prevail in the sixth century.

3.37 Standing Buddha of Cave 6 (inner room, rear wall), Yungang.

The Art of Luoyang, the Second Northern Wei Capital

In 494 Emperor Xiaowen (renamed Gaozu after his death) transferred the capital south to Luoyang, in Henan, against the wishes of a Tuoba faction that could not accept the Chinese orientation of the ruler and his court. (The dissidents even included the emperor's son, who was forced to take his own life in 497.) Although economic and strategic reasons may have influenced the choice of the new capital, undoubtedly cultural and historical associations were primary motives. The future capital of Luoyang was to occupy the very grounds where the ancient capitals of the Zhou and Eastern Han had once stood. The establishment of a new capital would symbolize that the Tuobas were equal in status to the Chinese and could rule from the heart of the northern central plains.

It took almost twenty years to build the new capital, which spread over an area 16 kilometers long and 11 kilometers wide. Only after the city was in place with its government buildings, court quarters, and six hundred thousand inhabitants did the ruler and elites pour their remaining energy and wealth into the construction of lavish monasteries and temples. These are all recorded in Yang Xuanzhi's *Record of the Monasteries of Luoyang (Luoyang jialan ji)*, 547–550.[62] At Pingcheng, there had never been competition for resources to build the city and the Yungang caves, whereas diverse interests coexisted at Luoyang. Building cave temples became secondary to fulfilling the emperor's dream of completing his new capital. As a result, only a handful of Northern Wei caves were created. The court barely managed to finish even one cave, the Central Binyang. Most of the Longmen caves were built during the subsequent Tang dynasty.

The Central Binyang was one of three caves started in 508 and the only one completed during the dynasty — probably in 523. It takes center stage among the caves sponsored by the dynasty because it reflects the Northern Wei style at its summit and the iconography in its mature phase. This style is characterized by angular and elongated body forms and an emphasis on linear and abstract ornamental motifs.

Emperor Xuanwu (r. 500–515) sponsored the Central Binyang Cave to commemorate his father, Emperor Gaozu (d. 499). The regent, Empress Dowager Hu, who played a prominent role in court politics and showed great generosity toward Buddhism, supervised the construction of the Central Binyang. In addition, Empress Dowager Hu sponsored the most lavish temples in Luoyang, such as the Eternal Peace (Yongning) Temple, which graced the capital with its impressive lacquered wood pagoda. The two unfinished caves included the Northern Binyang, built in honor of the empress dowager, and the Southern Binyang, planned for Emperor Xuanwu himself after his death in 515.

Several changes in the arrangement, iconography, and style of the images took place between the building of the Yungang caves and those at Luoyang. In contrast to Yungang, the large Central Binyang Cave (9.3 meters high, 11.4 meters wide, and 9.85 meters deep) lacks a central stupa pillar, but instead has three places of devotion: one against the rear wall and two against the side walls (fig. 3.38). The most important area, in the rear, is identified by a group of five figures: a central Buddha (6.45 meters high without the throne) sits majestically on a lion throne, assisted by two standing bodhisattvas and Buddha's youngest disciple, Ananda, and oldest, Kashyapa (fig. 3.39). The two side areas feature, more simply, a standing Buddha flanked by two bodhisattvas (fig. 3.40).

Chinese scholars generally identify the three Buddhas of the Central Binyang as Shakyamuni. But their hand positions, variations of the giving gesture (the left hand faces downward with two fingers pointing to the ground), suggest that they could be representations of Maitreya Buddha. This hand gesture is used in a Southern Qi stele dated 483 (see fig. 3.70) where the Buddha is identified as Maitreya. Conceivably the three Buddhas

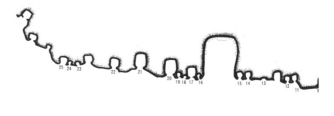

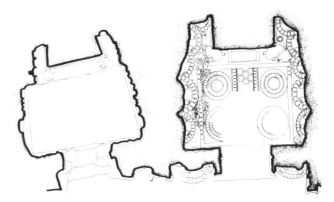

3.38 Plan of Central Binyang Cave, Longmen, Henan Province.

3.39 Pentad of Buddha, bodhisattvas, and disciples, limestone, Central Binyang Cave (rear wall). Northern Wei dynasty, 523.

3.40 Triad of Buddha and two bodhisattvas, limestone, Central Binyang Cave (side wall).

of the Central Binyang may represent the Maitreya Triple Assembly, which is recounted in sutras describing Maitreya's last reincarnation. This hypothesis is consistent with the existence of the Maitreya cult in pre–Northern Wei Gansu, which rested on the intense evangelism and translation work of the aforementioned Dao An (312–385) and his disciple Dharmaraksha, both devotees of Maitreya.

New formal concerns of the carvers in Luoyang are visible in the robes of the deities and in the arrangement and relationship between these robes and the body. The resulting ingenious formula represents the mature Northern Wei style. The Binyang Buddha's garment is no longer an official court costume (as in Yungang Cave 6), but is a monastic robe artfully draped over the body. When the Buddha is seated, this garment is tucked under him and displayed over the throne. The resulting overhang falls down in a cascade of controlled and multitiered arched patterns, a showcase of linear and abstract motifs that is characteristic of mature Northern Wei forms.

The bodies of the Buddhas and bodhisattvas are markedly flattened and elongated; they are now hidden under elaborately pleated and flaring skirts, which give the deities a look of imminent or arrested motion. The deities' faces are rectangular and elongated; their expression is softened by a smile. And the bodhisattvas wear crowns with elegant floral designs. Their costumes display refined touches such as scarves and jewelry crisscrossing the front of the body and two conspicuous disks on the shoulders, which clasp the robes.

The stone used for sculpture at Luoyang is a hard, dark gray limestone that tolerates sharp chiseling. Finely chiseled halos and aureoles back the images: the main Buddha's aureole stretches up and curves over the ceiling to merge with the carved lotus. Incised and low-relief carvings ornament the lateral walls and ceiling. On the walls are representations of divine beings and jataka tales set against a background of bejeweled hanging drapes. The ceiling is alive with rather angularly shaped celestials who carry trays of fruits and flowers while swiftly orbiting the huge, central lotus; their speed is conveyed by ribbons that flutter behind them (fig. 3.41). Even on the floor of this sumptuous cave are lotuses that were carved to lead worshipers to the main Buddha.

In Central Binyang craftsmen skillfully harmonized two contrasting aesthetic ideals: the formal religious images incorporated the recent developments in Northern Wei style, whereas the lively dynamic surface decor is purely Chinese in inspiration. The surface decor —

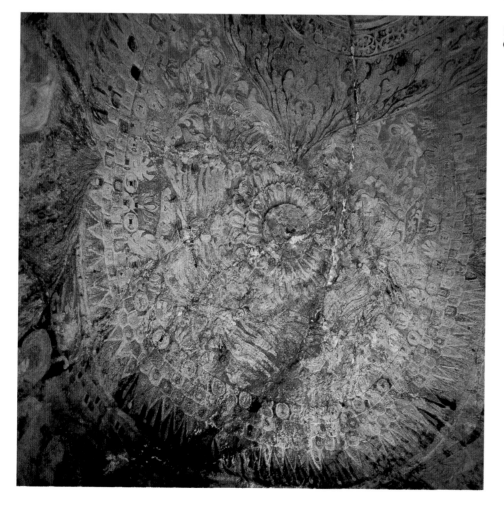

3.41 Ceiling of Central Binyang Cave, limestone.

originally painted in brilliant blue, red, and ochre, with a touch of gold — embodies an aesthetic different from that of the sculpture. Its sense of movement and multidimensional shapes are trademarks of the flamboyant art of the Warring States period.

The reliefs placed on either side of the cave entrance are accomplished creations of this period. Given their position, they were possibly the last in the cave to be completed. Placed on three levels, they represent (from top to bottom) the Manjushri-Vimalakirti debate, the Mahasattva jataka (the story of the bodhisattva prince, the future Shakyamuni, sacrificing himself to the tigers), and two extraordinary imperial processions.

The processions are of particular interest because they portray the splendor attained by the Northern Wei court at Luoyang. Both reliefs are no longer in situ: the emperor procession is now in The Metropolitan Museum of Art, New York, while the empress procession is in the Nelson-Atkins Museum of Art, Kansas City (figs. 3.42, 3.43). These reliefs likely commemorated historical events, namely the empress dowager's visit to the cave in 517 and, similarly, the emperor's presence at the consecration of the Central Binyang in 523. The emperor, empress, dignitaries, and ladies of the court all look gracious and solemn. Clad in Chinese court robes, these inhabitants of the newly built Luoyang appear genuinely Chinese. The two reliefs reflect an era in which the elite sought to emulate Han standards above all others. The reliefs are the most tangible evidence of the extent of sinification achieved by the Tuobas. The processions may have been inspired by the secular work of the Nanjing court painters, perhaps by similar masterpieces painted by the celebrated Gu Kaizhi (d. 406). When the low-relief, carved processions were covered with bright pigments and gold, they were remarkably similar to paintings.

The well-knit organization of the Central Binyang does not extend to the other Northern Wei caves of Longmen, even the three most important: Guyang, Lianhua, and Weizi. The Guyang Cave, in spite of its grand display of sculpture and impressive dimensions (11.10 meters high, 6.90 meters wide, and 13.55 meters deep), was not a product of imperial patronage, although several royal patrons and high officials sponsored the making of many images within the wall niches (fig. 3.44). Numerous inscriptions in the cave attest to the generosity of the patrons (the elite, the clergy, and Buddhist associations), whose largesse began as early as 495–498, as soon as the court had transferred to Luoyang.[63]

The individual Buddhas and bodhisattvas are chiefly representations of Shakyamuni and Maitreya, the prominent cultic figures of early Buddhism, rendered in the mature Northern Wei style. They have elongated and flattened bodies with narrow heads and pointy chins. The folds of their robes unfurl in a kind of controlled linear rhythm. The carver chiseled with great finesse and

3.42 Emperor procession, limestone, Central Binyang Cave. The Metropolitan Museum of Art, New York.

3.43 Empress procession, limestone with traces of color, Central Binyang Cave. 203.2 × 278.1 cm. The Nelson-Atkins Museum of Art, Kansas City, Missouri.

detail the large aureoles of the deities and the ornate frames of the niches. These inventive ornaments match the effects achieved in contemporary gilt bronzes.

During the last phase of the Northern Wei dynasty, the town of Gongxian County, Henan, was strategically important because it controlled the route to Taiyuan in Shanxi, another important military and political center of the dynasty. The Gongxian caves (located approximately sixty kilometers east of Longmen) occupy the spot where, according to the on-site Tang stele, dated 662, the Northern Wei emperor Xiaowen (r. 471–499) stopped on a stormy night to behold the landscape between the Yi and Luo Rivers. The majesty of the location induced him to create the Xixuan Temple at this location, as a precursor of the grottoes, which were probably built at the same time as the Binyang group.[64] The caves were undoubtedly completed before the year 528, when everyone in the royal house was massacred by Erzhu Rong, the leader of the dissident Tuoba faction.

The Gongxian complex reflects the waning of Northern Wei power. The complex is much smaller and

has far fewer caves than Yungang. Similarly, the glorious achievements of Longmen are superseded by less imposing, although quite accomplished, formal and structural effects. Gongxian reflects the beginning of a transitional political and artistic phase.

In addition to a monumental carving outside Cave 1 of a Buddha, two bodhisattvas, and two guardians, some of which is now missing, Gongxian consists of five caves: 1 and 2 were sponsored by Emperor Xuanwu and Empress Dowager Hu, who were the patrons of Central Binyang; 3 and 4 may have been built under the patronage of Emperor Xiaoming (r. 516–528) and his consort; 5 differs structurally and was probably completed by 538 (after the end of the dynasty). Whereas Cave 5 is a square chamber with three large niches on three walls, the other four caves use a central stupa-pillar construction, the formula first developed by the Liang in Gansu, appropriated by the Northern Wei after the unification, and adapted in Yungang (as in Caves 1 and 3). At Gongxian this central structure undergoes further modification: in Cave 3 it has two tiers, but in the remaining caves it includes only

3.45 Central pillar of Cave 1, limestone, Gongxian County, Henan Province. Northern Wei dynasty, ca. 525.

3.44 Interior of Guyang Cave, limestone, Longmen, Henan
Province. Northern Wei dynasty, started in 495–498.

3.46 Detail of Cave 4 ceiling, painted limestone, Gongxian County, Henan Province. Northern Wei dynasty, ca. 525.

one level. In either case, large niches have been opened at each of the four cardinal directions (fig. 3.45). The ceilings at Gongxian are coffered and decorated with refined carvings of lotuses, celestials, and newly reborn souls, all of which still retain traces of color (fig. 3.46).

Because of its influential patrons, Cave 1 is the largest (6 meters high, 5 meters wide, and 6.5 meters deep). Its importance is also apparent in the use of prominent religious and secular scenes modeled after those in the Central Binyang Cave. These scenes illustrate the Manjushri-Vimalakirti (Wenshu-Weimojie) debate, the miraculous joint manifestation of Prabhuta-

ratna and Shakyamuni based on the Lotus Sutra, and a fragmentary Parinirvana, themes that were popular in the decor of the three imperial sites. Cave 1 also features a long imperial procession that unfolds on three levels (fig. 3.47). (Similar processions are also present in Caves 3 and 4.) The processions follow the model of Longmen's Central Binyang, but the Gongxian version's overall effect is less flamboyant, with a sober elegance and touch of humanity. The Spirit Kings (Shenwang) carved on the dado of the shaft and walls (fig. 3.48) are reminiscent of those in the Central Binyang, where such carvings were first designed.[65]

3.47 Imperial procession, limestone, Cave 1 (entrance wall), Gongxian County, Henan Province. Northern Wei dynasty, ca. 525.

3.48 Spirit King, limestone dado frieze, central pillar of Cave 4, Gongxian County, Henan Province. Northern Wei dynasty, ca. 525.

The Spirit Kings — mythical, beastlike creatures, usually in a group of ten — embody the forces of nature and derive from the pre-Han text *Classic of Mountains and Water* (*Shanhai jing*). The sturdiness and corporeality of the Spirit Kings make them ideal supports for the architecture above. Their natural body shapes, and playful poses and facial expressions, signal a departure from the Northern Wei style of flat, linear, and abstract designs. The Spirit Kings became extremely popular in post-Wei art.

Gongxian sculpture embodies the Northern Wei style in its last stage of development. The images of Buddhas and bodhisattvas carved with great perfection display a softer modeling, with rounder contours. The suave smiles of Gongxian deities, too, make them seem gentler and more accessible. The cave temples of Gongxian carry the imprint of a dynastic work, but their execution on a smaller — albeit less stately — scale, where this somewhat attenuated Northern Wei style is featured, makes them more intimate and humanly accessible than those of Longmen.

The many multicolored fragments of clay sculpture — heads and torsos of bodhisattvas, donors, and monks — that once decorated the pagoda of the Yongning Temple in Luoyang, the most prominent of the Northern Wei monuments built in 519 under the sponsorship of Empress Dowager Hu, display an even gentler appearance than the Gongxian statuary (see figs. 4.7–4.10). The statuettes of the Yongning pagoda (unfortunately, none has survived intact) — which are marked by sweet, oval faces that grace elegant bodies with narrow waists — anticipate the Northern Qi style that followed.[66]

For seventy-five years, at the three Northern Wei imperial cave temples, the style favored by the Tuoba elite and the iconographies preached by their clerics were developed. During this time, Northern Wei style passed from a formative stage to its mature, transitional, and final stages. Because it was a prestigious, "dynastic" (imperially sponsored) style, it was taken as a model throughout the provinces. When erecting sites in other parts of China, undoubtedly one looked to Yungang and Longmen as guidelines. This was true for the Northern Caves (Beishiku) carved in the yellow sandstone of Fuzhongshan, at Sigou in the Qingyang district, northeast Gansu.[67]

The date for this site is given in an inscription at a sister site, the Southern Caves (Nanshiku), located fifty kilometers to the south in the Jingchuan district. A stele there identifies the patron of the Northern Caves site as the prefectural governor of Jingchuan, Xi Kangsheng, who had the northern site built in 510. Since the Northern Caves are quite similar to the Southern Caves, many have concluded that they were created at approximately the same time. The two sites, which postdate Yungang and are contemporary to Longmen, carry stylistic elements of both imperial projects. But local trends have

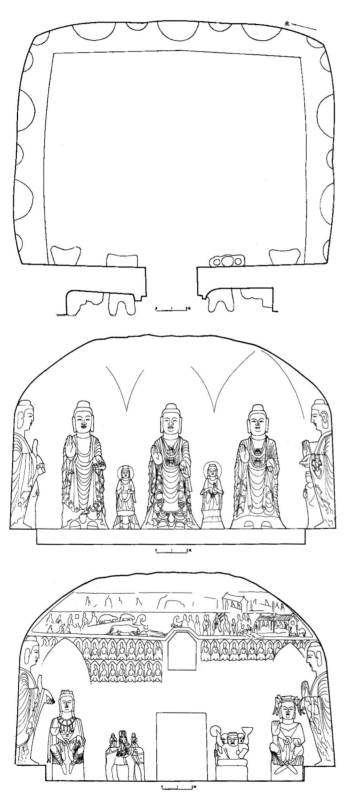

3.49 Plan and two schematic drawings of Cave 165, Northern Caves, Qingyang, Gansu Province.

3.50 Buddhas of Cave 165 (rear wall), sandstone, Northern Caves. Northern Wei dynasty, ca. 475.

influenced the dynastic formula, much as they have encouraged innovation in other independent images in stone, clay, and bronze.

Among the many Northern Wei caves, the well-preserved Cave 165 at Fuzhongshan stands out for its grand sculpture and impressive size (14 meters high, 21.7 meters wide, and 15.7 meters deep). In terms of layout and style, one can link Cave 165 to the Imperial Five at Yungang (fig. 3.49). The rectangular interior does not use the central stupa, but has a tall platform, reputedly added in Song time, running along the side and back walls. On this platform stand seven Buddhas, each 8 meters tall, attended by ten bodhisattvas, each about 4 meters in height (fig. 3.50). Along the entrance wall are four images (ranging from 3 to 4 meters in height), two on each side of the entrance: two bodhisattva Maitreyas rendered with slight variations of jewelry and leg postures, the bodhisattva Samantabhadra (Puxian) on an elephant, accompanied by two much smaller personages (fig. 3.51), and the three-headed, four-handed demigod Ashura (fig. 3.52).[68] Behind the

Buddhas are carved huge, unadorned aureoles. The upper sections of the walls, which slope inward to suggest a tentlike roof, carry jataka representations and the Thousand Buddhas (discussed later), all very damaged and barely distinguishable.

The iconography of the cave is unusual and not easily explained. While the group of seven Buddhas with Maitreya was anticipated in the Liang miniature pillars of Gansu and was also present in Yungang Cave 13 (south wall), the presence of two dissimilar Maitreyas, Samantabhadra, and Ashura is unique. The last two deities were to become prominent in the Buddhist iconography of the Tang, with Samantabhadra paired with Manjushri (Wenshu), and Ashura included among the eminent guardian figures called Demigods of the Eight Classes (Babu Tianlong).

Stylistically, the Northern Caves of the Northern Wei share features of the Luoyang dynastic model. A northwest influence, however, is also apparent in the more austere and even minimalist quality of the sculpture. The deities, like the seven Buddhas, resemble the Central Binyang Buddhas in modeling and mode of dress, although they do not have their refined execution. And the Buddha's head is more square and stern than in Luoyang. Yet the Buddhas of the two sites have the same hand gestures. Moreover, they are adorned with the same three-layered cloth embellished with cascading pleats. The bodhisattvas of the Northen Caves site and those of the Luoyang Central Binyang also display these stylistic differences. Both sets of bodhisattvas wear the standard Northern Wei costume and ornaments, but the modeling of the body and the head shape differ. The Northern Caves bodhisattvas have blocklike bodies, plainer surfaces, and squarish heads (like the Buddhas), surmounted by tall, simple headdresses (not crowns as in Luoyang) softened by lotus flowers. In short, the Northern Caves sculptors' stylistic approach is more sober and sturdy.

These basic traits of the northwest reemerged after the fall of the Wei, to form the Northern Zhou style (discussed later). The sculpture of this Gansu site is one of the first examples in the history of Chinese Buddhist art of local tastes modifying a dynastic style. By the time they had carved the Northern Caves sculpture, the carvers of northwest China (especially those of Shaanxi) had developed a peculiarly local style with angular, gaunt, formless bodies covered with robes defined by regular lines. Nonetheless, this style was not fully employed at Cave 165, which seems to have closer artistic ties to the imperially sponsored caves in the capital.

3.51 Samantabhadra (Puxian) bodhisattva on elephant, sandstone, Cave 165, Northern Caves.

Gilt Bronzes of the Northern Wei Dynasty

Under Emperor Xiaowen, during the Taihe era (477–499), production of gilt bronzes was particularly prolific, and superior standards were achieved. The major center of gilt bronze making remained Dingzhou in Hebei, which was so important that one can speak of a Hebei School.

The period between 450 and 500 produced three major types of images, which became prototypes for over a century: a Buddha image that Chinese scholars designate as Buddha Preaching the Law (Fo shuo Fa), the twin Shakyamuni and Duobao (Prabhutaratna) Buddhas and the bodhisattva Guanshiyin/Guanyin (Avalokiteshvara).[69]

The Buddha Preaching the Law type is depicted both standing and seated. The appellation derives from the Buddha's pose: the right hand is shown palm out and raised almost at shoulder level, while the left hand holds the robe. The Buddha's identity (whether standing or seated) oscillates between Shakyamuni and Maitreya, depending on the inscription carved on the pedestal. The Shakyamuni Buddha from Shijiazhuang (35.2 centimeters high and dated by inscription to 475) in the Hebei Provincial Museum is an excellent example of a standing Buddha Preaching the Law (fig. 3.53). The seated Buddha Preaching the Law is, instead, typically shown on a high pedestal and backed by a large aureole, which is cast separately from the otherwise one-piece image. The Buddha wears a monastic robe, leaving the right shoulder and part of the chest exposed. The gilt-bronze seated Shakyamuni, in the National Palace Museum, Taibei, is an outstanding example of the Fo shuo Fa type (fig. 3.54). The 40.3-centimeter-high image, dated 477, was made in Hebei. In addition to having all of the standard characteristics of this kind of icon, the pedestal is fashioned like Mount Sumeru with two lions halfway up and two kneeling adorers on each of the front corners. The attached aureole is richly decorated on both sides: in the front, the inner band contains seven small Buddhas (a reference to the Buddhas of the Past) surrounding the main Buddha, while the outer band features dramatic stylized flames darting toward the aureole's rim. On the back of the aureole, images are displayed on several levels. Starting from the top, the two Shakyamuni and Prabhutaratna Buddhas occupy the jeweled pagoda side by side; below them Vimalakirti and Manjushri engage in the famous debate; immediately beneath, Buddha presides in glory over

3.52 Three-headed, four-handed Ashura, sandstone, Cave 165, Northern Caves.

numerous standing and kneeling bodhisattvas, divine offerers, monks, and flying celestials; and the lowest levels depict the story from Buddha's last life — that is, the birth, the first seven steps, and the bath of the newborn.

This Buddha is related to the clay Buddhas of Maijishan, Cave 78 (see fig. 3.24), and also to the Yungang colossal Buddha of Cave 20, both of which preceded the bronze version. The bronze, however, represents a much higher level of artistic achievement. In particular, the piece achieves a rare balance between abstract surface decor and a sensitive naturalism in the body and face. The rich iconography unites the major Mahayana doctrines developed in the Gansu corridor with a few lingering Theravada teachings.

The second new image is a pair of Buddhas, seated side by side and not identical (how similar they are varies from work to work). The twin Buddha image is wholly indigenous to China and is seen throughout the three imperial cave sites. The common traits of this style are a conspicuous aureole with imagery carved on the back and a rather tall pedestal that carries an incised inscription.

The Shakyamuni and Prabhutaratna gilt bronze is a

superior example of the twin Buddha image, although the bronze's shape is unique. The 23.5-centimeter-tall bronze was made in Hebei, dated Northern Wei 489, and is now held in the Nezu Institute of Fine Arts, Tokyo (fig. 3.55). For this work, cast in one piece, the artisan used a very tall pedestal, placed the two deities under a cusped arch, and modeled a fairly flat plaque. In the upper front area are the two Buddhas variously attired and performing different hand gestures (the dhyana and the abhaya). A male and female donor, below the Buddhas, are quite noticeable for their size and their Tuoba costumes (the bronze was cast after the decree prohibiting native attire for the elite). They seem humble and pure as they each hold a lotus after placing their offerings below the deities.

On the reverse side of the aureole, a Buddha and two bodhisattvas are represented under a baldachin. Interestingly, their style of execution is superior to that used in the front. Indeed, the front possesses a beguiling "primitive" quality — an aspect that does not necessarily stem from a lack of skill, but may instead be a whimsical experiment of the artisan or the result of a patron's demand.

The third and last iconographic innovation of the second half of the fifth century is the standing bodhisattva Guanyin, the great compassionate one, who is typically represented with a lotus in the right hand and a bottle of ambrosia in the left (alternatively, the left may hold a scarf). The canonical source of Guanyin worship is chapter 25 of the Lotus Sutra. The sutra

3.53 Standing Buddha Preaching the Law (front and back), gilt bronze. Northern Wei dynasty, 475. Hebei Provincial Museum, Shijiazhuang.

extols the miraculous power of this savior, who appears in as many as thirty-three guises to rescue people from all types of perils, including fire, murder, robbery, shipwreck, and even poisonous snakes.

The initial visualization of this deity, as a lotus holder, may derive from India. It remained popular in China until the Tang dynasty. The Gansu corridor played an influential role in the popularization of Guanyin. An ill Liang king, Juqu Mengxun, was advised to recite chapter 25 of the sutra; he was cured, after which he became one of the earliest and most influential devotees of the deity. Excellent examples of Guanyin gilt bronzes are found in the early Maijishan caves.

A Lotus-holder Guanyin manufactured in Hebei and now in the Freer Gallery of Art, Washington, D.C.

(fig. 3.56), is one of the earliest extant Guanyin bronzes. The work, 23.1 centimeters high and dated to 453, is formed of two pieces — the figure and a detachable aureole, which consists almost entirely of leaping flames. The bejeweled Guanyin stands with feet wide apart on a pedestal-supported lotus. His costume is standard Northern Wei: a dhoti draped from waist to knees, a cape covering the shoulders and crossing in front of the body, and a long stole that seems swept back, as if by a gust of wind. (The billowing scarf motif is prominent in the clay sculptures and paintings of Gansu.) A crown elegantly complements the attire, and the standard lotus and bottle are also present.

The gilt bronzes executed in the first quarter of the sixth century demonstrate the continually evolving con-

3.54 Seated Shakyamuni Buddhas (front and back), gilt bronze, Hebei Province. Northern Wei dynasty, 477. National Palace Museum, Taibei, Taiwan.

3.55 Shakyamuni and Prabhutaratna (front and back), gilt bronze, Hebei Province. Northern Wei dynasty, 489. Nezu Institute of Fine Arts, Tokyo.

tent and style. Among numerous works from several centers of production of this period — Ningxia, Shaanxi, and Shandong — are two superb works of the Hebei School.[70] The lavish and brilliantly arranged images displayed on one of these gilt bronzes show the height of Buddhist metalwork artistry on the eve of the dynasty's fall; the other example is celebrated for its highly expressive use of a Northern Wei style.

The Maitreya altarpiece, 76.9 centimeters high and dated 524, was a product of Hebei, from the area of present-day Zhengding County, and is now in the collection of The Metropolitan Museum of Art, New York (fig. 3.57). Maitreya, the Buddha of the Future — as he is called in the inscription — is portrayed standing against the glittering background of an aureole. His hand gestures reassure the worshiper and convey the message that a wish shall be granted. Maitreya towers over the large, well-orchestrated group. Two standing bodhisattvas are shown at his sides; two others sit at his feet with pensive poses. Four offerers in Tuoba costume carry bowls in their hands. Two Thunderbolt Holders are placed as guardians at each corner of the altarpiece. Two lions sit on each side of the central incense burner

3.56 Lotus-holder Guanyin, gilt bronze, Hebei Province. Northern Wei dynasty, 453. 23.1 × 11.9 cm. Freer Gallery of Art, Smithsonian Institution, Washington, D.C.

3.57 Maitreya altarpiece, gilt bronze, Hebei Province. Northern Wei dynasty, 524. 76.9 cm. The Metropolitan Museum of Art, New York.

below the Buddha. Ten flying celestials (originally eleven), each with a musical instrument, are depicted as if just alighting on the rim of the large aureole. The images are placed on tiers, with each tier smaller than the one below. At the apex, a celestial with trailing garments swoops down. All of the holy participants seem caught in an imaginary triangle — the bound space of the heavenly realm. Tension, vigor, and movement enliven this magnificent and uncommonly large votive altarpiece, which a pious mother dedicated to the spiritual well-being of her deceased son. This all-encompassing work may be a miniature reproduction of an altar inside a contemporary temple in the capital.[71]

The second example, a 26-centimeter-tall representation of the twin Shakyamuni and Prabhutaratna Buddhas dated 518, was created in Hebei and now resides in

the Musée des Arts Asiatiques-Guimet, Paris (fig. 3.58). The two are seated side by side on a tall pedestal, each Buddha backed by his own aureole and leaning slightly toward the other, as if conversing.

In the mature Northern Wei style, surface embellishments rather than volume were the dominant concern. The appearance of the Buddhas is strikingly ethereal: their slim bodies with sloping shoulders seem to dissolve under the flowing robes. A lingering smile brightens the angular, gaunt faces (with their flat foreheads squared off at the sides, and pointed chins). The robe is a beautiful pattern of flat and slightly overlapping folds that form a cascade with sharply pointed ends projecting at the sides. One can almost read the tension of the age in this flamboyant work — a tension fed by the latent conflict between the Tuobas in power (who had metamorphosed themselves into Chinese) and those

3.58 Twin Buddhas Shakyamuni and Prabhutaratna, gilt bronze, Hebei Province. Northern Wei dynasty, 518. Musée des Arts Asiatiques-Guimet, Paris.

3.59 Rubbings of Wei Wenlang stele (front and back), limestone. Northern Wei dynasty, 424. Yaowangshan Museum, Yaoxian County, Shaanxi Province.

Tuobas who proudly clung to their native traditions. The Guimet bronze betrays the anxiety of a dynasty soon to end tragically.

In 528, the brilliance of Luoyang was destroyed by the revolt led by the nativist Tuoba dissident Erzhu Rong. The Tuobas who had been ignored by the court and who had stayed behind in the northern garrisons biding time rushed south to destroy Luoyang, now a hated symbol, and murdered the empress dowager and the infant emperor. The great effort of building the impressive city, a symbol of acculturation to Chinese mores that had been sponsored by a small elite, was in turn wiped away by the brutality of a few. Luoyang had lasted no longer than a quarter of a century. The dynasty's final destruction took place in 534 when it split to form the Eastern Wei (534–550) with its capital at Ye, Hebei (near present-day Handan), and the Western Wei (535–557) with its capital at Xi'an, Shaanxi, where the survivors of Luoyang regrouped.

Stone Steles of the Northern Wei

During the period of disunion, especially the century and a half marked by Northern Wei rule, a new genre of Buddhist devotional sculpture arose — that is, steles with carved images (*zaoxiangbei*). These works, tablets of varying size made of locally available stone, are carved with images and inscribed with the date, donor's name, and purpose. Although steles were a new genre in Buddhist art, they had been used since the Eastern Han in a Confucian and Daoist framework to record such important events as state edicts or the deaths of famous leaders.[72] And large steles erected in poor agricultural communities may have substituted for much more costly temples.

The most prolific period for stele making was 400–600: some two hundred works from this period are still extant in China, while many others are in Western collections. Steles are thus a sizable and relevant aspect of

Buddhist art. Shaanxi Province, more specifically the area of Yaoxian and Fuxian Counties, north of Xi'an, played a prominent role in stele production and created a distinctive school. Shaanxi, furthermore, was where Daoist art developed in China. The Wei Wenlang, dated 424, remains the earliest stele carved in northern China, although this date has recently been challenged. It is now kept in the Yaowangshan Museum, Yaoxiang Shaanxi (fig. 3.59). Rather crudely executed, this limestone stele, 124 centimeters high and about 70 centimeters wide, possibly reflects the coexistence and mutual influence of Daoism and Buddhism, which had emerged in the Gansu corridor during the fourth century. The inscription calls the stele a Buddhist-Daoist work, a claim further supported by the two images carved in the front niche. Although their damaged headdresses prevent conclusive identification, they may represent a Daoist and a Buddhist deity. On the back side is shown either Shakyamuni or Maitreya as a bodhisattva in a contemplative pose. Additional Buddhist references are carved on the sides. A cart pulled by an ox, a horseback rider, and a camel are portrayed on the front of the stele, and below these is a procession of several donors. The stele displays the traits of the Shaanxi style, discussed later.

Another work, the sandstone Daoist stele dated Northern Wei 515 and now in the Osaka Municipal Museum of Art, may appear to be a Buddhist product (fig. 3.60). In fact, just as Buddhism had appropriated Daoist concepts when initially spreading its doctrine to the Chinese, Daoism seized from Buddhism not only the idea of a canon but also the concept of using the figurative arts to create universal Daoist images. The Daoist sage Laozi, in the guise of the Supreme Lord Lao, or Taishang Laojun, sits like a Buddha assisted by two attending figures — perhaps Yin Xi and Liangzheng, the first people to receive his teaching. Laozi is further memorialized on the pedestal, where images of donors are burning incense. His countenance is very similar to that of a Buddha, and his throne is, in some works, a lion throne (like Buddha's), but there are, as in this instance, some basic differences. A Daoist usually is dressed as a Han official, holds a fan or fly whisk, sports a mustache, and wears a coronet. In this stele, too, animals such as intertwined hornless dragons (which carry a special symbolism for the Daoist believer) and the sun and moon were added to reinforce the link with Daoism.[73]

The last Daoist stele discussed here is of the deified Laozi, the founder of Daoism, seated to the left of the Jade Emperor (Yuhuang dadi; fig. 3.61). Three assistants stand behind them. Because of its style this work, dated

3.60 Laozi stele, sandstone, probably from Shaanxi Province. Northern Wei dynasty, 515. Osaka Municipal Museum of Art, Osaka.

Northern Wei 527, is ascribed to Shaanxi; it is part of the collection at the National Museum of China, Beijing. The inscription on the back of the stele, which measures 27.8 by 27.5 centimeters, explains that Wang Ashan was the primary donor. She is shown standing by an ox cart. The secondary patrons are her niece and her son, who are portrayed riding horses. The Wang Ashan stele cannot be mistaken for a Buddhist work: the Daoist characteristics are clearly defined.

The next two examples clarify the distinctive Shaanxi style, which was used for Daoist and Buddhist sculpture alike. The limestone bodhisattva Maitreya stele (86.9 centimeters high) from Xingping County, Shaanxi, dated Northern Wei 471, typifies the earliest format in northern China — a primary seated image on the front side and narrative scenes on the back (fig. 3.62) — rendered in the local Shaanxi idiom. A young-looking, plump-faced Maitreya, clasping a round jewel, is seated on a lion throne with crossed legs (similar to the version found in Cave 275 of the Northern Liang site Dunhuang; see fig. 3.17); his feet are supported by the Indian earth goddess Bhumidevi. The two-tiered throne features seated adorers and standing donors, now barely visible. The front of the all-encompassing aureole uses

3.61 Laozi and the Jade Emperor stele (front and back), limestone, Shaanxi Province. Northern Wei dynasty, 527. National Museum of China, Beijing.

bands of abstract darting flames and seated miniature Buddhas, while the superimposed halo displays scrolled leaves and vines in addition to the Buddhas. These motifs and their organization belong to the vocabulary of the contemporary gilt bronzes.

The back of the aureole displays numerous scenes of Shakyamuni's former and last lives (the conception, the birth, the prediction of the court diviner Ashita, the first bath, the seven jewels of the universal ruler, or Cakravartin, and the Buddha of the Past, Dipamkara) arranged within orderly cells on seven tiers. It is also possible that the narrative cycle refers to Maitreya's last incarnation.[74] The back of the pedestal carries a lengthy but fragmentary inscription explaining that the donor had the surname Jing and that he dedicated the work to his dead parents.

The use of Shakyamuni's stories in conjunction with the bodhisattva Maitreya reflects a tradition established by Liangzhou art and a general trend in early Buddhism in which the two deities were closely associated and at times visually interchanged. The choice of iconography is thus typical of northwestern China, including Shaanxi. Steles with the same iconographic themes from the central plains display Shakyamuni in front and fewer references to his life on the back.

The stringy drapery folds rendered with equally spaced grooves indicate the beginning of the Shaanxi style. As this feature evolved it became the trademark of the Shaanxi School. Before 500, as in this 471 stele, this distinctive style still used a certain roundness in its modeling; after 500, modeled works were renounced in favor of linear works in which the pattern was the most important feature.

The mature Shaanxi style is splendidly revealed in a four-sided stele that some scholars believe was derived from a stupa. Dated Northern Wei 501, the work, 58 centimeters tall and wide and 50 centimeters deep, was excavated at Zhajiazhai, Xi'an, and now resides in the local Beilin Museum (fig. 3.63). In each of the four directional niches sits a Buddha, each distinct from the others in hand gesture, pose, costume, and attendants. The stele was created in a Chang'an workshop and represents the pinnacle of Shaanxi refinement and inventiveness (note the playful figure supporting the columns). In this example, linearity triumphs over every other concern: tactile qualities are of no interest and bodies seem to exist only to support a cloth animated by controlled, fine lines that form intricate geometric patterns.

The mature phase of the Northern Wei style, which coincides with that of Luoyang, is also evident among

3.62 Seated Maitreya stele (front and back), limestone, Xingping County, Shaanxi Province. Northern Wei dynasty, 471. Beilin Museum, Xi'an.

3.63 Four-sided stele, limestone, found in Zhajiazhai, Xi'an. Northern Wei dynasty, 501. Beilin Museum, Xi'an. *Top row,* front and back.

northwest steles. A superb example of this mature phase is the stele in Maijishan Cave 133 (fig. 3.64). This work, which is 155 centimeters high and 76 centimeters wide, is not dated by inscription, but its style and iconography suggest the first quarter of the sixth century. In its main imagery, the work reflects the themes used at the dynastic sites (Yungang and Luoyang), per-

haps owing to the patron's taste. But the vivid and delightful vignettes on the side panels undoubtedly resonate with the aesthetic of Maijishan, which favored round bodies and soft contours.

An additional point of interest is the layout of the images. Only the front of the stele is carved with representations, and the space is divided according to the

3.64 Stele, painted stone, Cave 133, Maijishan caves, Tianshui, Gansu Province. Northern Wei dynasty, first quarter of the 6th century.

canonical importance of the scenes. Thus on the central axis we find three Mahayana themes, which are the leitmotif of Northern Wei Buddhist art. At the top are the twin Buddhas; the bodhisattva Maitreya occupies the center; and on the lowest level is Shakyamuni preaching and attended by two bodhisattvas and four Heavenly Kings (Lokapalas). With the exception of the second-from-the-bottom side panels, which show the Vimalakirti-Manjushri debate, all of the areas show stories from Shakyamuni's past and last lives, such as the Dipamkara Buddha prophecy, conception and birth, Mara's assault, and the Parinirvana. In short, the content of the stele sums up all the iconographic developments that took place in the northwest and spread to the central plains under the Northern Wei rulers. The content and composition of Buddhist steles like the Maijishan one suggest that this genre, which originated in the same region as the first embellished caves, may be an attempt to reproduce in miniature the iconography of such caves.

The artistic and iconographic approach to steles in the northeast — that is, metropolitan Luoyang and Henan, southern Shanxi, Hebei, and Shandong Provinces — is markedly different from that in the northwest. Two formats prevail: steles made of tall, rectangular slabs topped by as many as three pairs of intertwined dragons (their fronts embellished with reliefs neatly arranged in superimposed tiers, their backs carrying rows of donors); and steles with an imposing triad. In both types the style is that of dynastic Longmen.

The gray limestone monumental stele dated Northern Wei 529 and now in the Museum of Fine Arts, Boston, is a fine example of the first, tall type; it is 183 centimeters high (fig. 3.65). The style is unmistakably mature Northern Wei as seen in Luoyang: the figures are elongated, and crisp details executed in low relief animate the surface.[75]

The style is grandiose in both scale and subject. Three pairs of intertwined dragons at the top of the stele add an elegant, sinuous pattern to the stone surface. In front, they form an appropriate frame to the uppermost niche, where the newborn Buddha receives his first bath from the nine-headed dragon (naga). The central section of the stele, framed by a palmette border, is occupied by the main deity, the Shakyamuni Buddha, who is attended by a large group of bodhisattvas, disciples, guardians, and celestials, while the many donors are housed in small pavilions. Above the main niche are two rows of miniature Buddhas; below, in the two tall bands, are several donors beside the central incense

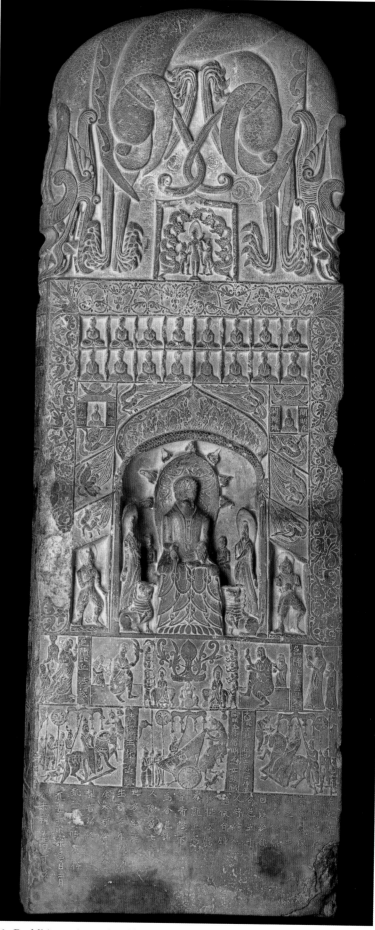

3.65 Buddhist votive stele with Buddhist figures and inscriptions, limestone. Northern Wei dynasty, 529. 191 × 67 cm. Museum of Fine Arts, Boston. Caroline Balch Allen Fund and Cranmere Nesmith Wallace Fund, 23.120.

3.66 Tian Yanhe stele, limestone. Northern Wei dynasty, ca. 525. Henan Province Museum, Zhengzhou.

burner, with a monk on each side. The inscription is on the lowest front section. The reverse and lateral sides are also carved, chiefly with rows of donors (six in the back), who by the inscription number fifty (as many as are carved on the monument) and belong to a devotional society; their listing by title displays a deep respect for hierarchy. Some of the side panels show acrobats — walking on stilts, performing somersaults — as are often seen in Han dynastic funerary art (more acrobats are placed in front near the incense burner).

The stele donated by Tian Yanhe represents the second type of northeast style (fig. 3.66). Originating in Henan, the sculpture, which is 96 centimeters high and 43.5 centimeters wide, illustrates the elegant formal artistic language of Longmen, especially that of the

Central Binyang Cave. The triad carved in the front unequivocally stresses the hierarchy of the Buddha and the two flanking bodhisattvas, and the deities, carved in the round, have been set cleverly against the finely worked, all-encompassing aureole. The leaf-shaped aureole, treated like a damasked surface, is teeming with lotus plants and abstract twisting flames, which are expressed with a finely controlled line.

The last example is an imposing stele, 3.1 meters high, ascribed to the Eastern Wei (534–550); it is one of the Buddhist reliefs among nearly three hundred pieces found in 1996 at the site of the former Longxing Temple, Qingzhou, Shandong (fig. 3.67).[76] This superb work, with remnants of paint and gilt on its surface, well represents the iconographic and aesthetic choices of Shandong despite missing sections of its huge aureole and base (fig. 3.68). The pedestal supporting the standing bodhisattvas — composed of luscious lotuses sprouting from the mouths of two winding dragons — is a prominent stylistic novelty. Also unusual is the reliquary stupa supported by two flying celestials at the stele summit. This stupa is called Ashokan in reference to the structure's origin in India during the reign of Emperor Ashoka (third century B.C.E.). In a single night Emperor Ashoka erected eighty-four thousand such stupas. Ashokan stupas later spread throughout Buddhist lands, arriving in the provinces of Zhejiang and Jiangsu especially during the administration of the pious Emperor Wu (r. 502–549) of the Liang dynasty, who styled himself on the model of his famous Indian predecessor. Ashokan stupas are single-storied square buildings characterized by acroteria; usually the roof is flat, but in this case a symbolic triple jewel rises from a dome. The use of this reliquary is indeed an iconographic novelty tied, moreover, to southern conventions. Uncommonly fine artistry shaped the composition of sinuous dragons spouting lotuses and of celestials balancing each other in midair, steadied by graceful trailing garments. The deeply cut forms emerge from the stones with exquisite ease and sensitivity.

The Buddhist steles carved between 450 and 535 thus show clear variations in style and can be attributed to specific schools using the Northern Wei style. In addition to the name of the donor(s), the steles' inscriptions frequently show the location, date, and purpose of the donation — which has allowed us to trace regional influences. The Shaanxi School was among the earliest production centers in northern China, supplying Daoist as well as Buddhist works; it was followed by the Henan School, notably at Luoyang, in the last phase of the

3.67 Stele triad (Buddha and bodhisattvas), gilded and painted limestone, from the discovery in 1996 at Longxing Temple, Qingzhou, Shandong Province. Eastern Wei dynasty. Qingzhou Municipal Museum.

3.68 Schematic drawing of stele triad from Longxing Temple, Qingzhou.

Northern Wei dynasty, and by that of Shandong. The imagery used in the steles was also influenced by the ecclesiastics residing in the major Buddhist centers: those of the northwest undoubtedly responded to the doctrinal work of the famous Kumarajiva and his predecessors. The most frequently used images were of great Mahayana themes of Manjushri-Vimalakirti, the twin Shakyamuni and Prabhutaratna Buddhas together with the complete cycle of Buddha's lives, and the worship of Maitreya. Such themes were passed on and further improved in the imperial cave temples. In turn, artisans adopted and reorganized these iconographic themes to complement the reduced format of the stone steles. The Qingzhou material generally shares the northern iconography but differs stylistically from the Northern Dynastic mode showing, instead, affinities to the southern style discussed later.

Buddhist Sculpture of the South: Sichuan Statuary

A passage from the *Treatise on Discerning the Correct Doctrine (Bianchenglun,* ca. 600) conveys the triumphant tone of Buddhism in southern China: "During the reign of the [Liu] Song...the distinguished members of the sangha [monastic community] and of wise worthies flourished like rice in the ear or like hemp, while jeweled monasteries and golden wheels were as thick as bamboo or reeds. The doctrine of Shakyamuni was triumphant...monks and nuns numbered 36,000."[77] While in 317 the north fell under the administration of non-Chinese, which led to ethnic tensions, the south enjoyed relative stability under Han Chinese rule, with Nanjing (known as Jianye, then Jiankang) as the capital. The administrators of the south were the Eastern Jin (317–420), the Liu Song (421–479), the Southern Qi (479–502), the Liang (502–557), and the Chen (557–589).

The culture of the south generated a distinctive type of Buddhism and Buddhist art. Under Emperor Wu of Liang, a generous patron and loyal practitioner of Buddhism, southern Buddhist art reached its zenith. Emperor Wu, known as the "imperial bodhisattva" for his unrivaled devotion, built temples and monasteries, discussed sutras and wrote commentaries on them, and practiced Buddhist precepts regardless of whether they enhanced his worldly powers.

Furthermore, an affluent court elite from the lower Yangzi basin and coastal area around Hangzhou had been educated in the Confucian tradition and were conversant in Daoist philosophy. As patrons they singled out monks bent on intellectual speculation and contemplation who, in turn, set up forms of devotionalism and images for worship that were unmatched in the north. Huiyuan (344–416) was one of the more prominent southern monks. He lived for thirty years on Mount Lu, Jiangxi, where he met with famous monks and literary personages to share his great knowledge of Buddhism and traditional Chinese thinking. On Mount Lu, he founded the Amitabha Buddha cult, discussed below.[78]

The geography of the south, which was vastly different from that of the north, also played an important role in the development of Buddhist art. Mercantile interests steadily developed a thriving commerce both along the Yangzi River and abroad with kingdoms along the South China Sea and Indian Ocean. These countries also paid tribute to the southern courts and offered them Buddhist images. As early as 405, embassies from what is now Sri Lanka had brought precious Buddhist images to Nanjing: "Under the [Eastern] Jin, early in Yixi (405–419), they first sent an ambassador to offer a jade image and some scriptures. It took him ten years to arrive. The image was four feet two inches high, the color of the jade pure and radiant, the fashioning of the forms unusual and distinctive, scarcely the work of a human artificer. This image throughout Jin and Song was in the Waguan Temple."[79] Funan (Cambodia) and what is now Malaysia also supplied extraordinarily crafted sandalwood images. Southern China was therefore exposed to a Buddhist art already transformed (by the southeast Asians) from the original Indian model. Consequently, its Buddhist sculpture evolved differently from that of the north, which was chiefly influenced by the art of central Asia.

Literary and historical sources carry abundant information on the Buddhist art fashioned in the capital and in the major centers of the south. We know in detail about the temples and the sculpture and paintings within them, as well as the identity of the patrons of those projects. These sources show that the makers of Buddhist art were not anonymous artisans as in the north, but well-known artists who commanded social prestige. Furthermore, the artist was spoken of with awe as if his genius placed him apart from ordinary mortals: "During the age of Jin, there was a man of the land of Qiao (Anhui) whose name was Dai Kui, courtesy name An Dao, whose air was pure, whose manner was far removed [from the ordinary understanding], and who dwelt in serene retirement in the old land of Wu.... With his subtle thought he saw through [everything], and such was his refinement that he could have been taken for a magician."[80] Dai Kui died in 396 after carving the most renowned sculpture in Nanjing, which was placed in the Waguan Temple. (Unfortunately, none of Dai Kui's works remain extant.) Although he worked with several different media, literary records credit Dai Kui with inventing large-scale lacquer images. Significantly, he is praised for achieving extraordinarily realistic effects, an accomplishment that we shall explore along with the Buddhist sculpture of Sichuan.

The wooden image in the Lingbao Temple, north of the mountains of Kuaiji, was fashioned by Dai Kui. He felt that since the images fashioned in middle antiquity were in general simple and severe, they were not capable of moving the hearts of those who might show them deference...as a result he wished to recarve the imposing form, hoping to approach the extreme of Reality.... Its effect was to make those who looked up to it worshipfully, whether religious or lay folk, feel as if they had met [the Buddha] in person.[81]

Of the copious artistic heritage of the Southern Dynasties, only a few gilt bronzes remain, and those Buddhist images executed in perishable materials (wood, lacquer, clay) are no longer extant. Moreover, in contrast to the north, the southern coastal areas do not hold many cave temples, largely because the terrain is less mountainous. Only two sites were carved out of rock during the Southern Qi dynasty, both dated to the late fifth century. One was a large carving project that was started in 489 in Jiangsu, at the Qixia Temple on Mount She. A retired scholar, a follower of Amitabha, initiated this work, called the Thousand Buddhas. The most important group of sculptures at the site includes a 9-meter-high Amitabha Buddha attended by two bodhisattvas. Unfortunately, the sculpture was severely damaged during the mid-nineteenth-century Taiping Rebellion, and subsequent restoration destroyed the carvings' original style. The other Southern Qi work is a monumental Maitreya carved on the side of Mount Shicheng, near Xinchang, Zhejiang Province. This project has also suffered irreparable damage and has lost much of its historical value. Su Bai has speculated that these two sites may have been influenced by Yungang, but the subject matter is distinctly southern.[82]

Because of the scarcity of extant art produced in the southern capital and in the coastal provinces under southern rule, we turn to the province of Sichuan, which holds the only extant evidence from this period. Annexed by the Eastern Jin in 347, Sichuan was an integral part of the southern regime. But whether the province's Buddhist sculpture reflects a Southern Dynasties influence or merely an indigenous choice is not clear.

Sichuan had a longstanding tradition of figurative art dating back to the Shang dynasty. As discussed earlier, the first evidence of proto-Buddhist art came from this province, yet after this initial flourishing in the second and third centuries, the making of Buddhist images drastically disappeared — for reasons still unknown — until the second part of the fifth century, when a wide net of trade routes connected Sichuan to numerous economic and cultural centers. More specifically in terms of Buddhism and its art, commercial routes enabled monks to travel in and out of Sichuan. Between 300 and 550, twenty clerics at least, some Sichuanese but mostly foreigners, passed through Sichuan on their way

east or west.[83] The Yangzi River served as a conduit of commerce and ideas between Chengdu, Sichuan's capital, the prosperous Jingzhou, in Hubei (also an important Buddhist center), and Nanjing. Southward from Chengdu, one route led through Yunnan, Burma, and Assam to India, the other through Yunnan, Guizhou, and Guangxi and ultimately to the southern seas. Finally, in the northwest, Sichuan also had access through Gansu to central Asian trade and culture. The Indian style of Buddhist art, acquired by contact with the southeast Asian cultures, became the most prominent in Sichuan.

Our investigation begins with the Maowen stele not only because it is the earliest extant work (483) but also, and more importantly, because it shows the style most in vogue at the time. This rectangular stele (171 centimeters high, 73 centimeters wide, and 21 centimeters thick) was damaged in the 1930s: the front and back central images were cut away to be sold to an art dealer. Local authorities prevented the sale and moved the remaining stone and its fragments to the Sichuan Provincial Museum of Chengdu, where it remains in storage.

A recently published reconstruction and reinterpretation of the stele (fig. 3.69) shows the stele with two main images: a seated Maitreya Buddha on the front and a standing Amitayus, to use another appellation of Amitabha (left incomplete), on the back (fig. 3.70).[84] According to the reconstruction, the four sides had small images (Buddhas, bodhisattvas, and Chan monks) placed in niches. The main inscription carved on the stele's left side carries the date and identifies as chief donor the monk Xuan Song, a prelate of the Western Liang in Gansu.

The technique used, a raised low relief, continues the linearity so popular in Han dynastic funerary art. The style, however, is quite innovative and influenced later Buddhist art of the north. Specifically, the cascade of the robe over the throne with its modulation of arched pleats, the use of the elegant sash, and the strong iconic character of the deity are prominent traits of the main Buddha of Central Binyang, Longmen (see fig. 3.39). Scholars have hypothesized that this fashion was adopted initially in Sichuan because of either an innovative monastic rule or a desire to imitate the robe of a southern court official. The similarity between the stele and the Central Binyang Buddha extends to the peculiar hand gesture, a variant of "giving" with two fingers extended.

The iconography is original in that it combines the two Buddhas, Amitayus and Maitreya, suggesting that in the south, unlike in the north, they were jointly worshiped. This striking combination unites Maitreya, whose cult was so prominent during the early stage of Buddhism, with Amitabha, who became a major cultic figure in later Tang Buddhism (ca. 700). Moreover, the presence of Amitabha Buddha in this late fifth-century art shows that devotionalism to him had already begun in Sichuan.

Southern Liang Sculpture from Wan Fo Temple and Xi'an Road, Chengdu

Ten Thousand Buddhas (Wan Fo) Temple, situated on the outskirts of Chengdu, was built during the Eastern Han, then repaired, remodeled, and renamed during successive dynasties. Between 200 and 250 pieces — steles and independent sculptures — have been retrieved during several periods of discovery. A few of the pieces are intact, but the majority are broken or damaged. Some works are exhibited in the Sichuan Provincial Museum, Chengdu, but most of the sculptures are kept in storage. Findings at the Wan Fo Temple site are of the utmost importance given the varied forms of the sculpture (steles and independent images) and the extended period that the works span — from the Southern Dynasties into the Tang dynasty. As recently as May 1995, nine Liang-period steles were found beneath Xi'an Road, Chengdu; they are iconographically and stylistically identical to the Wan Fo Temple carvings and so strengthen the assumption that in Sichuan a uniform style was thriving.[85]

The shape of the Liang steles is peculiar to southern Buddhist art, particularly in Sichuan: they are rectangular from the base to the section containing the images, then they gradually become round following the contour of the all-embracing aureole. Accompanying inscriptions refer to these steles as "images in niches" (kanxiang). The term suggests that the sculpture was placed in a recessed space, as if the maker wished to recreate the ambiance of a cave or of a temple niche.

The steles carved during the Liang (502–557) employ a uniform style named for a specific region, the Sichuan School style. The extent to which Sichuan art reflects Nanjing's remains unclear because Nanjing works are so rare. But one can regard Sichuan art as gravitating chiefly toward a southern, rather than a northern, aesthetic.

The Wan Fo Temple stele of Shakyamuni is one example. Made of dark gray sandstone (a medium common to steles), the stele measures 37 centimeters high, 30 centimeters wide, and 12.5 centimeters thick and is

dated Liang 523 (fig. 3.71). Its fairly small surface features many images. The central Shakyamuni on a lotus towers over all the others, his dominance further marked by two large lions at his feet. The remaining figures are four bodhisattvas; four monks placed on a higher, receding plane; two Heavenly Kings (the one carrying the stupa is Vaishravana, the guardian of the north) supported by brutish crouching figures on a lower level; and finally, in the front plane, a group of lively entertainers, musicians, and dancers. On the front of the broken aureole are fragments of narratives, possibly stories of Shakyamuni's lives; on the back are three bands. The lowest consists of the inscription, the middle is a scene of adoration placed in a natural setting, and the highest displays a procession of courtiers moving away from an alcove bed while its occupant (in the right corner) prepares to meet with a sylphlike figure. The meaning of this image is not clear.

The second Wan Fo Temple stele is of the bodhisattva Avalokiteshvara (Guanyin) — a donation of a monk (bhikshu) that is 44 centimeters high, 37 centimeters wide, and 15.5 centimeters thick and was created in 548 in the Liang dynasty (fig. 3.72). This opulent work was executed with great finesse and endowed with interesting stylistic and iconographic details. In lieu of Shakyamuni is a radiant Guanyin attended by four more manifestations of the same bodhisattva (five in all, confirmed Guanyins because of the Buddha in their crowns). The central Guanyin is guarded, as Shakyamuni is in the preceding work, by two powerful lions with their keepers. In the row behind the bodhisattvas are four proportionally smaller, smiling monks. Also in the group are two guardians standing on elephants with their mahouts, and a band of rowdy musicians below

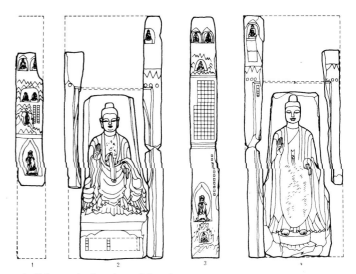

3.69 Schematic drawing of Southern Qi (483) stele from Maowen, Sichuan Province.

the gods. The front of the fragmented aureole displays portions of stories; in the back, beside the inscription, is a Buddha's adoration scene in a landscape.

The third stele, from Xi'an Road, is dated Liang 545 and was donated by the monk Zhang Yuan in memory of his deceased parents (fig. 3.73). The surface of this remarkably well-preserved stele, 43 centimeters high and 29.5 centimeters wide, still has extensive gilding. The work shows the twin Prabhutaratna and Shakyamuni Buddhas assisted by five bodhisattvas and two disciples, and they are guarded by two Heavenly Kings. The Buddhas' lotus thrones sprout from a vase guarded by two lions. The gilded bodies project the same rounded suppleness as the Wan Fo statuary, and the faces display the same vivaciousness and tenderness. The pointed, all-encompassing aureole shows in ascending order a Buddha seated, a Buddha assembly in a Pure Land, and numerous flying celestials, the two topmost supporting an Ashokan stupa reliquary at the apex. This reliquary is identical to that used in the aforementioned Qingzhou stele. Sichuan and Shandong clearly were inspired by the same source — visual and iconographic conventions established at the Liang capital, present-day Nanjing. The back of the stele has an inscription and a large scene of

3.70 Stele of Maitreya Buddha (front) and Amitayus Buddha (back), sandstone, Maowen. Southern Qi dynasty, 483. Sichuan Provincial Museum (storage), Chengdu.

3.71 Shakyamuni stele (*above,* front; *below,* back), sandstone with color, Wan Fo Temple, Chengdu, Sichuan Province. Southern Liang dynasty, 523. Sichuan Provincial Museum (storage), Chengdu.

3.72 Avalokiteshvara (Guanyin) stele, sandstone, Wan Fo Temple, Chengdu. Southern Liang dynasty, 548. Sichuan Provincial Museum, Chengdu.

Buddha preaching in a landscape setting, while eight male and female donors stand on either side of him.

The last example, also from the Xi'an Road findings, is a gilded image of a standing Ashoka-type Buddha that is 48 centimeters high and dated 551 (fig. 3.74). The sculpture's hands and most of the halo are lost. Significantly, the inscription states that this is an Ashokan image, an icon favored by the pious Indian emperor. The Ashokan stupa reliquary at the apex of the 545 stele is also linked to the same royal patron. As discussed earlier, vestiges of Emperor Ashoka's patronage kept appearing in Liang territory (especially Zhejiang and Jiangsu) during the period of disunion.

The style of all these artifacts is exclusively Sichuanese: note the sensuous, realistic modeling of the gracefully swaying bodies, the naturalism of their relaxed yet elegant poses, and the landscape setting chosen for the deities. Furthermore, a Sichuanese style is reflected in the friendly and vivacious expressions of the protagonists, the warm emotionalism permeating the entire group, and the inclusion of exotic components such as the band of foreign-looking musicians and elephants with their keepers.

Finally, the pictorial quality of the representations is uniquely Sichuanese. The adoration scenes take place in natural settings, where the narrative unfolds amid trees of various species and rolling hills suggestive of the local landscape. Carvers of northern steles (by the Shaanxi and Henan Schools) ignored these details in favor of more rigidly iconic and humanly detached effects.

Regarding the new developments in iconography, the substitution of Shakyamuni (stele 523) with the bodhisattva Savior Guanyin (stele 548) implies the equal status of the two deities in the eyes of the Sichuanese worshiper and thereby demonstrates the strength of the Guanyin cult. Undeniably, devotion to this bodhisattva was just as strong in the north, but its visualization did not portray an exclusive group of five Guanyins nor interpret Guanyin as Buddha.

Among the Wan Fo Temple remains in the round there are about sixteen larger-than-life freestanding images carved with great skill. This group is remarkable because most of the sculptures were created approximately during the time of the Liang dynasty, which was in power during the first half of the sixth century, using a variety of Indian styles — Gandharan, Gupta from Mathura, and Southern Gupta. The heterogeneity indicates that Sichuan artists were conversant with all of these styles and employed them according to their patrons' demands.

The standing Shakyamuni, dated Liang 529 — 1.58 meters tall and made of dark gray sandstone — is modeled on the Gupta aesthetic (fig. 3.75). But the adoption of two distinct patterns in the fall of the robe (curves for the right side, vertical grooves for the left) is reminiscent of the south Indian Gupta style of Amaravati. The blending of the two modes took place in what are now Indonesia and Vietnam and was adopted by the southern carvers of China. According to the inscription, the patron of this imposing statue was the prince of Poyang, alias Xiao Fan, the nephew of the Liang emperor Wu. The prince served as governor of Yizhou (present-day Chengdu).

The headless gray-sandstone Shakyamuni (1.27 meters high and dated Liang 537), fashioned according to yet another Indian style, the Gandharan, is also part of the Wan Fo Temple group (fig. 3.76). In this work, the carver conveyed the heavy fall of the robe and minimized the body forms, thereby achieving an overall effect quite dissimilar from that of the 529 Shakyamuni. The 537 sculpture, with its prominent display of the sash and the artificial arrangement of the robe, more closely resembles the mature Northern Wei Buddha images.

The most salient iconographic contribution of Sichuan to Buddhist art was the representation of the Pure Land of the Amitabha Buddha. In this respect,

3.73 Twin Buddhas stele, sandstone with gilt and color, found in 1995 at Xi'an Road, Chengdu. Southern Liang dynasty, 545. Chengdu Institute of Archaeology.

3.74 Ashoka-type Buddha (front and back), sandstone and gilt, found in 1995 at Xi'an Road, Chengdu. Southern Liang dynasty, 551. Chengdu Institute of Archaeology.

3.75 Standing Shakyamuni Buddha without head, sandstone, Wan Fo Temple, Chengdu. Southern Liang dynasty, 529. Sichuan Provincial Museum, Chengdu.

3.76 Standing Buddha without head, sandstone, Wan Fo Temple, Chengdu. Southern Liang dynasty, 537. Sichuan Provincial Museum, Chengdu.

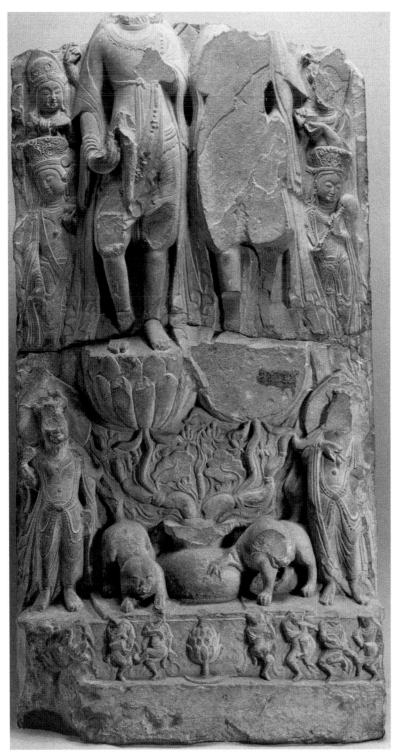

3.77 Fragmented stele with two bodhisattvas (front) and Pure Land
(back), sandstone, Wan Fo Temple, Chengdu. Southern Liang dynasty.
Sichuan Provincial Museum, Chengdu.

Sichuan outpaced other Chinese provinces and also acted independently of foreign models. One such scene is carved on the back of a Wan Fo Temple stele 1.19 centimeters high, 64.5 centimeters wide, and 24.8 centimeters thick. The sandstone stele displays on the front two fragmentary (headless) bodhisattvas attended by four smaller bodhisattvas (fig. 3.77). The two main deities, most likely Avalokiteshvara and Mahasthamaprapta (the canonical attendants of Amitabha), stand on two shapely lotuses. In the bottom frieze of the stele, as was customary, is a row of mirthful dancers. The distinctively Sichuanese ability to convey sensuously alive bodies and plants can still be enjoyed in spite of the fragmentary state of the work.

The stele carries further representations on the back and all around the frame. On the back, the Pure Land, or Paradise, is seen on the upper portion as a schematic garden. An alley of trees shaped like a triangle leads to the presiding Buddha and his assistant monks, while the blessed are sheltered by the trees. Several canals, placed along the perimeter, enliven the garden and function also as a "pond" of rebirth for Amitabha's devotees, who can be seen swimming among the lotuses. Two pavilions frame the sides of the garden, and in the distance numerous swaying trees evoke pleasant breezes. This vision is governed by spatial perspective, a device ignored in Chinese secular painting. It may have been adopted by Buddhist painters both to create a visual illusion and to facilitate meditational practices that centered on the Buddha, the focal point of the composition.

The Amidism cult appears to have originated in the south. Devotion to Amitabha Buddha began with the prelate Huiyuan of Mount Lu as early as 402, when he led his community in prayer to Amitabha. The patriarch advocated meditation on this deity as conducive to spiritual betterment.

No link has yet been established between the visualization of the Pure Land on Sichuan steles and a specific Sichuanese prelate, but its canonical sources are well known. There are three major sutras that discuss the Pure Land: the Larger Sukhavativyuha (Wuliangshoujing, Sanghavarman's translation, was written in 252), the Smaller Sukhavativyuha (Amituojing, Kumarajiva's translation from ca. 402), and the Amitayurdhyana (Guan Wuliang shoufo jing, Kalayashas' translation, completed in the early fifth century).[86]

The three texts are not identical. The first offers a description of the Pure Land, but also emphasizes gaining spiritual merit without totally relying on Amitabha's salvific power. The second text, in addition to describing the bliss of the Pure Land, promises salvation through faith and recitation of Amitabha's name and does not demand a more active role from the practitioner. The third text describes nine different degrees of rebirth in the Pure Land depending on the level of merit and emphasizes the role of meditation (a series of meditations are assigned by Shakyamuni Buddha to Queen Vaidehi, for whom the sutra is preached) as conducive to rebirth in Amitabha's paradise.

In the first two sutras, the description of Sukhavati (Amitabha's Pure Land) evokes a wondrous park with lovely trees and lofty pavilions, where scented breezes and pleasing sounds delight the inhabitants. These two Sukhavati sutras, thus, are the likely source of the Wan Fo Temple carving, where there is no reference to meditation (usually expressed through sixteen scenes surrounding the frame of the paradise, as in the Tang Pure Land frescoes at Dunhuang). In the stele's interpretation, Amitabha's main assistants, Avalokiteshvara and Mahasthamaprapta, are shown on the front. On the back, the Buddha welcomes his devotees to his celestial and pleasurable surroundings provided they have done good work — or at least cried out for him on their deathbed. Naturally, if the believers' striving has been minimal, they will not be allowed to participate in the paradisiacal gathering, but will have to await for rebirth within one of the lotuses growing in the transcendental pond, an essential feature of these surroundings. With a keenness for pictorial detail and remarkable compositional skills, the Sichuanese carver set a model for the rest of China: approximately forty years later (570) the northern carvers started an enduring artistic production on this theme.[87]

Using the Sichuanese evidence of the Liang dynasty — that retrieved from the Wan Fo Temple and more recently from the Xi'an Road — we can reconstruct the major southern stylistic and iconographic trends. This style differs from that of the north in its emphasis on realism and three-dimensionality in a humanized interpretation of the images. Sichuanese Buddhist sculpture of this period also placed the deities in natural settings, which can be regarded as an initial stage in the sculptural representation of landscape scenes. In terms of iconography, some Sichuan innovations during the Liang — including the pairing of the Amitabha and Maitreya Buddhas, the representation of Avalokiteshvara with the same marks of distinction used for Shakyamuni Buddha, and the path-breaking visualization of Amitabha's Pure Land — spread into other areas of China.

Northern Qi and Northern Zhou Style: A New Aesthetic

In the mid-sixth century the long rule of the Wei dynasty came to an end. Northern China was split in two: the east (comprising Hebei, Shandong, Henan, and parts of Anhui and Shanxi) fell under the Northern Qi dynasty (550–577), while the west (Shaanxi, Ningxia, Gansu, a portion of Shanxi, and the provinces of Sichuan and Hunan, which had formerly been part of the south but were annexed by the Western Wei in 553), became the territory of the Northern Zhou dynasty (555–581). In 582, the Northern Zhou (which had incorporated the Northern Qi in 577) was in turn conquered by the Sui dynasty. In 589 the Sui defeated the Chen, the last Southern Dynasty, and reunited China. These profound political changes corresponded in Buddhism to equally consequential artistic ones.

The Northern Qi style did not develop out of the Northern Wei, but was a complete departure from it. The rejection of the typically weightless forms and excessive tense linearity characteristic of the Wei style took place under the influence of the Gupta style (300–600) of India, the same style that had significantly shaped Southern Dynasties art during the first half of the sixth century.[88]

Gupta influence was not received from India through central Asia exclusively; it also came by a maritime route. Northern Qi artisans adopted the foreign style (examples were made at the two centers Sarnath and Mathura) of beautifully modeled and lightly clad bodies against oversized backdrops teeming with luscious, deeply cut vegetal scrolls. Moreover, Gupta heads with snail shell curls, lotuslike eyes, and voluptuous lips gracing elegant, sensitively modeled torsos became an alternative to the prevailing aesthetic.

This novel artistic approach was applied to the sculpture of the dynastic sites of Northern and Southern Xiangtangshan clustered on the Henan-Hebei border and to the sculpture of the Xiao Nanhai caves, near Anyang, Henan. This last site was not dynastic, but the patron, the prelate Seng Chou (481–560), had very close ties to the court. The site of Tianlongshan, Shanxi, also active at this time, will be considered for its Tang sculpture. Each of the three sites reflects innovations in style, structure, and iconography.[89]

Northern Xiangtangshan was likely founded by Emperor Wenxuan (r. 550–559) and completed by 572. Cave 7, the largest of the three extant caves, is generally thought to have been dedicated to the imperial founder.

It is a majestic and soaring space, 12 meters square, whose center is occupied by a massive (6.95 square meter) central shaft symbolic of a stupa (fig. 3.78). Three sides (excluding the back) have been fashioned as niches framed by powerful pillars that are supported by squatting guardian demons. Triads formed by a Buddha and two bodhisattvas occupy the interior of the niches. The base of the shaft displays reliefs of the Spirit Kings, a ubiquitous motif in Northern Qi art.

Despite the terrible damage inflicted to the images of Cave 7, one can still see that they exemplify the Northern Qi style. Under Gupta influence, the Buddhas of the central shaft exhibit more naturalistic and fuller body forms, embellished with unobtrusive and elegant surface patterns. In an early photo of the central pillar, we see the standing bodhisattva's superbly modeled body unencumbered by excessive drapes and jewels (fig. 3.79). Another example of Gupta influence is the standing Avalokiteshvara on the Sichuan stele dated to 548, during the Liang dynasty (see fig. 3.72). In both works, the diaphanous drapes enhance attractive bodies in contrapposto pose. The carver demonstrates a keen awareness of anatomical details and shifts the style toward naturalism.

The Xiangtangshan deities have been placed against large halos and aureoles filled with lushly vegetal scrolls whose intricate carving contrasts sharply with the smooth, unadorned bodies — a contrast derived from the Gupta aesthetic. Yet the Northern Qi style was an interpretation rather than an imitation of the Gupta. Northern Qi sculpture does not have the suppleness and convincing articulation of body parts of the Indian model, since the cylindrical bodies crowned by spherical heads (the ushnisha is barely indicated) are still too tied to geometric relationships with other parts of the sculpture.

Burial customs linked to stupa worship played a prominent role in Northern Qi dynastic art. The use of the stupa certainly was not a new development, but during this period its religious function took on added significance. It is generally believed that Emperor Wenxuan was buried in the back section of the central shaft (the stupa pillar) of Northern Xiangtangshan's Cave 7. Although at the dynastic sites of Yungang and the Longmen paired caves had been built in memory of the emperor and his family, the use of a cave temple as a burial site was unprecedented.

This innovation was related to religious concerns particular to Northern Qi times. The pervasive use of the stupa and of related decorative motifs in the Xiangtangshan caves (as in the side walls in Cave 7) was generated by the belief in *Mo Fa* (the doctrine of the Latter Days of the Law), which peaked after 550. The doctrine was based on a prophecy in Mahayana Buddhism that foretold the gradual decay and disappearance of Buddhism. Historical events prior to and during the Northern Qi (in particular, the Northern Wei and the Northern Zhou persecution of Buddhists in 574) contributed to a general feeling of impending doom. By placing the emperor in a tomb shaped as a stupa, a potent symbol of deterrence in Buddhism, the court and its Buddhist prelates may have sought to avert the waning of imperial power.

Likewise, important novelties in structure, style, and imagery can be seen in the caves of the Southern Xiangtangshan site built between 565 and 577 (after the Northern Xiangtangshan). The most apparent structural invention is the opening of the caves on two levels and the linking of the lower and upper parts to form a unit (for example, the lower Cave 1 is paired vertically with Cave 3) (fig. 3.80). Another striking structural change is the building of considerably smaller caves where three groups of images are displayed on the three walls (not the entrance wall). On the basis of the well-documented caves of Anyang, it seems that this innovative and more intimate layout, which became the favored structure during the Northern Qi, was determined by a specific type of worship — meditation.

Cave 7 of Southern Xiangtangshan is a model of these structural and stylistic changes. The facade suggests a wooden temple as inspiration: it has a three-bay simulated portico marked by four octagonal pillars styled after an Indian model; the pillars support an elaborate system of brackets linked to the tiled roof (fig. 3.81). The interior of the cave is a squarish space (3.6 meters by 3.4 meters), whose slightly curved ceiling displays a central lotus and swirling celestial musicians. Three shallow but wide niches host three different Buddhas: the figure in the rear wall may be the Vairocana Buddha (Bilushena), while Maitreya (whose feet are supported by a deity) and Amitabha reside in the lateral walls (fig. 3.82). (This particular triad was first used in the Anyang caves.) Two bodhisattvas and two monks assist each Buddha, and the Thousand Buddhas motif is employed as a background. The Spirit Kings adorn the tall pedestal, which runs along the lower walls.

The style employed in the sculpture of Cave 7 had evolved considerably from that of Northern Xiangtangshan. The scale is noticeably toned down, which means that a heroic quality was lost, but a sense of harmonious peacefulness took its place. The carver smoothed the images to make round contours but not quite precise forms. Geometric reduction still controls the cylindrical shapes crowned with spheroid heads, yet these images suggest an incipient naturalism. The attire has become noticeably simpler: the clothes cling to the body, forming unobtrusive pleats; the overhanging drapery of the seated Buddhas is discarded in favor of a transparent cloth that reveals the modeling of the legs underneath; and the heavy jewelry of the bodhisattvas is replaced with unobtrusive strands of beads and tassels indicated with incised, barely protruding lines. The artistry of these images inspires deep introspection and serenity.

The visual representation of the Pure Land occupies a special place among the iconographic innovations of the Northern Qi.[90] Undoubtedly, the anxiety caused by the Latter Days of the Law doctrine generated faith in the Pure Lands — of Maitreya and, even more, of Amitabha. It is still questionable whether representations of the Pure Lands were visual devices for meditation or whether they exalted the state of bliss attained in paradise.

At Southern Xiangtangshan, four reliefs from Caves 1 and 2 illustrate this nascent cult. The reliefs of Cave 1 are still in situ, but those of Cave 2 are now in the collection of the Freer Gallery of Art, Washington, D.C. Of those from Cave 2, one displays a gathering of Buddhas and bodhisattvas in an unidentified Pure Land; the other, 1.2 meters high and 3.3 meters long, depicts Sukhavati, the Land of Bliss, or Amitabha's Pure Land (fig. 3.83). Amitabha sits in the center accompanied by the bodhisattvas Avalokiteshvara and Mahasthamaprapta; together they watch over the pond of rebirth, where the blessed come to life again in the lotuses.

The setting, similar to that in the Liang relief from the Wan Fo Temple, Chengdu (see fig. 3.77, back), is that of a marvelous realm where divine and secular aspects are tightly interwoven. The spatial approach of the Northern Qi relief differs, however, from the Sichuanese in that it avoids depth; the artist opted instead for a horizontal layout that emphasizes the rebirth more than the Buddha group.

Carved less than half a century after the southern work, the Northern Qi relief uses the same textual sources (the two Sukhavati sutras), but a different stylistic language. The Southern Xiangtangshan paradise has a strongly exotic appeal, even more so than the Sichuan relief. The round bodies of the seemingly naked images are compactly arranged in a manner reminiscent of southeast Asian art.

3.78 Central pillar niche with Buddha and bodhisattva, limestone, Cave 7, Northern Xiangtangshan, Hebei Province. Northern Qi dynasty, ca. 572.

3.79 Central pillar niche with Buddha and bodhisattva, Cave 7, Northern Xiangtangshan. Photo by Tokiwa Daijō and Sekino Tadashi, 1937.

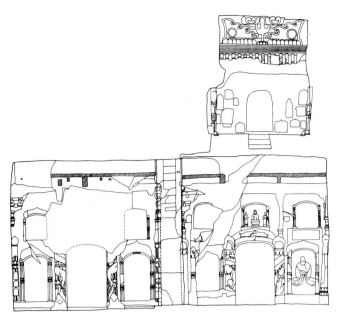

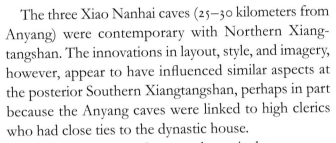

3.80 Plan of exterior of Caves 1, 2, and 3, Southern Xiangtangshan, Henan Province.

3.81 Schematic drawing of reconstruction of the facade of Cave 7, Southern Xiangtangshan.

The three Xiao Nanhai caves (25–30 kilometers from Anyang) were contemporary with Northern Xiangtangshan. The innovations in layout, style, and imagery, however, appear to have influenced similar aspects at the posterior Southern Xiangtangshan, perhaps in part because the Anyang caves were linked to high clerics who had close ties to the dynastic house.

Of the three caves, the central cave is the most representative, reflecting the beliefs of Seng Chou (481–560), who had imparted the bodhisattva vows to Emperor Wenxuan and was addressed at court as the "Erudite at the National University" on account of his vast learning. Hewn out of a massive square boulder, this cave, though small (approximately 1.7 meters deep and 1.4 meters wide), has a wealth of artistic and doctrinal content. The ceiling is shaped like a truncated pyramid with a conspicuous lotus at its apex, and the cave is laid out with the familiar three Buddha groups on three walls. Seng Chou's doctrinal preference for *Dilun* (a doctrine focused on the Avatamsaka Sutra, known in Chinese as Huayan) determined the choice of Vairocana as the main Buddha of the triad (he is featured on the rear wall); the others are Amitabha and Maitreya (fig. 3.84). The size of the cave and the use of iconographies favored by its patron, Seng Chou, suggest, furthermore, that he used this sacred space for meditation.

Two other striking innovations in this cave are the panels carved in low relief on the upper section of the lateral walls. The one on the east side (fig. 3.85) is a divine gathering, identified by inscription as "Maitreya Preaching the Law to the Sentient Beings." Its pendant on the western upper wall (fig. 3.86) is "Nine Modes of Rebirth in Amitabha's Pure Land," which describes the process of being reborn in accordance with one's acquired merits. Surprisingly, and in contrast to the Southern Xiangtangshan reliefs, this panel is derived from the Amitayurdhyana Sutra. Because of these two iconographies, the Buddhas shown below it are, without doubt, Maitreya (left) and Amitabha (right).

New developments in carving techniques also occurred during the Northern Qi. Artisans from Zhengding and Dingzhou Counties (near present-day Shijiazhuang, Hebei) working with local micaceous marble used perforation to create uncommonly intricate steles. The process was particularly effective in executing aureoles, which, as backdrops to the seated or standing images, were transformed into leafy screens with the lightness of lace. During this period, the favorite images were bodhisattvas (usually either Maitreya or Shakyamuni, sometimes both) in pensive poses, the pair Shakyamuni-Prabhutaratna, and Buddha groups. An excellent example was excavated in 1978 in Gaocheng, Hebei: a 77-centimeter-high Maitreya stele sponsored by a nun of the Jianzhong Temple in 562 and now stored at Longxing Temple, Zhengding County.[91] The front of the stele shows the paired Shakyamuni and Prabhutaratna under a perforated canopy formed by two intertwined trees (fig. 3.87). Two dragons wrap around the trunks as they ascend to the treetops. The leafy canopy is alive with numerous celestials and miniature Buddhas, and its apex is marked by a miniature stupa again hosting the famous pair below. Two disciples, two bodhisattvas, and two Heavenly Kings (placed on the lower level) are the attendants, but there are also several playful naked boys — for example, two hold the

Buddhas' feet, and two are hiding in the branches. The pedestal displays a central incense burner and two lively lions. Corresponding to the two frontal Buddhas are, at the back of the stele, two Maitreyas in pensive poses flanked by two monks and topped by celestials holding a precious jewel. Below the Maitreyas, on the pedestal, are a standing Buddha and four Spirit Kings. This exquisitely carved work was enhanced by extensive gilt and color, some of which remains visible today.

In the third quarter of the sixth century, while the Northern Qi artisans of the northeast employed innovative styles for their sculpture, northwestern craftsmen created a distinct artistic language. Although Northern Zhou sculpture is somewhat like that of the Northern Qi in that it is very compact and blocklike, its artisans developed quite different facial expressions, body forms, and body embellishments.

There are no known Northern Zhou provincial sites, but many caves, as well as numerous independently carved images, were sculpted during this period at the major provincial sites within Northern Zhou territory. The Northern Zhou grottoes at Xumishan, 55 kilometers northwest of Guyuan County, Ningxia, are outstanding. The most notable are Caves 45, 46, 48, 51, and

67. In Cave 51, the most grandiose, three seated Buddhas, each about 6 meters high, occupy the rear wall and project a masculine bravado and vigor (fig. 3.88). Their stocky physique is overlaid with simple but heavy robes with pleats. The Buddhas' squarish faces with large noses and thick lips give them a somber and unapproachable air. Northern Zhou Buddhas do not strive after the introspective serenity so characteristic of the Northern Qi Buddhas.[92]

The enormous (60 meters high) triad of sculptures at Lashaosi, Wushan County, Gansu, is another extraordinary and unique Northern Zhou work (fig. 3.89). According to the accompanying inscription, a distinguished Northern Zhou dignitary, Yu Chijiong, the governor of Qinzhou, sponsored the work, which was completed in 559. What is original about this sculpture, which consists of a Shakyamuni Buddha and his two bodhisattvas (all made of a stone core and an outer surface of clay that still retains traces of red, green, and white pigments), is the Buddha's unusual throne. It consists of six levels, with lotus leaves alternating with rows of elephants, deer, and lions. Moreover, the throne in the center contains a Buddha triad tucked in a niche, a tenth- or eleventh-century addition. The relief's sheer

3.82 Cave 7 (rear wall niche), painted limestone, Southern Xiangtangshan. Northern Qi dynasty, 565–577.

3.83 Amitabha's Pure Land, limestone with traces of color, Cave 2, Southern Xiangtangshan. Northern Qi dynasty, 565–572. 158.9 × 334.5 cm. Freer Gallery of Art, Smithsonian Institution, Washington, D.C.

size makes the style more schematized; nevertheless, it maintains the standard Northern Zhou characteristics of square faces, grave expressions, and bulky physiques.[93]

Cave 62 at Maijishan offers yet another interpretation of Northern Zhou style in Gansu. Eleven clay images (ranging from 90 to 112 centimeters in height) adorn the interior: three triads (one Buddha and two bodhisattvas) are aligned along the rear and side walls, while on each side of the entrance stand two monks (fig. 3.90). Maijishan clay images, regardless of when they were made, are always marked by a noticeable softness in their modeling and a gentle expression. Such characteristics here slightly alter, but do not eliminate, the weightiness and somber dignity of the Zhou aesthetic.

Whereas solemnity characterizes Northern Zhou Buddhas, opulence distinguishes the surface of the bodhisattvas. The bodhisattva Maitreya carved in yellow limestone (the stone typically used in Shaanxi sculpture) and housed in the Beilin Museum, Xi'an, is a good example of the Northern Zhou style (fig. 3.91). The heavily modeled body, about 2 meters tall, has an exorbitant amount of three-dimensional jewelry. The squarish face, however, retains the standard severe and gloomy expression.

The ostentatious ornamentation typical of the Northern Zhou is perhaps best exemplified, however, by the monumental standing bodhisattva, made of sandstone and standing approximately 5 meters high, in the collection of The Metropolitan Museum of Art, New York (fig. 3.92). Normally credited to the Northern Qi (the sculpture is not dated by inscription), the sculpture has features that favor a Northern Zhou attribution. With the exception of the back, which was kept bare, the sculptor concentrated on opulent surface decoration. Note the ostentatious necklace and crown of flowers, the beads crossing each other in front, and the elaborate pendant. (The multicolored patterns on the robe are possibly a Ming addition.)

While most Northern Zhou caves are located in China's northwest, Northern Zhou style was not an isolated geographical development. The annexation of territories to the north in 553, which made Sichuan part of the Northern Zhou, may have contributed to this particular style's formation. Why else would a seated bodhisattva without a head (fig. 3.93), part of the previously discussed Wan Fo Temple finds (from Chengdu, Sichuan Province, and dated Northern Zhou 567), be embellished in a Northern Zhou mode? This element of Northern Zhou style, in short, may have originated in Sichuan, while the sturdy and blocklike body pro-

3.84 Central Xiao Nanhai Cave (detail), limestone, near Anyang, Henan Province. Northern Qi dynasty, ca. 560.

3.85 Maitreya Buddha (detail), limestone, Central Xiao Nanhai Cave.

3.86 Amitabha's Pure Land (detail), limestone, Central Xiao Nanhai Cave.

3.87 Maitreya stele (front and back), marble with gilding and pigments, Gaocheng, Hebei Province. Northern Qi dynasty, 562.
Longxing Temple (storage), Zhengding Office of Cultural Properties and Preservation, Hebei Province.

3.88 Three Buddhas, sandstone, Cave 51 (rear wall), Xumishan, Ningxia Hui Autonomous Region. Northern Zhou dynasty.

3.89 Rock Cliff Buddhist group, painted sandstone, Lashaosi Cave Temple, Gansu Province. Northern Zhou dynasty, 559.

3.90 Triad of Buddha and two bodhisattvas, clay, Cave 62 (rear wall), Maijishan, Gansu Province. Northern Zhou dynasty.

portions and squarish face resulted from local artistic preferences.

Sichuanese influence on Northern Zhou style is also demonstrated by the monumental sculpture at the Huangze Monastery site in Guangyuan, Sichuan (fig. 3.94). This is not so surprising considering that Guangyuan, known as the Gate of Shu (Shu was the name of one ancient culture of Sichuan), served as a geographic conduit between this province and northwest China (Shaanxi and Gansu). The grandiose group — formed of Buddha (5.1 meters high) attended by Ananda and Kashyapa, two bodhisattvas, two guardians, and eight demigods, with a minuscule donor at Ananda's feet — seems to be a Northern Zhou monument. The Northern Zhou style is recognizable in the shape of the faces, the images' solemn expressions, and particularly the modeling of the bodhisattvas and their conspicuous and ponderous ornaments.

The production of Northern Qi and Northern Zhou art spanned little more than a quarter century (550–582) in northeastern and northwestern China, respectively. Yet within this chronological and spatial compression, profound stylistic and iconographic changes to Buddhist art occurred. The most important development was the rupture with the medieval aesthetic of the Northern Wei style and its replacement by a formal style based on rounder, smoother, and more naturalistic images — a style that was to pave the way for the realistic and worldly sculpture of the imperial Tang.

3.91 Seated Maitreya, limestone. Northern Zhou dynasty. Beilin Museum, Xi'an.

3.92 Standing bodhisattva, sandstone with traces of gilt and color. Northern Zhou dynasty. Height, 419.1 cm; width at base, 449.6 cm. The Metropolitan Museum of Art, New York.

3.93 Seated bodhisattva without head, sandstone, Wan Fo Temple, Chengdu. Northern Zhou dynasty, 567. Sichuan Provincial Museum, Chengdu.

3.94 Monumental niche at the Huangze Monastery, painted sandstone, Guangyuan, Sichuan Province. Northern Zhou dynasty.

3.95 Monumental Amitabha Buddha, marble, Hebei Province. Sui dynasty, 585. The British Museum, London.

Sui Statuary

As a result of the Sui unification of China in 589, the artistic achievements of the preceding quarter century were also merged. But the Sui style was not a mere synthesis of Northern Qi and Northern Zhou styles, because the artistic process was still evolving under the influence of various and complex regional trends. It is more accurate to state that characteristics that were latent in the two preceding styles were brought to full blossom by Sui carvers.[94] For example, the monumental marble Buddha Amitabha (5.78 meters high) in the British Museum, dated Sui 585 and originally dedicated to the Chongguang Temple of Hancui village, Hebei Province, is closely linked to the Northern Qi style of Hebei and yet expresses novel concerns (fig. 3.95).[95] There is a sober elegance in the surface embellishments — namely, the curving, stringlike folds that enliven the massive trunk. This style is also apparent in the refined patterns formed by the tucks of the bodice and by the pleats of the hem. The highly polished, abstract head projects an aura of deep calm and majesty. The imposing verticality and sparse, mirror-image decorative motifs are typical of northeastern Sui style. Although such traits were latent in the Northern Qi, they emerged fully under the new dynasty.

The stupendous Guanyin (Avalokiteshvara; 2.49 meters tall), carved in limestone and originally painted, does not have a date, but it is generally accepted as a Sui sculpture (fig. 3.96). Now in the Museum of Fine Arts, Boston, the statue was brought to the United States in 1915 from a Xi'an temple, and so was likely influenced by the Northern Zhou style. The deity soars majestically from a lotus pedestal guarded by four lions. In the raised left hand he holds several lotus pods; in the right, just one. Some of the major traits of Northern Zhou statuary are still present, like the dazzling array of jewels composed of lotus and pearl designs and studded medallions. Several other extravagant embellishments have been added as well, like mythical aquatic animals (*makara*) and side tassels with chimes. The headpiece that carries the Buddha, Guanyin's chief emblem, displays floral designs interwoven with rich jewels — an opulence of decoration reminiscent of the extreme Northern Zhou taste. But the grand serenity of the face and the regal body that leans to the side depart from the Northern Zhou style.

Indeed, Sui sculpture responded to regional preferences. For instance, the imposing statuary of Dunhuang Cave 427, which holds a 5-meter-tall Buddha (fig. 3.97) is

3.96 Guanyin, Bodhisattva of Compassion, limestone with traces of gilt and colors, Xi'an. Sui dynasty. 249 cm. Museum of Fine Arts, Boston. Francis Bartlett Donation, 15.254.

3.97 Buddhist triad, painted clay, Cave 427, Dunhuang, Gansu Province. Sui dynasty.

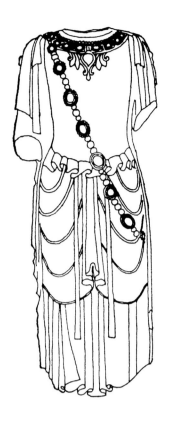
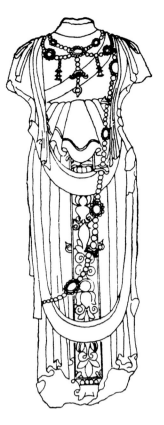
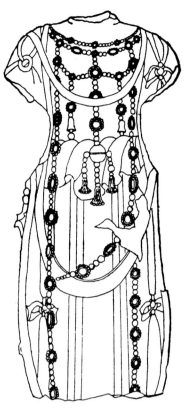

3.98 Schematic drawing of Sui-dynasty bodhisattvas from Zhucheng, Shandong Province.

not stylistically consonant with Northern Zhou sculpture. The simplified linear robes complementing smooth and round body forms and the round heads with benign faces are more akin to the Northern Qi style.

Further complicating matters is the fact that Sui works are among the numerous carvings found in Zhucheng, Shandong, in 1988 and 1990, and these perplexingly reflect the elaborate taste of Northern Zhou, which dominated the opposite end of China (fig. 3.98).[96] The reasons for such far-reaching stylistic connections are not clear.

The link between the Northern Qi and Sui styles is so strong that, for Qingzhou statuary, art historians find it challenging to date the findings. For example, Chinese scholars have labeled as Northern Qi a unique standing bodhisattva (136 centimeters high) that is completely carved in the round and almost intact (fig. 3.99). Yet its artistic conception appears to blend the opulent adornments of Northern Zhou and the Northern Qi suavity of facial expression and body forms — making it a Sui work. Equally arguable is the attribution to Northern Qi of imposing "Cosmological Buddhas" clad in monastic robes gilded and painted with cosmological themes (figs. 3.100, 3.101). Prior to the Qingzhou discovery, this type of image was represented in the West by a life-size stone statue in the Freer Gallery of Art, Washington, D.C., which was generally regarded as Sui.[97] Yet with the exception of the striking decoration of the robe, the Qingzhou Cosmological Buddha is

remarkably similar to the unadorned standing Buddha with a gilded robe that was discovered in the same area (fig. 3.102). This simpler-looking image, 63 centimeters high, is commonly considered Northern Qi because it perfectly embodies the Indian Gupta mode. Indeed, the division between the two styles is so blurred as to seem nonexistent.

Gilt bronzes of the era also show ties to one of two artistic lineages — Northern Zhou or Northern Qi. The gilt-bronze altarpiece dated Sui 593 is the most spectacular extant masterpiece of this epoch (fig. 3.103). Now in the Museum of Fine Arts, Boston, the 76.5-centimeter-tall sculpture represents Amitabha's Pure Land. To evoke these heavenly surroundings, luscious trees, ropes of pearls, dangling chimes, and celestials are carved around the deities. Amitabha appears on a jeweled lotus with two bodhisattvas: Guanyin holding a pomegranate and Dashizhi with hands clasped in prayer. Two of the four smaller images are the disciples Ananda and Kashyapa, the one wearing a crown is possibly a bodhisattva, while the fourth, with a conical headdress, is usually identified as a *pratyeka* Buddha who selfishly goes about his own enlightenment only (or, according to most recent scholarship, he represents the god Brahma). Lastly, two guardians brandishing thunderbolts appear in the lower corners.[98]

The two styles are perfectly blended in the shaping of the images: whereas the bodhisattvas are reminiscent of the Northern Zhou aesthetic (especially in their elab-

3.99 Standing bodhisattva (front and back), gilded and painted limestone, found in 1996 at Longxing Temple, Qingzhou, Shandong Province. Sui dynasty. Qingzhou Municipal Museum.

3.101 Detail of figure 3.100.

3.100 Cosmological Buddha with painted and gilded representations over the body, limestone, found in 1996 at Longxing Temple, Qingzhou. Sui dynasty. Qingzhou Municipal Museum.

orate ornamentation — note their exquisitely carved, filigree-like crowns) — the Buddha and the remaining images are more like the Northern Qi style in their simplicity and smoothness of modeling. The smiling and serene countenances of most of the protagonists and their elegantly natural bearings are quintessential Sui. The superb craftsmanship seen here rivals that of Hebei.

The very attractive but less flamboyant 32-centimeter-high altarpiece in the collection of the Freer Gallery of Art, Washington, D.C. (fig. 3.104), is dated Sui 597, but were it not for its inscription this work could be classified as Northern Qi because of its understated elegance. The inscription does not indicate where it was made, but it does inform us that sixteen ladies, some prominent at court, were the patrons of this trio, who look like Amitabha with his two canonical assistants holding flowers. The lithe figures of the bodhisattvas, their smiling miens, and the overall effect of the interaction of the three figures, however, confirm that they were made in the Sui period.

3.102 Standing Buddha fragment, gilded
limestone, found in 1996 at Longxing
Temple, Qingzhou. Northern Qi dynasty.
Qingzhou Municipal Museum.

3.103 Amitabha altarpiece, gilt bronze, probably from Xi'an. Sui dynasty, 593.
76.5 cm. Museum of Fine Arts, Boston. Gift of Mrs. W. Scott Fitz and Edward Jackson
Holmes, 22.407; in memory of his mother, Mrs. W. Scott Fitz, 47.1407-1412.

3.104 Amitabha altarpiece, gilt bronze. Sui dynasty, 597. 32.1 × 14.1 cm. Freer Gallery of Art, Smithsonian Institution, Washington, D.C.

Tang Art at the Northern Cosmopolitan Centers and Dunhuang

The Tang dynasty (618–907) was characterized by unprecedented expansion, unmatched political influence, and exceptional cultural efflorescence — as well as a peak in the production and development of Buddhist art. The Tang empire was enormous and stretched in all directions, toward central Asia, Korea, and southeast Asia. The capital of Chang'an (present-day Xi'an, Shaanxi) was regarded as one of the most cosmopolitan in Asia and attracted ambassadors, merchants, and visitors from all over the world. Interactions with international visitors taught the Chinese about other cultures and made them curious about foreign customs and achievements, and their own central role gave them a new self-confidence.

Imperial patronage was crucial to the creativity that distinguished the first 150 years of the dynasty. Emperor Gaozong (r. 650–683), Empress Wu Zetian (r. 684–704), and Emperor Xuanzong (r. 713–755) not only sponsored artistic projects but also fostered the growth of Buddhism itself by supporting eminent foreign monks and by encouraging Chinese monks to travel abroad to bring back the latest doctrinal developments. Once new texts became available, the monarchs supported the work of interpreting them.

Several prominent monks played critical roles in introducing novel Buddhist doctrines to China — doctrines whose associated icons crept into Buddhist art of the age. Xuanzang, for example, returned to Chang'an after sixteen years in India studying Buddhism in its native land. The sacred books, images, and iconographic sketches he brought back caused a sensation at court, and his travelogue *Record of the Western Regions* (*Da Tang Xiyu ji*) stirred the imagination not just of his contemporaries but of generations to follow.[99] In 695, too, responding to the invitation of Empress Wu, the monk Sikshananda arrived from Khotan with the Avatamsaka Sutra, which he then translated into Chinese. The empress herself contributed a preface to the translated text. And finally, in the first quarter of the eighth cen-

3.105 Vairocana and attendants, limestone, Fengxian Temple, Longmen, Henan Province. Tang dynasty, 675.

tury, the three Indian prelates Subhakarasimha, Amoghavajra, and Vajrabodhi arrived in the Tang capital as experts in Esoteric Buddhism, the latest and most theoretically challenging of the Buddhist schools. The celebration of Vairocana Buddha, the portrayal of arhats (*luohan*, worthy monks who were far advanced in their quest for enlightenment) linked to Contemplative Buddhism (Chan), and the many deities introduced to China by Esoteric teachers became prominent iconographic themes supported by the Tang court. These various beliefs lent inspiration to the sculpture (and painting) in metropolitan temples and religious caves.

As a result of the piety and largesse of Empress Wu, several outstanding caves were opened at Longmen embodying the new Tang style (and the patroness's doctrinal preferences). The imposing monumental sculpture of the Fengxian Temple, the heart of Longmen, was a grand project financed by the empress as early as 662 and completed in 675.[100] The huge central Buddha (17 meters high, including the pedestal) is Vairocana assisted by two regal bodhisattvas, the disciples Ananda and Kashyapa; two Lokapalas, or Heavenly Kings (the one holding the stupa being Vaishravana of the North); and two Thunderbolt Holders (Vajrapanis). It is a group of nine colossal images, widely spaced to form a semicircle (fig. 3.105).

In choosing this group of sculptures, the court had a very specific political goal: to draw a parallel between its own power and Buddhism. In the Brahma Net, or Brahmajala Sutra (a text belonging to the Huayan School), Vairocana represents the primordial Buddha, the one who creates and presides over all of the Buddhas in the infinitely large Buddhist cosmology.[101] The supremacy of one deity found its counterpoint in the Tang imperial bureaucracy, administered at the top by the emperor. The meaning of the stern yet dignified Buddha, the sumptuous attendant bodhisattvas, and the protective guardians becomes clearer in this context (figs. 3.106, 3.107).

Important stylistic changes also took place during this period. The Buddha, bodhisattvas, and monks seem less abstract than their Sui counterparts. The Tang have more gracefully joined body parts, and the figures thus seem more natural than the columnar Sui figures, yet the sheer monumentality of the Fengxian statues and their powerful symbolism prevented the use of outright realism. The penetrating expression of Vairocana Buddha carries a message of severe justice and suggests a remotely divine rather than human presence. The words that accompany the carving seemingly validate

this conjecture: "Truly I put my trust in Vairocana Buddha. In depicting his noble appearance the *lakshana* or holy marks [shape] an unmatched handsome face; His mercy and compassion are comparable to the greatness of sun and moon; when beholding this image and addressing one's prayer to it, one's wish will be fulfilled. The True Doctrine has flown over the East for over seven hundred years, yet this large Buddha niche is the greatest meritorious deed ever offered."[102] Carvers did, however, aspire to realism in their rendering of the expressive and dynamic guardians. The Heavenly Kings and Thunderbolt Holders have muscular builds, forceful poses, and expressive faces (see fig. 3.107).

The Huijian Cave, near the Fengxian Temple, was also linked to the imperial circle in that its sponsor, the abbot Huijian of the Fahai Temple of Chang'an who supervised its construction in 673, had close ties to the empress.[103] The choice of a seated Maitreya reflects the empress's strong support of the Maitreya cult. The style of this imposing Buddha — with his powerful chest and limbs discernible under the incised robes — successfully conveys the sense of a strong, naturally shaped body (fig. 3.108). The facial expression of this well-rounded head is dignified, but less distant than the Vairocana's. The Huijian Buddha reflects an idealized kind of realism.

The majestic Leigutai caves (no longer in their original setting) and the Kanjing Temple cave are some of the most notable caves sponsored by Empress Wu at Longmen. These late caves (690–704) were opened on the eastern side of the hill, across the Yi River. The Kanjing Temple was inspired by devotion to the arhats. These saintly personages were particularly revered by Chan Buddhists, although in later East Asian Buddhism the depiction of religious patriarchs became widespread in Tiantai, Esoteric, and Pure Land Schools (the Tiantai School, based on the Lotus Sutra, stresses that all sentient beings partake of Buddha nature).

Buddhism conceived the arhats as mortal but capable of amazing spiritual and physical deeds. Ostensibly they could read people's minds, hear at great distances, and move at remarkable speeds. These hermits, who reveled in the freedom of nature, appealed to those Chinese nostalgic for the Daoist sages.

Some of the best examples of Tang arhats are those carved on the walls of the Kanjing Temple. Here, twenty-nine arhats, all life-size (1.7 meters tall, on average), form an intriguing procession around the perimeter of the cave (fig. 3.109). They represent the great

3.106 Bodhisattva and disciple (detail), limestone, Fengxian Temple.

3.107 Heavenly King of the North Vaishravana and Thunderbolt Holder (detail), limestone, Fengxian Temple.

3.108 Buddha group, limestone, Huijian Cave (rear wall), Longmen, Henan Province. Tang dynasty, ca. 673–700.

3.109 Arhats, limestone, Kanjing Temple, Longmen. Tang dynasty, ca. 700.

patriarchs who had transmitted the Buddhist doctrine.[104] Each patriarch, starting with Mahakashyapa, is individually and realistically characterized: old, young, portly, skinny, withdrawn, sociable, dignified, lighthearted — even quite a few foreign-looking arhats can be seen. All are depicted interacting with each other in lifelike clarity.

A similar emphasis on realism is shown in a set of sixteen or eighteen arhats made of glazed clay originally found in caves of the Taihang Mountains, near Yixian County, in Hebei Province.[105] Of the original set six are in Western museums — a seventh, once in a German collection, was destroyed during World War II. The whereabouts of the remaining arhats is unknown. It is unclear exactly when and where the *sancai* (tricolor glazed pottery images) were made, but an earlier Tang date, within the eighth century, seems likely given the figures' strong stylistic, iconographic, and technical similarities with other Tang sculptures.

The two life-size seated arhats in The Metropolitan Museum of Art, New York, are renowned for their compelling realism (figs. 3.110, 3.111; see also fig. 4.37). They seem to be portraits of an introvert and extrovert, respectively. The older, who holds a scroll in his left hand, is deeply immersed in meditation, while, in sharp contrast, the younger arhat gazes searchingly at the world outside.

One compelling reason to consider these arhats Tang works is the use of the sancai technique. This technique demanded not only excellent skills but also a well-organized labor force and large kilns because the clay was fashioned over an iron armature and coated with an outer layer of finer clay, which in turn was covered with lead glazes (cream, rust, and green). These technological requisites for the sancai method became prominent at the height of the Tang and peaked by 750.

In addition to the monumental sculpture of Longmen, the empress sponsored the reliefs decorating the interior of the Seven Jewel Tower (Qibao Tai), one of the buildings in the Guangzhai Temple complex, Chang'an.[106] The Guangzhai Temple was established by the monarch in 677, but the tower was added later, shortly after 700. By the ninth century, the temple had ceased to exist and the reliefs were moved to the Baoqing, another Chang'an temple. At present only seven of the original thirty-two reliefs remain in Xi'an, still in the Baoqing Temple. The rest are in various Japanese and American collections. Because some of the reliefs carry the dates 703 and 704, the construction date for the tower has been ascribed to these years, at the end of the empress's reign.

The limestone reliefs, which are on average 1 meter high and 0.75 meters wide, are important for showing the Buddhist teachings favored by the ruler and the realistic style that pleased the court. They depict different settings for the same threesome (Amitabha, Maitreya, and the Jeweled Buddha [Bodhirui] as Vairocana): they gather, for example, under the shade of elegantly carved jeweled trees or floral canopies. Although the deities' faces communicate a kind of pure grace, their plump and soft bodies are exquisitely human (fig. 3.112). The bodhisattvas are posed with one hip thrust out and are adorned elegantly but simply, perhaps because of their minute proportions.

Among the reliefs are seven individual images of the eleven-headed bodhisattva Guanyin carved on taller and narrower stone slabs. Guanyin is an Esoteric image described in sutras translated as early as the Northern Zhou dynasty and later in sutras of the Tang such as the *Dharani Treatises* (*Duoloni jijing*), a collection of protective spells translated by the Indian monk Atigupta, probably in the mid-seventh century.

In the fragmentary Freer Gallery relief, Guanyin has ten small heads above the main head that look as though they are attached to the headdress (fig. 3.113). The distinctive expression of each face signifies, according to some canonical sources, the ten stages (*bhumi*) of perfection that indicate the bodhisattva's level of spiritual development. The deity on this panel displays a well-formed, supple body enhanced by skillfully executed robes and jewels. He embodies the kind of realism and refined taste associated with art of the early eighth century.

An exceptional statuette of a Nine-headed Guanyin (37.5 centimeters high) that was executed with superior craftsmanship from a single block of sandalwood proves the artisan's ability to interpret the same iconography in a different medium and in a reduced size (fig. 3.114). It is dated to 719. The use of sandalwood was a canonical requirement specified in the Sutra of the Dharani of the Eleven-headed Guanyin (Fo shuo shiyimian Guanshiyin shenzhou jing), translated by Yeshijuduo between 563 and 577. The statuette was brought to Japan in the early eighth century and is presently part of the Horyuji Temple's treasury.

3.110 Seated arhat, earthenware with tricolor glaze, Yixian County, Hebei Province. Tang dynasty, ca. 725; also ascribed to the Liao/Jin. 104.7 cm. The Metropolitan Museum of Art, New York.

3.111 Seated arhat, earthenware with tricolor glaze, Yixian County. Tang dynasty, ca. 725; also ascribed to the Liao/Jin. 127 cm. The Metropolitan Museum of Art, New York.

3.112 Buddhist triad, limestone architectural relief, from Seven Jewel Tower (Qibao Tai), originally part of Guangzhai Temple, Xi'an. Tang dynasty, 704. Tokyo National Museum.

3.113 Eleven-headed Guanyin, limestone architectural relief, from Seven Jewel Tower. Height, 108.8 cm; width, 37.7 cm; depth, 15.3 cm. Freer Gallery of Art, Smithsonian Institution, Washington, D.C.

3.114 Nine-headed Guanyin, sandalwood, probably made in Xi'an. Tang dynasty, 719. Treasury of the Horyuji Temple, Nara.

The Blending of Realism with Secularism

By the first quarter of the eighth century Tang sculpture was displaying not only realism but also a marked secularism (the image as a mirror of the refined opulence and sensuality of the court). The works were brilliantly conceived and flawlessly executed, as demonstrated by sculptures discovered in the Tianlongshan cave temples of Shanxi, and the Dunhuang caves of Gansu. The Tianlongshan cave temples (located approximately 40 kilometers southwest of Taiyuan, Shanxi) were first established during the Eastern Wei dynasty, but became particularly active during the reign of Emperor Xuanzong between 714 and 740. No inscription confirms this dating, nor are there records linking Tianlongshan to imperial sponsorship, but a prominent patron is likely because the sculptures are so exquisite, suggesting an affluent taste. Imperial patronage seems likely given that Empress Wu's father had been military governor of this commandery and that Taiyuan became the de facto northern capital under the empress.

The small sculptures in Tianlongshan were plundered in the early 1920s; at present the remaining statuary is extremely fragmentary. Caves 14, 17, 18, and 21 were particularly beautiful: their reliefs were placed in groups of five and seven all along the walls, forming an arc. The figures were shown sitting or standing at ease, interacting closely with each other.[107]

The art in Tianlongshan is more secular than that of any other Tang site of the early eighth century, to the extent that the holiness of the images is undermined. Tianlongshan Buddhas and bodhisattvas are clad in sheer, clinging garments that reveal soft, relaxed bodies (fig. 3.115). The vivid naturalism, the humanlike attitudes, and tranquil, dreamlike moods of these deities evoke the atmosphere of the court rather that that of a divine assembly.

The aesthetic of Tianlongshan with slight modifications is also embodied by the contemporary sculptures of Dunhuang. One example is Cave 45, ascribed to about 725 (fig. 3.116). Seven figures have been carved in the round: Buddha assisted by two monks, two bodhisattvas, and two Heavenly Kings. Each is rendered with supple and realistic modeling, with postures and countenances that create a sense of intimate interrelationship, and with highly refined clothing and jewelry. The audience is extended to include the bodhisattvas painted on the surrounding walls; this blending of three-dimensional and painted components creates an intriguing illusion.

Throughout the work, the divine harmonizes with the secular. Note the participants' humanlike expressions (especially the youthful, sweet-looking Ananda) and realistic, softly modeled bodies (the bodhisattvas in particular) barely covered by elegant drapes and jewels. Fascinating details include Buddha's robe caught in the pointed leaves of the lotus throne.

For further appreciation of this delicate, natural style, one can look ahead in time to the style shown in the sculpture of Cave 196, dated 893–894. By the late Tang, overpowering massiveness and a lack of emotion were predominant sculptural features. In Cave 196 the monumental bodhisattva (2.65 meters high), seated on a pedestal throne, displays an inflated chest and very rounded thighs (fig. 3.117). Although the sculpture has not reached the point of deformity, its style has reached a dead end.

Tang artisans of the earlier periods also applied their brilliant creativity to the execution of gilt bronzes. Exquisitely crafted and expertly conceived, these works are related to those of Tianlongshan in style. Several

3.115 Bodhisattva, sandstone, Cave 14, Tianlongshan, Shanxi Province. First half of the 8th century. Tokyo National Museum.

3.116 Buddha group, painted clay, Cave 45 (rear niche), Dunhuang, Gansu Province. Tang dynasty, ca. 725.

3.117 Seated bodhisattva, painted clay, Cave 196, Dunhuang. Tang dynasty, 893–894.

bronzes of Guanyin are contemporary with Tianlong-shan sculpture. Shown in strong contrapposto, the deity usually holds a bottle of ambrosia in one hand and a spray of willow in the other; at times, instead of holding the willow, Guanyin gingerly grasps the long ribbon hanging from his headdress.

The 37-centimeter-high Guanyin in the Sackler Museum, Cambridge, Massachusetts, typifies the worldly and realistic taste of the Tang (fig. 3.118). The perfectly round face is regally crowned by a weighty volute of hair; in the crown is also displayed Amitabha, Guanyin's spiritual father. The sensuously modeled body is draped with clingy, revealing robes, and the pronounced sway of the image has been emphasized with chains of jewelry slung across the figure, the movement of the cloth, and fluttering scarves.

A second example of the high Tang style is a seated Amitabha Buddha in the collection of The Metropolitan Museum of Art, New York (fig. 3.119). The 20.3-centimeter-high image, seated with interlocked legs, is dignified and somber. The slightly tilted head has elongated eyes, a small, fleshy mouth, and wavy hair forming large whorls that retain traces of indigo pigment. The hem of the robe is gathered to form fanlike pleats between the legs; a shawl is wrapped around the shoul-

ders. The facial expression, pose, modeling, and attire are all similar to those features of the Tianlongshan Buddhas. The smooth, bare chest contrasts with the textured diamonds and serpentine lines of the inner garment. The hands, lifelike and graceful, are perhaps the work's crowning achievement.

By contrast, the miniature bodhisattva (38.5 centimeters high), part of the treasury of the Famen Temple, Fufeng, discovered in 1987, eloquently exhibits the diverse stylistic and iconographic concerns accompanying the production of gilt bronzes in the ninth century (fig. 3.120). Made of gilded silver and decorated with over two hundred pearls, the exquisite statuette lacks the expressiveness of the earlier pieces and their humanized presence.[108] Its religious and artistic inspiration has reverted to the pre-Tang emotionless approach. The statuette portrays a sumptuously dressed and crowned bodhisattva kneeling and offering a golden tray shaped as a large lotus leaf. Fashioned in 871 by the order of Emperor Yizong (r. 860–874), the "bodhisattva offering the true body [of the Buddha]" displayed the Buddha's bone relic (*sarira*) for the emperor's worship. The imagery used to decorate the various sections of the pedestal (Sanskrit seed letters and multiheaded and multifaced deities) indicates how Esoteric teaching inspired the icon.

3.118 Standing bodhisattva Guanyin, gilt bronze. Tang dynasty, ca. 725. 37 cm. Arthur M. Sackler Museum, Harvard University Art Museums.

3.119 Seated Amitabha Buddha, gilt bronze. Tang dynasty, ca. 725. 20.3 cm. The Metropolitan Museum of Art, New York.

Esoteric Sculpture

In India, Esoteric or Tantric beliefs and iconography began to be systematized during the seventh century. Regarded as the supreme teaching of Buddha, this mystic or "True Word" (Chinese: *Zhenyan*) doctrine cannot be expressed in ordinary terms. Teachers secretly transmitted the doctrine to their pupils using set rituals and meditational practices. Such practices relied heavily on images (painting and sculpture), hand gestures, and the recitation of incantations.

The Sanskrit texts underlying the Esoteric doctrine were brought to China during the first half of the eighth century by three famous Indian monks — Subhakarasimha, Vajrabodhi, and Amoghavajra — who were well received at the court of Emperor Xuanzong (r. 713–756).[109] The ruler and the elite were attracted to Esoteric Buddhism by the magic overtones of its rituals and its exclusive status. The dazzling display of ritualistic implements may have also attracted commoners.

Esoteric Buddhism and its art suffered irreparable losses during the anti-Buddhist repression ordered by Emperor Wuzong (r. 840–846): its clergy, temples, and doctrine were left in shambles. As a result, prior to recent discoveries of Esoteric remains, examples of

3.121 Manjushri bodhisattva, marble with traces of gilding, Anguo Temple, Xi'an. Tang dynasty, ca. 750. Forest of Steles Museum, Xi'an.

3.120 Offering bodhisattva, gilded silver, Famen Temple, Fufeng, Shaanxi Province. Tang dynasty, 871. Museum of Famen Temple, Fufeng.

3.122 Two-armed Trailokyavijaya or Acala Vidyaraja, marble with traces of gilding, Anguo Temple, Xi'an. Tang dynasty, ca. 750. Forest of Steles Museum, Xi'an.

Chinese Esoteric sculpture from temples of the northern metropolitan centers were extremely rare: its very existence could be inferred only from the still extant statuary created in Japan from Chinese models.

The 1959 find of ten pieces of Esoteric sculpture likely belonging to the Anguo Temple, Chang'an, and the aforementioned reliquary deposit of the Famen Temple, Fufeng, remain our primary sources of information on Esoteric Buddhist images.[110] The Chang'an sculptures were discovered 10 meters belowground in northeastern Xi'an, in what was the Changle district of the Tang capital, where several imperial palaces were located. The Anguo Temple was thus literally situated in the shadow of the imperial court. Unfortunately, the statues — eight executed in white marble with traces of gilt and two in limestone — are not dated, but their style suggests that they were created between 750 and 770. Their uniform style and size (they are each about 1 meter tall) implies that they were part of a group.

Because images were considered essential for expressing the most difficult theological concepts of Esoteric Buddhism, the deities had to be sculpted, painted, or drawn according to strictly formulated rules. In other words, they had to be executed as described in the scriptures or as illustrated in collections of iconographic drawings, like the *Meditation on the Images of the Five Families of the Mandala* (*Wu bu xin guan*), compiled by Subhakarasimha. Adherence to iconographic rules concerning color selection and the rendering of implements and hand gestures was essential to guarantee the efficacy of the icon. Such strict requirements caused Esoteric statues to stand out conspicuously from earlier works.

The Anguo Temple statues that belong now to the Forest of Steles Museum, Xi'an, represent both benign and wrathful aspects of Esoteric Buddhist deities. The bodhisattva Manjushri (Wenshu; 74 centimeters high) embodies Wisdom; his implements, consequently, are a book placed on a lotus in his left hand and likely a sword, no longer extant, held in his right (fig. 3.121).

This sculpture establishes a type very different in physique, expression, and adornments from the non-Esoteric statuary of Tianlongshan and related sites. The face is full, marked by narrow eyes and deeply arched eyebrows, a moderately sized nose, and a tiny mouth. The expression is conspicuously haughty. The hair is gathered in a volutelike chignon, but in the back its luxuriant growth is perfectly arranged. The short and plump body is dressed in a tight bodice with tight sleeves ending in pleats and a dhoti tied with a noticeable knot between the breasts. The stole draped over the shoulders and falling on each side of the lotus seat is a remnant of Tianlongshan conventions. The painted counterparts to these images survive on the ceiling of the rear niche of Cave 148 at Dunhuang. The cave is dated by inscription to 776.

The sitting arrangement of the statue is another innovation. The bodhisattva rests in the lotus posture on a tall, elaborately carved lotus support that does not seem to follow any particular iconographic requirement (this construction was used for several Anguo Temple images). While maintaining the traditional hourglass, or Mount Sumeru, shape, the pedestal nonetheless shows substantial modifications. It consists of a round drum base, a middle section formed by lush three-dimensional foliage, and an upper section of overlapping lotus petals, occasionally decorated with a central rosette. The intricate construction and the depth of the carving suggest a lacquered wood model. The sheer sensuality of the vegetal forms harks back to the naturalness and realism of the first half of the eighth century.

The Vidyaraja, or King of Wisdom (72 centimeters high), perhaps a representation of a two-handed Trailokyavijaya or of Acala (Budong), the Immovable, one of the five emanations of the Esoteric Jina Buddhas, is a good example of a wrathful image from the Anguo Temple (fig. 3.122). One can assume that it is the deity Acala, the angry embodiment of Vairocana Buddha. The statue originally grasped a lasso in the left hand (now broken) and still brandishes a thunderbolt in the right. Seated on a rock formation, the sculpture is strikingly forceful and dynamic. The wide face has deeply embedded eyes, thick lips, and protruding fangs. Barely contained strength inflates the broad, naked chest that is sensuously adorned with a large pearl. The dynamic backward and somewhat twisted extension of the torso is accentuated by the outstretched right arm. The finely delineated hair, once painted crimson, stands like a bristling mane and is suggestive of flames (the canonical backdrop of Acala), an effect that increases the sense of uncontainable inner anger and impending action. The traditional frontal approach that for centuries dominated Chinese sculpture was broken in the making of this Esoteric sculpture, one of the most accomplished embodiments of religious realism. The Vidyaraja is stunning from all viewpoints.

The very high standard of execution shown by this group of Esoteric deities demonstrates that the development of Buddhist art did not mirror political events, and cautions against the hasty conclusion that Tang art started to decline after the An Lushan revolt of the 750s. The revolt undoubtedly dealt a blow to the political stability of Emperor Xuanzong's long reign, but it did not extinguish creativity in the religious arts. The Anguo Temple sculptures document that Buddhism was still a potent emotional force among artists, patrons, and believers. The connection of these works with a temple that is known to have been supported by members of the imperial house supports the inference that the statues were the result not only of princely patronage but also of princely devotion. In short, from the start of the dynasty until the mid-ninth century — the time of the suppression of Buddhism (840–846) — the production of Buddhist art expanded continuously.

The sociopolitical conditions that produced the Tang Buddhist art discussed here had changed by the mid-eighth century, when China's political might began to disintegrate and its territory shrank. Defeated by the Arabs at the Talas River in 751, China lost the heart of central Asia to Islam, as well as its supremacy over the Silk Road. The Chinese northwest was threatened by the Tibetans, who even conquered Dunhuang. In 756, the An Lushan revolt dealt a direct blow to Chang'an, the capital, and Emperor Xuanzong fled south to Yizhou, Sichuan's capital (present-day Chengdu). Peace was restored by 773, and one legacy of this political recovery was the making of Esoteric icons.

The political collapse of the dynasty and the persecution of Buddhists (840s) signaled a change in the locus of Buddhist art. The Huang Chao rebellion of the 870s pushed the court away from Chang'an; by 881, the court had taken shelter in Sichuan. The self-assuredness and flamboyance that characterized the first half of the dynasty had ended. Meanwhile, the southwest of China became a haven for Buddhism and a very productive and innovative center of Buddhist art.

Tang Buddhist Cave Temples of Sichuan

During the Tang, Sichuan became one of the most prolific regions for Buddhist art. Nurtured by centuries of figurative arts production and supported by relative political and economic stability, Sichuan sculpture reached maturity much as its northern counterpart did. Most importantly, the province continued as in earlier times to search for its own mode of expression rather than depend exclusively on the dynastic north for inspiration.

Sichuan contains over one hundred sites of Tang cliff sculpture spread over a broad area. One can, however, trace their development along the major tributaries of the Yangzi River that flow from north to south. Tang Buddhist sites occupied northern Sichuan (prominent sites included Guangyuan, Tongjiang, and Bazhong), central Sichuan, including Chongqing (exemplified by Zizhong, Anyue, and Dazu), and southern Sichuan (notably Leshan, Jiajiang, Qionglai, Renshou, and Pujiang). Overlooking terraced rice fields and tucked away in remote farmland, these sites are generally not easily accessible. Their placement was determined by the economic and cultural environment of their day.

Each site was further subdivided into several parts that held many sculptures. Thus thousands of cliff reliefs dot the red sandstone hills of Sichuan. This wealth of evidence is particularly important because it is often accompanied by dated inscriptions, enabling us to trace the chronological development of style and religious

3.123 Buddha Bodhirui Grotto, painted sandstone, Thousand Buddhas Cliff, Guangyuan, Sichuan Province. Tang dynasty, 711–712.

content. In contrast to Dunhuang, a self-contained and well-preserved monument of Buddhist art, Sichuan's cliffs resemble an open museum, exposed unfortunately to humanmade and natural hazards.

Northern Cliff Sculpture at Guangyuan and Bazhong

The Thousand Buddhas cliff in Guangyuan is about as large as Longmen.[111] Carving began by approximately 500, but the site is especially known for its Tang sculptures, made during the eighth and ninth centuries. Grottoes and niches were carved on stacked levels, and the sculptures of varying sizes number approximately ten thousand. The importance of Guangyuan can be traced to its twofold links to Chang'an. First, it was located on the Jinniu Road, so all traffic between Chang'an and Chengdu passed through it. And as several officials resided in Guangyuan because the family of Empress Wu administered it, the imperial house and Tang elite had close ties to the site through their patronage. Consequently, Buddhist art at Guangyuan reflects a northern influence, albeit with a local twist.

The large grotto (3.25 meters high, 4.1 meters wide, and 3.3 meters deep) called Bodhirui, from the name of its main Buddha, was a donation by the local governor Bi Zhonghua in 711–712 (fig. 3.123). Two monks, two bodhisattvas, two menacing guardians, and two kneeling donors accompany the conspicuously bejeweled Buddha sitting on a grand central altar.[112] The group is a prominent example of cult figures developed at the Tang capital, but with a stylistic interpretation very different from the northern one.

Bodhirui, the Jeweled Buddha, was considered a manifestation of Vairocana Buddha during the early phase of Esoteric Buddhism. The jeweled crown of Bodhirui, his touching-the-earth hand gesture, the presence of the two bodhisattvas Guanzizai and Jingang, and the use of two bodhi trees behind the throne are canonical requirements of the *Collection of Dharani Sutra* (*Dharani jijing*) translated by Atigupta. Carvers also used this iconography contemporaneously in the Leigutai caves at Longmen and in some of the reliefs of the Seven Jewel Tower (works sponsored by the empress), but the Guangyuan version displays strictly Sichuanese

3.124
Shakyamuni
and
Prabhutaratna
Grotto,
painted
sandstone,
Thousand
Buddhas
Cliff. Tang
dynasty,
ca. 720.

traits: namely, a unique interpretation of the central altar and the inclusion of additional personages along the side walls. It is possible that this altar replicates those used in Esoteric rituals (there are too few examples of Esoteric art to know for sure), but in no other part of China do we see such a construction formed by a platform plus a tall screen. Furthermore the screen uses bodhi trees as structural components — their canopy of leaves shelters some lesser gods, personifications of wind, rain, and thunder. To enrich this atmospheric structure, the artisans perforated the stone and created lifelike shadows that play on the group below. The ingenious interpretation and construction of the altar and the addition of five musicians to a group of spectators that includes twelve monks shows the local carvers' intent to anchor the divine scene firmly to earthly surroundings.

At this site, similar altars with screens are used in seven other grottoes and in connection with different main deities. Obviously they had a certain clerical and secular appeal. In the grotto called Shakyamuni and Prabhutaratna (2.2 meters high, 3 meters wide, and 3.6 meters deep), the two Buddhas are shown side by side on a tall altar against a leafy screen, which was left unfinished (fig. 3.124). The cave is thought to have been completed around 720. The refined elegance and perfection of High Tang style are seen in the Buddhas and bodhisattvas, but the courtly sensuality of northern

models (the Seven Jewel Tower reliefs, for instance) is tempered in this more sensitive and introspective Sichuan example.

In the screen's trees are the Demigods of the Eight Classes, whom we encountered in the monumental Northern Zhou niche at the Guangzi Temple, also in Guangyuan. These eight supernatural guardians, depicted with both human and superhuman features (multiple limbs and heads, as well as flamboyant headdresses adorned with snakes and birds), were extremely popular in Sichuan and most likely originated there. As such, they embody a picaresque theatricality that is totally alien to their northern siblings. The group that spills out of Grotto 8 (2.5 meters high, 2.1 meters wide, and 1.1 meters deep) in Shining Temple, a site farther south, near Bazhong, fittingly conveys the lively mood and antics of the eight protectors (fig. 3.125).[113]

Grotto 3 at the same Shining Temple exemplifies the Sichuan aesthetic sense, which humanized the sacred and charged forms with emotions (fig. 3.126). The grotto — which is 2.82 meters high, 1.65 meters wide, and 1.05 meters deep — displays two Buddhas, perhaps Shakyamuni and Maitreya, and their attendants (bodhisattvas, disciples, Vajrapani, even two children) densely crowding the limited space. In a highly unusual arrangement, the carvers placed one of the attending bodhisattvas, who looks straight out at the onlookers, between the two Buddhas. The centrality of the three

3.125 Grotto 8, Shining Temple, near Bazhong, Sichuan Province. Tang dynasty, ca. 725.

images is stressed by the unusual interplay of circular shapes, the halos and aureoles. These three icons are serene and expressive, round and soft, splendid creations of the High Tang (ca. 725). The rest of the group displayed along the side walls, in overlapping planes, are astonishingly animated in mien and pose. The tender presence of the children, one of them clinging to a monk's robe, firmly places the scene in the human realm. The viewer is also struck by the beauty and elegance of the carving, like the honeysuckle scroll that creeps all along the frame, reminiscent of the best floral borders of Chang'an steles. The northern taste had reached Bazhong via the imperial princes Li Shen, Li Ke, and Li Xian, who had been exiled there by the Empress Wu Zetian. These nobles and their retainers sought to re-create the cultural ambiance of the capital by patronizing Buddhist art and demanding that the Sichuanese carvers meet the metropolitan standards of Luoyang and Chang'an.

Central Cliff Sculpture at Anyue and Zizhong

Meanwhile, farther south, at Anyue and Zizhong, and closer to the Yangzi basin, religious sculpture was developing in purely indigenous ways. One prominent example is the monumental Parinirvana (25 meters long and 5 meters high) in the remote village of Miaoxiang,

in northern Anyue County (fig. 3.127). The site is built around a gully. Opposite the Parinirvana, carvers worked in additional niches and rock chambers. Led by the prelate Xuan Ying, who was highly respected in this area, pious benefactors (local and dynastic elite) had sutra texts extensively and systematically carved in stone. These inscriptions are dated and enable us to ascribe the making of the monumental Buddha to approximately 733, at the height of Tang style.[114]

The iconography is unique, displaying the outstretched Buddha as the focal point along with conflated events related to his final release. Above the supine body one sees Buddha preaching to a large audience of bodhisattvas, disciples, and the ubiquitous Demigods of the Eight Classes (fig. 3.128). At his feet stands a sorrowful (rather than the typically menacing) Vajrapani, and at his head, a Guanyin, while at his side the last convert, the venerable Brahmin Subhadra, or Ananda, tenderly holds the teacher's hand. The emotional involvement of the participants, as well as their unusual positioning, are all in keeping with Sichuanese taste.

The emphasis on making colossal recumbent, seated, and standing Buddhas can also be regarded as a prominent Sichuanese trend, one that accelerated during the Song dynasty.[115] To be sure, impressively large icons were built in the north, as the result of dynastic sponsorship,

3.126 Grotto 3, Shining Temple, near Bazhong. Tang dynasty, ca. 725.

but in Sichuan the donors were the local ecclesiastics and/or elite. When viewing such labor-intensive projects we are also reminded of the amount of wealth in the hands of local mercantile and agricultural interests.

The Anyue Parinirvana is but one of several monumental sculptures, namely the enormous Buddha of Tongnan (843–860), the half-bust Buddha of Renshou (late eighth century), and the well-known Maitreya Buddha of Leshan (fig. 3.129). Carved at the confluence of the Min and Dadu Rivers to protect sailors and their merchandise, the 70-meter-high Maitreya was started in the year 730 by the monk Haitong. A lack of funds delayed completion until 803, when the Leshan governor Wei Gao contributed the needed money.

In the early 1900s, the face of the Leshan Buddha was recut and its original Tang appearance was lost. The thick-set and schematized body also shows the ravages of time, but the aura of majesty remains intact. To understand the original style of the Leshan Maitreya, we have to look at its inspiration, namely the smaller-than-life-size seated Maitreya of Cave 135, at the nearby site of Jiajiang (fig. 3.130), which was created around 730. Around Buddha are two bodhisattvas as well as small seated Buddhas in floating clouds.

The pioneering Esoteric image of Guanyin as a thousand-handed, thousand-eyed bodhisattva remains one of Sichuan's most significant achievements. The boundless mercy and omnipotent power of this deity are made tangible by multiple arms projecting from Guanyin's body. The many carvings of Guanyin found throughout Sichuan are significant in that they differ in religious content from the paintings of Dunhuang; some of the carvings preceded the paintings.[116]

The Thousand-eyed, Thousand-handed Guanyin from Mount Zhonglong, in the northern hills of Zizhong, is the most prominent example of this image (fig. 3.131). There is no inscription to date it, but based on stylistic similarities to adjacent sculptures that are accompanied by dated inscriptions, it is probably Middle Tang (756–840). The sculpture, therefore, is the first known representation of its kind, anticipating similar Guanyins painted on the silk banners of Dunhuang.

The deity is shown seated (usually he is portrayed standing) in the middle of the horseshoe-shaped grotto (3.9 meters high, 4.2 meters wide, and 1.85 meters deep); his forty-two major hands hold canonical implements or make various symbolic gestures, or mudras, while his other hands lie outstretched behind him, forming a huge aureole. The canonical attendants (Buddhist and Hindu) are organized in tiers on the surrounding walls (fig. 3.132). Their systematic arrangement suggests a mandalic formation of a sacred Esoteric field. Fur-

3.127 Monumental Parinirvana, sandstone, Miaoxiang, Anyue County, Sichuan Province. Tang dynasty, ca. 733.

thermore, at each corner of the grotto are prominent carvings of two Great Kings of Wisdom (Vidyaraja), Thunderbolt Holders, Esoteric guardians par excellence. Multifaced and multihanded, framed within a flaming nimbus, the two seem poised to leap out of their enclosure.

The imagery was based on a number of different sacred texts, translated in Chang'an during the first half of the Tang, with the text by Baghavaddharma (ca. 650) being among the earliest translated, followed by the sutras translated by the famous Esoteric prelates of the *kaiyuan* era (713–741). These sources give specific instructions concerning the making of images and the types of ritual. The Zizhong artistic visualization, however, does not correspond exactly to the sacred texts (concerning the numerous attendants), suggesting that the carvers may have developed their own conventions and taken some liberties — a theory supported by the observation that the many images of this type found in Sichuan are by no means uniform. In short, the Sichuanese carvers possessed both the artistic and the doctrinal means to undertake such complex themes.

Southern Cliff Sculpture at Qionglai and Renshou

This Sichuanese artistic and religious independence is also seen in the interpretation of the Western Pure Land of Amitabha Buddha, the basis of another ex-

tremely popular cult in Sichuan. Copious scenes of paradise were painted contemporaneously at Dunhuang, but only in Sichuan do we find the sculptural versions. Numerous examples are available at virtually every Tang site. Among them is the relief in Qionglai, at Shisunshan, Cave 4 (3.5 meters high, 3 meters wide, and 3.05 meters deep), whose execution is ascribed to the eighth century (fig. 3.133).

The boldly innovative interpretation of this theme is the product of a carver uninhibited by dogmatic rules; it may, furthermore, be an adaptation of paintings that decorated a temple in Chengdu, the provincial capital. A three-leveled composition was devised corresponding to the paradisiacal setting, the heavenly assembly, and the pond of rebirth. All the towers of the upper level carved on the side and rear walls are inhabited by throngs of blessed people, walking from one tower to the next, climbing the staircases, and even sliding along the banisters. There are at least one hundred images of different sizes. Below the central triad of Amitabha and his assistants Avalokiteshvara and Mahasthamaprapta lies the pond of rebirth, marked by sturdy lotus plants that fan out to reach the threesome above. In the pond section in particular, the carver suited the text to his inspiration in a most unconventional fashion. Two large barges with gleeful passengers emerge from side tunnels to navigate the water of the pond. These extravagant additions underline the secularism and the exhilaration that pervade the entire scene. In the grotto's lower corners Manjushri and Samantabhadra — riding the lion and elephant, respectively — also participate in the paradise. Behind them lotus trees creep over the side walls carrying the reborn. With extraordinary inventiveness, the "conventional" northern Chinese representation of the western paradise — which stressed only the sacred and avoided the human content — has been radically transformed.

In the Niujiaozhai cliff of Renshou, which lies about 50 kilometers east of Qionglai, is another fascinating interpretation of Amitabha's Pure Land, a testimony to the wide range of thematic interpretations.[117] In niche 21 (approximately 1.5 meters tall and wide and about 0.5 meters deep), carved around 750, the paradise is alluded to through the lotus as a symbol of rebirth (fig. 3.134). Pliant lotus stems grow profusely from a central vase, filling the space and providing a seat to the triad and all of the blessed. The motif is eminently Indian, as it is profusely used in the Sanchi carvings, in those of Kanheri, and in the Ajanta murals. At the bottom of the niche, the deities stand in groups on arched

bridges, a cursory allusion to the architecture that played such a prominent role in Qionglai. With extraordinary finesse, the carver suggests the intricate arabesque of the lotus roots and stems growing in the water, transforming the hardness of the stone into a transparent cloth. In dealing with the Western Pure Land, the Sichuanese carvers moved away from the rather rigid iconic interpretation that characterizes the large frescoes of Dunhuang and favored instead a more fluid composition steeped in narrative details. No doubt the palaces and gardens that host the divine gatherings and their merrymaking reflected the contemporary Sichuan scene and its affluent society.

Sichuan more than any other part of China offers also the opportunity to study Daoist sculpture — which blossomed alongside the Buddhist, albeit in more limited numbers, from the Northern Zhou until the end of the Song. During the Tang, grottoes and niches of Daoist deities were made right next to those of Buddha, as in Jiange, Dongnan, and Renshou; exclusively Daoist sites were set up very rarely. At Yunüquan near Mianyang and at Xuanmiaoguan in Anyue County, however, most of the reliefs are Daoist. Although the content of the

3.128 Disciples (detail), sandstone, monumental Parinirvana, Miaoxiang.

3.130 Seated Maitreya, sandstone, Cave 135, Jiajiang, Sichuan Province. Tang dynasty, ca. 730.

3.129 Monumental seated Maitreya Buddha, sandstone, Leshan,
Sichuan Province. Begun in the Tang dynasty, 730.

3.131 Thousand-eyed, Thousand-handed Guanyin, painted sandstone, Zhonglongshan, Zizhong, Sichuan Province. Tang dynasty, 756–840.

3.132 Side attendants (detail), painted sandstone, Zhonglongshan.

3.133 Amitabha's Pure Land and side wall (detail), sandstone, Cave 4, Shisunshan, Qionglai, Sichuan Province. Tang dynasty, 8th century.

3.134 Amitabha's Pure Land, sandstone, niche 21, Niujiaozhai, Renshou, Sichuan Province. Tang dynasty, ca. 750.

3.135 Laojun, sandstone, Yunüquan, Mianyang, Sichuan Province. Tang dynasty, 7th century.

two religious systems is quite different, Daoist sculpture is deceptively close to Buddhist sculpture in appearance because the Daoist visual vocabulary was an adaptation and at times an outright appropriation of the Buddhist.

Two examples from the vicinity of Mianyang and Renshou clarify this artistic relationship between the two religious movements. The first is a rather modest, early Tang niche from Yunüquan, Mianyang.[118] In the small niche (about 60 centimeters high) is a representation of Laojun — the deified Laozi, the legendary philosopher and founder of Daoism from the late Zhou dynasty — and his two attendants (fig. 3.135). This sculpture has numerous characteristics that we normally associate with Buddhist icons, namely the nimbus, the lotus seat, the lion, and the arrangement of the trio. On the other hand, Laojun's and his assistants' garb resembles that of a Tang official rather than that of a Buddhist deity, while a bearded Laojun does not perform a mudra, but rests one hand on a three-legged stand (a common Daoist accoutrement) and holds a fan, also a requisite of "pure talk" (*qingtan*). This niche typifies the conflation of Buddhist and Daoist elements that was rather common during the Tang.

Niche 53 at Niujiaozhai, Renshou, presents a more complex iconography that carries important historical implications (fig. 3.136). This exceptional monument of twenty-six images, carved in 749, as the accompanying stele indicates, was likely generated by Emperor Xuanzong's active support for Daoism. By giving a record of imperial influence in forging novel Daoist iconography, this sculptural group alerts us once more to Sichuan's creative role in religious art. Literary records testify to the existence in Chang'an's Daoist temples of contemporary frescoes whose content paralleled that of Niujiaozhai's niche 53.[119]

Two Daoists, a high-ranking priest and a priestess, sponsored the imposing epiphany of deities that occupy the horseshoe-shaped niche (2.4 meters high, 2.8 meters wide, and 2.1 meters deep). At the center are the Three Pure Ones (Sanqing), the highest deities in the Daoist pantheon, the embodiment as well of the Three Lords of Treasure (Sanbaojun). Behind them are represented the Five Perfected Ones, who also are the equivalent of the Five Emperors. The union of the three and five gods was a theological development during Xuanzong's reign. Behind them are represented several Perfected Ones (Zhenren) of both genders, two astral deities identified by the sun and moon they carry, guardians (similar to the Buddhist Lokapala and Vajrapani), and Golden Lads and Jade Girls. The headless personage shown seated at right is difficult to identify (fig. 3.137). The art historian Jin Anning has proposed,

based on records asserting the propensity of the ruler to be included in such a group, that he is none other than Emperor Xuanzong himself.

Again we recognize the blending of Buddhist and Daoist characteristics, but we are also conscious that a distinctly Daoist formal language has emerged. The central trio framed by nimbuses brings to mind the Buddhas of Past, Present, and Future. Furthermore, their hand gesture is reminiscent of the touching-the-earth mudra. On the other hand, the beard, the coronet, and the costume are exclusively Daoist. The fusion of all these components forms a definitive Daoist style.

The independence of formal expression and the freedom in interpreting iconography inherent in the sculpture of Sichuan were propelled by the province's long tradition of figure making and also by the well-

3.136 Daoist gathering, sandstone, niche 53, Niujiaozhai, Renshou, Sichuan Province. Tang dynasty, 749.

developed tradition of Buddhism in Sichuan. Through the centuries, institutionalized Buddhism nurtured a local clergy well versed in doctrinal interpretation and confident enough to support the diffusion of new cultic images — like the Thousand-handed, Thousand-eyed Guanyin — or to modify those received from the dynastic centers (like Amitabha's Pure Land). Prominent local clerics, whose names were often carved next to sculptures, successfully channeled the wealth of patrons — members of the Sichuan administration and the mercantile class — into the production of grand monuments rivaling similar northern projects. The degree of excellence and the versatility of the carvers are also displayed in the abundant production of Daoist images. Most importantly, the Sichuan evidence has widened considerably the category of Tang art and has caused us to acknowledge that superb carving and exuberant inventiveness were not necessarily confined to those areas closest to dynastic power.

3.138 Standing Guanyin
with Rosary, sandstone,
Grotto 136, Beishan,
Dazu County, Chongqing.
Southern Song dynasty,
1142–1146.

Song Buddhist Cave Temples of Sichuan: The Merging of Secular and Spiritual

Our investigation of Song Buddhist art (960–1279) remains restricted to Sichuan because unlike China's northern provinces, which progressively fell under alien dynasties (the Liao, Western Xia, and Jin), Sichuan throughout the Song remained singularly Chinese. Consequently Sichuan art is purely Song in style and content. The province, furthermore, offers a rich body of fairly unresearched cliff sculptures (gilt bronzes being extremely rare) still in situ and often accompanied by inscriptions recording the date of their making, the sponsors, and even the carvers' identities.[120] Interestingly, cliff sculptures made during the Song, unlike those made during the Tang, are concentrated in central Sichuan (again, including Chongqing), in the counties of Anyue, Dazu, and Hechuan, and often occupy fortified hills.

Sichuan cliff reliefs undoubtedly reflect the momentous social and cultural transformations of this age: the impressive economic growth of the country, the surging population, and the emergence of an elite, the scholar-official class, that earned status through a competitive literary exam system. This affluent Song society was human-centered and leaned heavily on Confucianism, yet it was mindful of Buddhism and Daoism as harmonized in the Unity of the Three Teachings.

Particularly interesting are cliff sculptures in the two adjacent counties of Dazu and Anyue.[121] Dazu County includes a handful of very important Song sites (in Shimenshan, Miaogaoshan, Shizhuanshan, and Nanshan), among which Beishan and Baodingshan are the most famous. The Beishan site was a fortified hill; in 892, Wei Junjing, military governor of the area, began sponsoring its extensive carvings. These pious donations continued during the Song.

The ambitious layout and the excellent execution of Grotto 136 (4.1 meters wide and high and 6.8 meters deep), dated 1142–1146, make it the most prominent at Beishan. Its name, Grotto of the Revolving Wheel, derives from the structure placed in its forefront. Lining the perimeter of the grotto are the reliefs of Shakyamuni (rear wall) with the disciples Kashyapa and Ananda, the bodhisattvas Manjushri and Samantabhadra, and five additional manifestations of Guanyin, as well as images of guardians and donors.

The major stylistic traits of Grotto 136 are the femininity of the bodhisattva images and the astonishing detailing of their ornaments. These two characteristics apply as well to the aforementioned Song locations. The Guanyin with Rosary (1.95 meters high), standing on a lotus, is wrapped head to foot in a flowing outer robe, with one hand holding a rosary (fig. 3.138). The carving of the folds is sharp and angular, creating clean and streaming lines. The deity's fleshy, wide face and sumptuous attire suggest a feminine presence. The massive headpiece is embellished with a variety of intricate floral patterns and jewels. Richly embroidered hangings are fastened to the body; like a wondrous net they fall from the neck and both arms to below the knees.

In the same grotto, the bodhisattva Samantabhadra (Puxian), shown mounted on an elephant (total height 2.09 meters), exhibits the same aesthetic taste (fig. 3.139). This bodhisattva was particularly venerated in Sichuan because he was thought to reside on local Mount Emei, one of China's five sacred mountains. Elegantly garbed, the youthful androgynous image, with the head slightly inclined under the ponderous crown, elicits the impression of physical, rather than sacred, well-being. Samantabhadra's grace and beauty are effectively contrasted with the coarseness and rather dull expression of the elephant keeper. Samantabhadra seems to impersonate the accomplishments of the Song privileged class.

A different stylistic trend based on refined linear patterns distinguishes the depiction of Buddhas enclosed in shallow roundels. This particular format was very popular in the grand Baodingshan complex (discussed later) and its related monuments, as well as at the Bilu Cave and Mount Min sites in Anyue County. Figure 3.140 shows an architectural relief from the Daota pagoda (1175–1250), an octagonal, four-story monument in Dazu that stands about 10 meters tall. The Buddha (about 70 centimeters high) is executed with sharp linear incisions meandering over the surface in a sinuous, almost sensuous manner. The repetition and juxtaposition of oval rhythms is emphatic and elegant. The excessively tapered fingers are just one of the mannered traits of this style.

In the mature phase of Song art, style assumed an additional dimension: images became monumental, whereas the textural quality of their surfaces became somewhat less rich. As dynastic Song painters mastered the "monumental landscape" formula, the Sichuan sculptors further refined the language of colossal forms that had begun during the Tang. The carvers of Anyue County, who had been active for several generations (judging from the inscriptions accompanying their works), particularly favored this practice. Anyue County contains numerous important Song sites — Bilu Cave, Yuanjue Cave, Mount Min, and Kongquezhang, to

3.140 Buddha within oval, sandstone relief, Daota Pagoda, Dazu County, Chongqing. Southern Song dynasty, 1175–1250.

3.139 Samantabhadra (Puxian) bodhisattva, sandstone,
Grotto 136, Beishan.

3.141 Shakyamuni and two manifestations of Avalokiteshvara, painted sandstone, Mount Yunzhu, Anyue County, Sichuan Province. Northern Song dynasty, begun ca. 1100.

mention but a few. All of them have monumental sculptures.[122]

Representative reliefs are located at the Yuanjue (Complete Enlightenment) Cave site, on Mount Yunzhu, also a fortified hill near the town of Anyue. The three monumental deities (about 6 meters high) — Shakyamuni and two Avalokiteshvara manifestations (fig. 3.141), holder of the lotus and holders of the bottle and willow — were begun around 1100 with the patronage of different prominent local donors, whose images are also included in the niches.[123]

The three deities share a homogeneous style. An incisive, clean-cut carving technique defines the long drapes; the bodhisattvas wear imposing openwork crowns and jewelry that is opulent, though not as profuse as the jewelry in the Beishan reliefs. The heads of the bodhisattvas are quite different from the head of the Beishan bodhisattva: they are fuller and rounder, characterized by a smaller mouth with marked lips, a pronounced nose, abnormally elongated ears ending

with thick, pendulous lobes, and a very short neck. These facial traits resurface at Baodingshan, supporting the notion that Anyue carvings and style constituted the preliminary phase of the complex.[124]

Another fine example of Song monumentality is the sculpture of the Great Peacock (Mahamayuri), once part of the homonymous temple (no longer in existence) 55 kilometers south of the town of Anyue (fig. 3.142). This deity is associated with Esoteric teaching, which was extremely popular in Sichuan. The Great Peacock is the feminine embodiment of an extremely powerful incantation (*dharani*) spoken of in several sutras. She was thought to prevent physical and spiritual ills, as well as drought and flood.[125]

The goddess's supernatural power is alluded to by her four arms, which hold a tray of auspicious fruits, a peacock feather, and a lotus (the fourth arm is broken). This nobly portrayed bodhisattva (2.5 meters high) sits regally on a lotus aptly supported by a peacock and is flanked by two attendants. Small-scale stories illustrating the beneficial effects of the spell adorn the surrounding walls. But the artist seems to have brought all of his skills to bear on the goddess's expressive face, a superior version of the Anyue type surmounted by an imposing crown with a depiction of Amoghasiddhi Buddha. The Great Peacock in Anyue can be compared to similar but less outstanding reliefs executed at the sites of Beishan, Shimenshan, and Baodingshan, all dated 1175–1250.

The use of monumental sculpture at a given site underwent a radical transformation in the second half of the twelfth century: carvers not only created numerous colossal statues for a single location but also arranged them according to a doctrinal framework. No site in Sichuan better exemplifies this momentous change than Baodingshan.

Baodingshan (Summit of Treasures) in Dazu County, situated midway between Chongqing proper and Chengdu, is a grand sculptural complex based on the teachings of the major Buddhist schools, Theravada and Mahayana, active in this province during the Song dynasty. The three-dimensional scenes include salient episodes from Shakyamuni Buddha's last life, as well as images of Amitabha's Pure Land doctrine and teachings from the Huayan, Chan, Guanyin, and local Esoteric sects.

Generally when one thinks of the Baodingshan one pictures the large shoe-shaped display of thirty-one colossal sculptures (the tallest is 15 meters, the widest is 45 meters) inspired by the numerous Buddhist schools as well as by the wish to glorify a famous local Buddhist layman, Liu Benzun (855–939), regarded as the initiator of Sichuan Esoteric Buddhism (fig. 3.143). In addition to this "Large Baodingshan" section are the "Small Baodingshan," which displays on a reduced scale numerous scenes available in the large section, and carvings in the peripheral area. These three parts form a unique Buddhist sacred ground (most likely Esoteric in character), each with a specific doctrinal and ritual function. Because of textual references and stylistic connections to other dated works, it is commonly accepted that twenty-seven of the thirty-one representations at Large Baodingshan were created between 1175 and 1250 (Southern Song), under the leadership of a Dazu prelate, the monk Zhao Zhifeng (1159–1249) — even though at the site there is no specific reference to the founder, sponsors, or date of execution.

Here what may at first seem to be a mere sequence of monumental scenes is actually governed by an elaborately conceived system that aspires to include all of the major Buddhist doctrines — blending these Buddhist beliefs with contemporary attitudes of the upper and

3.142 The Great Peacock (Mahamayuri), sandstone, Kongque hamlet, Anyue County, Sichuan Province. Southern Song dynasty, 1175–1250.

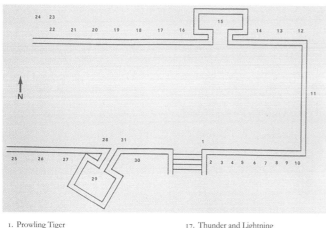

1. Prowling Tiger
2. Nine Protectors of the Law
3. Wheel of Reincarnation
4. Vast Jeweled Pavilion
5. Three Worthies of Huayan
6. Precious Relic Stupa
7. Vairocana Retreat
8. Thousand-handed, Thousand-eyed Avalokiteshvara
9. Manifested Walled City
10. Gathering of Men and Devas
11. Parinirvana
12. Birth of Shakyamuni
13. Nine Nagas Bathing Shakyamuni
14. Mahamayuri Vidyaraja, or Great Peacock
15. Bodhimanda, or Sacred Ground of Vairocana
16. Parents Bestowing Kindnesses on Their Children

17. Thunder and Lightning
18. Buddha Shakyamuni Repays His Parents' Kindness with Great Skillful Means
19. The Land of Bliss of Buddha Amitayus
20. Six Roots of Sensations
21. Hell Tribunals and Punishments
22. Ten Austerities of Liu Benzun, and the Vidyarajas
23. Daoist Triad
24. Two Daoist Gods
25. Two Daoist Goddesses
26. Stele Pagoda
27. Liu Benzun in His Perfected State
28. Roaring Lion
29. Grotto of Complete Enlightenment
30. Oxherding Parable
31. Two Licchavi Women

3.143 Plan of Baodingshan, Dazu County, Chongqing.

lower classes, as well as the pervasive neo-Confucian state doctrine.

For example, Confucian principles of filial piety deeply rooted in Chinese society are evident in the two scenes based on the spurious texts the Sutra on Repaying the Kindness of One's Father and Mother (Fumu enchong jing; fig. 3.144) and the Great Upaya Sutra of Requiting Kindness (Da fangbian Fo baoen jing). Inspired by contemporary life, the carvers adopted a less hieratic style and modeled their sculptures on real people of the time.

In the awesome portrayal of punishments in Hell, the tribunal of the ten kings led by the bodhisattva Dizang (Kshitigarbha; fig. 3.145) paralleled the contemporary bureaucracy, while the mechanical contraptions used to inflict the horrific punishments were directly inspired by the agrarian economy of Sichuan (fig. 3.146). Similarly, the Chan attainment of gradual enlightenment, symbolized by the ox-herding parable (the Northern Song version by the official Yang Jie), derives its imagery from local pastoral life (fig. 3.147). In short, in the execution of these ostensibly Buddhist scenes we see a subtle interweaving of religious and social values and of elite and popular attitudes widespread in Sichuan.

Sichuan carvers used narrative-based reliefs to attract and teach the local Buddhist audience. The marked pictorial quality of the scenes, as in the ox-herding parable, brings to maturity a characteristic of Sichuan carv-

ings during the preceding Tang. And given the carved inscriptions alongside the reliefs, it seems probable that the grandiose scenes were three-dimensional transformation pictures (bianxiang) used to instruct pilgrims and other visitors. Because of the all-inclusive content and the formal language, Baodingshan seems to have been unique in the broad spectrum of pilgrims it attracted. Moreover, by grounding these religious scenes unmistakably in Sichuan society, with elements of both the upper and the lower classes, carvers not only communicated directly and forcefully with the pilgrims but also effaced the boundary between sacred and secular.

The stately deities of Baodingshan built upon and, some believe, perfected the Anyue tradition. The carvers' full-size and half-bodied images suggest a visionary representation of, for instance, Shakyamuni, the main deity in figure 3.144. The ingenuity of the carvers is also evident in their use of the original shape of the boulders to model the expressive attitudes of the protagonists, people and animals, in the Chan tableau. Even a flowing spring and live wild plants are drawn into this naturalistic setting.

In typical Dazu style, bodies are harmoniously proportioned, while costumes and ornaments are kept fairly simple to create an impression of unassuming elegance. The bodhisattvas' heads, by contrast, are highly detailed and richly ornamented. The perfectly oval, unperturbed faces are slightly tilted under the weight of the opulent crowns. In this idealized, urbane portrayal of the divine figure, one that fits the humanism pervading Song culture, there is no trace of the realistic style employed during the Tang period.

The Chan complex at Laitan, located 45 kilometers northeast of Hechuan, was carved in the cliffs overlooking the Qujiang River. The numerous reliefs of varying sizes, 1,673 in all, are spread over three stories now incorporated within a wooden hall about 16 meters in height. The building belongs to the large Chan temple called Er Fo, Temple of the Two Buddhas. This fairly unknown complex is coeval with Baodingshan, but its execution served a totally different doctrinal purpose and employed its own formal language.[126] Based on several inscriptions accompanying the reliefs, one can date the site to the last quarter of the twelfth century. The Chan identification of the complex is confirmed by numerous in situ Ming and Qing steles, which thoroughly describe the iconography. The name of the founder, however, remains unknown.

The Hechuan project is a unique three-dimensional representation of the Chan doctrine and reminds us

3.144 Shakyamuni repays his parents' kindness, painted sandstone, Baodingshan. Southern Song dynasty, 1175–1250.

3.145 Dizang hell tribunals, painted sandstone, Baodingshan.

3.146 Punishments (detail), painted sandstone, Baodingshan.

that during the Song this school attained the status of a major, if not *the* major, institution of Buddhism. The sculptures ambitiously trace from the Song perspective the mythical beginning of Chan in India and its historical continuity in China. The central image of this omega-shaped site is a 12-meter-high Shakyamuni (fig. 3.148), backed by eighteen rows of small Buddhas (946 in all) and surrounded by ten bodhisattvas (2.40 meters high), Ananda and Mahakashyapa (4.45 meters high), and two flying worthies usually associated with Guanyin: Shancai (Sudhana) and the Dragon Princess (1.85 meters high). Fittingly, Shakyamuni and Mahakashyapa tower over all the other personages to signify the momentous founding of Chan in India. There, Buddha had addressed an immense audience and quizzically waved a flower without uttering a word, yet smiled to Mahakashyapa, who alone had received the dharma transmitted from mind to mind, from teacher to pupil.

Continuing this record of lineage, a paramount concern of Chan, three massive and foreign-looking images stand opposite to Shakyamuni (fig. 3.149). They are Bodhidharma, Subhuti (at 3.1 meters high, the

tallest of the three), and Maitreya. Each of these figures plays a significant role in the long chain of transmission. Subhuti ranks among the earliest Indian patriarchs; Bodhidharma was the last in India (the twenty-eighth) and brought the teaching to sixth-century China; and Maitreya, the ultimate receiver of the dharma, points to the future.

The group of patriarchs represented on the second level establishes the Chinese lineage. At 3.57 meters tall, Shakyamuni benevolently presides over the six Chinese patriarchs (1.50–1.75 meters high), namely Bodhidharma transplanted to Chinese soil, Huike, Zenxiu, Daoxin, Hongren, and Huineng (figs. 3.150, 3.151). Each is characterized according to the prolific Chan hagiography. Huike, for example, clearly lacks his left arm, which he offered to Bodhidharma as a token of his determination to be accepted as a disciple.

At the immediate right of this group stands a conspicuous personage, Sengqie, the monk from Sizhou, Jiangsu, who is bejeweled and wrapped head to foot in a monastic robe (fig. 3.152). The adornments may be justified by his true identity — he is a manifestation of

Guanyin. Sengqie arrived in China from the western lands in the 660s and resided chiefly in Sizhou, where the miracles he was said to have worked attracted many followers. Prior to his death in 710, he was summoned to the Tang court to receive the title of National Teacher. His nationwide fame is proven not only by his inclusion in the Hechuan pantheon and at a few other Sichuan locations but also by his painted image in Dunhuang Cave 72, Gansu, and his carved image on the Feilaifeng cliffs of Hangzhou, Zhejiang, and at Quanzhou, Fujian.[127]

The Indian and Chinese patriarchs are surrounded by a crowd of arhats depicted in every possible pose and size — indeed, many more than the canonical five hundred (fig. 3.153). Some of them are remarkably expressive and compelling, carved in a manner reminiscent of their Tang counterparts in Longmen (see fig. 3.109). For such pathos to exude from the great

patriarchs is rare among the generally idealized Song images.

Because the overwhelming majority of Hechuan reliefs are of monastic people, we are exposed to a formal language that is different from that of Dazu and Anyue. Yet the secular trend (that is, the characterization of the figures as real personages) so obvious in the Hechuan reliefs may have originated in the Chan milieu. Chan ecclesiastics of the Song preferred to emphasize the deeds and words of real rather than sacred or mythical people, so the portrayal of patriarchs and adepts, as in Hechuan, followed a more mundane style. Curiously, in spite of using a dissimilar formal language, the Baodingshan and the Hechuan reliefs both blur the boundary between sacred and secular. Indeed, at all the major Song sites, the viewer can see the melding of intellectual, social, and sectarian concerns, which convey the vigor and humanism of this age.

3.147 Pastoral life with oxen (detail), sandstone, Baodingshan.

3.148 Monumental Shakyamuni Buddha, gilded sandstone, Laitan, Hechuan County, Chongqing. Southern Song dynasty, 12th–13th century.

3.149 Bodhidharma and Subhuti, painted sandstone, Laitan.

3.150 Schematic drawing of Shakyamuni with the six Chan patriarchs, Laitan. Hechuan Cultural Relics Office.

3.151 Shakyamuni with the six Chan patriarchs, painted sandstone, Laitan.

3.152 Monk Sengqie (detail), painted sandstone, Laitan.

3.153 Group of arhats, painted sandstone, Laitan.

Tang and Song Buddhist Sculptures of Yunnan: Syncretism of a Frontier Kingdom

Buddhist art of the frontier area of Yunnan developed under the local Nanzhao (653–902) and Dali monarchies (937–1253), approximately coeval with the Tang and Song dynasties. Relatively independent politically from Chinese imperial rule and geographically linked to several peripheral cultures of Tibet and southeast Asia, Yunnanese Buddhist representations were influenced by numerous foreign elements that in turn were shaped by indigenous tastes and traditions. In Yunnan between 653 and 902 the Nanzhao evolved from a loosely tied and ethnically differentiated confederation of tribes into a cohesive power led by the Meng family, which represented the dominant Bai minority, of Tibeto-Burmese ethnic origin. The Nanzhao's center of power was the area around Lake Erhai in western Yunnan (in present-day Dali). Consolidation of power was rapid; by the mid-seventh century the six principalities were united, and during the eighth and ninth centuries the Nanzhao rulers were strong enough to resist the mighty Tang. The Nanzhao were allies of Tibet during the eighth century, but shifted their allegiance to China during the ninth. The alliance, however, proved short-lived, as frequent raids were waged against the Tang military governor of Sichuan; the most memorable raid was that of the winter of 828–829, when the capital, Chengdu, was stormed and pillaged and its craftsmen, high clergy, and laborers were dragged to Yunnan. The expansionist policies of the Nanzhao also led to war against the Pyu of what is now Myanmar, the Khmer of what is now Cambodia, and the Chinese protectorate of the southeast. After a brief interregnum, in 937 the Duan family took power, initiating the Dali monarchy, which lasted until the Mongol conquest.[128]

Buddhism's role in empowering a sovereign, and in legitimizing and guaranteeing the continuity of his rule, surfaced at the very inception of the Nanzhao monarchy. In Yunnanese art, these grounding principles were manifested in different ways.[129] First, in the major Buddhist monuments the rulers and their courts were always portrayed with vivid realism and reference to contemporary historical events. The royal presence not merely signified the faith of the patrons but expressed, above all, the recognition by the monarch that Buddhism was the source of his political power.

Shizhongsi Grotto, near Jianchuan, the Buddhist site 100 kilometers north of Dali opened by the Nanzhao dynasty in the ninth century, holds three representations of Nanzhao kings.[130] King Geluofeng (r. 748–779) is shown wearing an imposing headgear called a "dragon-cage" in the ninth-century text *Book of the Barbarians*

3.154 King Geluofeng and his court, sandstone relief, Shizhongshan, Jianchuan, Yunnan Province. Nanzhao kingdom / Tang dynasty, 9th century.

3.155 Schematic drawing of the pageant of King Shilong (detail), Boshenwahei, Xichang, Sichuan Province. Xichang Cultural Relics Office.

(*Manshu;* fig. 3.154). The king presides in full regalia over the court from his dragon throne. How fitting that Geluofeng's posture and demeanor resemble a Buddha's. Furthermore, the presence in the group of two officials in Tang court costume, on either side of the niche, recalls a similar arrangement in a Buddhist paradise setting, where the seated lateral figures are bodhisattvas.

From the Nanzhao outpost of Boshenwahei on the Liang Plateau (now in south Sichuan) originates the royal pageant of King Shilong (r. 859–877) and his retinue (4.8 meters high, 17.2 meters long; fig. 3.155).[131] At this site, the cavalcade is one among a majority of religious representations incised on large boulders. In the Jianchuan and Boshenwahei groups the proximity of the king to the deities and his portrayal in a scene reminiscent of a Buddhist gathering may even allude to the belief that the king was both temporal and divine, although this inference cannot be confirmed.

The use of Buddhism to legitimize royal power extended far beyond the inclusion of royalty in Buddhist monuments. Just as the Chinese emperor based his legitimacy on the Mandate of Heaven, the Yunnan monarchs grounded theirs on the will of Avalokiteshvara, or Guanyin. The possession of a special image (palladium) conferred legitimate power on the ruler. As the story is told in the scroll *Illustrated History of the Nanzhao Kingdom* (*Nanzhao guoshi tuzhuan,* dated 947 but actually a copy of a lost original painted in 899), an old monk, none other than Guanyin incarnate, arrived among the Meng tribe in the mid-seventh century, predicted their rise to the status of monarchs, and bestowed a special effigy of Guanyin as their tutelary deity.

The All Victorious Guanyin (Acuoye, 24 centimeters

3.156 The All-Victorious Guanyin (Acuoye), gold with silver aureole, Chongsheng Temple, Qianxun Pagoda, Dali, Yunnan Province. Nanzhao kingdom / Tang dynasty, 9th century. Yunnan Provincial Museum, Kunming.

high), fashioned in gold during the Nanzhao and found in 1978 inside the Qianxun pagoda of the Chongsheng Temple, Dali, is the most prominent example of the tutelary deity of the Nanzhao and Dali kingdoms (fig. 3.156).[132] As the enduring objectification of sanctioned power, this effigy of Guanyin was replicated through successive dynasties, always retaining its distinctive style. What mattered most was the continuity of that original myth.

Beliefs in a talismanic image symbolic of royal empowerment, the divinity of kings, and the divine nature of power were widespread among the major cultures of the southeast Asian continent and archipelago. These beliefs were practiced and potent Hindu and Buddhist images were worshiped in the Khmer kingdom of Cambodia, in the Champa kingdom of Vietnam, in the kingdoms of Indonesia, and in the kingdoms of Nanzhao and Dali contemporaneously.

The Acuoye Guanyin is distinctly non-Chinese in its facial traits; in the slender, completely frontal and rigid stance; in the arrangement of the clothing (the dhoti is gathered to form a median fold, and the girdle is tied in knots at the sides); and in the ornaments (diadem, earrings, necklace, and armlets). Instead, the Acuoye Guanyin reflects a southeast Asian influence. The pervasiveness of the cult of Avalokiteshvara in this region and the sharing of formal characteristics by several cultures make it difficult to distinguish which one of these styles Yunnan appropriated. But the comparison of the Nanzhao Guanyin executed in gold with a number of well-known Vietnamese (Cham) Avalokiteshvara bronzes convincingly points to present-day Vietnam as the chief source of inspiration. The transmission occurred during the ninth century, which was marked by the forceful political expansion of Nanzhao.

The prominence of Esoteric deities among the bronzes and cliff reliefs of Yunnan makes clear the importance of Esoteric teaching in the kingdom. The origins of Esoteric Buddhism in this region are still unclear; it probably spread from neighboring Tibet, given that the Esoteric Buddhism that developed in Yunnan was a local brand called *azhali,* which emphasized the crucial role played by the spiritual teacher (*acharya*).

The spiritual teachers were not required to respect fundamental monastic rules, such as celibacy; they carried on with their family life alongside their religious activity. Endowed with extraordinary powers, they often performed magical feats, such as delivering people and places from the threat of dragons or drying up bodies of water that had flooded cultivated fields. The acharya

Candragupta, the seminal Nanzhao Esoteric Buddhist, was reputed to have performed these miracles. In 839, this native of Magadha, India, came to Yunnan from Tibet. An azhali master, identified as Candragupta by Chinese scholars, is incised on a large boulder at Boshenwahei. Yunnanese azhali masters vividly recall the personality of great adepts (*mahasiddhas*), who, with their unconventional mysticism, contributed greatly to the development of Tibetan Buddhism. These eighty-four perfected beings are essentially a Tibetan product.[133]

Buddhist azhali masters became influential in Yunnan because of their compatibility with indigenous shamanism, which was widespread among the Bai and other local tribes. When spiritual teachers such as Candragupta became active in Yunnan, it was neither their Yogic skills nor their Esoteric knowledge that impressed the local people, but their magic, which was similar to that performed by indigenous shamans. The Yunnanese azhali became a new version of the Tibetan mahasiddha.

Tibetan Esoteric Buddhism also provided Yunnan with devotional icons, such as the demonic Mahakala — the Great Black God (Daheitian), who became a major tutelary deity of Nanzhao and Dali, second only in importance to Guanyin.[134] Mahakala was also the tutelary god of Ladakh, in the western Himalayas.

Mahakala is the Hindu god Bhairava, the angry manifestation of Shiva, lord of the cemeteries. An excellent representation is the snarling, triple-eyed Mahakala found at Shadeng village, in the Shizhong Mountains of Jianchuan. The statue, 2.7 meters tall, probably created during the ninth century, wears garlands of skulls and decapitated heads, with a crown of skulls atop his head and snakes tightly coiled around his upper arms and ankles (fig. 3.157). With his many hands he grasps numerous implements appropriate for an Esoteric deity (a lasso, a sword, and a three-pronged spear). Interestingly, the technique used, a combination of intaglio and incision, is similar to that employed in early Tibetan cliff reliefs, such as the allegedly eighth-century Nyethang Buddha outside Lhasa.

Indeed, transmission from Tibet is highly likely because Mahakala's presence is sporadic in central Asian art and entirely absent from northern China. We know that active Tibetan-Yunnanese exchanges occurred during this time because of the administrative presence of the Shilang principality, which paid allegiance to the Tibetans. During the eighth century, the principality controlled the area around Jianchuan (the location of the Shizhongshan dynastic site and the Shadeng village Mahakala). Similarly, until the ninth century, Tibetan

3.157 Mahakala, sandstone, Shadeng village, Jianchuan, Yunnan Province. Nanzhao kingdom / Tang dynasty, 9th century.

influence extended over the Boshenwahei site, where another image of Mahakala is etched on a boulder (fig. 3.158). Finally, the still-used trade route that links northwest Yunnan to central Tibet via the Li River facilitated contact between the two kingdoms. At Shadeng village, Yunnanese carvers paired the image of Mahakala with that of Vaishravana. This is not a single instance: the two deities are again represented together in the intaglio relief on a fortified hill at Santaishan, Wuding, about 150 kilometers northwest of Kunming (fig. 3.159). According to the accompanying inscription, these imposing images (the Vaishravana is 2.3 meters high; the Mahakala, 4 meters) were executed in the twelfth century, during the Dali administration. The two may have been represented together because Vaishravana, the guardian par excellence of the north, was transmitted to Yunnan from northern China, whereas Mahakala reached Yunnan from Tibet. By combining the two opposing deities, the Yunnanese expressed their desire to cover all bases, that is, to receive protection from dangers stemming from either direction.

3.158 Schematic drawing of Mahakala, Boshenwahei, Xichang, Sichuan Province. Xichang Cultural Relics Office.

The Dharani Pillar of Kunming

Made of red sandstone and over 8 meters tall, the dharani pillar of Kunming, which richly combines architecture and sculpture in three hundred images, is the most important work of the Dali period (fig. 3.160).[135] According to an inscription, the highest-ranking officials and clergy of the Dali administration from 1200 to 1220 were involved in establishing this burial monument. The name *dharani pillar* derives from magic spells incised on the surface. One of the most powerful is the spell included in the Sutra of the Honored and Victorious Dharani of Buddha's Ushnisha. The same scripture explains that the building of such a pillar enables one to be saved from evil reincarnations.

In the complexity of its theological content and the excellence of its art, the pillar is comparable to *A Long Scroll of Buddhist Images* (*Fan xiang tu*), painted around 1180 by Zhang Shengwen for the Dali ruler. But the theological content of the two works is different. The divergence leads to the conclusion that they were each inspired by different Esoteric schools. The combined imagery of the two masterpieces reveals the extent to which Buddhism flourished in this frontier kingdom.

The nine levels of the pillar are organized according to three major schemes (fig. 3.161). The lowest three tiers interpret notions of Buddhist cosmology: for example, the phenomenal world, with Mount Sumeru at its center, rises from the waters of the Great Ocean, which is inhabited by dragons (nagas; fig. 3.162). On the slopes of Sumeru are placed the guardians of the four directions (Lokapalas).

The second scheme, comprising tiers 4, 5, and 6, is a mandala (fig. 3.163). To express the drastic break with the world below, these three tiers are set up as a truncated pyramid whose corner figures (Vajrapani, Devas, and bodhisattvas) are not aligned with the Lokapalas. Tiers 4, 5, and 6 undoubtedly form a mandala, because their numerous deities respond to specific canonical rules governing their arrangement. Most of the Buddhas and bodhisattvas are identifiable. As members of Esoteric "families," they are all assigned a specific location and cardinal point. As members of a mandala, all the deities of the three tiers are emanations of Vairocana, who is not shown but alluded to in the central axis of the pillar.

The third scheme of the pillar, represented on the remaining tiers, interprets local burial practices of the Bai people, who were particularly influential in the Dali administration (fig. 3.164). It is revealing that in

3.159 Vaishravana and Mahakala, sandstone, Wuding, Yunnan Province. Nanzhao kingdom / Tang dynasty, 12th century.

this monument, as in the *Long Scroll*, the Yunnanese patrons mingled their local deities with orthodox Buddhist deities, thereby proudly acknowledging their roots and proclaiming unabashedly their sense of self-identity.

It is nearly impossible to know which scripture or combination of scriptures inspired the vertical mandala shown on the pillar, because we are unable to reconstruct the interpretive work of local ecclesiastics. One can, however, postulate that Yunnanese Esoteric teachings were here, as before, responding to Tibetan developments.[136]

Interestingly, the ingenious and well-knit construction of the pillar is made clear by the overhead view. The craftsmen used an intriguing alternation of superimposed shapes, chiefly variations of an octagon and a circle, with the exception of the double-cross layout of tier 7 (fig. 3.165). This complex arrangement, and the fact that the monument is a compendium of ongoing Buddhist beliefs, recalls the sophisticated spatial conception and theological concerns of Borobudur, sponsored by the ruling Shailendras of Java in about 800. Yunnan appears to have had knowledge of this grand project, because, just like at Borobudur, the Kunming dharani pillar shows the synthesis of monumental iconographic images and the arrangement of such images in a progression. Song China did not offer a comparable model.[137]

This frontier kingdom clearly took advantage of its contacts with other civilizations to enrich its own her-

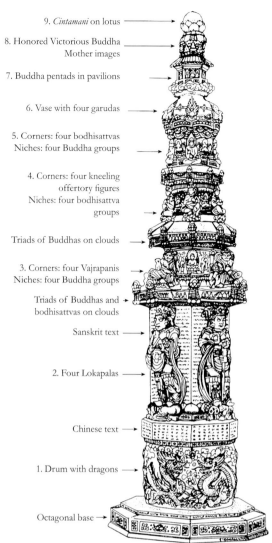

9. *Cintamani* on lotus

8. Honored Victorious Buddha Mother images

7. Buddha pentads in pavilions

6. Vase with four garudas

5. Corners: four bodhisattvas
Niches: four Buddha groups

4. Corners: four kneeling offertory figures
Niches: four bodhisattva groups

Triads of Buddhas on clouds

3. Corners: four Vajrapanis
Niches: four Buddha groups

Triads of Buddhas and bodhisattvas on clouds

Sanskrit text

2. Four Lokapalas

Chinese text

1. Drum with dragons

Octagonal base

3.161 Schematic drawing of dharani pillar, Kunming.

3.160 Dharani pillar, sandstone, Kunming, Yunnan Province. Dali kingdom / Song dynasty, 1200–1220.

3.162 Drum with dragons, sandstone, east side of dharani pillar, Kunming.

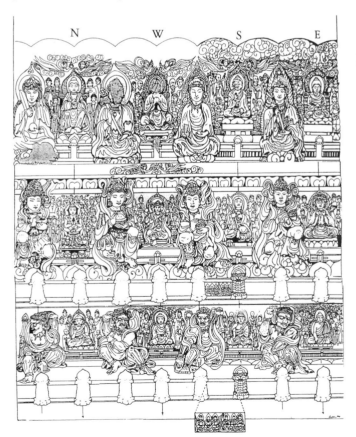

3.163 Schematic drawing of mandala configuration of dharani pillar, Kunming.

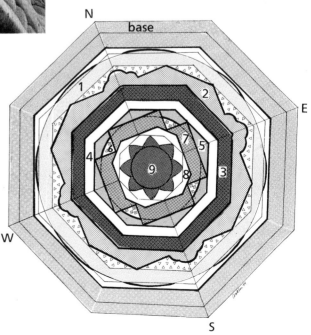

3.164 Burial deities of Bai people, sandstone, northeast side of dharani pillar, Kunming.

3.165 Schematic drawing of dharani pillar (overhead view), Kunming. The numbers match those in figure 3.161.

itage and shape its own style. There is also no doubt that the kingdoms of Nanzhao and Dali transformed the doctrines, rituals, iconography, and aesthetics they had appropriated into highly unusual art forms. In the dharani pillar, for example, the stylistic metamorphosis is so complete that it is difficult to recognize the original model (figs. 3.166, 3.167). Undoubtedly the sculpture does not look like contemporary Song works, and it is not possible to link it stylistically to the sculpture of any of the neighboring cultures. A purely Yunnanese style had evolved.

The next chapter will introduce the art executed during the Song period in other regions of China — those administered by the Song emperors and those that fell under the alien rule of the Tangut or Western Xia, Khitan Liao, and Jurchen Jin dynasties. Although contemporaneous with the Buddhist monuments of Sichuan and Yunnan, the Buddhist sculpture of northern and eastern China was distinctive in style and content.

3.166 Guardian, sandstone, north side of dharani pillar, Kunming.

3.167 Offering deity, sandstone, northeast side of dharani pillar, Kunming.

CHAPTER 4

From the Northern Song to the Qing

LI SONG

The establishment of the Northern Song dynasty in 960 brought an end to an era of bitter rivalry known as the period of Five Dynasties and Ten Kingdoms. For the next thousand years, through the Qing dynasty, the three great systems of belief in China — Buddhism, Daoism, and Confucianism — were all tolerated and accommodated by society at large; they even fused in essential ways. Imperial rulers gradually ceased to play them off against one another, particularly Daoism and Buddhism. Even when the rulers favored one religious sect, they found it politically useful to tolerate them all.[1] Their embrace of these religions greatly influenced the development of sculpture, as artists from each tradition incorporated themes, techniques, and materials used by the others.

Buddhism

In the two centuries before the Northern Song two events occurred that were devastating for Buddhist art. In 845 the Tang emperor Wuzong issued an imperial edict favoring Daoism that resulted in the destruction of some 45,000 Buddhist temples. Then in the tenth century Emperor Shizong of the Later Zhou, one of the Five Dynasties, directed that 3,336 Buddhist sanctuaries be destroyed and that all bronze Buddhist statues be confiscated to make coins. Also during this period large-scale grotto construction, a Buddhist

Full view of figure 4.46 (*opposite*) and detail of figure 4.13 (*above*)

tradition (adopted by Daoists) going back seven centuries in much of China, was largely confined to Dazu County in Chongqing during the Northern and Southern Dynasties and to Hangzhou during the Yuan dynasty.

Despite such challenges, Buddhism — and Buddhist art — survived. Immediately after ascending the throne, Emperor Shizong of the Later Zhou revoked an ordinance suppressing Buddhism, opening the way for a major revival in temple-building and the making of Buddhist statues. By the fifth year of the Northern Song emperor Zhenzong's reign (r. 998–1022), 40,000 Buddhist temples and sanctuaries existed in the country, housing 460,000 Buddhist monks and nuns.

For centuries considerable emphasis had been placed on the study of Buddhist doctrines and theory, from which different schools of Buddhism had emerged. By the Tang dynasty (618–907), a number of these had taken hold in China. Each showed notable Chinese characteristics while professing different Buddhist classics and doctrines and developed its own hierarchy and means of conversion. Several were of great importance to the development of Chinese sculpture. Tiantai (Heavenly Terrace), one of the oldest schools, much favored by the ruling classes through the Sui dynasty, regarded the Sutra of the Lotus of the True Law, which emphasizes the presence of the Buddha nature in all sentient beings, as the most important Buddhist text. The school was willing to accommodate various views and in its teachings stressed three modes: the gradual, the direct, and the final, or perfect. Emperor Wen of the Sui, a strong supporter of Tiantai, used it to legitimize his power, as did Empress Wu Zetian of the Tang.

The Pure Land (Jingtu) sect, by contrast, stressed the Pure Land Sutras, which focused on the western paradise, or Pure Land. Practitioners would chant the name of Amitabha (the Buddha of Measureless Light), believing that he offered the way to bring their souls to the Pure Land. A later, more populist school, Pure Land Buddhism inspired various visions of paradise through murals and taught meditation through visualization.

Chan (Zen) Buddhism was another school that grew increasingly popular after the Song. Like Pure Land a later school that spread as much among the common people as among the ruling classes, Chan stressed the importance of various physical and mental exercises to gain inner enlightenment. The increasing popularity of the arhats (luohan, "enlightened ones") may reflect its influence, and sculptural works in this era began to feature realistic depictions of individual monks.

The "Esoteric Vehicle," or Esoteric Buddhism (also called Lamaism), which came to China first from India, then from Tibet, drew on Indian texts which declare that everyone, though mired in profound ignorance, nonetheless retains the Buddha nature. In the Esoteric universe, populated by a myriad of male and female deities who represent various forces and energies, a wide range of activities and uses was necessary to break the karma of cause and effect: magic formulas, gestures, visualizations, diagrams (mandalas), incantations in Sanskrit, and sexually explicit imagery. It was these Esoteric Buddhist practices and beliefs in particular that proponents of Confucian ethics and morals criticized.

During the Song dynasty (960–1279), as Buddhism became an organic part of Chinese society, Buddhist ideas became increasingly fused with traditional Confucian doctrine. Indeed, Buddhist analytical thinking profoundly influenced the metaphysical philosophy of the Song Confucianists. As Confucianism became the guiding ethos of the scholar-bureaucrats and fertile soil for the growth of a belief system that took the "heavenly principles" as its starting point, neo-Confucianism flourished. Its development played an important role in sustaining traditional Chinese moral principles and ethics, as well as in consolidating imperial power.

Many Buddhist monks of the Song dynasty were well versed in Confucian classics, and some even sought common philosophical ground for Buddhism and Confucianism. Zhiyuan of the Tiantai School claimed that Buddhism and Confucianism arose from the same source and Confucianism was its base. In his view, Confucianism was a religion to improve learning and Buddhism a religion to purify the soul. Buddhism and Confucianism were different in language but identical in aim, he argued: both sought to promote good and eliminate evil. In A Guide to Religion (Fujiao bian) another monk, Qisong of the Yunmen School in the Song, compared Buddhism's doctrine of panca-gotrani (do not kill, steal, lie, drink, or commit adultery) with Confucianism's three cardinal rules (ruler guides subject, father guides son, husband guides wife) and five constant virtues (benevolence, righteousness, propriety, wisdom, and fidelity), maintaining that the sages of Buddhism and Confucianism had simply taken different approaches to the same ends. Qisong went to great lengths to promote filial piety, a central Confucian tenet that had long been seen as incompatible with the Buddhist ideal of becoming a monk and renouncing ties to the earthly realm. Qisong insisted that following such a path was actually the most meritorious way of demonstrating filial devotion.

Although there were still times during the Song when

Buddhism was suppressed by an emperor in favor of Daoism or vice versa, such tactics were no longer seen as necessary for the consolidation of imperial authority. An emperor might favor one faith or school over another, but by the Yuan dynasty a successful reign no longer required the exclusion of other faiths.

As Buddhism gained an ever more widespread following in the Song, its doctrines, idols, and religious practices became increasingly mixed with traditional folk beliefs. Adherents began to place greater faith in the worship of idols, the practice of vegetarianism, and prayer to the Buddha as a means to obtain justice in this life and enjoy a better fate in the next. Daoist deities and folk gods had entered the temples by now; Buddhist gods and Daoist immortals increasingly stood side by side. As a result, Buddhist statues became part of a complex pantheon of figures and forces. As Buddhism steered further from its earlier, Indian doctrines, the number of believers grew and thousands of Buddhist monasteries were built.

At the time of the Song, there were three other regimes in northern China, the Liao (907–1125), founded by the Khitans, the Jin (1115–1234), established by the Wanyan tribe of the Jurchens (Nüzhen), and the Western Xia (ca. 982–1227), founded by the Tanguts. The rulers of the three states were fervent Buddhists. They had Buddhist altars built in the imperial courts, both for worship and for initiating royal family members into the monkhood or nunhood. In the Liao dynasty, Buddhism thrived during the reigns of Emperors Shengzong, Xingzong, and Daozong. Esoteric Buddhism and the Huayan School (so called because it took the Buddhavatamsaka-mahavaipulya Sutra as its major classic), with its center on Mount Wutai, were the most vigorous, though imperial support for Esoteric Buddhism declined during the later years of the Liao. Not only were a great number of Buddhist temples and pagodas built, but social customs showed the influence of Buddhism as well; for example, women painted their faces with yellow powder because Buddhist statues were frequently painted yellow. During the Jin dynasty, Buddhism reached its zenith under Emperor Shizong (1161–1189), with Chan Buddhism the most dynamic of the schools. After the death of Emperor Zhangzong in 1208, however, Buddhism gradually declined as a result of corruption in the monastic circles. Tangut court patronage of Buddhism reached its peak in the late twelfth and early thirteenth centuries, when teachers of Esoteric Buddhist lineages from Tibet (mainly Kagyu) were invited to court and became imperial preceptors (*dishi*). Sculptures and paintings recovered from Kara Khoto, the Dunhuang and Yulin cave sites, as well as in the structures built close to the Tangut capital (present-day Yinchuan), show both Tibetan and Han Chinese stylistic characteristics and Buddhist themes.

Like the Tanguts before them, the Yuan imperial court (1271–1368) particularly favored Tibetan Esoteric Buddhism. Before the unification of China, Godan Khan had invited Sakya Pandita Kunga Gyaltsen (1181–1251), a famous master of the Sakya sect of Tibetan Buddhism, to appear in his court. Sakha Pandita was accompanied by his talented nephew, Chogyal Phagspa (1234–1280). Both of them impressed Godan Khan, but Chogyal Phagspa went on to play an important role at the court of Kublai Khan, who founded the Yuan dynasty. The khan granted Chogyal Phagspa the titles Imperial Tutor and Master of the Great Law, presented him with a jade seal, and gave him the power to oversee Buddhist affairs throughout the country and to lead government and religious affairs in Tibet. After he became Emperor Shizu, Kublai was initiated into Esoteric Buddhism along with his empress and concubines. Later this practice developed into a law: all Yuan emperors had to be initiated into Buddhism before ascending the throne.

Though the Yuan court favored the Esoteric School, it did not discriminate against other schools, which continued to develop. South of the Yangzi River, Chan Buddhism spread widely.

The outstanding feature of Buddhist sculpture in the Yuan dynasty was the introduction of Buddhist statues in the Tibetan style. Early in the dynasty, Anige (1244–1306), a young artist from the royal court of Nepal, led a group of artisans to Tibet to build a gold stupa (Buddhist funerary monument or pagoda). His work won him the respect of Chogyal Phagspa, who brought him to the Yuan capital, where the emperor eventually appointed him head of the department of craftsmen. Later Anige was commissioned to design and build Buddhist temples and pagodas, create and decorate Buddhist and Daoist statues, paint pictures for the emperor and empress, and construct astronomical instruments. Anige contributed greatly to the development of Buddhist art in China, and in 1278 he was granted various titles and made a high-ranking official in the court. Such was his fame that a Chinese sculptor named Liu Yuan was ordered by the court to study with him so that he too could make "western Buddhist statues" (statues in the style of Tibetan Buddhism). Liu Yuan excelled in the art, creating many of the Buddhist and Daoist statues in the important temples.[2]

Major Yuan Buddhist sculptures include a group of images carved on the cliffs of Feilaifeng (Flying-in Peak) in Hangzhou; a 5-meter-high bronze statue of Shakyamuni (the historical Buddha, or the Buddha of the Present) in Nirvana in the Shifang (Ten Direction) Pujue Temple in Beijing cast in 1321; and the marble bas-reliefs adorning the Juyong Gate north of Beijing on the way to the Great Wall at Badaling.

The construction of the gate, an imperially sponsored project (completed by 1354), was supervised by a minister appointed by Emperor Shun, and lamas of the Sakya sect took part in its design. The three stupas built in the Tibetan style on top of the surviving platform were destroyed in the early Ming dynasty. Now only the marble-clad foundation, in the form of an arch, remains. It is topped by the platform on which it used to stand, which later visitors often mistook for the pagoda itself. The foundation, 9.5 meters high, 26.5 meters wide, and 17.6 meters deep, is ornamented with finely carved marble balustrades and marble dragon heads for drainage (fig. 4.1). The passageway beneath the platform, which is carved both inside and out, features mandalas, Buddha images, guardians of the four directions, and the *Ushnishavijaya Dharani* (a prayer for longevity) written in various scripts. These themes were apparently designed to help people walking through receive Buddha's blessings and protect the Mongol Yuan state.

At the stone entrance to the arch, the lintel bends down diagonally on the left and right in the manner of the wooden frame of an old city gate. The bas-reliefs fronting the northern and southern arched entrances display on each side an elephant surmounted by a youth riding a mythical beast, while the apex of the arch shows a garuda (mythical bird) flanked by human-appearing nagas (serpents).

On the left and right walls just inside the entrance are the images of the Four Heavenly Kings (Tianwang, or Lokapalas) carved in relief, each 2.75 meters high and 3.65 meters wide. The Four Heavenly Kings are important guardians of Buddhist Law whose task is to repel threats to Buddhism. According to Buddhist scriptures, the four kings — Dhrtarastra, guardian of the east; Virudhaka, guardian of the south; Virupaksha, guardian of the west; and Vaishravana, guardian of the north — reside with their families halfway up Mount Sumeru, the center of the world, and guard the entire world.

The images inside the arch of the Juyong Gate of the awe-inspiring Heavenly Kings, dressed in armor with ribbons fluttering in the wind, are limited in size only by the height of the walls. Their size appears even more impressive because viewers need to stand underneath the arch to see them; they cannot step back to view the statues from a distance. The Four Heavenly Kings hold their characteristic items — sword, *pipa* (a four-stringed plucked instrument), honorific parasol, and coiled serpent — and sit flanked by smaller attendants and with their feet resting on ghosts or female demons.

The inside of the arch presents a mysterious and solemn Buddhist world. At the center of the vault appears a row of mandalas of the five directional Buddhas. Carved on the two sloping sides are Buddhas of the Ten Directions, all sitting cross-legged in meditation (fig. 4.2). The rest of the surface is filled with images of the Thousand Buddhas of the Bhadrakalpa (the contemporary period). The designs and images are carved with masterly skill in a precise, unified style that suggests the influence of the Sakya sect.[3] The principal and secondary subjects, as well as the many variations, not only achieve a decorative effect over a large area but also create a deeply religious atmosphere. Carved in the middle section of the passageway are the texts of the *Dharani Prayer of the Honored and Victorious Buddha (Ushnishvijaya Dharani)*, an abridged version of the Dharani Sutra of Tathagata, and *Records of Merits in the Construction of the Pagoda* in six languages: Sanskrit (Lanthsa), Tibetan, Phagspa, Uygur, Western Xia, and Han Chinese. The religious content and sculptural style of many of the carvings both inside and outside the passage can be identified with and closely compared to teachings and artwork of the contemporary Sakya sect in Tibet.

During the Ming dynasty (1368–1644), Buddhism received moderate encouragement. The Chan and Pure Land Schools remained in vogue, and it became fashionable to practice both at the same time. Tibetan Buddhism lost its luster in the Ming, though the Ming emperor Taizu continued the practice of granting Tibetan Buddhist monks who had served in the Yuan court such titles as Imperial Preceptor or State Preceptor. During the Yongle reign (1403–1424) alone, thirty-six Tibetan lamas were given the title Dharma King, Buddhists of Western Heaven, Supreme State Preceptor, and State Preceptor. Emperors Xianzong, Xiaozong, and Wuzong (who reigned successively from 1465 to 1521) also practiced Tibetan Buddhism. Emperor Wuzong, in particular, was well versed in Sanskrit and styled himself the Dharma King Daqing. Emperor Shizu of the Qing dynasty invited the fifth Dalai Lama to Beijing in 1652 and bestowed a title on him the following year. He also granted a title to Gushi Khan, a Mongol noble who

4.1 Relief sculpture, white marble, Juyong Gate, Changping district, Beijing. Yuan dynasty.

4.2 Bas-relief showing Amoghasiddhi, directional Buddha, white marble, Juyong Gate.

held de facto power in Tibet at that time. This helped strengthen the position of the Gelug sect of Tibetan Buddhism (a fifteenth-century branch whose adherents believed in the doctrine of successive reincarnated lamas), further integrating religious and political power, and enhanced the relation between the Qing imperial court and the local governments of Tibet and Mongolia. After the death of the fifth Dalai Lama, the construction within China of Tibetan-style temples and the production of Tibetan Buddhist art entered a new stage.

In the Qing dynasty (1644–1911), mudra (hand gesture), *asana* (posture), and proportion became extremely important in Esoteric Buddhist statues. These were set forth in the *Classic of Measurements for Making Buddhist Images* (*Zaoxiang liangdu jing*), which was translated from the Tibetan in 1742 by the Manchu Prince Gongbu Chabu, the minister in charge of foreign studies, to help standardize the creation of Buddhist statues in the hinterland of China.

During both the Ming and Qing dynasties, the number of Buddhist temples and believers continued to grow. In 1481 there were only 639 official temples inside and outside present-day Beijing. By 1667, however, statistics collected by the Board of Rites showed a total of 79,622 Buddhist temples across the country, with the number of monks and nuns reaching 118,907.

Daoism

Daoism reached the peak of its development during the Tang and Song dynasties, and many of China's rulers gave it great support and encouragement. The Tang imperial court was particularly fervent in its espousal of Daoism. The founder of Daoism, Laozi — whose surname (Li) was the same as that of the Tang imperial family — was identified as the direct ancestor of the emperors. Li Zhi (Emperor Gaozong) who ruled from 650 to 683, granted to Laozi the posthumous title Supreme Emperor Xuanyuan. Gaozong's empress, Wu Zetian, was not as enamored of Daoism. After she managed to usurp court power, dethrone two emperors in succession, and establish the so-called Great Zhou dynasty, she sought to weaken the theological foundation of the Li imperial family by stripping Laozi of his title and adopting Buddhism. Her efforts did not last, however: in 705, when Emperor Zhongzong ascended the throne and restored the Tang court, he also restored Laozi's title. The imperial favor shown toward Daoism culminated in the reign of Emperor Xuanzong, who published the Daoist canon. More glorious titles were posthumously awarded to Laozi, including Sage Ancestor and Great Sage Ancestor. By the time of Emperor Zhenzong of the Song dynasty, Laozi's posthumous title had been elevated to Emperor Hunyuan Shangde, the Supreme Master Lao. Laozi has been referred to by that title since then.

In the two Tang capitals of Chang'an and Luoyang, as well as in the seats of all the prefectures, temples to honor Laozi as Supreme Emperor Xuanyuan were built. In these temples, statues of Laozi were usually flanked by tablets dedicated to the five Tang emperors of the Li family: Gaozu, Taizong, Gaozong, Zhongzong, and Ruizong. Many believed that Laozi was the incarnation of Daode Tianzun (the Heavenly Worthy of the Way), one of the Three Pure Ones (Sanqing, the highest divine beings), and statues of Laozi as a Heavenly Worthy placed in these temples borrowed their presentation from Buddhist sculpture — suggesting that like Confucianism and Buddhism, Daoism and Buddhism also influenced each other at the time.

A stone stele featuring the image of a Heavenly Worthy carved in 687, now in the museum of Wuwei, Gansu Province, illustrates the influence of Buddhism. The image sits behind curtains with Daoist golden lads and jade girls standing on both sides, but with an overall "three-Buddha" arrangement of figures whose details resemble those of Buddhist art. Another example is the seated white marble Heavenly Worthy made in 719, now located in Taiyuan, Shanxi Province (see fig. 4.42). Wearing a loose ceremonial robe, with his hair piled up in the shape of a lotus and with a long beard divided into three strands, the figure rests his left hand on a low table and in his right holds a fan and a duster. Resembling a scholar-bureaucrat of ancient China, the statue shows the influence of ancient Buddhist sculpture.

The Song rulers of the Zhao family also sifted through the long list of Daoist deities to legitimize their rule, creating a new ancestor with their surname, Zhao: Zhao Xuanlang. Early in the reign of Emperor Zhenzong (1004), the Song court signed an infamous treaty that offered annual payments to the invading Khitans —

whom they had defeated. To divert public attention from the treaty and consolidate his rule, the emperor reported that he had been given a heavenly book and had seen Zhao Xuanlang in a dream. Zhao, he said, had told him that he, Emperor Zhao, had been sent down by the Jade Emperor (the leader of the Four Heavenly Emperors, who is in charge of the celestial way, or Dao) to look after the Zhao family and award Zhao Xuanlang the title Emperor Tianzun, the Sage Ancestor, and Zhao Xuanlang's wife that of Great Empress Yuantian, the Sage Ancestress. The creation of such husband-wife deities is unique to Chinese Daoism.

To substantiate the myth that his power came from Heaven, Emperor Zhenzong also ordered that Yuqing Zhaoying Palace be built in the capital city of Bianliang (present-day Kaifeng in Henan Province). Construction of the huge complex of 2,610 rooms continued day and night for seven years; it was not completed until 1014. Of great architectural beauty, the palace was also enormously costly: five thousand taels of silver were used to construct the statue of the Jade Emperor, and five thousand taels of gold were used to make each statue of Zhao Xuanlang and Emperor Zhenzong.

In the long list of Daoist deities, the Four Heavenly Emperors are second only to the Three Pure Ones: Yuanshi Tianzun (the Primordial Heavenly Worthy), Lingbao Tianzun (the Heavenly Worthy of the Sacred Jewel), and Daode Tianzun (the Heavenly Worthy of the Way), said to have derived from the three most fundamental qi (xuan, yuan, and shi) of the universe. The statues of the Jade Emperor, the Zhao family's ancestor god, and of the living sovereign were placed together in the Daoist temples to further sacralize imperial power.

Emperor Huizong of the Northern Song (r. 1101–1125), strongly favored Daoism over Buddhism; citing the Daoist Lin Lingsu, Huizong described himself as the incarnation of the older son of the Jade Emperor, named the Great Lord of Long Life. Conferring on himself a Daoist title (Lord of the Dao), Huizong made himself both the patriarch of Daoism and emperor of the country, adding a kind of papal power to his imperial sovereignty. In 1119 the emperor issued an edict changing the title of the Buddha to the Great Enlightened Golden Immortal and set out to assimilate and reform Buddhism into Daoism. Besides regarding all court officials as immortals, he ordered Buddhist monasteries changed into Daoist temples or palaces and ordered everyone to address monks and nuns as deshi (men of virtue) or nüde (women of virtue). Meanwhile, he issued orders that Daoist palaces and temples be constructed in scenic places and Daoist statues erected nationwide. Daoism thus received unparalleled political and material support throughout China.

Emperors Taizong, Zhenzong, and Huizong of the Northern Song dynasty tried repeatedly to organize the pantheon of Daoist deities. The imperial leaders sought to make a formal list of these gods, who had grown enormously in number as more and more folk deities were included. The emperors also sought to make the Daoist pantheon mirror the hierarchical imperial system of power and thus further consolidate their rule. Eventually, a long and complex list of Daoist deities was established, supplemented by corresponding rules for preaching, ceremonial rituals, and the construction of shrines. Chinese sculpture — not simply that done directly under Daoist inspiration — shows the deep influence of the imagery and requirements of this extraordinary pantheon.

As it developed, Daoism continued to borrow from Buddhist, as well as Confucian, teachings. In the Northern Song, numerous learned Daoists appeared, among them Chen Tuan and Zhang Boduan. Chen Tuan emphasized the philosophy of ultimatelessness and *neidan* (interior alchemy), which often went along with use of symbols and the Confucian *Book of Changes* (*Yijing*). Zhang Boduan emphasized the need to attain both physical and spiritual immortality, describing Buddhism, Daoism, and Confucianism as sharing the same goal. All of this influenced the theoretical development of Daoism and neo-Confucianism.

After the establishment of the Northern Song, *waidan* (exterior or laboratory alchemy) and the Daoist practice of using talismans gradually lost their hold. The quest for immortality through exterior alchemy, popular with several Tang emperors, declined. An emphasis on meditation reemerged, and new Daoist schools like Quanzhen, Taiyi, and Zhenda flourished in the Jin-controlled areas of northern China. Among the most important was the Quanzhen (Fundamental Truth) School established by Wang Zhe and his disciples, the Seven Immortals of the North — Ma Yu, Tan Chuduan, Liu Chuxuan, Qiu Chuji, Wang Chuyi, Hao Datong, and Sun Bu'er. The school sought to synthesize in an equal way the basic tenets of the three major belief systems — Buddhism, Daoism, and Confucianism — and called upon people to practice meditation without using external objects of faith, to eliminate passion, and to be tolerant, hard-working, and selfless.

In 1222, during the early Yuan dynasty, Qiu Chuji paid a visit to Genghis Khan to urge him to respect Heaven and love the people. Impressed by Qiu, the khan bestowed on him the title Divine Immortal and assured him that the Chinese would be spared the mass killings that the Mongols had inflicted on other peoples. Qiu was presented with a tiger-shaped tally and a book with the emperor's seal and entrusted to look after Daoist affairs throughout the country. Such imperial patronage helped Quanzhen Daoism spread throughout the country.

Toward the end of the Yuan dynasty, the Quanzhen School became unpopular as Daoist abbots and disciples became increasingly corrupt and the religion's conflict with Buddhism deepened. The imperial court repeatedly issued orders to burn Daoist books and engravings and to return temple land and properties acquired through illegal means to their original owners.

By the late Yuan, only two major schools, the Quanzhen and the Zhengyi, were active. The Zhengyi School (Way of Orthodox Unity), an old school that used talismans and had arisen again in the Yuan, thrived after the founding of the Ming dynasty, in part because most Ming emperors had an interest in divination and alchemy. (By contrast, the Quanzhen School lost favor and declined during the Ming.) Emperor Chengzu (r. 1403–1424) considered himself the incarnation of Zhenwu, a Daoist deity who had been elevated to a prominent position and whom Chengzu further promoted. He ordered a massive complex of palaces and temples built in the Wudang Mountains, Hubei Province, to worship both Zhenwu and the famous Daoist Zhang Sanfeng. Emperor Shizong (r. 1522–1566), the most pious Daoist emperor in history, gave himself several Daoist names and conferred posthumous Daoist titles on his parents. Many senior Daoists entered the Shizong court, becoming high-ranking officials. Daoism itself became widespread and ever more accepted during those years, in the cities as well as in rural areas.

The Qing imperial court, which favored Confucianism and Tibetan Buddhism, showed no interest in Daoist talismans and divination and set various constraints on Daoist activities. But while Daoism lost favor at court, its influence among the ordinary people expanded. Many secular gods were incorporated into the list of Daoist deities, and books advising people on how to do good deeds circulated widely. The tenets of Daoism and the idea of unity among the three beliefs continued to exert

4.3 Pillar with coiled dragon design, stone, Dacheng Hall, Confucian Temple, Qufu County, Shandong Province. Rebuilt in 1480 and 1500 and repaired in 1725.

4.4 Confucius meeting Laozi, stone, Wuliang Memorial Shrine, Jiaxiang County, Shandong Province. Eastern Han dynasty.

a wide and far-reaching influence on literature and the arts; they also deeply affected sculpture.

Confucianism and the Image of Confucius "the Sage"

Confucianism is a product of ancient Chinese culture, traditional religious beliefs, and thinking that emerged during the Eastern Zhou dynasty (770–256 B.C.E.). With the establishment of the Western Han dynasty (206 B.C.E.–9 C.E.), Confucianism became the religious ideology of the state, and a tradition that deified Confucius developed.[4] In 140 B.C.E., Emperor Wu accepted Dong Zhongshu's suggestion to "honor only Confucianism and reject all other schools of thought," and set up the Imperial College. Confucianism became the orthodox ideology of imperial China. The rise of neo-Confucianism during the Song and Ming dynasties led to further developments in Confucian theory.

Confucianism drew on a wide variety of traditional beliefs from ancient times previous to Confucius, prominent among them the worship of the Emperor of Boundless Heaven (Haotian Shangdi).[5] Because Confucianism was regarded as the state religion, sacrifices to the gods of Heaven, Earth, mountains, and rivers — as well as to ancestral gods — became the most important rituals performed in ancient China, and the "sons of Heaven" (emperors) alone had the honor of offering sacrifices to Heaven. Ritual offerings to honor Confucius, performed by emperors and others, were also important state ceremonies.

Sages hold the highest rank in Confucianism, and emperors were naturally regarded as such. Confucius came to be known as the "greatest sage of all sages." Thirteen classic books embodying Confucian beliefs, including the *Book of Changes, Book of Songs* (*Shijing*), *Book of Rites* (*Li ji*), and *Spring and Autumn Annals* (*Chun qiu*), are believed to have been annotated by Confucius himself, while the *Analects* (*Lunyu*) and *Mencius* (*Mengzi*) were collected and annotated by his disciples and later Confucian scholars.[6]

Most emperors found Confucianism useful as a way to justify their rule, and they awarded Confucius many posthumous honorifics. Duke Ai, the sovereign of the state of Lu (r. 494–477 B.C.E.) and Confucius's contemporary, referred to him as Nifu (an honorific roughly translated as "Confucius, Esquire") and granted him the rank of marquis. During the Western and Eastern Han, this rank was elevated to duke. During the reign of Emperor Wen in the Sui dynasty (581–604 C.E.), he was given the title Father Confucius the Great Teacher. In 657 Emperor Gaozong of the Tang changed his title to the Great Sage. Later, Confucius, like Laozi, was granted honorary monarchic titles: King Wenxuan (739), King Wenxuan the Greatest Sage (1012), and King Wenxuan the Greatest Sage with Perfect Completion (1308), the last remaining in use until the early Ming.[7] In addition, Confucius's major disciples were all posthumously made dukes and marquises.

The largest of the Confucian temples is located in Qufu County, Shandong Province, the birthplace of Confucius. Erected by Duke Ai of Lu, the temple was enlarged several times in later dynasties as the ceremo-

4.5 Shakyamuni Buddha, stone,
Greater Prajna Grotto, Anyue County,
Sichuan Province. Southern Song
dynasty, 1240.

4.6 Confucius and disciples, stone,
Cave 6, Mount Shizhuan, Dazu
grottoes, Dazu County, Chongqing.
Northern Song dynasty, 1082–1083,
1088.

nial rituals to honor Confucius increased. Beginning in the Song, emperors would take special trips to Qufu to make sacrifices to Confucius, using sacrificial implements crafted according to standards drawn up by the Imperial Department of Rites.

Covering a total area of 24.8 hectares, the temple now boasts 9 courtyards and 466 halls and side rooms. Numerous archways and doors are built along a long central corridor leading to the major hall, and all the architectural elements are laid out in accordance with standards for imperial palaces. The main room in the temple used to pay homage to Confucius is Dacheng (Great Achievement) Hall. A spacious nine-bay structure, this gigantic hall has double eaves and nine roof ridges. Under the roofs are twenty-eight stone pillars with carved coiling dragons in high relief (fig. 4.3), equivalent in standard to those in the Leng'an Hall in Changling mausoleum for the Ming emperor Chengzu in Beijing.

In the Song-dynasty statues of the great sage Confucius, the lesser sage Mencius, and the ten wise men (Confucius's main disciples) were enshrined in the central hall, while portraits of seventy-two major disciples and twenty-one leading Confucian scholars were painted on the wooden walls of the east and west side rooms. All these pictures have been destroyed.

Carved images of Confucius and his disciples first appeared in stone reliefs from the Eastern Han dynasty (fig. 4.4), while the practice of making statues of Confucius began in the Northern and Southern Dynasties (420–589). According to the epigraph "Li Zhongxuan Rebuilds the Tablets in the Confucian Temple" (*Li Zhongxuan chongxiu Kongzi miao bei*) carved on a stone stele, in 541 artisans were ordered to construct statues of Confucius and his ten disciples and decorate the statues with caps in the style used by Confucian scholars. Such decisions about dress remained sensitive issues: during the Tang dynasty, for example, arguments broke out over how Confucius's disciples should be attired. During the reign of Emperor Huizong of the Song (r. 1107–1125), it was ruled that the construction of Confucius's statue should follow the standards set for figures of emperors. The sage should wear a crown with twelve hanging tassels and hold an elongated jade tablet that signified imperial power. Most of the extant statues and images of Confucius thus depict either a long-bearded, elderly scholar wearing a cap, a long robe, and a sword, or a monarch arrayed in crown and sumptuous clothing. (After 1530, however, as Confucius's status changed from idol and king to Greatest Sage and

Teacher, statues of him became rare. The few we now see are mostly works of more recent times.)

During the Tang and Song dynasties, the practice of building temples to Confucius and his disciples was emulated in other aspects of social life. Temples of martial valor were built throughout the country to worship Jiang Ziya, a general who helped King Wu of the Western Zhou defeat King Zhou of the Shang and establish the Zhou dynasty. (Jiang was posthumously given the title King Wucheng in 674.) Modeled after the Confucian temple, the temple of martial valor enshrined the statues of "a lesser sage, ten wise men, and seventy-two disciples," all of whom were renowned strategists and generals in various dynasties. The list was subject to frequent changes; after the Song, the main god enshrined in the temple of martial valor changed quite a few times.[8]

The practice of bringing together Buddhist, Daoist, and Confucian sculptural images grew increasingly popular after the Song dynasty. Among the well-known examples are the images found in the grottoes in Anyue, Sichuan. The Greater Prajna Grotto, built in 1240 during the Southern Song dynasty, is 3.14 meters high, 3.22 meters deep, and 2.8 meters wide. Against the front wall are statues of a seated Shakyamuni and his two major disciples, Mahakashyapa and Ananda (fig. 4.5). Against the wall on the left are the statues of Laozi, with a long beard and wearing a long robe, and two attendants. By the wall on the right side are a sitting statue of Confucius flanked by two standing attendants. Confucius, looking imperial and flanked by his major disciples, wears a cap with tassels and a loose robe, holds a jade tablet, and has his feet on a low square stool.

Caves housing statues from all three religions are also found in grottoes around Fo'an Bridge, Shibi Temple, and Mount Shizhuan. Moreover, at Mount Shizhuan the three founders have been carved out of the wall in three adjacent caves. In the image of Confucius the hair is tied with a soft scarf; he wears a loose robe and boots and carries a feathered fan in his right hand. Flanking him on both sides are statues of ten disciples.[9] The three caves were built by Wen Weijian and his two sons, Wen Juyong and Wen Juli, in 1082–1083 and 1088 during the Northern Song dynasty (fig. 4.6).

During the Song, the age of the great grotto sculptures largely came to an end, and sculptural cave images were generally replaced by temple art. The sculptures that came to fill these places of worship reflected the deepening popularization of Buddhist and Daoist beliefs, their continued influence on each other and on Confucianism, and the ways popular folk faiths had shaped all three.

The Arrangement of Buddhist Temples

Although Buddhist temples in China, with their interior murals and pagodas, were partly inspired by the ancient grotto temples of India, they were even more profoundly influenced by native palatial buildings. When temple architects made the pagoda the major structure and placed it in the center of the temple, for example, they were following the traditional Chinese practice of placing the highest building in the center of an architectural complex. Such a layout directly influenced the design of cave temples during that time.

Of the earliest Buddhist temples only the ruins of the Yongning Temple in Luoyang can be verified. Erected in 519 under the auspices of the imperial court of the Northern Wei, it was an enormous Buddhist sanctuary. According to a contemporary account, *Record of the Monasteries of Luoyang* (*Luoyang jialan ji*), by Yang Xuanzhi, the layout of the Yongning Temple followed that of the famous Baima Temple, also in Luoyang, of the Eastern Han that featured a pagoda within the temple. Along the central south-north axis of the temple's rectangular layout were the south gate (in Chinese, "mountain gate"), a pagoda, a major Buddha hall, and the north gate. The left and right flanks were strictly symmetrical, and the entire complex was enclosed by thick walls forming a courtyard.

The towering, nine-storied wooden pagoda at the heart of the complex, once an important landmark of

4.7 Young woman with coiled hair, clay, excavated in 1980 from the base of Yongning Temple, Luoyang, Henan Province. Northern Wei dynasty. Luoyang Museum.

4.8 Young woman without coiled hair, clay, excavated in 1980 from the base of Yongning Temple. Northern Wei dynasty. Luoyang Museum.

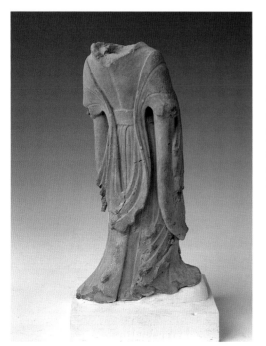

4.9 Figure, painted clay, excavated in 1980 from the base of Yongning Temple. Northern Wei dynasty. 19.1 cm. Luoyang Museum.

4.10 Head with dragon-design headgear, clay, excavated in 1980 from the base of Yongning Temple. Northern Wei dynasty. Luoyang Museum.

4.11 Wooden (Shakyamuni) Pagoda, Fogong Temple, Yingxian County, Shanxi Province. Liao dynasty, 1056. 6,730 cm.

4.12 Plan of Wooden (Shakyamuni) Pagoda, Fogong Temple, showing Buddhist images on each story.

the Northern Wei capital, "could be seen one hundred *li* away from the capital," and "in the long quiet windy night, bells over the pagoda [would] chime and their sound [could] be heard more than ten *li* away."[10] North of the pagoda was the hall devoted to the Buddha; enshrined there were a tall gilt-bronze statue of the Buddha and ten gilt-bronze Buddhist statues of medium height, together with embroidered and woven Buddhist images. The temple also had a thousand rooms in which the monks lived and meditated.

During these early years, the pagoda was typically the most outstanding architectural feature of the Buddhist temple complex. The Buddhist pagoda (stupa) originated in India. Created as a place to keep the relics of the Buddha, in China it also became a shrine in which the Buddha was worshiped.[11] A total of 1,560 pieces of broken painted sculptures were excavated from the base of the Yongning Temple pagoda, including large and medium-size statues from the shrines surrounding the central pillar and sculpted images of the Buddha, bodhisattvas, and attendants that had been attached to the niches around the pagoda. Although the images are in

fragments and cannot be restored, we can see that they were meticulously designed and carefully executed, showing the high level of sculptural artistry during the Northern Wei (figs. 4.7–4.10).

Starting in the Tang dynasty, a major hall devoted to the Buddha came to replace the pagoda as the center of a Buddhist temple. In some temples, pagodas were moved to the side; in others, separate courtyards were made for them. From the time of the Song dynasty, pagodas were placed at the back of the Buddha hall in a number of major temples. Nevertheless, pagodas continued to occupy a prominent position in the temple complexes because of their height and eye-catching designs, most of which fell into one of three styles: tower, multi-eave, or single-storied.

Extant are more than a hundred Buddhist pagodas built of various materials from the Northern and Southern Dynasties through to the Liao and Song. The Wooden Pagoda in Yingxian County, Shanxi Province,

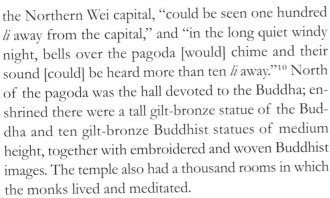

4.13 Buddhist figures, painted clay, in the main Buddha hall, Nanchan Temple, Mount Wutai, Shanxi Province. Tang dynasty.

is the largest and most magnificent. Also known as Shakyamuni Pagoda in Fogong Temple, it was built in 1056 (figs. 4.11, 4.12). Standing inside the major gate in front of the main worship hall, it is clearly the most important structure at the temple. An astonishing 67.3 meters high with a base platform 30 meters in diameter, it is an octagonal tower topped by a gold Kundika (ornate water vessel). The lower part is multistoried with double eaves.[12] From the outside, the structure appears to have five stories, although there are actually nine, visible from the inside. A complex, exquisite structure, the pagoda was ingeniously designed and built, with each story boasting more than sixty different bracket sets (*dougong*) inserted between the tops of the pillars and the crossbeams.

Buddhist statues were placed inside the spacious open stories, lending a solemn, majestic atmosphere. On the first floor the head of an 11-meter standing figure of the Buddha almost touches the ceiling; viewers have to crane their necks to take the whole figure in. On the third floor are statues of the Buddhas of the Four Directions, and on the fifth floor is a sitting statue of Shakyamuni, flanked by eight bodhisattvas. In 1974, when the Wooden Pagoda was repaired, other objects

were discovered, including the seven treasures of Buddhism (gold, silver, lapis lazuli, crystal, agate, rubies, and cornelian), a Buddhist relic, Buddhist scriptures, and paintings from the Liao dynasty.[13]

Shanxi Province is famous throughout China for having the largest number of extant ancient buildings, including the two remaining well-preserved Buddhist temples of the Tang dynasty, both on Mount Wutai: the Nanchan Temple, built in 782, and the Foguang Temple, built in 857. Although major changes were made to the layout of the two temples over the years, two major halls remain. Moreover, the Buddhist statues in these halls are also original works of the Tang, providing a clear example of the arrangement of Buddhist statues in temples at this time.

Nanchan Temple is not large compared to other temples built in the Tang dynasty, but its well-preserved sculpture displays the artistic level reached at the mid-Tang (fig. 4.13). The seventeen statues in the major hall are of different sizes, lined up on an inverted-U-shaped dais (fig. 4.14). These include figures of the Buddha (Shakyamuni), two disciples (Mahakashyapa and Ananda), and two bodhisattvas (Manjushri and Samantabhadra); four statues of attendants; and two

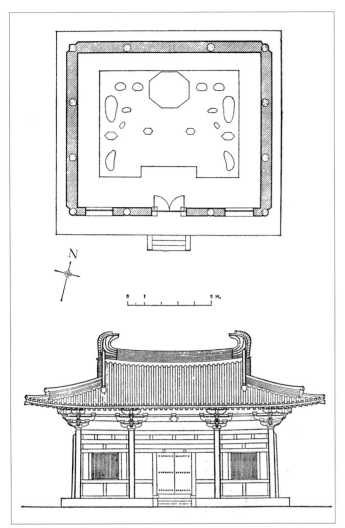

4.14 Plan and side elevation of the main Buddha hall, Nanchan Temple. Plan shows placement of statues.

statues of Heavenly Kings. In front on either side of the statue of Shakyamuni is a beautifully sculpted attendant bodhisattva with one knee on a lotus.[14]

The seventeen statues are variously adorned. The Buddha and the two bodhisattvas are gilded to stress their prominence, while the rest are painted and more realistically presented. The huge statue of Shakyamuni sits cross-legged on a Sumeru throne (a special Buddhist throne), which is adorned with the sculpted half-bodied images of a lion and a demigod. The Buddha's robe appears smooth and soft, falling down in pleats to cover the front of the throne. Over the huge halo behind the figure are sculpted images of a mythic bird, flying apsaras (celestials) in Han Chinese attire, and lotus flowers. The two bodhisattvas sit upright on lotus flowers, solemn yet elegant, and under them are their canonic mounts: on the left, Samantabhadra rides a white elephant in the company of ferocious demigods and a keeper, and on the right Manjushri rides a lion and is also accompanied by a group of demigods and a keeper. The elephant and lion seem ready to dash forward, and the keepers appear animated. The mixture of stillness and motion enlivens the otherwise solemn atmosphere.

From the Mogao and Longmen grottoes, we can see that the number of Buddhist statues placed in cave temples gradually increased during the Tang dynasty, from three in a cave to five and then nine (one Buddha, two disciples, two bodhisattvas, two heavenly guardians, and

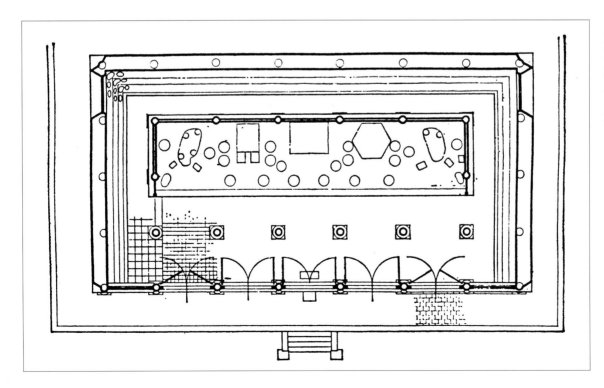

4.15 Plan of East Hall, Foguang Temple, Mount Wutai, Shanxi Province. Tang dynasty.

4.16 Buddhist figures, painted clay, East Hall, Foguang Temple.

two doorway guardians). The inverted-U-shaped dais, popular by the time of the later Tang and seen in the Nanchan Temple and elsewhere, replaced other seating arrangements for the major figures. Unlike those in earlier cave temples, the statues of demigods made during this period were placed in the gatehouse (the main, or mountain, gate) to guard the temple.

During the Tang, the Foguang Temple served as an important place of enlightenment for the Huayan School. Unfortunately, its Buddhist statues, as well as its major building, the Maitreya Hall, were destroyed in 845, when Buddhism was subject to suppression. Only the East Hall survived. Over the spacious fan-shaped dais standing in the center of the hall are thirty-six painted Buddhist statues in the Tang style. These statues lost much of their artistic value when they were repainted in the 1930s, but they remain in their original Tang arrangement, thereby providing a fine example of a group of Buddhist sculptures in the later Tang (fig. 4.15).[15]

Above the dais five standing statues are arranged in a line. In the middle is Shakyamuni, with Maitreya (the Buddha of the Future) to his left and Amitabha (the Buddha of Measureless Light) to his right (fig. 4.16). Their lotus-shaped seats are about 5.3 meters high, each flanked by four disciples or assistants with two attendant bodhisattvas in front, kneeling with one knee on a lotus flower. The group of sculptures displays two features seldom seen in Buddhist sculpture of later ages: Maitreya sits with his legs hanging down, and

assistant bodhisattvas holding different offerings are vividly depicted. Flanking the central group at the sides are sculpted statues of Manjushri (on the right) and Samantabhadra (left), each 4.8 meters high, together with their mounts.

Next to each sculpture are smaller statues of assistants, keepers, demigods, and other attendants. Two Heavenly Kings stand in front on both sides of the dais. In front of Samantabhadra is a statue of the warrior-like Skanda, a Hindu god who was adopted as a protector of Buddhism, and at the back are statues of two patrons: Ning Gongyu, a rich local woman who donated large sums of money to the temple, and the monk Yuancheng, who supervised reconstruction of the hall. The sizes of the statues vary according to their status in the Buddhist world. These five groups of sculpted statues are both independent from and related to one another. As a group, they create a feeling of mystery and awe.

Enshrined in Wanfo Hall, a wood-framed structure in Zhenguo Temple, Pingyao County, Shanxi Province, built in 936, is another group of eleven sculpted Buddhist statues (fig. 4.17). In addition to the statue of Shakyamuni, which was made later, there are statues of the Buddha, bodhisattvas, and Heavenly Kings, representing artistic styles similar to those seen in later sculptures of the Dunhuang grottoes.

Other sculptural works related to Buddhism that follow the iconographic, artistic, and compositional characteristics of the Tang style include twenty-nine

4.17 Figures, painted clay, Wanfo Hall, Zhenguo Temple, Pingyao County, Shanxi Province. Five Dynasties, 936.

4.18 Shakyamuni with kneeling bodhisattvas and disciple, painted clay, Hall for the Preservation of Excellent Teaching, Lower Huayan Temple, Datong, Shanxi Province. Liao dynasty, 1038.

Buddhist statues in the Hall for the Preservation of Excellent Teaching (Baojia jiaozang dian) of the Lower Huayan Temple in Datong, built in 1038 during the Liao dynasty (fig. 4.18).[16] As with those at the Nanchan Temple and in the East Hall of Foguang Temple, this group of statues stands on an inverted-U-shaped dais in the middle of the hall. The group includes three Buddhas (Shakyamuni, Maitreya, and Amitabha), four bodhisattvas (Manjushri, Samantabhadra, Avalokiteshvara, and Kshitigarbha), and their assistants. The group is further divided into three subgroups, each oriented toward one of the three Buddhas. The subgroups form a triangle, creating an animated, familial atmosphere that seems to transcend the bounds of Buddhism.

The inverted-U-shaped dais and the assistant bodhisattvas sitting on the lotuses clearly show the influence of the Tang style. In their arrangement, however, the sculptures do not follow the strict rules of Tang times. For example, both Shakyamuni and Amitabha are accompanied by disciples, whose images are similar to those of Mahakashyapa and Ananda, whereas Maitreya is flanked by four assistant bodhisattvas. Indeed, it is rare to see a Shakyamuni presented with Manjushri and Samantabhadra, an Amitabha together with Avalokiteshvara, a Maitreya with the bodhisattva Kshitigarbha, and the Four Heavenly Kings on the four sides of the dais.

All the statues in the Lower Huayan Temple are made of clay coated with lacquer using gold, red, and green pigments, giving them a simple and unadorned yet harmonious appearance. Some are almost 5 meters high. The bodhisattvas are plump and lifelike. Among the statues surrounding Maitreya one attendant bodhisattva in the outer ring is particularly beautiful: his palms are pressed together and his mouth is slightly open to expose his white teeth. In every sense, this is a masterpiece of sculpture (fig. 4.19).

Shanhua Temple, also in Datong, is the largest existing Buddhist temple with ties to the Liao and Jin dynasties. First built in the Tang, the temple was largely destroyed by invading Jin troops in 1112 and rebuilt by the monk Yuanman between 1128 and 1143. The Hall of Shakyamuni, built in the Liao, was among those renovated in the Jin, and some of its statues date from that time. Standing in a line on the dais in the central part of the hall are the Buddhas of the Five Cardinal Directions (north, south, east, and west, with Shakyamuni in the middle), with their disciples and assistant bodhisattvas,

4.19 Attendant bodhisattva, painted and lacquered clay, Hall for the Preservation of Excellent Teaching, Lower Huayan Temple. 302 cm.

4.20 Chandraprabha deva, painted clay, Shanhua Temple, Datong, Shanxi Province. Jin dynasty, 1128–1143. 390 cm.

4.21 Attendant deva, painted clay, Shanhua Temple. 360 cm.

and twenty-four devas (supernatural beings), all serving as guardians of Buddhist Law, adorning the east and west walls.[17] These statues best demonstrate the artistic level of Buddhist sculpture of the Liao and Jin dynasties. The five major Buddhas are similar in appearance; the only difference lies in their hand gestures. The halos and Sumeru throne are elaborately and beautifully executed, setting off the solemn, graceful lines in the Buddha sculptures. This gorgeous decoration had a far-reaching influence on later Buddhist statue making.

The devas are stunning. Each is depicted as having subtle spiritual and temperamental differences. Three female devas, for instance — Marici, Hariti, and Sarasvati — are presented as stately, beautiful, and awe-inspiring. Warriorlike devas such as Skanda sometimes appear bold and ferocious, sometimes merciful and amiable. Of devas in civilian official attire, such as Vayu and Varuna, the wind and water devas, some wear stern expressions, while others appear scholarly and refined. All the sculptures fit harmoniously into a single scene, perhaps sug-

gesting both their invincible, overarching might in protecting Buddhist Law and their great mercy and compassion toward all living creatures (figs. 4.20, 4.21).

This group of statues marks the beginning of a trend in Buddhist temple sculpture toward uniform stylization, simplified arrangement and composition of the statues, and exquisitely detailed halos and thrones. The sculpted devas, however, not only show the increasing variety of Buddhist gods; they also show that there was more room for artistic presentation and diversified arrangements of the Buddhist images in the temples. Images of devas became popular in later Buddhist sculpture and in paintings of the Ming dynasty. Two important examples are the twenty devas in the Hall of Shakyamuni of Upper Huayan Temple in Datong and the twenty-eight devas in the Dabei (Great Compassion) Hall of Dahui Temple in Beijing.

The largest surviving Buddhist temple structure from Liao and Jin times, the Hall of Shakyamuni in the Upper Huayan Temple of Datong was built in 1140.

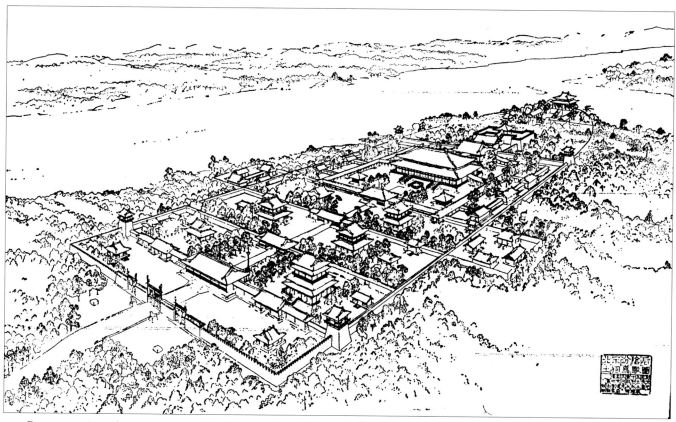

4.22 Reconstruction of the Houtu (God of the Earth) Temple in Fenyin, Wanrong County, Shanxi Province, as it would have appeared in 1137.

The original Buddhist statues were destroyed long ago; what we see now are sculptural works from the Ming dynasty. The statues are to some extent arranged like those in the Hall of Shakyamuni in the Shanhua Temple, described above. On the central dais stand the major statues of five Buddhas — the middle three made of wood, and the other two (as well as the bodhisattvas surrounding them) of clay. Standing along the side walls are statues of twenty devas. Although reminiscent of Jin works, they are artistically inferior.

Although the layout of Buddhist temples had always followed the same basic plan, the early, simpler temples with their one or two main courtyards and pagoda or main Buddha hall had gradually evolved into more elaborate complexes, filled with temples and subtemples grouped around innumerable courtyards. For the most part the layout of these later temples continued to be uniform. Inspired like the early temples by the organization of imperial palaces and residences of noble families (some temples in fact were originally residences of the aristocracy), Buddhist temples of the Song and later were also characterized by their use of closed spaces around a courtyard.

Set out on a south-north axis, along which big and small buildings were arranged symmetrically, most temples contained all or some of the following, in strict order: a first courtyard formed by the major, mountain gate, the Hall of the Heavenly Kings, and the bell and drum towers (sometimes with side halls), then a second courtyard, centered around the Hall of Shakyamuni and surrounded by halls for the various deities and disciples — the Zushi (Founder) Hall, the Sangharama Hall, the Bodhisattva Hall and the Kashyapa Hall. Larger temples might also have a towerlike building behind the Hall of Shakyamuni, such as the Avalokiteshvara Pavilion found in most major temples. (Statues and images enshrined in the temple halls varied to some extent by Buddhist school.) Reception rooms and the monks' living quarters were arranged along the east and west sides of the central axis. The mountain gate was also called the "three-door" gate, signifying the "three gates to the city of Nirvana," namely, gates to void, formlessness, and inactivity. Inside the gatehouse would be statues of two ferocious-looking gate guardians (*dvarapala*), naked to the waist.[18]

From the time of the Song dynasty, the Hall of Heavenly Kings was usually used to enshrine Maitreya, who was actually represented by the image of the monk Qici, or Budai (Hempen Sack), of the Five Dynasties. Legend has it that Qici wandered through the country carrying a hempen beggar's sack on his back; only at the time of his death, in 916, did he reveal his true identity

as Maitreya, the Buddha of the Future (purportedly Qici sat cross-legged on a rock in Yuelin Temple, chanting, "Maitreya, true Maitreya, simultaneously in a million forms; from time to time appearing among men, but by the men of the time unrecognized," which believers took as evidence of his incarnation).

Behind the statue of Maitreya would stand the statue of Skanda, while on the two sides would be the Four Heavenly Kings holding their traditional items: Dhrtarastra carries the pipa, Virupaksha a coiled serpent, Virudhaka a sword, and Vaishravana an honorific parasol. These statues would be modeled on famous military generals of the time, and all the heavenly guardians would be brightly armored, some depicted as ferocious and cruel, others as scholarly and graceful. Along with the Vajrapanis in the gatehouse, the Four Heavenly Kings and Skanda served to defend Buddhist Law and suppress demons and evil spirits.

The most important building in a Buddhist temple was always the Hall of Shakyamuni, commonly known as the Hall of the Great Hero. Here, "great hero" is a respectful reference to Shakyamuni's ability to avert calamity and suppress evil. The number of statues enshrined in the hall would vary — one, three, five, or seven. If there was only one statue in the hall, it was usually Shakyamuni, unless the temple had been built by the Pure Land School, in which case the statue would be Amitabha. When there were three statues in the hall, they would usually be Dipamkara (the Buddha of the Past), Shakyamuni (the historical Buddha, or the Buddha of the Present), and Maitreya (the Buddha of the Future); Shakyamuni was always in the center.

Depending on their familiarity with standard Buddhist iconography, viewers could distinguish one statue from another simply by looking at their hand gestures and the objects they held. In addition, different Buddhas would be grouped with specific attending bodhisattvas. For instance, Shakyamuni was usually placed with Manjushri and Samantabhadra to make a group called the Three Saints of the Huayan School, whereas Dipamkara was more often placed with Surya and Candra, and Amitabha with Avalokiteshvara and Mahasthamaprapta, called collectively the Three Saints of the West.

When a hall held five statues, they usually represented the Buddhas of the Five Cardinal Directions, as we have seen in the Hall of Shakyamuni in the Shanhua Temple, Datong. Sitting in the middle would be

4.23 Samantabhadra riding an elephant, bronze, Wannian Temple, Mount Emei, Sichuan Province. Northern Song dynasty, 980. 740 cm.

Shakyamuni; on his left would be the Buddhas of the South and the East (Ratnasambhava and Akshobhya), and on his right the Buddhas of the West and the North (Amitabha and Amoghasiddhi). They can be identified by their hand gestures.

An arrangement of seven statues was rare, but one appears in the Hall of Shakyamuni of Fengguo Temple in Yixian County, Liaoning Province, built in 1020. In addition to Shakyamuni the statues represent the other *manushi* Buddhas, the six Buddhas who had appeared prior to Shakyamuni Buddha: Vipashyin, Sikhin, Visvabhu, Krakucchanda, Kanakamuni, and Kashyapa.

Of the bodhisattvas attending the various Buddhas, three "great bodhisattvas" are revered above all others: Guanyin, or Avalokiteshvara, who, in one of his many forms, rides a lionlike animal; Manjushri, who rides a lion; and Samantabhadra, who rides a six-tusked white elephant. In some temples, these three have separate halls. In a few cases, they are worshiped along with the bodhisattva Kshitigarbha, or Dizang, who saves sentient beings from Hell.

As in the earlier temples, the large temples of the Song often featured a tall, centrally located building. In these temples, however, the focal point was no longer this building but the major hall housing statues of the Buddha. An example is the Longxing Temple in Zhengding County, Hebei Province. This temple contains standard features: a mountain gate, a Hall of Six Enlightenments, a Moni Hall, an altar for initiation into monkhood, a Hall of Skanda, a Hall of Amitabha, and several secondary buildings and courtyards on each side of the central axis. Toward the rear (the north end) of the temple stands the awe-inspiring Foxiang Pavilion. This three-storied tower holds a bronze Thousand-handed, Thousand-eyed Guanyin cast in 971 under the personal supervision of Emperor Taizu of the Northern Song. Since the mid-Tang, when construction of large Buddhist statues had become increasingly fashionable, multistoried buildings had frequently been built on the temple grounds to house them. Such structures gradually came to be built in the center of the complex. Meanwhile, the secondary temple buildings also grew higher. This increase in height was the major architectural innovation in Buddhist temples between the late Tang and the Northern Song.[19]

Like Buddhist temples, Daoist temples derived their main inspiration from imperial palaces, especially after the Song. A typical example is the Houtu (God of the Earth) Temple in Fenyin, Wanrong County, Shanxi Province. According to a plan carved on a stele to mark

4.24 Standing Thousand-handed, Thousand-eyed Guanyin, bronze, Dabei Pavilion, Longxing Temple, Zhengding County, Hebei Province. Northern Song dynasty, 971. 2,250 cm.

the completion of the temple in 1137, the major buildings of the temple are basically the same in scale and structure as those of the imperial palace in the Northern Song capital of Bianliang (present-day Kaifeng), in Henan Province (fig. 4.22).[20]

Another example is the Zhongyue Temple in Dengfeng County, Henan Province. According to a plan drawn in 1200, when the temple was rebuilt, the entire complex was modeled on traditional imperial palaces in China. Cut through the outer walls are, respectively, the Zhengyang Gate, the Donghua Gate, the Xihua Gate, and the rear gate, and a tower tops each of the four corners of the wall. To reach the inner city, a visitor would enter the Zhengyang Gate and pass along the central axis through three lower gates, three middle gates, and three upper gates. All the major buildings are within the inner city, and between the outer and inner walls are many courtyards, pools of water, monuments, and towers. The temple was overhauled during the Qing dynasty, but it retained eleven courtyards and more than four hundred rooms, making it the largest temple complex in Henan Province.

Built in the early years of the Northern Song dynasty, the Jinci Temple (see below) in Taiyuan, Shanxi Province, is unusual in that it combines garden scenery with temple buildings. In addition to the group of structures along the central axis centering on the Hall of the Sage Mother, many buildings on both sides were added by later generations. Consequently, the temple evolved to represent aspects of Buddhism, Daoism, and folk legends. Behind the halls, towers, and pavilions is a backdrop of green hills, and in front are limpid pools and streams. Such beautiful scenery was traditionally an important consideration for Daoists and Buddhist monks in the selection of sites for monasteries and temples.

Buddhist, Daoist, and Vernacular Sculpture in the Song Dynasty

During the Song dynasty several significant changes occurred in Chinese sculpture. Shifts in religious beliefs influenced almost every aspect of the way sculpture was conceived, used, and placed in the temples. Bodhisattvas gained unparalleled status in the religious beliefs of the Chinese; their importance is seen in the way the major bodhisattvas, Guanyin in particular, began to be set on their own, separate from the earlier groupings in which they had commonly been placed. Further, the Song marked the height of the sinification of Buddhism, which manifested itself in the greater realism of the sculpture, including a more feminine, gentle portrayal of Guanyin and a more lifelike rendering of arhats. The latest trend reflected both the successful spread of Chan Buddhism, with its emphasis on the role of individuals in achieving their own salvation, and the greater infusion of folk and secular concerns into religion,

which led to popular religious attitudes having a far less metaphysical approach.

Since the Tang dynasty, the worship of the bodhisattvas had gradually developed until individual bodhisattvas had become the focus for devotions alongside those directed toward the Buddha. In Sanskrit, *bodhi* means "enlightenment," and *sattva,* "living being" or "consciousness stream." In early Buddhism, as opposed to Mahayana Buddhism, the self-styled "Great Vehicle," *bodhisattva* refers to the historical Buddha — Shakyamuni in his previous existences. But in later Mahayana Buddhism the term refers to those who seek Buddhahood by systematically practicing the perfect virtues but renounce complete entry into Nirvana until all beings are saved. In Buddhist art, the bodhisattvas are usually Manjushri, Samantabhadra, Avalokiteshvara (Guanyin, whose image, with its "thousand" protective eyes and arms, was particularly popular), Mahasthamaprapta (Dashizhi in Chinese), Maitreya (believed to be currently in the Tushita Heaven, Maitreya will appear as an incarnated Buddha five thousand heavenly years after the Nirvana of Shakyamuni), and Kshitigarbha (Dizang). Many legends were created about the bodhisattvas, and four famous mountains are associated with them as sacred places. It is believed the bodhisattvas actually reside and manifest themselves in human form in these mountains, which became preaching centers after the Song. Most sacred is Mount Putuo in Zhejiang Province, which was associated with Guanyin (Avalokiteshvara) and boasted a magnificent complex of Buddhist temple buildings where grand religious activities were held regularly. Another is Mount Wutai, in northern Shanxi. In 980 Emperor Taizong of the Northern Song issued an imperial edict ordering Zhang Tingxun, a court official, to build a gilt-bronze statue of Manjushri to be enshrined at Mount Wutai in the Zhenrong Yuan (Temple of the True Face), which is now known as Pusa Ding (Bodhisattva Top). Mount Emei, another sacred site, is regarded as the center of preaching for Samantabhadra. A 62–metric ton bronze statue of Samantabhadra on a white elephant was placed in Wannian Temple there, also in 980 (fig. 4.23). The fourth sacred mountain, Mount Jiuhua in Qingyang County, Anhui Province, is associated with Dizang.

Of the four bodhisattvas associated with these sacred mountains, Guanyin was the most popular and influential. Originally also known in Chinese as Guanshiyin or Guanzizai, Guanyin had his name shortened in the early years of the Tang dynasty because it was forbidden for anyone to have a name that included a character used in the emperor's name (in this case, Emperor Taizong). The most important Buddhist classic that mentions Guanyin is the Lotus Sutra (Saddharmapundarika Sutra). Since Sui and Tang times, many texts of Esoteric Buddhism have appeared about Guanyin that have provided a basis for the images of Guanyin in Esoteric Buddhism.

Buddhist teachings claim that Guanyin is a bodhisattva of great compassion, with a boundless ability to help all sentient beings in times of danger and suffering and to grant such blessings as bestowing children on women. In the event of disaster or calamity, a person has only to chant his name and Guanyin will offer aid. Guanyin is believed to be able to appear in as many as thirty-three different forms, noble or humble, human or inhuman, and can protect sufferers from twelve major kinds of calamities. Throughout the ages, many books were written to preach his power, rooting the cult ever more deeply in Chinese society.

During the Tang and Song dynasties, Esoteric Buddhist sculptures of Guanyin became large in size, and generally sculptures of Guanyin became more feminine; in fact, Guanyin is often portrayed as a woman (for example, in the popular image of Guanyin gazing at the moon reflected in water). As the multihanded image of Guanyin became more prevalent, too, the pavilion that typically enshrined it became more central to temple architecture. The number of hands commonly ranged from four to eight, but sometimes there were forty-two, the number used to symbolize a thousand, each holding an eye in its palm (hence the name Thousand-handed and Thousand-eyed Guanyin). Guanyin can purportedly see every corner of the world with his thousand eyes, and with the thousand hands can extend help to all sufferers, wherever they may be. Though tradition has it that the Tang painter Yang Huizhi created the first thousand-handed, thousand-eyed image of Guanyin, it was not until the Song dynasty that it became widely popular.[21]

Such developments are evident in the major Song-dynasty statue of the Thousand-handed Guanyin in the Dabei (Great Compassion) Pavilion of Longxing Temple, Zhengding County, Hebei Province, cast in 971 (fig. 4.24). Erected on a lotus platform, the statue is 22 meters tall and was cast section by section from the bottom up. It has forty-two arms, which represent the thousand arms. The two main arms are brought together in front of the chest, while the rest extend from

4.25 Eleven-headed standing Guanyin, painted clay, Dule Temple, Tianjin, Jixian County, Hebei Province. Liao dynasty, 984. 1,600 cm.

4.26 Purple-Bamboo Guanyin, stone, Bilu Cave, Anyue grottoes, Sichuan Province. Song dynasty.

4.27 Water-Moon Guanyin, wood with paint. Northern Song dynasty. 241.3 × 165.1 cm. The Nelson-Atkins Museum of Art, Kansas City, Missouri.

4.28 Hanging sculpture of Guanyin, painted clay, Longxing Temple, Zhengding County, Hebei Province. Ming dynasty.

the back, twenty on each side, in all directions. These forty bronze arms were damaged in the eighteenth century; they were later replaced with wooden arms.

In the Dule Temple, Tianjin, the Guanyin Pavilion houses a 16-meter-high painted statue of a Guanyin with eleven heads, made in 984 (fig. 4.25). This statue of Guanyin wears as a crown nine faces in three tiers; the topmost part is adorned with a small head of Amitabha. According to the elaborate rules for depicting Buddhist figures, each of the faces shows Guanyin's response to the good or evil he sees; the various expressions include compassion, wrath, and pleasure.

In such large Guanyin statues of Esoteric Buddhism we can see the skill and craftsmanship of their makers in solving several key technical problems. One challenge

was designing the numerous arms in appropriate positions so that they would look natural, not awkward or misshapen. To tackle the problem the sculptors first took pains to proportion the two main arms to the body. They then arranged the dozens of other arms on the back and over the shoulders, making them fan out in all directions. In some statues the "thousand arms" are so meticulously designed and patterned that they form a halo around Guanyin's head.

Another technical obstacle was achieving a natural perspective for the viewer in the limited space of the building. Because the space in the front of the statue

4.29 Standing Guanyin, stone, Yanxia Cave, Hangzhou, Zhejiang Province. Early Northern Song dynasty.

was generally small and the statue huge, the view of the bodhisattva would appear distorted to the worshiper looking up at it. The designers solved the problem by building flights of steps that curled up around the statue, thus supplying several viewing spots at different heights. The objective was to have the statue generate a feeling of awe for viewers looking up from below and impress them with the deity's huge size in relation to the "universe" from their higher vantage point. In addition, the sculptors would tilt the statues forward slightly, with draperies flying behind, to generate a greater connection to and intimacy with the viewer.

As the image of Guanyin spread it became increasingly feminized, and many of the iconographic forms that were created for this new look reached their height in the Song. According to Buddhist scriptures, Guanyin can appear in various forms to help the distressed and deliver all living creatures from suffering. This characteristic freed artists to imagine Guanyin in many different settings and guises. The most popular images — some of which are not even based on Buddhist scriptures — depict Guanyin in the South Seas, as a white-robed master, as a "Water-Moon Guanyin," and with a willow wand. The Dazu and Anyue grottoes of Chongqing and Sichuan, for example, contain many types of beautifully designed and carved statues of Guanyin and other bodhisattvas in a feminine form. The Purple-Bamboo Guanyin in the Bilu Cave of the Anyue grottoes seems to resemble a noble lady tranquilly reclining against a background of bamboo (fig. 4.26). The deity's foot is placed on a lotus, and a vase rests close by. This image of Guanyin is almost certainly derived from the picture of the Water-Moon Guanyin created by the Tang painter Zhou Fang, but only in the Song did it become widespread among sculptured works (fig. 4.27).[22]

A similar feminized image of the bodhisattva can be seen in the hanging sculpture in the Moni Hall of Longxing Temple in Zhengding County, Hebei Province (fig. 4.28). Although a work of the Ming dynasty, this Guanyin image follows in the Song artistic tradition. The entire sculpture is attached to the fan-shaped wall behind the main pedestal, and the image of Guanyin is set against the background of Mount Putuo and surrounded by billowing waves. The image is graceful; Guanyin's head tilts slightly to one side, the right leg is bent and placed on the left knee, and his two arms rest naturally on his lap. In these statues the Song tendency toward realism is evident: both the hands and feet are smoothly sculpted, and the facial expressions are individualized (with Chinese, not Indian, features). These

works are fully sinicized and completely adapted to Chinese concerns and patterns. This image of Guanyin in the South Seas was often used to decorate the back walls of the main halls of Buddhist temples.

Most Guanyin statues follow more traditional models; they are either placed beside Amitabha together with Mahasthamaprapta or made into independent images for worship. Such traditional figures can be seen in almost every temple built in the Song dynasty, as well as in the Dazu and Anyue grottoes in Chongqing and Sichuan and the Yanxia Cave in Hangzhou (fig. 4.29). Iconographically, the sculptors primarily paid attention to depicting the crown and apparel rather than showing the lithe and graceful figure. In this way they sought to express the solemn and dignified air of a middle-aged woman. The face and dress again portray a realistic individual and, in so doing, lift Song sculpture to artistic greatness.

Arhat Statues

The arhat statues came into great favor in the Song dynasty. *Arhat,* a Sanskrit term meaning "enlightened or worthy ones," refers to persons who have attained the highest level of "no-more-learning" on the supramundane path. They possess the certainty that their defilements and passions have been extinguished and will not arise again in the future. Arhats are persons whose impurities have all been dissolved, whose wishes are fulfilled — who have laid down their burdens, attained their goals, and freed their minds through perfect understanding.

It is believed that before attaining his Nirvana, Shakyamuni selected Mahakashyapa and other disciples to stay in this world to preach Buddhist Law, initiate living beings into the Buddhist world, and extend blessings to the people. Buddhist classics give various figures for the number of people Shakyamuni asked to stay behind; in one work depicting Maitreya's arrival in this world, translated by the monk Dharmaraksha in the Jin dynasty (265–420), only four people are named, including Mahakashyapa. In another Mahayana classic, translated by the monk Daotai in the Northern Liang dynasty (421–460), the number is sixteen, which matches the number of arhats depicted in paintings and sculptures produced in later years. And starting in the late Tang and the Five Dynasties, the number increased — first to eighteen and finally to five hundred. No longer were only monks from India included; some famous Chinese monks and figures in Chinese folk legends were also among the chosen.

The Chinese names of the sixteen Indian arhats can be found in a Buddhist classic translated by the famous

Tang monk Xuanzang, who had lived in India for sixteen years to study Buddhist sutras. Their titles are found in the "Stone Inscription of Titles of Arhats in Qianming Temple, Jiangyin Military Command" erected by Gao Daosu, minister in charge of public works of the Southern Song dynasty, which is included in *Buddhist Sutras Collected and Added in the Great Ming (Daming xu zangjing)*. Even within the Buddhist canon, however, there are different lists of names. As a vehicle for artistic creation, particularly sculpture, the five hundred arhats remained popular after the Five Dynasties. In China, historical figures became arhats, as did many famous Chinese monks. And the arhats became yet another way in which Buddhism was sinicized. Many renowned Buddhist masters would have a troop of from five hundred to a thousand disciples, and the tradition that lists "five hundred arhats" is almost certainly an indirect reflection of this social phenomenon.[23]

Chinese Buddhist monks established and annotated a genealogy that would link their ancestors with patriarchs of Buddhism in ancient India. In the Song dynasty, for example, Qisong from the Yunmen (Cloud Gate) School wrote *The Genealogical System of Buddhism (Zheng zong ji)* and *A Table of Lineage of Buddhism (Dingzu pu)*, which together traced the lineage of twenty-eight patriarchs of Buddhism to Bodhidharma, a famous master who came to China from southern India during the Southern and Northern Dynasties. Although Bodhidharma is the twenty-eighth patriarch in the Indian lineage, he is regarded as the first patriarch of Chan Buddhism in China because he arrived there early, during the reign of Emperor Wu of the Liang (502–549).

The growing interest in arhats during the Tang and Song dynasties partly stemmed from the divisions within Buddhism and the development of various Buddhist schools. All these schools were eager to prove their orthodoxy by tracing their lineage to Shakyamuni. They expressed this heritage in their temples — and within these temples, arhats provided an iconographic bridge from Chinese folk patriarchs to the Indian founders of Buddhism. In the later Buddhist temples the Hall of Shakyamuni would be flanked on east and west by the Jialan (Sangharama) Hall and the Zushi (Founder) Hall (Bodhidharma Hall). In the Zushi Hall statues of the six patriarchs of Chan Buddhism, from Bodhidharma to Huineng, were enshrined. Their purpose was to establish a genealogical link with Mahakashyapa and Ananda, statues of whom appeared on both sides of Shakyamuni in the major hall. In addition, some of the Song rulers made specific use of arhat

images to enhance and legitimize their rule. Before Zhao Guangyi became Emperor Taizong (r. 976–997), he was given a painting of sixteen arhats by Qi Han, king of the Southern Tang. Sixteen days later he succeeded his older brother Zhao Kuangyin as emperor. Believing the arhats to have been an omen of his coronation, he named them the "auspicious arhats."[24]

The earliest known group sculpture of arhats is the collection of twenty-five relief images in the Eastern Hill Wanfo (Ten Thousand Buddha) Cave of the Longmen Grottoes in Luoyang. They were carved in the so-called Great Zhou dynasty (684–705), which was founded by Wu Zetian when she usurped power from the Li family during the Tang. Carved over three walls in the Kanjing (Sutra-Reading) Temple in the Eastern Hill are twenty-nine life-size, realistically presented arhats (see fig. 3.109).

The most outstanding example of Song-style arhats is in the Qianfo (Thousand-Buddha) Hall of Lingyan Temple in Changqing County, Shandong Province. Over a dais in the middle of Qianfo Hall, the most important structure of the temple, stand the statues of three Buddhas. The middle figure is Vairocana (the primordial Buddha, who creates and presides over all the other Buddhas), to its left is Bhaishajyaguru (Yaoshi in Chinese), and to its right, Shakyamuni. While the statue of Vairocana was a painted clay sculpture reinforced with ramie and rattan made during the Song, the statues of Bhaishajyaguru and Shakyamuni are works of the Ming dynasty cast in bronze. Set against the four walls as well as along the screen wall are several hundred Buddhist statues carved in wood and painted gold.

Running around the walls is an 80-centimeter-high platform on which the painted statues of forty arhats are placed. The statues are 145–165 centimeters high and lined up in a repeated pattern of seven sitting and five standing figures. The arrangement seems odd; and scholars further considered it unlikely that a thousand Buddha statues and forty arhats would have been created to share the same hall. The answer to the puzzle came in 1981, when restorers attempted to sort out and repair these arhats; it was found that they were not all made at the same time. Twenty-seven, of higher artistic quality, were sculpted around 1066 and originally belonged to a set of thirty-two arhats in Banzhou Hall, in the same temple. In 1328, during the Yuan dynasty, color was added to them. At some later point, Banzhou Hall collapsed, damaging some of the statues. Finally, in 1587, the remaining twenty-seven statues were moved to the renovated Qianfo Hall, and thirteen new arhats

4.30 Seated arhat, painted clay,
Lingyan Temple, Changqing
County, Shandong Province.
Song dynasty. Approx. 153 cm.

4.31 Seated arhat, painted clay,
Lingyan Temple. Approx. 151 cm.

4.32 Seated arhat, painted clay, Lingyan Temple. Approx. 155 cm.

sculpted to make a total of forty. The entire group was decorated for the last time in 1874. The current grouping of these statues, sculpted in different eras, in the same hall, thus provides the viewer with an ahistorical and somewhat random collection of some beautifully realistic statues (figs. 4.30–4.32).[25]

After its introduction to China by Bodhidharma, the Chan School increasingly flourished as it incorporated traditional Chinese philosophy. The Chan School advocated self-cultivation, working to realize one's own Buddha nature, and writings and rituals that were specific to its various subschools. By the time of Huineng (638–713), the sixth Chinese Chan patriarch, Chan had come to stress the idea that many of the common Mahayana ritualistic religious practices and the intellectual analysis of doctrine were not essential for attaining enlightenment. Instead it emphasized its own practices and discipline leading to intuitive awakening. The Chan masters also worked out various rules to restore monastic order. The *Rules for Life and Daily Routine of a Chan Monastery* (*Chanmen guishi,* renamed *Monastic Rules of Baizhang* [*Baizhang qinggui*]), written by a great Chan master of the Tang period while on Mount Baizhang, testifies to this successful effort. In accordance with these rules, long platforms were placed end to end in the halls of meditation, where the monks were commanded to sit in meditation (*dhyana:* sitting quietly free from worry and anxiety, concentrating on the teachings in the scriptures to attain enlightenment). The arhat statues in the Lingyan Temple represent monks meditating in accordance with these rules.

The arhats in Lingyan Temple are divided into two rows, to the east and west. The arhats at the head of each row sit in meditation. This practice demands that the observer sit in a particular posture, which is demonstrated by these two arhats: cross-legged, with back straight and upright. Other arhats also appear in the cross-legged posture, but their palms face each other. Possibly they are at the end of a lesson and are performing a finishing gesture, like the one frequently used at the end of Qigong exercises.

The arhats in the Lingyan Temple are mostly young

and middle-aged monks, some distinctly Chinese and others unmistakably Indian in attire and facial features. Some have the same facial expression; these probably came from the same mold or were copied from the same model. The arhats sculpted during the Song are artistically superior to the more formulaic Ming versions and show more individual traits. Perhaps the Song artisans drew on real models for inspiration. Generally, these Song arhats represent intelligent, competent, well-read monks of the time, appropriate to the monks of the Tang and Song dynasties, who were well versed in poetry, painting, astronomy, and mathematics.

The artists tried to capture the personality of each arhat through realistic renderings of facial expressions and hand and foot movements. Some of the arhats hold scarves and other objects in their hands; others appear to be doing needlework. Yet none of the figures seems overly concerned with such objects or pursuits; instead each seems to be musing on the world beyond. A few appear to be involved in heated debates; their robes are loosened as if they had become disheveled during intense discussions. This presentation of the inner world through physical features demonstrates the height of artistry of Song-dynasty sculpture.

Another group of arhat statues, created at about the same time and kept in Baosheng Temple in the town of Luzhi, Jiangsu Province, is presented in a completely different manner.[26] The eighteen statues were placed within a setting of seas and mountains that was cast on a gigantic sculpted wall (fig. 4.33). In 1927 a fire burned half the hall down, and only nine of the statues — along with fragments of the sculpted wall — survive. Renovation has restored the hall and the statues to close to their original appearance. *An Ode to the Arhats of the Baosheng Temple* (*Baosheng si luohan ge*), by Xi Shizhu of the Qing dynasty, describes the action shown in the mural and suggests some of the missing elements: "A monk sounds the clapper to arouse a dragon, while the other wields a Buddhist staff to harass a tiger. A monk captures a mountain demon single-handed, and a blue-headed arhat stares at cranes flying by overhead. A slender doe holds a flower in her mouth, and birds perch in their nests to watch, ignoring the wind. A goose listens attentively while the Buddha preaches, and a monkey turns its head in attention though the pine trees wave in disturbance."

4.33 Seated arhat, painted clay, Baosheng Temple, Luzhi, Suzhou County, Jiangsu Province. Song dynasty. Approx. 140 cm.

A description of a similar composition can be found in *An Ode to the Eighteen Great Arhats,* by Su Shi (1037–1101) of the Song dynasty, describing a sculptural work made by Zhang Xuan of the Former Shu kingdom. In the Song dynasty it was popular to present images of arhats against rocky mountains. In his *Picture of Sixteen Arhats,* Guanxiu (832–912) brought into prominence the rich imaginative possibilities in these painted figures. His arhats, perhaps monks of ancient India, are placed among rough rocks, their bodies almost grotesque and their facial expressions odd and contorted. The tormented expressions of pain, suffering, and death show Buddhist influence. A Song copy of the painting is now in the collection of the Japanese government.

Other tendencies in arhat sculpture are evident in the figures of the Baosheng Temple. Here the sculptures are clearly divided into two types: the Indian and the Chinese. In both image and attire the difference between them is obvious. The Indian arhats tend to have deep eyes, bushy eyebrows, high noses, and long beards, and their shoulders are covered by long robes with vertical folds, all characteristics of the sculptural tradition of ancient India, although occasionally one finds an Indian arhat wearing Han Chinese clothes. But the arhats in the Chinese style are invariably presented as learned monks through both their clothing and their individual expressions. Of the nine arhats that survived the fire, the most interesting to modern viewers are the Indian-style figure known as Nagasena and the Chinese-style figure known as Bodhidharma, presented as an old man deep in meditation. Sitting upright amid high mountains, the two enlightened beings project a sense of strong will and supernatural power.

Another important example of arhat sculpture is the group of the three great masters and eighteen arhats in the Dashi Hall in the rear courtyard of Chongqing Temple, Zhangzi County, Shanxi Province (figs. 4.34–4.36). These richly decorative figures all have exaggerated, animated expressions. Created during the reign of Emperor Shenzong (r. 1068–1085) of the Song dynasty, the best figures in this group are as good as those in the Lingyan Temple, where renovation workers found a cast-iron arhat in the belly of one of the statues. Somewhat similar in style are twenty-four painted arhat statues in Zizhu (Purple Bamboo) Nunnery, Dongshan Hill, Jiangsu Province. Of these, sixteen are believed to have been sculpted by the Southern Song folk sculptors Lei Chao and his wife. The remaining eight, including the statues of the monk Budai (Hempen Sack) and Guan Yu, are works by Qiu Mituo, a sculptor in the late Ming.

4.34 Seated arhat, painted clay, Chongqing Temple, Zhangzi County, Shanxi Province. Northern Song dynasty. Approx. 157 cm.

4.35 Seated arhat, painted clay, Chongqing Temple. Approx. 140 cm.

4.36 Seated arhat, painted clay, Chongqing Temple. Approx. 157 cm.

4.37 Seated arhat, earthenware with tricolor glaze, Yixian County, Hebei Province. Liao dynasty. 101.6 × 78.7 × 66 cm. The Nelson-Atkins Museum of Art, Kansas City, Missouri.

4.38 Seated arhat, wood, unearthed in 1963 from Nanhua Temple, Qujiang County, Guangdong Province. Northern Song dynasty, 1048. Approx. 54.5 cm. Palace Museum, Beijing.

Though many are vividly rendered, these arhat statues are somewhat inferior artistically to the Song statues.[27]

Arhat statues from this time were made from such materials as wood, bronze, iron, stone, pottery, and dried lacquer with ramie. Among them are the tricolor clay arhats of Bafowa in Yixian County, Hebei Province, which are now in private collections or held by museums in the United States, Great Britain, Canada, Japan, and Germany. Of particular artistic merit is an arhat of an old man in the collection of New York's Metropolitan Museum of Art and the statues of young arhats held there and in the collections of the University of Pennsylvania Museum and the Nelson-Atkins Museum of Art, Kansas City (fig. 4.37). All these statues succeed in manifesting the "supernatural bearing" of enlightened arhats. And thanks to the material from which they are made, the works have not needed much repair or renovation by later generations, and so are especially suggestive of the high artistic level in sculpting human figures achieved at this time.[28]

From the Five Dynasties to the Song, many groups of five hundred arhats were created. In the Greater Xiangguo Temple, the most important Buddhist sanctuary in the Northern Song capital of Bianliang, two groups of five hundred arhat sculptures can be found, in the Zisheng Tower and in the Mountain Gate Tower. One group was cast from iron (some say copper) in the Southern Tang period (937–975). Originally part of the Donglin Temple on Mount Lu, they were shipped to the Greater Xiangguo Temple by Cao Han, a court official in the early days of the Northern Song. The other group was cast from copper and moved to the temple from Yingchuan Prefecture in Henan in 1001. In 984 Emperor Taizong — the emperor who thought the number sixteen was a special omen — issued an imperial edict to cast 516 arhat statues for the Shouchang Temple in the Tiantai Mountains. During the reign of Emperor Zhenzong (r. 998–1022), Madame Yan, known as the "ingenious lady" for her superb skills in sculpture, sponsored and financed the sculpting of five hundred openwork arhat statues of sandalwood in Kanmen, Mount Ruilian. Five hundred arhat statues were made for Baiyun Temple, Huixian County, in Henan Province, in 1008; and in 1022 five hundred ramie-reinforced lacquer arhats were made for the eastern yard of the Greater Kaibao Temple in Bianliang. Toward the end of the Northern Song dynasty, such statue groups were constructed in Puzao Monastery, Xingtang County, Hebei, and Xiangcheng Palace, Langzhong, Sichuan. During the Southern Song years,

groups of five hundred arhats were constructed for both the Yunlin Temple and Jingci Temple in the capital city of Lin'an (present-day Hangzhou).

The earliest extant example of a group of five hundred arhats carved from wood was created between 1045 and 1048 during the reign of Emperor Renzong of the Song dynasty, and it is now kept in the Nanhua Temple, Qujiang County, Guangdong Province. Of the 360 statues that have been satisfactorily preserved, 159 have inscriptions on their bases. All are in a seated position, and each is carved from a single piece of wood. Though small in size, and although the craftsmanship varies, they make an impressive collection (fig. 4.38).

Statues of Historic Figures

From the Tang dynasty on, Buddhist temple sculpture has included images of eminent and learned monks who were themselves deified and worshiped as arhats and Buddhas. These figures — people of considerable historic significance — were usually portrayed not only as traditional Buddhist deities but as individuals in whose images sculptors sought to represent well-known features or character traits. This trend, peculiar to Chinese Buddhist sculpture, had considerable effect on the spread of Buddhism in China.

One of the first monks to be so deified was Huineng, the sixth patriarch of Chan Buddhism, who in 678 became abbot of the Nanhua Temple, birthplace and center of southern Chan Buddhism. When he died in 714, in Guo'en Temple in Xinzhou (now Xinxin), Guangdong Province, his disciples retrieved his remains and processed them with lacquered ramie to create a "true-body" statue for worship in the temple.

But in addition to this unique relic, many other images of Huineng began appearing throughout China, including a life-size cast-bronze statue in the Liuzu (Sixth) Patriarch Hall of Liurong Temple in Guangzhou. Built in 989, the statue portrays a thin monk with fine, delicate features sitting in deep meditation. Attired in beautiful clothes, he radiates a noble, dignified, and learned manner, very different from the earlier taut, unrestrained images of Huineng as a religious leader of boundless power and wisdom in such paintings as *The Sixth Patriarch Tearing Up the Scriptures* (*Liuzu sijing*) and *The Sixth Patriarch Cutting Bamboo Stems* (*Liuzu fazhu*) by Liang Kai (active thirteenth century).

Another learned monk who became the subject of religious sculpture after his deification was Sengqie, the Great Sage (or, in folk culture, Cultured Buddha) of Sizhou, who was born in a small state in central Asia.

4.39 The Great Sage of Sizhou (Sengqie), stone, Fowan Cave 177, North Hill, Dazu grottoes, Dazu County, Chongqing. Northern Song dynasty. 101 cm.

In the early years of the Tang dynasty Sengqie came to the town of Linhuai, in Jiangsu Province, where he built Puguangwang Temple. Held in high regard during his lifetime by Emperor Zhongzong, following his death in 710 Sengqie was proclaimed an incarnation of Guanyin, and worshipers called upon him to help prevent disasters. The worship of Sengqie flourished from the late Tang to the Northern Song, and statues and paintings of him appeared throughout the country — for example, the figures in the Dunhuang grottoes in Gansu, the Qianfo (Thousand-Buddha) Cliff grottoes, and the Dazu grottoes in Chongqing. Many Buddhist temples, such as the Greater Xiangguo Temple in Bianliang, contained separate courtyards dedicated to Sengqie's worship. The cult of Sengqie was particularly popular in areas along the Yangzi and Huai Rivers and the coast, where he was seen as the god of water.

Statues of Sengqie tend to be either enshrined alone or set together with images of the monks Baozhi and Fanghui. The standard image of Sengqie presents a monk sitting cross-legged with his eyes slightly closed, deep in meditation. He wears a monk's cap whose bands fall down over each shoulder. In Fowan Cave 177, North Hill, Dazu grottoes, Sengqie appears as the Great Sage of Sizhou, presented as an eminent middle-aged monk sitting behind a low table (fig. 4.39).[29]

Another popular figure in sculpture of the Song and later is the monk Qici, or Budai (Hempen Sack), of the Later Liang (tenth century), who, as we have seen, would typically be enshrined in the Hall of the Heavenly Kings as an incarnation of Maitreya. Often presented as a big-bellied laughing Buddha, Budai represented a reincarnation of Maitreya as a Chinese, not an Indian. The best work of Budai as the big-bellied Maitreya is the stone statue on Feilaifeng (Flying-in Peak) in Hangzhou that was carved in the Southern Song. Surrounded by a group of arhats, Budai-Maitreya here wears a broad smile as he sits with his fat belly exposed and a hand on his hempen beggar's sack (figs. 4.40, 4.41). The worship of both Sengqie and Budai evolved from the popular worship of Guanyin (Avalokiteshvara) and Maitreya.

Another example of a statue that presents the traits of a unique individual is the image of the Chan monk Daoji (1148–1209), from the Southern Song. Daoji was ordained in Lingyin Temple in Hangzhou and later moved to Jingci Temple, also in Hangzhou, where at one time there was a Hall of Master Ji to enshrine his statue. Folk legends have it that Daoji did not abide by the Buddhist commandments: he was fond of liquor and meat and behaved in a peculiar manner, for which

he was known among the people as "Mad Monk Ji" or "Living Buddha Master Ji." He usually appears as one of a group of five hundred arhats; presented as a sage monk with boundless supernatural power, he can be identified by his worn-out beggar's cap and shoes and his unruly behavior — an image derived from a popular book, *The Life of Master Ji*. In the group of five hundred arhats in Beijing's Biyun Temple, Ji appears squatting on a beam of the hall, as if he had arrived too late and found no other place.

As we can see by this example, Buddhist iconography was becoming more and more concerned with everyday life, moving away from earlier Indian influences, which were more involved with doctrine. The down-to-earth style seen in the Daoji image also reflected the growing importance of folk traditions for the Buddhist religion and the continued effort to popularize and humanize Buddhist figures and doctrines. Both Qici and Daoji were deified in part because of their unusual behavior — a phenomenon that was also evident in the sculpture of Daoist deities.

Daoist Sculpture: Heavenly Worthies and Laozi

As we saw earlier, Daoism's origins, philosophical import, interaction with folk religions and Buddhism, and lack of systematic doctrine all made it an extraordinarily complex and influential religious and artistic force. Its elaborate and sometimes confusing pantheon of gods and spirits provided many intriguing personalities who were immortalized in sculpture.

By the end of the Northern Song dynasty, the Daoist pantheon had pretty much been established, and certain standard images had emerged. The most important works from these years, and the most illustrative of this standardization, are statues of the Heavenly Worthies (Tianzun) and images of the Daoist founder, Laozi, along with several secular gods. In religious Daoism, "Heavenly Worthies" is the title accorded to the highest deities who inhabit the three highest heavens, that is, the Four Heavenly Emperors and the Three Pure Ones (Sanqing). A typical image of a Heavenly Worthy is the white marble statue described earlier that was sculpted in 719. A seated figure in a loose ceremonial robe with hair piled high in the shape of a lotus holding a fan and duster, the statue was created in the image of an ancient high-ranking official, clearly showing the influence of Buddhist sculpture (fig. 4.42).

The Four Heavenly Emperors are understood in various ways. As Chinese emperors chose one or another deity for special worship the identification and impor-

4.40 Maitreya Buddha (Budai), stone, Feilaifeng, Hangzhou, Zhejiang Province. Southern Song dynasty.

4.41 Arhats grouped with Maitreya Buddha, stone, Feilaifeng.

tance of the Four Heavenly Emperors changed, and their worship also changed along with their status. According to one version, the Four Emperors referred to are Emperor Yuhuang (the Jade Emperor), Emperor Ziwei of the North Pole, the Emperor of the Upper Gouchen Palace, and Emperor Huo of the Earth (whose original male image was later replaced by a female). According to another version, they are the heavenly emperors of the four poles, namely, Emperor Ziwei, Emperor Changsheng of the South Pole, Emperor Taiji of the West Pole, and Emperor Qinghua of the East Pole. Yet another version includes Emperor Tianqi of Mount Tai.

The transformation of Emperor Tianqi into one of the Four Heavenly Emperors suggests how various folk gods and beliefs were brought into the Daoist pantheon.

His ascension was directly linked to the deification of Mount Tai, located in Shandong Province and known as the Sacred Mountain in the East. Because Mount Tai was where emperors offered sacrifices to Heaven, it was deemed the most sacred of mountains, and its deity was proclaimed Emperor Tianqi (literally "as holy as Heaven") by Emperor Xuanzong of the Tang. During the Song and Yuan dynasties, Emperor Tianqi was given the title emperor and identified as the deity who regulates human affairs and determines the time of a person's birth and death. Temples were built throughout the country to worship him.

Like Tianqi, the Jade Emperor, the ruler of all heavenly and earthly affairs, was particularly revered in the Song. During the Southern Song, a grotto was built in Dazu to enshrine images of him and Tianqi, and he was proclaimed a Daoist deity during the reigns of Emperor Zhenzong and Emperor Huizong (1101–1125).

Yuhuang Temple, in Jincheng, Shanxi Province, was built in 1076. In the inner room of its major hall, the Hall of the Jade Emperor, sits a sculpted statue of the emperor holding a jade staff and attired in ceremonial robes. Lined up on the pedestals on both sides are sixty-two sculpted statues of ladies-in-waiting, boy servants, civilian officials, and military officers. Some of these figures were moved to the hall from temples that had been destroyed during a mutiny in the Jin period. Fortunately, their Song elegance has not been completely lost. Though the line-up is a bit confused, the intention of the artists is clear: to display the order of governance in Heaven through a realistic presentation of monarch-subject relations on earth.

The concept of the Three Pure Ones first appeared in the Southern and Northern Dynasties, and by Tang and Song times it had become very popular. After the establishment of the Song dynasty, the statues of the Three Pure Ones were usually worshiped together; Laozi was less frequently enshrined and tended to be worshiped separately. In these groupings Yuanshi Tianzun, the Primordial Heavenly Worthy, would take the central position, with Lingbao Tianzun (the Heavenly Worthy of the Sacred Jewel) on the left and Daode Tianzun (the Heavenly Worthy of the Way; Laozi) on the right. The images of Yuanshi Tianzun and Lingbao Tianzun, both derived from the figure used for Laozi, tend to be rather stylized. Yet they can leave an impression of boundless religious power in the hearts of Daoist followers when placed among the many Daoist divinities, beginning with the Four Heavenly Emperors in their ceremonial robes and including lesser deities

4.42 Heavenly Worthy, stone. Tang dynasty, 719. 305 cm. Shanxi Provincial Institute of Archaeology, Taiyuan.

arranged and attired in accordance with their hierarchical position, which was conceived of as matching the system of government in feudal China.

A relatively typical group of sculpted images of the Three Pure Ones is found in the Sanqing Grotto on the Southern Hill in Dazu, carved in the Southern Song between 1131 and 1140. Perhaps the most famous representations of the era, however, are the figures in Sanqing Hall in Xuanmiao Temple, Suzhou, although an attempted renovation has destroyed their original appearance.

The earliest Song sculpted image of Laozi appears on the Laojun Cliff in Sichuan Province. This figure, shown riding on the back of a black ox, is derived from legends describing how Laozi rode a black ox to Hangu

Pass, where he wrote the *Daodejing*, gave it to the general guarding the pass, and then continued on his way. Another Laozi shrine in Sichuan Province is on Mount Shizhuan. But the most important statue of Laozi is on Mount Qingyuan, Quanzhou, Fujian Province. Historical records say that in the Song dynasty a great Daoist complex, including a Beidou (Big Dipper) Hall and a Zhenjun (True Master) Hall, was built there. Today only a huge granite statue of Laozi (5-plus meters high, 7 meters wide, and 7 meters deep) survives. The detailed eyebrows, facial features, and beard give him the appearance of a wise, learned immortal (fig. 4.43).

Local and Folk Deities

In addition to the large array of Buddhist, Daoist, and Confucianist deities, there existed in Chinese society a wide-ranging and complex system of local and folk gods, and by the Song dynasty the worship of these gods had developed to an unprecedented degree. The origins of these gods can be traced back to much earlier religious beliefs in China. In pre-Qin times, worship of Heaven and ancestors brought about a combination of theocracy and imperial power. The emperors controlled the interaction between the world of human beings and the world of gods, and the gods themselves held different ranks according to the hierarchical system of human society. In the Zhou dynasty, for example, the sons of Heaven (sovereigns and emperors) presided over the sacrifices — to Heaven, earth, the gods of the four directions, the gods of mountains, and the gods of the family, the hearth, the door, and so forth.[30] Since the time of Emperor Wu of the Western Han, the content of traditional religion had tended to blend with the teachings of Confucianism. This eventually brought about an immense yet well-ordered official system of deities; deities not included in the government pantheon were considered false, and offerings to them were strictly prohibited.

As time went by the distinction between government rituals and folk beliefs became increasingly blurred. Some newly emerging folk gods and deified historical figures were either incorporated into the government-approved pantheon or turned into Buddhist, Daoist, and Confucian divinities. The others, the majority of the folk gods, were left to disappear on their own. Artistically, most of the government-designated gods are depicted wearing the ceremonial clothes of emperors or officials of various ranks; some are even accompanied by family members and attendants. By contrast, the folk gods are more freely depicted: some appear as ordinary people and wear commoners' clothes, and others appear in peculiar forms with both human and animal features.

Even those gods designated by the imperial government for worship were subject to changes in their positions, titles, and artistic representations. Throughout the various dynasties, rulers repeatedly issued orders to change and standardize the idols and rituals of worship, and debate broke out among the ruling classes about the titles and levels of the gods and the sacrifices that should be offered to them. Continual adjustments were made. Eventually, certain folk gods were granted the titles of emperor, prince, and duke. The Heavenly Emperor in folk legend, for instance, evolved into the Emperor of Boundless Heaven (Haotian Shangdi), who was incorporated into Confucianism; the ceremony to offer sacrifices to him became an important state ritual presided over by the emperor (who worshiped his own ancestors at the same time) and held atop either Mount Tai or Mount Song (the Sacred Mountain in the Middle, whose god was Emperor Tianzhong), thus incorporating Daoist beliefs as well.[31]

Sacrificial rituals to the god of land and grain were considered second in importance only to those to Heaven, Earth, and ancestors. Because the rituals were "for the good of all people," they were naturally officiated over by the emperor. For the performance of the rituals, only an altar to the god of land and grain was needed, and it was built with earth of five colors, representing the five elements — water, fire, earth, wood, and metal — that according to the ancient philosophers composed everything in the universe.[32] The Altar to the God of Land and Grain in Sun Zhongshan (Sun Yatsen) Park, Beijing, built in the Ming dynasty, was originally the place where emperors of the Ming and Qing dynasties offered sacrifices to the god and prayed for a good harvest. A stone pillar was erected at the heart of the altar to symbolize the god, though it has long since disappeared.

The Hall of the Sage Mother in Jinci Temple, Taiyuan, Shanxi Province, is a particularly well preserved example of well-funded art dedicated to exalted local deities — the preeminent extant palatial architecture of the Song dynasty.[33] It was dedicated to Yi Jiang, mother of Tang Shuyu, second son of King Wu of the Western Zhou dynasty (ca. 1046–771 B.C.E.). During Northern Song times, Yi Jiang was believed to be the Water Goddess of Shanxi and thus became one of the major idols for worship among numerous such gods housed in the Jinci Temple. The hall is 19 meters high, with a width of seven bays, a depth of six bays, and a double-eaved,

4.43 Laozi, granite, Mount Qingyuan, Quanzhou, Fujian Province. Song dynasty. 550 cm.

nine-ridge hipped roof. In front of the hall, pillars beneath the eaves support three-rafter beams, creating a wide verandah with extra open space for sacrifices to the Sage Mother. No pillars are used inside, leaving more space for the statues.

In the center of the hall is a brick pedestal on which the statue of the Sage Mother, the dominant figure, is placed together with six statues of ladies-in-waiting and female officials, which fan out in both directions and form the central group. The rest — thirty-six life-size statues of attendants, divided into three groups — stand along the walls on both sides.[34] Yi Jiang, the Sage Mother, is dressed in the ceremonial roles of an empress, appearing elegant and stately against a large screen painted in cloud-water patterns (figs. 4.44–4.45). Her seated posture, clothing, and ornaments clearly show the influence of Buddhist sculpture.

The central group — Yi Jiang on her throne with the screen at the back and her personal ladies-in-waiting around her — forms a sharp contrast to the other servants placed against the walls on both sides. In fact, the most skillfully executed work in the hall is not the statue of Yi Jiang but the figures of the servants, mostly ladies-in-waiting with an occasional eunuch or female official dressed in men's clothing (figs. 4.46–4.49). In these richly realistic, individualized painted sculptures, undoubtedly drawn from everyday life in the imperial palaces, we can see how Song sculptors successfully widened the conventions of religious sculpture. The personalities and feelings of different individuals appear through finely crafted details of clothing, facial features, movement, and expression. Although these statues, sculpted around 1087, were repaired and redecorated in a later generation, they retain their original Song look and charm.

The servants are divided into three age-groups —

young, middle-aged, and old. The young women all have an innocent appearance. Yet differences in personality have not been overlooked: some are radiant, others tranquil and confident, still others anxious or deep in thought. The middle-aged women are also portrayed in different ways: some are steady and confident, others self-restrained. The old are generally depicted as shrewd and conceited.

The painting of these sculptures has been used to particular effect. The techniques of painting sculpture in the round and those of highlighting relief sculpture have been combined to create the beautiful yet simple lines of the clothes. The paintwork not only accentuates the quality of the materials but gives movement and therefore life to the images.

In addition to the sculptured works in the Hall of the Sage Mother, Jinci Temple contains many smaller statues honoring a wide range of town and village gods. These local deities are somewhat comparable to the local magistrates, who were given the authority to keep order in their respective precincts. The origin of the town god goes back to pre-Qin times. The earliest temple dedicated to a town god was built in the Wuhu area, Anhui Province, in 239, during the Three Kingdoms period. In the Tang and Five Dynasties periods, the town god was granted official titles, and by the Song, the ceremony to offer sacrifices to the town god was listed as a function of the state. Now officials from the ancient past who were known for their good deeds were worshiped as town gods. Temples to such gods were built throughout the country. In line with the official hierarchy of the state, Emperor Taizu of the Ming dynasty further classified the gods of the national capital, the various prefectures, and the counties into four ranks and conferred appropriate titles on them.

Town gods are also regarded as deities in both Confucianism and Daoism. In temples built in the Ming and Qing dynasties, town gods are usually dressed in the manner of high-ranking officials and flanked by ox- and horse-headed demons as well as by White Wuchang and Black Wuchang, demons charged by the King of Hell with catching the souls of wrongdoers. Thus the temples to town gods usually also contain a statue of the King of Hell or, in a later adoption, King of Ten Hells.

The King of Hell, whose identity and worship draws on both Buddhist and Daoist traditions, looks after affairs in the netherworld. Originally called Yama, a figure in ancient Indian mythology, the king was later adopted into the Buddhist pantheon and renamed the King of Hell. In the Daoist belief derived from Chinese

folklore, the King of Hell became Emperor Tianqi, the god of Mount Tai, and later evolved into the King of Ten Hells (nine subsidiary kings preside over the other hells). According to Daoist belief, the main hell is located in Fengdu, Sichuan. There punishments are meted out for evil deeds performed in life, after which the evil souls are sent to various other hells to be tortured for their misdeeds.

Throughout Shanxi and elsewhere, temples built during the Ming dynasty enshrine statues of the King of Ten Hells and of judges in the netherworld who keep track of the merits and wrongdoings of the living.[35] These images all employ realism to emphasize the ghastliness of the punishments that await the wrongdoers in Hell (fig. 4.50). Originally some sort of mechanical device was even installed to move the figures within the various scenes in Hell.

As we have seen, a salient feature of Chinese belief is the way the line is blurred between human beings and gods. Many Chinese historical figures underwent various stages of posthumous deification. In commemoration of Sun Simiao, a renowned physician in the Tang dynasty, for example, later generations built a Temple of the King of Medicine in his native land, Yaoxian County in Shaanxi Province, and named the mountain on which he had often trekked to gather his medicinal herbs the Mountain of the King of Medicine.[36]

Among deities of this kind, Guan Yu holds the most prominent position. Guan Yu was a brilliant general in the kingdom of Shu during the Three Kingdoms period. In the late years of the Eastern Han, Liu Bei, king of Shu, launched an uprising under the pretext of safeguarding the rule of the Eastern Han court. Guan Yu, who took part in this rebellion, became Liu Bei's sworn brother. In 200, Liu Bei was defeated by Cao Cao, head of the kingdom of Wei, and Guan Yu was captured. Cao Cao treated his captive with great honor, awarding him the title marquis of Hanshouting. For several years Guan Yu served under him, but then, discovering the whereabouts of Liu Bei, he left Cao Cao to reunite with his "brother." Together Liu Bei and Guan Yu captured Western Shu (now Sichuan Province), and Liu Bei left Guan Yu to garrison Jingzhou in Hubei Province. Guan Yu won a series of military victories against the troops of the kingdom of Wei but finally suffered a fatal defeat during a sneak raid by troops under Sun Quan, the king of Wu, in which Guan Yu and his son were captured and executed.

Since the late Tang, stories about the Three Kingdoms have circulated widely among the populace through poetic drama and storytelling. In Song and Yuan times, plays set during the Three Kingdoms era were mainstays of the stage repertoire. With the appearance of *A Complete Collection of Stories of Three Kingdoms* (*Quanxiang Sanguozhi pinghua*) in the Yuan dynasty and *The Romance of the Three Kingdoms* (*Sanguozhi yanyi*), by Luo Guanzhong, in the Ming, the popularity of the era spread across China. Guan Yu became a symbol of both loyalty and virtue, and numerous temples were built in his honor. The most important are the temples in his birthplace, Xiexian County, Shanxi Province; Luoyang in Henan Province and Dangyang in Hubei Province, where his head and body are buried, respectively; and Chengdu, the old capital of the kingdom of Shu. As part of the widespread worship of Guan Yu, rulers of various later dynasties showered him with a number of elevated titles, worshiping him as a guardian of their rule. In Beijing alone, seven shrines for Guan Yu were built during the Qing dynasty in the fortifications of the city's nine gates.

In addition to the folk religions, Daoism, Buddhism and Confucianism incorporated Guan Yu into their pantheons of deities. Daoists revered him as the Sage of Martial Valor and Emperor Guan the Sage, while Buddhists ranked him as one of the Sangharama gods. In Shanxi, many Buddhist temples include a Sangharama Hall dedicated to Guan Yu (fig. 4.51). In western Liaoning, the hall dedicated to Guan Yu is the major structure of the temple, while secondary halls are used for worshiping the bodhisattvas, the king of medicine, the god of fire, and so on. Placing the traditional Confucian ethics of loyalty, filial piety, moral integrity, and righteousness at the core of such reverence — and making Buddhism an important but secondary aspect of the worship — reflects how far the syncretism of the three beliefs had come.

Guan Yu is usually depicted as a military general or king with a red face and a long, well-trimmed beard. (In traditional Chinese opera, red symbolizes great loyalty.) A popular setting for the sculpted image of Guan Yu shows him reading the Confucian classic *Spring and Autumn Annals* by candlelight together with his beloved son Guan Ping and favored lieutenant Zhou Cang. However, in the Ming-dynasty statue of Guan Yu from the Temple of Emperor Guan in Taiyuan (now in the Palace Museum, Beijing), Guan Yu appears as a middle-aged general in a black turban, with a golden face. He is fully armored and wears a green robe. The valiant military general has thus been transformed into a Confucian scholar, indicating the respect he evoked in later

generations and received in different modes of worship (fig. 4.52).

Another type of folk god is a provider of good fortune and blessings, such as a god of wealth or a goddess who delivers sons to sonless couples. The image of the god of wealth can be traced to Zhao Gongming, a character in the classical Ming novel *Canonization of the Gods* (*Fengshen yanyi*). The god of wealth has both a military and a civilian aspect: the god of military wealth refers to Zhao Gongming, whereas the civilian god of wealth is Fan Li, an able official under the king of Yue in the Eastern Zhou dynasty (770–256 B.C.E.) who was purportedly a wizard at financial affairs. Different stories were handed down over the centuries concerning the deity who delivers sons to sonless couples; in some, the god is male and is called Zhang Xian.

These various types of local, regional, and folk gods tend to retain their human auras. For instance, in some temples statues of father and son deities are put side by side for worship, such as Guan Yu and his son Guan Ping or Emperor Tianqi and his third son, Lord Bingling, the god of fire.[37] In other temples, mother and son are honored together, as in Jinci Temple. Its major hall was originally intended for the worship of Tang Shuyu, second son of King Wu of the Western Zhou dynasty. But as we have seen, it was later dedicated to the worship of his mother, Yi Jiang, the Sage Mother, while a secondary hall was built for him.[38] Similarly, behind the main hall dedicated to Laozi in Taiqing Palace in Luyi, Henan Province — believed to be the hometown of Laozi — was another hall in which his mother was worshiped.[39] These familial worships attest to the influence of folk belief on Daoism.

In some cases, husband and wife gods are housed and worshiped in the same temple. When Wu Zetian conferred the title King of Zhongtian (Central Heaven) on the god of Mount Song in 688, she also assigned him a wife, Lady Tianling. Later the two were promoted to the rank of emperor and empress. The kitchen god, too, known as the "head of the house," is often honored in household shrines with his wife, the goddess of the kitchen.

Not all of these gods are lofty or omnipotent. The village gods who took the form of old men were frequently objects of ridicule. And though the gods could offer protection to humans, they were also answerable to humans and might need to call on human help. It was humans who set the birthdays for the gods (including Daoist and Confucian gods), and different groups awarded different birthdays to the same god. When a

4.44 Group of ladies-in-waiting, painted clay, Hall of the Sage Mother, Jinci Temple, Taiyuan, Shanxi Province. Northern Song dynasty, ca. 1087. 161–174 cm.

4.45 Sage Mother, painted clay, Hall of the Sage Mother, Jinci Temple. 228 cm.

4.46 Standing lady-in-waiting, painted clay, Hall of the Sage Mother, Jinci Temple. 158 cm.

4.47 Standing lady-in-waiting, painted clay, Hall of the Sage Mother, Jinci Temple. 164 cm.

god did something wrong, he or she was subject to punishment. The world of immortals also had its dark side. In novels, folktales, and stage performances, town gods and judges of the netherworld often appeared imprisoned or were relieved of their posts for accepting bribes or bending laws. Though ranked as an emperor, Guan Yu was held accountable for local security and natural disasters. If a drought hit, for example, and prayers for rain proved ineffective, Guan Yu's disciples would take his wooden statues from the temple halls and place them in the scorching sun so that the god could personally experience the damage caused by the disaster.

These diverse qualities in the gods influenced the identity and appearance of sculpture in local temples. The folk world of gods and spirits is particularly important to the understanding of the profound undercurrent of vernacular belief that shaped Daoist, Buddhist, and Confucian imagery. After the Song, when Bud-

dhism had become fully sinicized and the interchange among the great belief systems increased, these systems were shaped by, and in turn influenced, popular religious beliefs and thus the portrayal, in thought and in sculpture, of the many Chinese folk gods.

Esoteric and Western Xia Images of the Yuan Dynasty

Tibetan Buddhism exerted a profound influence on religious art during and after the Yuan dynasty.[40] The monastically organized forms of Tibetan Buddhism (most notably, the Gelug lineage) place Esoteric Buddhist practices at the pinnacle of an ideology supported by a broad base of cultic Mahayana practices, by a philosophy based on the *Perfection of Wisdom* texts, and by a monastic life based on the *vinaya* traditions. Several

4.48 Standing lady-in-waiting, painted clay, Hall of the Sage Mother, Jinci Temple. 165 cm.

4.49 Standing lady-in-waiting (detail), painted clay, Hall of the Sage Mother, Jinci Temple. 165 cm.

important lineages developed, such as the Nyingma, Sakya, Kagyu, and Gelug, each with its own emphases, subschools, and lineages of teachers, but all integrating Esoteric Buddhist practices to one degree or another. Esoteric Buddhism, also known as the True Word, or Vajrayana, School of Buddhism, originated in India and shares features with Mahayana Buddhism, Brahmanism, Hinduism, and Indian folk beliefs. Soon after its emergence around the seventh century, it was transmitted to China; it also spread to Tibet, Gansu, Qinghai, Sichuan, Inner Mongolia, Yunnan, and other areas.

The early Esoteric Buddhists who reached China during the Tang dynasty revered Vairocana Buddha as Dharmakaya (Body of Truth, also translated One Undivided Truth) and believed that Vairocana Buddha passed on his secret teachings to his successors, first Vajrasattva and then Nagarjuna, Nagabodhi, Vajrabodhi, and Subhakarasimha. Subhakarasimha, Vajrabodhi, and

Amoghavajra brought Esoterism from India to China during the Kaiyuan reign (713–741) of the Tang dynasty and founded the School of Esoteric Buddhism in China, but it did not spread widely. The later teachings of Esoteric Buddhism in India were again brought to China during the Song. Although in China these Esoteric Buddhist teachings did not take much hold as a distinct school, they had a big impact on popular Buddhism. Esoteric Buddhism did, however, find fertile ground in the region of Tibet.

During the seventh century, the tribes on the Qinghai-Tibet Plateau were unified under Songtsen Gampo, the Tufan (Tibetan) king, who sent emissaries to foreign lands. The Tufan kings and armies encountered Buddhism as they made military conquests in the Nepalese and Indian territories, in the border lands of Kashmir, in central Asia, and also in western China. They brought back with them to Lhasa — already the

4.50 Judge of Hell, painted clay, Shuanglin Temple, Pingyao County, Shanxi Province. Ming dynasty.

4.51 Guan Yu as a Buddhist guardian god, painted clay, Sangharama Hall, Shuanglin Temple. Ming dynasty.

4.52 Guan Yu, painted clay, unearthed in 1958 from the Temple of God Guan Yu, Taiyuan, Shanxi Province. Ming dynasty. 168 cm. Palace Museum, Beijing.

capital — sophisticated ideas and instruments of culture. These included notions about writing and belief systems, including Buddhism. They also brought luxury items such as silk and precious Buddhist sculptures. Other Buddhist images, which came to Tibet through Songtsen Gampo's marriages, introduced further religious themes and deities at the court, to which Buddhism seems to have been largely confined in the early period.

Songtsen's first wife, a princess of Nepal, brought with her images of Aksobhya, Maitreya, and Tara. His second wife, Princess Wencheng of China, brought a statue of Shakyamuni. These images were enshrined in the Jokhang Monastery and Ramoche Temple of Lhasa, which were built for this purpose. During this era, too, translations of Buddhist scriptures began to appear, which initiated the large-scale spread of Buddhism into Tibet.

The new religion set off a fierce, sustained struggle within Tufan's ruling group. In the debate between the Esoteric adherents on the one hand and the followers of Bon and the Chan monks from the Han Chinese area on the other, the Esoteric School received the backing of the rulers and became established as the leading religious school in and around Tibet. The system of sangha was instituted. Under the patronage of the three successive Dharma Kings — Songtsen Gampo, Trisong Detsen, and Ralpachen — Esoteric Buddhism attained widespread popularity in the region. Movements to ban Buddhism followed, however; one occurred between 755 and 761, and the second was initiated by the last Tibetan king, Langdharma, in 841. At these times temples and monasteries were closed, murals and statues destroyed, Buddhist scriptures burned, and monks persecuted.

The spread of Buddhism in Tibet was thus disrupted for more than a hundred years. But in 978, with the support and participation of feudal rulers, Buddhism was brought back by believers who had gone underground in northern Amdo (present-day Qinghai) and in the western Tibetan kingdom of Gugé during the bans.

The most important sculptural works of Tibetan Buddhism in the interior of China are the groups of carved images on the Feilaifeng (Flying-in Peak), part of the West Lake scenic area on the outskirts of Hangzhou. The name of the peak (it is also known as the Divine Vulture Peak) was inspired by a myth. It is said that when the Indian monk Huili saw the peak in 326 he exclaimed, "This is a small peak of the Divine Vulture Mountain in India. Why has it flown here?" On the right cliff of the peak is the largest concentration of grottoes in China's southeastern coastal area, hewn between the tenth and fourteenth centuries. The sculptured images are found among the Qinglin, Yuru, Longhong, Shexue, and Huyuan grottoes cut into the cliff face. The earliest of these still extant are the Three Sages of the West carved by Teng Shaozong in 951, in the Later Zhou dynasty. There are more than 300 carved images still in existence on the peak, with 11 from the period of the Five Dynasties, more than 200 from the Song, and 110 or so from the Yuan.

Most of the images of the Song dynasty were carved during the Xianping era (998–1003) under Emperor Zhenzong. Many of them are of arhats, but there are also works that illustrate special themes, such as the "seventeenfold body of Vairocana Buddha," carved in relief by Hu Chengde in 1022; the three groups of reliefs of the Xianping period describing the pilgrimage of the monk Xuanzang to India in search of Buddhist scriptures; and the image described above of Budai (Hempen Sack) as Maitreya surrounded by eighteen arhats that was carved during the Southern Song period.

Of all of these images, those made during the Yuan dynasty are the largest, most finely carved, and most significant in the history of Chinese sculpture. Nearly half of the 110 or so Yuan images depict Esoteric themes. The inscriptions show that the early images were carved in 1282 and the rest ten years later. The most important are the images in the grottoes that were cut between 1285 and 1287 under the supervision of Yang Lianzhenjia, a married Tangut quasi-monastic practitioner of Tibetan-style Buddhism who found favor with Emperor Shizu. In 1277 Yang was made superintendent of Buddhism in the Yangzi Delta. In his new post he began pulling down the palaces of the Southern Song dynasty, digging up the mausoleums of the Song emperors, building temples and pagodas, and hewing grottoes throughout Hangzhou and elsewhere, seeking to destroy the kingly spirit generated by the geomantic layout of Lin'an (Hangzhou), the capital of the Southern Song dynasty. Once the old images had been destroyed, Yang set about replacing them with new ones and ordered the grotto images to be carved. These gilded, colorfully painted images have undergone repeated renovations over the centuries, although the long years of exposure have had their effect, and little remains of their original coloring. Some of the artwork was also damaged by people disgusted by Yang's destruction of the older images and offended by sculptures in the Tibetan style.

Buddhism in the Yuan dynasty was mainly influenced by the Sakya sect of Tibetan Buddhism. As already mentioned, Chogyal Phagspa, the Sakya master whom Kublai Khan had invited to oversee Buddhist affairs throughout Tibet, stayed on to instruct him and his family after the khan became Emperor Shizu. Supported by the court, the Sakya sect became the leading political-religious organization in the Tibet area. It was Chogyal Phagspa who introduced to the court Anige, the Nepalese sculptor who played a leading role in spreading the Indian style in religious sculpture throughout the region.

The Esoteric Buddhist images of the Yuan dynasty on Feilaifeng can be divided by subject into the following main categories: Buddhas, bodhisattvas, female deities, and guardians of the dharma. One Buddha group has the image of Vairocana at the center, flanked by Aksobhya Buddha in the east; Amitabha Buddha in the west; Ratnasambhava Buddha in the south; and Amoghasiddhi Buddha in the north. Together, these sculptures represent the Buddhas of the Five Directions, who are visualized both as a group and individually. They appear on the peak in more than one guise: sometimes they appear as conventional Buddhas and sometimes crowned and bejeweled like bodhisattvas.

The Shakyamuni Buddha in Niche 13, at the entrance of the Longhong Grotto, is shown sitting cross-legged on a lotus seat with coiled hair and an exposed right shoulder and with his right hand giving the touching-the-earth sign and his left holding a dharma wheel. In Han Chinese style, the image appears rather heavyset. But the thin, close-fitting vestment is more characteristic of the Indian style. The image of Amitayus, or Amitabha, in Niche 60 was carved under the supervision of Yang Lianzhenjia. It is presented with coiled hair, shoulder exposed, and hands together forming the gesture of meditation, with a bowl resting on top of them. Sitting cross-legged on his lotus seat, the figure, with the carefully carved folds in his clothes, oblate head nimbus, and inscription behind him in a Tibetan ornamental version of Sanskrit, is in the Tibetan style (fig. 4.53).

The group of three images of Amitayus with Tara and Manjushri bodhisattva in Niche 70 is different in composition from the group formed by Amitayus, Avalokiteshvara, and Mahasthamaprapta, the Three Sages of the West. Aksobhya in Niche 37 wears a crown, scarves, necklaces, and earrings. He sits cross-legged on a lotus seat with his right hand making the touching-the-earth gesture and the left resting in front of the stomach in the meditation gesture. The well-proportioned body is naked above the waist and bears distinct Indian features.

The Buddha whose image is enshrined in Niche 25 is a special Esoteric Buddhist figure known as Vajradhara. Among the distinctive features of this statue are his crown, the Vajra or adamantine thunderbolt, and the Vajra-handled bell he holds in his hands crossed in front of his chest.

Bodhisattvas form an important component of the Yuan-era Esoteric images on Feilaifeng. The images of the bodhisattvas Manjushri, Avalokiteshvara (Guanyin), and Vajrasattva, who are particularly important to the Sakya sect, all appear there. The Avalokiteshvara images take many forms, such as the four-handed Sadakshri and Simhanada (Lion-Roar) Avalokiteshvara. Among the themes that are distinctive to Tibetan Esoteric Buddhist imagery is Vajravidarana, who is particularly important in the Sakya lineage. In an image on the outer wall, he wears a five-petaled crown and is naked above the waist. He sits on a seat of five lotus flowers and holds the double Vajra in his right hand and a bell in his left. Between his brows is a third eye, and he sits in a relaxed, cross-legged posture (fig. 4.54). A wrathful form of Vajrapani bodhisattva appears in Niche 8. He is depicted with a stout body, naked above the waist and wearing a loincloth (dhoti). His right hand holds high the Vajra, and his left hand forms the gesture of admonition (fig. 4.55). In Tibetan Buddhism, wrathful bodhisattvas often have a terrifying aspect, reflecting their function as destroyers of obstacles. Compared to some contemporary Tibetan images, the wrathful deities at Feilaifeng are relatively restrained: although they look resolute, they do not look fearsome.

The female deity Sitatapatra, depicted in Niche 22, holds a special place in the Esoteric Buddhist pantheon. Distinguished by her great snow-white umbrella, she is particularly esteemed in the Sakya lineage and was highly venerated by the Yuan rulers because she was believed to be able to destroy armies and overcome disease and other disasters. Another female deity, the Marichi of Niches 41 and 50, is credited with the ability to bless those faithful to her. At Feilaifeng, Marichi, like the other female images, takes on a typically Indian appearance: she sits informally on a lotus seat with her left hand holding a stalk of grain, her right forming the gift-giving mudra, and her right foot resting on the back of a prostrate pig. She wears a crown, necklaces, and

4.53 Amitayus (Amitabha Buddha), stone, Niche 60, Feilaifeng, Hangzhou, Zhejiang Province. Yuan dynasty. 206 cm.

4.54 Vajravidarana bodhisattva, stone, Feilaifeng. Yuan dynasty. 210 × 170 cm.

scarves, and her exposed upper body shows that she has smooth skin and a slightly plump belly (fig. 4.56).

Vaishravana, one of the Four Heavenly Kings, is the most revered guardian of the dharma. In Niche 46 there is an outstanding sculpture of Vaishravana. Looking calm and brave, he rides on the back of a vividly chiseled black lion (fig. 4.57).

Among the other Esoteric Buddhist images of the Yuan dynasty in the Hangzhou area is the extraordinary over-lifesize sculpture of the Mahasiddha (Great Adept) Virupa in Niche 59 at Feilaifeng, sadly damaged. Big-bellied and in a relaxed posture, he is waited on by two maidens bearing wine. This refers to the famous miracle in which he stops the sun (to which he points) after striking an agreement with a tavern keeper to supply him with all the liquor he can drink until the sun sets (fig. 4.58). Another unusual Esoteric Buddhist figure is the great black deity Mahakala. Mahakala was highly revered in the court of the early Yuan, and his statue was placed in the palace and in all the Buddhist temples inside and outside the capital, although the group of Mahakala carvings in the Baocheng Temple in Hangzhou is the only one extant today. In this group Panjarnatha Mahakala (the Great Black One, Lord of the Pavilion) and attendants are all portrayed with extremely ferocious looks. Mahakala is short and plump;

his chest and stomach are exposed, and his hair stands on end in anger. Holding a skullcup in his left hand and resting his foot on the figure of a corpse, he is presented as a conqueror of demons (fig. 4.59).

In both architecture and sculpture, the works of the Yuan period tend to be elaborate, gorgeous, and refined. The Buddhist images, mandalas, texts of scriptures and prayers, and designs and friezes inside and outside the arch of the Juyong Gate, north of Beijing (see fig. 4.1), for example, combine relief and linear carvings and are exquisitely designed and skillfully executed in distinctive detail (figs. 4.60, 4.61). When compared with the fine works of the preceding period, they seem more gorgeous than forceful.[41]

Daoist Images of the Deities of the Twenty-Eight Lunar Mansions

The most important extant Daoist sculptures of the Yuan dynasty are the statues of the deities of the Twenty-Eight Lunar Mansions in the Longshan grottoes in Taiyuan and the Yuhuang Temple in Jincheng, both in Shanxi Province. The Longshan grottoes in Taiyuan were hewn before the founding of the Yuan dynasty, during the reign of Ogdai, the Mongol

4.55 Vajrapani bodhisattva, stone, Niche 8, Feilaifeng. Yuan dynasty. 160 cm.

4.56 Marichi, stone, Niche 41, Feilaifeng. Yuan dynasty.

4.57 Vaishravana, stone, Niche 46, Feilaifeng. Yuan dynasty.

4.58 Virupa, stone, Feilaifeng. Yuan dynasty.

4.59 Group of Mahakala images (detail), stone, Baocheng Temple, Hangzhou, Zhejiang Province. Yuan dynasty.

emperor Taizong (1229–1241). The grottoes of Long-shan were badly damaged during the later dynasties, and although their statues are not as finely rendered as the statues in the Buddhist grottoes, they are the only extant Daoist grottoes of the Yuan period.

The eight principal grottoes, containing more than forty statues, were created around 1236. The construction was supervised by the Daoist priest Song Defang (Daoist name Piyunzi), who was active in the Shanxi area as superintendent of religions. Under Emperor Taizong, Song Defang and his disciple Li Zhichang began to edit and collate Daoist classics in the Xuandu Temple in Pingyang (present-day Linfen), a task that took them eight years.

The Grottoes of the Three Pure Ones, the Three Emperors, and the Seven Immortals are the most important at Longshan. The images in these grottoes were carved to deify the early masters of the carvers' religious sect — for example, the Grotto of the Seven Immortals enshrines the images of the northern seven immortals of the Quanzhen School, and the Cloud-Draped (Piyun) Grotto, built by Li Zhiquan and Qin Zhi'an, honored their teacher Song Defang.

The largest of the eight grottoes is dedicated to the Three Pure Ones. The Primordial Heavenly Worthy is in the center with the Heavenly Worthy of the Sacred Jewel on his left and the Heavenly Worthy of the Way (Laozi) on his right. All are seated with their hands

4.60 Bas-relief showing Virudhaka, Heavenly King of the South, white marble, Juyong Gate, Changping district, Beijing. Yuan dynasty. Approx. 280 cm.

4.61 Bas-relief showing Vaishravana, Heavenly King of the North, white marble, Juyong Gate. Approx. 280 cm.

tucked into their sleeves and legs crossed. The lower hems of their ample robes hang down the front of their seats, and there are halos behind their heads and bodies. This style was obviously inspired by Buddhist images. Each Heavenly Worthy is flanked by two attendants, and on the left and right walls of the cave are three formally dressed figures who hold one hand cupped in the other in salute. The three are also seated, and boys and girls sit between them. From the inscriptions carved on the walls and the traces of color on the images, we can see that they were once lavishly gilded (fig. 4.62).

In the third grotto, the Woru, the figure of a Daoist priest — said to be Piyunzi — lies on a stone bed on his left side, with one leg on top of the other. This image clearly derives from the sculptural tradition of the Buddha in Nirvana. Indeed, most of the Daoist images in the Longshan grottoes are rather crudely executed and are derivative of Buddhist works. But some images were created by the Daoists themselves, such as one of the principal figures in the Grotto of the Three

Emperors, who is dressed in leaves and an animal skin; the cranes on the left and right walls inside the Grotto of the Seven Immortals, each of which features two dragons with a pearl above its head; and the cloud and dragon designs on the ceiling of the Grotto of the Three Pure Ones.

Yuhuang Temple in Jincheng is a very important Daoist construction. The three enclosed courtyards, one behind the other, enshrine carved images of the Jade Emperor, Three Officials, Four Sages, and Deities of the Nine Sources of Brightness, Twelve Zodiacal Constellations, and Twenty-Eight Lunar Mansions (fig. 4.63).[42]

The Twenty-Eight Lunar Mansions, zones of the sky demarcated by ancient astronomers to help in the observation of celestial bodies, were not represented by Daoist deities at first. They are the roughly twenty-eight stars on either side of the zodiacal belt and celestial equator; divided into four groups, the stars are represented by four creatures: the Green Dragon of the East, the Black Turtle of the North, the White Tiger of

4.62 Figures in the Grotto of the Three Pure Ones, stone, Longshan Daoist grottoes, Taiyuan, Shanxi Province. Yuan dynasty.

the West, and the Vermilion Bird of the South. In the Tang dynasty, Yuan Tiangang matched the Twenty-Eight Lunar Mansions with twenty-eight fantastically named creatures to mark specific zones. It was around the Song period that the Twenty-Eight Lunar Mansions were assigned to Daoist deities, whose images appear in the Yuan-dynasty painting *Picture of Homage* in the Three Pure Ones Hall of Yongle Temple (in Ruicheng, Shanxi Province). But the deities in the Yongle Temple wall painting are different from the unique representations in Jincheng: in Yongle Temple, each mansion, or astral zone, is indicated by a picture of a creature in a circular ornament on the crown.

By contrast, the sculptors of statues of the deities of the Twenty-Eight Lunar Mansions in Yuhuang Temple created a group of human figures with distinct and striking personalities. Perhaps because the subject had no religious restrictions, the artists seem to have given free rein to their imaginative impulses. The deities are portrayed as officials, men of letters, warriors, old men, and noble ladies — in short, ordinary people. They look kind-hearted or fierce, deep in thought or gentle. Although each has a unique character, they all exude the qualities of immortals and exhibit a noble bearing that inspires respect. Each figure has a corresponding creature on his left or right, such as the Morning Sun Mouse and the Winged Fire Snake (fig. 4.64).

The deities representing the constellations in the Hall of the Twelve Zodiacal Constellations in the Yuhuang Temple are similarly distinctive and expressive, though created in a different style. The Twelve Zodiacal Constellations, matched with corresponding creatures, were used by ancients as the twelve Earthly Branches in the system of Heavenly Stems and Earthly Branches for indicating the year, month, day, and hour. The deities are portrayed here as nobles and high officials, each holding a memorial tablet. Their corresponding creatures are painted on the circular ornaments on their crowns, which lack the official horizontal bar.

Images of Bodhisattvas and Arhats from the Ming and Qing Dynasties

The bodhisattva Guanyin continued to be a key figure of worship during the Ming and Qing periods, and statues of him were enshrined in temples throughout the country. In Beijing's Dahui (Great Wisdom) Temple, a large bronze statue of Guanyin cast in the Ming dynasty was originally enshrined in the Dabei (Great Com-

passion) Hall. It was removed by the Japanese and collaborationist authorities during the War of Resistance Against Japan (1937–1945) and replaced with a colorfully painted wooden image. Remaining in the hall are painted statues of the Thousand-handed Guanyin and his twenty-eight attendants, all works of the Ming dynasty (fig. 4.65).

The statues of the bodhisattvas Guanyin, Manjushri, and Samantabhadra in the Chongshan Temple in Taiyuan, Shanxi Province, are fine works of the early Ming period. Built by the Ming imperial clan in 1383, the temple was located in a magnificent complex of buildings originally composed of six great halls and eighteen courtyards. A fire in 1864 destroyed most of the buildings; only the Dabei Hall and the group of buildings in the rear courtyard survived.[43]

The three bodhisattvas, each 8.5 meters high and standing on a Sumeru platform, are sculpted in wood and clay, gilded, and gorgeously painted. The Thousand-handed Guanyin stands in the middle, Manjushri of a Thousand Arms and Alms Bowls is on the eastern side, and Samantabhadra of a Hundred Treasures, wearing a moonlike halo, is on the western side. All three images have solemn, respectful expressions. Although there is uniformity among the statues, they exhibit variations as well. Guanyin has the traditional forty-two arms; each of these (except for the two main arms) holds a religious object. But behind the statue, the "thousand arms and eyes" radiate powerfully in all directions. The halo behind Manjushri is also a compelling image: it too is presented with a thousand arms, each holding an alms bowl finely carved with the image of Shakyamuni. The longer arms stretch out like radiating rays and the seven rows of hands, each holding its bowl, are as beautiful as a garland. Manjushri's six main arms extend outward and upward from his chest. With the sleeves fluttering in the wind, they suggest a sequence of movements. Samantabhadra also wears a halo; it is carved in the shape of a full moon or wheel, in harmony with the overall shape of the two other statues. The three enormous statues demonstrate superb artistic skill. Although works of this size often look dull and lifeless, these statues are animated, in part because the folds of the long silk robes have been executed in natural, flowing lines (fig. 4.66).

Ming-dynasty carvers also created the beautiful wooden statue of the Guanyin of the Thousand Arms and Eyes that is enshrined in the Dabei Hall in Dahui Temple. The bodhisattva sits leisurely on an oddly shaped rock. The "thousand arms and eyes" are ar-

4.63 God of the constellation Wei, symbolized by a pheasant, painted clay, Yuhuang Temple, Jincheng, Shanxi Province. Yuan dynasty. 160 cm.

4.64 Winged fire snake, painted clay, Yuhuang Temple. 177 cm.

4.65 Twenty-eight attendants of the Thousand-handed Guanyin (detail), painted clay, Dabei Hall, Dahui Temple, Beijing. Ming dynasty.

ranged in four circles, once more resembling rays of light radiating from the body. In an ingenious break from the traditional style, the outer edge of the halo is carved with flame patterns.

Another large wooden statue of Guanyin of the Thousand Arms and Eyes can be found in the Puning Temple's Pavilion of Mahayana in Chengde, Hebei Province (see fig. 4.84). A representative work of the Qing, the statue is 22.28 meters high. It is similar in appearance to the Guanyin in the Longxing Temple in Zhengding County, Hebei Province (see fig. 4.24). Certain specific features of the statue, such as the white urna (Buddhist mark) carved between the eyebrows, are similar to those found on Buddhas. More important, the huge size of the statue, its mysterious multiple arms, and the surrounding religious atmosphere evoke feelings of awe from viewers.

But the most artistically sophisticated Ming images of Guanyin are the painted statues in the Shuanglin Temple, Pingyao County, Shanxi Province. Of the 2,052 statues in the temple, 1,566 are perfectly preserved. Among these, the Vajrapani and Four Heavenly Kings in the Hall of Devas, the sixteen arhats in the Hall of Arhats, and the Skanda in the Hall of the Thousand Buddhas are masterpieces of Ming Buddhist sculpture (fig. 4.67).

The most impressive figure is that of Guanyin, stat-

ues of whose various representations stand as the principal deity in the Hall of Arhats, the Hall of the Thousand Buddhas, and the Hall of Bodhisattvas. The best of all the different styles of Guanyin sculpture popular in the later period of Chinese Buddhism can be found in Shuanglin Temple. In the Hall of Arhats, a gilded Guanyin bodhisattva sits cross-legged on a seat of lotus petals with a Sumeru throne beneath him supported by viras (mighty men). This statue, with its finely carved halo, is typical of the holy Guanyin.

The statue of a feminine Guanyin in the Hall of the Thousand Buddhas is carved in a leisurely sitting position. The pose for this chief deity is almost exactly the same as that of the Guanyin of Purple Bamboo in Bilu Cave in Anyue (see fig. 4.26), Sichuan Province, demonstrating that the style had become standardized since the Song dynasty. The only difference is that this Guanyin's feet rest on a coiled dragon instead of a lotus flower.

The Guanyin in the Hall of Bodhisattvas is the most beautiful of the many-handed Guanyins. Presented as a lovely, graceful young woman, the bodhisattva has a charming face and wears beautiful clothes and ornaments. The arms are perfectly arranged behind the head and torso. Together with the fine texture of the skin and the graceful gestures of the hands, the twenty-plus arms give an impression of perfect artistic harmony (fig. 4.68).[44]

The image of Guanyin suspended on the rear wall of the Shakyamuni Hall is another striking work. Here the bodhisattva sits serenely on a red lotus petal in an expanse of rolling waves, surrounded by sixteen arhats. The delicate yet strong lotus petal contrasts with the turbulent waves to demonstrate the immense power of the bodhisattva (fig. 4.69).

Guanyin also appears as one of the eight bodhisattvas in the Hall of Heavenly Kings. In addition, two groups of five hundred bodhisattva images can be found on the walls of the Hall of the Thousand Buddhas and the Hall of Bodhisattvas. The bodhisattvas are positioned row upon row among rocks and clouds. The heads, made with molds, are small in proportion to the bodies, but the images are vivid and lifelike (fig. 4.70).[45]

Two groups of works that show an even closer meeting between the spiritual and human realms are the painted statues in Guanyin Hall in Changzhi, Shanxi Province, and the Temple of the Lesser Western Heaven, Thousand Buddhas Nunnery, in Xixian County, Shanxi Province. Both are works of the late Ming period. Because the creators of these images wished to fully illustrate the realm of the Buddha in their limited space, they sculpted miniature images with elaborate, exquisite detail and painted them in vivid colors.

The Guanyin Hall in the southwestern part of the city of Changzhi was built between 1581 and 1583. The principal deities are three bodhisattvas, which have been partially damaged. The southern and northern walls of the hall are covered from floor to ceiling with images sculpted both in the round and in high relief. Among the major images are those of sixteen arhats with their attendant and patron, twenty-four devas headed by Indra and the great Brahma, Manjushri and Samantabhadra (fig. 4.71). The rows of figures are separated by colorful clouds. Carved in the upper part of the hall are palace buildings with Daoist deities and Confucian philosophers, government officials carried in sedanchairs, and figures in mythological dramas.

The Hall of Shakyamuni in the Temple of the Lesser Western Heaven has an enormous 169.6 square meters of floor space. The carvings in this hall create a juxtaposition of lofty mountains with majestic palace buildings, all of which form a mysterious realm that combines the heavens and the human world. The statues enshrined in this hall are mainly images of Shakyamuni, Vairocana, Maitreya, Amitabha, Bhaishajyaguru, and assistant bodhisattvas (fig. 4.72). The five 3.2-meter-high Buddhas sit cross-legged in a row of interconnected large niches where the temple monks and disciples assembled.

Above the five Buddhas is the Western Heaven; depicted are a Buddhist gathering, the Hall of the Thousand Buddhas, the Golden World, and the Crystal World. The entire hall is supported by carved beams and painted rafters in gorgeous colors. On the lower part of the remaining wall space are images of the Ten Great Disciples standing on lotus flowers and waited on by attendants or young monks bearing food and drink. Above them, both inside and out, are the images of the Three Sages of the West, the Seven Buddhas of the Past, the Four Heavenly Kings, maharajas, and Kalinka (the two-headed bird). Mingled among them are also some Daoist images.

The buildings and sculptured images in the Temple of the Lesser Western Heaven portray an elaborate, sumptuous, aristocratic, and yet worldly realm of the Buddha. The sculptors were influenced more by dramas, novels, and folk culture than by Buddhist texts. This merging of folk tradition and Buddhist practice shaped Chinese sculpture throughout the Ming and Qing periods. During this time, in particular, the images of bodhisattvas were varied but harmonious in style. As we have seen, the Esoteric Buddhist image of Guanyin was the principal subject of large statuary. Although it was inspired by the sculptural art handed down from the Tang and Song dynasties, the Ming and Qing artists added their own innovations. For example, in creating the three bodhisattvas in the Dabei Hall in Chongshan Temple, they solved the technical problem of adding many arms to the body by using a decorative method of treatment (see fig. 4.66).

All the statues of Guanyin, a deity of profound influence among the ordinary people, had become feminized and increasingly closer in style to ordinary Han Chinese people and everyday life. The many-handed Guanyin and the Guanyin on a lotus petal were always presented as idealized images of beautiful women.

In addition to the statues in the temples and monasteries, many fine porcelain statuettes of Guanyin were made in the Yuan dynasty and later. The Dehua kiln in Fujian produced a statuette of Guanyin using the traditional painting method for depicting the folds of clothes. Its pure white celadon glazes present Guanyin as an embodiment of holiness and purity. It is not only an object of worship but also a noble ornament for a home (fig. 4.73).

But one can still find statues of bodhisattvas sculpted in the more or less traditional style in some temples and

monasteries in the Shanxi area. The four bodhisattvas in the Vairocana Hall of the Upper Guangsheng Temple in Hongdong County, for example, are portrayed as males with mustaches. They are riding on animals as their feet rest on lotus flowers — a Buddhist symbol — but their clothes resemble those of the Han Chinese people. By contrast, the Ming statues of Manjushri and Samantabhadra in the Hall of Three Sages of the Shanhua Temple wear crowns and are naked above the waist. Sitting cross-legged on lofty Sumeru thrones, they appear as dignified as the Buddha. There are also two Ming statues of Manjushri and Samantabhadra in the Xiantong Temple's Hall of Manjushri of a Thousand Alms Bowls in the town of Taihuai on Mount Wutai. The two bodhisattvas are richly depicted in the folk style as two aged monks. The fact that Manjushri holds a long-handled good-luck bar shows that the image was remolded to fit Chinese folk customs.

Although statues of arhats remained popular after the Song, few have been well preserved. Among the more important statues of the sixteen arhats with their attendant and patron are those coated with lacquer that were originally kept in Beijing's imperial palace and are now in the Hall of Shakyamuni in the Baima Temple, Luoyang, Henan Province (figs. 4.74–4.76), and those in the vestibule of the Hall of Shakyamuni in the Temple of Great Compassion in Beijing's Western Hills. Those in the Baima Temple are finely modeled, with colorfully painted draperies. The arhats at the Temple of Great Compassion, made of fine clay mixed with powder of camphor wood, are said to have been created by Liu Yuan, a disciple of Anige. The sixteen arhats of the Yuan dynasty in the Guanyin Hall of Green Lotus Temple in Jincheng, Shanxi Province, are made of clay gilded with golden leaves, close in style to works of the Song period.[46]

4.66 Thousand-handed
Guanyin and the Man-
jushri and Samanta-
bhadra bodhisattvas,
painted clay, Chong-
shan Temple, Taiyuan,
Shanxi Province. Ming
dynasty. Each, 850 cm.

Like the magnificent images of Guanyin, the painted wood-and-clay statues of the sixteen arhats with their attendants and patrons in the Shuanglin Temple in Pingyao County reached a new level in the depiction of character. These arhats, created during the Ming dynasty, are positioned in wooden niches carved with sets of beams and supporting brackets showing backgrounds of rocky cliffs. There is a door at the back of each niche through which the arhats pass. Significantly, they are portrayed as ordinary people. Later generations named them individually based on their most prominent characteristic (dumpy, talkative, sick, meditating, and so on; figs. 4.77, 4.78).

Most of the groups of five hundred arhats still in existence belong to the Qing period. Among the earlier ones are the gilded wooden statues of arhats and Buddhas in the Hall of Arhats built in 1748 in the Biyun (Azure Cloud) Temple on Fragrant Hill, Beijing. There are 508 statues in all. The life-size works are arranged in neat rows on Sumeru thrones, although in most cases their arrangement echoes the traditional presentation of arhat groups. They reveal nothing outstanding as far as the art of sculpture is concerned, but some are individuated: one of the statues is of an emperor in martial attire, said to be in the likeness of the Qianlong emperor.

Other important statues of the five hundred arhats are the clay figures in the Hall of Arhats of the Guiyuan Temple in Wuhan, Hubei Province, and in the Baoguang Temple in Xindu, Sichuan Province. These works draw on the images and activities of daily life. One arhat lounges lazily on a rattan chair reading a book with one foot in the air while another plays with a group of children. This human perspective receives what may be its fullest realization in the painted statues of five hundred arhats in the Qiongzhu Temple on Mount Yu'an, Yunnan Province. Made by the folk sculptor Li

4.67 Skanda, painted clay, Hall of the Thousand Buddhas, Shuanglin Temple, Pingyao County, Shanxi Province. Ming dynasty. 176 cm.

4.68 Multihanded Guanyin, painted clay, Hall of Bodhisattvas, Shuanglin Temple. 345 cm.

4.69 Guanyin bodhisattva on a lotus petal crossing the sea, painted clay, Shakyamuni Hall, Shuanglin Temple.

4.70 Wall sculpture of five hundred bodhisattvas (detail), painted clay, Hall of the Thousand Buddhas, Shuanglin Temple.

4.71 Relief wall sculpture of twelve *pratyeka* Buddhas and twenty-four devas (detail), painted clay, Guanyin Hall, Changzhi, Shanxi Province. Ming dynasty, 1581–1583. 66–98 cm.

4.72 Buddhist images, painted clay, Shakyamuni Hall, Temple of the Lesser Western Heaven (Xiaoxitian), Xixian County, Shanxi Province. Ming dynasty.

4.74 Arhat, painted mixed ramie fiber, Baima Temple, Luoyang, Henan Province. Yuan dynasty. 160 cm.

4.75 Arhat, painted mixed ramie fiber, Baima Temple. 160 cm.

4.76 Arhat, painted mixed ramie fiber, Baima Temple. 154 cm.

4.73 Guanyin, celadon. Yuan dynasty. 66 cm. National Museum of China, Beijing.

4.77 Seated arhat, painted clay, Hall of Bodhisattvas, Shuanglin Temple, Pingyao County, Shanxi Province. Ming dynasty.

4.78 Arhats, painted clay, Hall of Shakyamuni, Shuanglin Temple.

Guangxiu and his five assistants, who were commissioned by the temple's abbot in 1891, the statues took seven years to complete.

Although traditionally the crowd of arhats would be placed in one hall, the sculptors scattered the figures in this group among three halls: 68 are in the Hall of the Buddha, 216 in the Tiantailai Pavilion, and 216 in the Hall of Brahma's Voice. The meter-high statues are grouped according to different legends and flexibly arranged either in groups of three rows or in circles. The group that is crossing the ocean is so vividly sculpted that one can almost hear the sound of the crashing waves. The artists must have closely observed ordinary people to create such realistic — albeit often exaggerated — characters. They may also have drawn from the theater, especially the Sichuan Opera, for vivid stock characters. The arhats are portrayed as men from all walks of life; some are vulgar, wretched, crafty, or cunning. Materials such as hair for whiskers and beards and bamboo for walking sticks were used to enhance the realistic effect (fig. 4.79). Work of this idiosyncrasy was able to appear only at the end of the Qing dynasty, when society was sophisticated enough to tolerate complicated contradictions in religious images, and in an area like Yunnan, where orthodox religious ideas were not so prevalent.

4.79 Group of five hundred arhats (detail), painted clay, Qiongzhu Temple, Kunming, Yunnan Province. Qing dynasty, 1891.

sure of Mountain Resort. Of the Eight Outside Temples, the Puning Temple emulates the Samye Temple in Tibet; the Putuozongcheng Temple makes reference in its architecture to the Potala Palace, as does the Xumi Fushou Temple to the Tashilhumpo Temple; and the Anyuan Temple was understood as a replica of the Kulja Temple in Yili. Preserved in these temples — whose interiors combine Manchu, Han, Mongolian, and Tibetan features — are Tibeto-Chinese Buddhist murals, thangka paintings (paintings on cloth or woven tapestries), sculptures, and handicraft arts. There are thought to be as many as 55,161 sculptured images in the eight temples.

Because these were imperial temples, most of the statues embodied the characteristics of the Manchu court style that combined Mongolian and Tibetan themes and Chinese artistic methods. There are some huge sculptural works — for example, the images of the Guanyin of the Thousand Arms and Eyes and his attendants in the Pavilion of Mahayana in the Puning Temple, built in 1755. The statue of Guanyin was carved of five kinds of wood — pine, cypress, elm, linden, and spruce — and then gilded. Measuring 22.28 meters in height, with a waistline of 15 meters and weighing 110 metric tons, it is the world's largest wood-and-gold statue. This Guanyin has three eyes and wears a crown 1.53 meters high with a sitting image of Amitayus (Amitabha) on top of it. Constructed with the traditional forty-two arms, it has twenty-one arms on each side with an eye on each hand, and each hand holds a religious object. Though enormous and in Chinese rather than Tibetan style, the sculpture, which was covered with hemp and plaster before it was painted and gilded, is beautifully proportioned and dignified, the folds of the clothing falling in natural lines (fig. 4.84). Vasubandhu and Lakshmi, the attendants who stand on either side of Guanyin, are each 18 meters high and also carved in wood. Vasubandhu is depicted as an elderly man with bare arms, his hands joined in front of his chest and sandals on his feet. Lakshmi is dressed as a noble lady in a gorgeous robe decorated with gold flakes.

The Puren Temple, the oldest of the Eight Outside Temples, was built in 1713 by Mongolian princes to celebrate the sixtieth birthday of the Kangxi emperor. The statues of the three Buddhas and the sixteen arhats with their attendants and patrons in the temple were sculpted out of clay mixed with silk fibers, and they represent the early style of Qing statues. The Pule Temple, built in 1766, was intended as a place for receiving nobles from various northwest tribes when they came to pay

homage to the emperor. The front of the temple was made in the traditional Han temple style, and inside are statues of the Buddhas of the Three Periods, accompanied by Skanda and Budai (Hempen Sack) chiseled in wood and the Four Heavenly Kings modeled in clay. All the Buddhist statues are in the Han style that was popular during the Ming and Qing periods. They are magnificently ornamented but look rather stiff.

The buildings and sculptures behind the Zongyin Hall in the Pule Temple are in the Tibetan style. The principal structure is the Pavilion of Morning Sunlight, a copy of the Hall of Prayer for Good Harvest in Beijing's Temple of Heaven. In the pavilion is a mandala altar with Chakrasamvara embracing Vajravarahi enshrined on it (fig. 4.85). Chakrasamvara is an Esoteric Buddhist *yidam*, or meditation deity. A wrathful Buddha, he is portrayed with four heads, each with three eyes, and twelve arms; the two main arms hold his female consort, Vajravarahi. The image in the Pavilion of Morning Sunlight is cast in bronze. The complicated structure of the multiheaded, multihanded principal subject and the relationship between the two characters are well handled, and the textures are beautifully reproduced (fig. 4.86).

The Putuozongcheng Temple, built in 1767–1771 to celebrate the sixtieth birthday of the Qianlong emperor and the eightieth birthday of the empress dowager and to serve as a place for receiving visiting nobles from the ethnic minorities, is a gigantic complex. The statues of Magzor Gyalmo, Guhyasamaja, Shakyamuni, and the twelve attendant generals of Bhaishajyaguru in the temple were all cast under the supervision of the leading lama of the imperial palace's Zhongzheng Hall in the Forbidden City. The gilded copper statue of Magzor Gyalmo, the "Queen Who Turns Back Armies," was cast with more than 550 kilograms of copper as well as 1.6 kilograms of gold leaves. A deity for safeguarding the dharma, Magzor Gyalmo holds a staff in her raised right hand and is accompanied by *makara-* and lion-headed attendants. She is riding a mule across a sea punctuated by jagged rocks. Roaring flames are carved in the background, enhancing the feeling of movement and helping to create an awe-inspiring and mysterious religious atmosphere (fig. 4.87).

The principal Buddhist statues in the Eight Outside Temples in Chengde were produced by court artisans. But there are also a large number of gold and bronze Buddhist statues from this period that were delivered as tributes to the emperor by members of the Qing imperial clan and high monks in Tibet, Mongolia, and Xikang. Of these, the ones from Tibet are the finest.

4.84 Thousand-handed, Thousand-eyed Guanyin, painted wood, Puning Temple, Chengde, Hebei Province. Qing dynasty, 1755. 2,228 cm.

4.85 Mandala altar, wood, Pule Temple, Chengde, Hebei Province. Qing dynasty.

4.86 Chakrasamvara embracing Vajravarahi, wood, Pavilion of Morning Sunlight, Pule Temple.

4.87 Magzor Gyalmo, gilded copper, Putuozongcheng Temple, Chengde, Hebei Province. Qing dynasty, 1767–1771.

4.88 Amitayus, silver with gilt-bronze aureole, Putuozongcheng Temple.

On the Qianlong emperor's sixtieth birthday in 1770, representatives of various ethnic minorities presented him with a thousand statues of the Buddha of Measureless Light (Amitayus), which are all enshrined in the Cave of Thousand Buddhas in the Putuozongcheng Temple (fig. 4.88).[49]

Gilt-Bronze Statues in the Forbidden City

Tens of thousands of statues of Tibetan Buddhism were preserved in the Qing imperial palace. There were more than a dozen Buddhist shrines built inside the palace walls and thirty-five Tibetan Buddhist temples and shrines scattered throughout the inner quarters of the Forbidden City. In the center were ten buildings, among them Zhongzheng Hall, Baohua Hall, Fanzong Tower, and Yuhua Pavilion. The Yuhua Pavilion inside the Chunhua Gate, built in 1750, was the largest Tibetan Buddhist temple in the imperial palace. The temple was constructed by the third Zhangjia Khutukhtu, member of an incarnation lineage based in northern Amdon on the Mongol border, brought to the Forbidden City for his education. The temple is divided into four parts that correspond to the Tibetan Esoteric Buddhist text classification system: practice, action, Yoga, and supreme Yoga. Vajrabhairava, Guhyasamaja, and Chakrasamvara were the three principal statues enshrined in the temple.[50]

Most of the gilt-bronze Buddhist statues in the Qing palace had been either court commissions during the Yuan, Ming, and Qing dynasties or gifts from Mongolia, Tibet, Nepal, and other areas. A few were even earlier works. The gilt-bronze Tibetan Buddhist statues were cast in a wide variety of forms and styles. Because so few were inscribed, it is difficult to compare and date them, but one way of judging them is to note differences in form and style. Some works were clearly influenced by the Gandhara and Mathura art styles of India; indeed, the Tibetan or Chinese artists were so adroit in their sculptural skills and casting techniques that their copies of foreign statues are hard to distinguish from the originals.

The style introduced by the Nepalese sculptor Anige to the Yuan court combined the characteristics of classic Indian and Nepalese sculpture. It gradually became the dominant style of the Tibetan Buddhist statues. A good example of a Nepalese work of the ninth to tenth century is the gilt-bronze statuette of the Vajrapani bodhisattva, a gift preserved in the Qing imperial palace. The statuette, 28 centimeters tall, wears a three-lobed coronet inlaid with gems. Its slim figure is naked above the waist, with long hair flowing down its shoul-

ders, and a halo around the head carved in a flame pattern. The bodhisattva holds a Vajra bell, wears a skirt, and stands barefoot on a lotus pedestal (fig. 4.89).

The copper-gilt statuette of the bodhisattva Manjushri, dated by inscription to the ninth year of the Mongol Yuan Da-de reign (1305), is 18 centimeters high. The bodhisattva, shown as a youth with a slender figure, wears a five-lobed coronet, sits cross-legged on an upside-down lotus seat, and is naked above the waist. His earrings, necklace, bracelets, and belt are inlaid with coral, pearls, and turquoise. The hair ribbon in the back of his head curls upward, and the sprig of lotus flowers in his hand forms a symmetrical decoration. This superbly sculpted statuette is a representative work of the Nepalese style of Buddhist art (fig. 4.90).

The bodhisattva Manjushri is the subject of many gilt-bronze statues. Most of them portray Manjushri as a male bodhisattva, his hair tied in five knobs, holding a sword that represents wisdom and insight. Tsongkhapa, the founder of the Gelug sect, was regarded as an emanation of Manjushri. The largest gilt-bronze statue of Manjushri in the imperial palace is enshrined in the Fanyu Tower and was cast sometime between 1730 and 1799. This 113-centimeter-high Manjushri lounges carelessly, bedecked with ornaments.

The gilt-bronze statues that present White Tara as a seated female deity all have beautifully treated bodies and hands. The female figures often have a graceful, lithe posture and figure, and there is always a faint smile on their faces. The delicate hands and feet, smooth skin, and splendid ornaments are set off by the carefully carved and regularly shaped lotus seat (fig. 4.91).

Most of the gilt statues are made of bronze and overlaid with a thin layer of gold. But some statues are made entirely of either gold or silver. A small number, too, are cast in iron or sculpted in stone and then painted in color and inlaid with gold, silver, pearls, and gems. These are gorgeous examples of high-court art. The most precious of these sculptures are a standing statue of Maitreya and a sitting statue of Shakyamuni cast in pure gold during the Qing dynasty. In the resplendent, 50-centimeter-high statue, Maitreya wears a loose skirt and a coronet inlaid with large pearls. He is naked to the waist, although scarves and strings of pearls frame his body, and pierced designs of clouds, flowers, ewers, and dharma wheels appear on the left and right sides of the image (fig. 4.92).

The sitting statue of Shakyamuni is 45 centimeters high, although if we include the background halo and seat in the measurement, the overall height is 90.5 cen-

4.89 Vajrapani bodhisattva, gilt bronze, 9th–10th century. 28 cm. Palace Museum, Beijing.

4.90 Manjushri bodhisattva, copper gilt. Yuan dynasty, 1305. 18 cm. Palace Museum, Beijing.

4.91 White Tara, gilt bronze. Ming dynasty, 14th century. Palace Museum, Beijing.

4.92 Maitreya, gold with inlaid pearls. Qing dynasty. 50 cm. Palace Museum, Beijing.

4.93 Seated Shakyamuni, gold. Qing dynasty. 90.5 cm. Palace Museum, Beijing.

4.94 Vajrabhairava, red copper or red brass. Qing dynasty. 93 cm. Palace Museum, Beijing.

4.95 Guhyasamaja and consort, brass. Qing dynasty, 17th century. Palace Museum, Beijing.

4.96 Zhangjia Khutukhtu Rolpay Dorje, silver gilt. Qing dynasty, 1786. 75 cm. Palace Museum, Beijing.

timeters. Shakyamuni is shown turning the dharma wheel, with his right shoulder exposed and robes covering the rest of his body. The simply modeled Buddha contrasts dramatically with the finely carved halo and seat. The figure style emulates Kashmiri Buddhist sculptures of the ninth through eleventh centuries, exhibiting knowledge of archaic Indian sculpture on the part of the Qing artists and patrons. The skill with which the figures were made makes them stand out as masterpieces by any standard (fig. 4.93).

The depictions of a number of sculptures produced for the imperial palaces and temples, such as Hayagriva, for example, have multiple heads and arms. They have small skulls in their crowns and serpents as bracelets and carry various religious objects. Living creatures are being trampled under their feet. This kind of complex, detailed work was particularly difficult to design and cast. Although the sculptors had to observe the rules and measurements for making statues, they were free to portray the mood and arrange the details as they wished.

A copper statue of Vajrabhairava 93 centimeters high, cast during the Qianlong reign, has nine heads, each with a different facial expression, either benign or fierce. The principal head is that of a buffalo with two sharp horns; beneath is a short, heavy body with the stomach exposed. The right leg is bent and the left leg straight. The thirty-four arms and sixteen legs overlap one another and seem to be in motion, while a number of creatures writhe beneath his feet. Vajrabhairava is one of the principal meditation deities of the Gelug sect, and the multiplication of heads and limbs aims to show his ferocity in subduing obstacles to enlightenment and protecting good. Although the sculpture is complex, it is carefully planned; the result is a powerful and beautiful image (fig. 4.94). A sculpture of Guhyasamaja has an even more complicated structure.

It has six arms and three faces, with three eyes in each. Even the female consort sitting on Guhyasamaja's lap has six arms. Yet the sculptors seem to have effortlessly arranged the various members of the two subjects into a perfect whole (fig. 4.95).

There are also a number of gilt works that portray historically important monks, such as the silver-gilt statue of Zhangjia Khutukhtu Rolpay Dorje (1717–1786), a Tibetan Buddhist master who was closely associated with the Qianlong emperor and advised him on religious affairs. The statue was created by court artisans in the Qing palace in the year the monk passed away, and it has a sumptuous yet restrained appearance (fig. 4.96).[51]

Tibeto-Chinese sculpture formed one strand in the complex warp and weft of Chinese religious sculpture, which drew inspiration from Daoism, Chinese popular Buddhism, folk and local deities, and Tibetan Esoteric Buddhism. Although it is now relatively easy to distinguish the different strands on the basis of the contexts in which the sculptures were placed and are found — temples and shrines of their various orientations — in fact there was a circulation of motifs, along with attitudes and modes of figuration, that transcended differences.

For the most part, period styles seem to cut powerfully across religious and sectarian themes. Each period found innovative ways to express the supernatural through natural forms, exaggerating or diminishing physical features and resemblances, expanding or minimizing motifs recognizable from everyday life or exotic in origin. Sculptors at every turn also found ways to overcome the limits of their media to make towering figures of wood or exquisite porcelain miniatures, accumulating figures into dense complexes or isolating them by capitalizing on unusual outcroppings of natural stone. It is perhaps this consistent technical mastery of the Chinese sculptors that leaves the most lingering impression.

Epilogue

ANGELA FALCO HOWARD

China's sculptural heritage displays culturally distinct characteristics. The numerous genres explored here — the astonishing variety of objects coming to light from myriad tombs, the ponderous stone beasts and humans lining the Spirit Roads of successive emperors, the countless Buddhist and, to a lesser degree, Daoist and Confucian deities worshiped in caves and temples — indicate the need to rethink what *sculpture* means and to ponder how art was executed and what functions it filled. The definition of Chinese sculpture that emerges from this rethinking does not coincide with, nor does it have affinity with, the definition that Western art historians apply to Western sculpture.

We often think of sculpting as a physical labor in which, during the creative process, the artist frees the work by cutting and chiseling it away from a hard mass — stone or wood. With the exception of jade artifacts achieved through a process of abrasion — a cutting away — Chinese craftworkers began the art of modeling with clay, which requires joining parts to a base in an additive process. The sophisticated clay pots of the Neolithic period demonstrate the specialization in this technique that, in turn, made possible the great advances of the Bronze Age. This is probably why in China, unlike in other cultures, metal generally preceded stone as a medium, and the earliest sculptural objects coincided with extraordinary technological advances. Beautiful images resulted from the perfection of metallurgical skills; the application of complex methods of casting created art in the round. Mysterious bronze figures from Sanxingdui (Sichuan Province) manufactured around 1200 B.C.E., the maiden doubling as a lamp in the second-century B.C.E. tomb of Princess Dou Wan (Hebei Province), and warrior statues supporting an awesome rack of bells in the fifth-century tomb of Marquis Yi of Zeng (Hubei Province) are excellent examples of technology at the service of art.

When making a sculpture, the artist may either choose to imitate the surrounding world, thereby producing a work based on a model existing in life, or opt for nonrepresentation, thus creating an abstract work. Chinese sculptors generally favored abstraction over realism — with the important exception of sculptural works executed during the Tang dynasty, when realism took the arts by storm.

Why were Chinese sculptors drawn to abstraction? Their choice was grounded in the religious nature of most of their art. Believers needed to summon cosmic forces, which did not belong to the ordinary world, and those forces had to be portrayed in the abstract. Neolithic jades, the earliest three-dimensional art objects, represented totally imaginary figures, like the *zhulong,* or pig-dragon. During the Bronze Age, vessels became fantastic zoomorphs. During the period of disunion, the imperial tombs around Nanjing were protected by *bixie* and *qilin*—hornless winged creatures and unicorns. During the Song dynasty, when China was threatened at its northern borders, the imperial tombs were guarded by a mythic animal called the *jiaoduan.*

The attitude of patrons toward the art they supported forms another distinguishing trait of Chinese sculpture. Chinese patrons commissioned state ritual art that they would never see (at least not during their lifetime), art that was not intended for display in the open and that was not regarded as a complement to a home or a communal space. The army of terra-cotta warriors gathered in the underground necropolis of the First Emperor of Qin (d. 210 b.c.e.) remains the most ostentatious and monumental example of this kind. The reasons for such displays are connected to Chinese religious views of the afterlife, explored in the first two chapters of this book.

Sculpture — whether a response to the demands of state ritual or to those of Buddhist, Daoist, or Confucian congregations — was seldom conceived in terms of individual pieces and as a rule was collectively produced. Most of the time, statues or sculptural objects formed part of a large project or belonged to the lavish interior or exterior of a burial site, a cave temple, or a shrine. To build such complexes required the collaboration of workers, especially when deadlines were tight.

The scale of the sculptural works went hand in hand with yet another requirement. To achieve effectiveness, statuary had to be executed with meticulous respect for precedent. The stone guardians of an imperial Spirit Road, for instance, had to meet strict guidelines regarding their identity and hierarchical display, just as an image of Buddha or Laozi had to conform to unalterable specifications regarding body and costume.

The rigidity of the guidelines, in addition to the scale of the projects, took away the creative freedom and inspiration of the artist. The way sculpture was produced privileged the group over the individual. Consequently, in spite of the sophisticated artistry that Chinese sculpture displays in its various forms, even masterpieces were rarely credited to specific artists. Nevertheless, outstanding anonymous artists left us brilliant works, their artistic skills and inspiration undiminished.

In China, then, collective authorship prevailed over individual artistry; sculptors adhered to firm rules, merging function and aesthetic (if not allowing function to be the raison d'être of the work); sculpture was often a response to religious needs requiring abstract expression; and sculptors generally worked on the assumption that their creative endeavors were not intended for public display and admiration. Despite these indigenous constraints, Chinese sculpture is a fully realized art, not merely the creation of clever artisans. Its inventiveness, purpose, and brilliant execution are rooted in and nurtured by unique Chinese religious, intellectual, and practical choices.

White Tara, by Zanabazar, gilt bronze. Late 17th–early 18th century. 68.9 cm. Museum of Fine Arts, Ulaanbataar, Mongolia.

CHINESE SCULPTURE SITES

KAZAKHSTAN

KYRGYZSTAN

TAJIKISTAN

AFGHANISTAN

PAKISTAN

•130

•129

•101

NEPAL

BHUTAN

INDIA

BANGLADESH

•97

100• •99 •98

Bay of Bengal

75°E 90°E

45°E

30°E

0   500 KM

Lambert Conformal Conic Projection, SP 23N/45N

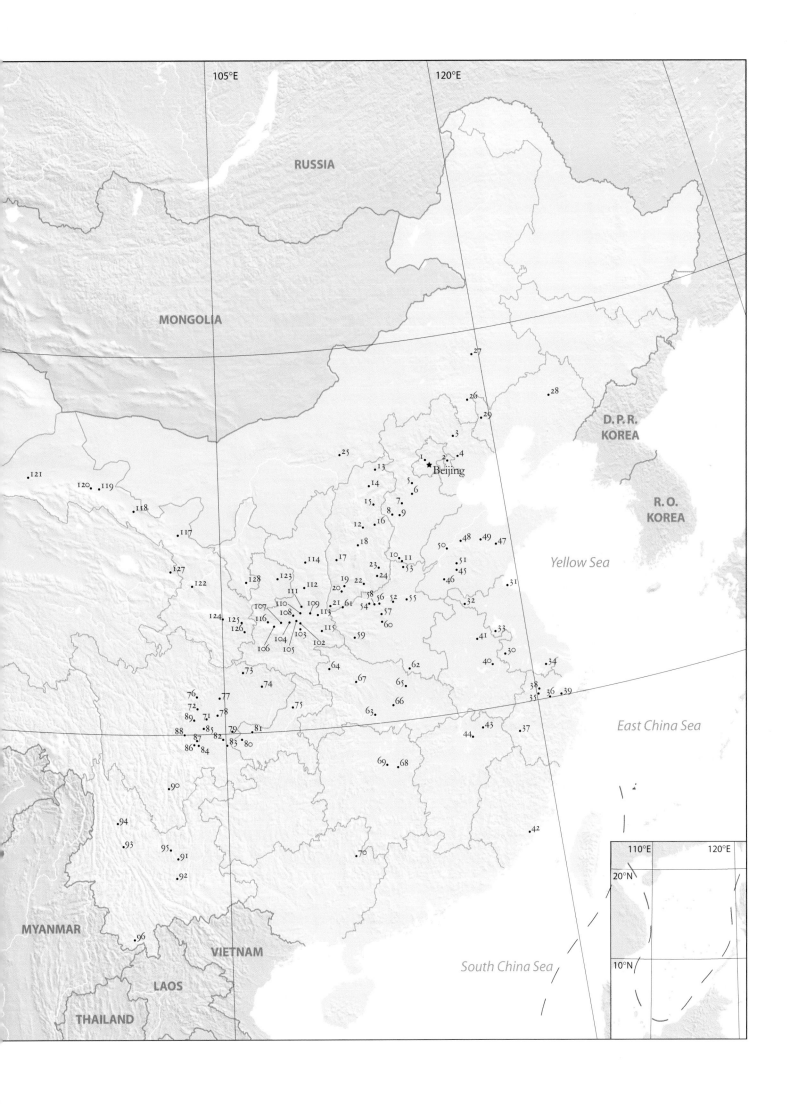

NOTES

Introduction by Li Song

1. See "Chahai yizhi fajue zai huo zhongda chengguo" (Major finds again achieved in the excavation of the Chahai ruins), *Zhongguo wenwu bao*, Mar. 19, 1995. *Dui* (piling) and *suo* (sculpting) represent specific ways of artistic modeling in early Chinese society. Three groups of patterns made with piled-up shells were discovered in Xishuipo Yangshao Culture ruins in Puyang, Henan Province, in 1987. The pattern of the dragon, which is much like the stylized dragons of later ages, is particularly impressive. Another dragon, a huge one composed of pebbles, was found in the Jiaodun ruins of Huangmei County, Hubei Province, in 1993. And two gigantic fish-dragon images made of rammed earth were discovered in 1998 in ancient ditches dug in Qingshuihe County, Inner Mongolia. All these images appear to have been created in the mid-fourth–mid-third millennium B.C.E.

2. An early source for this quotation is *Shi ji* (Historical records).

3. Sima Qian, *Shi ji: Qin Shihuang benji* (Historical records: Biography of the First Emperor of Qin), 2d ed. (Beijing: Zhonghua shuju, 1982), 223.

4. Ban Gu, *Han shu* (History of the Han), vol. 55: *Wei Qing, Huo Qubing zhuan* (Biographies of Wei Qing and Huo Qubing) (Beijing: Zhonghua shuju, 1962), 2471.

5. Specifically, under the supervision of the Dongyuan division of the Shaofu Department. Sima Biao, *Hou Han shu* (History of the Later Han) (Beijing: Zhonghua shuju,1965), 3589–3605. Starting in the Song, sculpture was put under the supervision of the Ministry of Industries. Tuo Tuo, *Song shi* (History of the Song) (Beijing: Zhonghua shuju, 1985), 3831–3899.

6. *Liaoning jiaoyu*, vol. 1 (1997): 157. The title of Zuo Qiuming's work is sometimes translated as "Spring and Autumn Annals."

7. Guo Ruoxu, *Huihua jianwen zhi*, vol. 1: *Lun Cao-Wu tifa*, in Pan Zhenggao, ed., *Tuhua jianwen zhi; Hua ji* (My experience in painting; Record of painting) (Hunan: Hunan meishu chubanshe, 2000).

8. See *Wudai Wang Chuzhi mu* (Tomb of Wang Chuzhi of the Five Dynasties) (Beijing: Wenwu chubanshe, 1998).

9. Li Zhuo, *Shang shu gu shi*: "Originally, Buddhist statues were modeled on images of foreigners and villagers, thus failing to win respect from the people. The current flowery and refined sculpture style started with Dai [Kui]."

10. There are a number of sources for this saying. An early one is Zhang Yanyuan's *Lidai minghua ji* (Record of famous paintings of successive dynasties), dated 847. See *Lidai minghua ji*, in *Congshu jicheng chubian* (Initial edition of a collection of various books) (Beijing: Shangwu yinshuguan, 1936).

11. Guo Ruoxu, *Huihua jianwen zhi*, vol. 1.

12. Dong You, *Guangchuan huaba*, in *Huapin congshu* (Series on painting) (Shanghai: Shanghai renmin meishu chubanshe, 1982). See Zhang Yanyuan, *Lidai minghua ji*.

13. For a biography of Yang Huizhi, see Liu Daochun, *Wudai minghua buyi*, in Pan Zhenggao, ed., *Songren huaping* (Comments on painting by people in the Song dynasty) (Hunan: Hunan meishu chubanshe, 1999), 110–111. With regard to sculpted mountain-water walls, see *Hua ji*, vol. 9, by Deng Chun of the Song dynasty: "In the central plains there were many sculpted mountain-water walls in the style created by [Yang] Huizhi. Seeing them, Guo Xi came up with some new ideas... He ordered the workers to throw mud on a wall and not worry about the unevenness. When the mud dried, he painted it randomly with ink, creating mountain peaks and valleys. Then he added towers, pavilions, and figures... This is called *yingbi* (shadow wall), and a great many people followed suit." Yingbi, then, is a kind of bas-relief combining painting with sculpture. The arhats sculpted on a wall in the Baosheng Temple in Luzhi, Jiangsu Province, in the Song dynasty (see fig. 4.33), fall into the category of high relief.

14. Liu Daochun, *Wudai minghua buyi*.

15. *Lüshi chunqiu Shen ying lan Li wei*, in *Ershi'er zi* (Twenty-two classics) (Shanghai: Shanghai guji chubanshe, 1986).

16. *Xiangjiang* refers to sculptors good at making statues of various kinds of people. *Xiang* refers to physiognomy, specifically to face reading as a form of fortune-telling. Painting and sculpting human figures require familiarity with the physical features of the people to be represented.

17. Both Dai Kui and Dai Yong were highly accomplished scholars. In the time of Emperor Xiaowu of the Eastern Jin, Dai Kui was repeatedly called to serve at court. Despite promises of high official posts, he refused. Later, Dai Yong also turned down repeated offers of high official positions at court. Both father and son are thus known as *zhengshi* (scholars solicited by the court).

18. *Yuandai huasu ji* (Beijing: Renmin meishu chubanshe, 1964). Originally a part of *Jingshi dadian: Gongdian* (Encyclopedia on administration of state affairs: Crafts) of the Yuan dynasty, it mainly comprised records of rules regarding materials to be used for paintings and sculptures for official use. The original work has been lost. The present book was extracted from *Yongle dadian* (Yongle encyclopedia) by the scholar Wen Tingshi and incorporated in *Guangcang xuejun congshu*, published in 1916.

Introduction by Angela Falco Howard

1. Ruth W. Dunnell, *The Great State of White and High: Buddhism and State Formation in Eleventh-Century Xia* (Honolulu: University of Hawai'i Press, 1996).

2. Alexander C. Soper, "Hsiang-Guo-Ssu: An Imperial Temple of Northern Sung," *Journal of the American Oriental Society* 68 (1948): 19–45.

3. Angela Falco Howard, *Summit of Treasures: Buddhist Cliff Sculpture of Dazu, Sichuan* (New York: Weatherhill, 2001).

4. Shi Jinbo, *Xi Xia Fojiao shilüe* (Yinchuan: Ningxia renmin chubanshe, 1988); Shi Jinbo et al., *Xi Xia wenwu* (Beijing: Wenwu chubanshe, 1988); Rob Linrothe, "Peripheral Visions: On Recent Finds of Tangut Buddhist Art," *Monumenta Serica* 43 (1995): 235–262.

5. Jing Anning, "The Portraits of Khubilai Khan and Chabi by Anige (1245–1306), a Nepali Artist at the Yuan Court," *Artibus Asiae* 54, 1–2 (1994): 49–86. For the history of the last three dynasties I relied on F. W. Mote, *Imperial China, 900–1800* (Cambridge: Harvard University Press, 1999).

6. Patricia Berger and Terese Tse Bartholomew et al., *Mongolia: The Legacy of Chinggis Khan* (San Francisco: Asian Art

Museum, 1995), 56–68; N. Tsultem, *The Eminent Mongolian Sculptor — G. Zanabazar* (Ulaanbataar: State Publishing House, 1982); Yang Boda, "Zhanabazha'er de liujintong zaoxiang yishu," *Gugong bowuyuan yuankan* 4 (1996): 59–65.

7. Anne Chayet, *Les temples de jahol et leurs modèles tibétains* (Paris: Edition recherche sur les civilizations, 1984); and Philippe Foret, *Mapping Chengde: The Qing Landscape Enterprise* (Honolulu: University of Hawai'i Press, 2000).

8. Wang Jiapeng, "Qingqong Zangchuan Fojiao wenhua kaocha," in *Qingdai gongshi congtan* (Beijing: Wenwu chubanshe, 1996), 58–71.

Chapter 1. From the Neolithic to the Han

1. The most famous examples of late Paleolithic ornaments are the 141 artifacts from Zhoukoudian on the outskirts of Beijing. Created circa 9000 to 8000 B.C.E., these include white stone beads, yellow-green oval pebbles, animal teeth, shells, and red-stained herring bones, all perforated.

2. David N. Keightley, "Archaeology and Mentality: The Making of China," *Representations* 18 (Spring 1987): 91–128. The northwestern tradition is also known as the Yangshao culture; the eastern tradition is also called the Longshan culture.

3. See K. C. Chang, *The Archaeology of Ancient China*, 4th ed. (New Haven: Yale University Press, 1986), 234–242.

4. See Yang Xiaoneng, *Sculpture of Prehistoric China* (Hong Kong: Tai Dao Publishing, 1988), 14, figs. 31, 32; Helmut Brinker, "On the Origin of the Human Image in Chinese Art," *Kaikodo Journal* (Spring 1997): 18–47, figs. 12, 40.

5. For further discussion of these two images, see Yang, *Sculpture of Prehistoric China*, figs. 104, 105; Brinker, "On the Origin of the Human Image," figs. 41, 42.

6. For illustrations, see Yang, *Sculpture of Prehistoric China*, figs. 33–34, 106–112.

7. For illustrations, see Yang, *Sculpture of Prehistoric China*, pls. 83, 84.

8. This vessel is 33 centimeters long, from Meiyan in Wuxian, Jiangsu Province. For an illustration, see Yang, *Sculpture of Prehistoric China*, pl. 7.

9. For illustrations, see Yang, *Sculpture of Prehistoric China*, figs. 49, 50.

10. There has been some debate about the figure's gender, and certain scholars consider the image either male or androgynous. For an illustration of the jar and a summary of the debate, see Jessica Rawson, ed., *Mysteries of Ancient China* (London: British Museum, 1996), no. 5:38.

11. One such image is found on a pottery jar in the Museum of Fine Arts, Boston. A similar example is from Shancheng, Minhe, Qinghai. See Yang, *Sculpture of Prehistoric China*, pl. 68.

12. *Baoji Beishouling* (The archaeological site at Beishouling in Baoji) (Beijing: Wenwu chubanshe, 1983), 75. See also Rawson, *Mysteries of Ancient China*, no. 2:35; Yang, *Sculpture of Prehistoric China*, pl. 5.

13. Representative works of this type include jars from Dadiwan and Sizui at Qin'an, Gansu. For Dadiwan jars, see *Wenwu* 11 (1979): 52–55, figs. 2, 3; for Sizui, see Yang, *Sculpture of Prehistoric China*, pl. 61. The famous examples of J. G. Andersson in the early twentieth century may have also come from Gansu: Yang, *Sculpture of Prehistoric China*, pls. 62,

64–66. Similar examples have been excavated at Liuwan in Ledu, Qinghai Province; see pl. 67. But a recent discovery indicates that this type of pottery vessel was also made in the South: a jar from Jiaxing, Zhejiang Province, has a tall body topped with a sculptured human head. See Wu Shichi, *Zhongguo yuanshi yishu* (Primitive art of China) (Beijing: Zijincheng chubanshe, 1996), pl. 12.

14. For this crucial transition in early Chinese art, see Wu Hung, *Monumentality in Early Chinese Art and Architecture* (Stanford: Stanford University Press, 1995), 24–44.

15. For illustration and more detailed discussion of Dawenkou axes, see Wu, *Monumentality in Early Chinese Art and Architecture*, 24–27, fig. 1.1.

16. For illustration, see Wu, *Monumentality in Early Chinese Art and Architecture*, fig. 1.33.

17. See Wu Hung, "Bird Motifs in Eastern Yi Art," *Orientations* 16, no. 10 (1985): 30–41.

18. For illustrations and a further discussion of these and other mask motifs, see Wu, *Monumentality in Early Chinese Art and Architecture*, 38–44; Brinker, "On the Origin of the Human Image in Chinese Art," 20–24.

19. See Angus Forsyth, "Five Chinese Jade Figures: A Study of the Development of Sculptural Form in Hongshan Neolithic Jade Working," *Orientations* 21, no. 5 (1990): 54–63. It has also been suggested that two stone sculptures of kneeling figures found at Naqitai in the Right Balin Banner in Inner Mongolia are Hongshan products (*Kaogu* 6 [1987]: 507–518), yet their forms show little resemblance to Honshan jade figures. Most unusually, the two figures have no definable facial features and wear peculiar headdresses in the shape of a pile of round disks.

20. For a discussion of the pig-dragon and other Hongshan images, see Elizabeth Childs-Johnson, "Jades of the Hongshan Culture: The Dragon and Fertility Cult Worship," *Arts asiatiques* 46 (1991): 82–95.

21. "Liaoning Niuheliang Hongshan wenhua 'Nüshen miao' yu jishizhong qun fajue jianbao" (A short report on the excavation of the "Temple of the Goddesses" and the stone heap tomb group of the Hongshan culture in Niuheliang, Liaoning), *Wenwu* 8 (1986): 1–17.

22. Sun Shoudao and Guo Dashun, "Niuheliang Hongshan wenhua nüshen touxiang de faxian yu yanjiu" (The discovery of and research on a goddess's head from Niuheliang of the Hongshan culture), *Wenwu* 8 (1986): 18–24.

23. Guo Dashun and Zhang Keju, "Liaoning sheng Kezuo xiang Dongshanzui Hongshan wenhua jianzhu qunzhi fajue jianbao" (A brief report on the excavation of the group architectural site of the Hongshan culture at Dongshanzui in Kezuo County, Liaoning Province), *Wenwu* 11 (1984): 1–11.

24. Che Lie, "The Ancestor Cult in Ancient China," in Rawson, *Mysteries of Ancient China*, 269–272; quotation from 270.

25. See Brinker, "On the Origin of the Human Image in Chinese Art," 29, fig. 18.

26. See Wu Hung, "Cong dixing bianhua he dili fenbu guancha Shandong diqu guwenhua de fazhan" (A study of ancient cultures of the Shandong region, in light of geographical distribution and topographical changes), in Su Bingqi, ed., *Kaoguxue wenhua lunji* (An anthology of Chinese archaeological and cultural studies) (Beijing: Wenwu chubanshe, 1987), 165–180.

27. See *Kaogu xuebao* 2 (1994): 191–229.

28. Some examples are illustrated in Rawson, *Mysteries of Ancient China,* nos. 12a–12h.

29. For a fuller discussion of the nature of the Chinese Bronze Age, see Wu, *Monumentality in Early Chinese Art and Architecture,* 63–75.

30. One of these *jue* is illustrated in Wen Fong, ed., *Great Bronze Age of China* (New York: Metropolitan Museum of Art, 1980), pl. 1.

31. This *ding* vessel is illustrated in Fong, *Great Bronze Age of China,* pl. 11. For other examples, see *Zhongguo qingtongqi quanji* (A comprehensive collection of Chinese bronzes), vol. 1, "Xia and Shang periods" (Beijing: Wenwu chubanshe, 1996), pls. 34–37, 46. The last example is from Xin'gan, Jiangxi Province, in south China.

32. For this development, see Jessica Rawson, *Chinese Bronzes: Art and Ritual* (London: British Museum, 1987), 26–29; Wu, *Monumentality in Early Chinese Art and Architecture,* 44–53.

33. *Yinxu Fu Hao mu* (The tomb of Lady Hao at Yinxu) (Beijing: Wenwu chubanshe, 1980). For a concise English introduction to this tomb and some excavated objects, see Fong, *Great Bronze Age of China,* 177–189.

34. See *Yinxu Fu Hao mu,* 31–100.

35. For these and other guang vessels from Fu Hao's tomb, see *Yinxu Fu Hao mu,* pls. 25–27.

36. This vessel (no. 1163) is illustrated in Fong, *Great Bronze Age of China,* pl. 30.

37. This vessel (no. 784) is illustrated in Fong, *Great Bronze Age of China,* pl. 29.

38. See *Yinxu Fu Hao mu,* 156–173. Some of these examples are illustrated in Fong, *Great Bronze Age of China,* pls. 34–36, 40.

39. For illustrations, see *Yinxu yuqi* (Jade carvings from the Yinxu) (Beijing: Wenwu chubanshe, 1982), pls. 52, 67.

40. For illustrations, see *Yinxu yuqi,* pls. 48, 49, 51, 109–111, 113.

41. See *Yinxu Fu Hao mu,* 151–156. The standing figure is also illustrated in Fong, *Great Bronze Age of China,* pl. 37.

42. For illustration, see *Yinxu yuqi,* pls. 98–100.

43. For illustrations, see *Yinxu yuqi,* pls. 109, 112, 113.

44. *Yinxu Fu Hao mu,* 151.

45. See Wu Hung, "The Great Beginning: Ancient Chinese Jades and the Origin of Ritual Art," in *Chinese Jades from the Mu-Fei Collection* (London: Bluett and Sons, 1990).

46. See Li Chi, *Anyang* (Seattle: University of Washington Press, 1977), 92–93, 220–225.

47. See *Yinxu Fu Hao mu,* 200–203.

48. For the excavation of the tomb, see K. C. Chang, *Shang Civilization* (New Haven: Yale University Press, 1980), 110–119.

49. See Li, *Anyang,* 213.

50. For a concise discussion of these images, see Yang Xiaoneng, *Sculpture of Xia and Shang China* (Hong Kong: Tai Dao, 1988), 13, pl. 2, figs. 58–61, 65–67, 86–93.

51. *Kaogu xuebao* 7 (1954), 24.

52. Wei Shuxun, "Anyang chutu de rentoufan" (A human-face mold unearthed at Anyang), *Kaogu* 5 (1959): 272.

53. See L. G. F. Huber, "Some Anyang Royal Bronzes: Remarks on Shang Bronze Decor," in G. Kuwayama, ed., *The Great Bronze Age of China: A Symposium* (Los Angeles: Los Angeles County Museum, 1980), 16–43; Wu, *Monumentality in Early Chinese Art and Architecture,* 56–58.

54. For illustrations, see Yang, *Sculpture of Xia and Shang China,* pls. 153, 161, 164.

55. For illustration, see Yang, *Sculpture of Xia and Shang China,* pl. 128.

56. For a general introduction to the Sanxingdui culture, see Qu Xiaoqiang, Li Dianxian, and Duan Yu, *Sanxingdui wenhua* (Sanxingdui culture) (Chengdu: Sichuan renmin chubanshe, 1993).

57. For archaeological excavations of the Sanxingdui site, see Ao Tianzhao and Liu Yutao, "Guanghan Sanxiangdui kaogu jilue" (A brief record of Guanghan archaeology), in Li Shaoming, Lin Xiang, and Xu Nanchuan, eds., *Ba Shu lishi, minzu, kaogu, wenhua* (History, ethnology, archaeology, and culture of the Ba and the Shu) (Chengdu: Ba Shu shushe, 1991), 331–338; "Guanghan Sanxingdui yizhi yihuo jisikeng fajue jianbao" (A brief report on the excavation of Sacrificial Pit 1 at Sanxingdui, Guanghan), *Wenwu* 10 (1987): 1–15; and "Guanghan Sanxingdui yizhi erhao jisikeng fajue jianbao" (A brief report on the excavation of Sacrificial Pit 2 at Sanxingdui, Guanghan), *Wenwu* 5 (1989): 1–20.

58. Zhao Dianzeng, "Sanxingdui kaogu faxian yu Ba Shu gushi yanjiu" (Archaeological finds at Sanxingdui and historical studies of Ba and Shu), *Sichuan wenwu,* special issue on Sanxingdui culture (1992): 3–12.

59. Chen Xiandan, "Guanghan Sanxingdui yizhi fajue gaikuang, chubu fenqi — jianlun 'zao Shu wenhua' de tezheng jiqi fazhan" (A general excavation report and preliminary periodization of the Sanxiangdui sites at Guanghan, with a discussion of the characteristics and development of early Shu culture), *Nanfang minzu kaogu* (Southern ethnology and archaeology), no. 2 (1989): 213–231; Wu Yi, "Chengdu Fangchijie chutu shidiao renxiang ji xiangguan wenti" (The sculpted stone human figure from Fangchijie in Chengdu and related problems), *Sichuan wenwu* (Sichuan cultural relics) 6 (1988): 18–22; Xu Pengzhang, "Woshi Fangchijie faxian guwenhua yizhi" (An ancient site found at Fangchijie in Chengdu), *Chengdu wenwu* (Chengdu cultural relics) 2 (1984): 89–91. For a fuller discussion of these images, see Wu Hung, "All About the Eyes: Two Groups of Sculptures from the Sanxingdui Culture," *Orientations* 28, no. 8 (1997): 58–66.

60. David Freedberg discusses numerous examples of both situations in his *Power of Images* (Chicago: University of Chicago Press, 1989).

61. Rawson, *Chinese Bronzes: Art and Ritual,* 36.

62. For examples, see *Zhongguo qingtongqi quanji* (A comprehensive collection of Chinese bronzes), vol. 5, "Western Zhou 1" (Beijing: Wenwu chubanshe, 1996), pls. 99–108.

63. This is the famous "Taibo you" in the Baihe Gallery in Japan. For an illustration, see *Zhongguo qingtongqi quanji,* vol. 5, "Western Zhou 1," pl. 176.

64. See *Shaanxi chutu Shang Zhou qingtongqi* (Shang and Zhou bronzes from Shaanxi Province), vol. 1 (Beijing: Wenwu chubanshe, 1979), pl. 167; *Zhongguo qingtongqi quanji,* vol. 5, "Western Zhou 1," pl. 165.

65. See Howard Rogers, ed., *China: Five Thousand Years* (New York: Guggenheim Museum, 1998), pl. 37.

66. Zhou bronze masks in both realistic and "abstract" styles have been found in Tomb 1193 at Liulihe near Beijing. See *Kaogu* 1 (1990): 30; *Kaogu* 12 (1992): 1112. A work from Tomb 451 at Pangjiagou near Luoyang exemplifies Western

Zhou chariot fittings with sculpted human images. See Rawson, *Mysteries of Ancient China,* 117.

67. See Wu, *Monumentality in Early Chinese Art and Architecture,* 53–63; Rawson, *Chinese Bronzes: Art and Ritual,* 38–45.

68. For information about and illustrations of the Li vessels, see *Shaanxi chutu Shang Zhou qingtongqi* (Shang and Zhou bronzes unearthed in Shaanxi Province), vol. 3 (Beijing: Wenwu chubanshe, 1980), pls. 193–197.

69. *Shaanxi chutu Shang Zhou qingtongqi,* vol. 2 (Beijing: Wenwu chubanshe, 1980), pl. 77; Gao Ciruo and Liu Mingke, "Baoji Rujiazhuang xin faxian tongqi jiaocang," *Kaogu yu wenwu* 4 (1990): 11–16.

70. *Zhou li zhushu* (An annotated *Rites of Zhou*), in Ruan Yuan, comp., *Shisanjing zhushu* (The annotated thirteen classics), 2 vols. (Beijing: Zhonghua shuju, 1980), vol. 1, p. 883.

71. Zhu Hua, "Wenxi Shangguocun gumuqun shijue" (An experimental excavation of a group of ancient tombs at Shangguo village in Wenxi), *San Jin kaogu* 1 (1994): 139–153. See also Lothar von Falkenhausen, "The Waning of the Bronze Age," in M. Loewe and E. Shaughnessy, eds., *The Cambridge History of Ancient China* (Cambridge: Cambridge University Press, 1999), 482–483.

72. These examples include a *he* vessel with two naked human figures as feet, a bronze casket carried by four naked kneeling figures, and a cylindrical container carried by three figures in a squatting posture. See Shanxi Provincial Institute of Archaeology, Department of Archaeology, Peking University, "Tianma-Qucun yizhi Beizhao Jinhou mudi disici faque" (The fourth excavation of the Jin royal cemetery at the Tianma-Qucun site in Beizhao), *Wenwu* 8 (1994): 4–21, figs. 24.2–24.3; Shanxi Provincial Institute of Archaeology, Department of Archaeology, Peking University, "Tianma-Qucun yizhi Beizhao Jinhou mudi disanci faque" (The third excavation of the Jin royal cemetery at the Tianma-Qucun site in Beizhao), *Wenwu* 8 (1994): 22–33, fig. 4.4.

73. For this cult, see Wu, "Bird Motifs in Eastern Yi Art," 30–41.

74. See Guolong Lai, "Uses of the Human Figure in Early Chinese Art," *Orientations* 30, no. 6 (1999): 49–55.

75. One of these two vessels is illustrated and discussed in Fong, *Great Bronze Age of China,* no. 67.

76. Some of these examples, dating from the mid-sixth century B.C.E., are found in Tomb 2 at Xichuan, Xiasi, Henan.

77. Rawson, *Mysteries of Ancient China,* 61–62.

78. The uncertainty is caused by different interpretations of the date 433 B.C.E. inscribed on a large bronze bell from the tomb, which was a gift from King Hui of Chu. Some scholars believe that Marquis Yi died in this year and the bell was a mortuary present from the ruler of a neighboring state. Other scholars consider that the bell was made while the marquis was still alive. See Qiu Xigui, "Tantan Suixian Zenghou Yi mu de wenzi ziliao" (On textual materials from the tomb of Marquis Yi of Zeng), *Wenwu* 7 (1979): 25–31; *Zenghou Yi mu* (The tomb of Marquis Yi of Zeng), 2 vols. (Beijing: Wenwu chubanshe, 1989), vol. 1, p. 461.

79. For Zeng bronzes, see Zhou Yongzhen, "Zengguo yu Zengguo tongqi" (The state of Zeng and Zeng bronzes), *Kaogu* 5 (1980): 436–443; Zeng Zhaoming and Li Jin, "Zengguo he Zengguo tongqi zongkao" (A synthetic study of the state of Zeng and Zeng bronzes), *Jianghan kaogu* 1 (1980): 69–84.

80. For a discussion of these rituals, see Yang Kuan, *Gushi xintan* (A new exploration of ancient history) (Beijing: Zhonghua shuju, 1965), 218–370.

81. See Zhu Jianhua, "Chu shu tanbi — lujiao lihe xuangu, lugu, huzuo niaojia gu kao," *Jianghan kaogu* 4 (1991): 83–86.

82. *Shanxi chutu wenwu* (Shanxi: Shanxi wenwu gongzuo yiyuanhui, 1980), nos. 87–89, 98, 103. See J. So, *Eastern Zhou Ritual Bronzes from the Arthur M. Sackler Collection* (New York: Arthur M. Sackler Foundation, 1995), 65.

83. For two excavated examples, see *Wenwu* 3 (1976), fig. 4; *Baoshan Chu mu,* 2 vols. (Beijing: Wenwu chubanshe, 1991), vol. 1, pp. 189–194.

84. For an illustration of this dragon image, see Umehara Sueji, *Sengoku shiki dōki no kenkyū* (A study of bronzes in Warring States styles) (Kyoto: Tōhō bunka gakuin Kyōtō kenkyūjo, 1936), fig. 80. For the remains of the *tai* platforms in Wuyang, see *Kaogu xuebao* 1 (1965): 88–95. For bronze door rings and other architectural remains from Laomu Tai, see *Hebei sheng chutu wenwu xuanji* (Beijing: Wenwu chubanshe, 1980), no. 115; Umehara Suiji, *Sengoku-shiki dōki no kenkyū* (Kyoto: Tōhō bunka gakuin Kyōtō kenkyūjo, 1936), pl. 79; Komai Kazuchika, "Eaves-Tiles with Double Dragon Designs of the State of Yan," in *Chūgoku kōkogaku ronsō* (Tokyo: Keiyūsha, 1974), 323–327.

85. For the excavation report, see *Wenwu* 1 (1979): 1–13. Exhibition catalogues of Zhongshan objects include *Chūgoku sengoku jidai no yū: Chūzan ōgoku bunbutsuten* (Tokyo: Tokyo National Museum, 1981) and Galeries nationales du Grand Palais, ed., *Zhongshan: Tombes des rois oubliés* (Paris: Association française d'action artistique, 1985).

86. For the history of Zhongshan, see Liu Laicheng and Li Xiaodong, "Shitan Zhanguo shiqi Zhongshanguo lishi shangde jige wenti," *Wenwu* 1 (1979): 32–36; Li Xueqin and Li Ling, "Pingshan sanqi yu Zhongshanguo shi de ruogan wenti," *Kaogu xuebao* 2 (1979): 147–170. The excavations of stone burials, gold earrings, and bronze daggers in the Zhongshan area prove that people who lived here continued the customs of the Di at least to the early Warring States period; see *Kaoguxue jikan* 5 (1987); *Kaogu* 11 (1984): 971–973; *Wenwu* 6 (1986): 20–24.

87. For the change in the center of ancestral worship from temple to tomb, see Wu, *Monumentality in Early Chinese Art and Architecture,* 79–121. For a discussion of the clan and lineage system during the Three Dynasties, see K. C. Chang, *Art, Myth, and Ritual* (Cambridge: Harvard University Press, 1983), 9–32.

88. For a discussion of the concept of ming qi and the early development of this art tradition, see Wu Hung, "Art and Architecture of the Warring States Period," in Loewe and Shaughnessy, *Cambridge History of Ancient China,* 727–744.

89. *Li ji,* 3 ("Tangong 1"), 1289; see J. Legge, trans.; Ch'u Chai and Winberg Chai, eds., *Li Chi: Book of Rites* (New Hyde Park, N.Y.: University Books, [1967]), vol. 1, p. 148.

90. See *Kaogu xuebao* 1 (1959): 54.

91. *Kaogu* 9 (1963): 461–473.

92. *Kaogu xuebao* 4 (1984): 504–507.

93. *Wenwu* 5 (1966): 33–55; Li, *Eastern Zhou and Qin Civilizations,* 422.

94. *Kaogu xuebao* 1 (1977): 73–104.

95. *Wenwu* 3 (1993): 1–7.

96. See Huang Zhanyue, *Zhongguo gudai de rensheng yu renxun* (Beijing: Wenwu chubanshe, 1990), 1–12.

97. *Xinyang Chu mu* (Chu tombs at Xinyang) (Beijing: Wenwu chubanshe, 1986), 18–20.

98. One exception is the figurines buried inside Tomb 7 at Niujiapo, Changzi. Quite large (67 centimeters high), they are made of wood, covered in black lacquer, and further painted with details of costumes. Their faces, however, which were originally made of clay, are now worn away. See *Kaogu xuebao* 4 (1984): 504–507. A limited number of clay figurines have been found in Hubei, a province between north and south China.

99. *Kaogu xuebao* 1 (1957): 116; *Huixian fajue baogao* (Beijing: Kexue chubanshe, 1956), 45; *Kaogu* 12 (1959): 656; 7 (1960): 71; 10 (1962): 516.

100. *Wenwu* 3 (1993): 1–7.

101. *Wenwu ziliao congkan* 3 (1980): 67–85.

102. See Jessica Rawson, *Ancient China: Art and Archaeology* (London: British Museum, 1980), 140. The museum registration number of this object is 1950.11–15.1.

103. For examples, see Zhang Zhengming and Pi Daojian, *Chu meishu tuji* (An illustrated catalogue of Chu art) (Changsha: Hubei meishu chubanshe, 1996), pls. 142–148.

104. For a typology of this object, see Chen Yaojun and Yuan Wenqing, "'Zhenmushou' luekao," *Jianghan kaogu* 3 (1983): 63–67.

105. See Qiu Donglian, "'Zhenmushou' biankao" (A critical examination of the "tomb guardian beast"), *Jianghan kaogu* 2 (1994): 54–59.

106. See *Wenwu* 5 (1966): 33–55.

107. For a concise introduction to lacquer, see Michael Knight, "So Fine a Luster: Chinese Lacquerwares," in Rogers, *China: Five Thousand Years,* 89–97.

108. See So, *Eastern Zhou Ritual Bronzes,* 52.

109. Chen Zhenyu, "Shilun Zhanguo shiqi Chuguo de qiqi shougongye," *Kaogu yu wenwu* 4 (1986): 77–85.

110. For examples, see Zhang and Pi, *Chu meishu tuji,* pl. 152.

111. For illustration, see Zhang and Pi, *Chu meishu tuji,* pl. 151.

112. For the development of jade carvings during the Eastern Zhou, see Jessica Rawson, *Chinese Jade, from the Neolithic to the Qing* (London: British Museum, 1995), 53–75.

113. *Luoyang chutu wenwu jicui* (Gems of cultural relics unearthed in Luoyang) (Beijing: Zhaohua chubanshe, 1990), no. 34.

114. See *Huixian fajue baogao,* 104, fig. 123, pl. 74.

115. Sima Qian, *Shi ji* (Historical records) (Beijing: Zhonghua shuju, 1959), 239; translation based on Yang Hsien-yi and Gladys Yang, *Selections from Records of the Historians* (Beijing: Foreign Languages Press, 1979), 168. Alternatively, the second sentence in this passage can be read as: "They were melted down to make Twelve Golden Men [to support] bronze bells." As Tang Chi has argued, this second reading is supported by archaeological finds, including the bell set from Leigudun Tomb 1 that is decorated with six sculpted human images. He has thus further distinguished the figurative images mentioned in *Shi ji* from another set of twelve bronze figures recorded in the *History of the Former Han* by Ban Gu, which were individual statues representing twelve giant barbarians. Tang Chi, "Qin ji Xi Han shiqi de diaosu yishu" (The art of sculpture during the Qin and Western Han period), in *Zhongguo meishu wuqiannian* (Five

thousand years of Chinese art), 8 vols. (Beijing: Renmin meishu chubanshe and others, 1991), vol. 3, "Diaosu shang" (Sculpture 1), 60–86, especially 62–63. But according to Ban Gu, this second set, also known as the Twelve Golden Men, was likewise commissioned by the First Emperor after the unification and made by melting down the bronze weapons collected from all over the country. It is difficult to imagine that this set is different from the Twelve Golden Men recorded by Sima Qian, which were made on the same occasion. I thus follow the traditional reading of the passage in the *Historical Records* in viewing the bronze bells and the twelve statues as two separate items.

116. It was common practice during the Eastern Zhou to represent one's enemies in sculpture; for example, it was recorded that a king of the Song made statues to represent the rulers of rival kingdoms. He arranged the figures in his palace as if they were all his servants, and humiliated them at will. In particular, having made a wooden statue to represent a king of Qin, the Song king shot it with arrows. See Liu Xiang, *Zhangguo ce* (Strategies of the Warring States) (Shanghai: Shangwu yinshuguan, 1933), vol. 3, p. 67.

117. For a discussion of the Nine Tripods, see Wu, *Monumentality in Early Chinese Art and Architecture,* 4–11.

118. For these records, see Shi Yan, "Qin zhi zhongjue jinren kao" (A study of the Qin bells and golden figures), *Jinling xuebao* 10, nos. 1–2 (1940); He Ziquan, *Qin Han shilüe* (A concise history of the Qin and Han) (Shanghai: Shanghai renmin chubanshe, 1955), 11; Tang Chi, "Qin ji Xi Han shiqi de diaosu yishu," 62–63; commentaries in Sima Qian, *Shi ji,* 240, n. 2.

119. Li Jian, ed., *Eternal China: Splendors from the First Dynasties* (Dayton, Ohio: Dayton Art Institute, 1998), 71.

120. For information about the excavation of these chariots, see Museum of the Terra-Cotta Army of the First Emperor of Qin and Shaanxi Provincial Institute of Archaeology, *Qin Shihuang tongchema fajue baogao* (A report on the excavation of the bronze chariots and horses unearthed from the First Emperor of Qin's mausoleum) (Beijing: Wenwu chubanshe, 1998).

121. For a comprehensive introduction to this chariot, see Yuan Zhongyi and Cheng Xuehua, "Qinling erhao tongchema" (No. 2 bronze chariot from the Qin mausoleum), in Archaeological Team of the Qin Figurines and Museum of the Terra-Cotta Army of the First Emperor of Qin, *Qinling erhao tongchema* (Xi'an: Kaogu yu wenwu chubanshe, 1983), 3–61.

122. See Yuan and Cheng, "Qinling erhao tongchema," 46–49.

123. For a discussion of the process, see Wu, *Monumentality in Early Chinese Art and Architecture,* 112–114.

124. English summaries of these excavations include Arthur Cotterell, *The First Emperor of China* (London: Penguin Books, 1981), 16–53; Robert Thorp, "An Archaeological Reconstruction of the Lishan Necropolis," in G. Kuwayama, ed., *The Great Bronze Age of China — A Symposium* (Los Angeles: Los Angeles County Museum), 72–83; *2001 Zhongguo zhongyao kaogu faxian* (Major archaeological discoveries in China in 2001) (Beijing: Wenwu chubanshe, 2002), 83–91. A summary of these archaeological excavations is Wan Xueli, *Qin Shihuangling yanjiu* (A study of the mausoleum of the First Emperor of Qin) (Shanghai: Shanghai renmin chubanshe, 1994).

125. Sima Qian, *Shi ji,* 265.

126. See *Qin Shihuangdi lingyuan kaogu baogao, 1999* (A report on the archaeological excavations in the mausoleum of the First Emperor of Qin, 1999) (Beijing: Kexue chubanshe, 2000).

127. This structure can be compared with the design of a royal funerary park of the Zhongshan kingdom during the Warring States period. According to this design, the Zhongshan funerary park was also surrounded by two walls. The central enclosure within the two walls was called the inner palace (*nei gong*); and the space between the two walls was called the middle palace (*zhong gong*). See Wu, *Monumentality in Early Chinese Art and Architecture,* 113–114. It is significant that in Beijing during the Ming and Qing dynasties, the emperor's Forbidden City was surrounded by an Imperial City. The identification of the central section of the Lishan Mausoleum as the First Emperor's inner court is also supported by the recent discovery of a group of "civil officials" southwest of the tumulus. With their hands tucked in their wide sleeves, these figures originally stood in a row in front of a chariot. Their stance and their close proximity to the emperor's grave suggest that they should be identified as "attendants in waiting." See *2001 Zhongguo zhongyao kaogu faxian,* 83–91.

128. Ruan Yuan, comp., *Shisanjing zhushu* (Beijing: Zhonghua shuju, 1980), 1253.

129. See Wu Hung, "Where Are They Going? Where Did They Come From? Chariots in Ancient Chinese Tomb Art," *Orientations* 29, no. 6 (1998): 22–31.

130. Wang, *Qin Shihuangling yanjiu,* 110.

131. See, for example, George Kuwayama, ed., *The Quest for Eternity* (Los Angeles: Los Angeles County Museum of Art, 1987), 102.

132. Wang Renbo, "General Comments on Chinese Funerary Sculpture," in Kuwayama, *Quest for Eternity,* 39–61, especially 41–44.

133. For information about the excavation of this pit, see Shaanxi Provincial Institute of Archaeology and Archaeological Team for Qin Funerary Figures, *Qin Shihuangling bingma yongkeng: Yihaokeng fajue baogao, 1974–1984* (A report on the excavation of warriors and horses: Pit 1 of the tomb of the First Emperor of Qin, 1974–1984), 2 vols. (Beijing: Wenwu chubanshe, 1988).

134. For information about the excavation of this pit, see Archaeological Team for Qin Funerary Figures, "Qin Shihuangling dongce di'erhao bingma yongkeng zuantan shijue jianbao" (Brief report on core samples and exploratory excavations of warriors and horses in Pit 2 on the east side of the tomb of the First Emperor of Qin), *Wenwu* 5 (1978): 1–19.

135. See *Imperial Tombs of China,* exh. cat. (Memphis, Tenn.: Memphis International Cultural Series, 1995), 77.

136. For information about the excavation of this pit, see Archaeological Team for Qin Funerary Figures, "Qin Shihuangling dongce disanhao bingma yongkeng qingli jianbao" (Brief report on the inspection of warriors and horses in Pit 3 on the east side of the tomb of the First Emperor of Qin), *Wenwu* 12 (1979): 1–12.

137. Ladislav Kesner, "Likeness of No One: (Re)presenting the First Emperor's Army," *Art Bulletin* 77, no. 1 (1995): 126, 129.

138. Kesner, "Likeness of No One," 126.

139. Sima Qian, *Shi ji,* 262. Translation based on Burton Watson, trans., *Records of the Great Historian: Qin Dynasty* (New York: Columbia University Press, 1993), 61.

140. For the construction of Chang'an, see Wu, *Monumentality in Early Chinese Art and Architecture,* chap. 3, "The Monumental City Chang'an," 143–188.

141. Sima Qian, *Shi ji,* 433.

142. For Emperor Wu's construction of the park and for its symbolism, see Wu, *Monumentality in Early Chinese Art and Architecture,* chap. 3, 170–174.

143. See Zhang Zongxiang, comp., *Jiaozheng Sanfu huangtu* (An edited and annotated version of *The Diagram of the Imperial District*) (Beijing: Gudian wenxue chubanshe, 1958).

144. According to *Guanfu guyu* (Ancient dialogues about the capital area) and *Sanfu gushi* (Stories about the three capital districts), as quoted in Zhang, *Jiaozheng Sanfu huangtu,* 32.

145. Tang Chi, "Xi Han shidiao Qianniu Zhinü bian" (On the Western Han stone sculpture of the Weaving Maid and Cowherd), *Wenwu* 2 (1979): 87–88.

146. See Ruan Yuan, ed., *Song zhu Chang'an zhi* (Records of Chang'an with Song Minqiu's commentary) (Xi'an: Chang'an xianzhi ju), vol. 3, p. 11a.

147. Sima Qian, *Shi ji,* 1369–1370.

148. Li He, "A Bronze Immortal Takes Leave of the Han" ("Jintong xianren ci Han ge"); quotation based on A. C. Graham's translation in *Poems of the Late T'ang* (Harmondsworth, England: Penguin, 1965), 106.

149. For a general study of this type of object, see Susan A. Erickson, "Boshanlu — Mountain Censers of the Western Han Period: A Topological and Iconological Analysis," *Archives of Asian Art* 45 (1992): 6–28.

150. *Xijing zaji* (Miscellaneous records of the western capital) (Shanghai: Shangwu yinshuguan, 1929), 6ab.

151. For a discussion of this myth, see Wu Hung, "Myth and Legend in Han Pictorial Art — A Structural Analysis of Bas-Reliefs from Sichuan," in Lucy Lim, ed., *Stories from China's Past: Han Art from Sichuan* (San Francisco: Chinese Cultural Foundation, 1987), 72–81, especially 76–77.

152. For information about its excavation, see "Shaanxi Maolin yihao wumingzhong yihao congzangkeng de fajue" (The excavation of Auxiliary Burial Pit 1 of unidentified Tomb 1 near the Maoling mausoleum in Shaanxi), *Wenwu* 9 (1982): 1–17.

153. Ban Gu, *Han shu,* 1067.

154. Yuan Anzhi, "Tan 'Yangxin jia' tongqi" (On the bronzes of the "Yangxin household"), *Wenwu* 9 (1982): 18–20.

155. See *Mancheng Han mu fajue baogao* (A report on the excavation of the Han tombs at Mancheng), 2 vols. (Beijing: Wenwu chubanshe, 1980), vol.1, pp. 255–261.

156. See Rawson, *Mysteries of Ancient China,* 84.

157. "Xi'an shi faxian yipi Handai tongqi he tong yuren" (The finding of a group of Han-dynasty bronzes and a bronze feathered figure in Xi'an), *Wenwu* 4 (1966): 7–8.

158. For illustration, see *Zhongguo yuqi quanji* (A comprehensive collection of Chinese jade objects), vol. 4, "Qin, Han — Nanbei chao" (The Qin and Han dynasties to the Northern and Southern Dynasties) (Shijiazhuang: Hebei meishu chubanshe, 1993), pl. 147.

159. For a fuller discussion of this belief and of related artistic expressions, see Wu Hung, "A Sanpan Shan Chariot Orna-

ment and the Xiangrui Design in Western Han Art," *Archives of Asian Art,* 37 (1984): 38–59, especially 47–48.

160. For the architectural layout of the Western Han royal mausoleums and "mausoleum towns," see Robert Thorp, "The Qin and Han Imperial Tombs and the Development of Mortuary Architecture," in Kuwayama, *Quest for Eternity,* 17–37, especially 21–26; Wu, *Monumentality of Early Chinese Art and Architecture,* 161–165.

161. "Xianyang Yangjiawan Han mu fajue jianbao" (Brief report on the excavation of the Han tomb at Yangjiawan, Xianyang), *Wenwu* 10 (1977): 10–21.

162. "Han Anling de kancha ji qi peizang mu zhong de caihui taoyong" (Investigation of the Han Anling mausoleum and the painted ceramic figures in its satellite tombs), *Kaogu* 5 (1981): 422–425.

163. See Wang Xueli, "The Pottery Figurines in Yangling Mausoleum of the Han Dynasty: Melodic Beauty of Pottery Sculpture," in Archaeological Team of Han Mausoleums and Archaeological Institute of Shaanxi Province, *The Coloured Figurines in Yangling Mausoleum of the Han in China,* in Chinese, English, and Japanese (Xi'an: China Shaanxi Travel and Tourism Press, 1992), 8–13.

164. See Susan Stewart, *On Longing: Narratives of the Miniature, the Gigantic, the Souvenir, the Collection* (Durham, N.C.: Duke University Press, 1993), 65.

165. "Xuzhou Beidongshan Xi Han mu fajue jianbao" (Brief report on the excavation of a Western Han tomb at Beidongshan in Xuzhou), *Wenwu* 2 (1988): 2–18, 68; Li Yinde, "The 'Underground Palace' of a Chu Prince at Beidongshan," *Orientations* 21, no. 10 (1990): 57–61.

166. Some examples excavated in Baijiakou near Xi'an are very similar to the one in The Metropolitan Museum of Art. For an illustration and information about this piece, see Rawson, *Mysteries of Ancient China,* 206.

167. Wang Xueli and Wu Zhenfeng, "Xi'an Renjiapo Hanling congzangkeng de fajue (Excavation of the pits for funerary objects accompanying a Han mausoleum at Renjiapo, Xi'an), *Kaogu* 2 (1976): 129–133, 75.

168. See Zhang Zibo and Wan Pizong, "Han Anling de kancha ji qi peizangmu zhong de caihui taoyong" (Investigation of the Anling mausoleum and the painted ceramic figurines in its satellite tombs), *Kaogu* 5 (1981): 422–423.

169. Cao Zhezhi and Sun Binggen, eds., *Zhongguo gudai yong* (Ancient figurines of China) (Shanghai: Shanghai wenhua chubanshe, 1996), 97–99.

170. See Cao and Sun, *Zhongguo gudai yong,* 96–97.

171. Wang, "Pottery Figurines in Yangling Mausoleum," 12.

172. Yin Shao (ca. 140–ca. 206), *Fengsu tongyi fu yiwen* (Explanations of social customs [along with fragments found in other texts]) (Beijing, 1943), vol. 1, p. 83. My translation here is based on those by Derk Bodde, "Myths of China," in Samuel Noah Kramer, *Mythologies of the Ancient World* (Garden City, N.Y.: Anchor Books, 1961), 64–65; and Anne Birrell, *Chinese Mythology: An Introduction* (Baltimore, Md.: Johns Hopkins University Press, 1993), 35.

173. Wang Kai, "Han Terra-Cotta Army in Xuzhou, *Orientations* 21, no. 10 (1990): 62–66.

174. "Shitan Ji'nan Wuyingshan chutu de Xi Han yuewu zaiji yanyin taoyong" (A tentative discussion of the ceramic figurines of musicians, dancers, acrobats, and banqueters

unearthed from a Western Han tomb at Wuyingshan, Ji'nan), *Wenwu* 5 (1972): 19–23.

175. The most complete report on this excavation is *Changsha Mawangdui yihao Han mu* (Mawangdui Tomb 1 in Changsha), 2 vols. (Beijing: Wenwu chubanshe, 1973). For an English summary, see David Buck, "The Han Dynasty Tomb at Mawangdui," *World Archaeology* 7, no. 1 (1975): 30–45.

176. According to the archaeological evidence, Mawangdui Tomb 1 was constructed after Mawangdui Tomb 3, belonging to Lady Dai's son, who died in 168 B.C.E. See "Mawangdui ersanhao Han mu fajue de zhuyao shouhuo" (The main achievements of the excavation of Mawangdui Tombs 2 and 3), *Kaogu* 1 (1975): 47.

177. Gao Ming has identified these two male images as the chief eunuchs in Lady Dai's family. "Changsha Mawangdui yihao mu 'guanren' yong" (The "Capped Men" figurines from Mawangdui Tomb 1 in Changsha), *Kaogu* 4 (1973): 255–257.

178. *Wenwu* 10 (1976): 31–37. The tomb also contained an inventory of the grave goods, written on seventy-four wooden strips. Sixteen of the strips describe the wooden servant figures. See *Wenwu* 10 (1976): 38–46.

179. "Lianyungang diqu de jizuo Han mu ji lingxing chutu de Handai muyong" (A number of Han tombs in the Lianyungang area and the unearthed wooden figurines), *Wenwu* 4 (1990): 58, 80–93; "Mianyang Yongxing Baoshan erhao Xi Han muguomu fajue jianbao" (Brief report on the excavation of Western Han wooden-chamber Tomb 2 at Baoshan, Yongxing, Mianyang), *Wenwu* 10 (1996): 13–29.

180. For a general introduction to Dian culture and art, see Zhang Zengqi, "Xunli duocai de Dian, Kunming qingtong wenhua" (The colorful and varied Dian and Kunming bronze cultures), in *Zhongguo qingtongqi quanji* (A comprehensive collection of Chinese bronzes), vol. 14, "Dian, Kunming" (Beijing: Wenwu chubanshe, 1993), 1–39.

181. For illustrations, see *Yunnan Jinning Shizhaishan gumu fajue baogao* (Report on the excavation of ancient tombs at Shizhaishan, Jinning, and Yunnan) (Beijing: Wenwu chubanshe, 1959); *Zhongguo qingtongqi quanji,* vol. 14.

182. For these finds, see Sun Shoudao, "'Xiongnu Xichagou wenhua' gumuqun de faxian" (The finding of a group of ancient tombs belonging to the "Xichagou culture of the Huns"), *Wenwu* 8–9 (1960); Gai Shanlin, "Neimenggu Zizhiqu Zhungar'erqi Sujigou chutu de yipi tongqi" (A group of bronzes unearthed at Sujigou in Zhungar Banner, Inner Mongolia), *Wenwu* 2 (1965); Wu En, "Woguo gudai dongwu wenshi" (Ancient Chinese animal designs), *Kaogu xuebao* 1 (1981): 45–61.

183. See Fong, *Great Bronze Age of China,* 326–327.

184. This is not to say that the ancient Chinese *never* used stone for sculptures. Marble sculptures were found in Shang royal tombs, for example, and a predynastic Qin royal tomb contained stone figurines; but these works were rarities and did not constitute an art tradition.

185. Ban Gu, *Han shu,* 2489.

186. A damaged statue later found at the site should have belonged to the same group. For a discussion of these works and related textual records, see Ann Paludan, *The Chinese Spirit Road* (New Haven: Yale University Press, 1991), 46–49.

187. Zheng Yan, "Barbarian Images in Han Period Art," *Orientations* 29, no. 6 (1998): 50–59, especially 55.

188. For a discussion of this historical movement, see Wu, *Monumentality in Early Chinese Art and Architecture,* 111–121.

189. Zhao Yi, *Gaiyu congkao* (Mesollenium) (Taibei: Shijie shuju, 1960), 32a–32b.

190. For a discussion of these inscriptions, see Wu, *Monumentality in Early Chinese Art and Architecture,* 192–201. For the relation between filial piety and mortuary art, see Martin Powers, *Art and Political Expression in Early China* (New Haven: Yale University Press, 1991), 42–43.

191. Wu Hung, "The Prince of Jade Revisited: Material Symbolism of Jade as Observed in the Mancheng Tombs," in Rosemary E. Scott, ed., *Chinese Jades,* Colloquies on Art and Archaeology in Asia, no. 18 (London: Percival David Foundation of Chinese Art, 1997), 147–170.

192. Li Daoyuan, *Shuijing zhu* (Annotated canon of waterways) (Shanghai: Shijie shuju, 1936), vol. 22, p. 276.

193. For an inventory and discussion of these structures, see Wu Hung, *Wu Liang Shrine: The Ideology of Early Chinese Pictorial Art* (Stanford: Stanford University Press, 1989), 3–30.

194. See *Ya'an dique wenwu zhi* (A record of cultural relics in the Ya'an area) (Chengdu: Ba Shu shushe, 1992), 82–85, 95, 106–107.

195. For a discussion of the structures of Eastern Han cemeteries, see Wu, *Monumentality in Early Chinese Art and Architecture,* 30–37.

196. For discussions of que towers, see Chen Mingda, "Handai de shique" (Stone que towers of the Han dynasty), *Wenwu* 12 (1961): 9–23; Paludan, *Chinese Spirit Road,* 31–40.

197. See Wilma Fairbank, "A Structural Key to Han Mural Art," *Harvard Journal of Asiatic Studies* 7, no. 1 (1942): 52–88.

198. For a comprehensive description of this tower, see Xu Wenbin et al., *Sichuan Handai shique* (Han-dynasty stone que towers in Sichuan) (Beijing: Wenwu chubanshe, 1992), 31–34; pls. 67–117.

199. Xu Weiyu, comp., *Lüshi chunqiu jishi* (Mr. Lü's Springs and Autumns with comprehensive commentaries) (Beijing: Zhonghua shuju, 1954), vol. 14, p. 6.

200. Sima Qian, *Shi ji,* 1459.

201. See Wu, *Monumentality in Early Chinese Art and Architecture,* 248; "Myths and Legends in Han Funerary Art" in Lucy Lim, ed., *Stories from China's Past* (San Francisco: Chinese Cultural Foundation, 1987), 75; Zhao Dianzeng and Yuan Shuguang, "Tian men kao" (On the "Heavenly Gate"), *Sichuan wenwu* 6 (1996): 3–11.

202. A pair of stone figures were located at Deng Feng in Henan and Fuping in Shaanxi. See Leigh Ashton, *An Introduction to the Study of Chinese Sculpture* (London: Ernest Been, 1924), pl. 4.

203. For illustrations, see Paludan, *Chinese Spirit Road,* figs. 41, 42.

204. See Wu Hung, "Beyond the Great Boundary: Funerary Narrative in Early Chinese Art," in John Hay, ed., *Boundaries in China* (London: Reaktion Books, 1994), 81–104.

205. Chen Shukui, ed., *Ya'an diqu wenwu zhi* (A record of cultural relics from the Ya'an region) (Chengdu: Ba Shu shushe, 1992), 96.

206. One such example is Mawangdui Tomb 1, which contained many beautiful tomb figures as well as a few crude figurines in rudimentary human shapes. The burial positions of the two types of figurines also differ: those of the first type were stored in the compartments surrounding the coffin chamber, while those of the second type were found inside the coffin chamber. See *Changsha Mawangdui yihao Han mu,* vol. 1, pp. 100–101. Another kind of semihuman figurine is the so-called Weng Zhong image, which is also given a nonfigurative, geometric treatment.

207. Feng Yan, *Feng shi jianwen lu* (Things heard and seen by Mr. Feng), cited in Liu Xingzhen, "Dong Han shiqi de diaosu yishu" (Art of sculpture during the Eastern Han period), in *Zhongguo meishu wuqiannian,* vol. 3, pp. 87–88.

208. See Paludan, *Chinese Spirit Road,* 45.

209. See Wu, "Myths and Legends in Han Funerary Art."

210. See Wilma Fairbank, "A Structural Key to Han Mural Art," 52–88.

211. See Xin Lixiang, "Han huaxiang shi de fenqu yu fenqi yanjiu" (A study of the geographical distribution and periodization of Han pictorial stone carvings), in Yu Weichao, ed., *Kaoguxue leixingxue de lilun yu shijian* (Theories and practices of archaeological typology) (Beijing: Wenwu chubanshe, 1989), 234–306, especially 238–242.

212. *Anqiu Dongjiazhuang Han huaxiang shimu* (Stone-relief tomb of the Han dynasty at Dongjiazhuang village, Anqiu County) (Ji'nan: Ji'nan chubanshe, 1992).

213. Liu Dunyuan, "Han huaxiangshi shang de yinshi nannü — Pingyin Mengzhuang Han mu shizhu jisi gewu tuxiang fenxi" (Sex in Han pictorial carvings — an analysis of images representing rituals and performances on the stone columns in a Han tomb at Mengzhuang in Pingyin), *Gugong wenwu yuekan* (National Palace Museum monthly of Chinese art), no. 141 (1994): 122–135. See also Zheng Yan, "Anqiu Dongjiazhuang lizhu diaoke tuxiang kao" (An examination of carved images on the columns in a Han tomb at Dongjiazhuang in Anqiu), *Jinian Shandong Daxue kaogu zhuanye chuangjian ershi zhounian wenji* (Papers commemorating the 20th anniversary of the Archaeology Department at Shandong University) (Ji'nan: Shandong Daxue, 1992), 397–413. Other discussions of the Anqiu carvings include Li Song, "You kaogu faxian yinchu de meishushi shang de jige wenti de sikao" (Speculating on several art historical problems raised by archaeological finds), *Meishu* (Fine arts) 1 (1986): 52–58; Yang Hong, "Zhongguo guwenwu zhong suojian renti zaoxing yishu" (Artistic representations of the human body in ancient China), *Wenwu* 1 (1987):59–65.

214. For the original architectural context of this carving, see Nanjing Museum, *Sichuan Pengshan Handai yamu* (Han-dynasty cliff tombs at Pengshan, Sichuan) (Beijing: Wenwu chubanshe, 1991), 19.

215. Chen Xiandan, "On the Designation 'Money Tree,'" *Orientations* 28, no. 8 (1997), 67–71.

216. For a general discussion of Eastern Han money tree and money tree bases, see Susan N. Erickson, "Money Trees of the Eastern Han Dynasty," *Bulletin of the Museum of Far Eastern Antiquities* 66 (1994): 5–115.

217. For illustrations and further discussion of this work, see Lim, *Stories from China's Past,* color plate 10, pl. 60.

218. For this and other types of performers as represented by Sichuan figurines, see Kenneth J. DeWoskin, "Music and Voices from the Han Tombs," in Lim, *Stories from China's Past,* 64–71.

219. For example, an exceptionally large model of a manor was excavated from a Western Han tomb at Yuzheng in Henan. See Rawson, *Mysteries of Ancient China,* 203–205.

220. This interpretation was first suggested to me by Cindy Hart Townsend, a doctoral candidate at the University of Chicago.

221. "Hebei Fucheng Sangzhuang Dong Han mu fajue baogao" (Report on the excavation of an Eastern Han tomb at Sangzhuang in Fucheng, Hebei), *Wenwu* 1 (1990): 19–30.

222. For a full discussion of this historical transformation in the Buddha's image, see Wu Hung, "Buddhist Elements in Early Chinese Art (2nd and 3rd Centuries A.D.)," *Artibus Asiae* 47, nos. 3–4 (1986): 263–347.

223. See Yu Weichao, "Dong Han Fojiao tuxiang kao" (A study of the Buddhist motifs of the Eastern Han), *Kaogu* 4 (1981): 346–358; Wu, "Buddhist Elements in Early Chinese Art," 263–347.

224. For such Indian examples, see Wu, "Buddhist Elements in Early Chinese Art," pls. 3, 4.

225. Nanjing Museum, *Sichuan Pengshan Handai yamu,* 36–37.

226. Yu, "Dong Han Fojiao tuxiang kao."

Chapter 2. From the Han to the Qing

1. Luoyang Cultural Relics Work Team, "Luoyang Cao Wei Zhengshi ba nian mu fajue baogao" (A report on the excavation of the tomb of the eighth year of the Zhengshi reign in the Wei period in Luoyang), *Kaogu* 4 (1959): 314–318.

2. Hubei Provincial Cultural Relics Administrative Committee, "Wuchang Lianxisi dongwu mu qingli baokao" (A report on the investigation of the Wu tomb in Lianxisi, Wuchang), *Kaogu* 4 (1959): 189–190.

3. Hubei Provincial Institute of Cultural Relics and Archaeology and Ezhou Museum, "Hubei Ezhou shi Tangjiaotou Liuchao mu" (The Six Dynasties tomb of Tangjiaotou, Ezhou, city of Hubei," *Kaogu* 11 (1996): 1–27. For further remarks on Buddhist statues in the tombs, see Yang Hong, "Ba Ezhou Sun Wu mu chutu taofoxiang" (A clay Buddha image from the tomb of Sun Wu at Ezhou, a postscript), *Kaogu* 11 (1996): 28–30.

4. Hubei Provincial Institute of Cultural Relics and Archaeology and Ezhou Museum, "Hubei Ezhou shi Tangjiaotou Liuchao mu."

5. Sichuan Provincial Cultural Relics Administrative Committee, "Sichuan Zhongxian Tujing Shu Han yamu" (Tombs of the Shu Kingdom period on cliff faces in Tujing, Zhongxian County, Sichuan Province), *Kaogu* 7 (1990): 49–95.

6. Second Group, Work Team of the Henan Province Culture Bureau, "Luoyang Jin mu de fajue" (Excavations of Jin-dynasty tombs in Luoyang), *Kaogu xuebao* 1 (1957): 169–185.

7. Hunan Museum, "Changsha liang Jin Nanchao Sui mu fajue baogao" (A Report on the excavation of tombs of the Western Jin, Eastern Jin, Sui, and Southern Dynasties in Changsha), *Wenwu* 3 (1959): 75–103.

8. Nanjing Museum, "Nanjing xiangshan 5, 6, 7 hao mu qingli baokao" (A report on clearing Tombs 5, 6, and 7 at Xiangshan, Nanjing), *Wenwu* 11 (1972): 23–41.

9. Li Jianzhao and Tu Sihua, "Nanjing Shimenkan xiang Liuchao mu qingli ji" (Record of the investigation of the Six Dynasties tomb in Shimenkan Township, Nanjing), *Kaogu tongxun* 9 (1958): 66–69.

10. Nanjing Museum, "Nanjing Fuguishan Dong Jin mu fajue baogao" (A report on the excavation of the Eastern Jin tomb at Fuguishan in Nanjing), *Kaogu* 4 (1966): 197–204.

11. Li Weiran, "Nanjing Fuguishan faxian Jin Gongdi Xuangong shijie" (A stone stele from the Xuangong palace of Emperor Gong of the Jin discovered in Fuguishan, Nanjing), *Kaogu* 6 (1961): 206.

12. Nanjing Municipal Cultural Relics Preservation Committee, Nanjing Museum, "Nanjing Xishanqiao Nanchao mu jiqi zhuanke bihua" (The Southern Dynasties tomb at the Xishanqiao in Nanjing and the brick carved murals in it), *Wenwu* 8–9 (1960): 37–42.

13. Zhang Yanyuan (Tang dynasty), *Lidai minghua ji* (Record of famous paintings of successive dynasties), vol. 7, *Zhongguo meishu lunzhu zhuankan* (Special issue of papers on Chinese fine art) (Beijing: Renmin meishu chubanshe, 1963), 150.

14. Nanjing Museum, "Nanjing Raohuamen Nanchao Liang mu fajue jianbao" (A report on the excavation of Liang tombs of the Southern Dynasties in Raohuamen, Nanjing), *Wenwu* 12 (1981): 14–23.

15. Nanjing Municipal Cultural Relics Administrative Committee, "Nanjing jiaoqu liangzuo Nanchao mu qingli jianbao" (A report on the investigation of two tombs of the Southern Dynasties in the suburbs of Nanjing), *Wenwu* 2 (1980): 612–613.

16. Wuzhou Museum of Guangxi, "Guangxi Cangwu Daoshui Nanchao mu" (Southern Dynasties tombs in Daoshui, Cangwu, Guangxi), *Wenwu* 12 (1981): 30–34; Cultural Relics Team of Guangxi Zhuang Autonomous Region, "Guangxi Yongfu xian Shouchen Nanchao mu" (Southern Dynasties tombs in Shouchen, Yongfu County, Guangxi), *Wenwu* 7 (1983): 612–613.

17. The term Sixteen Kingdoms refers to the political authorities established by peoples of Xiongnu, Xianbei, Xie, Shi, Qiang, Han, and so on, in north China from 304 to 439 C.E. The Xiongnu founded the Former Zhao (304–329), the Northern Liang (401–439), and the Xia (407–431); the Shi founded the Later Han (304–347), the Former Qin (351–394), and the Later Liang (386–403); the Xie founded the Later Zhao (319–350); the Xianbei founded the Former Yan (337–370) and the Later Yan (398–410); the Han founded the Former Liang (314–376), the Western Liang (400–420), and the Northern Yan (409–436); the Qiang founded the Later Qin (384–417).

18. Yang Hong, "Beichao taoyong de yuanliu, yanbian ji yingxiang" (The origin, evolution, and impact of Northern Dynasties clay figurines), in *Zhongguo kaoguxue yanjiu — jinian Xia Nai xiansheng kaogu 50 nian lunwen ji* (Study of Chinese archaeology — Collection in memory of Mr. Xia Nai for his fifty years of study of archaeology) (Beijing: Wenwu chubanshe, 1986), 269.

19. Shaanxi Provincial Cultural Relics Administrative Committee, "Xi'an nanjiao Caochangpo Beichao mu de fajue" (Excavation of Northern Dynasties tombs at Caochangpo in the suburbs of Xi'an), *Kaogu* 6 (1959): 285–287. The time of the burial determined by this report is somewhat too late. It should be during the period of the Sixteen Kingdoms. Similar clay figurines, including tomb guardian figures, from the Sixteen Kingdoms period have been found in recent years in Dongjia village, in the Weiyang district of Xi'an.

See *Kaogu yu wenwu* (Archaeology and cultural relics) 5 (1998), illustrations on front and back covers of the issue.

20. Guo Suxin, "Nei Mongu Hohhot Bei Wei mu" (The Northern Wei tomb in Hohhot, Inner Mongolia), *Wenwu* 5 (1977): 38–41.

21. Datong Museum of Shanxi Province, Shanxi Provincial Cultural Relics Work Team, "Shanxi Datong Shijiazhai Bei Wei Sima Jinlong mu" (Tombs of Sima Jinlong from the Northern Wei at Shijia village, Datong, Shanxi), *Wenwu* 3 (1972): 20–33.

22. Sima Jinlong's father was Sima Chuzhi, who was an eighth-generation descendant of Sima Kui, younger brother of Emperor Sima Yi of the Jin. When Liu Yu founded the Song to replace the Eastern Jin, Sima Chuzhi went, in 419, to the Northern Wei, who entrusted him with important posts. He took part in many battles and finally was given the title "King of Longya." He died in 464. Sima Jinlong was his son by Princess Henei. For details, see *Wei shu* (Beijing: Zhonghua shuju, 1974), chap. 37, "Sima Chuzhi zhuan" (Biography of Sima Chuzhi), 854–857.

23. See "Wei Lu zhuan," in Xiao Zixian, ed., *Nan Qi shu* (History of the Southern Qi), chap. 57 (Beijing: Zhonghua shuju, 1974).

24. Archaeological Institute of the Chinese Academy of Social Sciences, *Bei Wei Luoyang Yongning si 1979–1994 nian kaogu fajue baokao* (A report on the excavation of the Yongning Monastery of the Northern Wei in Luoyang, 1979–1994) (Beijing: Zhongguo dabaike quanshu chubanshe, 1996).

25. For further information on the construction of Yongning Monastery, see Yang Xuanzhi (Northern Wei), *Luoyang qielan ji*, ed. Fan Xiangyong (Beijing: Gudian wenxue chubanshe, 1958). For details about the statues inside the pagoda, see "Cui Guang zhuan," in *Wei shu*, chap. 67, p. 1495. There it is stated that Cui Guang sent a note, in the eighth month of the second year of the Shengui reign (519 C.E.), inviting the empress dowager to condescend to visit the Yongning Monastery and climb to the ninth floor to pay homage to the Buddha: "Though the statue has yet to be erected, it is a dwelling for immortals." From this we can conclude that the statue was erected around that time.

26. Su Bai, "Beichao zaoxing yishu zhong renwu xingxiang de bianhua" (Changes in images of human figures in the sculpture of the Northern Dynasties), in *Zhongguo shikusi yanjiu* (Study of Chinese grotto temples) (Beijing: Wenwu chubanshe, 1996), 351.

27. Luoyang Museum, "Luoyang Bei Wei Yuan Shao mu" (The tomb of Yuan Shao of the Northern Wei in Luoyang), *Kaogu* 4 (1973): 218–224.

28. The Eastern Wei capital was actually in a new city to the south of Ye of the original state of Wei. It is also known as the southern city of Ye. Institute of Archaeology of the Chinese Academy of Social Sciences, Yecheng Archaeological Team of the Hebei Provincial Institute of Cultural Relics, "Hebei Linzhang xian Yenancheng yizhi kantan yu fajue" (Exploration and excavation of the ruins of Yenancheng in Linzhang County, Hebei), *Kaogu* 3 (1997): 27–33.

29. For example, 1,064 terra-cotta figurines were unearthed in the burial of Princess Ru Ru from 550 C.E., during the Eastern Wei: Cixian Cultural Center, "Hebei Cixian Dongwei Ru Ru gongzhu mu fajue jianbao" (A brief report on the

excavation of the tomb of Princess Ru Ru of the Eastern Wei), *Wenwu* 4 (1984): 1–9.

30. Institute of Archaeology of the Chinese Academy of Social Sciences, Yecheng Archaeological Team of the Hebei Provincial Institute of Cultural Relics, "Hebei Cixian Chunzhang Beichao mu" (Northern Dynasties tombs of Chunzhang in Cixian, Hebei), *Kaogu* 7 (1990): 601–607.

31. For textual research indicating that the tune the elderly man dances to may be "High Cloud Dance," see Zhao Yonghong, "Nanbeichao hushou wudao yong kao" (Textual research on the figurine of a dancing Hu man of the Southern and Northern Dynasties), in *Han Tang yu bianjiang kaogu yanjiu* (Archaeological study of the Han and the Tang and frontiers) (Beijing: Zhongguo kexue chubanshe, 1994), 1:136–143. The elderly dancer has also been misunderstood by some to be a shaman.

32. Wang Kelin, "Bei Qi She Diluo mu" (She Diluo tomb of the Northern Qi), *Kaogu xuebao* 3 (1979): 377–402 (according to a line in the epitaph: "The king's name is Luo, self-styled Diluo," so the name of the deceased is She Diluo); Shanxi Provincial Institute of Archaeology, Taiyuan Municipal Cultural Relics Administrative Committee, "Taiyuan shi Bei Qi Lou Rui mu fajue jianbao" (A brief report on the excavation of the Lou Rui tomb of the Northern Qi in Taiyuan), *Wenwu* 10 (1983): 1–23.

33. Shaanxi Provincial Institute of Archaeology and Xianyang Municipal Institute of Archaeology, "Bei Zhou Wudi Xiaoling fajue jianbao" (A brief report on the excavation of the Xiaoling mausoleum of Emperor Wu of the Northern Zhou), *Kaogu yu wenwu* 2 (1997): 8–28.

34. Datong Museum of Shanxi Province, Shanxi Provincial Cultural Relics Team, "Datong Fangshan Bei Wei Yongguling" (The Yongguling mausoleum of the Northern Wei in Fangshan, Datong), *Wenwu* 7 (1978): 29–35.

35. Datong Museum of Shanxi Province, Shanxi Provincial Cultural Relics Team, "Shanxi Datong Shijiazhai Bei Wei Sima Jinlong mu" (The Sima Jinlong tomb from the Northern Wei in Shijia village, Datong, Shanxi), *Wenwu* 7 (1978): 21, 22, fig. 4.

36. Datong Museum of Shanxi Province, Shanxi Provincial Cultural Relics Team, "Shanxi Datong Shijiazhai Bei Wei Sima Jinlong mu," 24–25, including fig. 6, pl. 14, ills. 1, 2, and 4; Archaeological Finds Exhibition Team, *Wenhua dageming qijian chutu wenwu* (Cultural relics unearthed during the period of the Cultural Revolution) (Beijing: Wenwu chubanshe, 1973), vol. 1, pl. 146.

37. Huang Minglan, *Luoyang Bei Wei shisu shike xianhua ji* (A collection of secular pictures of the Northern Wei incised with lines, Luoyang) (Beijing, Renmin meishu chubanshe, 1987), 120, figs. 75–79.

38. Huang Minglan, "Xi Jin Pei Di he Bei Wei Yuan Wei liang mu shiling" (Notes on two tombs, of Pei Di of the Western Jin and Yuan Wei of the Northern Wei), *Wenwu* 1 (1982): 71–73.

39. See "Nanjing Fuguishan Dong Jin mu fajue baogao" (A report on the excavation of Eastern Jin tombs at Fuguishan in Nanjing), 117, in *Luoyang chutu shike shidi ji* (On-the-spot record of the excavation of stone carvings in Luoyang) (Xi'an: Dahua shubao gongyingshe, 1941).

40. Luoyang Museum, "Luoyang Bei Wei huaxiang shiguan" (Carvings on Northern Wei sarcophagi in Luoyang), *Kaogu* 3 (1980): 229–241.

41. Yao Qian and Gu Bing, *Liuchao yishu* (The art of the Six Dynasties) (Beijing: Wenwu chubanshe, 1981), pls. 180–182, 213–215.

42. Xia Mingcai, "Yidu Bei Qi shishi mu xianke huaxiang" (Stone chamber pictures incised with lines in the Northern Qi in Yidu), *Wenwu* 10 (1985): 49–54.

43. Shaanxi Institute of Archaeology, "Xi'an faxian de Bei Zhou An Jia mu" (The tomb of the priest An Jia of the Northern Zhou found in Xi'an), *Wenwu* 1 (2001): 4–26.

44. See the story by Zhang Yanyuan (Tang dynasty) about artists Dong Boren and Zhan Ziqian, *Lidai minghua ji* (Record of famous paintings of successive dynasties), vol. 8: "Initially Dong and Zhan entered the Sui at the same time. One was from Hebei, the other from the Yangzi River delta. They showed contempt for each other at first. Later each accepted the other's view." Cited in *Zhongguo meishu lunzhu congkan* (Beijing: Renmin meishu chubanshe, 1963).

45. Yellow River Reservoir Archaeological Team, "1956 nian qiu Henan Shanxian Liujiaqu Han-Tang muzang fajue jianbao" (A brief report on the excavation of burials of the Han and Tang dynasties in Liujiaqu, Shan County, Henan, in autumn 1956), *Kaogu tongxun* 4 (1957): 14–16, pl. 6.

46. Anyang Archaeological Team of the Institute of Archaeology of the Chinese Academy of Social Sciences, "Anyang Sui mu fajue baogao" (A report on the excavation of Sui tombs in Anyang), *Kaogu xuebao* 3 (1982): 369–406.

47. Shanxi Provincial Institute of Archaeology and Taiyuan Cultural Relics Administrative Committee, "Taiyuan Hulü Che mu fajue jianbao" (A brief report on the excavation of the Hulü Che tomb), *Wenwu* 10 (1992): 1–14.

48. Shanxi Provincial Institute of Archaeology and Taiyuan Cultural Relics Administrative Committee, "Taiyuan shi Bei Qi Lou Rui Sui Hulü Che mu fajue jianbao" (A brief report on the excavation of the Lou Rui tomb of the Northern Qi Hulü Che tomb of Sui in Taiyuan), *Wenwu* 10 (1983): 8, fig. 17.3, pl. 5, ill. 4.

49. Shaanxi Provincial Institute of Archaeology and Taiyuan Cultural Relics Administrative Committee, "Shaanxi sheng Sanyuan xian Shuangsheng cun Sui Li He mu qingli jianbao" (A brief report on the investigation of the Li He tomb of the Sui dynasty in Shuangsheng village, Sanyuan County, Shaanxi Province), *Wenwu* 1 (1966): 27–42.

50. Anyang Archaeological Team of the Institute of Archaeology of the Chinese Academy of Social Sciences, "Anyang Sui Zhang Sheng mu fajue ji" (The excavation of the Zhang Sheng tomb from the Sui dynasty in Anyang), *Kaogu* 10 (1959): 541–545.

51. Wang Qufei, "Sui mu chutu de 'Qianqiu Wansui' he qita" (Clay figurines of "Qianqiu Wansui" and others unearthed in the Sui tombs), *Kaogu* 3 (1979): 275–276. The twelve zodiac figurines have been excavated from the Sui tomb in Yuejiazui, Wuhan. Wuhan Cultural Relics Administrative Office, "Wuhan shi Donghu Yuejiazui Sui mu fajue jianbao" (A brief report on the excavation of the Sui tomb at Yuejiazhui in Donghu, Wuhan), *Kaogu* 9 (1983): 793–798.

52. Shaanxi Museum, Shaanxi Provincial Cultural Relics Administrative Committee, "Tang Li Shou mu fajue jian-bao" (A report on the excavation of the Li Shou tomb from the Tang dynasty), *Wenwu* 9 (1974): 71–88; Zhaoling Museum, "Tang Zhaoling Changle gongzhu mu" (The tomb of Princess Changle at the Zhao Ling mausoleum from the Tang dynasty), *Wenwu* 3 (1988): 10–30.

53. Sichuan Museum, "Sichuan Wanxian Tang mu" (The Tang-dynasty tomb in Wanxian County, Sichuan Province), *Kaogu xuebao* 4 (1980): 503–514.

54. Shaanxi Museum, Tang Tomb Excavation Team of the Culture and Education Bureau of Liquan County, "Tang Zheng Rentai mu fajue jianbao" (A brief report on the excavation of the tomb of Zheng Rentai from the Tang dynasty), *Wenwu* 7 (1972): 33–44.

55. Shaanxi Provincial Cultural Relics Administrative Committee, "Xi'an Yangtou zhen Tang Li Shuang mu de fajue" (The excavation of the tomb of Li Shuang from the Tang dynasty in Yangtou, Xi'an), *Wenwu* 3 (1959): 43–53.

56. Shaanxi Museum, Tang Tomb Excavation Team of the Culture and Education Bureau of Qianxian County, "Tang Zhanghuai taizi mu fajue jianbao" (A brief report on the excavation of the Tang tomb of Prince Zhanghuai), *Wenwu* 7 (1972): 13–25.

57. *Wenwu* 7 (1972): 26–32.

58. China Silicate Society, *Zhongguo taoci shi* (History of Chinese ceramics) (Beijing: Wenwu chubanshe, 1982), 214–216.

59. Shaanxi Provincial Cultural Relics Administrative Committee, *Shaanxi sheng chutu Tang yong xuanji* (Collection of Tang figurines unearthed in Shaanxi Province) (Beijing: Wenwu chubanshe, 1958), figs. 84–87.

60. See *Da Tang liu dian* (Six classics of the Great Tang) (Beijing: Zhonghua shuju, 1992), vol. 23, p. 597. Also see Du You (Tang dynasty), *Tong dian* (Beijing: Zhonghua shuju, 1984), vol. 46.

61. Wang Qufei, "Sishen, jinzi, gaoji" (Four deities, scarves, and tall coiffures), *Kaogu tongxun* 5 (1956): 54, n. 4.

62. Institute of Archaeology of the Chinese Academy of Social Sciences, *Tang Chang'an chengjiao Sui Tang mu* (Sui and Tang tombs in the outskirts of Tang Chang'an) (Beijing: Wenwu chubanshe, 1980), 56–65.

63. Xia Nai, "Xi'an Tang mu zhong chutu de jijian sancai tao-yong" (Several three-color pottery figurines unearthed at Tang tombs in Xi'an), in *Kaoguxue lunwen ji* (Collection of essays on archaeology) (Beijing: Kexue chubanshe, 1961).

64. Shaanxi Provincial Cultural Relics Administrative Committee, "Xi'an xijiao Zhongbaocun Tang mu qingli baogao" (A report on the investigation of the Tang tomb in Zhong-bao village in the western suburbs of Xi'an), *Kaogu* 3 (1960): 34–38.

65. Luoyang Museum, "Luoyang Guanlin 59 hao Tang mu" (Tang Tomb 59 in Guanlin, Luoyang), *Wenwu* 3 (1972): pl. 7.

66. Institute of Archaeology of the Chinese Academy of Social Sciences, *Tang Chang'an chengjiao Sui Tang mu*, 65–86, n. 21.

67. See *Wenwu* 1 (1966): 31–32, figs. 39, 41, and 44.

68. See *Wenwu* 1 (1966): 3–28, pls. 1–5.

69. Shanxi Provincial Institute of Archaeology, "Taiyuan Suidai Yu Hong mu qingli jianbao" (A brief report on the investigation of the Sui tomb of Yu Hong in Taiyuan), *Wenwu* 1 (2001): 27–52.

70. See Institute of Archaeology of the Chinese Academy of Social Sciences, *Tang Chang'an chengjiao Sui Tang mu*, 71–72, n. 10; 75–76, figs. 7–9, 31–33.

71. For further remarks concerning the incised pictures of female musicians and of musical instruments and other objects, see Sun Ji, "Tang Li Shou shiguo xianke 'shinü tu,' 'yuewu tu' sanji" (Notes on the incised pictures of "maid-servants" and "music and dance" on the outer stone coffin of Li Shou of the Tang), *Wenwu* 5 (1996): 33–49, and 6 (1996): 56–58. This article was later included in *Zhongguo shenghuo — Zhongguo gu wenwu yu dongxi wenhua jiaoliu zhong de ruogan wenti* (The sacred fire of China: A few issues concerning ancient Chinese cultural relics and the cultural exchange between East and West) (Shenyang: Liaojing jiaoyu chubanshe, 1996), 198–250.

72. Su Bai, "Xi'an diqu de Tang mu xingzhi" (Structures of Tang tombs in the area of Xi'an), *Wenwu* 12 (1995): 41–43.

73. Shaanxi Museum, Tang Tomb Excavation Team of the Culture and Education Bureau of Qianxian County, "Tang Zhanghuai taizi mu fajue jianbao" (A brief report on the excavation of the Tang tomb of Prince Zhanghuai), *Wenwu* 7 (1972): 15, 23, figs. 21, 22.

74. *Wenwu* 7 (1972): 27, fig. 2.

75. Shaanxi Provincial Cultural Relics Administrative Committee, "Tang Yongtai gongzhu mu fajue jianbao" (A brief report on the excavation of the tomb of Princess Yongtai), *Wenwu* 1 (1964): 7–33.

76. Shaanxi Provincial Cultural Relics Administrative Committee, "Chang'an xian Nanli Wangcun Tang Wei Jiong mu fajue jianbao" (A brief report on the excavation of the Tang tomb of Wei Jiong in Wangcun village, Nanli, Chang'an), *Wenwu* 8 (1959): 8–18; see Institute of Archaeology of the Chinese Academy of Social Sciences, *Tang Chang'an chengjiao Sui Tang mu*, n. 21, figs. 41–46.

77. See Institute of Archaeology of the Chinese Academy of Social Sciences, *Tang Chang'an chengjiao Sui Tang mu*, 38, n. 13.

78. Shaanxi Provincial Institute of Archaeology, *Tangdai Xue Jing mu fajue baogao* (A report on the excavation of the Tang tomb of Xue Jing) (Beijing: Kexue chubanshe, 2000).

79. Shaanxi Provincial Institute of Archaeology, Pucheng County Bureau of Culture, Sports, Broadcasting, and Television, "Tang Huizhuang taizi mu fajue jianbao" (A brief report on the excavation of the tomb of Huizhuang from the Tang dynasty), *Kaogu yu wenwu* 2 (1999): 3–22; Chen Anli and Ma Yongzhong, "Xi'an Wangjiafen Tangdai Tang'an gongzhu mu" (The Tang tomb of Princess Tang'an in Wangjiafen, Xi'an), *Wenwu* 9 (1991): 15–27.

80. Shaanxi Provincial Cultural Relics Administrative Committee, Zhaoling Cultural Relics Administrative Office, "Shaanxi Liquan Tang Zhang Shigui mu" (Tomb of Zhang Shigui from the Tang dynasty in Liquan), *Kaogu* 3 (1978): 168–178.

81. Zhaoling Cultural Relics Administrative Office, "Tang Yuchi Jingde mu fajue jianbao" (A brief report on the excavation of the tomb of Yuchi Jingde from the Tang dynasty), *Wenwu* 5 (1978): 20–25.

82. Tang Tomb Work Team of Shaanxi Provincial Institute of Archaeology, "Xi'an dongjiao Tang Yang Sixu mu qingli jianbao" (A brief report on the investigation of the tomb of Yang Sixu from the Tang dynasty in the eastern suburbs of Xi'an), *Kaogu* 1 (1960): 30–36.

83. Luo Feng, *Guyuan nanjiao Sui Tang mudi* (Sui and Tang burials in the southern suburbs of Guyuan) (Beijing: Wenwu chubanshe, 1996).

84. Ningxia Hui Autonomous Region Museum, "Ningxia Yanchi Tang mu fajue jianbao" (A brief report on the excavation of a Tang tomb in Yanchi, Ningxia), *Wenwu* 9 (1988): 43–56.

85. The term *Five Dynasties* refers to the Later Liang (907–923), Later Tang (923–936), Later Jin (936–946), Later Han (947–950), and Later Zhou (951–960), all established in north China in the period between 907 and 960. *Ten Kingdoms* refers to ten small powers established in the Yangzi River delta and the southwest of China during approximately the same period. They are states of Wu, the Southern Tang, Wu-Yue, the Shu, the Later Shu, the Southern Han, the Northern Han, Ming, Chu, and Jingnan (or Nanping).

86. Nanjing Museum, *Nantang er ling fajue baogao* (A report on the excavation of two mausoleums of the Southern Tang) (Beijing: Wenwu chubanshe, 1957); Zhejiang Provincial Cultural Relics Administrative Committee, "Hangzhou, Lin'an Wudai mu zhong de tianwen tu and mise ci" (An astronomical map and cream-colored porcelain unearthed in tombs from the Five Dynasties period in Hangzhou and Lin'an), *Kaogu* 3 (1973): 187–194; Zhejiang Museum, Hangzhou Cultural Relics Administrative Committee, "Zhejiang Lin'an Wantang Qian Kuan mu chutu tianwen tu ji 'guan' zi kuan baici" (The astronomical map and the white porcelain with the pattern of 官 unearthed in Lin'an, Zhejiang, in the tomb of Qian Kuan from the late Tang), *Wenwu* 12 (1979): 18–23; Suzhou Cultural Relics Administrative Committee, Wuxian County Cultural Relics Administrative Committee, "Suzhou Qizishan Wudai mu fajue jianbao" (A brief report on the excavation of Five Dynasties tombs at Qizishan in Suzhou), *Wenwu* 2 (1981): 37–45; Feng Hanji, *Qian Shu Wang Jian mu fajue baogao* (A report on the excavation of the tomb of Wang Jian from the Former Shu) (Beijing: Wenwu chubanshe, 1964); Chengdu Municipal Cultural Relics Administrative Office, "Hou Shu Meng Zhixiang mu yu Fu Qing zhang gongzhu muzhiming" (The tomb of Meng Zhixiang and the epitaph at the tomb of the eldest princess, Fuqing of the Later Shu), *Wenwu* 3 (1982): 15–20; Fujian Museum, "Wudai Mingguo Liu Hua mu fajue baogao" (A report on the excavation of the tomb of Liu Hua of the state of Min from the Five Dynasties period), *Wenwu* 1 (1975): 62–73.

87. Yi Shitong, "Zuigu de shike xingtu — Hangzhou Wu-Yue mu shike xingtu pingjie" (The most ancient carved stone astronomical map — Comments on the astronomical map incised on the Wu-Yue sarcophagus in Hangzhou), *Kaogu* 3 (1973): 153–157.

88. Archaeological Team of Chengdu Museum, "Wudai Hou Shu Sun Hanshao mu" (The tomb of Sun Hanshao of the Later Shu from the Five Dynasties period), *Wenwu* 5 (1991): 11–26; Chengdu Municipal Cultural Relics Administrative Office, "Chengdu shi dongjiao Hou Shu Zhang Qianzhao mu" (The tomb of Zhang Qianzhao of the Later Shu in the eastern suburbs of Chengdu municipality), *Wenwu* 3 (1982): 21–27.

89. Cultural Relics Work Team of Sichuan Museum, "Sichuan Pengshan Hou Shu Song Lin mu qingli jianbao" (A brief

report on the investigation of the tomb of Song Lin of the Later Shu in Pengshan, Sichuan), *Kaogu tongxun* 5 (1958): 18–26; Xu Pengzhang, Chen Jiuheng, and He Dezi, "Chengdu beijiao Zhandong xiang Gao Hui mu qingli jiaobao" (A brief report on the investigation of the tomb of Gao Hui in Zhandong township, northern suburbs of Chengdu), *Kaogu tongxun* 6 (1955): 39–42.

90. Hebei Provincial Institute of Cultural Relics, Baoding Cultural Relics Administrative Office, *Wudai Wang Chuzhi mu* (The tomb of Wang Chuzhi from the Five Dynasties period) (Beijing: Wenwu chubanshe, 1998).

91. Su Bai, "Guanyu Hebei sichu gumu de zhaji" (Notes on four ancient tombs of Hebei), *Wenwu* 9 (1996): 60.

92. Shandong Provincial Institute of Cultural Relics and Archaeology, "Linzi Beichao Cui Shi mu" (The tomb of the Cui family from the Northern Dynasties in Linzi), *Kaogu xuebao* 2 (1984): pl. 3 (6–7).

93. For further study of the "grave dragon" and "grave fish," see Xu Pingfang, "Tang Song muzang zhong de 'mingqi shensha' yu 'muyi' zhidu — du Dahan Yuanling muzang jing" (Spirit articles and the system of burial patterns of Tang and Song tombs — Notes on secret burial sutras of Yuanling mausoleum of the Great Han), *Kaogu* 2 (1963): 87–106.

94. Yangzhou Museum, "Jiangsu Hanjiang Caizhuang Wudai mu qingli jiaobao" (A report on the investigation of the tombs from the Five Dynasties period in Caizhuang village, Hanjiang, Jiangsu), *Kaogu* 8 (1980): 41–51.

95. See Institute of Archaeology of the Chinese Academy of Social Sciences, *Tang Chang'an chengjiao Sui Tang mu*, 92, n. 60.

96. Tang Yunming, "Hebei Shijiazhuang Bolin Song mu qingli jianbao" (A brief report on the investigation of the Song tomb in Bolin village, Shijiazhuang, Hebei), *Kaogu tongxun* 5 (1957): 64–67.

97. First Group of the Cultural Relics Work Team of the Henan Cultural Bureau, "Zhengzhou Nanguanwai Bei Song zhuan shi mu" (Brickwork tomb chambers of the Northern Song in Nanguanwai, Zhengzhou), *Wenwu cankao ziliao* 5 (1958): 52–54.

98. Su Bai, *Baisha Song mu* (The Song tomb in Baisha) (Beijing: Wenwu chubanshe, 1957).

99. Xu Pingfang, "Baisha Song mu zhong de zaju diaozuan" (Brick sculptures of zaju in the Song tomb of Baisha), *Wenwu* 9 (1960): 59–60.

100. Dong Xiang, "Yanshi xian Jiuliugou shuiku Song mu" (The Song tomb at the Jiuliugou reservoir in Yanshi County), *Wenwu* 9 (1959): 84–85.

101. For further information on brick sculptures of zaju, see Xu Pingfang, "Songdai de zaju diaozhuan" (Brick sculptures of zaju in the Song dynasty), *Wenwu* 5 (1960): 40–42.

102. Xu Pingfang, "Songdai muzang he jiaozang de fajue" (The excavation of burials and underground storage rooms of the Song dynasty), in *Xin Zhongguo de kaogu faxian he yanjiu* (Archaeological finds and research in New China) (Beijing: Wenwu chubanshe, 1984), 597–601.

103. Chen Zujun of Sichuan Provincial Institute of Cultural Relics and Archaeology, "1996 quanguo shida kaogu xin faxian zhi yi — Sichuan Huayin An Bing jiazu mudi" (One of the newly discovered ten most important archaeological finds in the country in 1996 — The An Bing clan burial ground in Huaying, Sichuan), *Zhongguo wenhua bao* 5–6 (1997): 12–26.

104. Sichuan Provincial Cultural Relics Administrative Committee, Pengshan County Cultural Center, "Nan Song Yu Gongzhu fufu hezang mu" (The joint tomb of Yu Gongzhu and his wife from the Southern Song), *Kaogu xuebao* 3 (1985): 383–402.

105. Xu Pingfang, "Song Yuan muzang de fajue" (Excavations of Song and Yuan tombs), in *Xin Zhongguo de kaogu faxian he yanjiu*, 605–607.

106. Houma Station, Shanxi Provincial Cultural Relics Administrative Committee, "Shanxi Houma Jin mu fajue jianbao" (A brief report on the excavation of the Jin tomb in Houma, Shanxi), *Kaogu* 12 (1961): 681–683. Houma Station, Shanxi Provincial Cultural Relics Administrative Committee, "Houma Jindai Dong shi mu jieshao" (Introduction to the Dong family tomb of the Jin in Houma), *Wenwu* 6 (1959): 50–55.

107. Zhou Yibai, "Houma Dong shi mu zhong wuge zhuanyong de yanjiu" (Study of the five brick figurines in the Dong family tomb in Houma), *Wenwu* 10 (1959): 50–52.

108. Archaeological Work Team, Henan Provincial Cultural Bureau, "Henan Fangcheng Yandiancun Song mu" (The Song tomb in Yandian village, Fangcheng, Henan), *Wenwu cankao ziliao* 11 (1958): 75–76; Liu Yusheng, Fangcheng County Cultural Center, "Henan sheng Fangcheng xian chutu Songdai shiyong" (Stone figurines unearthed in the Song tomb in Fangcheng County, Henan), *Wenwu* 8 (1983): 40–43.

109. Fujian Museum, "Fuzhou shi beijiao Yanzhishan Song mu qingli jianbao" (A brief report on the investigation of the Song tomb in Yanzhishan in the northern suburbs of Fuzhou), *Wenwu ziliao zhuankan* 2 (1978): 123–128.

110. Xie Ziyuan, "Minhou xian Huai'ancun de yizuo Song mu" (A Song tomb in Huai'an village, Minhou County), *Wenwu* 3 (1962): 59–60.

111. Fujian Museum, "Fujian Fuzhou jiaoqu qingli Nan song Zhu Zhu mu" (A report on the investigation of the Southern Song tomb of Zhu Zhu in the suburbs of Fuzhou, Fujian), *Wenwu* 9 (1987): 796–802.

112. Zeng Fan, "Fujian Lianjiang Song mu qingli jiaobao" (A report on the investigation of the Song tomb in Lianjiang, Fujian), *Kaogu tongxun* 5 (1958): 27–30.

113. Jiangxi Provincial Cultural Relics Administrative Committee, "Jiangxi Pengze Song mu" (The Song tomb in Pengze, Jiangxi), *Kaogu* 10 (1962): 539.

114. Peng Shifan, "Jingdezhen shijiao chutu Song ciyong" (Song porcelain figurines unearthed in the suburbs of Jingdezhen), *Kaogu* 2 (1977): 143–144.

115. Tang Shan, "Jiangxi Boyang faxian Songdai xiju yong" (Song figurines of dramatic performers discovered in Boyang, Jiangxi), *Kaogu* 4 (1979): 6–7.

116. Liu Nianzi, "Nan Song Raozhou ciyong xiaoyi" (Comments on the porcelain figurines of the Southern Song in Raozhou), *Wenwu* 4 (1979): 22–35.

117. Changping Cultural Relics Administrative Office, "Beijing Changping Chenzhuang Liao mu qingli baogao" (A report on the investigation of the Liao tomb in Chenzhuang village, Changping, Beijing), *Wenwu* 3 (1993): 68–77.

118. Xianyang Prefecture Cultural Relics Administrative Committee, "Shaanxi Huxian He shi mu chutu daliang Yuandai yong" (A large number of Yuan figurines unearthed in the burial ground of the He clan in Huxian County, Shaanxi), *Wenwu* 4 (1979): 10–22; Shaanxi Provincial Cultural Relics Administrative Committee, "Xi'an Qujiang Chixicun Yuan mu qingli baogao" (A report on the investigation of the Yuan tomb in Chixi village in Qujiang, Xi'an), *Wenwu cankao ziliao* 6 (1958): 57–61; Liu Bao'ai and Zhang Dewen, "Shaanxi Baoji Yuan mu" (Yuan tombs in Baoji, Shaanxi), *Wenwu* 2 (1992): 28–33.

119. Institute of Archaeology of the Chinese Academy of Social Sciences, Dingling Museum, Beijing Municipal Cultural Relics Work Team, *Dingling* (Dingling mausoleum) (Beijing: Wenwu chubanshe, 1990).

120. Shandong Museum, "Fajue Ming Zhu Tan mu jishi" (On-the-spot record of excavation of the tomb of Zhu Tan of the Ming), *Wenwu* 5 (1972): 25–36; Institute of Archaeology of the Chinese Academy of Social Sciences and Ming Tomb Excavation Team of Chengdu, Sichuan Museum, "Chengdu Fenghuangshan Ming mu" (The Ming tomb at Fenhuangshan, Chengdu), *Kaogu* 5 (1978): 307–313.

121. Jiangxi Museum, "Jiangxi Nancheng Ming Yiduan wang Zhu Hubin mu fajue baogao" (A report on the excavation of the Ming tomb of King Yiduan Zhu Hubin, in Nancheng, Jiangxi), *Wenwu* 3 (1973): 33–45; Jiangxi Provincial Cultural Relics Administrative Committee, "Jiangxi Nancheng Ming Yizhuang wang mu chutu wenwu" (Cultural relics unearthed in the Ming tomb of King Yizhuang in Nancheng, Jiangxi), *Wenwu* 1 (1959): 48–52.

122. Tianjin Cultural and Archaeological Excavation Work Team, "Hebei Fucheng Mingdai Liao Ji mu qingli baogao" (A report on the investigation of the tomb of Liao Ji of the Ming in Fucheng, Hebei), *Kaogu* 2 (1965): 73–79.

123. Shanghai Cultural Relics Preservation Committee, "Shanghai shi Luwan qu Ming Peng shi mu fajue jianbao" (A brief report on the excavation of the Ming burial ground of the Peng clan in the Luwan district of Shanghai), *Kaogu* 8 (1965): 425–434.

124. Yang Hao, "Qing chu Wu Liuqi mu jiqi xunzang yiwu" (The tomb of Wu Liuqi of the early Qing and its burial objects), *Wenwu* 2 (1982): 39–43.

125. *Wen xuan* (Selections of refined literature), compiled by Xiao Tong (Liang dynasty) (reprint, Beijing: Zhonghua shuju, 1977), vol. 44, Hu's engraved version, 617.

126. His order was issued in 218 (in the sixth lunar month of the twenty-third year of the Jian'an reign of the Wei dynasty). See "Biography of Emperor Wudi," in *Book of Wei, Records of the Three Kingdoms* (Beijing: Zhonghua shuju, 1959), 51.

127. Cao Pi, "Funeral System," in "Biography of Emperor Wendi," *Book of Wei*, 81–82.

128. Regarding the legend of Cao Cao's tomb, see *Yizhong* (The enigma of the tombs), vol. 26 in Tao Zongyi, *Nancun chuogeng lu* (Notes on quitting farming in Nancun village), in *Yuan-Ming shiliao biji congkan* (Beijing: Zhonghua shuju, 1980), 324. For one of the stories about the mystery surrounding Cao Cao's tomb, see *The Tomb of Cao Cao*, vol. 10 in Pu Songling, *Strange Stories from a Carefree Studio*, Serial Readers of Classical Chinese Literature (Beijing: Renmin wenxue, 1992), 1393.

129. Luoyang Work Team on Ancient Han and Wei Cities, Institute of Archaeology of the Chinese Academy of Social Sciences, "Xi Jin di ling kancha ji" (Records of a survey of imperial mausoleums of the Western Jin), *Kaogu* 12 (1984): 1096–1107.

130. For this imperial edict issued in 276 (the fourth year of the Xianning reign of Emperor Wu of the Jin), see "Li zhi" (Record of rites), in *Song shu* (Book of the Song) (Beijing: Zhonghua shuju, 1974), 407.

131. Huang Minglan, "Xi Jin sanqi changshi Han Shou mu mubiao ba" (Addendum to the epitaph for the tomb of Han Shou, gentleman cavalier attendant of the Western Jin), *Wenwu* 11 (1982): 65–69.

132. Beijing Cultural Relics Work Team, "Beijing xijiao faxian Handai shique qingli jianbao" (Bulletin on the investigation of the Han-dynasty stone gate towers discovered in the western suburbs of Beijing), *Wenwu* 11 (1964): 13–22.

133. Liu Xixiang and Zhang Yingzhao, "Bo'ai xian chutu de Jindai shizhu" (Jin-dynasty stone pillars unearthed in Bo'ai County), *Zhongyuan wenwu* 1 (1981): 63.

134. Emperor Yuan had issued an edict in 318 C.E. approving the erecting of a tombstone for Gu Rong; see "Li zhi," 407.

135. Luo Zongzhen, "Nanchao lingmu shike" (Stone sculpture from Southern Dynasties tombs), in the *Archaeology* volume, *Encyclopaedia Sinica* (Beijing: Zhongguo dabaike quanshu chubanshe, 1986), 344–345; Yao Qian and Gu Bing, *Liuchao yishu* (Arts of the Six Dynasties) (Beijing: Wenwu chubanshe, 1981).

136. Li Daoyuan (Northern Wei dynasty), *Shuijing zhu* (Annotated canon of waterways), condensed edition of four books (Shanghai: Commercial Press, n.d.), vol. 13, p. 128.

137. Luoyang Work Team on Ancient Han and Wei Cities, Institute of Archaeology of the Chinese Academy of Social Sciences and the Luoyang Ancient Tomb Museum, "Bei Wei Xuanwu di Jingling fajue baogao" (A report on the excavation of the tomb of Emperor Xuanwu of the Northern Wei at Jingling), *Kaogu* 9 (1994): 801–814.

138. Huang Minglan, "Luoyang Bei Wei Jingling weizhi de queding he Jingling weizhi de tuice" (The location of Jingling mausoleum of the Northern Wei and speculation on the location of Jingling mausoleum), *Wenwu* 7 (1978): 36–41.

139. Institute of Archaeology of the Chinese Academy of Social Sciences and Yecheng Archaeological Work Team of Hebei Provincial Cultural Relics Research Institute, "Hebei Cixian Wanzhang Beichao mu" (Tombs from the Northern Dynasties at Wanzhang in Cixian County, Hebei), *Kaogu* 7 (1990): 601–607.

140. He Zicheng, "'Guanzhong Tang shiba ling' diaocha ji" (Notes on a survey of eighteen Tang imperial mausoleums in central Shaanxi), in *Wenwu ziliao congkan* (Collection of reference materials on cultural relics), vol. 3 (n.d.), 53–60; Liu Qingzhu and Li Yufang, "Shaanxi Tangling diaocha baogao" (A report on an investigation of Tang mausoleums in Shaanxi), in *Wenwu ziliao congkan* 5 (1987): 216–263.

141. Shaanxi Provincial Institute of Archaeology, "Shunling kancha ji" (Notes on a survey of Shunling mausoleum of the Tang dynasty), *Wenwu* 1 (1964): 34–39.

142. Ruo Shi, "Tang Gongling diaocha jiyao" (Summary of a survey of the Gongling mausoleum of the Tang), *Wenwu* 3 (1985): 43–45; Second Group of the Henan Work Team

of the Institute of Archaeology of the Chinese Academy of Social Sciences and Yanshi County Cultural Relics Administrative Committee of Henan Province, "Tang Gongling shice jiyao" (Summary of a survey of Gongling mausoleum of the Tang), *Kaogu* 5 (1986): 458–462.

143. Shaanxi Provincial Cultural Relics Administrative Committee, "Tang Yongtai gongzhu mu fajue jianbao" (Bulletin on the excavation of the tomb of Princess Yongtai of the Tang), *Wenwu* 1 (1964): 7–33.

144. Qiu Xinggong followed Li Shimin in an expedition against Wang Shicong. When Saluzi, the horse that Li Shimin was riding, was injured by an arrow during the Battle of Mangshan near Luoyang, Qiu dispersed the enemy cavalry with arrows and dismounted to pull the arrow out of Saluzi. Then he helped Li Shimin onto his own horse, and, fighting on foot, he protected the future emperor until they reached the safety of their own base. To commemorate General Qiu's meritorious deed, an imperial edict was issued during the Zhenguan reign that a stone carving in the image of General Qiu Xinggong pulling an arrow out of the horse be erected in front of the stone gate tower to the Zhaoling mausoleum. See "The Biography of Qiu He, Together with the Biography of His Son Xinggong," in *Jiu Tang shu* (Old Book of Tang) (Beijing: Zhonghua shuju, 1975), 2327.

145. The two relief carvings that were shipped out of China are in the University of Pennsylvania Museum, Philadelphia. See Wang Shixiang, "Ji Meidi sougua woguo wenwu de qi da zhongxin" (Seven centers of U.S. imperialism for plundering cultural relics in China), *Wenwu cankao ziliao* 7 (1955): 49.

146. He Zhenghuang, "Jieshao Shanxi sheng bowuguan xinjian de shike yishu chenlie shi" (Introducing the newly built stone carving display room of the Shaanxi Museum), *Wenwu* 1 (1964): 47–48.

147. One of the stone tigers and one of the stone rhinoceroses are on display in the Stele Forest Museum of Xi'an.

148. The colophon of Xiao Tang Er is located below the neck of the stone tiger standing on the eastern side of the Spirit Path to the Xianling mausoleum.

149. Yang Chunyuan, "Yongji Pujin du yizhi" (Ruins of the Pujin ferry crossing at Yongji), in *Zhongguo kaoguxue nianjian: 1992* (China archaeology yearbook: 1992) (Beijing: Wenwu chubanshe, 1994), 166–167.

150. Wang Chengli and Cao Zhengrong, "Jilin Dunhua Liudingshan Bohai gu mu" (An ancient Bohai tomb at Liudingshan in Dunhua, Jilin), *Kaogu* 6 (1961): 298–301.

151. Wang Yi, "Zangwang mu—Xizang wenwu jian wen ji" (An eyewitness account of the tombs of Tibetan kings and Tibetan cultural artifacts [6]), *Kaogu* 4–5 (1961): 81–87; Su Bai, "Zang wang mu" (Tombs of Tibetan kings), in the *Archaeology* volume, *Encyclopaedia Sinica* (Beijing: Zhongguo dabaike quanshu chubanshe, 1986), 638; Cultural Relics Survey Team of the Tibetan Cultural Administrative Committee: "Tride Tsungtan bei qingli baogao" (Bulletin on a study of the stele dedicated to Tride Tsungtan), *Wenwu* 9 (1985): 73–76.

152. Henan Provincial Institute of Cultural Relics and Archaeology, *Bei Song huangling* (Imperial mausoleums of the Northern Song) (Zhengzhou: Zhongzhou guji chubanshe, 1997).

153. Chen Zhongchi, "Song Yongsiling pingmian ji shicangzi zhi chubu yanjiu" (An initial study of the plan of the Yongsi mausoleum of the Song and its stone figures), *Zhongguo yingzao xueshe huihan* (Collected journals of the China Construction Society), vol. 6, no. 3 (Beijing: n.p., 1936).

154. Chen Zengbi, "Ningbo Song yi yanjiu" (A study of a Song-dynasty chair of Ningbo), *Wenwu* 5 (1997): 42–48.

155. Tang Yuxian, "Liangjian diaoshi jingmei de Nan Song shima ji youguan shixiangsheng" (Two Southern Song stone horses with elaborate ornamentation, and the stone figures associated with them), *Wenwu* 8 (1999): 78–83.

156. Ningxia Institute of Cultural Relics and Archaeology, *Xi Xia ling* (Western Xia mausoleums) (Beijing: Dongfang chubanshe, 1995).

157. Ningxia Institute of Cultural Relics and Archaeology, *Xi Xia ling*, 152.

158. Zhou Jie, "Nei Menggu Zhao meng Liao Taizuling diaocha sanji" (Random notes on the survey of the mausoleum of Emperor Taizu of the Liao at the Ih Ju League in Inner Mongolia), *Kaogu* 5 (1966): 263–266.

159. Jilin Provincial Cultural Relics Work Team, "Wanyan Xiyin jiazu mu qun shidiao yishu chutan" (An initial study of the stone sculpture of the cemetery of the family of Wanyan Xiyin), *Wenwu* 3 (1982): 75–78.

160. Wang Jianying, *Ming zhongdu* (Central capital of the Ming) (Beijing: Zhonghua shuju, 1992).

161. Jiangsu Local Gazetteer Compilation Committee, "Ming Zuling" (The Zuling mausoleum of the Ming), in *Jiangsu sheng zhi wensu zhi* (Gazetteer of Jiangsu Province: Annals of cultural relics) (Nanjing: Jiangsu guji chubanshe, 1998), 147; Zhang Zhengxiang, "Ming Zuling" (The Zuling mausoleum of the Ming), *Kaogu* 8 (1963): 437–441.

162. Nanjing Museum, *Ming Xiaoling* (The Xiaoling mausoleum of the Ming) (Beijing: Wenwu chubanshe, 1981).

163. Zhao Qichang, "Ming shisan ling" (Thirteen tombs of the Ming), in the *Archaeology* volume, *Encyclopaedia Sinica* (Beijing: Zhongguo dabaike quanshu chubanshe, 1986), 336.

164. See Jiangsu Provincial Local Gazetteer Compilation Committee, *Jiangsu sheng difangzhi — kaogu* (Gazetteer of Jiangsu Province — archaeology) (Nanjing: Jiangsu guji chubanshe, 1998), 142–147.

Chapter 3. *From the Han to the Southern Song*

1. Hirakawa Akira, *A History of Indian Buddhism* (Honolulu: University of Hawai'i Press, 1990).

2. From the Prajnaparamita Sutra, as quoted in Tsukamoto Zenryū, *A History of Early Chinese Buddhism from Its Introduction to the Death of Hui-yüan*, 2 vols. (Tokyo: Kodansha International, 1985), 1: 18.

3. Jacques Gernet, *A History of Chinese Civilization* (Cambridge: Cambridge University Press, 1982), 117–128.

4. Benjamin I. Schwartz, *The World of Thought in Ancient China* (Cambridge: Harvard University Press, 1985), 56–135, 186–255.

5. Wu Hung, "Mapping Early Daoist Art: The Visual Culture of Wudoumi Dao," in Stephen Little, ed., *Taoism and the Arts of China* (Chicago: Art Institute of Chicago in association with University of California Press, 2000), 77–93.

6. Tsukamoto, *A History of Early Chinese Buddhism,* 1: 41, 60, 67–68.

7. For more on the image of the Queen Mother and the proto-Buddhist artifacts of southern China, see Wu Hung, *The Wu Liang Shrine: The Ideology of Early Chinese Pictorial Art* (Stanford: Stanford University Press, 1989), 108–141; Wu Hung, "Buddhist Elements in Early Chinese Art (Second and Third Centuries A.D.)," *Artibus Asiae* 47, nos. 3–4 (1986): 263–352; Jean M. James, "An Iconographic Study of Xiwangmu During the Han Dynasty," *Artibus Asiae* 55, nos. 1–2 (1995): 17–41.

8. Luo Yaling, "Leshanshi zhongqu Dong Han yanmode chosa shouhuo" (Results of the investigation of the Eastern Han cliff tomb at Leshan), *Sichuan wenwu* 6 (1991): 35–40; Tang Changshou, "Shiziwan Cliff Tomb No. 1," *Orientations* (September 1997): 72–77.

9. The sacred texts list thirty-two major marks *(lakshana)* and eighty minor marks, chiefly derivative from the Indian conception of royalty and impossible to be represented in toto. Besides the cranial protuberance, the artist singled out unnaturally elongated earlobes, the result of heavy jewelry worn by the Indian upper class, but also a likely reference to Buddha's supernatural hearing. A tuft of hair between the eyebrows *(urna,* in Sanskrit) is also a prominent mark that emanates light and inundates the universe to alert us whenever Buddha preaches. A prescribed golden body translates into an all-encompassing mandorla. Buddha's body is also perfectly proportioned and perfectly straight. Webbed hands and the Wheel of the Law appearing on the palms of hands and soles of feet are other less-common characteristics. For a discussion of the marks see Stella Kramrisch, "Emblems of the Universal Being," in Barbara Stoler Miller, ed., *Exploring India's Sacred Art* (Philadelphia: University of Pennsylvania Press, 1983), 130–140.

10. The symbolic hand gestures *(mudras)* are also numerous and meant to impart specific messages to the worshiper. Their growth and evolution go hand in hand with the doctrinal development of Buddhism. For a discussion of the most prominent mudras see E. Dale Saunders, *Mudra, a Study of Symbolic Gestures in Japanese Buddhist Sculpture* (New York: Pantheon Books, 1960).

11. The most recent and comprehensive study on money trees is by Susan N. Erickson, "Money Trees of the Eastern Han Dynasty," *Bulletin of the Museum of Far Eastern Antiquities* (Stockholm) 66 (1994): 5–115.

12. On Mianyang finds see He Zhiguo, "Sichuan Mianyang Hejiashan yihao Dong Han yamu qingli jianbao" (Preliminary report on the clearing of Eastern Han Cliff Tomb 1 at Hejiashan, Mianyang, Sichuan), *Wenwu* 3 (1991): 1–19; and He Zhiguo, "Shitan Mianyang chutu Dong Han Foxiang ji qi xiangguan wenti" (Exploratory talk on Eastern Han Buddhist images excavated in Mianyang and related questions), *Sichuan wenwu* 5 (1991): 23–30. On the possible link of Sichuan Han money trees to their Shang predecessors discovered in Sanxingdui, Guanghan County, see Chen Xiandan, "On the Designation 'Money Tree,'" *Orientations* (September 1997): 67–71. The 1994 finding of a money tree in Chengu County, southern Shaanxi, suggests the transmission of this artifact from Sichuan to neighboring regions; see Lo Erhu, "Shaanxi Chenggu chutu de qianshu Foxiang

ji qi yu Sichuan dichu de guanxi" (The money tree with Buddha images discovered in Chenggu, Shaanxi, and its relationship to Sichuan), *Wenwu* 12 (1998): 63–70.

13. On the Shenfang tile now in the Sichuan Provincial Museum, Chengdu, see Xie Zhicheng, "Sichuan Handai huaxiang zhuanshangde Fota tuxiang" (Buddhist stupa images on painted brick relief of the Han dynasty in Sichuan), *Sichuan wenwu* 4 (1987): 62–64.

14. Sichuan Provincial Cultural Relics Administrative Committee, "Sichuan Zhongxian Tujin Shu Han yamu" (Cliff tombs of the Shu Han kingdom at Tujing, Zhongxian, Sichuan), *Wenwu* 7 (1985): 49–95. A small clay Buddha image has also been found in a third-century Hubei tomb; see Yang Hong, "Ba Ezhou Sun Wu mu chushi tao Foxiang" (A clay Buddha image from the tomb of Sun Wu at Ezhou, a postscript), *Kaogu* 11 (1996): 28–30.

15. All the above proto-Buddhist artifacts have been analyzed by Wu Zhuo, "Sichuan zaoqi Fojiao yiwu jiqi niandai yu chuanbo tujing de kaocha" (An investigation of the artifacts of early Buddhism in Sichuan and their methods of dissemination), *Wenwu* 11 (1992): 40–50.

16. Wu Zhuo, "An investigation," 46–49; Zhong Enzheng, "Shitan gudai Sichuan yu Dongnanya wenming de guanxi" (Exploratory talks on the cultural rapport between ancient Sichuan and Southeast Asia), *Wenwu* 9 (1983): 73–81.

17. See Wu Hung, *Wu Liang Shrine,* 119–121.

18. Wu Hung, "Buddhist Elements," 273–283.

19. Numerous soul urns are illustrated in the Nanjing Museum catalogue *Fojiao chu chuan nanfang zhi lu* (The initial spread of Buddhism along the southern route) (Beijing: Wenwu chubanshe, 1993). For comprehensive studies on this artifact, see Kominami Ichiro, "Kokei no uchu" (The cosmos within a jar), *Tōhō gakuhō* 61 (1989): 165–221; Kominami Ichiro, "Shinteigo to Togo no bunka" (Aspects of eastern Wu culture as reflected in the *hunping* spirit bottles), *Tōhō gakuhō* 65 (1993): 223–311; Michèle Pirazzoli-t'Serstevens, "De l'efficacité plastique à la productivité: Les grès porcelaineux du Jiangnan aux IIIᵉ–IVᵉ siècles de notre ère," *T'oung pao* 84, 1–3 (1998): 21–61.

20. This interpretation was put forth by Ho Waikam, "Hunp'ing: The Urn of the Soul," *Bulletin of the Cleveland Museum of Art* 48, no. 2 (1961): 26–34.

21. See Susan L. Huntington, *The Art of Ancient India* (New York: Weatherhill, 1985), 134.

22. Tsukamoto, *History of Early Chinese Buddhism,* 1: 149 and 521*n.*

23. Wu Zhuo, "Investigation," 43.

24. Wu Hung, "Buddhist Elements," 292–302; Lianyungang Municipal Museum, *Haizhou shike: Jiangjun ya yanhua yu Kongwangshan moya zaoxiang* (Stone carvings of Haizhou: Boulder carvings of Jiangjun and the Moya Buddha of Mount Kongwang) (Beijing: Wenwu chubanshe, 1990).

25. Recent surveys on the Silk Route are Liu Xinru, *Ancient India and Ancient China: Trade and Religious Exchanges A.D. 1–600* (Delhi: Oxford India Paperback, 1994); Richard N. Frye, *The Heritage of Central Asia, from Antiquity to the Turkish Expansion* (Princeton, N.J.: Markus Wiener, 1996); Christoph Baumer, *Southern Silk Road: In the Footsteps of Sir Aurel Stein and Sven Hedin* (Bangkok: White Orchid Books, 2000).

26. W. L. Idema and Erik Zürcher, eds., *Thought and Law in Qin and Han China: Studies Presented to A. Hulsewe on Occasion of His Eightieth Birthday,* Han Buddhism and the Western Region Series, Sinica Leidensia 24 (Leiden: E. J. Brill, 1990), 158–182. The results of the most recent archaeological investigation of Khotan on the southern Silk Route are discussed in Corinne Debaine-Fracfort, Abdurassul Idriss, and Wang Binhua, "Agriculture irriguée et art bouddhique ancien au coeur du Taklamakan (Karadong, Xinjiang, IIe–IVe siècles)," *Arts asiatiques* 49 (1994): 34–52. A novel and revised synthesis of Buddhist art of the southern Silk Route is offered by Marylin Martin Rhie, *Early Buddhist Art of China and Central Asia,* vol. 1 (Leiden: E. J. Brill, 1999).

27. Angela F. Howard, "In Support of a New Chronology for the Kizil Mural Paintings, *Archives of Asian Art* 44 (1991): 68–83.

28. Su Bai, "Kezi'er bufen dongku jieduan huafen yu niandai deng wentide chubu tansuo daixu," in *Kezi'er shiku,* in *Zhongguo shiku* series (Beijing: Wenwu chubanshe, 1989), 1: 10–23.

29. The complex migration of numerous ethnic clans during this period is discussed by Wolfram Eberhard, *A History of China* (Berkeley: University of California Press, 1950), 110–174; a comprehensive account of the development of Buddhism in this period is found in Erik Zürcher, *The Buddhist Conquest of China* (Leiden: E. J. Brill, 1959).

30. Susanne Juhl, "Cultural Exchange in Northern Liang (396–439)," in Søren Clausen, Roy Starrs, and Anne Wedell-Wedellsborg, eds., *Cultural Encounters: China, Japan, and the West: Essays Commemorating Twenty-Five Years of East Asian Studies at the University of Aarhus* (Aarhus, Denmark: Aarhus University Press, 1995), 55–82; Alexander C. Soper, "Northern Liang and Northern Wei in Gansu," *Artibus Asiae* 21 (1958): 131–164; Zhang Xuerong and He Jingzhen, "Lun Liangzhou Fojiao ji Juqu Mengxun de zong Fo zun ru" (On the Buddhist religion in the Liangzhou area and Juqu Mengxun's belief in Buddhism and Confucianism), *Dunhuang yanjiu* 2 (1994): 98–110.

31. Alexander C. Soper, trans., *Literary Evidence for Early Buddhist Art in China* (Ascona, Switzerland: Artibus Asiae, 1959), 92.

32. Angela F. Howard, "Liang Patronage of Buddhist Art in the Gansu Corridor During the Fourth Century and the Transformation of a Central Asian Style," in Wu Hung, ed., *Between Han and Tang: Religious Art and Archaeology in a Transformative Period* (Beijing: Wenwu chubanshe, 2000), 235–272.

33. Su Bai, "Wuwei Tiantishan zaoqi shiku zanguan ji" (A visit to the early grottoes at Tiantishan, Wuwei), *Yanjing xuebao* 8 (2000): 215–225. The sites are partially illustrated in Gansu Provincial Institute of Cultural Relics and Archaeology, ed., *Hexi shiku* (Cave temples of the Hexi Corridor) (Beijing: Wenwu chubanshe, 1987).

34. Su Bai, "Liangzhou shiku yiji he 'Liangzhou moshi'" (Liangzhou cave temples and the 'Liangzhou style'), *Kaogu xuebao* 4 (1986): 435–446.

35. Tsukamoto, *History of Early Chinese Buddhism,* 2: 755.

36. From the *Wei shu* (Treatise on Buddhism and Daoism), trans. Leon Hurvitz, in Mizuno Seiichi and Nagahiro Toshio, *Yun-kang (Unkō sekkutsu): The Buddhist Cave-Temples of the Fifth Century A.D. in North China — Detailed Report of the Archaeological Survey by the Mission of the Tōhō Bunka Kenkyūjo,*

1938–1945, 16 vols. (two parts each) (Kyoto: Kyoto daigaku jimbun kagaku kenkyūjo, 1951–1956), 16 supplement: 57.

37. A stupa is the earliest and holiest Buddhist building. In pre-Buddhist India it was used as a royal burial in the shape of a large hemisphere. It was then adapted as a Buddhist monument containing some of the historical Buddha Shakyamuni's relics or remains. Over time the association between Buddha and stupa came to symbolize Buddha's final release from reincarnation or his Nirvana; hence it stood for his teaching. See Adrian Snodgrass, *The Symbolism of the Stupa,* Studies on Southeast Asia (Ithaca, N.Y.: Cornell University, 1985).

38. I discuss the miniature pillars and use this new terminology in "Liang Patronage of Buddhist Art in the Gansu Corridor During the Fourth Century and the Transformation of a Central Asian Style," in Wu, *Between Han and Tang,* 235–272.

39. H. Durt, K. Riboud, and T. Lai, "A propos de 'stupa miniatures' votifs du cinquième siècle découverts à Tourfan et au Gansu," *Arts asiatiques* 40 (1985): 92–107; Yin Guangming, "Dunhuangshi bowuguan cang sanjian Beiliang shita" (Three Northern Liang stone stupas in the collection of the Dunhuang Municipal Museum), *Wenwu* 11 (1991): 76–83; Huang Wenkun, "Shiliuguo de shikusi yu Dunhuang shiku yishu" (Cave temples of the Sixteen Kingdoms period and the art of the Dunhuang cave temples), *Wenwu* 5 (1992): 43–48.

40. The three caves are discussed in Roderick Whitfield, *Caves of the Singing Sands, Dunhuang: Buddhist Art from the Silk Road* (London: Textile and Art Publications, 1995), 2: 272–275.

41. The presence of a Buddha in the crown of the main image of Cave 275 does not challenge its identity as Maitreya. This usage is very rare (it occurs, for example, in a Maitreya carved in Yungang Cave 11). From the sixth century on, such a marker is used exclusively to represent the bodhisattva Avalokiteshvara/Guanyin. In the latter instance the Buddha in the crown is Amitabha, as stated in the canonical sources. I suggest that when used in conjunction with Maitreya, the Buddha is Shakyamuni. The bottle is the other implement that is shifted from Maitreya to Avalokiteshvara.

42. Dao An's catalogue is lost but can be reconstructed on the basis of the *Chu san zang jiji,* compiled by Seng Yu during the Southern Liang, as discussed in Tsukamoto, *History of Early Chinese Buddhism,* 2: 712–722.

43. I synthesize here the thorough study by Dong Yuxiang, ed., *Binglingsi 169 ku* (Binglingsi Monastery Cave 169) (Shenzhou: Haitian chubanshe, 1994).

44. Quoted in Dong Yuxiang, *Binglingsi 169 ku,* 16–17.

45. Shakyamuni preached the Lotus of the Wonderful Law on the Vulture Peak. The universality of Buddhism, the *upaya,* or skill-in-means doctrine applied in propagating Buddhism, the eternal nature of Buddha, and the compassionate mission of the bodhisattva (Guanyin in particular) are the major innovations of this sutra. Some narrative passages lent themselves to visual interpretation in medieval Buddhism: the episode of the Buddha of the Past Prabhutaratna (Duobao, or Many Jewels) miraculously manifesting himself inside a stupa before Shakyamuni's sermon is the earliest and most popular. The imagery of Guanyin (Savior from Perils) stems also from chapter twenty-five of the scripture. The Sutra Spoken by Vimalakirti (Vimalakirtinirdesa Sutra) cele-

brates the conduct and practice of Buddhism by the wise and liberal layman Vimalakirti of Vaishali and is critical of the narrow-mindedness of monastic circles. As Vimalakirti lies sick in his home, Buddha sends Manjushri, the bodhisattva of Wisdom, to inquire about his well-being (all the other disciples have declined to go, fearing the sharp tongue of the layman). Numerous witnesses, divine and secular, assemble to witness the debate. The two main protagonists discuss issues such as the power of the Buddha, the nature of his body, and, foremost, the doctrine of nonduality and insubstantiality. Miracles interrupt the dry sophistication of the debate, namely the appearance of a bowl of perfume to satisfy the hunger of the participants, the expansion of space to accommodate the arrival of thousands of thrones with their Buddhas, and the manifestation of a goddess who confounds the audience by changing gender with Shariputra, Shakyamuni's disciple. The myth of the learned layman who successfully argues Buddhist truths with Buddhist deities and clerics had a tremendous appeal to Chinese scholars. Lastly, the visualization of this sutra is exclusively Chinese.

46. It is relevant to clarify that the triad Amitabha, with the attendant bodhisattvas Avalokiteshvara and Mahasthamaprapta as depicted in niche 6 of Binglingsi, Cave 169, derives not from the Small Sukhavativyuha Sutra, but from the Longer Sukhavativyuha Sutra allegedly translated by Sanghavarman of the Cao Wei kingdom, thus also originating in China's northwest. The issue is discussed by Luis O. Gomez, *The Land of Bliss, the Paradise of the Buddha of Measureless Light* (Honolulu: University of Hawai'i Press, 1996).

47. Liu Huida, "Bei Wei shiku yu *chan*" (The Northern Wei cave temples and *chan*), *Kaogu xuebao* 3 (1978): 337–352, investigates *chan* in reference to Northern Wei grottoes.

48. I have relied especially on Dong Yuxiang, "Maijishan shiku de fenqi" (Classification of Maijishan grottoes), *Wenwu* 6 (1983): 18–30, and on Huang Wenkun, "Maijishan de lishi yu shiku" (History and the cave temples of Maijishan), *Wenwu* 3 (1989): 83–89.

49. This small group of images, many of which are in Japanese collections, was first investigated by Mizuno and Nagahiro, *Unkō sekkutsu* 2 (text): 77–88, and by Seiichi Mizuno, *Bronze and Stone Sculpture of China* (Tokyo: Nihon Keizai, 1960), 20–22. Among numerous recent Chinese studies see Li Jingjie, "Zaoqi jintong Fo puxi yanjiu" (Study of the genealogy of early gilt-bronze Buddhas), *Kaogu* 5 (1995): 451–465; among Japanese contributions see Matsubara Saburō, *Chūgoku Bukkyō chōkoku shiron* (Treatise on Chinese Buddhist sculpture), 2 vols. (Tokyo: Yoshikawa kobunkan heisei, 1995).

50. Marylin Martin Rhie, *Early Buddhist Art of China and Central Asia,* radically alters this chronology and dates the bronze to the second half of the second century A.D., during the Later Han dynasty, based mainly on stylistic comparison with a Kalchayan style Buddha, near Termez, in present-day Uzbekistan. See pp. 71–92.

51. Arthur F. Wright, *Studies in Chinese Buddhism,* ed. Robert Somers (New Haven: Yale University Press, 1990): 34–67.

52. *Special Exhibition, Gilt Bronze Buddhist Statues,* exh. cat. (Tokyo: National Museum, 1987), 80–81.

53. Mizuno Seiichi and Nagahiro Toshio, "The Yun-Kang Caves and Their Historical Background," *Unkō sekkutsu* 3 (text):

87–99; Su Bai, "Yungang shiku fenqi shilun" (Preliminary discussion on the chronological division/periodization of the Yungang caves), *Wenwu* 1 (1978): 25–38; James O. Caswell, *Written and Unwritten, a New History of the Buddhist Caves at Yungang* (Vancouver: University of British Columbia Press, 1988).

54. Su Bai, "Dongbei, Nei Menggu diqu de Xianbei yiji" (Xianbei Remains in Northeastern China and Inner Mongolia), *Wenwu* 11 (1977): 38–46; Adam T. Kessler, *Empires Beyond the Great Wall* (Los Angeles: Natural History Museum of Los Angeles County, 1993), 67–76.

55. I disagree with John Huntington's interpretation that the five Imperial caves form a mandalic arrangement generated by Esoteric teaching; see John Huntington, "The Iconography and Iconology of the Tan Yao Caves at Yungang," *Oriental Art* 32 (1986): 142–160.

56. I dissent with the opinion that the Buddha of Cave 18 is Vairocana (Chinese Lushena), offered by Matsumoto Seiichi; see Angela Falco Howard, *The Imagery of the Cosmological Buddha* (Leiden: E. J. Brill, 1986), 98.

57. Jessica Rawson, *Chinese Ornaments: The Lotus and the Dragon* (London: British Museum Publications, 1984), 39–62.

58. Alexander C. Soper, "Imperial Cave Chapels of the Northern Dynasties: Donors, Beneficiaries, Dates," *Artibus Asiae* 28 (1966): 241–246.

59. James Legge, trans., *A Record of Buddhistic Kingdoms* (reprint, New York: Dover Publications, 1965), 79; *Wei shu,* in Mizuno and Nagahiro, *Unkō sekkutsu* 16, supplement: 56–57.

60. A comprehensive list of all the pro-Chinese edicts is in W. J. F. Jenner, *Memories of Loyang: Yang Hsüan-chih and the Lost Capital (493–534)* (Oxford: Clarendon Press, 1982), 28–31, 58.

61. Alexander C. Soper, "South Chinese Influence on the Buddhist Art of the Six Dynasties Period," *Bulletin of the Museum of Far Eastern Antiquities* (Stockholm) 32 (1960): 58–72.

62. See the aforementioned translation in Jenner, *Memories of Loyang.*

63. Katherine R. Tsiang, "Disjunctures of Time, Text, and Imagery in Reconstructions of the Guyang," in Wu, *Between Han and Tang,* 313–348.

64. Ding Mingyi, *Gongxian Tianlong shan Anyang shuqu shiku si* (Cave temples at several locations in Gongxian, Tianlongshan, and Anyang), vol. 13 of Zhongguo meishu quanji bianji weiyuanhui, *Zhongguo meishu quanji* (Beijing: Wenwu chubanshe, 1989), 27.

65. Chang Qing, "Beichao shiku Shenwang diaoke shulue" (Review of Shenwang reliefs in the Northern Dynasties cave temples), *Kaogu* 12 (1994): 1127–1141.

66. Consider that the Yongning si images are carved in clay, a medium that lends itself to a softer modeling effect than stone. Institute of Archaeology of the Chinese Academy of Social Sciences, ed., *The Yongning Temple in Northern Wei Luoyang, Excavations in 1979–1994* (Beijing: Zhongguo dabaike quanshu chubanshe, 1996).

67. Gansu Provincial Cultural Relics Work Team, ed., *Qingyang Beishiku si* (The northern cave temples of Qingyang) (Beijing: Wenwu chubanshe, 1985).

68. In Vedic mythology Ashuras are "anti-gods," rivals and enemies of the Devas who dethroned them from the heavenly spheres. As demigods, they were absorbed in the Buddhist

pantheon, in the guise of guardians. The king of the Ashuras (probably represented in Cave 165) is usually shown with three faces, differently characterized, and four arms, two carrying sun and moon, two bow and arrow. When shown with six arms, the remaining two perform the *anjali,* or praying mudra.

69. Li Jingjie, "Zaoqi jintong Fo puxi yanjiu."

70. For Chinese scholarship on recent finds of gilt bronzes see Li Shaonan, "Shandong Boxing chushi bai yu jian Bei Wei zhi Suidai tong zaoxiang" (More than one hundred gilt-bronze images from Northern Wei to Sui time discovered in Boxing, Shandong), *Wenwu* 5 (1984): 21–31; Ding Mingyi, "Tan Shandong Boxing chushi de tong Fo Zaoxiang" (Discussion of bronze Buddhist images discovered in Boxing, Shandong), *Wenwu* 5 (1984): 32–43; Jin Hua and Wu Jianguo, "Shanxi Shouyang chushi yipi Dong Wei zhi Tangdai tong zaoxiang" (A group of bronze images from the Eastern Wei to the Tang dynasty unearthed in Shouyang, Shanxi), *Wenwu* 2 (1991): 1–13; Yecheng Archaeological Team and others, "Hebei Linzhang Yecheng yizhi chushi de Beichao tong zaoxiang" (Buddhist gilt bronzes of the Northern Dynasties from the ruins of Yecheng, Linzhang, Hebei), *Kaogu* 8 (1992): 741–744.

71. Gilt-bronze altarpieces with such ornate aureoles are discussed by Zhang Zhong, "Bei Wei jintong Fo beiguang feitian fenqi" (Chronology of Northern Dynasties Buddhist gilt bronzes with flying angels attached to the aureole), *Wenwu* 12 (1993): 47–53.

72. The most recent research on the subject is in Dorothy C. Wong, *Chinese Steles: Pre-Buddhist and Buddhist Use of a Symbolic Form* (Honolulu: University of Hawai'i Press, 2004).

73. Ding Mingyi, "Cong Qiang Dule jian Zhou Wenwang Fo dao zaoxiangbei kan Beichao Daojiao zaoxiangbei" (The Buddhist Daoist stele of King Wen of Zhou from Qiang Dule: A look at the Buddhist images of the Northern Dynasties), *Wenwu* 3 (1986): 52–62; Jean James, "Some Iconographic Problems in Early Daoist-Buddhist Sculptures in China," *Archives of Asian Art* 42 (1989): 71–76. For a discussion of more examples of early Daoist art from Shaanxi, see Little, *Taoism and the Arts of China*, 163–171.

74. This is the opinion of Roger Goepper in Helmut Brinker and Roger Goepper, *Kunstschätze aus China* (Zurich: Kunsthaus, 1980), 198–202.

75. A related stele is discussed in Zhou Zeng, "Bei Wei Xue Fenggui zaoxiangbei kao" (Investigation of the Northern Wei Xue Fenggui stele), *Wenwu* 8 (1990): 58–65.

76. National Museum of Chinese History, *Masterpieces of Buddhist Statuary from Qingzhou City,* exh. cat. (Beijing: Chinasight Fine Arts Co., 1999). The Qingzhou findings span the Northern and Eastern Wei, Northern Qi, and Sui periods (ca. 525–600).

77. Quoted in Tsukamoto, *Early Chinese Buddhism,* 1: 621.

78. Kenneth Ch'en, *Buddhism in China* (Princeton: Princeton University Press, 1964): 103–112.

79. Quoted from the *Nan shi* (History of the Southern Dynasties), vol. 78, in Tsukamoto, *Early Chinese Buddhism,* 1: 624.

80. Quoted from the *Fa yuan zhulin* (Pearl garden of the dharma forest), vol. 16, in Tsukamoto, *Early Chinese Buddhism,* 1: 626.

81. Quoted from the *Ji shenzhou sanbao gangtong lu* (Collections of miraculous tales on Buddhism in China), in Tsukamoto, *Early Chinese Buddhism,* 1: 625.

82. Both sites are discussed in Su Bai, "Nanchao kanxiang yiji chutan" (Preliminary investigation of remains of Buddha niches executed during the Southern Dynasties), *Kaogu xuebao* 4 (1989): 389–414.

83. Makita Tairyo, *Ryō kosoden sakuin* (Kyoto: Heirakuji shoten, 1972), 296–297.

84. Yuan Shuguang, "Sichuan Maowen Nan Qi Yongming zaoxiangbei ji youguan wenti" (The stone stele dated to the Southern Qi Yongming Era from Maowen, Sichuan, and related questions), *Wenwu* 2 (1992): 67–71. Dorothy C. Wong, "Four Sichuan Buddhist Steles and the Beginnings of Pure Land Imagery in China," *Archives of Asian Art* 51 (1998–1999): 56–79.

85. For a partial list of publications of the Wanfo Temple sculpture, see Liu Zhiyuan and Liu Tingbi, eds., *Chengdu Wanfosi shike yishu* (Rock-carving art of Wanfo Temple, Chengdu) (Shanghai: Gudian yishu chubanshe, 1958). The following are particularly thorough studies: Yuan Shuguang, "Chengdu Wanfo si chushi de Liangdai shike zaoxiang" (Liang-dynasty stone sculpture unearthed at the Wanfo Temple, Chengdu), *Sichuan wenwu* 3 (1991): 27–32; Li Sisheng, "Chengdu Wanfo si Liangdai zaoxiang yishu tese de xingcheng" (The formation of the style of the Liang-dynasty sculpture from the Wanfo Temple, Chengdu), *Dunhuang yanjiu* 3 (1992): 86–92; Chengdu Municipal Cultural Relics and Archaeological Work Team and Chengdu Municipal Institute of Cultural Relics and Archaeology, "Chengdu shi Xi'an lu Nanchao shike zaoxiang qingli jianbao" (Preliminary report of the retrieval of Southern Dynasties stone images on the Xi'an Road, Chengdu), *Wenwu* 11 (1998): 4–20.

86. The most recent studies on these three scriptures are Julian Pas, *The Vision of Sukhavati: Shan-dao's Commentary on the Kuan-wu-liang-shou Fo-ching* (Albany: State University of New York Press, 1995), and Luis O. Gomez, *The Land of Bliss: The Paradise of the Buddha of Measureless Light* (Honolulu: University of Hawai'i Press, 1996).

87. Among the Wanfo Temple reliefs there is also a fragmentary work that carries a representation of Mount Sumeru (front) and a Pure Land (back) that represents Maitreya's. The deity is shown in the upper portion as if in Tushita Heaven awaiting rebirth and below as a reborn Buddha in Ketumati preaching to the triple assembly (hence he is portrayed three times). This relief is a section of a large stele not dissimilar in construction from the one with the Amitabha Pure Land and is stylistically related to all the other Southern Liang works from the finding. I surmise that not only the Amitabha's but also the Maitreya's Paradise originated in Sichuan, as a logical result of the fact that the two Buddhas were jointly worshiped in the south, as shown in the 483 Maowen stele. This issue warrants further investigation.

88. The formation of the Northern Qi style arguably resulted from the acceleration of an artistic change that was already visible by the end of Wei, for instance in the clay images of the Yongning Temple's pagoda. This self-generated relaxation of Northern Wei traits was later pushed to an extreme by outside influences such as the Gupta, which had penetrated China chiefly through the sea route.

89. I have investigated Northern Qi cave-temple sculpture in Angela Falco Howard, "Buddhist Cave Sculpture of the Northern Qi Dynasty: Shaping a New Style, Formulating New Iconographies," *Archives of Asian Art* 35 (1996): 6–25. It contains the most recent Chinese and Western scholarship on the issue. See also Howard, "Reconstructing the Original Location of a Group of Sculptures in the University of Pennsylvania Museum," *Orientations* (February 2001): 32–39.

90. To be accurate one ought to mention the existence of a painted paradise scene, allegedly a Western Pure Land, in Western Wei Cave 127, Maijishan. See *Maijishan Caves,* Chūgoku sekkutsu series (Tokyo: Heibonsha; Beijing: Wenwu chubanshe, 1987), fig. 161.

91. Yang Boda, *Quyang Xiudesi chutu jinian zaoxiang de yishu fengge yu tezheng* (Style and characteristics of the dated sculpture unearthed at the Xiude Temple, Quyang) (Beijing: Gugong bowuyuan, 1960).

92. Ningxia Hui Autonomous Region Cultural Relics Committee, ed., *Xumishan shiku* (The Xumishan grottoes) (Beijing: Wenwu chubanshe, 1988).

93. Dong Yuxiang and Zang Zhijun, "Gansu Wushan Shuiliangdong shikuqun" (The Shuiliang group of caves on Mount Wushan, Gansu), *Wenwu* 5 (1985): 7–16.

94. Marylin M. Rhie, "Late Sui Buddhist Sculpture: A Chronology and Regional Analysis," *Archives of Asian Art* 35 (1982): 27–51.

95. Tanabe Saburosuke, "On the Sui Monumental Marble Buddha in the Collection of the British Museum," *Ars Buddhica* 129 (March 1989): 24–36.

96. Du Zaizhong and Han Gang, "Shandong Zhucheng Fojiao shizaoxiang" (Stone Buddhist sculpture from Zhucheng, Shandong), *Kaogu xuebao* 2 (1994): 231–262.

97. Howard, *Imagery of the Cosmological Buddha,* 3.

98. Kim La Na, "On the Buddhist Images with *Rahotsu* (Snail-like Curls of Hair) Among the Group of Seven Deities in Sixth-Century China," *Ars Buddhica* 219 (March 1995): 40–55. Bodhisattvas, monks, and *pratyekas* represent the three vehicles that were superseded by the Buddha vehicle alone preached in the Lotus Sutra. It is fitting that the three categories were amalgamated during the Sui period, which also coincided with the ascendancy of Tiantai, the school that took the Lotus Sutra as its centerpiece.

99. Sally Hovey Wriggins, *Xuanzang, a Buddhist Pilgrim on the Silk Road* (Boulder, Colo.: Westview Press, 1996).

100. Amy McNair, "Early Tang Imperial Patronage at Longmen," *Ars Orientalis* 4 (1994): 67 n.13.

101. Howard, *Imagery of the Cosmological Buddha,* 68–69.

102. Mizuno Seiichi, *Tōdai no Butsuzō chōkoku: Chūgoku no Bukkyō bijutsu* (Buddhist sculpture of the Tang dynasty: Buddhist art of China) (Tokyo: Heibonsha, 1968), 187–228, especially 200.

103. McNair, "Early Tang Imperial Patronage," 67.

104. The earliest depiction of twenty-four arhats as venerable patriarchs and protectors of the dharma is in the Dazhusheng cave on Mount Baoshan, Anyang, dated Sui 589. They were carved in the climate of the Latter Day of the Law (Mo Fa) belief pervasive of the second half of the sixth century; see Howard, "Buddhist Cave Sculpture," 20–23. Tang representations of the luohans stem from a different doctrinal background and increasingly gravitate toward Chan teaching.

These twenty-nine luohans are described in the *Lidai bao ji* (Precious record of the dharma through successive dynasties), a text completed by 750; the Kanjing group reflects, therefore, ongoing doctrinal concerns.

105. Their scriptural basis possibly is the *Record of the Abiding of the Dharma Spoken by the Great Arhat Nandimitra* (T.2030), short title *Record of the Abiding of the Law (Fa zhu ji),* translated into Chinese by 650. This sutra identifies sixteen luohans by name and by their characteristic implements, and it emphasizes their transcending powers and their goal of transmitter of the Law through time until the coming of Buddha Maitreya. Preservation of the dharma is therefore their primary task. With time the number of luohans increased to eighteen, then to one hundred, and, finally, to five hundred. Among articles on the provenance of the luohans I select Richard Smithies, "The Search for the Luohans of I-Chou (Yi Xian)," *Oriental Art* 29, no. 3 (Autumn 1984): 260–274 and, by the same author, "A Luohan from Yizhou in the University of Pennsylvania Museum," *Orientations* (February 2001): 51–56.

106. Yen Chuan-ying, "The Sculpture from the Tower of Seven Jewels: The Style, Patronage and Iconography of the T'ang Monument" (Ph.D. diss., Harvard University, 1986), 107.

107. A reconstruction of the caves by linking the sculpture now in Western and Japanese museums to their original setting (photographed in the 1920s by Tomura Taijirō and in the 1930s by Tokiwa Daijō and Sekino Tadashi) is by Harry Vanderstappen and Marylin Rhie, "The Sculpture of T'ien Lung Shan: Reconstruction and Dating," *Artibus Asiae* 26 (1965): 191–220.

108. Famen Temple Archaeological Team, *Famen si digong zhenbao* (Precious cultural relics in the crypt of the Famen Temple) (Xi'an: Shaanxi renmin meishu chubanshe, 1989).

109. Chou Yi-liang, "Tantrism in China," *Harvard Journal of Asiatic Studies* 8 (1944–1945): 241–332.

110. Cheng Xuehua, "Gilded and Painted Sculptures of the Tang Dynasty," *Wenwu* 7 (1961): 61–63; Brinker and Goepper, *Kunstschatze,* 212–222; Roderick Whitfield, "Esoteric Buddhist Elements in the Famensi Reliquary Deposit," *Asiatische Studien* 44, no. 2 (1990): 247–266.

111. Guangyuan Municipal Cultural Relics Administrative Office, "Guangyuan Qianfo ya shiku diaocha ji" (Survey of the Guangyuan cliff grottoes), *Wenwu* 6 (1990): 1–23.

112. Xing Jun, "Guangyuan Qianfo ya qu Tang mijiao zaoxiang xi" (Analysis of early Tang Esoteric images at the Thousand Buddhas Cliff, Guangyuan), *Wenwu* 6 (1990): 37–40; Luo Shiping, "Qianfo ya Lizhou bigong ji zaoxiang niandai kao" (Investigation of the date of Lizhou patronage and chronology of the sculpture at the Thousand Buddhas Cliff, Guangyuan), *Wenwu* 6 (1990): 34–36.

113. The Shining site used to be called Shuining (using the character for "water"), but the name has been recently changed to Shining (using the character for "beginning"). Sichuan Provincial Cultural Relics Administrative Committee, "Sichuan Bazhong Shuining si Tangdai moya zaoxiang" (Tang Cliff Sculpture at Shuining si in Bazhong, Sichuan), *Wenwu* 8 (1988): 14–18.

114. Peng Jiasheng, "Sichuan Anyue Wofo yuan diaocha" (Investigation of the Parinirvana Buddha temple in Anyue, Sichuan), *Wenwu* 8 (1988): 1–13; Fu Chengjin, "Anyue shiku

zhi Xuan Ying kao" (Investigation of Xuan Ying from the stone sculpture of Anyue), *Sichuan wenwu* 3 (1991): 48–49.

115. Zhou Junqi, "'Da xiang (Fo)' yanjiu" (Research on Large Images [Buddha]), *Sichuan wenwu* 5 (1995): 44–50.

116. Angela F. Howard, "Tang and Song Images of Guanyin from Sichuan," *Orientations* (January 1990): 49–57.

117. Deng Zhongyuan and Gao Junying, "Renshou xian Niujiaozhai moya zaoxiang" (The cliff sculpture of Niujiaozhai, Renshou County), *Sichuan wenwu* 5 (1990): 71–77.

118. Hu Wenhe, *Sichuan daojiao Fojiao shiku yishu* (Chengdu: Sichuan renmin chubanshe, 1994), 53–56.

119. Jin Anning, "Yongle Palace: The Transformation of the Daoist Pantheon During the Yuan Dynasty" (Ph.D. diss., Princeton University, 1994), 132–192.

120. Li Sisheng, ed., *Sichuan shiku diaosu* (Sichuan cave-temple sculpture), in vol. 12 of Zhongguo meishu quanji bianji weiyuanhui, *Zhongguo meishu quanji* (Beijing: Renmin meishu chubanshe, 1988).

121. Among the numerous Chinese publications on Dazu, I list the following books, omitting the articles: Dazu County Cultural Relics Preservation Office, ed., *Dazu shiku* (Cave temples of Dazu) (Beijing: Wenwu chubanshe, 1984); Hu Wenhe and Liu Zhangjiu, eds., *Dazu shike yanjiu* (Research on Dazu stone sculpture) (Chengdu: Sichuan sheng shehui kexueyuan chubanshe, 1985); Li Fangyin, *Dazu shiku yishu* (Cave-temple art of Dazu) (Chongqing: Chongqing chubanshe, 1990); Wang Qingyu, *Zhongguo Dazu shike* (Stone sculpture of Dazu, China) (Chongqing: Chongqing chubanshe, 1992).

122. Liu Zhangjiu, ed., *Anyue shiku yishu* (Cave-temple art of Anyue) (Chengdu: Sichuan renmin chubanshe, 1997), and Angela Falco Howard, *Summit of Treasures: Buddhist Cave Art of Dazu, China* (Trumbull, Conn.: Weatherhill, 2001).

123. The Guanyin with the lotus sponsored by the Yang family is dated 1099–1107 by the in situ stele inscription, the Xu patrons portrayed with Shakyamuni carry a 1098 date, and the Sun patrons next to the Guanyin with bottle and willow have dates spanning 1097–1153; I suggest that the carving of the monumental trio possibly required half a century (ca. 1100–1150) to complete. See Deng Zhijing, "Anyue Yuanjue dong 'Xifang san sheng' mincheng wenti tantao" (Inquiry into the issue of the term 'Three Worthies of the West' in the Yuanjue Grotto, Anyue), *Sichuan wenwu* 6 (1991): 34–35; Zhuan Chengjing, "Zai shuo Anyue Yuanjue dong moya zaoxiang" (Additional remarks on the cliff reliefs of the Yuanjue Grotto, Anyue), *Sichuan wenwu* 6 (1991): 36–40.

124. Chen Mingguan and Deng Jinzhi, "Shishu Dazu shike yu Anyue shike de guanxi (Examining the relationship between Dazu and Anyue sculpture), *Sichuan wenwu* (special issue, 1986): 79–83.

125. M. W. de Visser, "Die Pfauenkˆnigin in China und Japan," *Östasiatische Zeitschrift* 8 (1919–1920): 370–387.

126. Li Zheliang, "Shisuo ganjian de Laitan Chanzong shike yishu" (The relatively known Chan stone sculpture art of Laitan), *Sichuan wenwu* 2 (1995): 41–48.

127. Xu Pingfang, "Sengqie zaoxiang de faxian he Sengqie zong-pai" (The development of sculpture of Sengqie and the Sengqie sect), *Wenwu* 5 (1996): 50–58.

128. Charles Backus, *The Nan-Chao Kingdom and T'ang China's Southwestern Frontier* (Cambridge: Cambridge University Press, 1981).

129. Angela Falco Howard, "Buddhist Monuments of Yunnan: Eclectic Art of a Frontier Kingdom," in M. Hearn and J. Smith, eds., *Arts of the Song and Yuan* (New York: Metropolitan Museum of Art, 1996), 231–245.

130. Cultural Relics Bureau of Jianchuan County, Yunnan Province, ed., *Diannan guibao: Jianchuan Shizhongshan shiku* (A rare treasure in the south: The Shizhongshan grottoes in Jianchuan) (Kunming: Yunnan meishu chubanshe, 1998); Department of Archaeology of Peking University, Department of History of Yunnan University et al., "Jianchuan shiku 1999 nian kaogu diaocha jianbao" (Preliminary report of the 1999 archaeological investigation of the Jianchuan Grottoes), *Wenwu* 7 (2000): 71–84.

131. Stone Sculpture Investigation Group, "Liangshan Boshenwahei shike huaxiang diaocha jianbao" (Preliminary report on the investigation of petroglyphs at Boshenwahei, Liangshan), *Zhongguo lishi bowuguan guanli* 4 (1982): 128–136; Huang Chengzong, "Boshenwahei yanhua 'Chuxingtu' zhong de wangzhe shixi" (Discussion of the personage of the king in the "procession scene" carved on the Boshenwahei Cliff), *Sichuan wenwu* 4 (1992): 42–45.

132. Yunnan Provincial Cultural Relics Work Team, "Dali Chongsheng si santa zhuta shici he qingli" (Survey and clearing of the main pagoda from a group of three at the Chongsheng Temple), *Kaogu xuebao* 2 (1981): 245–267; and Albert Lutz, *Der Tempel der Drei Pagoden von Dali* (Zurich: Museum Rietberg, 1991).

133. I have explored this aspect in Angela F. Howard, "The Dharani Pillar of Kunming, Yunnan: A Legacy of Esoteric Buddhism and Burial Rites of the Bai People in the Kingdom of Dali (937–1253)," *Artibus Asiae* 57, nos. 1–2 (1997): 33–72.

134. Lee Yu-min, "An Iconographic Study of Mahakala Imagery in Yunnan — from the Ninth to Thirteenth Centuries," in *"Iconography and Style" in Buddhist Art Historical Studies* (Kobe: Kobe University, 1995), 99–117.

135. For an in-depth discussion of this monument see Howard, "Dharani Pillar."

136. Although one cannot determine a specific Tibetan source for the pillar's mandala or the effigy of the Yunnan Mahakala, or assert that a lineage transmission existed between Tibet and Yunnan, it is nevertheless correct that Yunnan was part of a wider geographic area surrounding Tibet. Tibet's doctrinal and artistic achievements had a great influence on the cultures within this area. As one of these cultures, Yunnan manipulated and recreated the received influence. Thus, in the doctrine and the art of the two countries, we find common but not identical factors.

137. I have often used the word *syncretism* to express the idea that the art and practice of the Buddhist religion of this frontier state, because of geographic and historical circumstances, were influenced to varying degrees by several neighboring regions. Of course, the Chinese central plains, as the most powerful neighbor, exercised a very strong influence, but the role of Himalayan cultures, which we are now beginning to grasp, should not be underestimated, especially in the transmission of Esoteric Buddhism. Similarly, we have become

aware that several major Southeast Asian countries (those of Java, the Malay peninsula, Vietnam, and Cambodia) entertained active cultural exchanges with Yunnan. The exchanges are tangibly manifest, for instance in the shaping of the Avalokiteshvara icon and in the role of palladia it assumed for the Nanzhao and Dali monarchy.

Chapter 4. *From the Northern Song to the Qing*

1. See Peng Lin, Qi Jixiang, and Fan Chuyun, eds., *Zhonghua wenming shi* (A history of Chinese civilization) (Shijiazhuang: Hebei jiaoyu chubanshe,1994), vol. 6, chap. 4 (The Western Xia dynasty), chap. 6 (The Liao dynasty), chap. 7 (The Jin dynasty), and chap. 10 (The Song dynasty).

2. See *Yuandai huasu ji* (Records of painting and sculpture in the Yuan dynasty) (Beijing: Renmin meishu chubanshe, 1964).

3. Su Bai, "Juyong guan guojie ta kao gao" (A study of the Juyong Gate at Juyong Pass), in Su Bai, ed., *Zangchuan Fojiao siyuan kaogu* (Archaeological studies of Tibetan Buddhist temples) (Beijing: Wenwu chubanshe, 1996).

4. See Sima Qian, *Shi ji* (Historical records), 2d ed. (Beijing: Zhonghua shuju, 1982); and *Hanfeizi* (Shenyang: Liaoning jiaoyu chubanshe, 1997).

5. The title was first seen in the *Rites of Zhou,* and it was by this title that the deity was worshipped by early Confucians. At the end of Northern Song, the title was changed to Jade Emperor. In the early years of the Southern Song Daoists came to worship the Jade Emperor as well.

6. For Confucianism, see related entries in Ren Jiyu, ed., *Zongjiao da cidian* (A comprehensive dictionary of religion) (Shanghai: Shanghai cishu chubanshe, 1998).

7. Tuo Tuo et al., *Song shi* (History of the Song) (Beijing: Zhonghua shuju, 1986).

8. Tuo Tuo et al., *Song shi.* During the Yuan dynasty the idol worshiped in the temple of martial valor was still Jiang Ziya, but in the Ming it was replaced by Guan Yu, a great general under Liu Bei, king of the Shu kingdom in the Three Kingdoms period.

9. The "ten wise men" (ten main disciples of Confucius) are: Yan Yuan, Min Wenqian, Ran Boniu, Zhong Gong, Zai Wo, Zi Gong, Ran You, Ji Lu, Zi You, and Zi Xia. Yan Yuan was later replaced by Zeng Shen, who was later replaced by Zi Zhang, as both Yan Yuan and Zeng Shen were moved to stand by the side of Confucius in the major shrine.

10. Yang Pazhi [Xuanzhi], *Luoyang qielan ji* (Records of Buddhist monasteries in Luoyang), vol. 1 (Shanghai: Shanghai shu-dian, 2000). See also Institute of Archaeology of the Chinese Academy of Social Sciences, *Bei Wei Luoyang Yongning si — 1979–1984 nian kaogu fajue baogao* (Yongning Temple of the Northern Wei in Luoyang: A report on archaeological excavations, 1979–1994) (Beijing: Zhongguo dabaike quanshu chubanshe, 1996).

11. Fan Ye, *Hou Han shu* (History of the Later Han) (Beijing: Zhonghua shuju, 1965).

12. Sun Ji, "Zhongguo zaoqi gaoceng fota zaoxing zhi yuanyuan" (Origin of high-rise Buddhist pagodas in the early years in China), in Sun Ji, *Zhongguo shenghuo — Zhongguo gu wenwu yu dongxi wenhua jiaoliu zhong de ruogan wenti* (The sacred fire of China: A few issues concerning ancient Chinese cultural

relics and the cultural exchange between East and West) (Shenyang: Liaojing jiaoyu chubanshe, 1996),

13. Chen Mingda, *Yingxian muta* (The Wooden Pagoda in Yingxian County) (Beijing: Wenwu chubanshe, 1966). See also "Shanxi Yingxian Fogong si muta nei faxian Liaodai zhengui wenwu" (Rare cultural relics of the Liao dynasty found in the Wooden Pagoda in Fogong Temple, Yingxian County, Shanxi), *Wenwu* 6 (1982).

14. Chen Mingda et al., "Liannian lai Shanxi sheng xin faxian de gu jianzhu — Nanchan si" (Nanchan Temple: An ancient building newly found in Shanxi Province in the past two years), *Wenwu cankao ziliao* 11 (1954): 42.

15. See Liang Sicheng, *Ji Wutai shan Foguang si de jianzhu* (A note on the architecture of Foguang Temple on Mount Wutai), *Wenwu cankao ziliao* 5–6 (1953).

16. The scriptures of the Liao and Jin dynasties that used to be kept in the hall are lost; all that remain are those printed in the Ming and Qing. Over the walls inside the hall are thirty-eight well-built multistoried chambers for keeping scriptures. An arched bridge extends from the central part of the chambers, leading to the attic.

17. The practice of enshrining statues of the various devas in Chinese Buddhist temples goes back several centuries. Yet there are different opinions about how they are lined up. After studying the twenty-four devas in the Shanhua Temple, Jin Weinuo concluded, "Mahabrahma leads the group on the left, followed in order by Pancika, the sun deva, Skanda, Prthivi, the fire deva, Marici, Dhrtarastra, Virudhaka, Hariti, the Deep-Sand General, and Yamaraja. Heading the right row is Shakra devanam Indra, and he is then followed by Isana, Candra, Rakshara, Bodhidharma, the wind deva, Sarasvati, Vaishravana, Virupaksha, Lakshmi, Guhyapati, and the water deva." See "Lun Shanxi Fojiao caisu" (On painted Buddhist sculpture in Shanxi), in Research Institute of Chinese Buddhism, Shanxi Provincial Bureau of Cultural Relics, *Shanxi Fojiao caisu* (Painted Buddhist sculptures in Shanxi) (Beijing: Zhongguo Fojiao wenhua chuban youxian gongsi, 1991).

18. Bai Huawen, "Zhongguo Fojiao siyuan diantang dianxing peizhi — Shanmen, dabiong baodian jiji dongxi peidian" (The mountain gate, the Hall of Shakyamuni, and the east-west lateral buildings: A typical layout of Chinese Buddhist temples," in *Fojiao yu Zhongguo wenhua* (Buddhism and Chinese culture) (Beijing: Zhonghua shuju, 1988).

19. See Cheng Jizhong, "Longxing Temple," *Wenwu* 1 (1979). The article contains the full text carved on a stone stele erected in the temple in the Northern Song, which recorded in detail when and how the bronze Buddha statue was cast and how many people participated in the project, thus providing an important historical text for studying the making of large bronze statues in ancient China.

20. See Liu Dunzhen et al., eds., *Zhongguo gudai jianzhu shi* (A history of ancient Chinese architecture), chap. 6, "Architecture of the Song, Liao, and Jin dynasties" (Beijing: Zhongguo jianzhu gongye chubanshe, 1980).

21. See Zhang Yanyuan, *Lidai minghua ji* (Record of famous paintings of successive dynasties), vol. 10: "Zhou Fang succeeded in creating the water-moon image of the bodhisattva that appears dignified," in *Huashi congshu* (Complete collec-

tion on the history of painting) (Shanghai: Shanghai renmin meishu chubanshe, 1963).

22. See Zhou Shoujia, "Shiliu luohan shiba luohan he wubai luohan" (Sixteen arhats, eighteen arhats, and five hundred arhats)," in *Zhou Shujia Foxue lunzhu ji* (A collection of treatises on Buddhism by Zhou Shujia) (Beijing: Zhonghua shuju, 1991).

23. Guo Ruoxu, *Tuhua jianwen zhi* (Anecdotes on painting), vol. 3 (reprint, Shanghai: Shanghai renmin meishu chubanshe, 1964).

24. See Zhang Heyun, "Changqing Lingyan si gudai diaosu kao" (A study of the ancient sculpture in Lingyan Temple in Changqing County), *Wenwu* 12 (1959); Ji'nan Municipal Cultural Relics Administrative Institute, Ji'nan Municipal Museum, and Changqing Lingyan Temple Cultural Relics Administrative Office, "Shandong Changqing Lingyan si luohan de suzhi niandai ji youguan wenti" (Some questions regarding the chronology of the arhat statues in Lingyan Temple, Changqing, Shandong), *Wenwu* 3 (1984); and Hu Jigao, "Shandong Changqing Lingyan si caisu luohan xiang de xiufu" (Repair of the painted arhat statues in Lingyan Temple, Changqing, Shandong), *Wenwu* 11 (1983).

25. Hu Jigao, Shi Xiaolong, and Zhao Guifang, "Wuxian Luzhi Baosheng si caisu luohan xiang de baohu" (Protection of painted arhat statues in Baosheng Temple, Luzhi Town, Wu County), *Zhongguo wenwu bao*, April–May 1999.

26. Art History Teaching and Research Group of East China School of Fine Arts, "Dongting Dongshan Zijin'an gusu luohan kaocha ji" (An investigation of the arhat statues sculpted in ancient times in Zijin Nunnery, Eastern Hill, Dongting), *Wenwu cankao ziliao* 9 (1955); Zijin Nunnery of Wu County in Jiangsu, ed., *Zijin'an gu su luohan* (Ancient statues of arhats in Zijin Nunnery) (Shanghai: Shanghai renmin meishu chubanshe, 1993).

27. Jin Shen, ed., *Fojiao diaosu mingpin tulu* (A catalogue of famous Buddhist sculptures) (Beijing: Beijing gongyi meishu chubanshe, 1995).

28. Guangdong Provincial Museum, ed., *Nanhua si* (Nanhua Temple) (Beijing: Wenwu chubanshe, 1990).

29. Luo Shiping, "Dunhuang Sizhou Sengqie jingxiang yu Sizhou heshang xinyang" (The statue of the monk Sengqie of Sizhou in the Dunhuang grottoes and worship of the Sizhou monk), *Meishu yanjiu* 1 (1993); Xu Pingfang, "Sengqie zaoxiang de faxian he Sengqie chongbai" (The discovery of the statue of Sengqie and the worship of Sengqie), *Wenwu* 5 (1996).

30. See *Li ji* (Book of rites) (reprint, Shanghai: Shanghai guji chubanshe, 1987), 21: "The emperor offers sacrifices to Heaven, the four lands, the mountains, and the plains."

31. Before the Tang dynasty, the ceremonies for emperors to offer sacrifices to Heaven were all held on top of Mount Tai. When Wu Zetian ascended the throne, she moved the ceremony to Mount Song, which was named a sacred mountain. In 696 the god of Mount Song was granted the title "Emperor Tianzhong of the Sacred Mountain" when Wu went to the top of the mountain to preside personally over the sacrifice-offering ceremony. By the time of Emperor Xuanzong of the Tang, the ceremony was moved back to Mount Tai, which was then given the title "Emperor Tianqi." The last emperor to offer sacrifices to Heaven and

confer titles on the sacred mountains was Zhenzong of the Northern Song. In 1008 he journeyed to Mount Tai, and later, in the fourth year of the reign, he went to Fenyin in Shanxi to offer sacrifices to the god of the earth. Apart from Mount Tai and Mount Song, there are three other so-called sacred mountains: Mount Hua in Hunan Province (the Sacred Mountain in the South), Mount Heng in Shaanxi Province (the Sacred Mountain in the West), and Mount Heng in Shanxi Province (the Sacred Mountain in the North). The gods of the three mountains are called, respectively, the Heavenly King Jin, Heavenly King Si, and Heavenly King An.

32. Zhang Tingyu et al., *Ming shi* (A history of the Ming) (Beijing: Zhonghua shuju, 1974), 1285.

33. See Liang Sicheng and Lin Huiyin, "Jin-Fen gu jianzhu yucha jilüe: Taiyuan xian Jinci" (An initial study of ancient architecture in Shanxi: Jinci Temple in Taiyuan County," *Zhongguo Yingzao Xueshe huikan* 5, no. 3 (1935); Liu Dunzhen, ed., *Zhongguo gudai jianzhu shi* (A history of ancient Chinese architecture) (Beijing: Zhongguo jianzhu gongye, 1980), chap. 6, sec. 4; Peng Hai, "Jinci Shengmu dian kance shouhuo — Shengmu dian chuangjian niandai xi" (Achievements from a survey of the Hall of the Sage Mother in Jinci Temple: Study of the date of construction of the Hall of the Sage Mother), *Wenwu* 1 (1996).

34. See *Zhongguo Jinci Song su* (Song-dynasty sculpture in Jinci Temple, China) (Taiyuan: Shanxi renmin chubanshe, 1993): "Of the forty-three statues in the Hall of the Sage Mother, those of the servants put by the sides of the Sage Mother Yi Jiang are works of the Ming dynasty. The craftsmanship is inferior."

35. The kings of the ten hells are named, respectively, King of Taiguang, King of Chujiang, King of Songdi, King of Wuguan, King of Hell (Yamaraja), King of Biancheng, King of Mount Tai, King of Equality, King of Cities and Towns, and King of Transmigration. The expression "kings of ten hells" first appeared at the end of the Tang, and their images are most often seen in temples built in Shanxi during the Ming.

36. There are a number of temples to the king of medicine scattered throughout China. But the deities in them vary: although some honor Sun Simiao, others enshrine the legendary ancient chief Shennong ("Divine Farmer") or the famous physician Bian Que, of the Warring States period (476–221 B.C.E.)

37. According to one legend, the god of fire, known as Lord Bingling, is the third son of Emperor Tianqi. The title was granted by an emperor in 1008, in the Northern Song dynasty. Another legend identifies the god of fire as Wang Lingguan, a Daoist alchemist in the Song. His image is usually sculpted with a red face and three eyes, dressed in armor, and holding a cudgel. A third story claims that the god of fire is Zhu Rong, the legendary figure of the red lord in ancient times.

38. Peng Hai, "Jinci Shengmu dian kance shouhuo."

39. The Taiqing Palace was originally called the Temple of Laozi when it was built in 165. In the reign of Emperor Xuanzong of the Tang, it was renamed Taiqing Palace, and the hall dedicated to Laozi's mother, Madame Li, was renamed Dongxiao Palace. During the reign of Emperor

Zhenzong of the Song, the temple was expanded, and Laozi's mother was given the title Queen Mother Primordial. The ruins can still be seen.

40. See Peng Lin et al., *Zhonghua wenming shi,* vol. 7; Zhongguo Fojiao xiehui, ed., *Zhongguo Fojiao* (Chinese Buddhism), (Beijing: Zhishi chubanshe, 1980); Li Jicheng, *Zangchuan Fojiao* (Tibetan Buddhism) (Beijing: Xinhua chubanshe, 1991); Su Bai, "Yuandai Hangzhou de Zangchuan mijiao jiqi youguan yizhi" (Tibetan Buddhism in Hangzhou during the Yuan dynasty and related sites), in *Zangchuan Fojiao siyuan kaogu* (Archaeology of temples of Tibetan Buddhism) (Beijing: Wenwu chubanshe, 1996); Yang Boda, "Xiuli duocai de Yuan Ming Qing diaosu" (The elegant and colorful sculptures of the Yuan, Ming, and Qing dynasties), in *Zhongguo meishushi quanji, Yuan Ming Qing diaosu juan* (Encyclopedia of Chinese art, volume on the sculpture of the Yuan, Ming, and Qing dynasties) (Beijing: Renmin meishu chubanshe, 1999); and Wang Yaogong, "Yuandai Hangzhou Fojiao Mizong zaoxiang zhi yanjiu" (A study of Esoteric Buddhist sculptures of the Yuan dynasty in Hangzhou), *Meishu jiaoliu* 4 (1993).

41. Su Bai, "Juyong guan guojie ta kao gao."

42. Gong Senhao, "Jincheng Yuhuang miao de Daojiao diaosu" (Daoist sculptures in Yuhuang Temple in Jincheng), *Zhongguo yishu* 1.

43. Yang Boda, "Xiuli duocai de Yuan Ming Qing diaosu."

44. Research Institute of Chinese Buddhism, Shanxi Provincial Bureau of Cultural Relics, *Shanxi Fojiao caisu.*

45. *Shuanglin si caisu* (Painted sculptures in the Shuanglin Temple) (Tianjin: Tianjin renmin meishu chubanshe, 1999).

46. *Zhongguo mingsheng cidian* (Dictionary of famous and historical sites in China), 2d ed. (Shanghai: Shanghai cishu, 1986).

47. Su Bai, *Zangchuan Fojiao siyuan kaogu;* Jin Weinuo and Luo Shiping, *Zhongguo zongjiao meishu shi* (A history of Chinese religious art) (Nanchang: Jiangxi meishu chubanshe, 1995); Peng Lin et al., *Zhongguo wenming shi,* vols. 8–10.

48. See Gongbu Chabu, *Zaoxiang liangdu jing fu xubu* (Classic of measurements for making Buddhist images, with supplement) (Jinling: Jinling Sculpture Carving Department, 1874); and Menla Donzhu, "Rulai foshen liang ming zhe bao lun" (A clear explanation of the measurements of the statue of Tathagata), and Duma Gexi, "Caihui gongxu mingjian" (References on the coloring and painting process), both in *Xizang Fojiao caihui caisu yishu* (The art of Tibetan Buddhist colored painting and colored sculpture), translated and annotated by Luo Bingfen (Beijing: Zhongguo zangxue, 1997).

49. *Zangchuan Fojiao zaoxiang: Chengde Waibamiao cang* (Statues of Tibetan Buddhism: Preserved in the Eight Outside Temples in Chengde) (Tianjin: Tianjin renmin meishu chubanshe, 1995); Yang Boda, "Xiuli duocai de Yuan Ming Qing diaosu."

50. Patricia Berger, *Empire of Emptiness: Buddhist Art and Political Authority in Qing China* (Honolulu: University of Hawai'i Press, 2003), 97–104.

51. Wang Jiapeng, *Zangchuan Fojiao jintong foxiang tudian* (An illustrated manual of gilt-bronze statues of Tibetan Buddhism) (Beijing: Wenwu chubanshe, 1996).

FURTHER READINGS

Introduction by Li Song

Ban Gu 班固. *Han shu* 汉书 (History of the Han). Beijing: Zhonghua shuju, 1962.

Dong You 董逌. *Guangchuan huaba* 广川画跋 (Painting criticism by Guangchuan). In *Huapin congshu* 画品丛书 (Series on painting). Shanghai: Shanghai renmin meishu chubanshe, 1982.

Ren Jiyu 任继愈, Zhuo Xinping 卓新平, and He Guanghu 何光沪, eds. *Zongjiao da cidian* 宗教大辞典 (A comprehensive dictionary of religion). Shanghai: Shanghai cishu chubanshe, 1998.

Sima Biao 司马彪. *Hou Han shu* 后汉书 (History of the Later Han). Beijing: Zhonghua shuju, 1965.

Sima Qian 司马迁. *Shi ji* 史记 (Historical records). Beijing: Zhonghua shuju, 1982.

Song Lian 宋濂 et al. *Yuan shi* 元史 (History of the Yuan). Beijing: Zhonghua shuju, 1976.

Tuo Tuo 脱脱. *Song shi* 宋史 (History of the Song). Beijing: Zhonghua shuju, 1962.

Yuandai huasu ji 元代画塑记 (Record of painting and sculpture in the Yuan dynasty). Beijing: Renmin meishu chubanshe, 1964. Originally written in the Yuan dynasty by an unknown author.

Zhang Yanyuan 张彦远. *Lidai minghua ji* 历代名画记 (Records of famous paintings through the dynasties). In *Congshu jicheng chubian* 丛书集成初编 (Initial edition of a collection of various books). Beijing: Shangwu yinshuguan, 1936.

Introduction by Angela Falco Howard

Berger, Patricia, and Terese Tse Bartholomew et al. *Mongolia: The Legacy of Chinggis Khan.* San Francisco: Asian Art Museum of San Francisco, 1995.

Chayet, Anne. *Les temples de Jahol et leur modèles tibetains.* Paris: Edition recherche sur les civilizations, 1984.

Clark, Walter Eugene. *Two Lamaist Pantheons.* Harvard-Yenching Monograph Series, nos. 3–4. Cambridge: Harvard University Press, 1937.

Foret, Philippe. *Mapping Chengde: The Qing Landscape Enterprise.* Honolulu: University of Hawai'i Press, 2000.

Karmay, Heather. *Early Sino-Tibetan Art.* Warminster, England: Aris and Phillips, 1975.

Mote, F. W. *Imperial China, 900–1800.* Cambridge: Harvard University Press, 1999.

Shi Jinbo 史金波. *Xi Xia Fojiao shilüe* 西夏佛教史略 (An outline history of Buddhism in the Western Xia). Yinchuan: Ningxia renmin chubanshe, 1988.

Shi Jinbo et al. *Xi Xia wenwu* 西夏文物 (Cultural relics of the Western Xia). Beijing: Wenwu chubanshe, 1988.

Tsultem, N. *The Eminent Mongolian Sculptor—G. Zanabazar.* Ulaanbataar: State Publishing House, 1982.

Wang Jiapeng 王家鹏. "Qingqong Zangchuan Fojiao wenhua kaocha" 清宫藏传佛教文化考察 (A cultural study of Tibetan Buddhism in the Qing court). In *Qingdai gongshi congkan* 清代宫室丛刊 (Conference on Qing-dynasty palace history). Beijing: Wenwu chubanshe, 1996.

Chapter 1. From the Neolithic to the Han

Anqiu xian wenhuaju, Anqiu xian bowuguan 安丘县文化局、安丘县博物馆 (Bureau of Culture of Anqiu County, Museum of Anqiu County), ed. *Anqiu Dongjiazhuang Han huaxiang shimu* 安丘董家庄汉画像石墓 (Stone-relief tomb of the Han dynasty at Dongjiazhuang village, Anqiu County). Ji'nan: Ji'nan chubanshe, 1992.

Ashton, Leigh. *An Introduction to the Study of Chinese Sculpture.* London: Ernest Benn, 1924.

Baoshan Chu mu 包山楚墓 (The Chu tombs at Baoshan). 2 vols. Beijing: Wenwu chubanshe, 1991.

Birrell, Anne. *Chinese Mythology: An Introduction.* Baltimore, Md.: Johns Hopkins University Press, 1993.

Brinker, Helmut. "On the Origin of the Human Image in Chinese Art." *Kaikodo Journal* (Spring 1997): 18–47.

Chang, Kwang-chih. *The Archaeology of Ancient China.* 4th ed. New Haven: Yale University Press, 1986.

———. *Art, Myth, and Ritual.* Cambridge: Harvard University Press, 1983.

———. *Shang Civilization.* New Haven: Yale University Press, 1980.

Chen Shukui 陈蜀奎, ed. *Ya'an diqu wenwu zhi* 雅安地区文物志 (A record of cultural relics from the Ya'an region). Chengdu: Ba Shu shushe, 1992.

Chinese Jades from the Mu-Fei Collection. London: Bluett and Sons, 1990.

Fong, Wen, ed. *The Great Bronze Age of China: An Exhibition from the People's Republic of China.* New York: Metropolitan Museum of Art, 1980.

Freedberg, David. *Power of Images.* Chicago: University of Chicago Press, 1989.

Galeries nationales du Grand Palais, ed. *Zhongshan: Tombes des rois oubliés.* Paris: Association française d'action artistique, 1985.

Hay, John, ed. *Boundaries in China.* London: Reaktion Books, 1994.

Hebei sheng bowuguan wenwu guanlichu 河北省博物馆、文物管理处 (Administration of Cultural Relics of Hebei Provincial Museum), ed. *Hebei sheng chutu wenwu xuanji* 河北省出土文物选集 (A selection of cultural relics unearthed in Hebei Province). Beijing: Wenwu chubanshe, 1980.

Huang Zhanyue 黄展岳. *Zhongguo gudai de rensheng yu renxun* 中国古代的人牲与人殉 (Human sacrifices in ancient China). Beijing: Wenwu chubanshe, 1990.

Kramer, Samuel Noah. *Mythologies of the Ancient World.* Garden City, N.Y.: Anchor Books, 1961.

Kuwayama, George, ed. *The Great Bronze Age of China: A Symposium.* Los Angeles: Los Angeles County Museum, 1980.

———, ed. *The Quest for Eternity*. Los Angeles: Los Angeles County Museum of Art, 1987.

Li, Chi [Li Ji]. *Anyang*. Seattle: University of Washington Press, 1977.

Li Daoyuan 郦道元. *Shuijing zhu* 水经注 (Annotated canon of waterways). Shanghai: Shijie shuju, 1936.

Li Shaoming 李绍明 et al., eds. *Ba Shu lishi, minzu, kaogu, wenhua* 巴蜀历史民族考古文化 (History, ethnology, archaeology, and culture of the Ba and the Shu [Sichuan]). Chengdu: Ba Shu shushe, 1991.

Li Xueqin. *Eastern Zhou and Qin Civilizations*. Translated by Kwang-chih Chang. New Haven: Yale University Press, 1985.

Lim, Lucy, ed. *Stories from China's Past: Han Art from Sichuan*. San Francisco: Chinese Cultural Foundation, 1987.

Loewe, M., and E. Shaughnessy, eds. *The Cambridge History of Ancient China*. Cambridge: Cambridge University Press, 1999.

Luoyang wenwu gongzuodui 洛阳文物工作队 (Luoyang Cultural Relics Work Team), ed. *Luoyang chutu wenwu jicui* 洛阳出土文物集萃 (Gems of cultural relics unearthed in Luoyang). Beijing: Zhaohua chubanshe, 1990.

Nanjing bowuguan 南京博物馆 (Nanjing Museum). *Sichuan Pengshan Handai yamu* 四川彭山汉代崖墓 (Han-dynasty cliff tombs at Pengshan, Sichuan). Beijing: Wenwu chubanshe, 1991.

Paludan, Ann. *The Chinese Spirit Road: The Classical Tradition of Stone Tomb Statuary*. New Haven: Yale University Press, 1991.

Powers, Martin. *Art and Political Expression in Early China*. New Haven: Yale University Press, 1991.

Qu Xiaoqiang 屈小强 et al. *Sanxingdui wenhua* 三星堆文化 (Sanxingdui culture). Chengdu: Sichuan renmin chubanshe, 1993.

Rawson, Jessica. *Ancient China: Art and Archaeology*. London: British Museum, 1980.

———. *Chinese Bronzes: Art and Ritual*. London: British Museum, 1987.

———, ed. *Mysteries of Ancient China*. London: British Museum, 1996.

Rogers, Howard, ed. *China: Five Thousand Years*. New York: Guggenheim Museum, 1998.

Ruan Yuan 阮元, comp. *Shisanjing zhushu* 十三经注疏 (The annotated thirteen classics). 2 vols. Beijing: Zhonghua shuju, 1980.

Shaanxi chutu Shang Zhou qingtongqi 陕西出土商周青铜器 (Shang and Zhou bronzes from Shaanxi Province). Beijing: Wenwu chubanshe, 1979.

Shaanxi sheng kaogu yanjiusuo Hanmu kaogu gongzuodui 陕西省考古研究所汉墓考古工作队 (Archaeological Team on Han Mausoleums and the Shaanxi Provincial Institute of Archaeology). *Zhongguo Han Yangling caiyong* 中国汉阳陵彩俑 (The colored figurines in the Han-dynasty Yangling mausoleum of China). Xi'an: Zhongguo Shaanxi lüyou chubanshe, 1992.

Sima Qian 司马迁. *Shi ji* 史记 (Historical records). Beijing: Zhonghua shuju, 1959.

So, Jenny. *Eastern Zhou Ritual Bronzes from the Arthur M. Sackler Collection*. New York: Arthur M. Sackler Foundation, 1995.

Su Bingqi 苏秉琦, ed. *Kaoguxue wenhua lunji* 考古学文化论集 (An anthology of Chinese archaeological and cultural studies). Beijing: Wenwu chubanshe, 1987.

Wan Xueli 王学礼. *Qin Shihuang ling yanjiu* 秦始皇陵研究 (A study of the mausoleum of the First Emperor of Qin). Shanghai: Shanghai renmin chubanshe, 1994.

Wu Hung. *Monumentality in Early Chinese Art and Architecture*. Stanford, Calif.: Stanford University Press, 1995.

———. *The Wu Liang Shrine: The Ideology of Early Chinese Pictorial Art*. Stanford, Calif.: Stanford University Press, 1989.

Wu Shichi 吴诗池. *Zhongguo yuanshi yishu* 中国原始艺术 (Primitive art of China). Beijing: Zijincheng chubanshe, 1996.

Xinyang Chu mu 信阳楚墓 (Chu tombs in Xinyang). Beijing: Wenwu chubanshe, 1986.

Xu Weiyu 许维遹, comp. *Lüshi chunqiu jishi* 吕氏春秋集释 (*Mr. Lu's Springs and Autumns* with comprehensive commentaries). Beijing: Zhonghua shuju, 1954.

Xu Wenbin 徐文彬 et al. *Sichuan Handai shique* 四川汉代石阙 (Han-dynasty stone *que* towers in Sichuan). Beijing: Wenwu chubanshe, 1992.

Yang Hsien-yi and Gladys Yang. *Selections from Records of the Historians*. Beijing: Foreign Languages Press, 1979.

Yang Kuan 杨宽. *Gushi xintan* 古史新探 (A new exploration of ancient history). Beijing: Zhonghua shuju, 1965.

Yang Xiaoneng. *Sculpture of Prehistoric China*. Hong Kong: Tai Dao Publishing, 1988.

———. *Sculpture of Xia and Shang China*. Hong Kong: Tai Dao Publishing, 1988.

Yinxu Fu Hao mu 殷墟妇好墓 (The tomb of Lady Hao at Yinxu). Beijing: Wenwu chubanshe, 1980.

Yinxu yuqi 殷墟玉器 (Jade carvings from Yinxu). Beijing: Wenwu chubanshe, 1982.

Yu Weichao 俞伟超, ed. *Kaoguxue leixingxue de lilun yu shijian* 考古学类型学的理论与实践 (Theories and practices of archaeological typology). Beijing: Wenwu chubanshe, 1989.

Zhang Zengqi 张增祺. "Xunli duocai de Dian, Kunming qingtong wenhua" 绚丽多彩的滇, 昆明青铜文化 (The colorful and varied Dian and Kunming bronze cultures). In *Zhongguo qingtongqi quanji* 中国青铜器全集 (A comprehensive collection of Chinese bronzes). Beijing: Wenwu chubanshe, 1993.

Zhang Zhengming 张正明 and Pi Daojian 皮道坚. *Chu meishu tuji* 楚美术图集 (An illustrated catalogue of Chu art). Changsha: Hubei meishu chubanshe, 1996.

Zhang Zongxiang 张宗祥, comp. *Jiaozheng Sanfu huangtu* 校正三辅黄图 (An edited and annotated version of *The Diagram of the Imperial District*). Beijing: Gudian wenxue chubanshe, 1958.

Zhongguo qingtongqi quanji 中国青铜器全集 (A comprehensive collection of Chinese bronzes). Beijing: Wenwu chubanshe, 1996.

Zhongguo shehui kexuayuan kaogu yanjiusuo 中国社会科学院考古研究所 (Institute of Archaeology of the Chinese Academy of Social Sciences), ed. *Baoji Beishouling* 宝鸡北首岭 (The archaeological site at Beishouling in Baoji). Beijing: Wenwu chubanshe, 1983.

Zhongguo yuqi quanji 中国玉器全集 (A comprehensive collection of Chinese jade objects). Shijiazhuang: Hebei meishu chubanshe, 1993.

Chapter 2. From the Han to the Qing

Cao Zhezhi 曹者祉 and Sun Binggen 孙秉根, eds. *Zhongguo gudai yong* 中国古代俑 (Ancient figurines of China). Shanghai: Shanghai wenhua chubanshe, 1996.

Du You 杜佑. *Tong dian* 通典 (Universal ceremonial codes). Photo offset edition. Beijing: Zhonghua shuju, 1984.

Feng Hanji 冯汉骥. *Qian Shu Wang Jian mu fajue baogao* 前蜀王建墓发掘报告 (A report on the excavation of the tomb of Wang Jian of the Former Shu). Beijing: Wenwu chubanshe, 1964.

Henan sheng wenwu kaogu yanjiusuo 河南省文物考古研究所 (Henan Provincial Institute of Cultural Relics and Archaeology). *Bei Song huangling* 北宋皇陵 (Imperial mausoleums of the Northern Song). Zhengzhou: Zhongzhou guji chubanshe, 1997.

Huang Minglan 黄明兰. *Luoyang Bei Wei shisu shike xianhua ji* 洛阳北魏世俗石刻线画集 (A collection of secular pictures of the Northern Wei incised with lines, Luoyang). Beijing: Renmin meishu chubanshe, 1987.

Imperial Tombs of China. Exh. cat. Memphis, Tenn.: Memphis International Cultural Series, 1995.

Jiangsu sheng difangzhi bianzuan weiyuanhui 江苏省地方志编纂委员会 (Jiangsu Local Gazetteer Compilation Committee). *Jiangsu sheng wenwu zhi* 江苏省志·文物志 (Gazetteer of Jiangsu Province: Annals of cultural relics). Nanjing: Jiangsu guji chubanshe, 1998.

Jiu Tang shu 旧唐书 (Old book of Tang). Collated and punctuated edition. Beijing: Zhonghua shuju, 1975.

Luo Feng 罗丰. *Guyuan nanjiao Sui Tang mudi* 固原南郊隋唐墓地 (Sui and Tang burials in the southern suburbs of Guyuan). Beijing: Wenwu chubanshe, 1996.

Nanjing bowuguan 南京博物馆 (Nanjing Museum). *Ming Xiaoling* 明孝陵 (The Xiaoling mausoleum of the Ming). Beijing: Wenwu chubanshe, 1981.

———. *Nantang er ling fajue baogao* 南唐二陵发掘报告 (Report on the excavation of two Southern Tang mausoleums). Beijing: Wenwu chubanshe, 1957.

Ningxia wenwu kaogu suo 宁夏文物考古所 (Ningxia Institute of Cultural Relics and Archaeology). *Xi Xia ling* 西夏陵 (Western Xia mausoleums). Beijing: Dongfang chubanshe, 1995.

Shaanxi sheng kaogu yanjiusuo 陕西省考古研究所 (Shaanxi Provincial Institute of Archaeology). *Tangdai Xue Jing mu fajue baogao* 唐代薛儆墓发掘报告 (A report on the excavation of the Tang tomb of Xue Jing). Beijing: Kexue chubanshe, 2000.

Shaanxi sheng wenwu guanli weiyuanhui 陕西省文物管理委员会 (Shaanxi Provincial Cultural Relics Administrative Committee). *Shaanxi sheng chutu Tang yong xuanji* 陕西省出土唐俑选集 (Collection of Tang figurines unearthed in Shaanxi Province). Beijing: Wenwu chubanshe, 1958.

Stewart, Susan. *On Longing: Narratives of the Miniature, the Gigantic, the Souvenir—The Collection*. Durham, N.C.: Duke University Press, 1993.

Su Bai 宿白. *Baisha Song mu* 白沙宋墓 (The Song tomb in Baisha). Beijing: Wenwu chubanshe, 1957.

———. "Zang wang mu" 藏王墓 (Tombs of Tibetan kings). In *Encyclopaedia Sinica* 中国大百科全书. Beijing: Zhongguo dabaike quanshu chubanshe, 1986.

Tao Zongyi 陶宗仪. "Nancun chuogeng lu" 南村辍耕录 (Notes on quitting farming in Nancun village). In *Yuan-Ming shiliao biji congkan* 元明史料笔记丛刊 (A collection of historical data and book notes of the Yuan and Ming dynasties). Beijing: Zhonghua shuju, 1980.

Wang Jianying 王剑英. *Ming Zhongdu* 明中都 (Central capital of the Ming). Beijing: Zhonghua shuju, 1992.

Wei Shou 魏收, ed. *Wei shu* 魏书 (Book of the Wei). Collated and punctuated edition. Beijing: Zhonghua shuju, 1959.

Xia Nai 夏鼐. "Xi'an Tang mu zhong chutu de jijian sancai taoyong" 西安唐墓中出土的几件三彩陶俑 (Several three-color pottery figurines unearthed at Tang tombs in Xi'an). In *Kaoguxue lunwen ji* 考古学论文集 (Collection of essays on archaeology). Beijing: Kexue chubanshe, 1961.

Xiao Tong 萧统, comp. *Wen xuan* 文选 (Selections of refined literature). Hu Kejia's [1869] edition. Reprint, Beijing: Zhonghua shuju, 1977.

Xiao Zixian 萧子显, ed. *Nan Qi shu* 南齐书 (History of the Southern Qi). Collated and punctuated edition. Beijing: Zhonghua shuju, 1974.

Xu Pingfang 徐苹芳. "Songdai muzang he jiaozang de fajue" 宋代墓葬和窖藏的发掘 (The excavation of burials and underground storage rooms of the Song dynasty). In *Xin Zhongguo de kaogu faxian he yanjiu* 新中国的考古发现和研究 (Archaeological finds and research in New China). Beijing: Wenwu chubanshe, 1984.

Yang Chunyuan 杨纯渊. *Yongji Pujin du yizhi* 永济蒲津渡遗址 (Ruins of the Pujin ferry crossing at Yongji). In *Zhongguo kaoguxue nianjian: 1992* 中国考古学年鉴: 1992 (China archaeology yearbook: 1992). Beijing: Wenwu chubanshe, 1994.

Yang Hong 杨泓. "Bei chao taoyong de yuanliu, yanbian ji yingxiang" 北朝陶俑的源流、演变及影响 (The origin, evolution, and impact of Northern Dynasties clay figurines). In *Zhongguo kaoguxue yanjiu—jinian Xia Nai xiansheng kaogu 50 nian lunwen ji* 中国考古学研究——纪念夏鼐先生考古五十年论文集 (Study of Chinese archaeology—Collection in memory of Mr. Xia Nai for his fifty years of study of archaeology). Beijing: Wenwu chubanshe, 1986.

Yang Xuanzhi 杨衒之. *Luoyang qielan ji* 洛阳伽蓝记 (Buddhist monasteries in Luoyang). Edited by Fan Xiangyong. Beijing: Gudian wenxue chubanshe, 1958.

Yao Qian 姚迁 and Gu Bing 古兵. *Liuchao yishu* 六朝艺术 (The art of the Six Dynasties). Beijing: Wenwu chubanshe, 1981.

Zhang Yanyuan 张彦远. *Lidai minghua ji* 历代名画记 (Record of famous paintings of successive dynasties). Beijing: Renmin meishu chubanshe, 1963.

Zhongguo guisanyan xuehui 中国硅酸盐学会 (China Silicate Society), ed. *Zhongguo taoci shi* 中国陶瓷史 (History of Chinese ceramics). Beijing: Wenwu chubanshe, 1982.

Zhongguo shehui kexuayuan kaogu yanjiusuo 中国社会科学院考古研究所 (Institute of Archaeology of the Chinese Academy of Social Sciences). *Tang Chang'an chengjiao Sui Tang mu* 唐长安城郊隋唐墓 (Sui and Tang tombs from the Tang dynasty in the outskirts of Chang'an). Beijing: Wenwu chubanshe, 1980.

———, Dingling Museum, Beijing Municipal Cultural Relics Work Team. *Dingling* 定陵 (Dingling mausoleum). Beijing: Wenwu chubanshe, 1990.

Chapter 3. From the Han to the Southern Song

Abe, Stanley K. *Ordinary Images.* Chicago: University of Chicago Press, 2002.

Backus, Charles. *The Nan-Chao Kingdom and T'ang China's Southwestern Frontier.* Cambridge: Cambridge University Press, 1981.

Baumer, Christoph. *Southern Silk Road: In the Footsteps of Sir Aurel Stein and Sven Hedin.* Bangkok: White Orchid Books, 2000.

Caswell, James O. *Written and Unwritten: A New History of the Buddhist Caves at Yungang.* Vancouver: University of British Columbia Press, 1988.

Ch'en, Kenneth. *Buddhism in China.* Princeton, N.J.: Princeton University Press, 1964.

Clausen, Søren, Roy Starrs, and Anne Wedell-Wedellsborg, eds. *Cultural Encounters: China, Japan, and the West. Essays Commemorating Twenty-Five Years of East Asian Studies at the University of Aarhus.* Aarhus, Denmark: Aarhus University Press, 1995.

Dazu xian wenwu baoguansuo 大足县文物保管所 (Dazu County Cultural Relics Preservation Office), ed. *Dazu shiku* 大足石窟 (Cave temples of Dazu). Beijing: Wenwu chubanshe, 1984.

Dong Yuxiang 董玉祥, ed. *Binglingsi 169 ku* 炳灵寺 169 窟 (Binglingsi Monastery Cave 169). Shenzhou: Haitian chubanshe, 1994.

Gansu sheng wenwu gongzuodui Qingyang beishiku si wenguansuo甘肃省文物工作队庆阳北石窟寺文管所 (Administration of Cultural Relics of the Northern Grottoes of Qingyang, Gansu Provincial Cultural Relics Work Team), ed. *Qingyang Beishiku si*庆阳北石窟寺 (The northern cave temples of Qingyang). Beijing: Wenwu chubanshe, 1985.

Gansu sheng wenwu kaogu yanjiusuo甘肃省文物考古研究所 (Gansu Provincial Institute of Cultural Relics and Archaeology), ed. *Hexi shiku* 河西石窟 (Cave temples of the Hexi Corridor). Beijing: Wenwu chubanshe, 1987.

Gernet, Jacques. *A History of Chinese Civilization.* Translated by J. R. Foster. Cambridge: Cambridge University Press, 1982.

Gomez, Luis O. *The Land of Bliss: The Paradise of the Buddha of Measureless Light.* Honolulu: University of Hawai'i Press, 1996.

Henan sheng wenwu yanjiusuo 河南省文物研究所 (Institute of Cultural Relics of Henan Province), ed. *Zhongguo shiku* 中国石窟 (Grottoes in China). Beijing: Wenwu chubanshe, 1989.

Hirakawa, Akira. *A History of Indian Buddhism: From Sākyamuni to Early Mahāyāna.* Translated by Paul Groner. Honolulu: University of Hawai'i Press, 1990.

Howard, Angela Falco. *Buddhist Monuments of Yunnan: Eclectic Art of a Frontier Kingdom, Arts of the Song and Yuan.* Edited by M. Hearn and J. Smith. New York: Metropolitan Museum of Art, 1996.

———. *The Imagery of the Cosmological Buddha.* Leiden: E. J. Brill, 1986.

———. *Summit of Treasures: Buddhist Cave Art of Dazu, China.* Trumbull, Conn.: Weatherhill, 2001.

Hu Wenhe 胡文和. *Sichuan Daojiao Fojiao shiku yishu* 四川道教佛教石窟艺术 (Daoist and Buddhist cave-temple art of Sichuan). Chengdu: Sichuan renmin chubanshe, 1994.

Hu Wenhe 胡文和 and Liu Zhangjiu 刘长久, eds. *Dazu shike yanjiu* 大足石刻研究 (Research on Dazu stone sculpture). Chengdu: Sichuan sheng shehui kexueyuan chubanshe, 1985.

Huntington, Susan L. *The Art of Ancient India.* New York: Weatherhill, 1985.

Jenner, W. J. F. *Memories of Loyang: Yang Hsüan-chih and the Lost Capital (493–534).* Oxford: Clarendon Press, 1982.

Jin Anning 金安宁. "Yongle Palace: The Transformation of the Daoist Pantheon During the Yuan Dynasty." Ph.D. diss., Princeton University, 1994.

Kessler, Adam T. *Empires Beyond the Great Wall.* Los Angeles: Natural History Museum of Los Angeles County, 1993.

Legge, James, trans. *A Record of Buddhistic Kingdoms: Being an Account by the Chinese Monk Fâ-hien of His Travels in India and Ceylon (A.D. 399–414) in Search of the Buddhist Books of Discipline.* Reprint, New York: Dover Publications, 1965.

Li Fangyin 黎方银. *Dazu shiku yishu* 大足石窟艺术 (Cave-temple art of Dazu). Chongqing: Chongqing chubanshe, 1990.

Lianyungang shi bowuguan 连云港市博物馆 (Lianyungang Municipal Museum). *Haizhou shike: Jiangjun ya yanhua yu Kongwangshan moya zaoxiang* 海州石刻：将军崖岩画与孔望山摩崖造像 (Stone carvings of Haizhou: Boulder carvings of Jiangjun Cliff and the Moya Buddha of Mount Kongwang). Beijing: Wenwu chubanshe, 1990.

Little, Stephen, ed. *Taoism and the Arts of China.* Chicago: Art Institute of Chicago in association with the University of California Press, 2000.

Liu Changjiu 刘长久. *Zhongguo xinan shiku yishu* 中国西南石窟艺术 (Grotto art of southwest China). Chengdu: Sichuan renmin chubanshe, 1998.

Liu Xinru. *Ancient India and Ancient China: Trade and Religious Exchanges A.D. 1–600.* Delhi: Oxford University Press, Oxford India Paperback, 1994.

Liu Zhiyuan 刘志远and Liu Tingbi 刘廷壁, eds. *Chengdu Wanfosi shike yishu* 成都万佛寺石刻艺术 (Rock-carving art of Wanfo Temple, Chengdu). Shanghai: Gudian yishu chubanshe, 1958.

Lutz, Albert. *Der Tempel der Drei Pagoden von Dali.* Zurich: Museum Rietberg, 1991.

Makita Tairyo 牧田谛亮. *Ryō kosoden sakuin* 梁高僧传索引. Kyoto: Heirakuji shoten, 1972.

Miller, Barbara Stoler, ed. *Exploring India's Sacred Art.* Philadelphia: University of Pennsylvania Press, 1983.

Mizuno, Seiichi. *Bronze and Stone Sculpture of China: From the Yin to the T'ang dynasty.* Translated from the Japanese by Yuichi Kajiyama and Burton Watson. Tokyo: Nihon keizai shimbunsha, 1960.

——— 水野清一. *Tōdai no Butsuzō chōkoku: Chūgoku no Bukkyō bijutsu* 中国の佛教美术 (Buddhist sculpture of the Tang dynasty: Buddhist art of China). Tokyo: Heibonsha, 1968.

Nanjing bowuguan 南京博物馆 (Nanjing Museum). *Fojiao chu chuan nanfang zhi lu* 佛教初传南方之路 (The initial spread of Buddhism along the southern route). Beijing: Wenwu chubanshe, 1993.

Ningxia Huizu zizhiqu wenwu guanli weiyuanhui 宁夏回族自治区文物管理委员会 (Ningxia Hui Autonomous Region Cultural Relics Committee), ed. *Xumishan shiku* 须弥山石窟 (The Xumishan grottoes). Beijing: Wenwu chubanshe, 1988.

Pas, Julian. *The Vision of Sukhavati: Shan-dao's Commentary on the Kuan-wu-liang-shou Fo-ching*. Albany: State University of New York Press, 1995.

Rawson, Jessica. *Chinese Ornaments: The Lotus and the Dragon*. London: British Museum, 1984.

Rhie, Marylin M. *Early Buddhist Art of China and Central Asia*. Vol. 1. Leiden: E. J. Brill, 1999.

Saunders, E. Dale. *Mudra, a Study of Symbolic Gestures in Japanese Buddhist Sculpture*. New York: Pantheon Books, 1960.

Schumann, H. W. *The Historical Buddha*. London: Arkana and Penguin Books, 1989.

Schwartz, Benjamin I. *The World of Thought in Ancient China*. Cambridge: Harvard University Press, 1985.

Snodgrass, Adrian. *The Symbolism of the Stupa*. Studies on Southeast Asia. Ithaca, N.Y.: Cornell University, 1985.

Soper, Alexander C. *Literary Evidence for Early Buddhist Art in China*. Ascona, Switzerland: Artibus Asiae, 1959.

Tsukamoto, Zenryū. *A History of Early Chinese Buddhism: From Its Introduction to the Death of Hui-yüan*. Translated from the Japanese by Leon Hurvitz. 2 vols. Tokyo: Kodansha International, 1985.

Wang Qingyu 王庆宇. *Zhongguo Dazu shike* 中国大足石刻 (Stone sculpture of Dazu, China). Chongqing: Chongqing chubanshe, 1992.

Whitfield, Roderick. *Caves of the Singing Sands, Dunhuang: Buddhist Art from the Silk Road*. 2 vols. London: Textile and Art Publications, 1995.

Wong, Dorothy C. "The Beginnings of the Buddhist Stele Tradition in China." Ph.D. diss., Harvard University, 1995.

———. *Chinese Steles: Pre-Buddhist and Buddhist Use of a Symbolic Form*. Honolulu: University of Hawai'i Press, 2004.

Wriggins, Sally Hovey. *Xuanzang, a Buddhist Pilgrim on the Silk Road*. Boulder, Colo.: Westview Press, 1996.

Wright, Arthur F. *Studies in Chinese Buddhism*. Edited by Robert Somers. New Haven: Yale University Press, 1990.

Wu Hung. *The Wu Liang Shrine: The Ideology of Early Chinese Pictorial Art*. Stanford, Calif.: Stanford University Press, 1989.

———, ed. *Between Han and Tang: Religious Art and Archaeology in a Transformative Period*. Beijing: Wenwu chubanshe, 2000.

Yang Boda 杨伯达. *Quyang Xiudesi chutu jinian zaoxiang de yishu fengge yu tezheng* 曲阳修德寺造像的艺术风格与特征 (Style and characteristics of the dated sculpture unearthed at the Xiude Temple, Quyang). Beijing: Gugong bowuyuan, 1960.

Yunnan sheng Jianchuan wenwusuo 云南省剑川文物局 (Cultural Relics Bureau of Jianchuan County, Yunnan Province), ed. *Diannan guibao: Jianchuan shizhongshan shiku* 滇南瑰宝：剑川石钟山石窟 (A rare treasure in the south: The Shizhongshan grottoes in Jianchuan). Kunming: Yunnan meishu chubanshe, 1998.

Zhongguo meishu quanji bianji weiyuanhui 中国美术全集编辑委员会 (Committee for a Complete Collection of Chinese Fine Art), ed. *Zhongguo meishu quanji* 中国美术全集 (Collection of Chinese art). Each volume has a different publisher.

Zhongguo shehui kexuayuan kaogu yanjiusuo 中国社会科学院考古研究所 (Institute of Archaeology of the Chinese Academy of Social Sciences), ed. *The Yongning Temple in Northern Wei Luoyang: Excavations in 1979–1994*. Beijing: Zhongguo dabaike quanshu chubanshe, 1996.

Zürcher, Erik. *The Buddhist Conquest of China: The Spread and Adaptation of Buddhism in Early Medieval China*. Leiden: E. J. Brill, 1959.

Chapter 4. From the Northern Song to the Qing

Chen Mingda 陈明达. *Yingxian muta* 应县木塔 (The Wooden Pagoda in Yingxian County). Beijing: Wenwu chubanshe, 1966.

Guangdong sheng bowuguan 广东省博物馆 (Guangdong Provincial Museum), ed. *Nanhua si* 南华寺 (Nanhua Temple). Beijing: Wenwu chubanshe, 1990.

Jin Shen 金申, ed. *Fojiao diaosu mingpin tulu* 佛教雕塑名品图录 (A catalogue of famous Buddhist sculptures). Beijing: Beijing gongyi meishu chubanshe, 1995.

Jin Weinuo 金维诺 and Luo Shiping 罗世平. *Zhongguo zongjiao meishu shi* 中国宗教美术史 (A history of Chinese religious art). Nanchang: Jiangxi meishu chubanshe, 1995.

Li ji 礼记 (Book of rites). Reprint, Shanghai: Shanghai guji chubanshe, 1987.

Li Jicheng 李冀诚. *Zangchuan Fojiao* 藏传佛教 (Tibetan Buddhism). Beijing: Xinhua chubanshe, 1991.

Liu Dunzhen 刘敦桢 et al., eds. *Zhongguo gudai jianzhu shi* 中国古代建筑史 (A history of ancient Chinese architecture). Beijing: Zhongguo jianzhu gongye chubanshe, 1980.

Peng Lin 彭林, Qi Jixiang 齐吉祥, and Fan Chuyun 范楚云, eds. *Zhonghua wenming shi* 中华文明史 (A history of Chinese civilization). Vol. 1. Shijiazhuang: Hebei jiaoyu chubanshe, 1994.

Ren Jiyu 任继愈, ed. *Zongjiao da cidian* 宗教大辞典 (A comprehensive dictionary of religion). Shanghai: Shanghai cishu chubanshe, 1998.

Shuanglin si caisu 双林寺彩塑 (Painted sculptures in the Shuanglin Temple). Tianjin: Tianjin renmin meishu chubanshe, 1999.

Su Bai 宿白, ed. *Zangchuan Fojiao siyuan kaogu* 藏传佛教寺院考古 (Archaeological studies of Tibetan Buddhist temples). Beijing: Wenwu chubanshe, 1996.

Sun Ji 孙机. "Zhongguo zaoqi gaoceng Fota zaoxing zhi yuanyuan" 中国早期高层佛塔造型之渊源 (Origin of high-rise Buddhist pagodas in the early years in China). In Sun Ji, *Zhongguo sheng huo—Zhongguo gu wenwu yu dongxi wenhua jiaoliu zhong de ruogan wenti* 中国圣火——中国古文物与东西文化交流中的若干问题 (The sacred fire of

China: A few issues concerning ancient Chinese cultural relics and the cultural exchange between East and West). Shenyang: Liaoning jiaoyu chubanshe, 1996.

Wang Jiapeng 王家鹏. *Zangchuan Fojiao jintong foxiang tudian* 藏传佛教金铜佛像图典 (An illustrated manual of gilt-bronze statues of Tibetan Buddhism). Beijing: Wenwu chubanshe, 1996.

Wenhuabu wenwuju 文化部文物局 (Bureau of Cultural Relics of the Ministry of Culture), ed. *Zhongguo mingsheng cidian* 中国名胜辞典 (Dictionary of famous and historical sites in China). Shanghai: Shanghai cishu chubanshe, 1986.

Xizang Budala gong 西藏布达拉宫 (The Potala Palace in Tibet). Beijing: Wenwu chubanshe, 1996.

Yuandai huasu ji 元代画塑记 (Records of painting and sculpture in the Yuan dynasty). Beijing: Renmin meishu chubanshe, 1964.

Zangchuan Fojiao zaoxiang: Chengde Waibamiao cang 藏传佛教造像：承德外八庙藏 (Statues of Tibetan Buddhism: Preserved in the Eight Outside Temples in Chengde). Tianjin: Tianjin renmin meishu chubanshe, 1995.

Zhang Tingyu 张廷玉 et al. *Ming shi* 明史 (A history of the Ming). Beijing: Zhonghua shuju, 1974.

Zhongguo Fojiao xiehui 中国佛教协会 (Chinese Buddhist Association), ed. *Zhongguo Fojiao* 中国佛教 (Chinese Buddhism). Beijing: Zhishi chubanshe, 1980.

Zhongguo Fojiao yanjiusuo, Shanxi sheng wenwuju 中国佛教研究所，山西省文物局 (Research Institute of Chinese Buddhism, Shanxi Provincial Bureau of Cultural Relics). *Shanxi Fojiao caisu* 山西佛教彩塑 (Painted Buddhist sculptures in Shanxi). Beijing: Zhongguo Fojiao wenhua chuban youxian gongsi, 1991.

Zhongguo Jinci Song su 中国晋祠宋塑 (Song-dynasty sculpture in Jinci Temple, China). Taiyuan: Shanxi renmin chubanshe, 1993.

Zhongguo shehui kexuayuan kaogu yanjiusuo 中国社会科学院考古研究所 (Institute of Archaeology of the Chinese Academy of Social Sciences). *Bei Wei Luoyang Yongning si—1979–1984 nian kaogu fajue baogao* 北魏洛阳永宁寺—1979–1994 年考古发掘报告 (Yongning Temple of the Northern Wei in Luoyang: A report on archaeological excavations, 1979–1994). Beijing: Zhongguo dabaike quanshu chubanshe, 1996.

Zhou Shujia 周叔迦. *Zhou Shujia Foxue lunzhu ji* 周叔迦佛学论著集 (A collection of treatises on Buddhism by Zhou Shujia). Beijing: Zhonghua shuju, 1991.

CONTRIBUTORS

ANGELA FALCO HOWARD is professor of Asian art at Rutgers University, New Brunswick, New Jersey, and was formerly special consultant in Chinese Buddhist art to the Department of Asian Art, Metropolitan Museum of Art, New York. Her work includes *The Imagery of the Cosmological Buddha* (1986) and *Summit of Treasures: Buddhist Cave Art of Dazu, China* (2001).

LI SONG, former editor of *Fine Art Studies* (*Meishu yanjiu*), was editor in chief of the volume on sculpture in the *Encyclopedia of China* (*Zhongguo dabaike quanshu: Meishu juan, diaosu,* 1991) and the volumes on the Xia, Shang, and Zhou dynasties in the *History of Fine Arts* (*Zhongguo meishu shi: Xia-Shang-Zhou,* 2002). He is the author of *Li Keran: Study of a Twentieth-Century Chinese Artist* (*Ershi shiji Zhongguo huajia yanjiu congshu—Li Keran,* 1995).

WU HUNG is the Harrie A. Vanderstappen Distinguished Service Professor in Chinese Art History and director of the Center for the Art of East Asia at the University of Chicago. His major publications include *The Wu Liang Shrine: The Ideology of Early Chinese Pictorial Art* (1989), *Monumentality in Early Chinese Art and Architecture* (1995), *The Double Screen: Medium and Representation in Chinese Painting* (1996), and *Remaking Beijing: Tiananmen Square and the Creation of a Political Space* (2005).

YANG HONG is professor and research fellow at the Institute of Archaeology at the Chinese Academy of Social Sciences and senior editor of the journal *Cultural Relics* (*Wenwu*). He is the author of *Ancient Chinese Weapons* (*Zhongguo gu bingqi luncong,* 1986), *A Half-Century of Fine Arts in Archaeology: A History of Archaeological Finds in China* (*Meishu kaogu ban shiji: Zhongguo meishu kaogu faxian shi,* 1997), and *Archaeological Finds of Buddhist Art of the Han and Tang Dynasties* (*Han-Tang meishu kaogu he Fojiao yishu,* 2000).

ACKNOWLEDGMENTS

From conception on, this book presented many challenges, and only the collaborative involvement of scores of talented and dedicated professionals made publication possible. Too many people contributed for us to name them all, but we thank each and every one.

A great many institutions contributed to the making of the book. We owe special thanks to the institutions in the People's Republic of China that provided photographs: the Palace Museum, Cultural Relics Press, China Pictorial, the National Museum of China, the Museum of Qingzhou in Shandong Province, the Museum of Shaanxi History, and the Cultural Relics Research Institute of Hebei Province. In addition, we thank the following individuals: Yang Hong, Luo Zhongmin, Luo Xiaoxing, Wei Jun, Liu Chungen, Sun Shuming, Wang Chunshu, Sun Yongxue, Lan Peijin, Chen Zhi'an, Wang Lu, Jin Yongmiao, Wu Xinyu, Zhou Qinjun, Yan Xinfa, Zhang Baoxi, Chen Zonglie, Li Jinyun, Chen Keyin, Jiang Cong, Guo Qun, Yan Xinzhi, Sun Lizhi, Yu Bingwen, Tao Zhenggang, Wang Dajun, Di Xianghua, Zhao Qi, Liang Dacai, Wu Jian, Li Xucheng, Wei Xuefeng, Xie Jun, Zhang Keqing, Gao Gao, Li Chunsheng, Bai Liang, Dong Ruicheng, Yu Ning, Wang Zhengbao, Gao Chunrui, Cheng Qinhua, Zhaxi Cedain, Qu Weibo, Hu Chui, Liu Jiayi, Jiang Xueliang, Hu Baoyu, Xia Juxian, Yang Weiqing, Zhang Hui, Wu Tianwen, Ma Zhichao, Zhao Keming, Wang Huaixin, Cheng Dongdong, and Cui Jinglian.

The staff of the Department of The Culture & Civilization of China at Foreign Languages Press worked diligently on the manuscript, checked translations, attended carefully to the smallest details, and answered questions from their Yale University Press colleagues, who are grateful for the excellent help. Liao Pin, senior editor, worked with skill, dedication, and good cheer to edit the Chinese text and handle many complex aspects of the art, with expert help from Cheng Qinhua and Yu Bingqing at the later stages. Sun Shuming assisted in collecting the needed photographs and in ensuring their proper placement in the text. Sun Haiyu assisted in coordinating work on the manuscript in the early stages. Zhou Daguang helped in the initial discussions about writing the book and coordinated the early work of the Chinese authors. We thank them all.

Several people lent their expertise with the translations of the Chinese texts into English and, in some cases, offered advice on how to deal with complex and thorny issues. We thank Tang Bowen, Ling Yuan, and Wang Mingjie for their diligent and careful work, often performed under tight deadlines. A team of editors, photo editors, and translators at Foreign Languages Press worked on this project over the years, and we are grateful for their contributions.

At Yale University Press another team was involved in producing this book. John G. Ryden, director emeritus of Yale University Press, supported this book from the beginning and gave valuable advice about The Culture & Civilization of China series as well as this particular project. James Peck, former executive director of The Culture & Civilization of China, helped design the contents of this volume together with Chinese and Western scholars and specialists and contributed significantly to the preparation of the manuscript. There is no way to adequately thank him. Jonathan Brent, editorial director of Yale University Press, offered crucial assistance in the final stages. Janyce P. Siress, development associate, was series recordkeeper and facilitator par excellence.

Mary Pasti, managing editor of The Culture & Civilization of China at Yale University Press, cheerfully coordinated the editorial work at the Press, edited part of the manuscript, and handled the endless rounds of page proof with scrupulous attention to detail. Susan Abel, Susan Laity, and Jeffrey Schier painstakingly edited the chapters, improving them in countless ways. Julie Carlson skillfully shaped an earlier version of the text. Millie Piekos and Chris Dakin, among others, helped check the page proofs and caught innumerable errors. Ching-Jung Chen helped with some translations at the American end, as did Quincy Howe and Mei Guan.

Julianne Griffin, special projects manager at Yale University Press, brought much specialized knowledge, years of art-book experience, and dogged determination to the extraordinarily demanding task of producing this book. John Long, photo editor, handled several complex photographic and artwork problems. Rita Powell, Alice Lovejoy, and Alisha Butler tracked innumerable details concerning production and the cataloguing of the art. Peter Wang, president of Redstone, Inc., advised on the artwork and scanned some of the art. Jerry Kelly designed the book and the jacket with artistry and resourcefulness, often under extremely tight deadlines. Angela Taormina typeset round after round of hideously marked-up page proofs with patience and skill. David Goodrich of Birdtrack Press expertly typeset the Chinese characters. Anandaroop Roy drew the beautiful maps. Bill Nelson re-rendered two finely detailed drawings from the *Classic of Measurements for Making Buddhist Images* and figure 1.30.

Angela Falco Howard, one of the authors, contributed her time and expertise far beyond expectation. She tirelessly checked and rechecked text and art and answered thousands of questions. Her commitment to excellence and willingness to be constantly on call made it possible to continue work on this book, and we are immeasurably grateful to her. We are also deeply indebted to Rob Linrothe, who dealt handily with some tricky passages on Himalayan art and supplied three illustrations. His constructive criticism helped improve the book in important ways.

The Editorial Advisory Boards for The Culture & Civilization of China in the People's Republic of China and in the United States have been a significant and continuing source of support and excellent advice. We are especially grateful for the guidance and help of James C. Y. Watt, Brooke Russell Astor Chairman, Department of Asian Art, The Metropolitan Museum of Art, a longtime friend of The Culture & Civilization of China. We also appreciate the warm support of Ambassador J. Stapleton Roy and Mr. Ronnie C. Chan, vice chairs of the International Advisory Board.

Ambassador Joseph Verner Reed, under-secretary-general of the United Nations and senior adviser to The Culture & Civilization of China, has generously contributed his time and wisdom. His expertise in foreign diplomacy helped make this volume a reality. Cynthia A. Forbes, consultant to, and director of development for, The Culture & Civilization of China, worked with Ambassador Reed to successfully raise funds for the series and coordinated communication among our generous financial supporters.

Huang Youyi, vice president of the China International Publishing Group and coordinating director of The Culture & Civilization of China, deserves our profound thanks. His vision, commitment, unsparing efforts, and unconditional support of this project made publication possible.

Finally, let us thank Zhao Qizheng, former director general of the Information Office of the State Council; Cai Mingzhao, president of the China International Publishing Group and vice minister of the Information Office of the State Council of the People's Republic of China; and John E. Donatich, director of Yale University Press. Their unstinting support and unswerving belief in the cooperative spirit of this project made all the difference.

Taiping Chang Knechtges
Executive Editor
The Culture & Civilization of China
Yale University Press

Li Zhenguo
Deputy Editor in Chief
Foreign Languages Press

ILLUSTRATION CREDITS

Illustrations are courtesy of Foreign Languages Press, Beijing, unless otherwise specified.

Chapter 1. From the Neolithic to the Han

1.7. Courtesy of the Arthur M. Sackler Museum, Harvard University Art Museums, Bequest of Grenville L. Winthrop, [1943.52.103]. Photograph credit: Michael Nedzweski and Junius Beebe; © President and Fellows of Harvard College.

1.10–1.11. Courtesy of the Institute of History and Philology, Academia Sinica, Taibei, Taiwan.

1.12. Asian Art Museum of San Francisco, The Avery Brundage Collection, Chong-Moon Lee Center for Asian Art and Culture (B60 B1+).

1.16. The Art Institute of Chicago, Edward and Louise B. Sonnenchein Collection, 1950.671. Three-quarter view (E27682). Photograph © The Art Institute of Chicago. All Rights Reserved.

1.23. *Xinyang Chu mu* (Beijing: Wenwu chubanshe, 1986), fig. 15.

1.30. Drawn by Bill Nelson.

1.34. Adapted from *Awakened: Qin's Terra-Cotta* Army (Xi'an: Shaanxi Travel and Tourism Press, 2001).

1.39. Courtesy, Wu Hung.

1.46. The Metropolitan Museum of Art, Charlotte C. and John C. Weber Collection, Gift of Charlotte C. and John C. Weber, 1992 (1992.165.19). Photograph by Seth Joel. Photograph © 1988 The Metropolitan Museum of Art.

1.53. Courtesy, Wu Hung.

Chapter 2. From the Han to the Qing

2.20. "Episode from Stories of Filial Piety," The Nelson-Atkins Museum of Art, Kansas City, Missouri. (Purchase: Nelson Trust) 33-1543/2.

2.21. *Offering shrine with engraved figures and inscriptions.* Chinese, Northern Wei dynasty, early 6th century A.D. Limestone with engraved pictorial scenes. Courtesy, Museum of Fine Arts, Boston. Reproduced with permission. © 2002 Museum of Fine Arts, Boston. All Rights Reserved. Photograph © 2006 Museum of Fine Arts, Boston.

2.71. University of Pennsylvania Museum (neg. T4-171c, object C395).

Chapter 3. From the Han to the Southern Song

Map 3.1. Drawn by Anandaroop Roy.

Map 3.2. Drawn by Anandaroop Roy. Adapted from Gansu sheng wenwu kaogu yanjiusuo, ed., *Hexi shiku* (Beijing: Wenwu chubanshe, 1987), p. 2.

3.1–3.2. Photographs by Angela Falco Howard.

3.3. *Zhongguo wenwu jinghua* (Beijing: Wenwu chubanshe, 1997), pl. 82.

3.4. *Wenwu,* no. 3 (1991), p. 6, fig. 19.

3.5. *Wenwu,* no. 7 (1985), p. 74, fig. 59.

3.6. Wu Hung, *The Wu Liang Shrine: The Ideology of Early Chinese Pictoral Art* (Stanford, Calif.: Stanford University Press, 1989), p. 120, fig. 49.

3.7. Nanjing bowuguan, *Fojiao chu chuan nanfang zhi lu* (Beijing: Wenwu chubanshe, 1980), pl. 80.

3.12. Gansu sheng wenwu kaogu yanjiusuo, *Hexi shiku,* p. 5, fig. 4.

3.15. Gansu sheng bowuguan, *Sichou zhi lu* (Yongchang, 1994), p. 94.

3.17. *Dunhuang Mogao ku,* in *Zhongguo shiku* series (Beijing: Wenwu chubanshe, 1980), vol. 1, pl. 11.

3.18. Dong Yuxiang, ed., *Binglingsi 169 ku* (Shenzhou: Haitian chubanshe, 1994), p. 2, fig. 2.

3.20. *Binglingsi shiku,* in *Zhongguo shiku* series (Beijing: Wenwu chubanshe, 1986), pl. 17.

3.22–3.23. Dong Yuxiang, *Binglingsi 169 ku,* p. 5, fig. 8; p. 8, fig. 12.

3.24–3.25. *Maijishan shiku,* in *Zhongguo shiku* series (Beijing: Wenwu chubanshe, 1987), pls. 3, 25.

3.26. Seiichi Mizuno, *Bronze and Stone Sculpture of China: From the Yin to the Tang Dynasty,* trans. Yuichi Kajiyama and Burton Watson (Tokyo: Nihon Keizai, 1960), color pl. 6.

3.27. Courtesy of the Arthur M. Sackler Museum, Harvard University Art Museums, Bequest of Grenville L. Winthrop. Photograph: Michael Nedzweski and Junius Beebe; © President and Fellows of Harvard College.

3.28. Asian Art Museum of San Francisco, The Avery Brundage Collection, Chong-Moon Lee Center for Asian Art and Culture (B60 B1034).

3.30. The Metropolitan Museum of Art, John Stewart Kennedy Fund, 1926 (26.123). Photograph © 1983 The Metropolitan Museum of Art.

3.34. *Yungang shiku* (Beijing: Wenwu chubanshe, 1991), pl. 28.

3.38. *Ryūmon sekkutsu,* Chūgoku sekkutsu series (Tokyo: Heibonsha, 1987), vol. 1, p. 288.

3.42. "The Emperor and His Court as Donors," The Metropolitan Museum of Art, Fletcher Fund, 1935 (35.146). Photograph © 2000 The Metropolitan Museum of Art.

3.43. "The Empress as Donor with Attendants," The Nelson-Atkins Museum of Art, Kansas City, Missouri. (Purchase: Nelson Trust) 40-38.

3.45–3.48. *Gongxian shiku,* in *Zhongguo shiku* series (Beijing: Wenwu chubanshe, 1983), pls. 3, 23, 4, 173.

3.49. Gansu sheng kaogudui (Archaeological Team of Gansu Province) et al., eds., *Qinyang Beishikusi* (Beijing: Wenwu chubanshe, 1985), p. 7 (plan), pp. 8–9 (drawings).

3.50–3.52. *Binglingsi deng shiku diaosu,* vol. 9 of *Zhongguo meishu quanji* (Beijing: Xinhua shudian, 1988), pls. 42, 48, 49.

3.54. The Collection of the National Palace Museum, Taibei.

3.55. Mizuno, *Bronze and Stone Sculpture of China,* color pl. 9 (front), monochrome pl. 105 (back).

3.56. "Standing figure of Padmapani in relief against a flaming mandorla; inscription of thirty-two characters incised on four-legged base," Freer Gallery of Art, Smithsonian Institution, Washington, D.C.: Gift of Charles Lang Freer, F1909.266. Photograph by John Tsantes.

3.57. The Metropolitan Museum of Art, Rogers Fund, 1938 (38.158.1a–n). Photograph by Lynton Gardiner. Photograph © 1989 The Metropolitan Museum of Art.

3.58. "The Buddhas Shakyamuni and Prabhutaratna," Musée des Arts Asiatiques-Guimet, Paris (EO 2604). Photograph: Thierry Olivier, © Réunion des Musées Nationaux / Art Resource, N.Y.

3.60. Yamaguchi Collection, Osaka Municipal Museum of Art.

3.62–3.63. *Wei Jin Nanbeichao diaosu*, vol. 3 of *Zhongguo meishu quanji* (Beijing: Xinhua shudian, 1988), pls. 69, 70–71.

3.64. *Maijishan shiku*, pl. 95.

3.65. *Buddhist votive stele with carved Buddhist figures and inscriptions* Chinese, Northern Wei dynasty, A.D. 529. Photograph © 2006 Museum of Fine Arts, Boston.

3.66. *Wei Jin Nanbeichao diaosu*, pl. 79.

3.67. *Masterpieces of Buddhist Statuary from Qingzhou City,* exh. cat. (Beijing: Chinasight Fine Arts Co., 1999), p. 57.

3.68. *Wenwu,* no. 5 (2000), p. 57, fig. 15.

3.69. *Wenwu,* no. 2 (1992), p. 68, fig. 1.

3.70. *Shiji guobao,* exh. cat. (Beijing, 2001), pp. 178–179.

3.71–3.72. *Wei Jin Nanbeichao diaosu,* vol. 3, pls. 54–55, 58.

3.73-3.74. *The Treasures of a Nation,* exh. cat. (Beijing: Morning Glory Publishers, 1999), pls. 187, 190.

3.75. Art Exhibitions China, Beijing.

3.76–3.77 (front). *Shiji guobao,* pp. 181, 186.

3.77 (back). Art Exhibitions China, Beijing.

3.79. Tokiwa Daijō and Sekino Tadashi, *Shina Bukkyō shiseki,* 6 vols. (Tokyo: Bukkyō shiseki kenkyūkai, 1926–1938), vol. 5, p. 104.

3.80–3.81. *Wenwu,* no. 5 (1992), p. 2, fig. 3; p. 23, fig. 3.

3.83. "Western Paradise," Freer Gallery of Art, Smithsonian Institution, Washington D.C. Purchase, F1921.2.

3.88. *Xumishan shiku neirong zonglu* (Beijing: Wenwu chebanshe, 1997), p. 191, pl. 12.

3.89. *Binglingsi deng shiku diaosu,* pls. 74, 75.

3.90. *Maijishan shiku,* pl. 218.

3.91. Wang Ziyun, *Shaanxi gudai shi diaoke* (Xi'an: Shaanxi renmin chubanshe, 1985), pl. 75.

3.92. The Metropolitan Museum of Art, The Sackler Collections, Purchase, Sackler Fund, 1965 (65.19.4). Photograph © 1998 The Metropolitan Museum of Art.

3.93. Courtesy of the Sichuan Provincial Museum, Chengdu.

3.95. © The British Museum.

3.96. *Guanyin, Bodhisattva of Compassion.* Chinese, Northern Zhou or Sui dynasty, about A.D. 580. Carved limestone with traces of polychrome and gilding, 249 × 71 cm. Courtesy, Museum of Fine Arts, Boston. Reproduced with permission. © Museum of Fine Arts, Boston. All Rights Reserved. Photograph © 2006 Museum of Fine Arts, Boston.

3.97. *Dunhuang shiku,* in *Zhongguo shiku* series (Beijing: Wenwu chubanshe, 1981), vol. 2, pl. 51.

3.98. *Kaogu xuebao,* no. 2 (1994): p. 250, fig. 14.

3.99–3.100, 3.102. *Masterpieces of Buddhist Statuary from Qingzhou City,* pp. 132–133, 114–115, 111.

3.103. *Altarpiece with Amitabha and Attendants.* Chinese, Sui dynasty, dated A.D. 593. Cast bronze. Courtesy, Museum of Fine Arts, Boston. Reproduced with permission. © Museum of Fine Arts, Boston. All Rights Reserved. Photograph © 2006 Museum of Fine Arts, Boston.

3.104. "Buddhist Altarpiece," Freer Gallery of Art, Smithsonian Institution, Washington, D.C.: Gift of Charles Lang Freer, F1914.21.

3.108. *Longmen shiku* (Beijing: Wenwu chubanshe, 1992), vol. 2, pl. 87.

3.110. "Seated Lohan," The Metropolitan Museum of Art, Frederick C. Hewitt Fund, 1921 (21.76). Photograph by Lynton Gardiner. Photograph © 1989 The Metropolitan Museum of Art.

3.111. "Seated Lohan," The Metropolitan Museum of Art, Fletcher Fund, 1920 (20.114). Photograph by Lynton Gardiner. Photograph © 1989 The Metropolitan Museum of Art.

3.112. Tokyo National Museum. Image: TNM Image Archives. Source: http://TnmArchives.jp/.

3.113. Freer Gallery of Art, Smithsonian Institution, Washington D.C.: Gift of Charles Lang Freer, F1909.98.

3.115. Collection of the Tokyo National Museum.

3.116. *Dunhuang shiku,* vol. 3, pl. 124.

3.118. "Standing Bodhisattva Avalokitesvara (Guanyin Pusa)," Courtesy of the Arthur M. Sackler Museum, Harvard University Art Museums, Bequest of Grenville L. Winthrop (1943.54.61). Photograph: Michael Nedzweski and Junius Beebe; © President and Fellows of Harvard College.

3.119. The Metropolitan Museum of Art, Rogers Fund, 1943 (43.24.3). Photograph © 1995 The Metropolitan Museum of Art.

3.125. Photograph by Chen Jing.

3.130. Photograph by Chen Jing.

3.143. Drawn by Anandaroop Roy after an original drawing by Li Qiang. Courtesy, Angela Falco Howard.

3.150. Courtesy of the Hechuan Cultural Relics Office.

3.153. Photograph by Chen Jing.

3.155. Courtesy of the Xichang Cultural Relics Office.

3.158. Courtesy of the Xichang Cultural Relics Office.

3.161. Drawn by Karen Conklin. Courtesy, Angela Falco Howard.

3.162. Photograph by Luo Zhewen.

3.163. Drawn by Karen Conklin. Courtesy, Angela Falco Howard.

3.164. Photograph by Liu Jianhua.

3.165. Adapted from a drawing by Karen Conklin. Courtesy, Angela Falco Howard.

3.166. Photograph by Liu Jianhua.

Chapter 4. From the Northern Song to the Qing

4.27. "The Water and Moon Guanyin Bodhisattva," The Nelson-Atkins Museum of Art, Kansas City, Missouri. (Purchase: Nelson Trust) 34-10.

4.37. The Nelson-Atkins Museum of Art, Kansas City, Missouri. (Purchase: Nelson Trust) 34-6.

4.56. Photograph by Rob Linrothe.

4.58. Photograph by Rob Linrothe.

4.59. Photograph by Xie Jinsheng.

4.82–4.83. Redrawn by Bill Nelson.

Page After Epilogue

White Tara (Sk. Sitatara), by Zanabazar, from Patricia Berger and Terese Tse Bartholomew et al., *Mongolia: The Legacy of Chinggis Khan* (San Francisco: Asian Art Museum of San Francisco, 1995), p. 387. Photograph by Kazuhiro Tsuruta.

INDEX

Page numbers in *italics* indicate illustrations.

Arthur M. Sackler Museum, Cambridge, Massachusetts
hats, 109, 114, 128
head of warrior (Qin bronze), 50, *51*
Heavenly Kings, 379–380. *See also* Hall of Heavenly Kings; Heavenly Worthies
Tang, 128, 130, *132*, 139, 299, *303*, 372, 373
tomb guardian figure, 132
Yuan, *420, 421*
Heavenly Song of the Moon Palace (Jin dynasty), *377*
Heavenly Worthies. *See also* Laozi; Three Pure Ones
Daoist sculptures, 399–*402*
as Daoist term, 399
Grotto of Three Pure Ones (Longshan), 420, *422*
Tang sculpture, 363, *402*
Hebei Provincial Bureau of Cultural Relics, *146*
Hebei Provincial Institute of Archaeology and Cultural Relics, *42, 48, 101*
Hebei Provincial Museum, Shijiazhuang, *69, 71*, 149, *249, 250*
Hebei Research Institute of Cultural Relics, *43*
Hebei School, and Northern Wei gilt bronzes, 252, *253, 254–255*
Hechuan Cultural Relics Office, *343*
Hechuan reliefs (Song dynasty), 336, 338–340, *341–344*
He clan, tomb of, *156*
Hejiashan, Mianyang, Sichuan (Eastern Han sculpture), *205*
Helima (Fifth Karmapa), 13
Hell, 405
Henan Museum, and Sui figurines, *125, 126*
Henan Province Museum, *262*
Henan Provincial Institute of Cultural Relics and Archaeology, *39*
Henan School, 262–263
Hexi corridor, 222
Buddhist art and, 212
map, *211*
high-court art (Qing dynasty), 451, *455*, 460, *460*
high-relief decoration, 19
historical figures
as deities, 405
statues of, 397–399, *398, 459*, 460
History of the Later Han (Hou Han shu), 203
History of the Wei (Weishu; Wei Shou), 215, 230
Hohhot, Inner Mongolia Autonomous Region, and Northern Wei figurines, 113
Hongmao Hill, Shimenkan, Nanjing, 109–110
Hongshan culture, 21–23, *22*
Hong Zicheng, tomb of, 155
honor guard figurines, 108
Ming, *157, 159*
Northern Wei, 114
horse sculpture. *See also* bronze horses; stone horses
blue horse figurines, 133

Saluzi (Valiant purple-haired horse) relief carving, 171, *173*
Tang figurines, 128, *129, 130*, 133, *136*
Western Han, *83*
winged horses (Tang dynasty), 174, 175, *178*
Xia kingdom, 170
Yuan, 156
horse-shaped vessel (Zhou), 35–*36*
Horyuji Temple, Treasury of the, and Tang artifact, 303, *308*
Houma City, Shanxi, and Jin carvings, *153*
Houtu (God of the Earth) Temple, Fenyin, Wanrong County, Shanxi, *379*, 381
Howard, Angela Falco, 8, 461–462
Hu, Empress Dowager (Northern Wei ruler), 115, 237, 241, 246
Huang Chao rebellion, 315
Huangling mausoleum, 188
Huangpu village, Wanrong County, Shaanxi, 142–143
Huangze Monastery, Guangyuan, Sichuan, 286, *289*
Huayan School, 359, 373
Huayan Temple, Datong, Shanxi, 378
Buddhist statues (Liao dynasty), *375*, 376
hu bronze sculptures, 37–38
Hu Chengde (sculptor), 412
Hui, Emperor (Western Jin), 160
tomb of, 74
Huijian Cave, Longmen, Henan, 299, *301*
Huili (Indian monk), 412
Huineng (Chan patriarch), 397
Huiyuan (monk), 264
Huiyun of Mount Lu, 273
Huizhuang, Prince, 143
Huizong, Emperor (Northern Song dynasty), 364, 368
Daoism and, 363–364, 402
Hulü Che, tomb of, *124–125*
human-headed vessels (Neolithic period), 19–20
human images, 112
Ming stone sculpture, 192–193
Northern Dynasties tomb sculpture, 170
Northern Song stone men, 182, *184, 185*
Northern Wei sculpture, 113
Shu figurines, 108
Warring States sculpture, 40–41
Western Jin figurines, 108–109, 109, *110*
Zhou bronzes, 36–37
human sacrifices
Dian sculpture and, 81
grave figurines and, 43
Lishan Mausoleum and, 55, 57, 67
types of victims, 43
Hunan Province. *See also* Changsha, Hunan
bronze manufacturing, 35
Mawangdui Tomb I, 76, *80*–81
Western Jin figurines, 109
Hunan Provincial Museum, *80*
hunping (soul urns), 207
Huo Qubing, tomb of, 2, 8, 82–*83*, 169, 170, 171
Hu people, 114–115
husband-and-wife deities, 363

Huxian County, Xi'an, *156*

iconography, 336
Anyue cliff sculpture (Tang dynasty), 318
Buddha identification, 381
early seated Buddha in Hebei, 227
Eastern Han animal statues, 89–90
Esoteric statues, 314
everyday life and, 399
Guangyuan cliff sculpture, 316–318
Guanyin images, 388
Kunming dharani pillar, 350
Liangzhou art, 214–215
Northern Wei caves, 247
Northern Wei gilt bronzes, 249–251
Northern Wei stone steles, 261
Sichuan statuary, 265, 269, 321, 328–329
Tang Buddhist art, 299, 303
Tang gilt bronzes, 312
Xi'an Road artifacts (Liang dynasty), 267–269
Xiao Nanhi caves, 278–279
Yungang cave temple, 231, 233
Zizhong cliff sculpture, 320
Illustrated History of the Nanzhao Kingdom (Nanzhao guoshi tuzhuan), 346
"images in niches" (*kanxiang*), 266
imaginary creature, 39, 169, 462
immortality, 364
Buddhist sculpture and, 103
Eastern Han and, 94, *96*, 97
Han funerary sculpture and, 74, 76
Song brick sculpture and, 152
Wu sculpture and, 68–72
Imperial Five, 230–236
imperial palaces, 2, 382, 444
imperial patronage
foreign inspiration and, 7
influence of, 9–10
Quanzhen Daoism and, 364
Tang Buddhist art and, 298
Tianlongshan and, 309
Yuan, 364
imperial power
arhat images and, 389
Buddhist art in Tang dynasty and, 299
Confucianism and, 366
Duan family and, 345–347
pre-Qin, 403
Imperial Preceptors, and guidelines, 12
imperial procession, and Northern Wei relief carving, 244, *245*
India. *See also* foreign influences
arhats, 388–389
Buddhist art style, 265, 451, *453*
origins of Buddhism, 201–202
Indo-Iranian painting style, 211
"indoor" images, and Western Han tomb sculpture, 76
Inner Mongolia Autonomous Region Museum, *113*
inner-tomb sculpture, 106
inscriptions, 228
Ashoka-type Buddha (Liang dynasty), 268

Prabhutaratna and Shakyamuni. *See* twin Buddhas

Prabhutaratna Grotto, Thousand Buddhas cliff (Tang dynasty), *317*

pradakshina (rite of circumambulation), 211

pratyeka Buddha, 293

prehistoric cultures, and religious differences, 18–24

prismatic tube (*cong*), 21, *22*

processions. *See also* Spirit Path
    Ming Spirit Path, 193, 197
    Northern Wei relief carving, *240, 241*
    Song brick sculpture, 152
    Tang, 128, *129*, 130, 176
    Yuan funerary sculpture, 156

proto-Buddhist art
    in coastal provinces, 206–208
    in Sichuan, 201–206

public sculpture, in Eastern Han dynasty, 84

Pujin ferry crossing, Yongji County, Shanxi, 175

Pule Temple, Chengde, Hebei, 445
    Pavilion of Morning Sunlight, 445, *448*
    Qing mandala altar, 445, *447*

Puning Temple, Chengde, Hebei, and Guanyin image (Qing dynasty), 426, *446*

Pure Land of the Amitabha Buddha. *See also* Amitabha Buddha; Pure Lands
    Northern Qi representation, 275, 278, 280, *280*
    Sichuan representations, 269, 272, 273, 320–321, *326, 327*
    Southern Liang, *272*, 273, 275
    Southern Xiangtangshan site, 280
    stele at Wan Fo Temple, Chengdu, *272*, 273, 275
    Sui gilt-bronze altarpiece, 293, 295, *296*
    Tang cliff sculpture, 320–321, *326, 327*
    Xiao Nanhai Cave, Anyang, *282*

Pure Lands, 219, 220
    canonical sources on, 273
    idea of, 202
    Jingtu school of Buddhism and, 358
    visualization of, 273

Puren Temple, Chengde, Hebei, 445

Purple-Bamboo Guanyin (Song statue), *384*, 388

Pusa Ding (Bodhisattva Top), 382

Putuozongcheng Temple, Chengde, Hebei, 445, *449, 450*, 451

Puxian. *See* Samantabhadra bodhisattva

Puzao Monastery, Xingtang County, Hebei, 397

Qian family of the Wu-Yue, mausoleums of, 144, 148

Qianfo (Thousand-Buddha) Cliff grottoes, 399

Qianling mausoleum (Emperor Gaozong), 170, 171, 174–175, *176–178*

Qianling Mausoleum Museum, *142*

Qianlong emperor. *See* Gaozong, Emperor

Qianqiu Wansui (Longevity) figurines, 125, *127*

Qianxian County, Shaanxi, 128, 142

Qian Yuanguan, tomb of, 143, 144

Qian Yuanliao (King Guangling of Wu-Yue), 148

Qiaoling mausoleum (Emperor Ruizong), 170, 175, *179*

Qiaolin village, Pucheng County, Shaanxi, 143

Qici (monk), 380, 399, *400, 401*

Qifu rulers (Western Qin dynasty), 219

qilin (mythical creature), 169, 462

Qin dynasty, 49–67. *See also* Lishan Mausoleum
    bronze casting, 50–54, *51, 52, 53*
    Buddhist art, 219–223
    Gansu and, 219
    head of warrior (bronze), 50, *51*
    imperial power and, 67, 403
    laws, 211
    realism and, 58, 59
    regional style and, 61, 67
    sectional construction, 53–54, 58, 61
    Xianbei people (Tuoba clan) and, 219

Qing dynasty, 451. *See also* Forbidden City, Beijing
    artistic innovation and, 13–14
    Buddhist sculpture, 362
    Daoism and, 364
    imperial patronage, 9
    Spirit Path stone sculpture, *194–196*, 197
    Tibetan Buddhist statues, 442, 443–451, *447, 448, 449, 450*, 460

qingtan ("pure talk"), 328

Qingyang, Princess, tomb of, 2

Qingzhou, Shandong
    dating of statuary from, 293
    Longxing Temple artifacts, 262, *263*, 293, *294, 295, 296*

Qingzhou Municipal Museum, *263, 294, 295, 296*

Qin Shihuang (First Emperor of Qin), tomb of, 2. *See also* Lishan Mausoleum; Qin dynasty

Qinyang County, Henan, and Northern Dynasties funerary sculpture, 119–*120*

Qin Zhi'an (Daoist), 420

Qionglai, Sichuan, and Tang cliff sculpture, 320–321, *326*

Qiongzhu Temple, Mount Yu'an, Yunnan, and painted arhat statues, 429, *440*

Qisong (monk), 358

Qiu Chuji (Daoist), 364

Qiu Mituo (sculptor), 393

Qiu Xinggong, General, 171

Qizi Hill, Suzhou, 148

Quanzhen (Fundamental Truth) Daoism, 364, 420

Queen Mother of the West (Xiwangmu), 9, 93–94, 97
    cult of, 203–205
    images of, 203, *204*

que gate, 86–88, *87*, 90

Quyang County, Hebei, 146
    marble relief, *146, 147*

Quzhou Municipal Museum, Zhejiang, *208*, *263*

realism. *See also* abstraction; naturalism
    Buddhist sculpture of Sichuan and, 264
    Daoist iconography, 4
    Dian sculpture and, 81
    Esoteric sculpture and, 315
    Five Dynasties relief carving and, 146, 147
    Ming statues of local deities and, 405
    Neolithic sculpture and, 23
    Northern Wei figurines and, 113, 115
    Qin figures and, 58, 59, 440
    secularism and, 309–312
    Shang bronzes and, 28–29
    Sichuan style and, 268, 273
    Song funerary sculpture and, 182
    Song religious sculpture and, 12, 336, 382, 388, *390*, 391, 393
    southern innovations and, 10–11
    Sui and, 124
    Tang Buddhist art and, 299, *303*
    Tang funerary sculpture and, 4, 10–11, 128, 141, 171, 174, 461
    Warring States sculpture and, 44–45
    Western Han sculpture and, 76, 79, 81, 100
    Western Jin and, 109
    Zhou sculpture and, 38, 40

"reality"
    posthumous, 61, 67
    Western Han and, 74

Record of the Monasteries of Luoyang (Luoyang jialan ji; Yang Xuanzhi), 237, 269

Record of the Western Regions (Xuanzang), 298

Records of the Huayang Kingdom (Huayang-guo zhi), 31

regional styles
    interactions among, 23–24
    Qin underground army and, 61, 67
    Shang, 29–33
    Sui, 124–125
    Tang, 127–128
    Western Han tomb figurines and, 79–81
    Zhou grave figurines and, 44–45

relief carving. *See also* brick relief sculpture; line carvings; stone steles
    Central Binyang caves, *239, 240*
    Eastern Han graveyards, 86, *87–88*
    Eastern Han stone sarcophagi, 90
    Five Dynasties funerary sculpture, 143–145
    Han stone sculpture, 82, 83
    Northern Dynasties tombsites, 119–122, *120, 121, 123*
    Northern Song stone sculpture, 184–185, *187*
    Northern Wei caves, 244
    painting and, 4
    proto-Buddhist art, 203, *204*

religious art
    abstraction and, 461–462
    decorative coloring, 5
    government and, 3
    images of founders, 3–4
    secular tradition and, 7–8
    task of, 3

Renshou, Sichuan, and Tang cliff sculpture,